vegetarian
times

everything vegan

Edited by Mary Margaret Chappell

WILEY

John Wiley & Sons, Inc.

WITHDRAWN

Published by John Wiley & Sons, Inc., Hoboken, New Jersey
Published simultaneously in Canada

For general information on our other products and services or for technical support, please contact our Customer Care Department within the United States at (800) 762–2974, outside the United States at (317) 572–3993 or fax (317) 572–4002.

Wiley also publishes its books in a variety of electronic formats. Some content that appears in print may not be available in electronic books. For more information about Wiley products, visit our web site at www.wiley.com.

Library of Congress Cataloging-in-Publication Data
Vegetarian times everything vegan.
    p. cm.

  Includes index.
  ISBN 978-0-470-54788-5 (cloth)
  ISBN 978-0-470-94677-6 (ebk);
  ISBN 978-0-470-94678-7 (ebk);
  ISBN 978-0-470-94680-0 (ebk)
1. Vegan cookery. 2. Vegetarian cookery. I. Vegetarian times.
II. Title: Everything vegan.
  TX837.V427147 2010
  641.5'636--dc22
                        2010000777

Printed in the United States of America
10 9 8 7 6 5 4 3 2 1

contents

acknowledgments

There are many voices and visions that go into putting together a magazine like Vegetarian Times and a book like this one.

It all starts with the recipe developers who create fresh, healthy recipes month after month. Robin Asbell, Ann Gentry, Myra Kornfeld, Donna Meadows, Rochelle Palermo, Nicole Palitti, Victoria Abbott Riccardi, Joyce Sangirardi, Melynda Saldenais, and Elliott Prag keep things tasty for us and came up with the recipes you'll find on the following pages.

Fiona Kennedy and Maggie Patinelli, our recipe testers and frequent recipe contributors, have logged hundreds of hours in the kitchen to make sure each and every recipe works as it is supposed to, occasionally adding a little of this or that to make each dish the best it can possibly be.

The beautiful images that accompany the recipes are taken by supertalented photographers who bring the VT vision to life each month. Thank you Beatriz Da Costa, Andrea Gómez, Jacqueline Hopkins, Richard Jung, John Kelly, Amy Neunsinger, Lisa Romerein, and Dasha Wright for making the dishes look so tempting and delicious.

At Wiley, Anne Ficklen, Cecily McAndrews, Amy Zarkos, and Kevin Watt not only guided this book through all the editorial hoops on the path to publication, but also they were instrumental in creating a cookbook that has the tone and feel of the magazine.

Without Healthy Living Group General Manager Pat Fox or VT's literary agent, Mary Ann Naples, this book never would have reached the Wiley people—or anyone else! They tirelessly championed the concept long before the first word was on a page.

Finally special thanks go out to VT magazine staffers Gabrielle Harradine, Scott Hyers, Don Rice, Jolia Sidona Allen, Amy Spitalnick, and Anna Roberts. In addition to their invaluable input, their collaborative efforts on everything from tasting recipes (really fun) to typing up lists and fact checking pages (really boring) made this book possible.

introduction

The term "vegan" has come to mean so much more than its dictionary definition of someone who eats no animal products or dairy. Sure, a person can be vegan, but these days, so can a bakery, a music festival, a fashion trend, a pair of shoes—even lipstick and nail polish. "Vegan" is also used as a synonym for "animal-friendly" and "cruelty-free" in environmental movements and often implies a wider concern for protecting the earth.

When it refers to food, what "vegan" ultimately implies is a choice. It can be a lifestyle choice for personal or political reasons. It can be a diet choice for health reasons. It can even be a meal choice for someone who selects a vegan entrée in a conventional eatery simply because it sounds appetizing. All those choices have one thing in common: a decision to enjoy delicious, health-giving foods.

This book was written to help you reaffirm your vegan choice—no matter what the context. (Though we probably can't help you with a shoe size or the right lipstick hue.) What better guide could you have for discovering everything vegan cuisine has to offer than *Vegetarian Times*, a publication that's been creating, testing, and tasting vegan food for over 35 years? The more than 250 recipes on the following pages range from the simple (Maple-Mustard Sauce, p. 313: two ingredients, stir... voilà! A vegan alternative to honey-mustard sauce!) to the sublime (Vietnamese Hot Pot, p. 240, a party dish that our editors scored a perfect 10). There are soups that warm, salads that wow, one-pot meals that make weeknight dinners a breeze, greens dishes, grains dishes, desserts... all with the VT editors' seal of approval.

And we're a picky bunch. Not only do our recipes have to be superlatively tasty, but they must also be simple enough for a novice cook and creative enough to entice experienced foodies. Most of all, each and every recipe has to meet our stringent requirements for health and nutrition—which is why you'll find nutritional information after them all.

Just for a second, let's take the term "vegan" out of the cookbook title. What's left? A collection of easy, innovative, delicious, and health-giving recipes that just happen to be made without using any animal products or dairy. Good choice, huh?

MARY MARGARET CHAPPELL
FOOD EDITOR

THE HEALTH POWER OF VEGAN FOODS

foreword by NEAL D. BARNARD, MD

Whether vegan foods are inspired by Mediterranean, Asian, or any of a hundred other traditions, they boast delightful flavors and aromas. They are animal-friendly and kind to the environment.

But perhaps the broadest appeal of vegan dishes comes from what they do for your health. When you fill your plate with vegetables, fruits, whole grains, and legumes, and skip the cholesterol, fat, and other undesirables that animal products harbor, you've got a menu that is unmatched in health-promoting power.

For decades, researchers have been measuring the health benefits of various diets. One group that has lent itself to intensive study is the Seventh-Day Adventists. Adventist religious tenets call for avoiding tobacco, alcohol, caffeine, and meat. But while most Adventists follow the first three rules pretty well, only about half avoid meat. The rest are modest meat-eaters. That creates a perfect natural experiment, allowing scientists to see the effects of meat-eating in an otherwise health-conscious population.

In 1960, when the Adventist Mortality Study began tracking the health of 24,673 adults, it became clear that vegetarians were much less likely to be overweight compared with people who ate even rather small amounts of meat. The vegetarians in the study were also much less likely to develop diabetes.[1]

But it was not until four decades later that results for vegans could be teased apart from those of other vegetarians. In the Adventist Health Study 2, which included 60,903 participants, vegans were by far the slimmest group, with a body weight right smack in the middle of the healthy range. Lacto-ovo-vegetarians were a bit heavier, and participants who included fish in their diets were heavier still. "Semi-vegetarians"—those who had meat less than once a week, but more than once per month—weighed more than fish-eaters, and frequent meat-eaters were teetering on the edge of obesity.[2]

Diabetes risk followed exactly the same gradient, affecting only 2.9 percent of vegans, compared with nearly 8 percent of nonvegetarians, with the other diet groups falling in between.[2]

Researchers have studied European populations in the same way. In the European Prospective Investigation into Cancer and Nutrition, vegans were once again the slimmest group, red meat–eaters the heaviest, with lacto-ovo-vegetarians and fish-eaters falling in between.[3]

Because vegan diets have essentially no cholesterol or animal fat, they are powerful cholesterol-lowering diets. At the University of Toronto, David Jenkins, MD, PhD, showed just how powerful. Beginning with a basic vegan diet, he asked volunteers to favor foods with a cholesterol-lowering effect, such as oat bran, nuts, soy products, and certain plant sterols. The combination of a vegan diet paired with cholesterol-lowering foods reduced LDL ("bad") cholesterol by nearly 30 percent in four weeks, which was similar to the power of cholesterol-lowering drugs.[6]

Studies conducted by the Physicians' Committee for Responsible Medicine (PCRM) show that low-fat vegan diets have similarly dramatic effects. In 2005, PCRM reported the results of a study involving a group of postmenopausal women who had been struggling with weight problems. The volunteers had tried every diet you can imagine, and felt stuck—nothing they did could take the weight off and keep it off. As the study began, we assigned half the participants to a low-fat vegan diet; the other half began a more conventional low-fat diet. By 14 weeks, the difference between the two groups was clear. The vegans had lost, on average, one pound per week, while the control group had lost slightly more than half that amount.[7] The PCRM researchers continued to track their weight. While the control group regained its lost weight, the vegan group did not—even after two years of follow-up.[8]

What was especially remarkable was why the vegan group lost weight. Part of the credit goes to the fact that vegan diets have no animal fat. Since every gram of fat has nine calories (compared with carbohydrates, which have only four), skipping high-fat items means skipping the most calorie-dense foods. Also, foods from plant sources are fiber-rich. Because fiber holds water and fills your stomach, it tricks your brain into thinking you are eating a large amount of food when in fact your calorie intake is modest.

But there is one more compelling reason for this weight loss: Vegan foods boost your metabolism for a few hours after every meal. In the weight-loss study described above, we brought the participants into the laboratory. Using a special mask that fits over the nose and mouth, we were able to measure their metabolism. This is because the amount of oxygen a person takes in and the carbon dioxide he or she breathes out shows how fast the body is burning calories. We did this test before and after a meal.

After the participants had been on a vegan diet for 14 weeks, their after-meal calorie-burn was measurably faster. The effect was modest, but it occurred after every breakfast, lunch, and dinner. More of the calories they consumed were burned off as body heat rather than being stored as fat.

So vegan diets have fewer calories to start with, they satisfy your appetite before you've overdone it, and they ramp up your metabolism for a few hours after every meal.

A DIET SOLUTION FOR TYPE 2 DIABETES

Starting in 2003, the National Institutes of Health funded our research team to test a similar diet for diabetes. Among people who kept their medications and exercise constant, a low-fat vegan diet controlled blood sugar much better than a more conventional diabetes diet.[9] The vegan diet also lowered participants' cholesterol and helped them lose weight. Many participants were able to reduce their medications or even eliminate them. Tracked over the long run, the benefits of the vegan diet still held.[10]

Vegan diets have many other advantages, from reducing menstrual cramps and premenstrual syndrome to improving arthritis pain and migraines. All in all, it is a remarkably healthful way to go.

In 2009, the American Dietetic Association reaffirmed its strong support for vegetarian and vegan diets. In its official position paper, the ADA wrote that vegan diets are not just nutritionally adequate; they bring a wide variety of health benefits.[11]

THE VITAMIN GAP

Some people may think natural foods ought to provide all nutrition needed for a vegan diet, without having to rely on supplements. I agree, in principle. But we are not in anything like a natural environment. Just as being indoors deprives us of the sunlight that normally produces vitamin D, modern life also means a vitamin B12 supplement is essential for vegans—and a good idea for everyone else, too.

A healthy diet means including a reliable source of vitamin B12 in your routine.

Vitamin B12 is essential for the blood and central nervous system. Because vitamin B12 is not made by plants or animals, but by bacteria, and because the best food sources of vitamin B12 are animal products, it can be hard for vegetarians and vegans to get the recommended amount. Nevertheless, a daily multiple vitamin will do the job, providing you with enough vitamin B12, as will fortified foods (e.g., fortified soymilk, cereals, etc.).

⇒ BE A MODEL VEGAN ⇐

If you are new to a vegan diet, let me offer one piece of advice: be a good example. Watch what you eat. Base your menus on a variety of vegetables, fruits, whole grains, and beans. Potato chips, sodas, and other junk foods may be free of animal products, but if you rely on them to stay away from meat and dairy, the health benefits will be limited. When you stick to a well-balanced vegan diet, your body is an advertisement to the world that veganism is not just an ethical way of eating, but that it is the optimal choice for your waistline and every other part of you.

As you page through the recipes in this book, you can almost taste the healthy power they have. I hope you enjoy them and all the wonderful benefits they bring.

REFERENCES

1. Snowdon DA, Phillips RL. Does a vegetarian diet reduce the occurrence of diabetes? Am J Publ Health 1985;75:507-12.

2. Tonstad S, et al. Type of vegetarian diet, body weight and prevalence of type 2 diabetes. Diabetes Care 2009;32:791-6.

3. Spencer EA, et al. Diet and body mass index in 38,000 EPIC-Oxford meat-eaters, fish-eaters, vegetarians, and vegans. Int J Obesity 2003;27:728-34.

4. Ornish D, Weidner G, Fair WR, et al. Intensive lifestyle changes may affect the progression of prostate cancer. J Urol 2005;174:1065-9.

5. Esselstyn CB Jr. Updating a 12-year experience with arrest and reversal therapy for coronary heart disease (an overdue requiem for palliative cardiology). Am J Cardiol 1999;84:339-41.

6. Jenkins DJ, Kendall CW, Marchie A, et al. Direct comparison of a dietary portfolio of cholesterol-lowering foods with a statin in hypercholesterolemic participants. Am J Clin Nutr. 2005;81:380-387.

7. Barnard ND, Scialli AR, Turner-McGrievy G, Lanou AJ, Glass J. The effects of a low-fat, plant-based dietary intervention on body weight, metabolism, and insulin sensitivity. Am J Med 2005;118:991-997.

8. Turner-McGrievy GM, Barnard ND, Scialli AR. A two-year randomized weight loss trial comparing a vegan diet to a more moderate low-fat diet. Obesity 2007;15:2276-81.

9. Barnard ND, Cohen J, Jenkins DJ, Turner-McGrievy G, Gloede L, Jaster B, Seidl K, Green AA, Talpers S. A low-fat, vegan diet improves glycemic control and cardiovascular risk factors in a randomized clinical trial in individuals with type 2 diabetes. Diabetes Care 2006;29:1777-1783.

10. Barnard ND, Cohen J, Jenkins DJ, Turner-McGrievy G, Gloede L, Green A, Ferdowsian H. A low-fat vegan diet and a conventional diabetes diet in the treatment of type 2 diabetes: a randomized, controlled, 74-week clinical trial. Am J Clin Nutr 2009;89(suppl):1588S-96S.

11. American Dietetic Association. Position of the American Dietetic Association . Vegetarian diets. J Am Diet Assoc. 2009;109:1266-82.

COOKING AND PREP TERMS

Most of the recipes in this book have self-explanatory cooking instructions,
but in case you want to double-check that you're doing something right or refer to what
a term means, we've included this handy guide.

Baking

Cooking foods with dry heat in
an oven. Always preheat the oven
at least 10 minutes before baking
foods; low temperatures can alter
the results of recipes. When baking
more than one item at a time (say,
two trays of cookies), leave space
between the items so that the hot air
circulates and cooks the food evenly.

Blanching

Dipping fruits or vegetables into
rapidly boiling water for a few
seconds to a couple of minutes,
then dunking them into cold water
immediately afterward. Blanching
is used to loosen peach and tomato
skins; lightly cook vegetables, such as
broccoli and asparagus, to set their
vibrant colors; and get fresh produce
ready for freezing.

Braising

Foods are sautéed in a little oil, then
simmered in liquid to produce rich,
velvety dishes with loads of flavor.

Broiling

Cooking with high heat from above.
The secret to broiling success is to
preheat the broiler well and have the
oven rack in the topmost position.
Then keep a watchful eye to make
sure foods don't burn.

Chiffonading

Slicing leafy greens into thin strips.

Chopping

Cutting food into bite-size or smaller
pieces with downward movements
(chops) of a knife.

Cubing

Cutting fruits or vegetables into
cubes or cubelike shapes.

Dicing

Cutting fruits or vegetables into small
($\frac{1}{4}$-inch or smaller) cubes.

Deep-Frying

Not a technique we use often, but
still a good one to know. Deep-frying
is done in a pot that is filled one-third
to half full with oil, then heated to
375°F. Food is lowered into the oil in

small batches (to keep the temperature from dropping) and cooked until golden brown. Draining deep-fried foods on a paper-towel-lined plate keeps them from getting soggy.

Deglazing
Adding a liquid—wine, broth, water, alcohol—to ingredients in a skillet or saucepan to loosen any bits (which happen to hold lots of flavor) stuck to the bottom of the pan, bringing the flavors together.

Folding
Gently incorporating one mixture into another using a spatula or wooden spoon.

Julienning
Cutting fruits or vegetables into thin matchsticks with a knife or mandoline.

Mincing
Cutting into tiny pieces. This term is most often used for garlic and ginger, and occasionally onions or shallots.

Poaching
Cooking foods in simmering, not boiling, water.

Puréeing
Blending ingredients into a smooth, thick paste. Food processors, blenders, and hand blenders can be used to purée.

Roasting
Like baking, roasting uses dry oven heat to cook foods. The oven temperature is generally high because the idea is for foods to brown, crisp up, and caramelize on the outside.

Sautéing
Cooking foods in a small amount of oil over medium to medium-high heat. "Sauté" comes from the French word meaning "to jump"; you want to make the food jump in the pan—so shake or stir it often.

Simmering
Cooking a liquid over medium to medium-low heat to allow it to bubble but not be at a rolling boil.

Steaming
Cooking foods using steam from boiling water in the bottom of a covered pot or saucepan. Foods are placed in a steamer or steamer basket to prevent them from coming in direct contact with the boiling water.

Stir-Frying
Stir-frying is a stove-top technique for cooking foods in a small amount of oil or fat using a wok or skillet.

MENU IDEAS

Whether you realize it or not, every dining occasion has a theme. That theme may be a wedding reception for 200, a romantic dinner for two, Thanksgiving for the whole family, or "whatever-I-can-grab-from-the-fridge-and-make in-30-minutes," but there is always some unifying objective that brings recipes together to make a meal. Here are some meal themes we've fleshed out using the recipes in this book. Use them as a guideline, a starting point, or a springboard for your own cooking imagination.

REASONS TO CELEBRATE

Thanksgiving Feast

Roasted Vegetable Cornucopias with Gravy, p. 198

Taste of Autumn Salad, p. 72

Chestnut Stuffing, p. 195

Double Cranberry Chutney, p. 312

Cranberry-Cherry Lattice Pie, p. 291

Christmas Dinner

Rich and Creamy Eggnog, p. 45

Cranberry-Pecan Salad, p. 73

Winter Squash with Spicy Maple Chestnuts, p. 194

Green Beans with Walnuts and Shallot Crisps, p. 191

Pomegranate-Pineapple Granita, p. 298

Thumbprint Cookies, Kourabiedes, Snickerdoodles, Iced Ginger Gems, p. 267, 269, 270, 274

New Year's Eve Dinner Party

New World Party Mix, p. 32

"Wild" Mushroom Soup with Sage Croutons, p. 221

Twice-Cooked Polenta Wedges with Black-Eyed Pea Salsa, p. 121

Triple Nut Chocolate Tart, p. 290

New Year's Day Brunch

Twice-Cooked Polenta Wedges with Black-Eyed Pea Salsa, p. 121

Southwestern Tofu Scramble, p. 132

Tempeh Bacon, p. 148

Morning Glory Loaf, p. 264

Super Bowl Sunday Get-Together

Root Vegetable Chili Soup, p. 235

Double-Corn Cornbread, p. 260

Taste of Autumn Salad, p. 72

Chinese New Year Supper

Avocado Vietnamese Summer Rolls, p. 28

Fiery Tofu with Red Chiles, Orange, and Ginger, p. 135

Chinese Broccoli with Black Bean Sauce, p. 190

East-West Risotto, p. 112

Mardi Gras Buffet

Seitan Jambalaya, p. 164

Deep South Slaw, p. 79

Garlic Bread, p. 253

Vanilla Pound Cake with Lime Glaze, p. 282

Valentine's Day Tête à Tête

Roasted Apple-Potato Soup, p. 228

Crispy Tofu Hearts, p. 142

Beet Green–Tangerine Salad, p. 81

Chocolate Truffles, p. 280

St. Patrick's Day Dinner

Sunset Sweet Potato Drop Biscuits, p. 257

Irish Stew, p. 248

Colcannon, p. 174

Three-Cherry Crumble, p. 296

Passover Seder

Quinoa and Spinach Soup, p. 224

Sephardic Stuffed Cabbage, p. 170

Baked Leek and Sweet Potato Gratin, p. 178

Roasted Strawberry Compote with Vanilla Bean, p. 281

Easter Dinner

Roasted Garlic Hummus, p. 6

Muhammara, p. 7

Spring Vegetable Stew with Soft Polenta, p. 245

Radicchio, Radish, and Fennel Salad, p. 68

Vanilla Pound Cake with Lime Glaze, p. 282

Cinco de Mayo Celebration

Homemade Salsa, p. 318

Mango Salsa, p. 319

Oaxacan Clayudas, p. 29

Refried Beans, p. 205

Mexican Rice, p. 119

Chili sin (Without) Carne, p. 249

Mother's Day Brunch

Cold Carrot-Ginger Bisque, p. 217

Orzo with Peas and Asparagus, p. 97

Lebanese Chickpea Croquettes, p. 23

Tofu Custard Tart with Fresh Fruit, p. 294

GLOBAL GOODNESS

EVERYDAY OCCASIONS

Sunday Breakfast
Creamy Breakfast Quinoa with Dried
    Fruit, p. 126

Tofu Frittata with Zucchini and
    Onion, p. 133

Toast with Easy Kiwi Jam, p. 322

Bag Lunch
Paprika Cauliflower Pita Pockets, p. 52

Corn and Mung Bean Salad, p. 76

The Heart Healthiest Chocolate Chip
    Cookies in the World, p. 276

Weeknight Dinner
Seitan with Shiitake Mushrooms,
    p. 160

Sunshine Spinach Salad, p. 66

Peanut Butter–Coconut Ice Cream,
    p. 299

starters

If you've ever ordered a round of appetizers to share as a meal, packed hors d'oeuvres leftovers for lunch, or turned a bowl of hummus into a light supper with veggies and crackers, then you know starters are no longer just before-the-meal party fare. These little bites are perhaps the most delicious introduction to vegan cuisine around. Many conventional offerings, such as bruschetta, hummus, dips, and (our favorite "wow" starter) steamed artichokes, are naturally vegan—so there are no food substitutions or cooking alterations involved. Starters are usually light, often easy, and generally well-loved by omnivores, who probably won't even notice there's no meat or dairy in the mix.

Roasted Red Pepper Crostini with Balsamic Reduction

SERVES 6

When allowed to reduce, or cook down, balsamic vinegar becomes a thick, slightly sweet syrup. Here, a balsamic reduction is used to flavor an herb-laced roasted red pepper topping and then add a finishing touch to crostini.

3 Tbs. pine nuts

3 large red bell peppers

1 red or green jalapeño chile

3 tsp. olive oil, divided

1 ½ Tbs. chopped fresh parsley

1 ½ Tbs. chopped fresh mint

3 cloves garlic, minced (1 Tbs.)

½ cup balsamic vinegar

1 Tbs. agave nectar

6 ⅓ -inch-thick slices ciabatta bread, toasted

1. Toast pine nuts in skillet over medium heat 3 to 4 minutes, or until browned, shaking pan constantly.

2. Preheat broiler. Coat bell peppers and jalapeño with 1 tsp. oil. Broil on baking sheet, 15 minutes, or until blackened on all sides. Transfer to bowl, cover, and cool.

3. Peel and seed bell peppers and jalapeño. Slice bell peppers into thin strips, finely chop jalapeño; transfer both to bowl. Stir in pine nuts, parsley, mint, garlic, and remaining 2 tsp. oil. Season with black pepper.

4. Bring vinegar and agave nectar to a simmer in saucepan over medium heat. Cook 10 minutes, stirring occasionally. Stir 1 Tbs. balsamic syrup into pepper mixture. Marinate pepper mixture 30 minutes. Top bread slices with pepper mixture, and drizzle with remaining balsamic reduction.

PER SERVING: 133 CAL; 3 G PROT; 5 G TOTAL FAT (1 G SAT FAT); 21 G CARB; 0 MG CHOL; 103 MG SOD; 2 G FIBER; 10 G SUGARS

Wild Mushroom Bruschetta

SERVES 4

The topping for these toasts can be made well ahead and warmed just before serving. The mushroom types listed are just suggestions—feel free to experiment with other varieties you find at the farmers' market or local supermarket.

1 Tbs. canola oil

2 small shallots, finely chopped (2 Tbs.)

1 clove garlic, minced (1 tsp.)

2 cups button mushrooms, diced

1 cup shiitake mushrooms, stems removed and diced

1 cup cremini mushrooms, trimmed and diced

2 Tbs. chopped fresh parsley, divided

1 Tbs. dry sherry

1 medium baguette, sliced into ½-inch-thick rounds

2 Tbs. olive oil

1. Preheat oven to 325°F.

2. Heat canola oil in skillet over medium heat. Sauté shallots and garlic in oil 3 minutes, or until light brown. Add all mushrooms, and cook 5 to 7 minutes, or until soft. Stir in 1 Tbs. parsley and sherry, reduce heat to low, and simmer 10 minutes. Season with salt and pepper.

3. Meanwhile, brush both sides of bread slices with olive oil; place on baking sheet, and bake 5 minutes, or until crisp. Top toasted bread slices with mushroom mixture. Garnish with remaining parsley.

PER SERVING: 312 CAL; 9 G PROT; 11.5 G TOTAL FAT (1.5 G SAT FAT); 39 G CARB; 0 MG CHOL; 520 MG SOD; 2 G FIBER; 3 G SUGARS

Storage Hint: Mushrooms

Think paper, not plastic, when it comes to storing mushrooms (especially the delicate varieties from farmers' markets) in the fridge. Paper bags allow mushrooms to breathe, while plastic traps moisture that can wilt a batch of mushrooms and make them dark and slimy. Paper bags also protect the delicate fungi from light.

Wine-Braised Leeks over Garlic Toast

SERVES 4

This is a fork-and-knife toast that's something between a soup and stew. It's light, but filling, and it makes a wonderful appetizer or even a main lunch course. Gentle braising renders the garlic and leeks earthy and sweet.

8 small leeks, white and pale green parts only, halved lengthwise

12 cloves garlic, peeled, divided

½ cup pitted, oil-cured black olives

1 cup low-sodium vegetable broth

1 cup dry white wine

2 Tbs. minced fresh thyme

1 ½ Tbs. olive oil

4 1-inch-thick slices whole-grain bread, cut from 8-inch round loaf

¼ cup chopped fresh parsley, for garnish

Prep Talk: Save That Day-Old Bread

The best toasts are those made with, slightly stale bread that won't fall apart once toppings have been added. Simply slice the bread, brush slices with olive oil, and rub with a clove of garlic, then toast in a 325°F oven 5 to 10 minutes. Cool, and store up to 1 month.

1. Preheat oven to 450°F. Arrange leek halves, cut-side down, in 13- × 9-inch baking dish. Set aside 1 clove garlic (for rubbing on toasts); scatter remaining garlic and olives over leeks. Pour broth and wine over leeks, olives, and garlic; sprinkle with thyme; drizzle with oil; and season with salt and pepper, if desired. Cover dish with foil, and bake 30 minutes. Remove foil, and bake 40 minutes more to brown and tenderize leeks.

2. Toast bread slices until golden. Cut reserved garlic clove in half and rub over each piece of toast. Lay out 4 shallow bowls. Place 1 slice garlic-rubbed toast in each bowl, and top with one-quarter of braised leek mixture. Drizzle cooking juices over each dish, and garnish with parsley.

PER SERVING: 322 CAL; 10 G PROT; 9 G TOTAL FAT (1 G SAT FAT); 51 G CARB; 0 MG CHOL; 420 MG SOD; 8 G FIBER; 11 G SUGARS

Roasted Garlic Hummus

MAKES 3 CUPS

This creamy-zesty dip has more than 40 cloves of garlic in it. Roasting the garlic softens the cloves to a smooth, slightly sweet pulp that doesn't overwhelm other flavors or give off that typical garlicky aroma. And if you're looking for a way to dress up store-bought hummus, you can just roast the garlic cloves and stir them in.

4 to 5 heads garlic

¼ plus 1 Tbs. cup olive oil, divided, plus more for drizzling

3 cups cooked chickpeas, or 1 28-oz. can chickpeas, rinsed and drained

½ cup fresh lemon juice

3 Tbs. tahini

Success Secret: The Creamiest Hummus Ever

When cooking dried chickpeas for hummus, add 1 teaspoon baking soda to the cooking water. Baking soda helps break down the chickpeas when they're blended for hummus that's creamy and smooth.

1. Preheat oven to 350°F. Cut tops from garlic heads to reveal tips of cloves. Place garlic heads on large sheet of foil, and drizzle with 1 Tbs. oil. Wrap tightly in foil, and bake 30 minutes, or until garlic heads feel soft through foil. Cool in foil.

2. Purée chickpeas 1 minute in bowl of food processor, or until finely chopped. Add lemon juice, ¼ cup oil, tahini, and ½ cup water. Blend chickpea mixture 2 to 3 minutes, or until smooth.

3. Squeeze roasted garlic pulp from each clove into chickpea mixture in food processor. Pulse hummus several times to combine. Season with salt and pepper. Spread in thin layer on large plate, and drizzle with olive oil.

PER ¼-CUP SERVING: 168 CAL; 5 G PROT; 8.5 G TOTAL FAT (1 G SAT FAT); 20 G CARB; 0 MG CHOL; 184 MG SOD; 3 G FIBER; ⊲1 G SUGARS

SERVING SUGGESTION

Try a light, fruity rosé wine with Mediterranean appetizers such as hummus, muhammara, dolmades, and tapenade.

Muhammara

MAKES 2 CUPS

This purée made from roasted red peppers and toasted walnuts is as addictive as its Middle Eastern cousin, hummus. Pomegranate syrup, an ingredient found in gourmet stores and Middle Eastern markets, adds a hint of sweetness.

2 cups raw walnuts (6 oz.)

3 large red bell peppers (1 ½ lb.)

4 Tbs. olive oil, divided

4 cloves garlic, sliced

2 tsp. salt

2 Tbs. pomegranate syrup

Prep Talk: Pomegranate Syrup Substitution

Don't happen to have pomegranate syrup in your pantry? Substitute reduced pomegranate juice. Simply simmer 2 cups pomegranate juice uncovered in a small saucepan over low heat until it is reduced to ¼ cup.

1. Preheat oven to 375°F. Spread walnuts on baking sheet, and toast 10 to 12 minutes, or until light brown and fragrant. Cool.

2. Meanwhile, place bell peppers on separate baking sheet in oven. Roast 1 hour, or until skins are black all over, turning occasionally. Transfer bell peppers to bowl, and cover with plate to steam 15 minutes. Cool bell peppers on plate, then rub off blackened skins and remove seeds.

3. Heat 2 Tbs. oil in small skillet over medium heat; add garlic, and sauté 1 minute. Remove from heat, and allow garlic and oil to cool.

4. Purée bell peppers, walnuts, garlic, remaining 2 Tbs. oil, salt, and pomegranate syrup in food processor until smooth. Season with salt and black pepper. Transfer to small serving bowl.

PER ⅓-CUP SERVING: 320 CAL; 5 G PROT; 28 G TOTAL FAT (3 G SAT FAT); 17 G CARB; 0 MG CHOL; 780 MG SOD; 4 G FIBER; 11 G SUGARS

Red Lentil–Pecan Pâté

MAKES 2 CUPS

The pale orange color of this red lentil pâté looks spectacular when surrounded by crackers, gherkin pickles, apple slices, and vegetable sticks.

1 cup dried red lentils

1 bay leaf

1 Tbs. olive oil

1 medium onion, diced (1 ½ cups)

3 cloves garlic, minced (1 Tbs.)

½ tsp. chopped fresh thyme

½ tsp. chopped fresh sage

½ cup toasted chopped pecans

2 Tbs. mirin (rice wine)

1 Tbs. white miso

1 tsp. umeboshi (sour plum) paste or sherry vinegar

½ tsp. salt

½ tsp. ground black pepper

1. Bring lentils, bay leaf, and 2 cups water to a boil, reduce heat to medium-low, and simmer, covered, 20 minutes, or until lentils are soft. Cool, then remove bay leaf.

2. Heat oil in skillet over medium heat. Add onion, and sauté 5 to 7 minutes. Reduce heat to low, and cook onion 15 to 20 minutes more, or until browned, stirring occasionally. If onion starts to stick, stir in Tbs. water. Add garlic, thyme, and sage, and cook 1 minute more.

3. Place mixture in food processor with the remaining ingredients. Purée until smooth. Chill 2 hours, or store up to 3 days in fridge.

PER 1-TBS. SERVING: 45 CAL; 2 G PROT; 2 G TOTAL FAT (0 G SAT FAT); 5 G CARB; 0 MG CHOL; 73 MG SOD; 1 G FIBER; 1 G SUGARS

Buy and Try: Umeboshi Paste

This Japanese condiment, made with dried pickled plums, is the Worcestershire sauce of the vegan world (even though you can now find vegan Worcestershire sauce). Tangy and salty with a rich, full-bodied flavor, it's a fantastic flavor booster

French Onion Dip

No artificial seasonings, colors, or sodium-laced instant mixes here!
All the flavor comes from oven-roasted onions, a dash of soy sauce, and dried
thyme. Serve with potato chips, of course.

1 medium onion, cut into ½-inch-thick slices

1 Tbs. olive oil

1 Tbs. balsamic vinegar

1 tsp. salt

¼ tsp. ground black pepper

1 12-oz. container vegan sour cream

½ tsp. low-sodium soy sauce

½ tsp. dried thyme

1. Preheat oven to 450°F. Toss together onion, oil, vinegar, salt, and pepper on baking sheet. Bake 18 minutes, or until onion slices are browned. Transfer onion to bowl, and cool.

2. Coarsely chop onion slices, and return to bowl; stir in sour cream, soy sauce, and thyme. Season with salt and pepper.

PER 1-TBS. SERVING: 20 CAL; 1 G PROT; 2 G TOTAL FAT (0.5 G SAT FAT); 1 G CARB; 0 MG CHOL; 129 MG SOD; 1 G FIBER; 0 G SUGARS

Dip Tip

While guests often "expect" to see dips as hors d'oeuvres, one way to make them a standout starter is to replace the carrot and celery sticks with other veggies, and ditch the crackers and chips for different crispy snackables. Here is a list of a few to try:

Turnip slices

Fresh fennel wedges

Jicama sticks

Belgian endive leaves

Yellow squash rounds

Trimmed green onions

Fruit slices

Plantain or banana chips

Grissini (thin Italian breadsticks)

Vegetable chips

Melba rounds (remember those?)

Cinnamon-raisin bread triangles (trust us)

Flavored lavash or other flat bread triangles

Eggplant Caviar

MAKES 3 CUPS

This colorful spread gets its fresh taste from finely chopped onions
and a splash of red wine vinegar. It will keep for up to a week in the fridge
and makes a great hostess gift. Serve on crackers or pita wedges,
by itself, or with vegan cream cheese.

2 medium eggplants (1 ½ lb.)

1 large red bell pepper

1 large yellow bell pepper

1 small onion, finely chopped (1 cup)

2 ½ Tbs. red wine vinegar

Success Secret:
Blacken, Don't Burn

For perfectly roasted whole eggplant and
bell peppers, don't be afraid to blacken
them until they blister. This guarantees
the flesh inside will be tender and makes
the skin easy to remove, but it won't burn
the high-moisture veggies themselves.

1. Preheat oven to broil. Prick eggplants several times with fork. Place eggplants and bell peppers on baking sheet. Broil 20 to 25 minutes, or until eggplants and peppers are blackened on all sides, turning occasionally. Place bell peppers in plastic bag to cool and steam skins. Cool eggplant and bell peppers 20 minutes, or until easy to handle.

2. Peel and coarsely chop eggplants, then place in large bowl. Peel and remove core and seeds from bell peppers. Chop into ¼-inch dice, and add to bowl with eggplant. Stir in onion and vinegar. Season with salt and black pepper.

PER 2-TBS. SERVING: 13 CAL; 1 G PROT; 0 G TOTAL FAT (0 G SAT FAT); 3 G CARB; 0 MG CHOL; 25 MG SOD; 1 G FIBER; 1 G SUGARS

Garlicky Spinach Dip

MAKES 3 CUPS

This dip is based on a Greek meze called skorthalia, which is often served with hummus. It gets its creaminess and body from soaked bread rather than dairy or nondairy alternatives.

1 cup coarsely chopped raw walnuts, plus more for garnish, optional

1 cup cubed French bread, preferably stale

1 10-oz. pkg. frozen chopped spinach, thawed

5 cloves garlic, minced (1 ½ Tbs.)

½ cup olive oil, plus more for garnish, if desired

2 Tbs. fresh lemon juice

1 ½ tsp. light brown sugar

1. Preheat oven to 350°F. Spread walnuts on baking sheet, and toast 7 to 10 minutes, or until light brown and fragrant. Cool 10 minutes.

2. Meanwhile, place bread cubes in bowl, and cover with ½ cup cold water. Let stand 5 to 7 minutes, then drain. Squeeze to remove excess water. Place bread, toasted walnuts, spinach, and garlic in food processor, and purée 2 minutes, or until smooth. Add oil, lemon juice, and sugar, and season with salt and pepper. Purée until combined.

3. Spread dip in shallow plate, drizzle with oil, and sprinkle with walnuts, if desired.

PER ¼-CUP SERVING: 166 CAL; 3 G PROT; 15.5 G TOTAL FAT (2 G SAT FAT); 6 G CARB; 0 MG CHOL; 92 MG SOD; 2 G FIBER; 1 G SUGARS

Prep Talk: Toasting Nuts

Why do we always (well, more often than not) call for toasting nuts before using them in recipes? Because that quick trip to the oven brings out so much flavor and can even reclaim nuts that have gotten soft or stale with storage. If you want to get ahead of the game, toast a big batch (1 cup or more) of nuts at a time, then save whatever you don't use in an airtight container for future recipes.

Black Olive Tapenade

MAKES ³/4 CUP

Tapenade is an olive spread from Provence that's traditionally made
with finely chopped olives, garlic, and capers (and anchovies,
in classic recipes, but we'd rather not mention them). In this version,
white beans help lighten the fat and calorie counts and lower the sodium.
Serve with crackers or rounds of French bread.

¼ cup pitted, dry-cured black olives

¼ cup canned white beans, rinsed and drained

2 tsp. chopped onions

1 tsp. capers, rinsed and drained

1 clove garlic, chopped (1 tsp.)

1 Tbs. fresh lemon juice

1 tsp. olive oil

1. Place olives, beans, onions, capers, and garlic and in bowl of food processor or blender and pulse until paste forms. Add lemon juice and oil, and process until smooth.

2. Transfer mixture to bowl. Cover, and refrigerate 1 day before serving for flavors to blend. (Tapenade will keep refrigerated up to 2 weeks.)

PER 1-TBS. SERVING: 18 CAL; 0 G PROT; 1 G TOTAL FAT (0 G SAT FAT); 2 G CARB; 0 MG CHOL; 106 MG SOD; 0 G FIBER; ‹1 G SUGARS

Prep Talk: Pretty Pinwheels

Tired of the dip look? Try this party presentation. Spread smooth dips (such as tapenade) on flat bread (such as lavash), then roll into a cylinder. Slice the cylinder into ½-inch-thick rounds, and … presto! Beautiful, bite-size pinwheels you can serve on a platter.

Artichoke Tapenade

MAKES ³/₄ CUP

This creamy spread is also a specialty from Provence, where it's sold in markets alongside olive tapenades. Serve with sliced baguette rounds or pita wedges.

4 fresh globe artichoke bottoms, steamed, or canned artichoke bottoms

6 pitted green olives

2 Tbs. olive oil

2 Tbs. fresh lemon juice

2 Tbs. grated vegan Parmesan cheese, optional

1 clove garlic, minced (1 tsp.)

Place all ingredients in bowl of food processor with 2 Tbs. water. Purée until smooth, adding 1 Tbs. or more water to obtain desired consistency.

PER 2-TBS. SERVING: 55 CAL; 1 G PROT; 5 G TOTAL FAT (0.5 G SAT FAT); 2 G CARB; 0 MG CHOL; 73 MG SOD; 1 G FIBER; 0 G SUGARS

Buy and Try: Canned Artichoke Bottoms

It may require keen eyes to find them, but canned artichoke bottoms are sold in many supermarkets. They're a great pantry item to have on hand to add to pizzas and salads and have less fat and sodium than marinated artichoke hearts.

Roasted Asparagus Tapenade

MAKES 1 CUP

Here, roasted asparagus replaces the olives for a fresh version that tastes of spring. This is a great recipe to make when you want to use up a bunch of asparagus that's been sitting in the fridge a little too long.

1 medium head garlic

2 Tbs. plus 1 tsp. olive oil, divided

1 lb. asparagus, trimmed

¼ cup pine nuts

1 Tbs. fresh lemon juice

½ tsp. freshly grated lemon zest

1. Preheat oven to 375°F. Line baking sheet with parchment paper. Peel excess papery skin from garlic head. Slice top off so that tips of cloves appear, and place on 6-inch square of foil. Drizzle with 1 tsp. oil, and sprinkle with salt. Wrap foil around garlic head, and bake 45 minutes, or until softened and golden. Cool 5 minutes, then squeeze garlic out of cloves.

2. Meanwhile, toss asparagus with remaining 2 Tbs. oil in bowl on prepared baking sheet, and roast 20 minutes, or until tender; shake baking sheet occasionally. Cool and chop.

3. Toast pine nuts in dry skillet over medium heat 3 minutes, or until lightly golden.

4. Place half of asparagus in food processor with garlic, pine nuts, and lemon juice. Process until smooth. Transfer to bowl, and stir in lemon zest and remaining asparagus. Season with salt and pepper.

PER ¼ -CUP SERVING: 151 CAL; 3 G PROT; 14 G TOTAL FAT (1.5 G SAT FAT); 6 G CARB; 0 MG CHOL; 155 MG SOD; 2 G FIBER; 1 G SUGARS

Cheese, Please!

Ask any vegan what he or she misses most from an omnivorous diet
and the answer will probably be cheese. As the so-so store-bought imitations prove,
it's hard to re-create the creamy goodness of cheese using only plant-based products.
That's why we at VT are pretty proud of the following vegan
cheese offerings. They are incredible. Easy to make, pretty to serve,
and utterly up to our cheese-lover standards.

Chive and Walnut "Cheese" Bites

MAKES 28 BITES

When you look down the ingredients list, it doesn't look like there's a whole lot to these mini cheese balls. But just the right combination of nuts, herbs, and spices turns tofu cream cheese into something special.

1 ½ cups raw walnuts, divided

16 oz. vegan cream cheese, softened

1 cup finely chopped fresh chives (4 bunches), divided

½ small shallot, minced (1 Tbs.)

¼ tsp. smoked paprika

1. Preheat oven to 350°F. Spread walnuts on baking sheet, and bake 8 to 10 minutes, or until fragrant. Cool, and finely grind in food processor.

2. Stir together cream cheese, 3 Tbs. chives, shallot, paprika, and 3 Tbs. walnuts until smooth. Season with salt and pepper. Scoop mixture into 2 tsp.-size balls. Roll half in remaining chives and half in remaining walnuts. Serve immediately.

PER PIECE: 88 CAL; 2 G PROT; 8.5 G TOTAL FAT (1.5 G SAT FAT); 2 G CARB; 0 MG CHOL; 98 MG SOD; 1 G FIBER; ◂1 G SUGARS

Shopping Savvy: Paprika

Sweet or Hungarian paprika is the most common type found and used in the United States; it's added to soups and stews for color and flavor or sprinkled on dishes to add a bright, delicately flavored finishing touch. Smoked or Spanish paprika has a more pronounced flavor. While sweet or smoked paprika can be used interchangeably in recipes, the choice you make will vary the flavor.

Cheddar Cheeze

MAKES 1 1-LB. BLOCK

Pine nuts are so small and tender that they don't need to be soaked before using to make this cheese. Agar flakes lend firmness and sliceability and eliminate the need for a straining step. Try adding other ingredients, such as chopped jalapeño chiles, cumin or caraway seeds, or a dash of smoked paprika.

1 ¼ cups unsweetened plain soymilk

¼ cup agar flakes

½ cup pine nuts

⅓ cup canola oil

¼ cup fresh lemon juice

3 Tbs. dry white wine

3 cloves garlic, peeled

2 tsp. granulated onion

1 ¼ tsp. salt

¾ tsp. ground black pepper

1. Line 2- to 3-cup rectangular (or whatever shape you prefer) container with 2 layers cheesecloth, allowing cheesecloth to hang over sides.

2. Whisk together soymilk and agar flakes in saucepan. Bring to a simmer over medium heat, and cook 8 minutes, or until agar dissolves completely and mixture is thick, stirring frequently.

3. Blend pine nuts, oil, lemon juice, wine, garlic, granulated onion, salt, and pepper in blender or food processor 5 minutes, or until smooth, scraping down sides frequently. Add soymilk mixture, and blend 2 minutes more, or until smooth. Transfer mixture to cheesecloth-lined container; smooth top. Fold overhanging cheesecloth over cheese. Refrigerate 1 hour, or until firm. Unwrap, slice, and serve.

PER 1-OZ. SERVING: 167 CAL; 3 G PROT; 16 G TOTAL FAT (1 G SAT FAT); 5 G CARB; 0 MG CHOL; 522 MG SOD; 1 G FIBER; 1 G SUGARS

Success Secret: Agar Flakes

Gelatin, made from pig or cattle feet, is a no-no in the veg-o-sphere. Agar flakes (made from seaweed) are the jelling alternative. Agar flakes need time to dissolve in hot liquids, so be patient, and stir often. After 10 minutes, strain out any remaining flakes floating in the mixture so the final recipe will be perfectly smooth.

Pepper-Crusted Cashew "Goat" Cheese

MAKES 1 10-OZ. ROUND

Cashews become creamy when blended, which makes them perfect for this cheese. It's aged at room temperature, then baked until dry to the touch.

¾ cup raw unsalted cashews

6 Tbs. canola oil

¼ cup fresh lemon juice

1 Tbs. tahini

1 ¼ tsp. salt

1 tsp. cracked black peppercorns or coarsely ground black pepper

Prep Talk: Reusing Cheesecloth

To ready cheesecloth for reuse, fill the sink with cold water, add a drop of dishwashing liquid, and wash the way you would a hand-washable garment. Rinse well, and hang to dry.

1. Soak cashews overnight in large bowl of cold water. Drain; rinse under cold water; drain again. Purée cashews, oil, lemon juice, tahini, salt, and 2 Tbs. water in food processor 6 minutes, or until creamy.

2. Place large strainer over bowl and line with triple layer of cheesecloth. Spoon cashew mixture into cheesecloth. Fold sides of cloth over cheese, and form into oval loaf. Twist ends of cloth and secure with rubber bands. Set in strainer over bowl, and let stand 12 hours at room temperature. Chill.

3. Preheat oven to 200°F. Line baking sheet with parchment paper. Unwrap cheese, and scrape into 7-inch-long log on cheesecloth. Rewrap, and twist ends to secure. Place on prepared baking sheet. Bake 35 minutes, or until cheese becomes set on outside but still soft, turning occasionally. Cool, and chill.

4. Unwrap cheese. Sprinkle with peppercorns, and press to adhere.

PER 1-OZ. SERVING: 140 CAL; 2 G PROT; 14 G TOTAL FAT (2 G SAT FAT); 4 G CARB; 0 MG CHOL; 293 MG SOD; 1 G FIBER; 0 G SUGARS

Almond "Feta" Cheese with Herb Oil

MAKES 1 10-OZ. ROUND

Blanched almonds give this creamy-crumbly cheese a rich texture. Unbaked, it will be smooth and spreadable. Baking will make it crumbly, like feta cheese.

1 cup whole blanched almonds

¼ cup fresh lemon juice

¼ cup plus 3 Tbs. olive oil, divided

1 clove garlic, peeled

1 ¼ tsp. salt

1 Tbs. thyme leaves

1 tsp. rosemary leaves

1. Soak almonds in large bowl of cold water 24 hours. Drain, rinse almonds under cold water, and drain again.

2. Purée almonds, lemon juice, 3 Tbs. oil, garlic, salt, and ½ cup water in food processor 6 minutes, or until creamy.

3. Place large strainer over bowl, and line with triple layer of cheesecloth. Spoon almond mixture into cheese-cloth. Bring corners of cloth together, and twist around cheese, forming into ball and squeezing to extract moisture. Secure with rubber band. Chill overnight. Discard liquid.

4. Preheat oven to 200°F. Line baking sheet with parchment paper. Unwrap cheese, and transfer to prepared baking sheet. Flatten to form ¾-inch-thick round. Bake 40 minutes, or until top is firm. Cool, then chill.

5. Warm remaining ¼ cup oil, thyme, and rosemary in saucepan over medium-low heat 2 minutes, or until very hot but not simmering. Cool. Drizzle herb oil over cheese just before serving.

PER 1-OZ. SERVING: 170 CAL; 3 G PROT; 17 G TOTAL FAT (2 G SAT FAT); 4 G CARB; 0 MG CHOL; 295 MG SOD; 2 G FIBER; ◄1 G SUGARS

Vegetable Tempura with Chile Sauce

There's really no way to make "light" tempura, but this recipe lets you re-create all that crispy, deep-fried goodness of Japanese restaurant tempura without the risk of cross-contamination from other nonvegan ingredients cooked in the fryer. Seltzer water keeps the rice flour batter light as air, and ground flaxseed replaces the eggs traditionally used to help hold things together.

CHILE SAUCE

1 green onion, minced

1 Tbs. chile-garlic sauce

1 Tbs. low-sodium soy sauce

1 Tbs. rice vinegar

1 tsp. toasted sesame oil

TEMPURA

1 qt. plus ¼ cup canola oil

1 Tbs. ground flaxseed

2 tsp. salt

2 ½ cups chilled seltzer water

2 ½ cups white rice flour, divided, plus more for dredging

3 avocados, peeled, pitted, and each cut into 6 wedges

2 small red bell peppers, cut into strips

1 medium zucchini, cut into ¼-inch-thick rounds

1. To make Chile Sauce: Combine all ingredients plus 1 Tbs. water in small bowl.

2. To make Tempura: Heat 1 qt. oil to 375°F in wok or large saucepan over medium-high heat. Combine flaxseed with ¼ cup water in large bowl. Let stand 5 minutes, or until mixture is slightly thickened. Stir in remaining ¼ cup oil and salt. Mix in seltzer. Add 1 ¼ cups rice flour, and stir until batter forms.

3. Working in batches, dredge avocado wedges, bell pepper strips, and zucchini rounds in remaining 1 ¼ cups rice flour to lightly coat, then dip in batter to coat. Immediately place battered vegetables in hot oil, and fry 3 minutes, or until coating is crisp and pale golden. Transfer to paper-towel-lined baking sheet, using slotted spoon to drain. Serve hot with Chile Sauce for dipping.

PER SERVING: 483 CAL; 6 G PROT; 24 G TOTAL FAT (2 G SAT FAT); 63 G CARB; 0 MG CHOL; 948 MG SOD; 7 G FIBER; 2 G SUGARS

Lebanese Chickpea Croquettes

SERVES 6

These easy-to-make croquettes combine chickpeas with a blend of
Middle Eastern spices—sumac, cumin, and coriander. Serve the dish with the
Tzatziki Sauce (p. 318) for a fresh, bright contrast of flavors.

2 14-oz. cans chickpeas,
rinsed and drained

½ cup breadcrumbs

¼ cup olive oil

8 sun-dried tomatoes packed in oil
(2 oz.), drained and finely chopped

2 Tbs. ground sumac, optional

1 Tbs. ground coriander

1 Tbs. ground cumin

3 cloves garlic, minced (1 Tbs.)

½ cup all-purpose flour

2 Tbs. canola oil, for frying

1. Pulse chickpeas, breadcrumbs, olive oil, tomatoes, sumac, if using, coriander, cumin, and garlic in food processor until roughly puréed. Season with salt and pepper.

2. Roll mixture into walnut-size patties with your hands. (Mixture should make 18 medium-size croquettes or 24 smaller ones.) Dredge croquettes in flour, and shake off any excess.

3. Heat canola oil in skillet over medium-low heat, and add half of croquettes. Brown croquettes 2 minutes per side. Repeat with remaining croquettes.

PER SERVING. 372 CAL; 10 G PROT; 17 G TOTAL FAT
(2 G SAT FAT); 47 G CARB; 0 MG CHOL; 542 MG SOD;
8 G FIBER; <1 G SUGARS

Buy and Try: Sumac

Deep purple sumac powder has an herbal, slightly sour flavor and is
used in Middle Eastern cooking to add a tangy accent to foods.
Use it to season anything with chickpeas and you can't go wrong.
Or sprinkle it over salads, soups, and stews for a colorful finishing touch.

Dolmades *(Stuffed Grape Leaves)*

MAKES 24 DOLMADES

Once you've discovered how easy it is to stuff your own grape leaves, you'll want to make this appetizer all the time.

2 Tbs. olive oil

1 medium onion, finely chopped (1 ½ cups)

½ cup long-grain white rice

¼ cup pine nuts

¼ cup dried currants or raisins

⅛ tsp. ground cinnamon

1 bay leaf

¼ cup chopped fresh parsley, stems reserved

3 Tbs. chopped fresh mint, stems reserved

1 16-oz. jar preserved grape leaves, rinsed and patted dry

¼ cup fresh lemon juice

1. Heat oil in skillet over medium heat. Add onion, and sauté 5 minutes. Stir in rice and pine nuts, and sauté 3 minutes more. Add currants, cinnamon, bay leaf, and 1 cup water. Cover, reduce heat to medium-low, and simmer 15 minutes. Remove from heat, and stir in parsley and mint.

2. Cut stems from grape leaves. Line large pot with 3 or 4 leaves. Place parsley and mint stems on bottom.

3. Place 1 grape leaf smooth-side down on work surface and set heaping teaspoon of filling near base of stem end of leaf. Fold end and sides over filling, and roll toward leaf point. Set seam-side down in pot. Repeat with remaining leaves and filling, and layer on top of one another.

4. Add lemon juice and 1 cup water, cover with 3 grape leaves, and invert plate on top. Cover, and bring to a boil. Reduce heat to medium-low, and simmer 45 minutes. Remove from heat, and let stand 2 hours. Serve warm or at room temperature.

PER DOLMA: 47 CAL; 1 G PROT; 2 G TOTAL FAT (1 G SAT FAT); 6 G CARB; 0 MG CHOL; 140 MG SOD; 1 G FIBER; 2 G SUGARS

Success Secret: Filled Foods

To keep dolmades and other filled foods from cracking while cooking, don't over-stuff them. Here, 1 teaspoon is plenty of rice to make plump stuffed grape leaves.

Warm Pitas with Dukka

SERVES 8

Dukka is an Egyptian spice mix that contains toasted nuts and is served with pita bread and olive oil. Guests dip the pita into the olive oil and then into the spice mix. Leftover dukka can be sprinkled on roasted cauliflower, tossed with pasta, or stirred into yogurt to make a sauce.

1 cup whole raw almonds

¼ cup raw sesame seeds

3 Tbs. coriander seeds

2 Tbs. cumin seeds

½ tsp. dried thyme

½ tsp. Aleppo pepper or chili powder

4 fresh pita bread rounds

Olive oil, for serving

1. Preheat oven to 350°F. Place almonds on baking sheet, and roast in oven 13 to 15 minutes, or until fragrant. Transfer nuts to cool baking sheet. Heat skillet over medium heat, and add sesame seeds, coriander, cumin, thyme, and Aleppo pepper. Cook 3 to 4 minutes, or until spices are fragrant. Place almonds and spices in food processor and pulse until mixture resembles coarse sand (do not overprocess or mixture will become almond butter).

2. Meanwhile, heat pita rounds on baking sheet 5 minutes, or until warm. Slice pitas into triangles, and serve with dukka and oil.

PER SERVING: 206 CAL; 7 G PROT; 10.5 G TOTAL FAT (1 G SAT FAT); 23 G CARB; 0 MG CHOL; 166 MG SOD; 4 G FIBER; 1 G SUGARS

Success Secret: Toasting Seasonings

Western cooks are so used to just adding a pinch of this spice or a teaspoon of that, and we often overlook how much better the seasonings can be if they're lightly toasted before using. To use the technique with any whole spices, place them in a pan over medium or medium-low heat, and cook 2 to 4 minutes, shaking and swirling the pan constantly.

Sunny Raw Nori Rolls

SERVES 8

Blended, soaked sunflower seeds replace cooked rice in this colorful
veggie "sushi." For the filling, you can substitute your favorite raw veggies,
including jicama, radish, daikon, burdock, or even raw pickles!

2 cups hulled raw sunflower seeds

8 green onions,
light and dark green parts, divided

¼ cup cilantro leaves

¼ cup fresh lemon juice

2 Tbs. Bragg Liquid Aminos

4 cloves garlic (4 tsp.)

6 small collard green leaves,
tough stems removed

8 sheets untoasted nori

2 medium carrots, cut into thin strips

1 medium cucumber, peeled, seeded,
and cut into thin strips

1 medium avocado, peeled, pitted,
and thinly sliced

1 8-oz. container daikon sprouts or
sunflower sprouts

Raw brown sesame seeds,
for garnish, optional

1. Soak sunflower seeds in large bowl of cold water 4 hours. Rinse, and drain.

2. Transfer sunflower seeds to food processor, and add 2 green onions, cilantro, lemon juice, liquid aminos, garlic, and ¼ cup water. Purée until creamy. Set aside.

3. Cut collard green leaves to half the size of nori sheets.

4. Lay 1 nori sheet, rough side up, on cutting board. Place collard leaf piece on nori sheet, covering half of sheet nearest you. Spread 2 Tbs. sunflower seed mixture on collard green with spatula. Stack carrot strip, cucumber strip, avocado slice, green onion, and daikon sprouts in narrow line 1 inch from long edge of nori sheet. Fold nori sheet over vegetables, and roll sheet away from you as tightly as possible. Dab edge of nori sheet with water to seal and close. Repeat with remaining ingredients. Cut each roll into 6 bite-size pieces with serrated knife.

PER SERVING (6 PIECES): 359 CAL; 13 G PROT; 29.5 G
TOTAL FAT (3 G SAT FAT); 18 G CARB; 0 MG CHOL; 249
MG SOD; 8 G FIBER; 3 G SUGARS

Avocado Vietnamese Summer Rolls

MAKES 12 MEDIUM ROLLS

If you've ever enthusiastically ordered a summer roll in an Asian restaurant only to be let down by a mouthful of bland, tasteless rice noodles that need a dunk in sauce to be edible, you'll appreciate this flavor-packed version.

SUMMER ROLLS

3 oz. rice noodles

3 shiitake mushroom caps, sliced

2 Tbs. low-sodium soy sauce

12 rice paper wrappers

1 5.5-oz. pkg. vegan turkey slices, cut into thin strips

1 small cucumber (1 cup)

2 small carrots (1 cup)

1 avocado, diced (1 cup)

1 cup basil leaves, chopped

1 cup coarsely chopped fresh cilantro

½ small red onion, minced (½ cup)

½ cup unsalted peanuts, chopped

2 tsp. chili oil

DIPPING SAUCE

1 cup rice wine vinegar

1 green onion, minced

1. To make Summer Rolls: Submerge rice noodles in warm water 8 to 10 minutes, until soft and clear. Drain, and cut noodles into 2-inch pieces. Set aside. Toss mushrooms with soy sauce in bowl, and set aside.

2. Submerge 1 spring roll wrapper in large bowl of cold water 2 to 3 minutes, or until softened. Lay wrapper flat on work surface and arrange, mushrooms, noodles, turkey strips, cucumber, carrots, avocado, basil, cilantro, onion, and peanuts in log shape in center of wrapper. Sprinkle with chili oil, and roll wrapper like burrito, folding ends to seal.

3. To make Dipping Sauce: Combine vinegar and green onion in small bowl. Serve Spring Rolls, whole or halved, with Dipping Sauce.

PER ROLL: 234 CAL; 7 G PROT; 6.5 G TOTAL FAT (1 G SAT FAT); 38 G CARB; 0 MG CHOL; 168 MG SOD; 3 G FIBER; 2 G SUGARS

Oaxacan Clayudas

SERVES 8

Clayudas are a Mexican dish that has a lot in common with pizza. Tortillas are slathered with a spicy black bean purée (the same way a pizza gets spread with tomato sauce), baked, then sprinkled with various toppings.

1 Tbs. canola oil

1 small white onion, diced (1 cup)

1 clove garlic, minced (1 tsp.)

1 tsp. ground cumin

1 15-oz. can black beans, rinsed and drained

1 canned chipotle chile in adobo sauce, drained

½ tsp. light brown sugar

4 8-inch flour tortillas

8 oz. slaw mix

½ cup chopped fresh cilantro

2 Tbs. fresh lime juice

1. Preheat oven to 450°F. Heat oil in saucepan over medium-high heat. Add onion, and cook 5 minutes, or until translucent. Add garlic and cumin, and cook 1 minute more. Place onion mixture in blender with beans, chipotle chile, sugar, and 3 Tbs. water. Blend until smooth. Season with salt and pepper, if desired.

2. Place 2 tortillas each on 2 baking sheets. Spread bean mixture on tortillas, and bake 5 to 7 minutes, or until edges become golden.

3. Toss slaw in bowl with cilantro and lime juice. Season with salt and pepper, if desired. Top each clayuda with slaw, and cut into triangles.

PER SERVING: 157 CAL; 6 G PROT; 4 G TOTAL FAT (0.5 G SAT FAT); 25 G CARB; 0 MG CHOL; 436 MG SOD; 5 G FIBER; 2 G SUGARS

Storage Hint: Chipotles in Adobo

Chipotle chiles in adobo sauce come three to four per can, but most recipes call for using only one or two of the tart, spicy chiles. What to do with the rest? Drain, and freeze in a resealable plastic bag for future use.

Perfect Steamed Artichokes à la Française

SERVES 4

Leave it to the French to gild the lily—or the thistle (artichokes are members of the thistle family). Instead of just cooking artichokes in boiling salted water, they add a bay leaf and a clove of garlic, which help make fresh artichokes taste even sweeter. Serve with a light vinaigrette and Tarragon Mayonnaise (p. 314) as they do in la belle France, or mix things up with Raspberry-Sesame Vinaigrette (p. 314) or Jalapeño Orange Dipping Sauce (p. 316).

4 globe artichokes

1 medium lemon, halved

1 bay leaf

1 clove garlic, peeled

Chopped fresh parsley, for garnish, optional

Prep Talk: Trimming Artichokes

Before trimming, break the stem from the bottom of the artichoke with your hands (this pulls fibrous strands out of the tender artichoke bottom). Then use scissors to trim away tough leaves and tips.

1. Cut stem ends off artichokes, and trim off pointed leaf tops with scissors. Rub cut parts with lemon half.

2. Fill large pot with 2 inches water, and add bay leaf and garlic clove. Squeeze juice from lemon halves into water, and place steamer basket in pot. Set artichokes top down in steamer basket, cover, and bring water to a boil. Reduce heat to medium, and steam artichokes, covered, 45 to 50 minutes, or until a bottom leaf from each base pulls away easily. Cool to room temperature. Sprinkle with parsley, if using.

PER SERVING: 64 CAL; 3 G PROT; 0.5 G TOTAL FAT (0 G SAT FAT); 14 G CARB; 0 MG CHOL; 72 MG SOD; 10 G FIBER; 1 G SUGARS

SERVING SUGGESTION

Artichokes are notorious for being difficult to match with a vintage. To marry the flavors of a wine with an artichoke, serve a dry white or rosé wine or even Champagne.

New World Party Mix

MAKES 1 CUP

Sure, roasted peanuts are delish with cocktails, but when you want to add a little elegance (without taking away from the crunchy-salty fix), this party mix is just the ticket. Cocoa nibs are cocoa beans that have been roasted and crushed into small bits—here they add a hint of chocolate flavor without any sweetness.

½ cup hulled raw pepitas
(pumpkin seeds)

⅛ tsp. olive oil

¼ cup pine nuts

¼ cup dried cranberries

¼ cup cocoa nibs

¼ tsp. cayenne pepper

¼ tsp. salt

1. Toss pumpkin seeds in small bowl with oil until coated. Spread seeds in skillet, and heat over medium-high heat. Cook 3 minutes, shaking skillet constantly, or until most of pumpkin seeds swell and pop. Transfer to bowl.

2. Add pine nuts to skillet, and cook 30 seconds, shaking skillet constantly, or until golden flecks appear. Transfer to bowl with pumpkin seeds. Stir in dried cranberries, cocoa nibs, cayenne pepper, and salt, and mix thoroughly. Season with more salt, if desired.

PER ¼ -CUP SERVING: 161 CAL; 5 G PROT; 13 G TOTAL FAT (1.5 G SAT FAT); 9 G CARB; 0 MG CHOL; 99 MG SOD; 1 G FIBER; 3 G SUGARS

Buy and Try: Pepitas

Pepitas, or pumpkin seeds, are sold both raw and roasted and provide a good source of protein and magnesium. Keep them on hand to eat as a snack or sprinkle over salads like nuts.

drinks

Perfection. That's what any drink recipe needs to be—because when a smoothie is so-so or a cocktail doesn't knock your socks off, you just go back to buying a bottled fruit drink or serving wine. So, rather than offer a compendium of beverage concoctions, this chapter gives you a small but perfect selection of smoothies and sippers you'll want to make again and again.

Basic Smoothie Base

SERVES 2

Bananas and silken tofu provide a one-two punch of fiber and protein
and give smoothies dairy-free richness. For thicker smoothies, add more ice cubes
or freeze your fresh fruit before blending it.

1 ripe banana

1/2 cup soft silken tofu (4 oz.),
drained

2 Tbs. pure maple syrup

6 ice cubes

Place banana, tofu, maple syrup, and
ice in blender with one of the ingredient combinations below, and process
until smooth. Pour into 2 glasses, and
serve.

PER SERVING: 220 CAL; 6 G PROT; 2 G TOTAL FAT
(0 G SAT FAT); 46 G CARB; 0 MG CHOL; 15 MG SOD;
2 G FIBER; 34 G SUGARS

Take Five

Whip up a different smoothie every weekday morning with these fresh add-in ideas
that go with our Basic Smoothie Base.

QUICK & EASY Add 1 cup fruit juice
of choice and ½ cup fresh or frozen
fruit.

BRIGHT-EYED & BERRY-LACED Add
1 cup pomegranate-blueberry juice
and ½ cup frozen strawberries.

RAZZLE-DAZZLE RASPBERRY Add 1
cup orange juice, ½ cup frozen raspberries, and 2 tsp. lime juice.

TROPICAL TREAT Add ¾ cup mango
juice, ½ cup frozen peaches, ¼ cup
mango sorbet, and 2 Tbs. lime juice.

CRANTASTIC CREATION Omit syrup
from base and add ¾ cup cranberry
juice, ½ cup frozen cranberries, and
¼ cup plus 2 Tbs. cranberry juice
concentrate.

Prep Talk: Freezing Bananas

Prefreeze peeled bananas in resealable
plastic bags, and break into chunks
before blending into smoothies that are
thick and rich, not watery.

Frozen Hot Chocolate Smoothie

SERVES 4

Doesn't a chocolate milkshake sound good for breakfast? How about one
that tastes like hot chocolate? Here's a recipe you can sip on guilt-free.
The creamy, chocolaty concoction is rich in potassium (from the bananas),
calcium (from the soymilk), and magnesium (from the cocoa), three minerals
that strengthen brain function and reduce fatigue for a superhealthy
start to a busy day.

2 ripe bananas, peeled and frozen

2 cups chocolate soymilk

8 ice cubes

1 tsp. unsweetened cocoa powder

½ tsp. ground cinnamon

Place all ingredients in blender, and
blend until smooth. Pour into 4 tall
glasses, and serve.

PER SERVING: 126 CAL; 3 G PROT; 2 G TOTAL FAT
(0.5 G SAT FAT), 25 G CARB; 0 MG CHOL; 38 MG SOD;
2 G FIBER; 17 G SUGARS

....

Success Secret: Dutch-Processed Cocoa Powder

....

For smoothies, Dutch-processed or alkalized cocoa powder is the best choice
because of its smooth taste (it has been treated with an alkali to neutralize the natural
acids in cocoa) and easy dissolvability. Natural cocoa powder will also work,
but its flavor can be bitter and chalky when used raw in recipes.

Avocado Frappé Smoothie

SERVES 1

In the Philippines, this pale green drink is made with sweetened
condensed milk, but soymilk and a little brown sugar work just as well.
Make it for breakfast, have it as a postworkout refresher, or multiply
the recipe and blend a batch for a sweet, cool snack after a day at the beach.

¼ ripe medium avocado

3 Tbs. packed light brown sugar

¾ cup unsweetened plain soymilk

4 ice cubes

2 tsp. fresh lime juice

Place all ingredients in blender, and
blend until smooth. Pour into tall
glass, and serve.

PER SERVING: 313 CAL; 7 G PROT; 12 G TOTAL FAT
(2 G SAT FAT); 48 G CARB; 0 MG CHOL; 121 MG SOD;
2 G FIBER; ‹1 G SUGARS

Shopping Savvy: Avocados

When buying avocados for creamy recipes like guacamole or this smoothie, pick small,
nubbly Hass avocados that have ripened to a blackish-brown and give slightly
when gently squeezed. Smooth-skinned avocado varieties like Fuerte have a firmer
texture that makes them better used as slices or cubes.

Chai Cooler Smoothie

SERVES 2

You just can't beat those prepared chai drinks for rich spicy flavor,
but the sugary sweetness is a bit overpowering (not to mention high in calories).
The solution? This smoothie dilutes the prepared mix with banana
and plain soymilk. We've done the measuring for perfect proportions
so that you don't have to guess.

¾ cup prepared chai mix, chilled

¾ cup unsweetened plain soymilk,
chilled

½ ripe banana, sliced and frozen

Place all ingredients in blender,
and blend until smooth. Pour into
2 glasses and serve.

PER SERVING: 117 CAL; 4 G PROT; 2 G TOTAL FAT
(0 G SAT FAT); 20 G CARB; 0 MG CHOL; 81 MG SOD;
1 G FIBER; 14 G SUGARS

Sorrel Drink

Bright and spicy, this ruby-hued drink is a Jamaican favorite. Red hibiscus flowers, also called sorrel or flor de Jamaica, can be found in Caribbean groceries. They are a common ingredient in herbal tea bags, such as Celestial Seasonings' Red Zinger, which will also work in this recipe.

SORREL DRINK

3 cups dried sorrel or dried red hibiscus flowers, or 5 Red Zinger tea bags

1 4-inch cinnamon stick

10 whole cloves

¼ tsp. crushed allspice

2 3-inch pieces peeled fresh ginger

SIMPLE SYRUP

1 cup sugar

1 cup water

1. To make Sorrel Drink: Bring all ingredients and 4 cups water to a boil in saucepan. Reduce heat to medium-low, and simmer 10 minutes. Cool, strain, and chill.

2. To make Simple Syrup: Bring sugar and water to a boil in small saucepan. Stir to dissolve sugar, and simmer 1 minute. Cool.

3. Pour drink over ice. Serve with pitcher of simple syrup for guests to sweeten drinks to taste.

PER SERVING: 33 CAL; 0 G PROT; 0 G TOTAL FAT (0 G SAT FAT); 8 G CARB; 0 MG CHOL; 0 MG SOD; 0 G FIBER; 8 G SUGARS

Homemade Ginger Ale

MAKES 4 CUPS SYRUP TO SERVE 8

You haven't tasted ginger ale until you've had a glass of this brew . . .
you'll never go back to the canned stuff again! The fresh ginger adds zip
without being too spicy. And besides being totally irresistible,
it's super-simple to make and keeps up to 2 weeks in the fridge.

2 cups packed light brown sugar

8 oz. fresh ginger, cut into ¼-inch
thick rounds

1 cinnamon stick

Pinch of cayenne pepper

Sparkling water

1. Bring sugar, ginger, cinnamon stick, and 2 cups water to a boil in large saucepan. Simmer 5 minutes, then remove from heat, and stir in cayenne pepper. Let cool.

2. Strain liquid into small pitcher, and discard ginger and cinnamon. Cover, and refrigerate until ready to use.

3. To serve: Ladle ½ cup ginger syrup into tumbler filled with ice. Top with ¾ cup sparkling water, and stir.

PER SERVING: 103 CAL; 0 G PROT; 0 G TOTAL FAT
(0 G SAT FAT); 27 G CARB; 0 MG CHOL; 12 MG SOD;
0 G FIBER; 25 G SUGARS

. . . .

Shopping Savvy: Fresh Ginger

. . . .

Look for fresh gingerroot with skin that is pale brown and smooth, not dried or wrinkly—
older, dried-out ginger can be stringy.

Watermelon Slushies (for Grown-Ups)

SERVES 4

The next time you buy a big watermelon, cut half into chunks and freeze so you can whip up these cocktails at a moment's notice.

1 small seedless watermelon, cubed (about 4 cups)

½ cup vodka

¼ cup fresh lime juice

¼ cup confectioners' sugar

1. Place watermelon cubes in shallow baking dish. Freeze 4 hours, or until solid. Transfer frozen cubes to resealable plastic bag if making ahead.

2. Blend frozen watermelon cubes, vodka, lime juice, and sugar in blender until smooth. Pour into 4 glasses, and serve immediately.

PER SERVING: 143 CAL; 1 G PROT; 0.5 G TOTAL FAT (0 G SAT FAT); 20 G CARB; 0 MG CHOL; 2 MG SOD; 1 G FIBER; 17 G SUGARS

Shopping Savvy: Watermelons

There's nothing like a perfectly sweet, juicy watermelon on a hot summer day... and nothing more disappointing when you slice into a fruit that's tasteless and mealy. To make sure the watermelon you choose is ripe and ready, look for a pale, ripening spot on one side, which means the fruit was allowed to ripen fully in the field.

Three Citrus Basil Cocktail

SERVES 6

Got a bounty of fresh basil in your garden? Try this refreshing summer cocktail made with a sweet syrup infused with fresh basil sprigs. We've called for gin, but you could also use rum, tequila, or vodka. Or, for a nonalcoholic option, substitute seltzer water for the gin.

⅔ cup sugar

4 large sprigs basil (½ cup firmly packed), plus more for garnish

⅔ cup fresh lime juice

⅓ cup fresh lemon juice (1 large lemon)

⅓ cup fresh orange juice (1 small orange)

2 Tbs. frozen raspberries

1 cup gin

1. Bring sugar and ⅓ cup water to a simmer in saucepan. Stir in basil, and remove from heat. Let steep 30 minutes.

2. Pour lime juice, lemon juice, orange juice, and raspberries into blender. Strain basil syrup into blender, pressing on basil leaves. Blend until smooth, and strain into pitcher. Stir in gin.

3. Divide among 6 glasses filled with ice, and garnish with basil sprigs.

PER SERVING: 213 CAL; 1 G PROT; 0 G TOTAL FAT (0 G SAT FAT); 27 G CARB; 0 MG CHOL; 1 MG SOD; 1 G FIBER; 24 G SUGARS

....

Prep Talk: Double and Simple Syrups

Double syrups, made by simmering two parts sugar to one part water, are often used to make cocktails because they sweeten them without diluting the alcohol. Simple syrup, made from one part sugar and one part water, has a less concentrated sweetness—it's used to sweeten nonalcoholic beverages like coffee, tea, Sorrel Drink, and Homemade Ginger Ale.

Dutch-Style Mulled Wine

SERVES 4

Bisschopswijn, a hot mulled wine flavored with oranges, cinnamon, and cloves, is served during the holidays in the Netherlands. We've added chamomile tea to the traditional recipe to help balance the tang that comes from simmering the wine.

12 whole cloves

1 orange, quartered

1 750-ml. bottle full-bodied red wine, such as red Zinfandel

¾ cup sugar

2 cinnamon sticks

1 chamomile tea bag

Orange slices and whole cloves, for garnish

1. Insert 3 cloves into skin of each orange quarter. Place orange quarters, wine, sugar, and cinnamon sticks in large saucepan, and heat until wine is steaming but not boiling. Reduce heat to low, cover, and let steam 30 minutes.

2. Steep tea bag in 1 cup boiling water 5 minutes. Remove tea bag, and stir tea into wine mixture. Serve in cups, garnished with orange slices pierced with cloves.

PER SERVING: 261 CAL; 0 G PROT; 0 G TOTAL FAT (0 G SAT FAT); 44 G CARB; 0 MG CHOL; 6 MG SOD; 0 G FIBER; 40 G SUGARS

Shopping Savvy: Chamomile Tea

All chamomile teas are not created equal—cheaper varieties can taste bitter and grassy rather than sweetly herbal. Buy a high-quality brand, or look for whole chamomile flowers in the bulk section of natural food stores.

Rich and Creamy Eggnog

SERVES 8

Sure, you can buy quarts of soymilk eggnog as soon as Thanksgiving rolls around, but for a real holiday treat, try this thick homemade version. A touch of ground turmeric gives it a creamy color without affecting the flavor.

2 10.5-oz. pkgs. soft silken tofu, drained

16 oz. vanilla soymilk or rice milk

1 Tbs. plus 1 tsp. vanilla extract

¼ cup sugar

2 Tbs. light brown sugar

¼ tsp. ground turmeric

½ to 1 cup rum or brandy, optional

Ground nutmeg, for garnish

Blend tofu, soymilk, vanilla, sugars, and rum, if using, in blender or food processor until smooth. Chill 2 hours, or overnight. Serve sprinkled with nutmeg.

PER SERVING: 110 CAL; 5 G PROT; 3 G TOTAL FAT (½ G SAT FAT); 15 G CARB; 0 MG CHOL; 55 MG SOD; 0 G FIBER; 13 G SUGARS

. . . .

Prep Talk: Eggnog

Eggnog—particularly when it's spiked with alcohol—is one of those drinks that tastes best after a day of rest. The chilling time allows the flavors of the spices to develop and tames the bite of the liquor so that it tastes smooth and rich with just a touch of rum or brandy flavor.

Vegan Wine-Pairing Guide

What's the first thing most people learn about wine pairing? "Red with meat, white with chicken or fish." But what about when the main dish is roasted veggies or a spicy stir-fry?

White or red? There's no wrong answer. Sweetness, acidity, and robustness are better indicators than old-school wine-pairing rules when choosing a wine to go with food. Try sparkling wine with tofu and bean dishes, a dry or full-bodied white wine with pasta. And don't forget rosé. Dry rosés made from traditional red wine grapes, such as Pinot Noir and Syrah, are an easy choice because they go well with a variety of vegetarian dishes and don't overpower the fresh flavors.

Think locally (even when you buy globally). In Europe all the wines and foods grew up together, so look for wines from the same or similar regions as the food you are eating. An herb-laced Mediterranean ragoût will naturally go well with a hearty wine from Spain, Italy, or Southern France. But don't rule out Californian, South African, Australian, or Argentinean options just because your meal is French or Italian. Wines that come from similar climates can match the food just as well.

Pair accordingly A weeknight pasta dish probably doesn't warrant uncorking a pricey vintage. A young table wine won't stand up to a gourmet entrée as well as a more complex wine, even if the table wine is from the right region. And it's harder to appreciate the nuances in an expensive Bordeaux when it's sipped with a quick supper.

Delicate to delicate, and robust to robust Light, fruity wines go best with subtly flavored dishes. Bold-tasting foods pair perfectly with big-flavored wines.

Sweet tempers heat Indian and Thai cuisines have no wine-accompaniment heritage, but that doesn't mean you have to forgo serving wine with your favorite curry or pad thai. The ripe fruit and residual sugars in sweet white wines help tame the heat and bring out the other flavors in spicy dishes. A California Viognier or a German Riesling couldn't be produced much farther away from Mumbai or the River Kwai, but these wine choices will bring out the sweetness of the vegetables in Indian and Asian dishes.

Trust your taste buds Don't overthink your food-wine combinations—and understand the built-in preferences you have—everyone's taste buds are different. Try choosing a different type of wine every time you buy a bottle over the course of a year. Take notes, and the following year you'll know your preferences so well that you won't have to wonder what to buy.

WINE-PAIRING CHEAT SHEET

Entire books are devoted to wine pairing and selection, so there's no way we can fit in all the info they cover. The following list will help you match wines with favorite veg cuisines—and go beyond popular favorites like Merlot and Chardonnay.

Japanese
White: Grüner Veltliner, Riesling

Red: Shiraz, Viognier

Sparkling: Cava, Champagne, Prosecco

Italian
White: Arneis, Côtes du Rhône, Greco di Tufo, Pinot Grigio, Sauvignon Blanc, Verdicchio, Viognier

Red: Barbera, Barolo, Beaujolais, Chianti, Gamay, Nebbiolo

Mexican
White: California Riesling, Chenin Blanc

Red: Châteauneuf-du-Pape, Malbec, Tempranillo, Zinfandel

Thai and Indian
White: Gewürztraminer, Sylvaner, Viognier

Red: Beaujolais, Mourvèdre, Pinot Noir

Eastern Mediterranean (Greek, Israeli, North African, and Lebanese)
White: Chenin Blanc, Roussanne, Verdicchio, Viognier

Red: Pinot Noir, Syrah

Sparkling: Crémant d'Alsace, Crémant de Bourgogne

burgers and sandwiches

Anybody can slap a few ingredients on a bun or between a couple of slices of bread, but when a burger or sandwich has a balance of freshness, flavors, and textures, it's practically an art form. From tasty tartines and paprika-laced pita pockets to comfort food favorites like Reubens and meatloaf sandwiches, with three different homemade veggie burgers thrown into the mix, these offerings are mealtime masterpieces.

White Bean and Watercress Tartines

SERVES 6

A classic Italian combo—white beans, roasted peppers, and watercress—
gets the tartine treatment here, meaning it's turned into an open-face sandwich
that you eat with a knife and fork. If the bean purée seems too thick to spread,
add a couple of tablespoons of water to thin it out when blending.

1 14-oz. can cannellini beans,
rinsed and drained

2 Tbs. fresh lemon juice

1 Tbs. freshly grated lemon zest

2 cloves garlic, peeled

1 ½ cups watercress,
tough stems removed

1 jarred roasted red bell pepper,
drained and thinly sliced

½ small red onion, thinly sliced
(¼ cup)

1 tsp. balsamic vinegar

½ tsp. olive oil

6 thick slices sourdough bread,
walnut bread, or olive bread, toasted

1. Purée beans, lemon juice, lemon
zest, and garlic in blender or food
processor until smooth.

2. Toss together watercress, roasted
red bell pepper, onion, vinegar, and oil
in bowl.

3. Spread each toast slice with 2 Tbs.
cannellini bean mixture. Arrange
watercress mixture on top.

PER SERVING: 193 CAL; 8 G PROT; 1 G TOTAL FAT
(0 G SAT FAT); 37 G CARB; 0 MG CHOL; 438 MG SOD;
4 G FIBER; 2 G SUGARS

Shopping Savvy: Watercress

Watercress may have a robust, peppery
flavor, but its leaves are delicate and
easily torn. Look for fresh watercress
that looks fluffy and full and has leaves
without creases, tears, or holes.
For bargain prices, shop Asian markets
where watercress is sometimes sold in
inexpensive bunches.

Veggie Club Sandwiches

SERVES 4

Classic club sandwiches are meat-laden, mayonnaise-slathered, three-layer creations that contain enough fat and calories for an entire day. Here, veg fillings and a creamy arugula spread lighten the load without compromising flavor.

½ cup vegan mayonnaise

¼ cup chopped arugula

12 slices toasted whole-wheat sourdough bread, divided

1 cup radish sprouts

2 medium tomatoes, sliced ½-inch thick (8 slices)

8 slices low-fat vegan bacon strips, cooked

1 medium avocado, peeled, pitted, and sliced

12 slices vegan smoked chicken

1. Combine mayonnaise and arugula in medium bowl. Spread on 4 slices bread.

2. Divide radish sprouts over spread. Top each with 1 tomato slice and 2 bacon strips. Add a second layer of toast to each sandwich, and top each with 1 more tomato slice, then avocado and chicken. Spread remaining mayonnaise over remaining 4 toast slices, and place over chicken. Secure sandwiches with decorative toothpicks, and cut into 4 triangles.

PER SERVING: 628 CAL; 24 G PROT; 30.5 G TOTAL FAT (3.5 G SAT FAT); 57 G CARB; 0 MG CHOL; 763 MG SOD; 10 G FIBER; 9 G SUGARS

Shopping Savvy: Sprouts

Want to know which sprouts suit your tastes? Check out these flavor profiles.

ALFALFA, CLOVER, QUINOA wispy and sweet with a delicate crunch

ARUGULA, RADISH, BROCCOLI, LEEK, MUSTARD, FENUGREEK tiny and tender with a peppery bite

DRIED BEANS, PEAS, LENTILS crunchy, chewy, with a beanlike quality

PUMPKIN, SUNFLOWER SEEDS slightly nutty and crunchy

BARLEY, BUCKWHEAT starchy and slightly sweet

Paprika Cauliflower Pita Pockets

SERVES 4

Steamed cauliflower has a chewy, meaty texture that makes it a perfect vegetable sandwich filling when you want something hearty but healthy that's delicious hot or cold. Try topping with tomatoes, chopped black olives, and some fresh baby greens.

1 large head cauliflower (2 lb.), cut into bite-size florets

3 Tbs. olive oil

2 Tbs. sweet paprika

½ tsp. ground black pepper

½ tsp. salt

1 small red onion, diced (1 cup)

1 clove garlic, minced (1 tsp.)

½ cup low-sodium vegetable broth

2 Tbs. fresh lemon juice

4 pita bread rounds, halved and warmed

1. Steam cauliflower 7 to 9 minutes, or until tender.

2. Heat oil, paprika, pepper, and salt in nonstick skillet over medium-low heat 2 minutes, or until fragrant, stirring constantly. Add onion and garlic, and sauté 2 minutes more. Stir in broth and cauliflower, and simmer 3 minutes. Remove from heat, and stir in lemon juice. Serve in pita halves.

PER SERVING: 318 CAL; 9 G PROT; 11.5 G TOTAL FAT (1.5 G SAT FAT); 46 G CARB; 0 MG CHOL; 663 MG SOD; 6 G FIBER; 6 G SUGARS

Prep Talk: Fast Florets

To quickly cut a cauliflower head into florets, trim away leaves, cut away the core, then cut through the thick stalks (without cutting into the florets) and pull apart so you have four quarters. Cut thick stem from each quarter— these can be saved for soups or purées— then pull away florets.

Tempeh Reubens

Now here's a sandwich you can really sink your teeth into. Thinly sliced tempeh simmered in a flavorful broth makes a great sandwich "meat" in this deli classic. The seasoned tempeh will keep up to a week in its liquid, so you may want to make a bigger batch to be used in weekday lunches.

TEMPEH

¼ cup Bragg Liquid Aminos

1 small onion, quartered

2 cloves garlic, peeled

1 bay leaf

1 8-oz. pkg. tempeh, thinly sliced

DRESSING

¼ cup vegan mayonnaise

3 Tbs. relish

2 Tbs. ketchup

SANDWICHES

16 slices rye bread

5 oz. vegan Monterey Jack cheese, sliced

2 cups sauerkraut

1. To make Tempeh: Combine liquid aminos, onion, garlic, bay leaf, and 2 cups water in saucepan over medium heat. Add tempeh slices, and bring to a simmer. Reduce heat to medium-low, and simmer 20 minutes. Cover, and let tempeh cool in broth.

2. To make Thousand Island Dressing: Stir together mayonnaise, relish, and ketchup in small bowl.

3. To make Sandwiches: Toast bread. Drain tempeh, and discard liquid, onion, garlic, and bay leaf. Place 3 slices tempeh on 8 bread slices. Top with cheese slices. Broil 3 to 5 minutes, or until cheese has melted. Top each sandwich with ¼ cup sauerkraut. Spread remaining toasted bread slices with dressing. Place tops on sandwiches, and slice in half.

PER SERVING: 276 CAL; 14 G PROT; 9 G TOTAL FAT (1 G SAT FAT); 33 G CARB; 0 MG CHOL; 971 MG SOD; 6 G FIBER; 3 G SUGARS

Meatless "Meatloaf" Sandwiches

MAKES 1 LOAF (8 SLICES)

This meatloaf probably belongs in the entrée section, but it makes such delicious sandwiches that we couldn't resist putting it here. Try it as an open-face sandwich topped with Speedy Red Sauce (p. 307) or Holiday Gravy (p. 308), or make a Dagwood sandwich with a thick slathering of grainy mustard and some pickles.

¼ cup raw walnut pieces

2 medium stalks celery, finely chopped (1 cup)

½ medium onion, finely chopped (¾ cup)

2 green onions, thinly sliced (about ⅓ cup)

2 cloves garlic, minced (2 tsp.)

1 10-oz. pkg. firm tofu, drained

1 12-oz. pkg. soy crumbles

1 ¼ cups quick-cooking oats

3 Tbs. low-sodium soy sauce

2 Tbs. ketchup, plus additional 2 Tbs. for topping

1 Tbs. Dijon mustard

2 tsp. dried parsley, or 2 Tbs. chopped fresh parsley

1 tsp. poultry seasoning

1. Preheat oven to 350°F. Grind walnuts to powder in food processor. Set aside. Coat medium skillet with cooking spray and place over medium heat. Add celery, onion, green onions, and garlic, and sauté 4 to 5 minutes, or until vegetables are tender. Remove from heat, and cool.

2. Mash tofu in bowl. Stir in ground walnuts, vegetables, soy crumbles, oats, soy sauce, ketchup, mustard, parsley, and poultry seasoning. Season with salt and pepper.

3. Coat 9- × 5-inch loaf pan with cooking spray and spoon mixture into pan, lightly packing in. Spread thin layer of ketchup over top of loaf, and bake 55 to 60 minutes, or until toothpick inserted in center comes out clean. Cool, then wrap in plastic wrap and refrigerate until ready to slice for sandwiches.

PER SERVING: 219 CAL; 16 G PROT; 11 G TOTAL FAT (2 G SAT FAT); 16 G CARB; 0 MG CHOL; 613 MG SOD; 5 G FIBER; 3 G SUGARS

Creepy Halloween "Finger" Sandwiches

SERVES 13

For kids and kids at heart, these "fingers" make the perfect light supper on Halloween night. You can also serve them with dipping bowls of blood (ketchup) and green slime (prepared pesto). Try the lentil spread on regular sandwiches throughout the year, too.

1 cup raw walnut pieces

1 ½ cups dried brown lentils, rinsed and picked through

¼ cup low-sodium vegetable broth or water

2 Tbs. olive oil

3 small cloves garlic, peeled

2 tsp. chili powder

2 tsp. fresh lemon juice

1 ½ tsp. ground cumin

1 tsp. salt

8 cups baby spinach, chopped

13 whole-wheat hot dog buns

1 small cucumber, cut into 13 diagonal slices

1 7-oz. jar roasted red bell peppers, drained, cut into thin strips

Low-fat vegan mayonnaise, for decoration, optional

1. Preheat oven to 350°F. Place walnuts on baking sheet, and bake 10 minutes, or until browned and fragrant. Cool.

2. Bring lentils and 4 cups water to a boil in saucepan. Reduce heat, cover, and simmer 40 minutes, or until lentils are tender and most of water is absorbed. Drain.

3. Purée lentils, walnuts, broth, oil, garlic, chili powder, lemon juice, cumin, and salt in food processor. Transfer to bowl, and cool 20 minutes, or until barely warm. Stir in spinach.

4. Spread ⅓ cup lentil mixture inside each hot dog bun. Close bun, and gently squeeze so filling mounds up in long "finger" shape along sides. Place one cucumber slice on end of each bun to resemble fingernail. Place 2 strips roasted red pepper on either side of filling in bun to outline "finger" shape. Draw joints and wrinkles with mayonnaise, if desired.

PER SERVING: 279 CAL; 12 G PROT; 10.5 G TOTAL FAT (1 G SAT FAT); 39 G CARB; 0 MG CHOL; 445 MG SOD; 10 G FIBER; 6 G SUGARS

Pulled "Pork" BBQ Sandwiches

SERVES 6

The sauce in these sandwiches may taste like an old family recipe that
has been simmered for days, but the simple ingredients and short cooking time
make it easy to whip up whenever you have a craving for 'cue.

2 Tbs. olive oil

1 small onion, chopped (1 cup)

12 cloves garlic, minced (¼ cup)

1 15-oz. can tomato sauce

1 Tbs. prepared horseradish

2 tsp. molasses

2 tsp. cider vinegar

1 tsp. freshly grated lemon zest

2 8-oz. pkgs. seitan, shredded

6 sandwich rolls

Deep South Slaw
(p. 79) or Collard Green Coleslaw
(p. 81), for serving, optional

Hot sauce, for serving

1. Heat oil in saucepan over medium
heat. Add onion, and sauté 7 minutes,
or until soft. Add garlic, and cook 1
minute more.

2. Stir in tomato sauce, and cook
3 minutes. Add horseradish,
molasses, vinegar, lemon zest, and
½ cup water, and simmer over low
heat 30 minutes, stirring occasionally.
Fold in seitan.

3. Fill rolls with seitan mixture, and
top with coleslaw, if desired. Serve
with hot sauce.

PER SERVING: 307 CAL; 27 G PROT; 7.5 G TOTAL FAT
(1.5 G SAT FAT); 35 G CARB; 0 MG CHOL; 602 MG SOD;
3 G FIBER; 8 G SUGARS

Prep Talk: Mincing Garlic

To make light work of mincing garlic, invest in a self-cleaning garlic press.
Many models let you skip the step of peeling the garlic and also produce a fine paste,
so your hands won't smell even after you've minced a whole head.

Tempeh-Mushroom Burgers

SERVES 8

The secret ingredient in these patties is grated beet, which keeps them juicy and makes them look like "real" burgers. Crumbled tempeh gives them texture, while a miso-flavored seitan base holds them together.

¼ cup white miso (Japanese soybean paste)

2 8-oz. pkgs. tempeh, grated

3 Tbs. canola oil, divided

½ cup vital wheat gluten

2 Tbs. guar gum

1 portobello mushroom, stem removed and grated (¾ cup)

1 small beet, grated (¾ cup)

1 small onion, grated (½ cup)

1 small carrot, grated (½ cup)

½ cup fresh or frozen corn kernels

½ medium green bell pepper, finely chopped (⅓ cup)

½ medium red bell pepper, finely chopped (⅓ cup)

2 cloves garlic, minced (2 tsp.)

1. Preheat oven to 350°F. Coat baking sheet with cooking spray.

2. Dilute miso in ¼ cup water in bowl. Stir in tempeh and 1 ½ Tbs. oil. Stir in wheat gluten and guar gum.

3. Mound tempeh mixture on prepared baking sheet. Cover with foil, and bake 20 minutes, or until heated through.

4. Heat remaining 1 ½ Tbs. oil in skillet over medium heat. Add mushroom, beet, onion, carrot, corn, bell peppers and garlic. Sauté 10 minutes, or until vegetables are tender.

5. Pulse vegetables and tempeh mixture in food processor 6 or 7 times or until just blended (do not overblend).

6. Shape tempeh mixture into 8 patties. Cover with plastic wrap, and refrigerate 4 hours, or overnight, to blend flavors.

7. Preheat grill to medium. Brush burgers and grill rack with oil. Grill 8 to 10 minutes per side.

PER SERVING: 218 CAL; 20 G PROT; 9 G TOTAL FAT (1.5 G SAT FAT); 14 G CARB; 0 MG CHOL; 259 MG SOD; 6 G FIBER; 3 G SUGARS

Gluten-Free Veggie Burgers

SERVES 4

Simple, speedy, and satisfying, this patty recipe is made with TVP (textured vegetable protein), which can be found in the bulk section of natural food stores. These burgers get their flavor from dulse, dried seaweed flakes that are a good source of B vitamins and iron. For that authentic burger flavor, serve topped with lettuce, tomato, and condiments.

1 cup TVP
(textured vegetable protein)

½ oz. dulse, rinsed and finely chopped

1 Tbs. ground flaxseed

¼ cup ketchup

4 tsp. cornstarch

1 Tbs. horseradish-flavored mustard

2 Tbs. canola oil

4 8-inch corn tortillas, warmed

1. Combine TVP and dulse In large bowl. Add 1 cup boiling water, stir to combine, and set aside. Combine flaxseed and 2 Tbs. hot water in separate bowl. Let stand 5 minutes.

2. Stir flax mixture into TVP mixture. Add ketchup, cornstarch, and mustard.

3. Heat oil in nonstick skillet over medium heat. Using ½-cup measure, scoop and shape 4 patties. Fry 3 to 5 minutes on each side, or until golden and crispy. Serve on corn tortillas.

PER SERVING: 277 CAL; 15 G PROT; 9.5 G TOTAL FAT (0.5 G SAT FAT); 33 G CARB; 0 MG CHOL; 310 MG SOD; 7 G FIBER; 7 G SUGARS

Grilled Portobello Mushroom Burgers

SERVES 6

Portobello mushrooms have been called the steak of the vegetarian world because of their hearty flavor and texture. A marinade made with a medium-bodied red wine makes these mushroom burgers juicy as well as meaty. And unlike other burgers, they're even good cold.

6 large portobello mushrooms, stems and gills removed

2 cups Syrah

2 small shallots, chopped (¼ cup)

1 clove garlic, chopped (1 tsp.)

8 black peppercorns

2 sprigs thyme

6 toasted whole-wheat hamburger buns

Vegan mayonnaise, onions, tomatoes, and arugula, for serving

1. Poke holes all over mushrooms, making sure not to break them. Place in large glass baking dish.

2. Combine wine, shallots, garlic, peppercorns, and thyme in small saucepan, and season with salt. Bring to a boil. Reduce heat to medium-low, and simmer 5 minutes. Pour wine mixture over mushrooms, and stir to coat. Cover, and marinate 2 hours.

3. Preheat grill or broiler. Remove mushrooms from marinade, and discard liquid. Grill mushrooms 5 minutes on each side, or until browned and juicy. Serve on buns with burger fixings.

PER SERVING: 166 CAL; 7 G PROT; 2 G TOTAL FAT (0.5 G SAT FAT); 29 G CARB; 0 MG CHOL; 216 MG SOD; 3 G FIBER; 5 G SUGARS

Shopping Savvy: Portobello Mushrooms

When buying portobello mushrooms, choose mushrooms that are smooth and brown on top with gills that look dry, not wet or sticky. And don't throw out those stems and gills! Use them to make mushroom broth by covering with water and simmering 20 to 30 minutes.

SERVING SUGGESTION

These meaty veggie burgers need bold flavor to bring out their best, so serve them with a fruity white or full-bodied red wine.

Greek-Style Lentil Burgers

SERVES 8

Laced with Mediterranean flavors, these thick, chewy burgers are always a hit at cookouts. Freezing the burgers once they've been shaped makes them hold together on the grill. Serve with Tzatziki Sauce (p. 318)—delicious!

BURGERS

½ cup dried lentils

2 Tbs. olive oil

1 small onion, chopped (about 1 cup)

½ red bell pepper, diced (½ cup)

4 cloves garlic, minced (about 4 tsp.)

1 15-oz. can chickpeas, rinsed and drained

1 cup loosely packed parsley leaves

½ cup pitted kalamata olives

2 large eggs

2 tsp. ground cumin

1 tsp. ground coriander

1 tsp. salt

½ tsp. ground black pepper

1 cup plain breadcrumbs

¾ cup grated carrots

½ tsp. baking powder

1. Cook lentils according to package directions. Drain. Set aside.

2. Heat oil in skillet over medium heat. Add onion and bell pepper, and sauté 7 minutes. Stir in garlic.

3. Blend chickpeas, parsley, olives, eggs, cumin, coriander, salt, and pepper in food processor 2 minutes, or until smooth. Stir chickpea mixture, breadcrumbs, carrots, and baking powder into lentils. Shape into 8 patties. Layer patties between plastic wrap and freeze.

4. Preheat grill to high. Brush frozen patties with oil, and cook 6 minutes on each side. Serve burgers with Tzatziki Sauce.

PER BURGER: 248 CAL; 10 G PROT; 10 G TOTAL FAT (1 G SAT FAT); 30 G CARB; 55 G CHOL; 656 MG SODIUM; 7 G FIBER; 4 G SUGARS

salads

Here's a little insider *Vegetarian Times* secret: our recipes not only need to be delicious, but they also have to be bright and varied. Why? Because for food to look appetizing in magazine photos, it has to "pop" on the page. There needs to be color, contrast, and a combination of shapes and textures so that readers aren't just looking at a big, monochromatic blob—no matter how delicious that blob might be. This visual requirement turns out to be a major taste asset when it comes to salads. The results are innovative, interesting creations like those that follow here.

Greens Glossary

Know your greens,
from arugula to watercress.

ARUGULA, also known as rocket, grows wild in the Mediterranean and in China. The easily cultivated peppery-nutty green has become hugely popular. The more mature leaves are very strongly flavored; enjoy them sautéed. Use the tender leaves in salads.

BELGIAN ENDIVE'S mineral-rich, compact oval heads are members of the chicory family (along with radicchio and escarole) and are grown in the dark so that the leaves remain creamy white. Red endive is a cross between radicchio and Belgian endive.

LIMESTONE LETTUCE, also known as Bibb or Boston lettuce, has mild flavor and tender "buttery" leaves (it's sometimes called butter lettuce). The soft leaves require a delicate touch when handling.

LOLLA ROSA is a bronze lettuce with red edges and frilly and deeply curly leaves. It's described as having a super "lettuce" flavor.

MÂCHE or corn salad has the mildest flavor and the softest texture of any salad green. The leaves form pretty rosettes. It's best eaten very lightly dressed.

MIZUNA or mizuna mustard is an earthy-sweet, mild mustard green. The leaves are delicate and pretty, and it is often planted as an ornamental.

RADICCHIO Deep red purple leaves form compact round heads. One head yields many leaves. The Italian green radicchio adds beautiful color, and a distinctive, slightly bitter flavor to salads.

SPINACH An old favorite that originated in Persia. High in iron and calcium, the tender baby leaves are best for salads. For convenience, buy packages of prewashed baby spinach.

RED MUSTARD or gai choy is an Asian mustard. It has finer foliage than common mustard but has the same spicy flavor. The copper-colored leaves are very pretty in salads.

TATSOI or rosette bok choy is a small, dark green, spoon-shaped leaf. It is related to bok choy. Rich in calcium and vitamins, it's as delicious in stir-fries as it is in salads.

WATERCRESS has a pleasant pungent flavor. It grows wild in streams and lakes and is cultivated as well. Related to mustard, the pretty leaves are good in salads and are often used as garnish.

HERBS with tender, nonoily leaves, such as basil, tarragon, parsley, chervil, dill, and tarragon, make excellent additions to the salad bowl.

SPROUTS, such as mung, pea, broccoli, and sunflower, are another great way to add flavor and texture as well as nutrients.

Salad-Making Tips

PURCHASE For best quality and variety, try to buy your greens directly from growers at farmers' markets. Better yet, cultivate your own. Many seed companies offer seeds for unusual varieties unavailable at the market. Nothing beats the flavor of fresh-picked homegrown salad greens and sprouts.

For convenience or "salad emergencies," keep a bag of prepared salad greens on hand. The prewashed baby spinach leaves are very good quality.

CLEAN Wash greens in cold water. Delicate, sandy greens can be soaked in the sink or a large bowl to remove grit and dirt. Sturdier greens can be washed in a water-filled salad spinner. Compact heads of lettuce such as radicchio and Belgian endive require only a quick rinse.

DRY Invest in a salad spinner to effectively dry greens without bruising them. Dry greens as thoroughly as possible so as not to dilute your dressing. In a pinch, try layering greens between clean kitchen towels and roll lightly.

KEEP Store washed greens wrapped in a clean tea towel or paper towel in a reusable plastic bag or container. Make sure that your refrigerator is not too cold. Lettuce and greens freeze easily and once frozen are ruined. Undressed salads can be kept fresh until serving in a bowl wrapped tightly with plastic wrap and refrigerated.

DRESS Don't ruin a beautiful salad with too much dressing. A light dressing allows the flavors of the salad vegetables to come through. Start with a small amount just to lightly coat the salad. Guests can always drizzle individual salad with more dressing, if desired, after serving.

SERVE Serving salad on chilled plates keeps it cold and adds an elegant touch. Green salads don't keep. Be sure to serve soon after dressing.

Sunshine Spinach Salad

SERVES 6

This crunchy salad looks and tastes special, though it's no harder to put together than a garden-variety tossed salad. Fresh orange juice and orange fans add a dash of sunshine and a dose of vitamin C. If you can't find pepitas (pumpkin seeds), substitute pine nuts or sunflower seeds.

DRESSING

½ cup fresh orange juice

1 large shallot, finely chopped (¼ cup)

3 Tbs. olive oil

2 Tbs. sherry vinegar

2 tsp. Dijon mustard

1 tsp. agave nectar

½ tsp. salt

¼ tsp. ground black pepper

SALAD

3 navel oranges

10 cups baby spinach (9 oz.)

1 ½ cups sliced radishes (1 bunch)

3 medium avocados, peeled, pitted, and sliced

¼ cup toasted hulled pepitas (pumpkin seeds)

1. To make Dressing: Place all ingredients in jar with lid or medium bowl. Shake or whisk to blend.

2. To make Salad: Peel oranges with sharp knife, removing white pith. Quarter and slice into fans. Toss spinach, radishes, and half of dressing in large salad bowl. Top with orange segments and avocados. Drizzle with remaining dressing, and sprinkle with pumpkin seeds.

PER SERVING: 299 CAL; 7 G PROT; 21.5 G TOTAL FAT (3 G SAT FAT); 26 G CARB; 0 MG CHOL; 322 MG SOD; 9 G FIBER; 10 G SUGARS

Shopping Savvy: Shallots

Because the turnover for shallots in most supermarkets is not high, squeeze them before buying to make sure they are firm and dry, not soft. Mushy shallots could be moldy inside or may also have begun to germinate in the bin.

Sugar Snap Pea Salad
with Lemon-Mint Vinaigrette

SERVES 4

Now that sugar snap peas are available year-round in most supermarkets, this salad lets you get a fresh taste of spring even when it's cold outside. To keep the sugar snap peas bright green, toss them with the vinaigrette just before serving.

LEMON-MINT VINAIGRETTE

¼ cup olive oil

3 Tbs. chopped fresh mint

2 Tbs. fresh lemon juice

1 Tbs. minced shallot

1 tsp. Dijon mustard

½ tsp. sugar

SALAD

1 lb. sugar snap peas, trimmed

⅓ cup chopped unsalted pistachios

1. To make Lemon-Mint Vinaigrette: Whisk together all ingredients in small bowl. Set aside.

2. To make Salad: Cook sugar snap peas in boiling water 2 minutes, or until bright green. Drain. Toss peas with 3 Tbs. lemon-mint vinaigrette. Stir in pistachios.

PER SERVING: 169 CAL; 5 G PROT; 12 G TOTAL FAT (1.5 G SAT FAT); 12 G CARB; 0 MG CHOL; 167 MG SOD; 4 G FIBER; 5 G SUGARS

. . . .

Storage Hint: Vinaigrettes

. . . .

Most homemade vinaigrettes and non-cream-based salad dressings will keep for weeks in the fridge, so double the amounts and store in resealable jars. Use as a dip or on salads.

Radicchio, Radish, and Fennel Salad

SERVES 8

This salad is a godsend in winter and early spring, when even the iceberg lettuce looks a little worse for wear in the produce aisle. All its freshness and crunch come from cold-weather salad fixings.

SALAD

½ cup pine nuts

1 large head radicchio (6 oz.), quartered and thinly shredded

6 small radishes, thinly sliced

1 small fennel bulb (6 oz.), trimmed, halved, and thinly sliced

1 large cucumber, sliced into ¼-inch matchsticks

DRESSING

½ cup mint leaves

¼ cup fresh lemon juice

¼ cup olive oil

2 Tbs. pure maple syrup

1 ½ Tbs. Dijon mustard

1. To make Salad: Toast pine nuts in skillet over medium heat 5 minutes, or until golden brown. Transfer to plate to cool.

2. Combine radicchio, radishes, fennel, and cucumber in large bowl.

3. To make Dressing: Purée mint, lemon juice, oil, maple syrup, and mustard in blender until smooth. Season with salt and pepper. Add dressing to salad; toss to coat, and garnish with toasted pine nuts.

PER SERVING: 154 CAL; 2 G PROT; 12.5 G TOTAL FAT (1.5 G SAT FAT); 10 G CARB; 0 MG CHOL; 166 MG SOD; 2 G FIBER; 4 G SUGARS

Spicy Fig and Artichoke Salad

SERVES 6

Savor fresh figs with a sweet-and-spicy salad that makes a perfect light meal.

SALAD

1 Tbs. plus 1 tsp. olive oil, divided

1 small red onion, thinly sliced (1 cup)

3 cloves garlic, thinly sliced

1 6.5-oz. jar marinated artichoke
hearts, rinsed, drained,
and halved lengthwise

1 jarred roasted red bell pepper,
drained and thinly sliced

¼ tsp. chili powder

2 bunches watercress,
tough stems removed

10 fresh figs, trimmed and halved

½ cup chopped pecans

2 green onions, thinly sliced (¼ cup)

DRESSING

¼ cup olive oil

3 Tbs. fresh lime juice

2 tsp. red wine vinegar

2 tsp. brown rice syrup

1. To make Salad: Heat 1 tsp. oil in skillet over medium heat. Add onion and garlic, and sauté 2 minutes. Add pinch of salt, and sauté 1 minute more. Stir in artichoke hearts and red pepper, and sauté 2 minutes, or until heated through. Transfer to bowl.

2. Heat remaining 1 Tbs. oil and chili powder in same skillet over medium heat, stirring to combine. Lay figs cut-side down in oil, and cook 2 minutes. Transfer to plate.

3. To make Dressing: Whisk together oil, lime juice, vinegar, and rice syrup. Season with salt and pepper.

4. Place watercress on platter. Top with artichoke mixture, and drizzle with 3 Tbs. dressing. Add figs, sprinkle with pecans and green onions, and pass remaining dressing.

PER SERVING: 224 CAL; 2 G PROT; 14.5 G TOTAL FAT
(1.5 G SAT FAT); 24 G CARB; 0 MG CHOL; 240 MG SOD;
5 G FIBER; 9 G SUGARS

Italian Garden Salad
with Artichokes and Fava Beans

SERVES 6

Mention fava beans and fresh artichokes to a foodie and the wistful look
he or she gets is all the explanation you need for how wonderful this salad is.
Frozen artichoke hearts and fava beans will also work in this recipe
when the veggies are no longer in season.

VINAIGRETTE

¼ cup fresh lemon juice

¼ cup olive oil

½ cup finely chopped red onion

2 Tbs. chopped fresh rosemary

3 cloves garlic, minced (1 Tbs.)

SALAD

1 cup fava beans

16 baby artichokes, trimmed and
halved

½ lemon

1 medium red bell pepper, chopped
(1 cup)

1 small fennel bulb (6 oz.), trimmed
and thinly sliced

1 cup halved red grape tomatoes

¼ cup pine nuts

1. To make Vinaigrette: Whisk together lemon juice and oil in bowl. Whisk
in onion, rosemary, and garlic. Season
with salt and pepper.

2. To make Salad: Bring large pot
of salted water to a boil. Add fava
beans, and cook 3 minutes. Remove
with slotted spoon, and rinse under
cold water. Drain, and peel off outer
shells of fava beans. Add artichokes
and lemon half to boiling water.
Simmer 15 minutes, or until tender.
Drain. Add artichokes and fava beans
to vinaigrette in bowl. Stir in bell pepper, fennel, tomatoes, and pine nuts.
Serve warm or at room temperature.

PER SERVING: 223 CAL; 6 G PROT; 13.5 G TOTAL FAT
(1.5 G SAT FAT); 24 G CARB; 0 MG CHOL; 290 MG SOD;
13 G FIBER; 5 G SUGARS

....
Success Secret: Fennel Fronds
....

Save the green, wispy leaves from
the fennel bulb and sprinkle into the
salad for extra flavor.

Taste of Autumn Salad

Beets, fennel, and "bitter" salad greens like watercress and radicchio go together in this composed salad that can be served tossed or spread out on a platter.

CRACKED BLACK PEPPER DRESSING

¼ cup fresh lemon juice

¼ cup olive oil

½ tsp. salt

½ tsp. cracked black pepper

½ tsp. ground fennel seed

SALAD

3 medium beets (8 oz.)

1 Tbs. red wine vinegar or cider vinegar

1 small fennel bulb (6 oz.), trimmed

6 medium oranges

6 cups watercress and/or mixed field greens (6 oz.), coarsely chopped

1 small head radicchio (4 oz.), thinly sliced

½ small red onion, thinly sliced (¼ cup)

16 pitted kalamata olives, halved

1. To make Cracked Black Pepper Dressing: Whisk together all dressing ingredients in bowl or shake in jar.

2. To make Salad: Cook beets in boiling water 20 to 30 minutes, or until easily pierced with knife. Drain and cool. Cut off stem ends, and rub off peel. Cut beets into thin wedges. Toss beets with vinegar in bowl, cover, and chill.

3. Cut fennel in half lengthwise, and thinly slice each half into semicircles. Transfer to separate bowl. Cut peel from oranges, and cut orange sections from pith. Do this over bowl of fennel slices, squeezing extra juice into bowl and adding orange sections. Cover, and chill.

4. Combine greens, radicchio, and onion on large platter. Top with fennel and oranges, then beets and olives. Drizzle 2 to 3 Tbs. dressing over salad. Serve remaining dressing on side.

PER SERVING: 167 CAL; 3 G PROT; 9 G TOTAL FAT (1 G SAT FAT); 21 G CARB; 0 MG CHOL; 332 MG SOD; 5 G FIBER; 12 G SUGARS

Cranberry-Pecan Salad

SERVES 4

Holiday salads should stay light and simple—like this one—so they don't clash with the richer foods they're served with. The vinaigrette for this salad is made with unsweetened cranberry juice rather than vinegar for a seasonal twist, but you could also replace the juice with red wine vinegar or lemon juice.

CRANBERRY VINAIGRETTE

2 Tbs. unsweetened cranberry juice

1 Tbs. Dijon mustard

1 Tbs. canola oil

1 Tbs. walnut or hazelnut oil

1 small shallot, finely chopped (2 Tbs.)

SALAD

4 cups arugula

⅔ cup dried cranberries

⅓ cup chopped toasted pecans

1. To make Cranberry Vinaigrette: Whisk together cranberry juice and mustard in small bowl. Whisk in canola and walnut oils until smooth. Stir in shallot, and season with pepper.

2. To make Salad: Toss arugula, cranberries, and pecans with vinaigrette.

PER SERVING: 207 CAL; 2 G PROT; 14.5 G TOTAL FAT (1 G SAT FAT); 21 G CARB; 0 MG CHOL; 242 MG SOD; 2 G FIBER; 15 G SUGARS

Buy and Try: Unsweetened Cranberry Juice

One of the biggest complaints about bottled cranberry juice is the high sugar content: a 1-cup serving contains more than 130 calories, beating out a sugary soft drink! For an easy version that delivers a higher concentration of cranberry juice and a lot less sugar, follow these easy steps:

Mix 1 cup unsweetened cranberry juice with ¼ cup plus 2 Tbs. agave nectar in heatproof, 1-qt. measuring cup. Add a 2-inch cinnamon stick to juice mixture. Stir in 4 cups boiling water. Cool, and enjoy.

Roasted Vegetable Salad

SERVES 6

Planning a cookout? Make room on the grill for some roasted vegetables and you can have this salad ready to go for a meal the next day. The vegetables can also be roasted under the oven broiler. Serve on a bed of salad greens, or use the roasted vegetables to make a hearty, healthy sandwich.

3 Tbs. canola oil

1 serrano chile, seeded and chopped (2 tsp.)

2 cloves garlic, minced (2 tsp.)

1 tsp. minced fresh ginger

1 medium sweet onion, such as Walla Walla or Vidalia, sliced (1 ½ cups)

1 medium red bell pepper, sliced (1 ½ cups)

1 medium eggplant (12 oz.), sliced lengthwise

1 medium yellow squash (8 oz.), sliced lengthwise

3 medium portobello mushroom caps (8 oz.), gills removed

¼ cup coarsely chopped fresh parsley

2 Tbs. fresh lime juice

1. Preheat broiler or grill. Coat baking sheet with cooking spray, if broiling. Combine oil, serrano chile, garlic, and ginger in large bowl. Season with salt and pepper. Add onion, bell pepper, eggplant, squash, and mushroom caps; toss to coat.

2. Place vegetables on prepared baking sheet or grill, and broil or grill 8 to 12 minutes, or until cooked through, turning once. Transfer to platter or bowl.

3. Sprinkle vegetables with parsley and lime juice, and season with salt and pepper.

PER SERVING: 118 CAL; 3 G PROT; 7.5 G TOTAL FAT (0.5 G SAT FAT); 13 G CARB; 0 MG CHOL; 396 MG SOD; 4 G FIBER; 5 G SUGARS

Prep Talk: Serrano Chiles

Can't find serrano chiles? Jalapeño chiles will also work, as will ½ teaspoon red pepper flakes.

Pita Panzanella

SERVES 4

Panzanella is an Italian bread salad that's traditionally made with cubed bread, basil, and tomatoes. Here, the concept gets a cold-weather makeover that calls for frozen veggies and pita bread tossed in a light, lemony dressing.

PANZANELLA

2 Tbs. olive oil

2 whole wheat pita bread rounds, each cut into 8 triangles

4 cups frozen artichoke hearts

1 ½ cups frozen shelled fava beans

1 ½ cups frozen peas

LEMON-MINT DRESSING

¼ cup olive oil

¼ cup chopped fresh mint

2 Tbs. fresh lemon juice

4 tsp. freshly grated lemon zest

2 cloves garlic, minced (2 tsp.)

1. To make the Panzanella: Heat oil in skillet over high heat. Add pita triangles, and toast 1 minute on each side, or until slightly brown and crisp.

2. Place artichoke hearts in glass dish, cover with plastic wrap, and microwave on high power 4 to 5 minutes, stirring halfway through. Drain, and place in bowl. Microwave fava beans in same glass dish, covered with plastic wrap, on high power 5 to 7 minutes, stirring halfway through. Drain, and add to artichokes. Microwave peas in same glass dish on high power, 3 to 4 minutes, stirring midway. Drain, and add to artichokes and fava beans.

3. To make Lemon-Mint Dressing: Whisk together all ingredients in bowl. Season with salt and pepper. Add dressing and toasted pita triangles to artichoke mixture, and toss to coat. Let stand 5 minutes before serving.

PER SERVING: 472 CAL; 17 G PROT; 22.5 G TOTAL FAT (3.5 G SAT FAT); 57 G CARB; 0 MG CHOL; 365 MG SOD; 19 G FIBER; 7 G SUGARS

....

Storage Hint: Stale Bread

Got leftover bread that's lost the softness it needs to be sandwich-worthy? Put it in a resealable plastic bag and place in the freezer for future use in salads.

Corn and Mung Bean Salad

SERVES 6

In Asian cuisines, mung beans are used whole, ground into flour, or sprouted for bean sprouts. Their texture is similar to black-eyed peas, and their pale green color is a nice addition to salads like this one.

1 cup dried mung beans, rinsed and picked through

1 ½ cups fresh corn kernels or 1 cup frozen corn kernels, thawed

1 bunch green onions, finely chopped (½ cup)

¼ cup fresh lime juice

¼ cup plain gomashio

1. Soak beans in bowl of cold water 5 hours, or overnight.

2. Drain beans. Place them in saucepan, and cover with cold water. Bring to a boil. Reduce heat to medium-low, and simmer 15 to 20 minutes, or until beans are soft but not mushy. Drain and rinse under cold water.

3. Transfer to bowl. Stir in corn, green onions, lime juice, and gomashio. Season with salt and pepper. Chill before serving.

PER SERVING: 166 CAL; 7 G PROT; 3 G TOTAL FAT (1 G SAT FAT); 25 G CARB; 0 MG CHOL; 341 MG SOD; 7 G FIBER; 3 G SUGARS

Buy and Try: Gomashio

Gomashio, the Japanese seasoning made of seaweed, sesame seeds, and salt, can be sprinkled on soup, rice, omelets—even popcorn! Or use it to season salads and vegetable dishes.

Sea Palm Salad

SERVES 8

Looking for something surprising, savory, and authentically Asian
to serve with a stir-fry? This salad is the ticket. A fine-strand seaweed,
sea palm adds taste and crunch to salads.

1 1-oz. pkg. sea palm fronds, rinsed well and drained

2 Tbs. white miso (Japanese soybean paste)

2 Tbs. cider vinegar

1 Tbs. low-sodium soy sauce

1 medium cucumber, peeled, seeded, and sliced

1 cup sliced radishes (12 to 15)

¼ cup finely diced red onion

1. Soak sea palm fronds in large bowl of cold water 30 minutes, or until softened. Drain sea palm fronds Transfer to saucepan, and cover with water. Bring water to a boil, reduce heat to medium, and simmer 20 minutes. Drain, and rinse under cold water.

2. Whisk together miso, vinegar, and soy sauce in large bowl. Add cucumber, radishes, onion, and sea palm fronds, and toss to coat.

PER SERVING: 28 CAL; 2 G PROT; 0 G TOTAL FAT
(0 G SAT FAT); 5 G CARB; 0 MG CHOL; 264 MG SOD;
2 G FIBER; 3 G SUGARS

....

Prep Talk: Sea Palm

....

If you can't find sea palm, try this salad with dulse or cooked, sliced wakame, which are equally delectable sea vegetables.

Mock Green Papaya Salad

SERVES 8

Because green papayas can be hard to find even in Asian grocery stores, this twist on a traditional Thai recipe calls for tart green apples instead.

6 Granny Smith apples, peeled and grated (6 cups)

¼ cup plus 2 Tbs. fresh lime juice, divided

1 bunch green onions, chopped (1 cup)

2 cloves garlic, minced (2 tsp.)

2 tsp. low-sodium soy sauce

1 tsp. sambal oelek (chili paste)

1 cup cherry tomatoes, halved

1 5-oz. bag watercress, tough stems removed, or arugula

1. Toss grated apples with 2 Tbs. lime juice in large bowl to keep from browning. Stir in green onions.

2. Whisk together remaining ¼ cup lime juice, garlic, soy sauce, and chili paste in small bowl. Add to grated apples, and toss to combine. Stir in cherry tomatoes, and serve over watercress.

PER SERVING: 61 CAL; 1 G PROT; 1 G TOTAL FAT (0 G SAT FAT); 16 G CARB; 0 MG CHOL; 64 MG SOD; 2 G FIBER; 11 G SUGARS

Buy and Try: Sambal Oelek

Sambal oelek, a chili paste from Southeast Asia, can be found with the hot sauces in many supermarkets or ordered online. It can be used to add spice to soups, stews, and salad dressings. Or if you and your family like to add hot sauce to your food at the table, put out a jar during meals.

Deep South Slaw

SERVES 8

The key to perfect coleslaw is a creamy base, a hint of sweetness,
a touch of tangy vinegar, and, in the case of Cajun versions, a little kick
from hot sauce or cayenne pepper.

1 small head green cabbage, thinly sliced (4 cups)

2 medium carrots, grated

1 medium red bell pepper, thinly sliced (1 cup)

3 Tbs. vegan mayonnaise

2 Tbs. whole-grain mustard

1 Tbs. cider vinegar

1 Tbs. sugar

½ tsp. salt

¼ tsp. cayenne pepper

½ cup fresh parsley, chopped

1. Combine cabbage, carrots, and bell pepper in large bowl.

2. Whisk together mayonnaise, mustard, vinegar, sugar, salt, and cayenne pepper in small bowl. Pour mayonnaise mixture over cabbage mixture, and toss to coat. Chill well. Sprinkle with parsley before serving.

PER SERVING: 50 CAL; 1 G PROT; 2 G TOTAL FAT (1 G SAT FAT); 7 G CARB; 0 MG CHOL; 299 MG SOD; 2 G FIBER; 3 G SUGARS

....
Prep Talk: Slicing Cabbage
....

To slice cabbage for slaw, cut the cabbage head into quarters, then slice each quarter lengthwise. The layers of leaves will fall away into thin, crunchy strands that hold up to coleslaw dressings.

Collard Green Coleslaw

SERVES 8

The hot dressing poured over this salad slightly wilts the greens without cooking them. Chilling the salad lets the flavors develop. Serve as a side dish, or use instead of lettuce to top vegetarian barbecue. Other greens to try in this recipe: Swiss chard, beet greens, or flat-leaf kale.

8 oz. collard greens, tough stems removed (8 leaves)

3 medium carrots, grated (2 cups)

1 medium onion, grated (1 cup)

1 medium red bell pepper, diced (1 cup)

½ cup rice or cider vinegar

⅓ cup sugar

¼ cup canola oil

1 tsp. powdered mustard

1 tsp. celery seeds

½ tsp. salt

¼ tsp. ground black pepper

1. Stack 3 or 4 collard leaves flat on work surface. Roll tightly into a cylinder, hold together, and thinly slice to make narrow strips. Coarsely chop strips once sliced. Repeat with remaining collard leaves, and transfer to large bowl. Stir in carrots, onion, and bell pepper.

2. Whisk together vinegar, sugar, oil, mustard, celery seeds, salt, and black pepper in small saucepan, and bring to a boil, whisking to dissolve sugar. Remove from heat, and pour hot vinegar mixture over collard and vegetable mixture. Stir to coat vegetables with dressing. Season with salt and black pepper, if desired. Cover, and chill 4 hours or overnight.

PER SERVING: 136 CAL; 1 G PROT; 7 G TOTAL FAT (0.5 G SAT FAT); 17 G CARB; 0 MG CHOL; 172 MG SOD; 2 G FIBER; 12 G SUGARS

Buy and Try: Celery Seeds

Tiny, dark brown celery seeds have a mild, sweet flavor. Use them to season salad dressings, fresh pickles, dips, and sandwich spreads.

Roasted Beets and Parsnips
with Black Olives and Oranges

SERVES 4

Fresh orange slices add a juicy tang to this warm salad that's a light meal when served with creamy polenta. For added color, try using golden beets along with the red ones.

4 medium beets, peeled and diced (3 ½ cups)

4 medium parsnips, peeled and cut into matchsticks (2 cups)

1 small fennel bulb, trimmed and cut into bite-size wedges (¾ cup)

3 Tbs. garlic-infused olive oil, divided

8 cups baby arugula (8 oz.)

2 oranges, peeled and sectioned, each section thinly sliced

½ cup pitted kalamata olives, coarsely chopped

2 Tbs. balsamic vinegar

1. Preheat oven to 450°F. Place beets, parsnips, and fennel in large bowl. Add 2 Tbs. oil, and toss to coat. Season with salt and pepper, if desired, and evenly scatter vegetables on baking sheet. Roast vegetables 20 minutes, turning 2 or 3 times with spatula. Increase oven temperature to 500°F. Roast vegetables 10 minutes more, or until tender.

2. Place arugula, orange slices, and olives in large salad bowl. Add roasted vegetables, balsamic vinegar, and remaining 1 Tbs. oil. Toss well to mix, and season with salt and pepper, if desired.

PER SERVING: 261 CAL; 4 G PROT; 15 G TOTAL FAT (2 G SAT FAT); 31 G CARB; 0 MG CHOL; 461 MG SOD; 7 G FIBER; 16 G SUGARS

....

Buy and Try:
Golden and Candy Cane Beets

....

For showstopping salads, give golden and candy cane beets (a variety with red and white rings) a try. They can be prepared in the same way as red beets and tend to be a bit less sweet.

Beet Green–Tangerine Salad

SERVES 8

Don't throw those leafy beet tops away! Beet greens make buying fresh beets a two-in-one bargain because the leaves look, taste, and can be prepared like Swiss chard. Other greens to try in this recipe: Swiss chard, spinach, or flat-leaf kale.

HORSERADISH-TANGERINE DRESSING

¼ cup olive oil

¼ cup fresh tangerine juice

2 Tbs. cider vinegar

2 Tbs. prepared horseradish

BEET GREEN SALAD

2 large beets, peeled and grated (4 cups)

2 large shallots, chopped (½ cup)

¼ cup dried cranberries

3 cups beet greens, tough stems removed and torn into bite-size pieces

1 bunch watercress, tough stems removed

2 tangerines, peeled, halved, and thinly sliced

¼ cup toasted chopped pecans, for garnish

1. To make Horseradish-Tangerine Dressing: Whisk together oil, tangerine juice, vinegar, and horseradish in small bowl.

2. To make Beet Green Salad: Toss beets, shallots, and cranberries with ⅓ cup dressing in medium bowl. Season with salt and pepper, if desired.

3. Toss beet greens and watercress with remaining dressing in large bowl, and divide among serving plates. Top each serving with ½ cup grated beet mixture and tangerine slices. Sprinkle with pecans.

PER SERVING: 140 CAL; 2 G PROT; 10 G TOTAL FAT (1 G SAT FAT); 14 G CARB; 0 MG CHOL; 146 MG SOD; 3 G FIBER; 9 G SUGARS

Potato and Edamame Salad

SERVES 4

A simple potato salad gets a fresh, protein-packed twist from frozen shelled edamame (soybeans). If you're not a cabbage fan, substitute 2 cups fresh baby spinach—just stir the leaves in at the same time you add the tomatoes.

1 12-oz. pkg. frozen shelled edamame

1 cup finely shredded green cabbage (4 oz.)

16 small red, purple, fingerling, or new potatoes (1 lb.), halved

1 pint cherry tomatoes, halved

¼ cup olive oil

3 Tbs. red wine vinegar

4 cups baby greens

1. Bring pot of lightly salted water to a boil. Blanch edamame 3 minutes in boiling water, then transfer to medium bowl with strainer or slotted spoon. Blanch cabbage in same pot of boiling water 1 minute, and transfer in same bowl.

2. Drop potatoes in boiling water, reduce heat to medium, and cook 10 minutes, or until tender. Drain, and add to edamame mixture. Cool 5 minutes. Stir in tomatoes, and toss with oil and vinegar. Season with salt and pepper, if desired. Serve warm or chilled on a bed of baby greens.

PER SERVING. 351 CAL; 13 G PROT; 2 G TOTAL FAT (17.5 G SAT FAT); 37 G CARB; 0 MG CHOL; 330 MG SOD; 9 G FIBER; 6 G SUGARS

Prep Talk: Cooking Potatoes

If you plan to use several different varieties of potatoes in a salad, be sure to cook each variety separately. Cooking times can vary, and colorful types like purple and red-fleshed potatoes may bleed.

Sweet Potato Salad with Apple and Avocado

SERVES 6

More a meal than a side dish, this potato salad gets its protein from avocado and pumpkin seeds, both good sources of essential fatty acids. Nutrient-rich corn and diced apple give it crunch. Try serving it over a bed of spinach or arugula.

1 lb. sweet potatoes, peeled and cut into ½-inch cubes

1 cup frozen corn

¼ cup raw hulled pepitas (pumpkin seeds)

1 medium red apple, peeled, cored, and diced (1 cup)

½ small onion, finely chopped (½ cup)

¼ cup chopped fresh cilantro

¼ cup fresh lime juice

2 Tbs. olive oil

½ avocado, finely diced

1. Place sweet potatoes in large sauce-pan, and cover with water. Bring to a boil, and cook 3 minutes. Add corn, and cook 1 to 2 minutes more, or until potatoes are tender. Drain in colander and rinse under cold water to cool. Drain well.

2. Toast pumpkin seeds in dry skillet over medium-high heat 3 to 4 minutes, or until seeds begin to pop. Transfer to plate, and cool.

3. Combine apple, onion, cilantro, and lime juice in large bowl. Stir in sweet potatoes, corn, and oil, and season with salt and pepper, if desired. Stir in avocado and toasted pumpkin seeds just before serving.

PER SERVING: 179 CAL; 3 G PROT; 9 G TOTAL FAT (1 G SAT FAT); 23 G CARB; 0 MG CHOL; 117 MG SOD; 4 G FIBER; 8 G SUGARS

Prep Talk: Sweet Potatoes

Some sweet potato varieties brown quickly once cut (like apples), so have a large bowl of water on hand to place cubes or slices in once they're sliced. The water prevents browning.

Roasted Portobello-Potato Salad

SERVES 4

This potato salad comes together quickly when you roast the potatoes and mushrooms at the same time.

1 ½ lb. Yukon gold potatoes, peeled and cut into 1-inch chunks

3 Tbs. olive oil, divided

4 medium portobello mushrooms, stems removed

1 Tbs. sherry vinegar

⅓ cup chopped fresh parsley

2 cloves garlic, minced (2 tsp.)

1 tsp. freshly grated lemon zest

Success Secret: Flavored Oils

A quick drizzle of a flavored oil (truffle, walnut, garlic, etc.) just before serving adds an ultra-elegant touch and will have tasters raving.

1. Preheat oven to 425°F. Coat 2 baking sheets with cooking spray. Toss potatoes with 2 Tbs. oil in bowl, and season with salt and pepper. Transfer to a prepared baking sheet. Place mushrooms stem side up on second baking sheet. Whisk remaining 1 Tbs. oil with vinegar in small bowl, and brush over mushrooms. Season with salt and pepper. Roast mushrooms and potatoes 30 to 35 minutes, or until potatoes are golden and mushrooms are tender. Cool 10 minutes.

2. Slice mushrooms into 1-inch wedges. Toss with potatoes, parsley, garlic, and lemon zest in large bowl. Serve warm or at room temperature.

PER SERVING: 272 CAL; 7 G PROT; 10.5 G TOTAL FAT (1.5 G SAT FAT); 37 G CARB; 0 MG CHOL; 312 MG SOD; 4 G FIBER; 2 G SUGARS

pasta and noodles

What's the dinner most people make when there's not much time to cook? Pasta. The comfort food they crave when they're hungry, tired, or stressed? Pasta. The first meal they turn to when they go vegan or veg? You guessed it. Pasta. But just because pasta (or noodles, if you make the dish Asian) is an easy, anytime, please-everyone option doesn't mean it has to take on a ho-hum, everyday role in your meal rotations. You can make Spaghetti with Sautéed Leeks, White Beans, and Walnuts (p. 90) or Penne with Caramelized Cauliflower (p. 92) in less than half an hour, for example. In fact, most of the pasta and noodle recipes in this chapter can be made in 30 minutes or less. And they're anything but boring.

Spaghetti with Sautéed Leeks, White Beans, and Walnuts

SERVES 4

This recipe should be labeled "sauce with pasta" because of the generous serving of chunky leek-and-white-bean sauce that is ladled over spaghetti.

1 Tbs. olive oil

3 medium leeks, white and pale green parts only, chopped (6 cups)

1 medium yellow bell pepper, thinly sliced (1 cup)

¼ tsp. red pepper flakes

1 15-oz. can cannellini beans, rinsed and drained

1 cup low-sodium vegetable broth

3 cloves garlic, minced (1 Tbs.)

12 oz. whole-wheat spaghetti

3 oz. crumbled vegan feta cheese (¾ cup), optional

⅓ cup chopped toasted walnuts

1. Heat oil in large saucepan over medium-high heat. Add leeks, bell pepper, and red pepper flakes; sauté 10 minutes, or until vegetables begin to brown. Stir in beans, broth, and garlic. Reduce heat to low, and simmer 5 minutes. Season with salt and pepper, if desired.

2. Meanwhile, cook spaghetti in a large pot of boiling salted water according to package directions until al dente. Drain. Divide spaghetti among 4 bowls or plates. Spoon sauce over each serving of pasta, and sprinkle with feta, if desired, and walnuts.

PER SERVING: 569 CAL; 20 G PROT; 12 G TOTAL FAT (1 G SAT FAT); 103 G CARB; 0 MG CHOL; 524 MG SOD; 19 G FIBER; 11 G SUGARS

Prep Talk: Cleaning Leeks

Leeks can be very sandy and gritty because of the way they grow. To get rid of all the grit from leeks, cut them in half, chop, then dunk the pieces in a large bowl of cold water. Shake the chopped leeks around—the dirt will sink to the bottom of the bowl. Scoop out leek pieces with a strainer, drain, and then use.

Quinoa Fettuccine in Mushroom Broth with Truffle Oil

SERVES 4

Truffle oil adds a luxurious flavor to the rich, brothy sauce that coats slightly nutty-flavored, gluten-free quinoa fettuccine. If you don't have truffle oil on hand, try the recipe with walnut oil or a good-quality olive oil.

1 oz. dried porcini mushrooms (1 cup)

2 Tbs. olive oil

12 oz. shiitake mushrooms, stems removed and thinly sliced

½ cup finely chopped shallots

3 cloves garlic, minced (1 Tbs.)

1 cup dry white wine

½ cup frozen peas

1 Tbs. chopped fresh parsley

3 tsp. truffle oil, divided

8 oz. gluten-free quinoa fettuccine

1. Cover porcini mushrooms with 3 cups boiling water in bowl. Soak 30 minutes. Drain mushrooms; reserve soaking liquid.

2. Heat oil in skillet over medium-high heat. Add shiitake and porcini mushrooms, shallots, and garlic. Sauté 5 minutes. Add wine and porcini soaking liquid, and simmer 10 minutes. Add peas, and simmer 2 minutes more. Stir in parsley and 1 tsp. truffle oil. Season with salt and pepper.

3. Cook fettuccine in large pot of boiling salted water according to package directions. Drain pasta, and toss with mushroom sauce. Drizzle ½ tsp. truffle oil over each serving.

PER SERVING: 379 CAL; 9 G PROT; 13 G TOTAL FAT (1.5 G SAT FAT); 57 G CARB; 0 MG CHOL; 324 MG SOD; 6 G FIBER; 9 G SUGARS

Buy and Try: Truffle Oil

Once you've tasted how even a tiny drizzle of truffle oil can transform pasta or mashed potatoes, you'll be sold. Black truffle oil is slightly less expensive and has a stronger, more pronounced flavor, so you can use less.

SERVING SUGGESTION

Truffle oil demands a light touch when paired with wine. Aim for something fruity and fresh, like a Syrah or a Côtes du Rhône.

Penne with Caramelized Cauliflower

SERVES 6

Tired of tomato sauce with your pasta? This classic Italian recipe is a hearty alternative to spaghetti with marinara. The roasted cauliflower can also be served sans pasta as a delicious side dish.

4 Tbs. olive oil, divided, plus more for greasing baking sheet

1 small head cauliflower (1 lb.), cut into ¼-inch slices

1 cup parsley leaves

1 Tbs. freshly grated lemon zest

1 Tbs. capers, rinsed and drained

1 lb. penne rigate

½ tsp. red pepper flakes

Grated vegan Parmesan cheese, for garnish, optional

Prep Talk: Caramelizing Vegetables

Caramelizing vegetables doesn't mean turning them into dessert. Rather, it refers to what happens when they're cooked over high heat. As the natural sugars in vegetables come out, they brown and "caramelize," adding a depth of flavor and sweetness.

1. Place oven rack in highest position, and preheat oven to 475°F. Grease baking sheet with oil. Toss cauliflower with 2 Tbs. oil on prepared baking sheet. Season with salt and pepper, and spread in single layer. Roast 18 to 20 minutes, or until cauliflower pieces are browned.

2. Meanwhile, pulse parsley, lemon zest, and remaining 2 Tbs. oil in food processor until chunky sauce forms. Add capers, and pulse until capers are coarsely chopped.

3. Cook penne in large pot of boiling salted water according to package directions until al dente. Drain, and reserve ½ cup cooking water. Toss pasta with cauliflower, parsley sauce, and red pepper flakes in large serving bowl, adding reserved cooking water if sauce seems too thick. Sprinkle with Parmesan cheese, if desired.

PER SERVING: 447 CAL; 13 G PROT; 17 G TOTAL FAT (3 G SAT FAT); 59 G CARB; 0 MG CHOL; 212 MG SOD; 3 G FIBER; 5 G SUGARS

Fresh Tomato Farfalle

SERVES 6

Here's a quick pasta recipe that is perfect for summer-ripe beefsteaks
or colorful heirloom tomatoes. A dash of ground cumin gives it a little kick
and chickpeas add protein.

¼ cup fresh lime juice

3 Tbs. olive oil

1 Tbs. freshly grated lime zest

1 tsp. ground cumin

2 lb. tomatoes, cut into bite-size
pieces (5 cups)

1 15-oz. can chickpeas,
rinsed and drained

½ cup torn basil leaves

9 oz. farfalle

1 ¼ cups fresh or frozen corn kernels

1. Combine lime juice, oil, lime zest, and cumin in large bowl. Add tomatoes, chickpeas, and basil, and toss to coat. Set aside.

2. Cook pasta in large pot of boiling salted water according to package directions until al dente. Add corn to pasta water 2 minutes before end of cooking time. Drain, and toss with tomato mixture. Serve warm or at room temperature.

PER SERVING: 362 CAL; 12 G PROT; 9 G TOTAL FAT (1 G SAT FAT); 61 G CARB; 0 MG CHOL; 352 MG SOD; 7 G FIBER; 6 G SUGARS

SERVING SUGGESTION
Fresh tomato sauce equals Chianti, baby! Or at least a no-fuss, inexpensive Italian wine.

Spaghetti with Roasted Broccoli "Pesto"

SERVES 4

Roasting broccoli gives it a rich flavor and causes tiny florets to fall off the stalks, which coat the spaghetti and give it the look of pesto.

3 lb. broccoli, cut into bite-size florets

3 Tbs. olive oil, divided

¼ cup fresh lemon juice

6 cloves garlic, minced (2 Tbs.)

1 Tbs. freshly grated lemon zest

½ tsp. ground black pepper

8 oz. spaghetti

2 Tbs. grated vegan Parmesan cheese, optional

2 Tbs. toasted pine nuts

Success Secret: Gluten-Free Pasta

If you're making this sauce with a gluten-free pasta, we recommend choosing one made with rice, potato, and soy. The sauce is perfect for the delicate texture of soy spaghetti, which must be handled carefully to keep it from breaking.

1. Preheat oven to 450°F. Coat large baking sheet with cooking spray. Toss broccoli and 2 Tbs. oil on baking sheet, and season with salt and pepper. Roast broccoli 35 minutes, or until beginning to brown, turning after 20 minutes.

2. Meanwhile, combine lemon juice, garlic, lemon zest, pepper, and remaining 1 Tbs. oil in large bowl. Cook spaghetti in large pot of boiling salted water according to package directions until al dente. Drain spaghetti, and reserve 1 cup cooking water. Transfer spaghetti to bowl with lemon mixture, and toss to coat.

3. Coarsely chop broccoli, and toss with spaghetti mixture, adding enough reserved cooking liquid to moisten as needed. Season with salt, and sprinkle with Parmesan, if using, and pine nuts.

PER SERVING: 390 CAL; 13 G PROT; 14 G TOTAL FAT (1.5 G SAT FAT); 59 G CARB; 0 MG CHOL; 375 MG SOD; 9 G FIBER; 4 G SUGARS

Fettuccine with Three-Herb Pesto, Black Kale, and Oyster Mushrooms

SERVES 6

Here's a recipe to make after a trip to the farmers' market, where you're likely to find black kale, oyster mushrooms, and small bouquets of fresh herbs. If you can't find the specialty ingredients, curly kale and button mushrooms will also work here.

¾ cup parsley leaves

¼ cup raw walnuts

5 cloves garlic, divided

1 Tbs. thyme leaves, plus 2 large sprigs, divided

1 tsp. finely chopped fresh rosemary, plus 2 large sprigs, divided

4 Tbs. olive oil, divided

8 oz. black kale, coarsely chopped

12 oz. dried tagliatelle or fettuccine

1 ¼ lb. oyster mushrooms, halved

1 large onion, chopped (2 cups)

1 cup low-sodium vegetable broth

1. Blend parsley, walnuts, 3 garlic cloves, thyme leaves, and chopped rosemary in food processor until finely chopped. Add 3 Tbs. oil, and blend until smooth. Set aside.

2. Cook kale in large pot of boiling water 5 minutes, or until tender. Remove kale with large sieve, and drain. Add pasta, remaining 2 garlic cloves, and thyme and rosemary sprigs to boiling water, and cook according to package directions. Reserve 1 cup cooking water, then drain pasta.

3. Meanwhile, heat remaining 1 Tbs. oil in pot over medium-high heat. Add mushrooms and onion, and sauté 12 minutes, or until golden. Add pesto, and sauté 2 minutes. Add broth, and simmer 2 minutes, or until liquid is reduced by half.

4. Add kale and pasta to mushroom mixture, and toss to coat. Stir in reserved cooking water, if desired.

PER SERVING: 391 CAL; 13 G PROT; 13 G TOTAL FAT (2 G SAT FAT); 59 G CARB; 0 MG CHOL; 62 MG SOD; 6 G FIBER; 6 G SUGARS

Success Secret: Pasta Cooking Water

Adding a little of the cooking water for pasta helps stretch a sauce (without piling on extra fat or calories) and keep the noodles moist and delicious.

Orzo with Peas and Asparagus

SERVES 6

Serve this pasta dish hot as a main dish or cold as a salad. Feel free to use any vegetables you have on hand in place of the peas and asparagus—just be sure to cut them into small pieces to blend well with the orzo.

ORZO

8 oz. orzo

2 medium shallots, finely chopped (½ cup)

8 oz. mushrooms, quartered

1 lb. asparagus, trimmed and cut into ½-inch pieces

1 cup frozen peas

½ cup finely chopped toasted walnuts, optional

VINAIGRETTE

3 Tbs. red wine vinegar

2 Tbs. olive oil

2 tsp. whole-grain mustard

1 ½ tsp. brown sugar

1. To make Orzo: Cook pasta according to package directions. Rinse under cold water, and drain.

2. Coat nonstick skillet with cooking spray, and place over medium heat. Add shallots, and cook 3 to 4 minutes. Raise heat to medium-high, add mushrooms, and cook 5 minutes. Add asparagus, and cook 4 minutes more. Stir in peas, season with salt and pepper, and remove from heat.

3. To make Vinaigrette: Whisk together all ingredients in bowl. Stir in pasta. Sprinkle with walnuts, if desired

PER SERVING: 229 CAL; 9 G PROT; 5.5 G TOTAL FAT (1 G SAT FAT); 39 G CARB; 0 MG CHOL; 261 MG SOD; 4 G FIBER; 6 G SUGARS

Buy and Try: Whole-Grain Mustard

Whole-grain mustard has less bite than Dijon or yellow mustard, making it a wonderful addition to salads and sandwiches when you want more delicate flavors to come through.

Stir-Fried Udon with Bok Choy

SERVES 4

Japanese udon are thick, round, chewy noodles that hold up well
in stir-fries and salads. If you can't find udon noodles, replace them
with cooked spaghetti or linguine.

1 8-oz. pkg. udon noodles,
rinsed and drained

2 Tbs. olive oil

3 cloves garlic, thinly sliced

1 tsp. minced fresh ginger

⅛ tsp. red pepper flakes

1 medium carrot, cut into matchsticks
(½ cup)

1 8-oz. pkg. Asian-flavored baked
tofu, cut into matchsticks

1 medium head bok choy, cut into
1-inch pieces (3 cups)

2 tsp. low-sodium soy sauce

2 Tbs. fresh lemon juice

1. Cook udon noodles according to package directions. Drain.

2. Heat oil, garlic, ginger, and red pepper flakes in skillet or wok over medium heat 1 minute. Add carrot, and stir-fry 2 minutes. Add tofu, and stir-fry 1 minute. Add bok choy, and stir-fry 5 minutes, or until greens wilt. Fold in udon noodles and soy sauce, and cook 3 minutes. Sprinkle with lemon juice.

PER SERVING: 406 CAL; 23 G PROT; 14.5 G TOTAL FAT
(2 G SAT FAT); 47 G CARB; 0 MG CHOL; 492 MG SOD;
5 G FIBER; 3 G SUGARS

Prep Talk: Making Matchsticks

To cut carrots into thin matchsticks, start
by cutting each carrot into 2-inch pieces.
Cut each piece into thin slices lengthwise,
then stack slices and cut into matchsticks.

Chilled Noodle Salad with Mango

SERVES 6

This is a twist on the Vietnamese Bun Thit Nuong noodle dish. Rice stick noodles
have a very short cooking time, making them ideal for summery dishes.

DRESSING

½ cup light brown sugar

⅓ cup fresh lime juice

¼ cup low-sodium soy sauce

2 cloves garlic, minced (2 tsp.)

1 red jalapeño chile, finely chopped

SALAD

1 large carrot, cut into thin strips

8 oz. dried rice-stick noodles

1 ½ cups thinly sliced leaf lettuce

½ cup thinly sliced basil leaves

½ cup thinly sliced mint leaves

½ English cucumber, halved
lengthwise, thinly sliced (1 cup)

1 cup bean sprouts

1 green onion, thinly sliced (2 Tbs.)

1 large ripe mango, peeled, pitted,
and thinly sliced (1 cup)

½ cup cilantro leaves

½ cup crushed peanuts, optional

1. To make Dressing: Warm all
ingredients in saucepan over low
heat until sugar dissolves, stirring
occasionally. Cool.

2. To make Salad: Soak noodles in
hot water 15 minutes. Drain, and
set aside.

3. Cook carrot in pot of boiling water
30 seconds. Transfer to colander with
slotted spoon, and rinse under cold
water. Add noodles to water and cook
5 minutes, stirring frequently. Transfer to colander with carrots, and rinse
under cold water. Drain, and chill.

4. Toss noodle mixture with lettuce,
basil, mint, and ½ cup dressing.
Divide among 4 bowls. Top with
cucumber slices, bean sprouts, and
green onion. Arrange mango slices
on top, and drizzle with remaining
dressing. Sprinkle with cilantro and
peanuts, if desired.

PER SERVING: 269 CAL; 6 G PROT; 0.5 TOTAL FAT
(0 G SAT FAT); 62 G CARB; 0 MG CHOL; 359 MG SOD;
3 G FIBER; 26 G SUGARS

Soba Salad with Miso Vinaigrette

SERVES 8

Once the vegetable slicing is done, this dish goes together in no time.
The recipe calls for a colorful carrots and radicchio, but feel free to substitute
cucumber, arugula, sliced zucchini, blanched green beans or any of
your favorite vegetables. We offer a range of amounts for miso in this recipe,
depending on how intense you like the flavor.

8 oz. soba noodles

1–2 Tbs. white miso paste

1 Tbs. toasted sesame oil

1 Tbs. rice vinegar

1 tsp. pickled ginger

2 carrots, cut into matchsticks

1 head radicchio, thinly sliced

2 green onions, chopped

1 ½ sheets toasted nori, cut into thin strips

2 Tbs. toasted sesame seeds

1. Cook soba noodles according to package directions. Rinse under cold water, drain, and place in large bowl.

2. Blend miso, sesame oil, rice vinegar, pickled ginger, and 3 Tbs. water in blender until smooth. Stir carrots, radicchio, green onions, nori, sesame seeds, and miso mixture into soba noodles. Serve cold.

PER SERVING: CALORIES: 151, PROTEIN: 5G, TOTAL FAT: 3.5G, SATURATED FAT: 0.5G, CARBS: 26G, CHOLESTEROL: MG, SODIUM: 164MG, FIBER: 3G, SUGARS: 3G

Shopping Savvy:
Soba Noodles

If you love soba noodles, shop for them at Asian groceries. They are a fraction of the cost they go for at high-end grocery stores and often you have a selection of sizes and flavors.

Vegetable Gyoza and Edamame Succotash

SERVES 4

Here, prepared frozen dumplings, or gyoza, are stir-fried with frozen edamame succotash and topped with a black bean sauce for a spicy main dish. If you can't find edamame succotash in your freezer section, feel free to use any regular frozen succotash.

CHILI-SOY DRESSING

3 Tbs. rice vinegar

1 Tbs. low-sodium soy sauce

1 Tbs. toasted sesame oil

2 tsp. rinsed and chopped dried fermented black beans, or 1 tsp. black bean sauce

1 clove garlic, minced (1 tsp.)

1 tsp. chili oil

GYOZA SUCCOTASH

2 tsp. canola oil, divided

8 frozen vegetable gyoza

1 16-oz. pkg. frozen edamame succotash mix

¼ cup chopped fresh cilantro

2 green onions, chopped (¼ cup)

1. To make Chili-Soy Dressing: Whisk together all ingredients in small bowl.

2. To make Gyoza Succotash: Heat 1 tsp. oil in large nonstick skillet over medium-high heat, and add gyoza. Cook 3 to 4 minutes, or until browned on bottoms. Add ¼ cup water to pan, cover, and cook 3 to 4 minutes more. Transfer gyoza to plate, and pour remaining 1 tsp. oil in pan.

3. Add succotash, and sauté vegetables 5 minutes, or until crisp-tender. Remove pan from heat, and stir in cilantro, green onions, gyoza, and dressing.

PER SERVING: 261 CAL; 11 G PROT; 12 G TOTAL FAT (1 G SAT FAT); 31 G CARB; 0 MG CHOL; 306 MG SOD; 6 G FIBER; 2 G SUGARS

Buy and Try: Gyoza

Gyoza are crescent-shaped Japanese dumplings (sometimes called pot stickers) that can be steamed or pan-fried and are usually served as an appetizer.

Ultimate Vegan Lasagna

This is the cheese-free, noodle-icious, rich and hearty lasagna you've been dreaming of. A blend of tofu and vegan cream cheese makes a creamy substitute for the ricotta usually layered in lasagna, and a homemade tomato sauce pulls everything together.

FILLING

2 tsp. olive oil

2 medium onions, chopped (2 cups)

3 cloves garlic, minced (1 Tbs.)

1 10-oz. bag fresh baby spinach

2 12-oz. pkgs. firm tofu, drained

1 8-oz. pkg. vegan cream cheese

½ cup chopped fresh basil

¼ cup nutritional yeast

LASAGNA

5 ½ cups Speedy Red Sauce (p. 307)

12 uncooked whole-wheat lasagna noodles

12 oz. vegan Italian sausage links, cut into thin rounds, or vegan sausage crumbles, broken apart

1 cup shredded vegan mozzarella cheese (3 oz.)

1. To make Filling: Preheat oven to 375°F. Heat oil in skillet over medium-high heat. Sauté onions and garlic in oil 4 to 5 minutes, or until golden. Add spinach, and cook 2 to 3 minutes, or until wilted. Transfer to bowl of food processor. Add tofu, cream cheese, basil, and nutritional yeast, and blend until smooth. Season with salt and pepper.

2. Spread one-quarter of Speedy Red Sauce on bottom of 13- × 9-inch baking dish. Cover with 4 or 5 noodles, then half of filling, and ladle on another one-quarter of sauce. Repeat layer of noodles and remaining filling. Spread sausage evenly over top, and top with one-quarter of sauce. Finish with final layer of noodles and remaining sauce. Sprinkle with mozzarella. Cover with foil, and bake 30 minutes. Uncover, and bake 15 to 20 minutes more, or until noodles are tender and topping is melted. Let stand 10 minutes before serving.

PER SERVING: 508 CAL; 33 G PROT; 19 G TOTAL FAT (3 G SAT FAT); 60 G CARB; 0 MG CHOL; 817 MG SOD; 13 G FIBER; 10 G SUGARS

rice and whole grains

Saying vegetarians and vegans eat a lot of rice and whole grains is such a cliché—but the stereotype is really something to wear as a badge of honor. Long before omnivores discovered that whole grains were a delicious, filling, and healthy addition to their diet, the veg world was building whole meals around bowls of rice and plates of bulgur. Vegan cuisine has helped turn grain-based recipes into gourmet dishes worthy of high-end eateries. Some, like Forbidden Rice Stove-Top Bibimbap (p. 108), East-West Risotto (p. 112), and Casablanca Quinoa Salad (p. 125) take their inspiration from global cuisines, while others, like Basmati and Wild Rice over Acorn Squash (p. 110) and Twice-Cooked Polenta Wedges with Black-Eyed Pea Salsa (p. 121), are 100 percent American. Serving them—as well as other recipes in this chapter— will do any cook proud.

Confetti Rice Salad

SERVES 6

Seeds, beans, and finely chopped veggies add color and crunch to a rice dish. This is an exceptionally good salad to take on picnics.

1 cup long-grain white rice

1 tsp. cumin seeds

1 clove garlic, lightly crushed

½ tsp. salt

1 small orange bell pepper, finely chopped (1 cup)

1 15-oz. can black beans, rinsed and drained

1 large tomato, chopped (1 ½ cups)

1 cup fresh or frozen corn kernels

⅔ cup chopped green onions (1 bunch)

¼ cup fresh lime juice

3 Tbs. olive oil

½ cup roasted, unsalted sunflower seeds, optional

½ avocado, diced, optional

1. Combine rice, cumin, and 2 cups water in saucepan. Add garlic and salt, cover, and bring to a simmer. Reduce heat to medium-low, and cook 15 minutes, or until rice is tender and most of water is absorbed. Remove from heat, sprinkle bell pepper on top, cover, and cool rice in pan.

2. Transfer rice to large bowl, and remove garlic clove. Stir in beans, tomato, corn, green onions, lime juice, and oil. Season with salt and black pepper. Fold in sunflower seeds and avocado, if desired. Serve at room temperature.

PER SERVING 291 CAL; 8 G PROT; 8 G TOTAL FAT (1 G SAT FAT); 48 G CARB; 0 MG CHOL; 365 MG SOD; 7 G FIBER; 4 G SUGARS

Success Secret: Bell Peppers

By adding the bell pepper pieces to the hot cooked rice in this recipe, it allows you to lightly steam them, making them more tender and easier to digest.

Forbidden Rice Stove-Top Bibimbap

SERVES 8

Bibimbap is a Korean rice dish traditionally served in a hot stone bowl that crisps up the rice on the bottom. Here, you get the same taste and texture by cooking chewy Chinese black or "forbidden" rice in sesame oil in a hot skillet or wok. Once the rice is cooked, it goes together quickly.

1 ½ cups Chinese black rice, rinsed and drained

1 Tbs. plus 1 tsp. sesame oil, plus more for drizzling

1 16-oz. pkg. frozen vegetable blend with edamame

8 green onions, cut into 1-inch lengths (½ cup)

1 cup kimchee, coarsely chopped

....
Buy and Try: Kimchee
....

Kimchee is a Korean pickled cabbage dish that's usually served as a condiment. It can be used in salads, soups, and rice dishes to give them a spicy, tangy kick.

1. Bring rice and 3 cups water to a boil in medium saucepan. Cover, and cook 30 minutes, or until rice has absorbed all water. Remove from heat, and season with salt and pepper, if desired.

2. Heat 1 tsp. oil in wok or large skillet over medium-high heat. Add frozen veggies and green onions, and stir-fry 5 to 6 minutes, or until vegetables are tender and beginning to brown. Stir in kimchee, and cook 2 to 3 minutes more, or until heated through. Transfer to bowl, and season with salt and pepper, if desired. Keep warm.

3. Add remaining 1 Tbs. oil to wok or large skillet. Stir in rice, and cook 5 to 7 minutes, or until rice on bottom begins to crisp and smells nutty, stirring once or twice. Serve vegetable mixture over rice.

PER SERVING: 189 CAL; 7 G PROT; 5 G TOTAL FAT (1 G SAT FAT); 31 G CARB; 0 MG CHOL; 477 MG SOD; 4 G FIBER; 2 G SUGARS

SERVING SUGGESTION
A light, crisp lager beer helps tame the spice and vinegary tang of Korean food.

Guidelines for Choosing Rice

Sure, bulgur is nifty and quinoa is cool, but rice remains our No. 1 grain—
the daily staple for more than half the world's population
(can you imagine Mexican or Chinese food without it?). But with so
many varieties available these days, choosing rice can be a bit daunting.
This guide makes grabbing the right kind as easy as boiling water.

LONG-GRAIN
Cooks up light and fluffy with distinct grains
Try: fragrant jasmine, basmati, Texmati (basmati crossed with American long-grain), and hearty, nutty Wehani
Best in: pilafs, fried rice, Indian recipes, and steamed side dishes

MEDIUM-GRAIN
Shorter and softer than long-grain; sticky when cool
Try: Spanish paella rice and Chinese black or "forbidden" rice
Best in: rice and beans, casseroles, and Mediterranean dishes

SHORT-GRAIN
Soft, creamy and sticky when cooked (chopstick-friendly!)
Try: Arborio or risotto rice, sushi rice, and Bhutanese red rice
Best in: rice pudding, risotto, sushi, and stir-fry sides

Basmati and Wild Rice over Acorn Squash

SERVES 8

This is a fantastic one-dish dinner party entrée.

SQUASH

1 Tbs. olive oil

1 tsp. pure maple syrup

1 tsp. low-sodium soy sauce

¼ tsp. ground cinnamon

2 acorn squash (2 lb.), quartered

RICE

¼ cup pine nuts

1 ½ cups basmati–wild rice mix

1 Tbs. olive oil

1 small red onion, diced (¾ cup)

2 cloves garlic, minced (2 tsp.)

VEGETABLES

2 Tbs. olive oil

1 small fennel bulb, cut into chunks

2 cups baby carrots, halved

2 cups sugar snap peas

1 Tbs. capers, rinsed and drained

⅓ cup chopped fresh parsley

1. To make Squash: Preheat oven to 350°F. Coat baking sheet with cooking spray. Whisk together oil, maple syrup, soy sauce, cinnamon, and 2 Tbs. water in bowl. Brush squash with syrup mixture, and place on prepared baking sheet. Bake 30 to 40 minutes, or until squash is soft.

2. To make Rice: Toast pine nuts in skillet over medium-low heat 3 to 5 minutes. Cook rice according to package directions. Heat oil in skillet over medium heat. Sauté onion and garlic in oil 5 minutes. Stir in rice and pine nuts, and season with salt and pepper.

3. To make Vegetables: Heat oil in Dutch oven over medium heat. Sauté fennel in oil 10 minutes. Add carrots, and sauté 5 minutes more. Add 2 cups water, cover, and steam 10 to 15 minutes. Add peas, and steam 2 to 3 minutes more. Stir in capers.

4. To serve: Place 1 squash wedge on each plate. Spoon rice into center of each squash quarter, and top with vegetables. Sprinkle with parsley.

PER SERVING: 295 CAL; 6 G PROT; 10 G TOTAL FAT (1 G SAT FAT); 47 G CARB; 0 MG CHOL; 313 MG SOD; 6 G FIBER; 8 G SUGARS

East-West Risotto

SERVES 6

Sushi rice is a short-grain starchy rice that works just like Italian Arborio to thicken this Asian-flavored dish. It even tastes good cold as a take-along lunch.

3 Tbs. low-sodium white miso (Japanese soybean paste)

2 Tbs. vegetable oil, divided

3 medium Japanese eggplant (1 lb.), cut into ½-inch dice

1 Tbs. minced fresh ginger

3 cloves garlic, minced (1 Tbs.)

1½ cups short-grain sushi rice

⅔ cup sake or dry white wine

1 lb. baby bok choy, cut into 1-inch pieces

6 green onions, sliced (1 cup), white and light green parts

6 oz. shiitake mushrooms, stems removed and sliced

1¼ tsp. toasted sesame oil

Buy and Try: Japanese Eggplant

Thin, pale violet Japanese eggplant is more tender and has a more delicate flavor than the common deep purple variety. There's no need to salt it—Japanese eggplant rarely tastes bitter.

1. Whisk together miso and 6 cups water in large glass measuring cup. Heat 5 minutes in microwave, or until boiling. Stir well.

2. Heat 1 Tbs. oil in Dutch oven over medium-high heat. Add eggplant, and cook 6 to 8 minutes, or until browned, stirring occasionally. Transfer to bowl.

3. Heat remaining 1 Tbs. oil in same skillet over medium-high heat. Add ginger and garlic, and sauté 30 seconds. Add rice, and cook 2 minutes, stirring constantly. Add sake, and cook 1 to 2 minutes. Add ½ cup miso broth; cook and stir until broth is almost absorbed. Continue adding broth, ½ cup at a time, and cook 8 minutes.

4. Stir in bok choy, and cook 3 to 4 minutes, or until wilted. Add green onions and mushrooms, and cook 10 minutes, adding liquid ½ cup at a time. Stir in eggplant and cook 2 minutes, or until rice is tender. Stir in sesame oil, and season with salt and pepper.

PER SERVING: 325 CAL; 7 G PROT; 6 G TOTAL FAT (1 G SAT FAT); 55 G CARB; 0 MG CHOL; 386 MG SOD; 6 G FIBER; 6 G SUGARS

Butternut Squash Risotto with Pesto

SERVES 6

Most people avoid making risotto because it requires a lot of stirring.
But really, if you do the stirring while you're getting things ready for supper
(stir, pull out the plates, stir, grab the silverware, stir ...), the time flies.

3 cups low-sodium vegetable broth

¼ cup Arugula Pesto (p. 309) or
vegan basil pesto, divided

1 cup chopped fresh or frozen onion

1 ½ cups Arborio rice

3 cups fresh or frozen cubed
butternut squash (1 small squash)

Buy and Try:
Frozen Butternut Squash

Here's a convenience food to add to your
shopping list: cubed butternut squash,
which is now sold fresh or frozen at
supermarkets and natural grocers. The
precut cubes and prepared pesto make
this recipe ideal for busy weeknights or
impromptu dinner parties.

1. Bring broth and 2 cups water to a
boil in large saucepan; turn off heat.

2. Heat 1 Tbs. pesto in saucepan
over medium heat. Add onion, and
sauté 5 minutes. Stir in rice, followed
by ½ cup hot broth. When rice has
absorbed broth, add another ½ cup.
Continue adding broth in this manner
5 minutes.

3. Stir in squash, and season with salt
and pepper. Resume adding broth,
½ cup at a time, until rice has absorbed all liquid. (This should take
about 15 minutes.) Remove from heat,
and stir in 1 Tbs. pesto. Spoon risotto
into 6 plates and top each with 1 tsp.
pesto.

PER SERVING: 290 CAL; 5 G PROT; 16 G TOTAL FAT
(2 G SAT FAT); 33 G CARB; 0 MG CHOL; 78 MG SOD;
4 G FIBER; 4 G SUGARS

Vegetable Paella with Tofu

SERVES 6

Traditional paella pans are round, shallow metal pans that let the
rice and vegetables cook evenly without getting mushy. A wok will do the job
just as well; the wide mouth lets liquid evaporate, so the rice cooks
and the other ingredients steam rather than boil.

2 Tbs. olive oil

2 7-oz. pkgs. spicy marinated tofu, diced

8 oz. cremini mushrooms, sliced

2 large carrots, diced (1 cup)

1 cup fresh or frozen corn kernels

1 14-oz. can chopped tomatoes, drained

4 cloves garlic, minced (4 tsp.)

1 cup short-grain brown rice

⅛ tsp. saffron, crumbled

1 cup fresh or frozen peas, thawed

¼ cup fresh lemon juice

3 green onions, thinly sliced

1. Heat oil in wok over medium-high heat. Add tofu, and season with salt. Sauté 10 minutes, or until tofu is browned. Add mushrooms, and sauté 4 to 5 minutes, or until mushrooms begin to brown.

2. Stir in carrots, corn, tomatoes, and garlic, and sauté 2 minutes more. Stir in rice, 2¼ cups water, and saffron. Bring paella to a boil. Reduce heat to medium-low, cover with wok lid, and simmer 40 minutes, or until all liquid is absorbed. Add peas on surface (do not stir yet), cover, and allow peas to steam 1 to 2 minutes. Remove wok from heat, and stir in lemon juice and green onions. Season with salt and pepper.

PER SERVING: 375 CAL; 22 G PROT; 12.5 G TOTAL FAT (2 G SAT FAT); 45 G CARB; 0 MG CHOL; 569 MG SOD; 6 G FIBER; 5 G SUGARS

Prep Talk: Woks

Pull out that wok for big batches of grain dishes like paella. The sloped sides make it easier to stir and toss without spilling.

SERVING SUGGESTION

Spanish wines are considered a bargain in wine circles, and paella's a good dish to give them a try. Argentinean wines will also go well with paella.

Maki Garden Rolls

SERVES 6

Isn't it great that sushi is no longer synonymous with raw fish? Serve with soy sauce, wasabi, and pickled ginger.

RICE

1 ½ cups short-grain white rice or sushi rice, rinsed and drained

1 Tbs. sake

2 ½ Tbs. rice vinegar

1 ½ tsp. sugar

¾ tsp. coarse salt or kosher salt

FILLING

⅔ cup low-sodium vegetable broth

3 Tbs. low-sodium soy sauce

1 Tbs. mirin (rice wine)

12 green beans, trimmed

1 small carrot, cut into matchsticks

10 medium shiitake mushrooms, stems removed

3 sheets nori seaweed, toasted

3 tsp. toasted sesame seeds

1 cup daikon radish sprouts

1. To make Rice: Bring rice, 1 ⅔ cups water, and sake to a boil in saucepan. Reduce heat to low, cover, and simmer 10 minutes. Cool 10 minutes.

2. Whisk together vinegar, sugar, and salt in bowl. Stir rice into vinegar mixture. Cover with damp cloth, and cool.

3. To make Filling: Bring broth, soy sauce, and mirin to a boil in skillet. Add green beans and carrot, cover, and simmer 6 minutes. Transfer to plate. Add mushrooms, cover, and simmer 4 minutes, turning once. Cool, and slice.

4. Place 1 nori sheet shiny-side down on sushi mat, wax paper, or clean kitchen towel. Spread one-third rice over nori, leaving 1-inch border at top edge. Sprinkle with 1 tsp. sesame seeds. Arrange vegetables on rice. Dampen top edge of nori with water; roll up, and press edge to seal. Repeat with remaining ingredients. Cut rolls into 8 pieces.

PER SERVING (4 PIECES): 275 CAL; 6 G PROT; 2 G TOTAL FAT (0.5 G SAT FAT); 57 G CARB; 0 MG CHOL; 530 MG SOD; 4 G FIBER; 4 G SUGARS

Scattered Brown Rice Sushi Bowls

SERVES 4

Sushi flavor without all the sushi-rolling work! This recipe makes
a beautiful one-bowl meal in the summer when you crave something
cool but filling. Although brown rice rarely makes an appearance
in Japanese cuisine, it offers a nutty, fiber-rich alternative.

SUSHI RICE

1 ⅓ cups short-grain brown rice,
rinsed and drained

1 Tbs. sake

2 ½ Tbs. rice vinegar

1 ½ tsp. sugar

¾ tsp. coarse salt or kosher salt

TOPPING

2 Tbs. low-sodium soy sauce

2 Tbs. toasted sesame oil, divided

¼ tsp. wasabi paste

2 12-oz. pkgs. smoked tofu, drained
and cut into bite-size pieces

2 cups frozen baby peas, thawed

2 cups frozen corn kernels, thawed

2 Tbs. minced pickled ginger

2 green onions, thinly sliced

1. To make Sushi Rice: Bring rice,
1 ⅔ cups water, and sake to a boil in
saucepan. Reduce heat to low, cover,
and simmer 10 minutes. Let rest 10
minutes off heat.

2. Whisk together vinegar, sugar, and
salt in bowl. Transfer rice to large
bowl, and drizzle half of vinegar over
rice, cutting through with wooden
spoon. Continue adding until vinegar
is absorbed. Cover with damp cloth,
and cool.

3. To make Topping: Whisk together
soy sauce, 1 Tbs. water, 1 Tbs. oil, and
wasabi in bowl.

4. Heat remaining 1 Tbs. oil in skillet
over medium heat. Add tofu, and
sauté 5 minutes, or until crisp. To
serve: Pack ¾ cup rice into 4 bowls.
Top with peas, corn, ginger, onions,
and tofu. Drizzle with soy sauce
mixture.

PER SERVING: 617 CAL; 29 G PROT; 19 G TOTAL FAT
(2 G SAT FAT); 80 G CARB; 0 MG CHOL; 852 MG SOD;
8 G FIBER; 7 G SUGARS

Mexican Rice

SERVES 4

Planning a Mexican fiesta? Don't forget the side of rice. This version of Mexican rice goes together quickly and tastes just as good reheated as it does hot out of the pan. For extra protein, stir in a can of rinsed, drained black beans just before serving.

1 Tbs. olive oil

1 cup instant brown rice

1 cup frozen corn

1 cup frozen peas

8 green onions, chopped (½ cup)

3 cloves garlic, minced (1 Tbs.)

1 tsp. ground cumin

½ tsp. dried oregano

2 Tbs. tomato paste

1. Heat oil in saucepan over medium-high heat. Add rice, and sauté 3 to 4 minutes, or until beginning to brown. Add corn, peas, green onions, garlic, cumin, and oregano, and sauté 1 minute.

2. Spoon tomato paste in 2-cup measuring cup. Add enough boiling water to make 2 cups, and stir to combine. Pour tomato paste mixture into rice, and season with salt and pepper. Reduce heat to medium-low, cover, and simmer 15 minutes, or until all liquid is absorbed. Remove from heat, and fluff with fork just before serving.

PER SERVING. 190 CAL; 6 G PROT; 4.5 G TOTAL FAT (0.5 G SAT FAT); 32 G CARB; 0 MG CHOL; 427 MG SOD; 5 G FIBER; 4 G SUGARS

Barley Risotto with Spinach and Tofu

SERVES 6

Barley's taken a back seat to trendier grains like spelt, wheat berries, millet, and kamut, but it's time it got it's place on the stove. The chewy texture and quick cooking time make it an ideal choice for a risotto-style main dish.

3 no-salt-added vegetable bouillon cubes

2 cups quick-cooking barley

2 Tbs. olive oil, divided

3 large shallots, chopped (1 cup)

⅔ cup dry white wine

½ cup oil-packed sun-dried tomatoes, drained and sliced

12 oz. baby spinach (8 cups)

1 8-oz. pkg. baked garlic-herb tofu, cubed

3 Tbs. grated vegan Parmesan cheese

3 Tbs. chopped fresh chives

1. Place bouillon cubes and 6 cups water in large glass measuring cup, and heat in microwave 5 minutes, or until boiling. Stir to combine.

2. Toast barley in skillet over medium-high heat 5 minutes, stirring often. Transfer to bowl.

3. In same skillet, heat 1 Tbs. oil over medium heat. Add shallots, and sauté 4 minutes, stirring often. Return barley to pan and cook 2 minutes, stirring often. Stir in wine, and cook 3 minutes, or until liquid is almost completely absorbed. Add ½ cup bouillon and tomatoes, and cook 4 minutes, or until liquid is absorbed, stirring constantly. Add spinach a few handfuls at a time, and cook until spinach is wilted. Continue adding bouillon ½ cup at a time, and stir and cook 5 minutes, allowing barley to absorb most of liquid before adding more. Stir in tofu, and cook 8 minutes, or until barley is tender. Stir in remaining 1 Tbs. oil, Parmesan, and chives.

PER SERVING: 373 CAL; 18 G PROT; 11.5 G TOTAL FAT (2 G SAT FAT); 54 G CARB; 0 MG CHOL; 366 MG SOD; 9 G FIBER; 2 G SUGARS

Twice-Cooked Polenta Wedges
with Black-Eyed Pea Salsa

SERVES 6

Any Southerner will tell you that on New Year's Day you've got to eat greens and black-eyed peas to have luck in the coming year. Here's a dish that gets them all in. You can make polenta with another Southern classic—yellow cornmeal.

POLENTA

1 large sweet onion, chopped (1 ½ cups)

2 large cloves garlic, peeled

1 cup polenta

1 16-oz. pkg. frozen mixed greens

Chopped fresh cilantro, for garnish, optional

SALSA

4 cups grape tomatoes, halved

2 15-oz. cans black-eyed peas, rinsed and drained

1 large sweet onion, chopped (1 ½ cups)

4 small jalapeño chiles, seeded and chopped

2 cloves garlic, minced (2 tsp.)

⅛ tsp. red pepper flakes

1. To make Polenta: Coat 9-inch pie plate with cooking spray. Steam onion and garlic in steamer basket 10 to 15 minutes, or until soft.

2. Bring 3 cups lightly salted water to a boil. Stir in polenta, and cook 5 minutes, or until thick and creamy, stirring often. Set aside. Cook frozen greens according to package directions. Drain, and squeeze dry.

3. Mash garlic in large bowl; stir in polenta, greens, and onion, and season with salt and pepper. Spread in prepared pie plate. Chill 2 hours, then cut into wedges

4. To make Salsa: Combine all ingredients in bowl.

5. Cut polenta into 6 wedges. Coat skillet with cooking spray. Sauté polenta wedges 3 to 4 minutes on each side, or until crispy at edges. Transfer to plates, and top with salsa. Sprinkle with cilantro, if desired.

PER SERVING: 286 CAL; 14 G PROT; 3.5 G TOTAL FAT (1 G SAT FAT); 52 G CARB; 0 MG CHOL; 555 MG SOD; 11 G FIBER; 8 G SUGARS

Slow Cooker Irish Oatmeal

There's no question that steel-cut oats are superior in flavor to
instant oatmeal, but the extended cooking time, obligatory stirring, and sticky
pot to clean can put off even the most loyal oatmeal enthusiast.
Using a slow cooker eliminates the stove-top surveillance and mess.
Plus, the oatmeal can be kept warm for late risers.

4 cups vanilla soymilk

1 ¾ cups steel-cut oats

½ cup dried cherries or raisins

½ cup plus 3 Tbs. pure maple syrup

½ tsp. salt

¼ tsp. ground allspice

½ cup blueberries, for garnish,
optional

⅓ cup chopped pecans, for garnish,
optional

1. Coat 4-quart slow cooker with cooking spray. Combine soymilk, oats, dried cherries, ½ cup maple syrup, salt, allspice, and 4 cups water in slow cooker. Cook on high 2 to 4 hours.

2. Turn off slow cooker, and stir in 3 Tbs. maple syrup. Add water as necessary to achieve desired thickness. Serve garnished with blueberries and pecans, if desired.

PER SERVING: 290 CAL; 8 G PROT; 5 G TOTAL FAT (0 G SAT FAT); 53 G CARB; 0 MG CHOL; 196 MG SOD; 10 G FIBER; 23 G SUGARS

Shopping Savvy: Steel-Cut Oats

Unlike old-fashioned or quick-cooking oats, which have been presteamed and flattened, Irish or steel-cut oats are rice-shaped oat groats that have been cut into small pieces. They take longer to cook, but their creamy texture is well worth the time.

Casablanca Quinoa Salad

SERVES 4

No, quinoa, a South American grain, is not a North African staple. In this light winter salad it stands in for couscous, adding fiber and protein.

⅓ cup sliced almonds

1 cup quinoa, rinsed

¼ tsp. salt

⅓ cup dried apricots, diced

⅓ cup raisins

⅓ cup fresh orange juice

1 small shallot, finely chopped (2 Tbs.)

2 Tbs. chopped fresh parsley

2 Tbs. chopped fresh cilantro

2 Tbs. chopped fresh mint

1 Tbs. freshly grated orange zest

½ tsp. ground cumin

½ tsp. ground coriander

2 Tbs. olive oil

2 oranges, peeled and sectioned, for garnish

1. Toast almonds 4 to 5 minutes in dry skillet or toaster oven, or until pale brown and fragrant, stirring often.

2. Bring 2 cups water to a boil in medium saucepan. Add quinoa and salt, reduce heat to medium-low, and simmer 15 minutes, or until tender and almost all water is absorbed. Drain, then transfer to large bowl. Toss with apricots and raisins.

3. Whisk together orange juice, shallot, parsley, cilantro, mint, orange zest, cumin, and coriander. Whisk in oil. Pour dressing over quinoa, and toss to coat. Garnish with orange slices and toasted almonds.

PER SERVING: 383 CAL; 9 G PROT; 13.5 G TOTAL FAT (1.5 G SAT FAT); 61 G CARB; 0 MG CHOL; 161 MG SOD; 7 G FIBER; 22 G SUGARS

Success Secret: Rinsing Quinoa

There are many grains you can get away with not rinsing—quinoa isn't one of them. It has a natural coating that can make the cooked grains sticky and bitter if not washed off.

Creamy Breakfast Quinoa with Dried Fruit

SERVES 4

Need a switch from oatmeal in the morning? Try quinoa as a hot cereal.
The complex carbohydrates in quinoa provide sustained energy
throughout the morning. And unlike some brands of oatmeal, there's no risk
of cross-contamination with wheat products.

1 ½ cups vanilla soymilk,
plus more for serving

¼ tsp. salt

1 cup quinoa, rinsed

½ cup dried cranberries,
dried cherries, or raisins

2 Tbs. maple sugar or sugar

1 tsp. ground cinnamon

½ tsp. ground ginger

¼ tsp. ground allspice or
ground cloves

¼ tsp. ground nutmeg

½ cup chopped toasted pecans,
for sprinkling

1. Bring soymilk, salt, and 1 cup water to a boil in saucepan. Stir in quinoa and cranberries, and reduce heat to medium-low. Simmer 15 to 20 minutes, or until liquid is absorbed and grains are tender, stirring occasionally.

2. Remove from heat, and stir in maple sugar, cinnamon, ginger, allspice, and nutmeg. Serve warm, topped with more soymilk and pecans.

PER SERVING: 362 CAL; 10 G PROT; 15 G TOTAL FAT (1 G SAT FAT); 50 G CARB; 0 MG CHOL; 185 MG SOD; 6 G FIBER; 17 G SUGARS

Prep Talk: Sugar and Spice

For fast assembly in the morning, premix a big batch of the sugar and spices, store in a jar, and simply scoop ¼ cup of the mixture to flavor the hot cereal.

Savory Tofu and Vegetables over Tomato Couscous

SERVES 4

Steaming couscous with a can of chopped tomatoes adds flavor and color without any extra work. Top the mixture with a hearty combination of tofu and vegetables and you've got a tasty one-dish supper.

1 6-oz. jar marinated artichoke hearts

1 14-oz. pkg. extra-firm tofu, drained and cubed

1 tsp. ground cumin

1 tsp. ground black pepper, divided

2 Tbs. olive oil

4 medium carrots, thinly sliced (1 ½ cups)

2 medium leeks, white and pale green parts only, thinly sliced (1 ½ cups)

1 14.5-oz. can diced tomatoes

1 cup whole-wheat couscous

2 cloves garlic, minced (2 tsp.)

1. Combine artichokes and liquid, tofu, cumin, and ¾ tsp. pepper in nonstick skillet. Cook over high heat 5 minutes or until liquid evaporates, stirring constantly. Transfer to bowl, and set aside.

2. Heat oil in same skillet over medium-high heat. Add carrots, leeks, and remaining ¼ tsp. pepper. Cook 10 minutes, or until carrots are tender and leeks are lightly browned.

3. Meanwhile, bring tomatoes and liquid and ⅔ cup water to a boil in saucepan. Stir in couscous, cover, and remove from heat. Let stand 5 minutes, then fluff with fork.

4. Add garlic and reserved tofu mixture to vegetable mixture in skillet. Cook 3 minutes over medium heat, or until heated through and garlic is fragrant. Serve tofu and vegetables over tomato couscous.

PER SERVING: 372 CAL; 18 G PROT; 16 G TOTAL FAT (1.5 G SAT FAT); 47 G CARB; 0 MG CHOL; 310 MG SOD; 10 G FIBER; 9 G SUGARS

Bulgur with Curried Potatoes and Peas

SERVES 6

Most often used to make tabbouleh, a Middle Eastern salad, bulgur is a form of whole wheat that has been precooked, dried, and ground. Curry powders can vary in spiciness, so feel free to use more or less according to your taste.

¾ cup bulgur

2 medium red potatoes, diced (2 cups)

2 Tbs. minced fresh ginger

1 Tbs. red curry powder

1 cup frozen peas

1. Bring 1 ½ cups water to a boil in medium saucepan. Add bulgur; season with salt, if desired. Remove from heat, cover, and let stand 30 minutes.

2. Meanwhile, coat large nonstick skillet with cooking spray. Heat over medium-high heat, and add potatoes. Cook 12 to 13 minutes, or until beginning to brown. Stir in ginger and curry powder, and cook 3 minutes more. Stir in peas, and cook 2 minutes more, or until heated through. Toss potato mixture with bulgur in large serving bowl. Season with salt and pepper, if desired.

PER SERVING: 120 CAL; 5 G PROT; 0.5 G TOTAL FAT (0 G SAT FAT); 26 G CARB; 0 MG CHOL; 264 MG SOD; 6 G FIBER; 2 G SUGARS

Lemony Bulgur with Asparagus and Spinach

SERVES 4

This versatile recipe is easily adapted to showcase vegetables throughout the seasons. Feel free to substitute green beans or sliced zucchini for the asparagus. Serve warm or chilled.

1 cup medium-ground bulgur

¼ cup plus 1 tsp. olive oil, divided

3 cloves garlic, minced (1 Tbs.), divided

1 lb. asparagus, trimmed and cut into ½-inch pieces (2 cups)

1 10-oz. bag baby spinach, coarsely chopped

2 Tbs. fresh lemon juice

1 Tbs. freshly grated lemon zest

⅓ cup chopped raw walnuts

8 basil leaves, thinly sliced

8 mint leaves, thinly sliced

1. Place bulgur in large bowl, and pour 3 cups boiling water over it; cover, and let stand 20 to 30 minutes, or until bulgur is tender. Drain, and set aside.

2. Meanwhile, heat 1 tsp. oil in large skillet over medium heat. Add 2 tsp. garlic, and cook 1 minute. Add asparagus and ½ cup water. Cover, and cook 5 to 6 minutes. Add spinach, and cook 3 to 4 minutes, or until just wilted, tossing occasionally with tongs. Season with salt, if desired.

3. Whisk together remaining ¼ cup oil with lemon juice, lemon zest, and remaining 1 tsp. garlic. Season with salt and pepper, if desired.

4. Fluff bulgur with fork. Fold in spinach mixture. Stir in walnuts, basil, mint, and olive oil mixture.

PER SERVING: 371 CAL; 10 G PROT; 22 G TOTAL FAT (3 G SAT FAT); 41 G CARB; 0 MG CHOL; 425 MG SOD; 13 G FIBER; 2 G SUGARS

Prep Talk: Chiffonade

To thinly slice fresh herbs (also called "chiffonade"), pile several leaves on top of each other, roll tightly into a cylinder, and slice.

Orange Israeli Couscous with Carrots and Raisins

SERVES 6

Technically, couscous may not be a grain, but it has a grainlike texture that's satisfyingly chewy. You can also try substituting vegetable broth or tomato or carrot juice for the orange juice for more savory results.

1 ⅓ cups Israeli couscous

1 cup plus 1 Tbs. no-pulp orange juice

3 medium carrots, grated (1 ½ cups)

½ cup raisins

1 tsp. ground cumin

1. Coat medium saucepan with cooking spray, and heat over medium heat. Add couscous, and toast 4 minutes, or until pale brown, stirring frequently. Add 1 cup orange juice and 1 cup water; season with salt and pepper, if desired; and bring to a boil.

2. Reduce heat to low, cover, and simmer 12 minutes, or until liquid is absorbed. Remove from heat, and steam, covered, 5 minutes. Stir in remaining 1 Tbs. orange juice, carrots, raisins, and cumin. Serve warm or at room temperature.

PER SERVING: 191 CAL; 4 G PROT; 0.5 G TOTAL FAT (0 G SAT FAT); 43 G CARB; 0 MG CHOL; 218 MG SOD; 3 G FIBER; 14 G SUGARs

tofu, tempeh, and seitan

Unless you were raised vegetarian or vegan from infancy or had parents who were really adventurous in the kitchen, there was probably a time you didn't know that tempeh (pronounced TEM-pay) refers to more than a town in Arizona, seitan isn't just a devilish spelling mistake, and tofu doesn't have to be tasteless hippie health food. As you tried recipes with plant-based proteins, you may have mistaken tofu for a cheese substitute, botched an attempt to prepare tempeh (a nubbly soybean cake), or overcooked seitan (pronounced SAY-tan), a meat substitute made from wheat. But like everything, practice makes perfect. The luscious tofu, tempeh, and seitan dishes here open up a world of cooking possibilities—and will give you the confidence to prepare (and pronounce!) these ingredients in mixed company.

Southwestern Tofu Scramble

SERVES 6

Ground turmeric gives this egg-free scramble a golden hue.
Leftovers (if any) make a great sandwich filling. Feel free to adjust the fillings
to your breakfast preferences.

1 medium red bell pepper, diced (1 cup)

1 small carrot, diced (½ cup)

4 green onions, chopped (½ cup)

1 clove garlic, minced (1 tsp.)

½ tsp. ground cumin

¼ tsp. ground turmeric

1 14-oz. pkg. firm tofu, drained and crumbled

½ tsp. hot sauce

2 Tbs. chopped fresh cilantro

Prepared salsa, for garnish

Heat large nonstick skillet over medium heat and coat with cooking spray. Add bell pepper and carrot, and cook 7 minutes, or until just tender. Stir in green onions, garlic, cumin, and turmeric, and cook 1 minute more. Add tofu and hot sauce, and cook 5 minutes, or until heated through and all liquid has cooked off, stirring often. Stir in cilantro, and serve with salsa.

PER SERVING: 113 CAL; 11 G PROT; 6 G TOTAL FAT (1 G SAT FAT); 6 G CARB; 0 MG CHOL; 32 MG SOD; 3 G FIBER; 2 G SUGARS

Success Secret: Hot Sauce

Hot sauce doesn't just add spice to dishes; the tang of the vinegar it's made with also helps highlight other flavors. So the next time a recipe tastes a little blah, try a drop of hot sauce. You'll be amazed at what it can do without tasting, well, hot.

Tofu Frittata with Zucchini and Onion

SERVES 8

Brunch is ready whenever you are with a frittata that can be assembled the night before.

2 Tbs. olive oil

1 small red onion, diced (¾ cup)

2 small carrots, diced (1 cup)

5 green onions, chopped (¾ cup)

1 small zucchini, diced (¾ cup)

1 12-oz. pkg. extra-firm tofu, drained

3 Tbs. grated vegan mozzarella cheese

3 Tbs. low-sodium soy sauce

6 medium plum tomatoes, sliced

Speedy Substitution: Grated Carrots and Zucchini

Not a fan of slicing and dicing? Grate the carrots and zucchini in a food processor or with a box grater, then use in the frittata.

1. Preheat oven to 375°F. Coat 10-inch casserole dish or 24-cup minimuffin tin with cooking spray.

2. Heat oil in skillet over medium heat. Sauté red onion 3 to 4 minutes, or until soft. Add carrots, green onions, and zucchini, and sauté 2 minutes. Season with salt and pepper and cook 5 minutes more, or until vegetables are crisp-tender. Remove from heat.

3. Process tofu, mozzarella, and soy sauce 2 minutes in food processor, or until smooth and thick. Stir tofu mixture into vegetable mixture, and spoon into prepared casserole dish or muffin tin. (Recipe can be made ahead up to this point, and baked the next day.) Arrange tomato slices on top of frittata. Bake 40 to 45 minutes for large frittata, 25 to 30 minutes for mini frittatas, or until top is firm to the touch. Let stand 10 minutes before serving.

PER SERVING: 102 CAL; 6 G PROT; 6.5 G TOTAL FAT (1 G SAT FAT); 7 G CARB; 0 MG CHOL; 547 MG SOD; 2 G FIBER; 3 G SUGARS

Tofu 101

The best way to think of tofu, or bean curd (as it's known in Chinese), is as a kind of soymilk cheese. Soybeans are soaked and cooked in water, then pressed to make a soymilk base. A coagulant is added to the soymilk, which turns it into cottage cheese–like curds. The curds are then pressed and drained to form white cakes—the pressing and draining time determines how firm the resulting tofu will be.

EXTRA-FIRM This dense, sturdy block is the highest in protein, fat, and calcium because it's had more moisture pressed out. Because it holds its shape when sliced or diced, extra-firm tofu is best for sautéing, grilling, or baking.

FIRM Look no further for a nondairy cheese substitute. Firm tofu marinated in your favorite salad dressing makes a great sandwich or casserole filling. Cubes of firm tofu work well in stir-fries, too.

SOFT While you have to have a light touch to keep cubes of soft tofu from turning to crumbles, the tender bean curd is great in tofu scrambles or as a substitute for soft ricotta cheese. Puréed soft tofu has the consistency of sour cream and can be used to replace eggs in baked goods (¼ cup per egg).

SILKEN The coagulant used separates this type of tofu from soft. Melt-in-your-mouth and custardlike, silken tofu can add protein to smoothies and be used to make creamy puddings and dips.

Fiery Tofu with Red Chiles, Orange, and Ginger

SERVES 6

Many store-bought Asian sauces are laden with salt and sugar. The homemade version used to coat the tofu here calls for fresh ingredients and just a touch of reduced-sodium tamari. Serve this savory dish over brown rice.

18 oz. extra-firm tofu, drained and halved lengthwise

⅓ cup fresh orange juice

⅓ cup fresh lime juice

⅓ cup pure maple syrup

6 dried chiles de arbol or Thai bird chiles, divided

4 large cloves garlic, minced (1 Tbs.)

2 Tbs. minced fresh ginger

2 Tbs. freshly grated orange zest

3 tsp. canola oil, divided

1 medium onion, sliced (1 ½ cups)

2 Tbs. chopped fresh cilantro

1 Tbs. low-sodium soy sauce

1. Line plate with paper towels. Place tofu on paper towels, cover with more paper towels, and top with another plate and heavy can. Let drain 15 minutes. Cut into ¼-inch cubes.

2. Meanwhile, blend orange juice, lime juice, maple syrup, 3 chiles, garlic, ginger, and orange zest in bowl.

3. Heat 2 tsp. oil in large nonstick skillet over high heat. Add remaining 3 chiles, and sauté 2 minutes, or until toasted. Transfer to plate. Add tofu to same pan, and sauté 10 minutes, or until golden brown. Transfer to plate with chiles. Add onion and remaining 1 tsp. oil to pan, and sauté 5 minutes, or until onion is golden and beginning to soften. Return tofu and chiles to pan. Stir in chile sauce, cilantro, and soy sauce, and reduce heat to medium. Simmer 20 minutes, or until onion is very tender, liquid evaporates, and sauce coats tofu, stirring occasionally.

PER SERVING: 184 CAL; 10 G PROT; 7 G TOTAL FAT (1 G SAT FAT); 22 G CARB; 0 MG CHOL; 124 MG SOD; 2 G FIBER; 14 G SUGARS

Buy and Try: Chiles de Arbol

Chiles de arbol and Thai bird chiles both have quite a kick, so go sparingly when cooking with them at first. Using them whole lets you control the heat better than with chopped fresh or dried chiles.

Broiled Tofu and Steamed Mustard Greens with Spicy Mango Sauce

SERVES 8

Mustard greens have a peppery flavor that complements the sweet and spicy sauce here, but you could use any steamed greens as the base for this entrée.

2 Tbs. canola oil

1 small onion, quartered and thinly sliced (½ cup)

1 small red bell pepper, coarsely chopped (½ cup)

¾ cup hot mango chutney

1 medium tomato, coarsely chopped (¾ cup)

2 16-oz. pkgs. extra-firm tofu, drained and patted dry

2 12-oz. bunches mustard greens, thick stems removed

Success Secret: Handling Tofu

Tofu is very fragile before it's been cooked, so use a wide spatula to transfer it from work surface to baking pan or skillet.

1. Heat oil in saucepan over medium heat. Add onion and bell pepper, cover, and cook 10 to 15 minutes, stirring occasionally. Stir in mango chutney and tomato. Cover, and simmer 5 minutes more.

2. Preheat oven to broil. Coat baking sheet with cooking spray. Halve each tofu block horizontally to make pieces the size of sandwich bread. Cut each tofu piece into 4 triangles. Brush each triangle on both sides with mango mixture and place on prepared baking sheet. Broil 4 to 5 minutes. Flip and brush with more mango mixture. Broil 4 to 5 minutes more, or until browned.

3. Bring 1 cup water to a boil in large pot. Add mustard greens, cover, and steam 5 to 7 minutes, turning occasionally with tongs.

4. Divide mustard greens among plates. Top each serving with 2 tofu triangles, and drizzle with ¼ cup mango sauce.

PER SERVING: 246 CAL; 14 G PROT; 10 G TOTAL FAT (1 G SAT FAT); 29 G CARB; 0 MG CHOL; 490 MG SOD; 5 G FIBER; 22 G SUGARS

Tofu Cutlets with Cilantro Pesto

These cutlets are a homemade version of baked tofu you find in the supermarkets.

CUTLETS

1 16-oz. pkg. extra-firm tofu, drained

¼ cup low-sodium soy sauce

¼ cup low-sodium vegetable broth

1 Tbs. rice vinegar

1 Tbs. agave nectar

1 Tbs. toasted sesame oil

3 Tbs. nutritional yeast

PESTO

1 cup cilantro leaves

2 slices fresh ginger, peeled

2 Tbs. toasted cashews

1 Tbs. rice vinegar

1 tsp. toasted sesame oil

¼ tsp. salt

1. To make Cutlets: Wrap tofu in clean kitchen towel; press under cutting board. Let stand 2 hours to drain. Unwrap tofu, and cut widthwise into 8 slices. Place slices in single layer in container with lid.

2. Bring soy sauce, vegetable broth, vinegar, agave nectar, and oil to boil in saucepan, then pour mixture over tofu slices. Cover, and refrigerate overnight, turning pieces at least once.

3. Preheat oven to 400°F. Coat baking sheet with cooking spray. Remove tofu slices from marinade, sprinkle with nutritional yeast, and place on prepared baking sheet. Bake 20 minutes, turn slices, and bake 20 minutes more, or until browned.

4. To make Pesto: Pulse cilantro, ginger, and cashews in food processor until finely minced. Add vinegar, oil, and salt. Process until smooth.

5. Crisscross 2 tofu slices on each plate. Top each serving with 1 Tbs. cilantro pesto.

PER SERVING: 206 CAL; 16 G PROT; 11.5 G TOTAL FAT (1.5 G SAT FAT); 11 G CARB; 0 MG CHOL; 561 MG SOD; 3 G FIBER; 4 G SUGARS

Prep Talk: Freezing Tofu

For chewier, meatier cutlets, try freezing the tofu beforehand, then proceed with the draining step.

Tofu Baked with Peanut Sauce

SERVES 6

Plain ol' peanut butter can be turned into a savory African-inspired sauce with the addition of canned tomatoes, hot sauce, and frozen veggies. Serve over brown rice or couscous.

2 12-oz. pkgs. extra-firm tofu, drained and cut into ½-inch-thick slices

1 Tbs. vegetable oil

1 small onion, finely chopped (¾ cup)

½ cup diced canned tomatoes, drained

1 Tbs. tomato paste

1 ½ tsp. chile-garlic sauce

½ tsp. dried thyme

½ cup creamy peanut butter

½ cup frozen okra slices

1. Preheat oven to 350°F. Coat 13- × 9-inch baking dish with cooking spray, and place tofu slices on bottom.

2. Heat oil in saucepan over medium heat. Sauté onion in oil 5 to 7 minutes, or until translucent. Add tomatoes, tomato paste, chile-garlic sauce, and thyme, and sauté 1 to 2 minutes, or until tomato paste begins to darken. Stir in peanut butter, okra, and 1 cup water, and bring to a simmer.

3. Pour peanut sauce over sliced tofu, cover with foil, and bake 5 to 7 minutes. Remove foil, and bake 5 minutes more, or until heated through.

PER SERVING: 269 CAL; 17 G PROT; 20 G TOTAL FAT (3 G SAT FAT); 11 G CARB; 0 MG CHOL; 182 MG SOD; 3 G FIBER; 5 G SUGARS

Prep Talk: Okra Substitution

If you're not an okra fan, substitute frozen cut green beans.

Tofu with Olives and Preserved Lemon

SERVES 4

Today, preserved lemons are available at many grocers and specialty markets, although they are easy to make at home (see opposite page). Add them to spicy stews and soups, and use leftover brine to add a citrus boost to vinaigrettes.

3 Tbs. vegetable oil

1 ½ lb. extra-firm tofu, drained and cut into 1-inch cubes

1 small onion, finely chopped (½ cup)

3 cloves garlic, minced (1 Tbs.)

1 tsp. ground ginger

1 tsp. ground cinnamon

2 cups low-sodium vegetable broth

1 preserved lemon (opposite page)

⅔ cup pitted green olives

3 Tbs. finely chopped fresh parsley

1. Heat oil in large skillet over medium heat. Sear tofu, turning occasionally, until golden and crisp on all sides, about 5 minutes. Remove from pan and drain on paper-towel-lined plate.

2. Sauté onion and garlic in same skillet 2 to 3 minutes, or until onion is soft. Stir in ginger and cinnamon, then add broth and tofu. Cover and simmer 15 to 20 minutes, stirring once.

3. Rinse preserved lemon under cold water, discard pulp, and cut peel into small pieces. Stir into tofu mixture with olives and parsley. Season with salt and pepper.

PER SERVING: 315 CAL; 18 G PROT; 22 G TOTAL FAT (2.5 G SAT FAT); 13 G CARB; 0 MG CHOL; 510 MG SOD; 5 G FIBER; 3 G SUGARS

Success Secret: Searing Tofu

Be patient when searing tofu cubes and give it a chance (2 to 3 minutes) to brown before turning. This helps prevent the tofu from falling apart or crumbling when you turn it.

SERVING SUGGESTION
Reach for rosé when serving Moroccan and North African dishes like this one. Its light, fresh flavor (and low alcohol content) lets the flavors of the vegetables shine through.

Preserved Lemons

MAKES 5 LEMONS

Use preserved lemons to season soups, stews, North African dishes like couscous or tagines, Greek dishes, and roasted vegetables.

5 organic lemons, washed and dried

⅔ cup salt, divided

2 Tbs. fresh lemon juice

5 whole cardamom pods

1 bay leaf

1 or 2 dried red chiles

Success Secret: Preserved Lemons as Gifts

Preserved lemons are pricey. Double or triple this recipe to make gourmet gifts to share at holiday time.

1. Stand each lemon on end and slice vertically into 4 wedges, but leave base of lemon uncut. Fill each lemon with 1 Tbs. salt, and place in 1-qt. glass jar with lid.

2. Cover lemons with 2 cups boiling water. Add remaining salt, lemon juice, cardamom pods, bay leaf, and chiles.

3. Seal jar tightly, shake to mix, and store a minimum of 3 days (though 1 month is better) before using.

PER LEMON: 26 CAL; <1 G PROT; 0 G TOTAL FAT (0 G SAT FAT); 9 G CARB; 0 MG CHOL; 472 MG SOD; 4 G FIBER; 2 G SUGARS

Crispy Tofu Hearts

We heart tofu—and tofu hearts you, too! Oven-fried tofu hearts with a homemade vegetable topping make a cute entrée for Valentine's Day. Or, you can use different-shaped cookie cutters to suit any occasion.

STEW

1 Tbs. olive oil

1 medium onion, chopped (1 cup)

3 cloves garlic, minced (1 Tbs.)

2 medium red bell peppers, chopped (2 cups)

1 medium eggplant, chopped (2 cups)

2 cups low-sodium vegetable broth

1 Tbs. red wine vinegar

½ cup basil leaves, cut into strips

TOFU HEARTS

½ cup polenta or coarse yellow cornmeal

1 tsp. dried Italian seasoning

½ tsp. red pepper flakes

2 12-oz. pkgs. extra-firm tofu, drained and sliced in half lengthwise

1 Tbs. olive oil

1. **To make Stew:** Heat oil in skillet over medium heat. Add onion and garlic, and sauté 7 minutes. Add bell peppers, eggplant, broth, vinegar, and 2 cups water. Cover, reduce heat to medium-low, and simmer 1 hour.

2. **To make Tofu Hearts:** Preheat oven to 400°F. Combine polenta, Italian seasoning, and red pepper flakes on plate. Coat baking dish with cooking spray. Cut each tofu half with heart-shaped cutter, and brush with oil. Dredge in polenta mixture. Transfer to prepared baking dish. Bake 30 minutes, or until browned. Stir basil into stew, and spoon onto plates. Set tofu hearts on top.

PER SERVING: 332 CAL; 18 G PROT; 16.5 G TOTAL FAT (2 G SAT FAT); 32 G CARB; 0 MG CHOL; 562 MG SOD; 6 G FIBER; 9 G SUGARS

Storage Hint: Leftover Tofu

Wrap any extra tofu in plastic wrap or return to its original packaging and cover with water, then refrigerate for up to 2 days. For longer storage, freeze the tofu wrapped in plastic wrap.

Chilled Tofu Salad with Ginger, Green Onions, Asparagus, and Sesame

SERVES 4

The combination of cool, custardy tofu with a tart sesame vinaigrette makes for a refreshing low-fat lunch. Feel free to substitute other diced steamed vegetables, such as zucchini, snap peas, or green beans, for the asparagus.

VINAIGRETTE

4 Tbs. low-sodium soy sauce

3 Tbs. mirin (rice wine)

2 Tbs. seasoned rice vinegar

½ tsp. toasted sesame oil

¼ tsp. chili oil

TOFU SALAD

12 oz. asparagus, trimmed

20 oz. silken tofu, drained and cut into 2-inch squares (8 squares total)

2 green onions, minced (¼ cup)

2 tsp. grated fresh ginger

3 Tbs. toasted sesame seeds

1. To make Vinaigrette: Combine all ingredients in small bowl, and stir to combine. Set aside.

2. To make Tofu Salad: Place asparagus in microwave-safe dish with ¼ cup water; cook on high 45 to 60 seconds, or until crisp-tender. Rinse asparagus under cold water, drain, and wrap in paper towels to dry. Slice into ¼-inch coins. Divide asparagus among 4 shallow bowls.

3. Center 2 pieces tofu atop asparagus in each bowl. Mound green onions and ginger atop tofu, and sprinkle sesame seeds over each dish. Drizzle 2 Tbs. vinaigrette around tofu.

PER SERVING: 185 CAL; 10 G PROT; 8 G TOTAL FAT (0.5 G SAT FAT); 15 G CARB; 0 MG CHOL; 759 MG SOD; 1 G FIBER; 10 G SUGARS

Prep Talk: Grating Ginger

To grate fresh ginger, peel a piece with a vegetable peeler or the side of a spoon, then grate on the smallest holes of a box grater. Better still, use a Microplane zester or a ceramic ginger grater (available in Asian stores for about $5). Use the fine pulp, and discard any stringy fibers.

Barbecued Tofu and Corn Salad
with Cilantro Vinaigrette

SERVES 6

This hearty salad offers all the flavor of a backyard barbecue even when you're miles from the nearest grill.

CILANTRO VINAIGRETTE

1 cup cilantro leaves

½ cup vegetable oil

¼ cup fresh lime juice

¼ cup fresh orange juice

1 Tbs. agave nectar

2 cloves garlic, minced (2 tsp.)

Dash hot sauce

SALAD

1 16-oz. pkg. extra-firm tofu, drained and cut into ½-inch-thick slices

½ cup prepared barbecue sauce

1 cup fresh or frozen corn kernels, thawed

1 cup canned pinto beans, rinsed and drained

⅓ cup diced red bell pepper

¼ cup finely diced red onion

1 medium head romaine lettuce, torn (4 cups)

1. To make Cilantro Vinaigrette: Place all ingredients in blender, and process until smooth. Season with salt and black pepper.

2. To make Salad: Heat grill pan or skillet over medium-high heat. Brush tofu with barbecue sauce, and grill or sear 3 to 4 minutes per side. Cool, and cut into squares.

3. Toss tofu, corn, beans, bell pepper, and onion with vinaigrette in large plastic container. Place lettuce in large bowl. Toss lettuce with tofu mixture just before serving.

PER SERVING: 351 CAL; 10 G PROT; 23 G TOTAL FAT (2 G SAT FAT); 27 G CARB; 0 MG CHOL; 379 MG SOD; 4 G FIBER; 13 G SUGARS

Prep Talk: Cilantro Substitution

Don't like cilantro? (Some people find its flavor to be soapy.) Substitute fresh parsley or basil. The flavor will be different (but that's what you want), but the recipe can stay the same.

Grilled Sesame-Tofu Skewers
with Ginger Peanut Sauce

As a party appetizer or a cookout entrée, these easy-to-make skewers can't be beat because they can be passed around and eaten without utensils.

½ cup fresh orange juice

4 Tbs. low-sodium soy sauce, divided

1 Tbs. toasted sesame oil

2 cloves garlic, minced (2 tsp.), divided

½ tsp. red pepper flakes

1 12-oz. pkg. extra-firm smoked tofu, cut into 16 cubes

¼ cup creamy peanut butter

3 Tbs. grated fresh ginger

2 Tbs. light brown sugar

Prep Talk: Toothpick Skewers

Instead of threading the barbecued tofu onto skewers, spear it onto soaked toothpicks, and broil as directed.

1. Combine orange juice, 2 Tbs. soy sauce, sesame oil, 1 tsp. garlic, and red pepper flakes. Let stand 15 minutes at room temperature. Stir in tofu, cover, and marinate 1 hour or overnight, stirring occasionally.

2. Soak 16 wood skewers in cold water 30 minutes. Preheat grill or oven broiler. If using broiler, coat broiler pan with cooking spray. Drain tofu, and thread on skewers. Place on broiler pan, if using. Grill or broil 5 to 7 minutes, or until lightly browned on all sides, turning occasionally.

3. Whisk together peanut butter, remaining 1 tsp. garlic, ginger, sugar, remaining 2 Tbs. soy sauce, and ⅓ cup warm water to make thick sauce. Serve skewers with dipping sauce.

PER SERVING: 121 CAL; 7 G PROT; 7 G TOTAL FAT (1 G SAT FAT); 8 G CARB; 0 MG CHOL; 245 MG SOD; 1 G FIBER; 4 G SUGARS

Tempeh 101

Tempeh is an Indonesian staple made from partially cooked, fermented soybeans that are pressed into cakes. Made with minimal processing and just four ingredients—soybeans, rice (or another grain), water and a fermenting agent— the nubbly, nutty-flavored ingredient is essentially a whole food. With some brands containing up to 12 grams of fiber per serving, tempeh can be an excellent source of fiber along with being the perfect meat substitute to use in stews, turnover fillings and vegan bacon, just to name a few.

HOW IT'S USED Tempeh cakes can be sliced or cubed, then marinated and baked, grilled or deep-fried. You can also crumble tempeh for chili or chop and shape into burgers. For easy slicing, freeze tempeh one hour to chill thoroughly. When the soybean cake is warm, it tends to crumble. To soften tempeh and help it absorb flavors, steam or simmer in a marinade, broth or sauce at least 15 minutes. Unopened packages of tempeh can be refrigerated up to two weeks or frozen up to three months.

LOOK FOR Packaged blocks in refrigerated sections of supermarkets. Tempeh should have few or no black spots, which appear when it is exposed to air. (You can still eat it with spots; the taste will just be stronger.) Flavored tempeh—often fermented with wild rice, vegetables or herbs—is delicious on sandwiches or in recipes where the flavors complement the other ingredients.

Tempeh Bacon

MAKES 24 SLICES

This simple recipe can be assembled the night before and prepared in the morning for a weekend breakfast or brunch. Or use it for a BLT with baby greens and summer-ripe tomatoes. The tempeh strips can be left marinating in the fridge 2 to 3 days. Just be sure to eat the bacon as soon as it's cooked—otherwise, it may lose its crispness.

1 8-oz. pkg. tempeh, sliced into 24 very thin slices

¼ cup low-sodium soy sauce

2 Tbs. apple cider vinegar

1 tsp. light brown sugar

½ tsp. ground cumin

½ tsp. ancho chile powder

2 tsp. liquid smoke, optional

1 Tbs. canola oil

Smoked paprika, optional

Buy and Try: Liquid Smoke

Get a whiff of a bottle of liquid smoke—it smells like a barbecue joint. The all-natural, vinegar-based seasoning can give veg recipes smokehouse flavor without the beef or pork.

1. Lay tempeh slices in 2 13- × 9-inch baking dishes. Bring soy sauce, vinegar, sugar, cumin, ancho chile powder, and ½ cup water to a boil in small saucepan. Boil 1 minute, then remove from heat, and stir in liquid smoke, if using. Pour over tempeh slices. Let cool, then cover and chill 2 hours, or overnight.

2. Preheat oven to 300°F. Line 2 baking sheets with parchment paper. Carefully transfer tempeh slices to prepared baking sheets, and discard marinade.

3. Brush tempeh slices with oil, and sprinkle with paprika, if desired. Bake 10 to 15 minutes, or until beginning to brown. Flip tempeh slices, brush with oil, and bake 5 to 7 minutes more, or until crisp and dark brown.

PER SLICE: 24 CAL; 2 G PROT; 1.5 G TOTAL FAT (0.5 G SAT FAT); 1 G CARB; 0 MG CHOL; 31 MG SOD; <1 G FIBER; 0 G SUGARS

Tempeh Bourguignonne

SERVES 4

Forget beef. Tempeh does the job better when it comes to absorbing all the flavors of this rich, simmered French stew. Serve over rice.

2 cups medium-bodied red wine, such as Pinot Noir

1 8-oz. pkg. tempeh, cut into 1-inch cubes

1 small onion, chopped (1 cup)

1 large carrot, cut into ½-inch dice (1 cup)

3 cloves garlic, chopped (1 Tbs.)

3 Tbs. olive oil, divided

½ tsp. herbes de Provence

1 bay leaf

1 Tbs. balsamic vinegar

2 Tbs. tomato paste

7 oz. sliced shiitake mushrooms (4 cups), stems trimmed

Chopped fresh parsley, for garnish

1. Combine wine, tempeh, onion, carrot, garlic, 1 Tbs. oil, herbes de Provence, and bay leaf in bowl. Cover, and refrigerate 1 hour. Strain and reserve marinade.

2. Heat remaining 2 Tbs. oil in Dutch oven over medium-high heat. Add tempeh and vegetables, and cook 5 to 7 minutes, or until tempeh cubes are browned. Add vinegar, and stir to coat evenly. Add tomato paste, and cook 1 minute. Stir in reserved marinade. Reduce heat to medium low, cover, and simmer 30 minutes, or until carrots are tender. Add mushrooms and ¾ cup water, and simmer 10 minutes, or until tender. Remove bay leaf. Season with salt and pepper. Sprinkle with parsley.

PER SERVING: 269 CAL; 14 G PROT; 13 G TOTAL FAT (2 G SAT FAT); 24 G CARB; 0 MG CHOL; 338 MG SOD; 6 G FIBER; 9 G SUGARS

Prep Talk: Slicing Tempeh

Place tempeh in freezer one hour to chill thouroughly and make slicing and dicing easier. When it is warm, it tends to crumble

Jamaican Tempeh Patties

MAKES 12 PATTIES

Spicy Jamaican patties are savory turnovers filled with a variety of ingredients. Make these for a party—then watch them disappear.

CRUST

3 cups all-purpose flour

1 Tbs. curry powder

¾ tsp. salt

½ tsp. baking powder

4 oz. nonhydrogenated margarine, cut into pieces

FILLING

1 Tbs. canola oil

1 small onion, finely chopped (1 cup)

3 cloves garlic, minced (1 Tbs.)

1 8-oz. pkg. tempeh, crumbled

2 tsp. curry powder

2 tsp. chili powder

1 tsp. dried oregano

1 tsp. dried thyme

½ tsp. ground allspice

¼ cup dark rum, optional

½ cup chopped green onions (8)

1. To make Crust: Combine flour, curry powder, salt, and baking powder in food processor. Add margarine, and pulse until mixture resembles coarse meal. Add ¾ cup cold water; process until dough forms. Wrap in plastic wrap, and refrigerate 1 hour.

2. To make Filling: Heat oil in skillet over medium heat. Add onion, and sauté 7 minutes. Stir in garlic, and cook 30 seconds. Add tempeh, curry powder, chili powder, oregano, thyme, allspice, and 1 ½ cups water. Reduce heat to medium-low, and simmer 15 minutes. Stir in rum, if desired, and cook until liquid has evaporated. Cool, then stir in green onions.

3. Preheat oven to 400°F, and coat baking sheet with cooking spray. Roll out dough to ⅛-inch thickness. Cut into 6-inch circles. Brush edges of circles with water, and place 1 ½ Tbs. filling in centers. Fold circles in half, sealing edges with fork tines. Place on prepared baking sheet, and bake 20 to 25 minutes, or until golden.

PER PATTY: 259 CAL; 7 G PROT; 13 G TOTAL FAT (4.5 G SAT FAT); 28 G CARB; 0 MG CHOL; 328 MG SOD; 2 G FIBER; 1 G SUGARS

Thai Golden Curry

SERVES 8

Coconut milk and fruit are what distinguish Thai curries from their Indian and Asian cousins. Frozen mango cubes can be found in the freezer section of most large supermarkets and work well in this dish if you can't find fresh.

¼ cup olive oil

2 8-oz. pkgs. tempeh, cubed

2 medium red onions, cut into ½-inch dice (1 cup)

2 yellow bell peppers, cut into ½-inch dice (1 cup)

¼ cup minced fresh ginger

2 14-oz. cans light coconut milk

2 large mangoes, peeled, pitted, and cut into ¾-inch cubes, divided (2 cups)

1 cup unsweetened pineapple juice

2 Tbs. curry powder

1 tsp. salt

¼ cup chopped fresh chives, for garnish

4 cups cooked brown rice

1. Heat oil in skillet over medium-high heat. Add tempeh, and cook 1 to 2 minutes per side, or until lightly golden. Transfer to plate.

2. Reduce heat to medium. Add onions and bell peppers to skillet, and sauté 4 minutes, or until softened. Add ginger, and sauté 30 seconds.

3. Stir in coconut milk, 1 cup mangoes, pineapple juice, curry powder, salt, and tempeh. Cover, and bring to a boil. Reduce heat to medium-low, and simmer 5 minutes. Uncover, and simmer 10 minutes more, or until thickened, stirring occasionally. Top with remaining mango cubes and chives, and serve over rice.

PER SERVING: 438 CAL; 15 G PROT; 23 G TOTAL FAT (7.5 G SAT FAT); 46 G CARB; 0 MG CHOL; 310 MG SOD; 4 G FIBER; 11 G SUGARS

Success Secret: Canned Coconut Milk

Shake cans of coconut milk well before opening to reincorporate the thick coconut cream that can rise to the top.

Tempeh Larb

SERVES 8

Crumbly tempeh is a perfect substitute for the minced meat used in Thai larb salads because of its texture and ability to soak up the flavors of the sauce.

LARB

2 8-oz. pkgs. tempeh

2 tsp. fresh minced ginger

¼ cup canola or peanut oil

16 iceberg lettuce leaves

LARB SAUCE

½ cup fresh lime juice

3 Tbs. low-sodium soy sauce

1 ½ tsp. sugar

1 medium red onion, thinly sliced (1 ½ cups)

½ cup chopped fresh cilantro

½ tsp. or more red pepper flakes

2 tsp. minced fresh ginger

16 mint leaves

1. To make Larb: Steam tempeh in steamer 20 minutes. Cool, and cut each block into quarters. Pulse tempeh in blender or food processor until crumbly. Add ginger, and process until combined.

2. Heat oil in large nonstick skillet over medium-high heat. Add tempeh, and cook 8 to 10 minutes, or until golden brown and dry, stirring often.

3. To make Larb Sauce: Combine lime juice, soy sauce, and sugar in large bowl. Add tempeh, onion, cilantro, red pepper flakes, and ginger, and toss to combine. Fill each lettuce leaf with about 2 Tbs. tempeh mixture. Top each with 1 mint leaf, and serve.

PER SERVING: 200 CAL; 12 G PROT; 13.5 G TOTAL FAT (2 G SAT FAT); 12 G CARB; 0 MG CHOL; 504 MG SOD; 1 G FIBER; 4 G SUGARS

Success Secret: Larb Sauce

Use Larb Sauce as a dip for dumplings, summer rolls, and egg rolls, or try as a spicy-sweet salad dressing.

Kung Pao Tempeh Triangles

"Kung Pao" refers to a spicy Szechuan Chinese seasoning for stir-fry dishes.
Serve this easy-to-prepare entrée with stir-fried vegetables
and steamed brown rice or soba noodles.

⅓ cup pure maple syrup

⅓ cup brown rice syrup

⅓ cup low-sodium tamari or
soy sauce

2 Tbs. toasted sesame oil

1 clove garlic, minced (1 tsp.)

1 tsp. red pepper flakes

1 tsp. paprika

½ tsp. minced fresh ginger

½ tsp. chili powder

¼ tsp. cayenne pepper

2 8-oz. pkgs. 5-grain tempeh,
sliced in half widthwise,
each half cut into 4 triangles

1. Whisk together maple syrup, rice syrup, tamari, oil, garlic, red pepper flakes, paprika, ginger, chili powder, cayenne pepper, and 2 Tbs. water in glass baking dish. Arrange tempeh triangles in marinade, and turn to coat. Cover, and marinate in refrigerator 4 hours, or overnight, turning occasionally.

2. Preheat broiler. Line broiler pan with foil. Transfer tempeh pieces to broiler pan, and reserve marinade. Broil tempeh 3 minutes on each side, or until triangles are golden brown and heated through, brushing tops with reserved marinade when turned. Bring remaining marinade to a boil in saucepan. Serve tempeh triangles drizzled with sauce from marinade.

PER SERVING: 476 CAL; 24 G PROT; 19.5 G TOTAL FAT (3.5 G SAT FAT); 56 G CARB; 0 MG CHOL; 985 MG SOD; 1 G FIBER; 31 G SUGARS

Success Secret: Marinated Tempeh

Marinating tempeh before cooking helps moisten and tenderize it in addition to letting it soak in flavor.

Seitan 101

Seitan, sometimes called "wheat meat" originated in China as a Buddhist meat alternative. In fact, most mock meat offerings in vegetarian Chinese restaurants are made using seitan. Seitan is prepared by kneading a dough of high-gluten flour (sold as vital wheat gluten), water and seasonings. The dough is cut into smaller pieces and simmered in liquid for a firm, chewy texture. Because gluten is the insoluble protein component of wheat grains, seitan is high in protein, while remaining low in fat and calories.

HOW IT'S USED Prepared seitan is probably the easiest meat substitute to use as well as the most appealing because its taste and texture are so close to meat. To cook with prepared seitan, give it a quick rinse to remove the high-sodium broth (you don't have to do this with homemade seitan), then pat dry with paper towels. Tear into bite-sized pieces with your hands, pull apart with a fork or cube or slice with a knife. Cook seitan just long enough to heat through; overcooking can make it tough and rubbery.

LOOK FOR Tubs or boxed packages of seitan near or in refrigerated sections of supermarkets. Because seitan has a shorter shelf life than tofu or tempeh, so be sure to check the expiration date if you're planning on buying ahead. You can also make your own seitan using vital wheat gluten, a flourlike product sold in many supermarkets.

Homemade Seitan

MAKES 4 CUPS

Seitan is essentially a dough made with vital wheat gluten, a high-protein wheat flour, and liquid. The dough can be rinsed or poached to become a chewy meat substitute that can be added to many different dishes. We've added light seasonings to this recipe so that it will work in any dish, but feel free to play around with flavors and textures.

2 cups vital wheat gluten

2 Tbs. nutritional yeast

3 cups low-sodium vegetable broth, divided

4 Tbs. reduced-sodium soy sauce, divided

½ small onion

1 clove garlic, crushed

1. Combine vital wheat gluten and nutritional yeast in large bowl. Stir in 1 cup broth or water and 2 Tbs. soy sauce until thick dough forms, adding more broth or water if necessary. Knead dough in bowl with wooden spoon 2 to 3 minutes, or until dough is elastic and easy to handle. Roll dough into wide log, and either shape into 8 or 10 cutlets, or cut into 6 pieces.

2. Place seitan dough in large saucepan, and add remaining 2 cups broth, remaining soy sauce, garlic clove and onion, adding enough water to cover seitan pieces. Cover saucepan, and bring to a boil over medium heat. Reduce heat to medium-low, and simmer 30 to 45 minutes, or until seitan pieces are firm. Remove from heat, and cool in broth. Use in any recipe calling for seitan.

"Meat" Balls and Spaghetti

SERVES 6

This recipe is really all about the meatless meatballs,
so we reworded its name a bit. The meatball "dough" is a flavored
homemade seitan with added chickpeas for chunkiness.

1 cup cooked chickpeas

2 Tbs. olive oil, plus more for frying

½ cup vital wheat gluten

½ cup breadcrumbs

2 Tbs. reduced-sodium tamari
or soy sauce

2 cloves garlic, minced (2 tsp.)

½ tsp. fresh lemon juice

½ tsp. dried thyme

½ tsp. dried basil

½ tsp. dried oregano

½ tsp. rubbed sage

12 oz. spaghetti

1 14-oz. jar pasta sauce

1. Mash chickpeas and 2 Tbs. oil in large bowl, leaving some lumps. Stir in wheat gluten, breadcrumbs, tamari, garlic, lemon juice, herbs, and ¼ cup water. Knead by hand 3 to 4 minutes, or until wheat gluten begins to form strands and all ingredients are well incorporated. Shape into 1 ½-inch balls.

2. Cook pasta according to package directions until al dente; warm pasta sauce in saucepan.

3. Meanwhile, heat oil in large skillet over medium heat. Sauté meatballs 7 minutes, or until browned. Drain on paper-towel-lined plate; serve over pasta and sauce.

PER SERVING: 493 CAL; 23 G PROT; 15.5 G TOTAL FAT
(2 G SAT FAT); 66 G CARB; 0 MG CHOL; 669 MG SOD;
11 G FIBER; 11 G SUGARS

Seitan Satay with Peanut Sauce

SERVES 8

Spicy peanut sauce and lemon wedges add flavor to this vegan
version of an Indonesian favorite.

SATAY

¼ cup low-sodium soy sauce

2 Tbs. toasted sesame oil

1 ½ tsp. grated fresh ginger

1 lb. seitan, rinsed, drained, and
cut into chunks

2 medium cucumbers, peeled and
quartered lengthwise

Lemon wedges, for garnish

SAUCE

½ cup creamy peanut butter

2 Tbs. tahini

2 Tbs. low-sodium soy sauce

1 Tbs. toasted sesame oil

1 tsp. hot sesame oil

1 tsp. minced fresh ginger

1. To make Satay: Combine soy sauce,
sesame oil, and ginger in resealable
plastic bag. Add seitan; seal, and
shake to coat. Refrigerate
1 hour, or overnight.

2. Preheat oven to 375°F. Coat baking
sheet with cooking spray. Drain seitan,
and thread onto skewers. Place on
prepared baking sheet, and bake 10 to
15 minutes, or until seitan is browned.

3. To make Sauce: Blend all ingredients and ½ cup water in blender until
smooth. Transfer to serving bowl.

4. Place cucumber quarters on serving plates. Set satay on top. Garnish
with lemon wedges, and pass peanut
sauce for dipping.

PER SERVING: 223 CAL; 21 G PROT; 13.5 G TOTAL FAT
(2.5 G SAT FAT); 8 G CARB; 0 MG CHOL; 276 MG SOD;
2 G FIBER; 2 G SUGARS

Speedy Substitution: Tahini

No tahini (a Middle Eastern sesame seed
paste) in the house? Replace it with 2 Tbs.
peanut butter and a little more sesame oil.

Seitan with Shiitake Mushrooms

SERVES 6

There's really nothing to this quick entrée, and yet the results are so satisfying when served over brown rice or steamed whole grains.

1 Tbs. sesame oil

3 medium onions, cut into thick half-moons (3 cups)

¼ tsp. salt

16 oz. seitan, cut into 1-inch strips

3 cups sliced shiitake mushrooms, stems removed

1 ½ Tbs. kudzu, cornstarch, or arrowroot powder

2 Tbs. low-sodium soy sauce

1. Heat oil in large skillet over medium-low heat. Add onions and salt, and sauté 10 minutes, or until onions are translucent. Add seitan, and cook 5 minutes more.

2. Stir in mushrooms and 1 ¾ cups water. Dissolve kudzu in ¼ cup water, then add to skillet along with soy sauce.

3. Simmer 5 to 10 minutes, or until mushrooms are tender.

PER SERVING: 159 CAL; 22 G PROT; 2.5 G TOTAL FAT (0.5 G SAT FAT); 14 G CARB; 0 MG CHOL; 279 MG SOD; 2 G FIBER; 3 G SUGARS

Success Secret: Jazz It Up

To jazz up this basic entrée, try stirring in 1 tsp. Dijon mustard or miso paste.

Curried Seitan Salad Pita Pockets

SERVES 4

Chewy seitan makes a satisfying replacement for chicken in this sandwich option.
Try the salad as a sandwich, or serve it on a bed of greens for a light supper.
And at the height of tomato season, use it to fill hollowed-out beefsteak or
heirloom tomatoes for an elegant entrée.

⅓ cup vegan mayonnaise

2 Tbs. Major Grey's chutney

2 tsp. curry powder

1 8-oz. pkg. seitan, rinsed, drained,
and coarsely chopped

¼ cup frozen peas, thawed

3 Tbs. chopped red onion

3 Tbs. chopped, roasted cashews,
salted

2 Tbs. dried currants

2 cups shredded romaine lettuce

4 thin slices tomato

4 pita bread rounds, halved

Combine mayonnaise, chutney, and
curry in bowl. Add seitan, peas, red
onion, cashews, and currants. Season
with salt and pepper. Divide seitan
salad, lettuce, and tomato among
pita pockets.

PER SERVING: 445 CAL; 23 G PROT; 16 G TOTAL FAT
(2 G SAT FAT), 52 G CARB; 0 MG CHOL; 607 MG SOD;
4 G FIBER; 10 G SUGARS

Success Secret:
Preventing Soggy Pita Pockets

To keep the pita pockets from getting
soggy, line the sides with the shredded
lettuce, and place the tomato slices and
seitan salad in the center.

Braised Seitan Cutlets in Mushroom and Red Wine Sauce

SERVES 2

Want to whip up an elegant entrée with on-hand ingredients? Try a meal of seitan cutlets cooked to perfection in a mustardy red wine sauce. This recipe is for two servings, but you could easily double or triple it for a dinner party.

1 8-oz. pkg. seitan, rinsed, drained, and halved into 2 thin cutlets

1 Tbs. all-purpose flour

1 Tbs. olive oil

4 oz. button mushrooms, sliced

¼ cup chopped onion

2 cloves garlic, minced (2 tsp.)

½ cup red wine

1 tsp. Dijon mustard

½ tsp. dried thyme

1 tsp. cornstarch

½ cup low-sodium vegetable broth

¼ cup chopped fresh parsley

1. Coat seitan pieces in flour. Heat oil in large skillet or Dutch oven over medium-high heat. Add seitan, and cook 1 to 2 minutes on each side, pressing pieces down to brown evenly. Remove seitan from skillet, and keep warm.

2. Add mushrooms, onion, and garlic to skillet. Sauté 7 to 10 minutes, or until softened and lightly browned. Whisk together wine, mustard, and thyme in measuring cup. Add to mushroom mixture; season with salt and pepper, if desired; and cook 2 to 3 minutes, or until slightly thickened. Whisk together cornstarch and vegetable broth in same measuring cup, then add to mushroom mixture. Simmer 2 to 3 minutes, or until thickened, stirring constantly. Place seitan cutlets on plates, top with mushroom sauce, and sprinkle with parsley.

PER SERVING: 260 CAL; 34 G PROT; 7 G TOTAL FAT (1 G SAT FAT); 16 G CARB; 0 MG CHOL; 399 MG SOD; 3 G FIBER; 3 G SUGARS

Prep Talk: Rinsing Seitan

Rinsing and draining seitan removes some of the salty broth it is packaged in, lowering its sodium content.

Seitan Jambalaya

Cajun cooks all have their seasoning mixes they use in gumbos and jambalayas, so feel free to play around with the quantities of the spices listed.

SEASONING MIX

1 tsp. ground cumin

1 tsp. chili powder

½ tsp. dried thyme

½ tsp. dried sage

½ tsp. celery seeds

¼ tsp. ground white pepper

⅛ tsp. cayenne pepper

1 tsp. salt

JAMBALAYA

1 cup canned whole peeled tomatoes

12-oz. seitan, rinsed and drained

2 ¾ cups low-sodium vegetable broth

1 cup brown rice

1 Tbs. olive oil

½ cup chopped onion

½ cup chopped red bell pepper

½ cup chopped celery

2 cloves garlic, minced (2 tsp.)

1. To make Seasoning Mix: Stir together all ingredients in small bowl.

2. To make Jambalaya: Preheat oven to 400°F. Drain tomatoes, reserving liquid, and coarsely chop. Set aside. Place seitan in food processor, and pulse on/off 12 times or until seitan is shredded. Set aside.

3. Bring broth and reserved tomato liquid to a boil in 4-qt. Dutch oven over medium-high heat. Add rice, return to a boil. Cover, reduce heat, and simmer 20 minutes. Meanwhile, heat oil in skillet over medium-high heat. Add onion, and cook 2 minutes. Stir in bell pepper, celery, garlic, and seasoning mix. Add tomatoes, then seitan and cook 3 minutes.

4. Transfer vegetables to rice, and stir to combine. Cover, and place in oven. Bake 30 to 45 minutes, or until liquid is completely absorbed. Let stand 5 minutes before serving.

PER SERVING: 352 CAL; 28 G PROT; 5 G TOTAL FAT (1 G SAT FAT); 49 G CARB; 0 MG CHOL; 835 MG SOD; 6 G FIBER; 5 G SUGARS

vegetables

Step into a farmers' market or stop at a roadside stand any time of year—yes, even winter—and the vibrant colors, the complex textures, the fresh-grown scents are enough to cast a spell over any shopper.

A good vegetable recipe lets you taste and relive that magical experience even when your weekly shopping gets done in a grocery store. It enchants diners and makes them crave seconds. And every once in a while, it has the power to transform a picky eater into a turnip green lover (Spicy Sausage and Turnip Green Ragoût, p. 167), turn a French fry fan into an oven fry aficionado (Garlicky Oven Fries, p. 175), or make a tentative cook reach out of his or her comfort zone and go gourmet (Carciofi alla Romana, p. 188).

North Indian Spiced Cabbage, Fennel, and Onions

Fennel bulb and fennel seed are both used here to give this warming side dish a subtle anise flavor and to tame the pungency of the cabbage.

3 Tbs. vegetable oil

1 tsp. fennel seeds

1 tsp. cumin seeds

1 large fennel bulb (10 to 12 oz.), trimmed, halved, and thinly sliced (4 cups)

1 large onion, halved and sliced into half-moons (2 cups)

1 medium head green cabbage (1 ½ lb.), cored and thinly sliced (8 cups)

¼ tsp. cayenne pepper

1 15-oz. can chickpeas, rinsed and drained

2 Tbs. fresh lemon juice

1 tsp. garam masala or curry powder

1. Heat oil in cast iron skillet over medium-high heat. Add fennel seeds and cumin seeds, and sauté 30 seconds. Add fennel and onion, and season with salt, if desired. Sauté 5 minutes.

2. Carefully pile cabbage into pan, cover, and cook 15 minutes, or until cabbage has cooked down, stirring often. Add cayenne pepper, reduce heat to medium-low, cover, and cook 20 to 30 minutes, or until vegetables are browned and caramelized. Stir in chickpeas, lemon juice, and garam masala, and cook 5 minutes more, or until chickpeas are heated through.

PER SERVING: 205 CAL; 6 G PROT; 8 G TOTAL FAT (1 G SAT FAT); 30 G CARB; 0 MG CHOL; 385 MG SOD; 8 G FIBER; 2 G SUGARS

Buy and Try: Fennel Seeds

In addition to adding a smoky anise flavor to dishes, fennel seed makes a great, tummy-soothing herbal tea when you steep 1 teaspoon in a cup of hot water.

Spicy Sausage and Turnip Green Ragoût

SERVES 4

Turnip greens have a peppery bite when raw and develop a slightly smoky taste when cooked. Other tasty greens to try in this recipe include curly kale, mustard greens, or collard greens. Serve over rice or steamed whole grains.

3 Tbs. olive oil, divided

4 vegan Mexican chipotle sausages (1 lb.), halved and cut into ½-inch slices

1 lb. sliced button or cremini mushrooms

2 medium onions, coarsely chopped (3 cups)

2 medium yellow bell peppers, cut into 1-inch pieces (3 cups)

12 cups coarsely chopped turnip greens (1 lb.)

2 large russet potatoes, peeled and cut into 1-inch pieces

4 cups cooked brown rice

1. Heat 1 Tbs. oil in large pot or Dutch oven over medium heat. Add sausage slices, and cook 5 to 7 minutes, or until browned, turning often. Transfer to paper-towel-lined plate, and set aside.

2. Heat remaining 2 Tbs. oil in same pot over medium heat. Add mushrooms, onions, and bell peppers, and sauté 7 to 10 minutes, or until vegetables are soft and mushrooms begin to brown. Add turnip greens, potatoes, and 2 cups water, and season with salt and black pepper, if desired. Cook 20 to 25 minutes, or until greens are soft and potatoes are cooked through.

3. Stir in sausage, and cook 2 to 3 minutes more, or until heated through. Serve over rice.

PER SERVING: 140 CAL; 2 G PROT; 109 G TOTAL FAT (1 G SAT FAT); 14 G CARB; 0 MG CHOL; 146 MG SOD; 3 G FIBER; 9 G SUGARS

....
Success Secret: Sausage
....

The spiciness of this dish depends on the type of sausage you choose—for a milder stew, substitute Italian-style vegan sausage for chipotle-style.

Hoppin' John with Collard Greens

SERVES 4

Southern cooks put cruets of vinegar and bottles of vinegar-based hot sauce (like Tabasco and Texas Pete) on the table for guests to doctor up this classic New Year's dish with tangy flavor. But don't limit this recipe to January dinners—it's delicious year-round.

¼ cup apple cider vinegar, divided

2 Tbs. agave nectar

3 tsp. olive oil, divided

1 tsp. chili powder, divided

1 tsp. salt, divided

1 large bunch collard greens, tough stems removed and chopped

4 slices low-fat vegan bacon strips, chopped

1 small onion, chopped (¾ cup)

3 medium stalks celery, chopped (¾ cup)

2 cloves garlic, minced (2 tsp.)

1 ½ cups cooked long-grain white rice

1 15.5-oz. can black-eyed peas, rinsed and drained

1. Whisk together 2 Tbs. vinegar, agave nectar, 1 tsp. oil, ½ tsp. chili powder, and ½ tsp. salt; set aside.

2. Cook collard greens in pot of boiling salted water 15 minutes. Drain, reserving ½ cup liquid.

3. Meanwhile, heat remaining 2 tsp. oil in large skillet over medium heat. Add bacon, onion, celery, garlic, and remaining ½ tsp. chili powder. Cook 8 minutes, or until translucent. Add collard greens, vinegar-agave nectar mixture, ¼ cup reserved cooking liquid, remaining 2 Tbs. vinegar, and remaining ½ tsp. salt. Cover, and cook 10 minutes, or until greens are tender. Transfer to serving platter.

4. Add rice and beans to skillet. Stir in remaining ¼ cup cooking liquid, and cook 3 minutes, or until heated through. Serve rice and beans over greens.

PER SERVING: 291 CAL; 12 G PROT; 6 G TOTAL FAT (0.5 G SAT FAT); 51 G CARB; 0 MG CHOL; 723 MG SOD; 8 G FIBER; 12 G SUGARS

Steamed Greens with Sliced Leeks

SERVES 6

Even though the vegetables in this simple recipe are cooked until just tender, the dish reheats well; so feel free to make it ahead, then warm just before serving.

3 Tbs. olive oil

6 large leeks, white parts only, thinly sliced (1 ½ cups)

3 bunches Swiss chard, collard greens, or beet greens (12 oz.), tough stems removed and coarsely chopped

3 cloves garlic, minced (1 Tbs.)

Heat oil in large skillet over medium heat. Add leeks, and sauté 5 minutes, or until soft. Reduce heat to low; add Swiss chard and garlic. Cover pan, and steam greens 7 to 9 minutes, or until wilted and tender.

PER SERVING: 132 CAL; 4 G PROT; 8 G TOTAL FAT (1 G SAT FAT); 16 G CARB; 0 MG CHOL; 638 MG SOD; 4 G FIBER; 4 G SUGARS

Shopping Savvy: Buying Bitter Greens

Choose bunches of collards, kale, Swiss chard, or other leafy greens that are bright and perky, not wilted. Avoid bunches with yellowing leaves or dried, tough stems, which means they have been in storage too long.

Sephardic Stuffed Cabbage

SERVES 6

This is like the one served on Jewish holidays—minus the meat.

CABBAGE

14 large savoy cabbage leaves

1 8-oz. pkg. tempeh

8-oz. cremini mushrooms

2 Tbs. olive oil

2 small onions, finely diced (2 cups)

2 cloves garlic, minced (2 tsp.)

2 tsp. paprika

2 tsp. ground cumin

1 14-oz. can plum tomatoes, drained and coarsely chopped

⅛ tsp. cayenne pepper

TOMATO SAUCE

2 Tbs. olive oil

2 cloves garlic, minced (2 tsp.)

1 tsp. ground cumin

1 tsp. paprika

2 8-oz. cans tomato sauce

½ cup chopped fresh parsley

2 Tbs. chopped fresh cilantro

1. To make Cabbage: Preheat oven to 350°F. Blanch cabbage leaves in pot of boiling water 2 minutes. Drain, and rinse under cold water. Remove vein at base of each leaf, and pat dry.

2. Pulse tempeh and mushrooms in food processor until coarsely ground. Heat oil in skillet over medium heat. Add onions, and sauté 7 minutes. Add garlic, paprika, cumin, and tempeh mixture, and sauté 5 minutes. Add tomatoes, and cook 10 minutes more. Stir in cayenne pepper, and season with salt and pepper. Set aside.

3. To make Tomato Sauce: Heat oil in saucepan over medium heat. Add garlic, cumin, and paprika, and cook 2 minutes. Stir in tomato sauce and 1 cup water. Simmer 10 minutes, then add parsley and cilantro. Season with salt and pepper, and pour into 13- × 9-inch baking dish.

4. Spoon 2 Tbs. tempeh mixture on base of each cabbage leaf. Fold sides around filling, and roll. Place seam-side down in baking dish. Bake 30 minutes, or until sauce is bubbling.

PER SERVING: 247 CAL; 12 G PROT; 14 G TOTAL FAT (2 G SAT FAT); 23 G CARB; 0 MG CHOL; 671 MG SOD; 6 G FIBER; 8 G SUGARS

Sweet-and-Sour Red Cabbage
with Apples and Tempeh

SERVES 8

Apples and cabbage are a common combination in German recipes.
If you can't find chestnuts, try this dish with chopped walnuts or pecans.

1 ½ Tbs. olive oil, divided

1 8-oz. pkg. tempeh

1 Tbs. low-sodium soy sauce

2 large sweet-tart apples, such as
Gala, Idared, or Rome, peeled, cored,
and chopped

1 large red onion, chopped (2 cups)

1 medium red cabbage (2 lb.), thinly
sliced (8 cups)

½ cup apple cider

⅓ cup balsamic vinegar

3 ½ Tbs. dark brown sugar

1 ½ cups cooked chestnuts, chopped

1. Heat 1 ½ tsp. oil in skillet over medium heat. Add tempeh, and sauté 4 minutes, or until browned. Stir in soy sauce and ½ cup water. Simmer 5 minutes, or until liquid is absorbed, turning occasionally. Cool, and cut tempeh into small squares.

2. Heat remaining 1 Tbs. oil in large skillet over medium-high heat. Add apples and onion, and sauté 12 minutes. Stir in cabbage, cider, vinegar, and sugar. Reduce heat to medium, and partially cover. Cook 25 minutes, or until cabbage is tender, stirring occasionally. Stir in tempeh and chestnuts, and season with salt and pepper.

PER SERVING: 242 CAL; 8 G PROT; 6.5 G TOTAL FAT
(1 G SAT FAT); 41 G CARB; 0 MG CHOL; 391 MG SOD;
5 G FIBER; 21 G SUGARS

....

Success Secret:
Preparing in Advance

....

When making this dish ahead,
use white cabbage instead of red.
Red cabbage tends to turn
a brownish color when cooled.

Callaloo with Hot Pepper Vinegar

SERVES 8

Callaloo refers to amaranth, a leafy vegetable cooked the same way greens are cooked in the southern United States. For a similar taste and texture, we made this Jamaican dish using a half-and-half mix of collard greens and spinach.

CALLALOO

3 Tbs. canola oil

1 large onion, thinly sliced (2 cups)

1 lb. collard greens, tough stems removed and chopped

1 lb. spinach, tough stems removed

5 cloves garlic, minced (1 ½ Tbs.)

HOT PEPPER VINEGAR

½ cup finely diced red bell pepper

½ cup finely diced yellow bell pepper

½ to 1 Scotch bonnet chile, minced

½ cup cider vinegar

½ tsp. sugar

1. To make Callaloo: Heat oil in large pot over medium heat. Add onion, and sauté 5 to 7 minutes, or until beginning to brown.

2. Add collard greens, spinach, and garlic; cover, and increase heat to medium-high. Cook 7 to 10 minutes, stirring often with tongs, or until greens wilt. Add 2 cups water, and season with salt and pepper. Cover, reduce heat to medium-low, and cook 45 minutes, or until greens are tender. Season again with salt and pepper.

3. To make Hot Pepper Vinegar: Combine bell peppers and Scotch bonnet chile in 2-cup glass measuring cup. Stir together vinegar, sugar, and ½ cup water in small saucepan. Bring vinegar mixture to a boil, then pour over peppers. Cool.

4. To serve: Top each serving of callaloo with pepper vinegar.

PER SERVING: 97 CAL; 3 G PROT; 5.5 G TOTAL FAT (0.5 G SAT FAT); 10 G CARB; 0 MG CHOL; 191 MG SOD; 4 G FIBER; 3 G SUGARS

Prep Talk: Handling Chiles

When using fresh hot chiles like Scotch bonnets or habaneros, slip on a pair of kitchen gloves to slice them. This will prevent any burning juices from getting on your hands.

Colcannon

This ultra-Irish dish gets a modern-day makeover with purple potatoes, garlic, and shiitake mushrooms to reflect all the delicious new options found in farmers' markets around Ireland today.

1 lb. purple potatoes

1 lb. kale, tough stems removed

2 to 3 Tbs. olive oil

10 oz. shiitake mushrooms, stems removed and sliced (3 cups)

3 cloves garlic, chopped (1 Tbs.)

1 cup unsweetened rice milk, warmed

1. Boil potatoes in large pot of water 15 to 20 minutes, or until very tender. Drain, and return to pot. Heat potatoes over medium heat 1 to 2 minutes to steam off excess water, and set aside.

2. Meanwhile, bring large pot of salted water to a boil. Add kale, and cook 5 minutes. Drain, and set aside.

3. Heat oil in skillet over medium heat. Add mushrooms and garlic, and sauté 5 to 7 minutes, or until mushrooms are soft. Stir in kale, and cook 1 minute more, or until hot. Season with salt and pepper.

4. Mash rice milk into potatoes until soft, but still chunky. Fold in kale mixture, and serve.

PER SERVING: 184 CAL; 4 G PROT; 7 G TOTAL FAT (1 G SAT FAT); 30 G CARB; 0 MG CHOL; 406 MG SOD; 4 G FIBER; 5 G SUGARS

SERVING SUGGESTION
Beer would be the obvious choice to go with this Irish dish, but we also we recommend hard cider. Or if cider's too sweet, try a Snakebite, a drink made with half beer, half hard cider.

Garlicky Oven Fries

SERVES 4

Crispy on the outside, tender and fluffy on the inside, these potato wedges are the answer to any French fry urge—minus the fat and calories of deep-frying. A last-minute sprinkling of garlic and parsley boosts flavor so that you don't need as much salt to season them.

1 ½ lb. russet potatoes, peeled and cut into ¼-inch-thick wedges

2 tsp. canola oil

2 tsp. olive oil

4 cloves garlic, coarsely chopped

1 Tbs. chopped fresh parsley

....

Success Secret: Presoaking Potatoes
....

Presoaking potato slices in hot water helps remove excess starch so that they brown and crisp like oil-cooked fries.

1. Place oven rack in lowest position, and preheat oven to 475°F. Coat baking sheet with cooking spray. Soak potatoes in bowl of hot water 10 minutes. Drain, pat dry, and return to dry bowl.

2. Meanwhile, heat canola oil, olive oil, and garlic in saucepan over medium-low heat. Cook garlic 2 minutes, or until it begins to brown. Transfer garlic to small bowl with slotted spoon.

3. Pour oil over potatoes, and toss to coat. Season with salt and pepper. Arrange potatoes in single layer on prepared baking sheet. Bake 20 minutes, or until potatoes are golden on bottom. Turn, and bake 10 minutes more, or until golden and crisp.

4. Meanwhile, stir parsley into reserved garlic; sprinkle over fries. Season with salt and pepper, and serve immediately.

PER SERVING: 167 CAL; 3 G PROT; 4.5 G TOTAL FAT (0.5 G SAT FAT); 29 G CARB; 0 MG CHOL; 298 MG SOD; 2 G FIBER; 5 G SUGARS

Curried Potatoes

Mmm…starch and spice! (Plus a little protein from black beans.)
This versatile recipe can be a stellar side dish or a filling main course when
served on a bed of wilted spinach.

1 ½ Tbs. vegetable oil

2 medium onions, diced (3 cups)

3 cloves garlic, minced (1 Tbs.)

4 large Yukon gold potatoes, peeled
and cut into chunks

3 medium carrots, cut into 2-inch
pieces (1 cup)

3 Tbs. Madras curry powder

1 15-oz. can black beans

3 medium tomatoes, coarsely
chopped (1 ½ cups)

1 cup low-sodium vegetable broth

2 jalapeño chiles, seeded and finely
chopped (¼ cup)

1 tsp. balsamic vinegar

1. Heat oil in large skillet over medium heat. Add onions and garlic, and cook 5 to 7 minutes, or until onions are soft and translucent. Stir in potatoes, carrots, and curry powder, and cook 4 minutes.

2. Add beans and liquid, tomatoes, broth, jalapeños, vinegar, and 1 cup water; season with salt and pepper. Cover and simmer 45 minutes, or until potatoes are flaky and carrots are cooked through, stirring occasionally.

PER SERVING: 282 CAL; 9 G PROT; 4 G TOTAL FAT (0.5 G SAT FAT); 55 G CARB; 0 MG CHOL; 499 MG SOD; 10 G FIBER; 9 G SUGARS

Speedy Substitution: Canned Tomatoes

If fresh tomatoes aren't in season, replace them with a 15-oz. can diced tomatoes and use only ¾ cup vegetable broth.

Shopping Savvy: Yukon Gold Potatoes

Yukon golds are an excellent all-purpose potato choice because they both stay firm when cooked in stews and become creamy when mashed or blended. Their yellow hue and buttery flavor make them look as appetizing as they taste, too.

Baked Leek and Sweet Potato Gratin

SERVES 8

Sautéed leeks add a milder, sweeter flavor than onions to this hearty sweet potato dish, which can also be served with a salad as a light main course.

1 ½ Tbs. olive oil, divided

3 medium leeks, white and pale green parts only, chopped (6 cups)

3 cloves garlic, minced (1 Tbs.)

3 Tbs. chopped fresh rosemary, divided

2 medium sweet potatoes (2 lb.), peeled and thinly sliced

⅓ cup low-sodium vegetable broth

3 Tbs. seasoned Italian breadcrumbs

Success Secret:
Don't Undercook Casseroles

With gratins and casseroles, overcooking is always better than undercooking. So if this gratin looks a little pale after the recommended cooking time, don't hesitate to leave it in the oven 5 to 15 minutes longer. The browned, crispy bits that form on top and around the edges are the best part!

1. Preheat oven to 450°F. Coat 10-inch round pan with cooking spray.

2. Heat 1 Tbs. oil in nonstick skillet over medium-high heat. Add leeks, garlic, and 1 ½ Tbs. rosemary; sauté 8 minutes, or until softened. Season with salt and pepper, if desired.

3. Arrange one-third sweet potato slices over bottom of prepared pan, overlapping slightly. Spread half of leek mixture on top. Arrange another one-third sweet potato slices over leeks; top with remaining leeks, followed by remaining sweet potatoes. Drizzle broth over dish. Cover pan with foil, and bake 35 minutes.

4. Stir together breadcrumbs, remaining 1 ½ tsp. oil, and remaining 1 ½ Tbs. rosemary in small bowl. Remove foil from gratin, and sprinkle with breadcrumb mixture. Bake, uncovered, 15 minutes, or until breadcrumbs are browned and crisp. Let gratin cool slightly before cutting into wedges.

PER SERVING: 143 CAL; 3 G PROT; 3 G TOTAL FAT (◂1 G SAT FAT); 28 G CARB; 0 MG CHOL; 402 MG SOD; 4 G FIBER; 8 G SUGARS

Roasted Sweet Potato Wedges with Broccoli

SERVES 4

Place this colorful dish on a big platter and watch it disappear. Even broccoli haters will love the vegetable's rich flavor when it's roasted at high heat.

4 cups bite-size broccoli florets, halved lengthwise

2 small sweet potatoes (1 lb.), peeled, each cut into 16 wedges

6 green onions, each cut into 4 segments

3 Tbs. toasted sesame oil, divided

¼ tsp. coarse salt

2 Tbs. fresh orange juice

2 Tbs. low-sodium tamari or soy sauce

1 Tbs. rice vinegar

1 Tbs. mirin (rice wine)

1 Tbs. toasted sesame seeds

2 tsp. grated fresh ginger

1 clove garlic, minced (1 tsp.)

6 cups baby spinach (8 oz.)

1. Preheat oven to 450°F. Place broccoli, sweet potatoes, and green onions in large bowl. Add 2 Tbs. oil and salt; toss well to coat. Spread vegetables on baking sheet, and roast 20 minutes, turning with spatula 2 or 3 times. Increase oven temperature to 500°F. Roast vegetables 10 minutes more, or until tender and browned.

2. Meanwhile, whisk together orange juice, tamari, vinegar, mirin, sesame seeds, ginger, garlic, and remaining 1 Tbs. oil in small bowl. Place spinach in large serving bowl, add roasted vegetables and orange juice mixture, and toss well to mix.

PER SERVING: 248 CAL; 7 G PROT; 12 G TOTAL FAT (1.5 G SAT FAT); 31 G CARB; 0 MG CHOL; 607 MG SOD; 8 G FIBER; 8 G SUGARS

Success Secret: Preheat Oven

Get the oven good and hot (preheat it for at least 15 minutes) before roasting sweet potatoes. This helps sear them on the outside so that they get crisp, not soggy.

Vegan Moussaka

SERVES 12

Moussaka, a potato dish? Mashed potatoes replace cream sauce and ground lentils replace lamb in a casserole that serves a crowd.

5 large russet potatoes (3 ½ lb.), peeled and cut into chunks

4 cloves garlic, peeled

¼ cup plus 2 Tbs. olive oil, divided

1 large onion, chopped (1 ½ cups)

3 Tbs. dried oregano

2 15-oz. cans chopped tomatoes, drained

⅔ cup dried green or brown lentils, rinsed and picked through

1 bay leaf

1 cinnamon stick

2 medium eggplants (2 lbs.), thinly sliced

2 small zucchini (1 lb.), thinly sliced

3 medium tomatoes (1 lb.), thinly sliced

1. Cook potatoes and garlic in boiling salted water 10 minutes. Drain, and reserve cooking liquid. Mash with ¼ cup oil and 2 cups cooking liquid.

2. Heat remaining oil in saucepan over medium heat. Add onion and oregano, and sauté 5 minutes. Add tomatoes, lentils, bay leaf, cinnamon stick, and 3 cups potato cooking liquid. Cover and simmer 45 minutes. Remove bay leaf and cinnamon, and purée in food processor. Season with salt and pepper.

3. Place eggplant slices on baking sheet, and sprinkle with salt. Let stand 30 minutes. Rinse, and pat dry.

4. Preheat oven to 350°F. Coat 13- x 9-inch baking dish with cooking spray. Spoon 1 ½ cups lentil mixture into bottom. Top with eggplant, followed by zucchini and tomatoes. Spoon 2 cups lentil mixture over top. Spread half of potatoes over lentil mixture. Repeat layering, ending with potatoes. Bake 1 ½ hours, or until top is browned.

PER SERVING: 274 CAL; 7 G PROT; 8.5 G TOTAL FAT (1 G SAT FAT); 46 G CARB; 0 MG CHOL; 587 MG SOD; 12 G FIBER; 9 G SUGARS

Potato Latkes

SERVES 4

Potato pancakes aren't just for Hanukkah. They are also great for party appetizers (when you make them small), kid-friendly dinners, and Sunday night suppers. Use the largest holes on the grater you choose (box or food processor) so that the potatoes retain some texture after they're cooked. Serve with vegan sour cream or applesauce.

2 large potatoes (1 ½ lb.), peeled, grated, and squeezed dry

1 medium yellow onion, chopped (1 ¼ cups)

¼ cup all-purpose flour

2 Tbs. whole-grain or Dijon mustard

1 tsp. baking powder

¼ cup canola oil, divided, for frying

1. Combine potatoes, onion, flour, mustard, and baking powder in large bowl. Season with salt and pepper. Heat 1 Tbs. oil in large skillet over medium heat. Scoop ½ cup potato mixture into skillet and spread into ⅛-inch-thick patty. Repeat. Fry patties 3 to 4 minutes per side, or until golden brown. Cook remaining latkes in batches of 2, adding 1 Tbs. oil to skillet each time.

2. To drain, transfer latkes to wire rack on top of baking sheet lined with newspaper. Place latkes on pan in low oven to keep warm.

PER SERVING: 241 CAL; 4 G PROT; 8 G TOTAL FAT (5 G SAT FAT); 40 G CARB; 0 MG CHOL; 372 MG SOD; 3 G FIBER; 5 G SUGARS

Prep Talk:
Draining Grated Potatoes

To eliminate the liquid from grated potatoes, roll them in a clean dishtowel, then twist the ends of the towel and squeeze tightly.

Pickled Daikon Cubes with Carrots and Jalapeños

MAKES 3 ½ CUPS

This recipe is inspired by the daikon kimchee pickles that are served at the start of a Korean meal. These pickles are great served on the side or sliced up in sandwiches or salads.

1 small daikon radish, peeled and cut into ½-inch cubes (2 ¼ cups)

2 small carrots, cut into ¼-inch rounds (1 cup)

½ small sweet onion, thinly sliced (½ cup)

1 small red jalapeño chile, thinly sliced (1 Tbs.)

1 clove garlic, lightly crushed

2 tsp. salt

1 cup apple cider vinegar

¼ cup sugar

1. Place daikon, carrots, onion, jalapeño, and garlic in large bowl and toss with salt. Let stand 1 hour, and then drain well. Transfer to 4-cup jar or plastic container.

2. Bring vinegar, sugar, and ½ cup water to a simmer in small saucepan over high heat. Stir until sugar dissolves. Pour vinegar mixture over vegetables. Cover, and refrigerate 3 hours.

PER SERVING (1/2 CUP): 26 CAL, 1 G PROT; 0.5 G TOTAL FAT (0 G SAT FAT); 4 G CARB; 0 MG CHOL; 180 MG SOD; 1 G FIBER; 2 G SUGARS

....

Success Secret

....

Pickled Daikon Cubes can be eaten as soon as they're chilled, but the flavors improve after a few days.

Fresh Cucumber Pickles

MAKES 1 QUART

For backyard gardeners who get a bumper crop of cucumbers
in the summer, this is a cool, tasty way to repurpose them without
having to can them or put them into another tossed salad.
Otherwise, it is a great year-round side dish. The pickles stay fresh and crisp
for several days, if you can manage to keep them around that long.

2 medium cucumbers, peeled, halved,
and cut into ⅛-inch-thick slices

1 cup cider vinegar

3 Tbs. sugar

1 clove garlic, lightly crushed

1 tsp. whole coriander seeds

1 tsp. kosher salt

¾ tsp. yellow mustard seeds

¼ tsp. red pepper flakes

7 whole black peppercorns

Combine all ingredients in 1-qt. plastic
storage container with lid. Cover, and
shake to coat. Refrigerate 4 hours, or
overnight.

PER SERVING (¼ CUP): 6 CAL; 1 G PROT; 0 G TOTAL
FAT (0 G SAT FAT); 1 G CARB; 0 MG CHOL; 81 MG SOD;
1 G FIBER; 1 G SUGARS

Success Secret:
To Peel or Not to Peel

If the cucumbers are untreated and
organically grown, you can leave the peel
on when making these pickles.

Edamame Succotash

SERVES 6

Fresh green soybeans (edamame) offer a great variation on a
classic dish, standing in for traditional lima beans. For an elegant twist,
serve the succotash in hollowed-out tomatoes.

2 tsp. vegetable oil

½ cup chopped red bell pepper

¼ cup chopped onion

2 cloves garlic, minced

1 ½ cups fresh or frozen shelled
edamame

2 cups fresh or frozen corn kernels

3 Tbs. dry white wine or low-sodium
vegetable broth

½ tsp. salt

¼ tsp. ground black pepper

2 Tbs. chopped fresh parsley

1 Tbs. chopped fresh basil, or
1 ½ tsp. dried basil

1. Heat oil in large nonstick skillet over medium heat. Add bell pepper, onion, and garlic, and cook, stirring frequently, 2 minutes. Stir in edamame, corn, and wine; cook 4 minutes, stirring frequently.

2. Remove pan from heat. Stir in salt, black pepper, parsley and basil.

PER SERVING· 140 CAL; 8 G PROT; 5 G TOTAL FAT (0 G SAT FAT); 18 G CARB; 0 MG CHOL; 200 MG SOD; 4 G FIBER; 3 G SUGARS

....

Speedy Substitutions:
Dried Herbs

....

When replacing fresh herbs with dried, divide the amount in half. Dried herbs are more potent and will have a slightly different flavor.

Asparagus with Vegan Hollandaise

SERVES 6

Classic hollandaise sauce is mostly egg yolks and butter, so off-limits for vegans. Seasoned silken tofu gives you the same creamy consistency, and there's no worry about the sauce curdling or turning. This version can be made ahead and reheated by stirring over low heat until just warm.

½ cup silken tofu, drained

2 Tbs. fresh lemon juice

1 Tbs. nutritional yeast

½ tsp. salt

⅛ tsp. cayenne pepper

⅛ tsp. ground turmeric

2 Tbs. corn oil

2 lb. asparagus, trimmed

1. Heat tofu on plate in microwave 30 to 45 seconds, or until warmed through. Transfer to food processor, and purée until smooth. Add lemon juice, nutritional yeast, salt, cayenne pepper, and turmeric; pulse until well combined. With food processor running, add oil in steady stream to finish sauce.

2. Steam asparagus 2 minutes, or until crisp-tender. Drain, and serve with sauce.

PER SERVING: 73 CAL; 3 G PROT; 5.5 G TOTAL FAT (0.5 G SAT FAT); 5 G CARB; 0 MG CHOL; 206 MG SOD; 2 G FIBER; 1 G SUGARS

Shopping Savvy: Asparagus

Look for bunches of asparagus that are all the same size with tightly closed tips. Same-size asparagus cook more evenly, and the tight tips are a sign of freshness.

Carciofi alla Romana
(Roman-Style Braised Artichokes)

SERVES 4

Make this recipe once and preparing fresh artichokes will never feel like a chore again.

1 cup parsley leaves

1 Tbs. freshly grated lemon zest

2 cloves garlic, peeled

2 Tbs. olive oil

¼ tsp. salt

⅛ tsp. ground black pepper

½ cup fresh lemon juice

4 large globe artichokes with stems

Storage Hint

Fresh artichokes need to stay cool to prevent them from browning or yellowing. Stored in the fridge, they will often keep up to 2 weeks.

1. Pulse parsley, lemon zest, and garlic in food processor until finely chopped. Add oil, salt, and pepper, and pulse until paste forms. Set aside.

2. Combine lemon juice and 6 cups water in bowl. Trim outer leaves of each artichoke until cone of pale green leaves appears. Cut off 1 inch of central cone of leaves. Trim away first 3 rows of outer leaves at base of artichoke, and pare down stem to white center. Pull out pointed leaves in center. Scrape out hairy choke with spoon. Dunk in lemon water.

3. Drain artichokes, reserving 2 cups lemon water. Rub parsley mixture all over artichokes, and place stem-side up in Dutch oven. Add reserved lemon water and enough water to come 1 inch up sides of artichokes. Cover, and bring to a boil. Reduce heat to medium-low, and simmer 30 to 45 minutes, or until very tender. Serve warm or at room temperature drizzled with pan juices.

PER SERVING: 147 CAL; 6 G PROT; 7 G TOTAL FAT (1 G SAT FAT); 20 G CARB; 0 MG CHOL; 307 MG SOD; 9 G FIBER; 2 G SUGARS

Spicy Sautéed Oyster Mushrooms

SERVES 4

More and more chefs are taking mushrooms out of sauces
and using them in light side dishes like this quick sauté. You can also serve
it over rice and beans as an entrée.

2 Tbs. olive oil

1 medium shallot, finely chopped
(3 Tbs.)

1 jalapeño chile, seeded and minced
(2 Tbs.)

1 clove garlic, minced (1 tsp.)

1 ¼ lb. oyster mushrooms, trimmed
and chopped

2 tsp. fresh lime juice

2 Tbs. chopped fresh cilantro

Heat oil in large skillet over medium-high heat. Add shallot, jalapeño, and garlic, and sauté 2 to 3 minutes. Add mushrooms, and sauté 7 to 9 minutes, or until liquid released by mushrooms has cooked off and mushrooms begin to brown. Stir in lime juice, and season with salt and pepper. Remove from heat and toss with cilantro. Serve warm.

PER SERVING: 193 CAL; 7 G PROT; 7.5 G TOTAL FAT (1 G SAT FAT); 25 G CARB; 0 MG CHOL; 213 MG SOD; 4 G FIBER; 5 G SUGARS

Success Secret: Jalapeño Chiles

When mincing or slicing jalapeños, take a small taste to see how hot they are. Jalapeño chiles can vary widely in potency from mild to superhot, so you may have to adjust the amount used accordingly.

Chinese Broccoli with Black Bean Sauce

SERVES 4

Chinese take-out fans will recognize this vegetable classic. Salty-sweet black bean–garlic sauce can be found in Asian grocery stores and well-stocked supermarkets. Try it on other steamed vegetables as well.

1 ½ lb. Chinese broccoli, trimmed and stalks peeled

2 Tbs. canola oil

2 cloves garlic, minced (2 tsp.)

1 ½ Tbs. black bean–garlic sauce

½ tsp. sugar

Buy and Try: Chinese Broccoli

Chinese broccoli looks and tastes like a cross between broccoli and broccoli rabe. It has a slight bitterness that pairs well with the sweetness in Asian sauces.

1. Bring large pot of water to a boil. Blanch broccoli 1 to 2 minutes, or until bright green. Rinse under cold water to stop cooking, and drain well.

2. Heat oil in nonstick skillet over medium-high heat. Add broccoli, and sauté 2 to 3 minutes. Add garlic, and cook 1 minute, or until fragrant. Stir in black bean sauce and sugar, and sauté 2 to 3 minutes more, or until broccoli is crisp-tender.

PER SERVING: 130 CAL; 4 G PROT; 8 G TOTAL FAT (0.5 G SAT FAT); 13 G CARB; 0 MG CHOL; 141 MG SOD; 3 G FIBER; 1 G SUGARS

Green Beans with Walnuts and Shallot Crisps

SERVES 8

This recipe is an elegant twist on the green bean casserole served in many households at Thanksgiving. Shallot crisps are the star attraction here and can be made in advance. In a tightly sealed jar, they will keep at room temperature for 2 weeks—but you'd better hide the jar.

SHALLOT CRISPS

5 large shallots (8 oz.), sliced into thin rings

½ cup vegetable oil

GREEN BEANS

2 lb. green beans, trimmed

3 Tbs. apple cider vinegar

3 Tbs. Dijon mustard

3 Tbs. vegetable oil

3 Tbs. pure maple syrup

1 cup toasted chopped walnuts (8 oz.)

1. To make Shallot Crisps: Spread shallot rings on paper towel, sprinkle with salt, and cover with another paper towel. Let stand 10 minutes. Blot excess moisture from shallots.

2. Heat oil in small saucepan over medium heat. Add shallots, and fry 2 to 4 minutes, or until golden brown, stirring frequently. Pour shallots and oil through fine-mesh strainer, or remove shallots with slotted spoon. Spread shallots on paper towels to drain and cool. Discard oil. Store shallots in jar, if desired.

3. To make Green Beans: Cook beans in large pot of boiling salted water 5 to 8 minutes, or until just tender. Drain. Whisk together vinegar, mustard, oil, and maple syrup in serving bowl. Add green beans, and toss to coat. Season with salt and pepper. Top with shallot crisps and walnuts.

PER SERVING: 253 CAL; 5 G PROT; 18 G TOTAL FAT (1.5 G SAT FAT); 22 G CARB; 0 MG CHOL; 291 MG SOD; 5 G FIBER; 9 G SUGARS

Prep Talk:
Trimming Green Beans

Speed up the trimming process for green beans by skipping the snapping. Instead, line green beans up on a cutting board and trim stems in one movement with a large chef's knife.

Best-Ever Basic Roasted Veggie Recipe

SERVES 4

Can you ever make enough roasted vegetables? Not when you're talking about this versatile recipe. Hot, they can be served over rice, pasta, or whole grains. Leftovers can go into salads, sandwiches, tofu scrambles, and frittatas.

2 cups bite-size cauliflower florets, halved lengthwise

2 cups halved Brussels sprouts

2 medium carrots, cut into sticks

1 medium yam or sweet potato (8 oz.), diced

3 Tbs. garlic-infused olive oil, divided

1 Tbs. chopped fresh rosemary

2 tsp. chopped fresh thyme

2 Tbs. chopped fresh parsley

2 tsp. fresh lemon juice

Preheat oven to 450°F. Line baking sheet with parchment paper. Place cauliflower, Brussels sprouts, carrots, and yam in large bowl. Add 2 Tbs. oil, rosemary, and thyme, and toss to coat. Season with salt and pepper. Scatter vegetables evenly on baking sheet, and roast 20 minutes, turning 2 or 3 times with spatula. Increase oven temperature to 500°F, and roast vegetables 10 minutes more, or until tender. Transfer vegetables to large serving bowl, and add parsley, lemon juice, and remaining 1 Tbs. oil. Toss to mix, and serve.

PER SERVING: 164 CAL; 3 G PROT; 11 G TOTAL FAT (1.5 G SAT FAT); 16 G CARB; 0 MG CHOL; 343 MG SOD; 5 G FIBER; 6 G SUGARS

Success Secret: Size of Vegetables for Roasting

Slice and cube all vegetables for roasting so that they are approximately the same size. That way, they will all be done at the same time and there are no worries about burning or sticking.

Winter Squash with Spicy Maple Chestnuts

SERVES 6

Sugar and spice and everything nice—that's what this cold weather vegetable dish is full of. It's lightly sweetened with maple syrup and gets a hit of spicy heat from red pepper flakes.

2 lb. butternut squash or other winter squash, peeled, seeded, and diced (8 cups)

1 medium red onion, cut into small wedges

3 Tbs. olive oil, divided

3 Tbs. pure maple syrup

1 ½ Tbs. rice vinegar

½ tsp. red pepper flakes

1 15-oz. jar cooked, peeled chestnuts (1 ½ cups)

¼ cup chopped fresh chives

1. Preheat oven to 450°F. Combine squash, onion, and 2 Tbs. oil in large bowl, and toss to coat. Season vegetables with salt and pepper, if desired, and scatter evenly on baking sheet. Roast vegetables 20 minutes, turning 2 or 3 times with spatula.

2. Meanwhile, whisk together remaining 1 Tbs. oil, maple syrup, vinegar, and red pepper flakes in small bowl. Season with salt and pepper, if desired. Place chestnuts in medium bowl, and add 1 Tbs. maple syrup mixture. Toss to coat.

3. Increase oven temperature to 500°F. Scatter chestnuts among squash and onion wedges. Roast vegetables 10 minutes more, or until tender. Transfer vegetable-nut mixture to large serving bowl, drizzle with remaining maple syrup mixture, add chives, and toss to mix.

PER SERVING: 278 CAL; 3 G PROT; 8 G TOTAL FAT (1 G SAT FAT); 51 G CARB; 0 MG CHOL; 202 MG SOD; 6 G FIBER; 15 G SUGARS

Storage Hint: Chestnuts

Around the holidays, cooked, peeled chestnuts show up in jars in specialty shops and some grocery stores, so it's a good time to stock up.

Chestnut Stuffing

SERVES 10

OK, so stuffing isn't exactly a vegetable. But it is a side dish that's served with vegetables. This old-fashioned recipe will impress holiday guests with its rich, nutty flavor and homey feel.

1 tsp. vegetable oil

1 lb. soy sausage crumbles

1 tsp. rubbed sage

5 Tbs. nonhydrogenated margarine, divided

2 medium onions, diced (2 cups)

1 ½ cups diced celery

1 large fennel bulb, diced (1 cup)

½ cup dry white wine

1 15-oz. jar cooked, peeled chestnuts, chopped (2 ½ cups)

1 lb. loaf whole-wheat bread, cubed (8 cups)

¼ cup chopped fresh parsley

2 Tbs. chopped fresh thyme

3 cups low-sodium vegetable broth

1. Preheat oven to 375°F. Coat 4-qt. baking dish with cooking spray. Heat oil in large skillet over medium heat. Add sausage crumbles and sage, and cook 7 to 9 minutes, or until sausage is browned. Drain on paper-towel-lined plate.

2. Melt 3 Tbs. margarine in same skillet; add onions, celery, and fennel; and cook 5 to 7 minutes, or until vegetables are soft. Deglaze pan with wine, and add chestnuts. Cook 2 to 3 minutes, or until most of liquid has evaporated.

3. Place bread cubes in bowl. Stir in onion mixture, then sausage crumbles. Mix in parsley and thyme, and season with pepper. Stir in broth, adding more if necessary without making stuffing too wet. Spoon stuffing into prepared baking dish, and dot top with remaining 2 Tbs. margarine. Cover with foil and bake 30 minutes. Remove foil and bake 30 to 40 minutes longer, or until top is browned and crisp.

PER SERVING: 347 CAL; 16 G PROT; 10.5 G TOTAL FAT (3 G SAT FAT); 47 G CARB; 0 MG CHOL; 531 MG SOD; 8 G FIBER; 9 G SUGARS

Storage Hint: Freeze Chestnuts

Freeze chestnuts in resealable plastic bags for future use.

Brussels Sprouts with Walnuts and Dried Cranberries

SERVES 6

These seared, then steamed, Brussels sprouts have all the earmarks of a holiday side dish, but they are well worth eating during the other cold weather months when Brussels sprouts are in season.

½ cup coarsely chopped raw walnuts

2 tsp. olive oil

1 ½ lb. Brussels sprouts, trimmed and halved

2 medium shallots, halved and sliced (¼ cup)

1 clove garlic, minced (1 tsp.)

¼ cup coarsely chopped dried cranberries

1 Tbs. agave nectar

1 Tbs. walnut oil

1. Heat large skillet over medium-high heat. Add walnuts, and toast 3 to 4 minutes, or until fragrant. Transfer to plate, and set aside.

2. Wipe out skillet, and return to heat. Add olive oil, and swirl skillet to coat bottom. Add Brussels sprouts, and cook 5 minutes, or until browned, stirring occasionally. Add shallots and garlic, and cook 1 minute more.

3. Stir in cranberries, agave nectar, and 1 cup water. Partially cover pot, reduce heat to medium, and simmer 5 to 7 minutes, or until most of liquid has evaporated and Brussels sprouts are just tender but not soft. Transfer to serving bowl. Stir in walnut oil and toasted walnuts, and season with salt and pepper, if desired.

PER SERVING: 172 CAL; 5 G PROT; 11 G TOTAL FAT (1 G SAT FAT); 19 G CARB; 0 MG CHOL; 124 MG SOD; 5 G FIBER; 9 G SUGARS

Prep Talk: Trimming Brussels Sprouts

To trim Brussels sprouts, simply cut a thin sliver off the base. Halve, or leave smaller sprouts whole.

Roasted Vegetable Cornucopias with Gravy

Easy enough for kids to help make, elegant enough for a Thanksgiving celebration, these wow-worthy cornucopias will take you back to the times you made horns of plenty in grade school.

CORNUCOPIAS

1 17.3-oz. pkg. frozen puff pastry, thawed

ROASTED VEGETABLES

2 cups cauliflower florets

2 cups baby zucchini, or 8 oz. regular zucchini, halved and cut into 1 ½-inch chunks

2 cups baby pattypan squash, or 8 oz. regular pattypan squash, cut into 1 ½-inch chunks

1 cup baby carrots

12 purple pearl onions, peeled and halved

6 oz. cremini mushrooms, trimmed

¼ cup olive oil

2 Tbs. chopped fresh sage

2 Tbs. chopped fresh marjoram

1 Tbs. chopped fresh thyme

1 tsp. salt

¼ tsp. ground black pepper

⅔ cup Holiday Gravy (p. 308)

1. Preheat oven to 425°F. Coat 2 baking sheets with cooking spray.

2. To make Cornucopias: Tear off 8 18-inch-long sheets of heavy-duty foil. Fold each sheet into quarters. Roll each quarter into cone; bend "tail" if desired. Coat each con with cooking spray.

3. Place 1 puff pastry sheet on lightly floured work surface. Refrigerate second sheet until ready to use. Gently pull ends of puff pastry to stretch it out to 10 inches wide. Cut pastry sheet into 20 ½-inch strips. Loosely wrap 1 strip around pointed end of first foil cone, and spiral strip around cone, overlapping edges as you wrap. When strip runs out, brush end with water, then press on second strip to adhere. Continue wrapping cone with 4 more pastry strips, "gluing" them with water as you go. Repeat with remaining strips and cones and remaining pastry sheet.

4. Place cones on their sides on 1 baking sheet. Bake 20 to 25 minutes, or until golden brown. Cool on baking sheet.

5. To make Roasted Vegetables: Increase oven heat to 450°F. Toss together all vegetables, oil, sage, marjoram, thyme, salt, and pepper in large bowl. Spread vegetables on second baking sheet. Roast 30 to 35 minutes, or until vegetables are browned and tender, turning every 10 minutes to make sure they cook evenly. Transfer to large bowl.

6. To assemble Cornucopias: Gently pull foil cones away from insides of cooled cornucopias, and discard. Toss vegetables with gravy. Spoon into cornucopias, and serve.

PER SERVING: 402 CAL; 7 G PROT; 26 G TOTAL FAT (4 G SAT FAT); 37 G CARB; 0 MG CHOL; 557 MG SOD; 3 G FIBER; 4 G SUGARS

easy beans and lentils

If we were to put all of the recipes in this book that call for beans and lentils into one chapter, that chapter would probably take up three-quarters of the book. But these recipes are all supersimple, super-satisfying, very beany, and very lentil-y offerings that belong in a chapter all their own.

Chickpea Tacos

SERVES 4

Turns out, tacos don't have to be hot to be delicious. The chickpea-avocado mash used as a filling here is prepared and served at room temperature. (It makes a great sandwich spread as well.)

1 avocado, peeled, pitted, and diced

1 15-oz. can chickpeas, rinsed and drained

3 Tbs. chopped fresh cilantro

4 tsp. fresh lime juice

1 clove garlic, minced (1 tsp.)

8 corn taco shells

2 cups baby salad greens

1 cup prepared salsa (medium or hot)

½ cup vegan sour cream

1. Place avocado in small bowl, and mash with fork. Stir in chickpeas, cilantro, lime juice, and garlic; season with salt and pepper.

2. Set taco shells in napkin-lined basket. Place salad greens, salsa, and sour cream in separate bowls, and set out alongside chickpea-avocado mash.

3. To serve, let each person build tacos by filling each shell with ¼ cup chickpea-avocado mash, some greens, salsa, and sour cream.

PER SERVING: 402 CAL; 11 G PROT; 19 G TOTAL FAT (4 G SAT FAT); 51 G CARB; 0 MG CHOL; 800 MG SOD, 10 G FIBER; 2 G SUGARS

Shopping Savvy: Taco Shells

Because the fat content of taco shells can vary, look for brands that contain approximately 6 grams or fewer per shell.

Chickpea Stew with Couscous

SERVES 6

Prepared creamy soups like butternut squash, corn, and potato-leek make great bases for hearty stews that sneak an extra veggie serving past picky eaters.

2 Tbs. olive oil

1 medium carrot, diced (¾ cup)

1 small onion, diced (1 cup)

½ red bell pepper, chopped (½ cup)

1 Tbs. cumin seeds

1 bay leaf, crumbled

2 16-oz. cans chickpeas, rinsed and drained, divided

1 32-oz. container butternut squash soup, divided

1 ½ cups couscous

1. Heat oil in saucepan over medium heat. Sauté carrot in oil 3 to 5 minutes, or until softened. Add onion and bell pepper, and sauté 3 to 5 minutes more, or until soft. Stir in cumin seeds and bay leaf.

2. Purée ¾ cup chickpeas and ¾ cup butternut squash soup in blender until smooth. Add to carrot mixture along with remaining chickpeas and soup. Simmer 15 to 20 minutes. Remove bay leaf and season with salt and black pepper.

3. Meanwhile, place couscous in heat-proof bowl, and stir in 1 ½ cups boiling water. Cover, and let stand 3 to 5 minutes, or until all liquid is absorbed. Fluff couscous with fork. Divide couscous among 6 shallow bowls. Ladle chickpea stew around couscous in each bowl.

PER SERVING: 480 CAL; 15 G PROT; 8 G TOTAL FAT (1 G SAT FAT); 87 G CARB; 0 MG CHOL; 645 MG SOD; 11 G FIBER; 11 G SUGARS

Guidelines for Cooking Beans and Legumes

Legumes	Presoak	Cooking Time
ADZUKI BEANS	YES	1 TO 1 ½ HOURS
BLACK BEANS	YES	1 TO 2 HOURS
BLACK-EYED PEAS	YES	1 TO 1 ½ HOURS
CANNELLINI BEANS	YES	1 TO 2 HOURS
CHICKPEAS	YES	2 ½ TO 3 HOURS
CRANBERRY BEANS	YES	1 TO 2 HOURS
FAVA BEANS	YES	1 ½ TO 2 HOURS
FAVA BEANS, SKINS REMOVED	YES	40 TO 50 MIN.
GREAT NORTHERN BEANS	YES	1 TO 2 HOURS
KIDNEY BEANS	YES	1 ½ TO 2 HOURS
LENTILS (BROWN)	NO	30 MIN. TO 1 HOUR
LENTILS (GREEN)	NO	30 TO 45 MIN.
LENTILS (RED)	NO	20 TO 30 MIN.
LIMA BEANS (SMALL)	YES	45 MIN. TO 1 ½ HOURS
LIMA BEANS (LARGE)	YES	1 TO 1 ½ HOURS
MUNG BEANS	NO	1 HOUR
NAVY BEANS	YES	1 TO 2 HOURS
PINK BEANS	YES	1 TO 2 HOURS
PINTO BEANS	YES	1 TO 2 HOURS
RED BEANS	YES	1 ½ TO 2 HOURS
SOYBEANS	YES	3 TO 4 HOURS
SPLIT PEAS (GREEN)	NO	45 MIN. TO 1 HOUR
SPLIT PEAS (YELLOW)	NO	45 MIN. TO 1 ½ HOURS

Refried Beans

Making Mexican for dinner? Don't forget the refried beans. This recipe is so good that you may find yourself eating it with a spoon—no chips or salsa necessary. Serve these refried beans with chips, slather on tortillas and top with vegan cheese for quesadillas, or pair with the Southwestern Tofu Scramble (p. 132) for a vegan version of huevos rancheros.

2 15-oz. cans pinto beans

1 Tbs. olive oil

5 green onions, white and pale green parts only, chopped (¼ cup)

1 Tbs. ground cumin

2 cloves garlic, minced (2 tsp.)

1 Tbs. fresh lime juice

2 tsp. freshly grated lime zest

4 Tbs. chopped fresh cilantro, for garnish

....

Success Secret:
Lime Zest and Juice
....

This meat-free bean dish gets a lift from lime zest and juice. Try adding a tablespoon or two of juice and a teaspoon of zest to other Tex-Mex dishes that taste like they're missing something.

1. Mash pinto beans and liquid with potato masher in large bowl. Leave some beans whole, or mash until smooth if you prefer a creamier texture.

2. Heat oil in large nonstick skillet over medium heat. Add green onions, cumin, and garlic, and cook 1 minute, stirring frequently. Stir in mashed beans (mixture will be soupy). Increase heat to medium-high, and cook beans 10 minutes, or until they thicken and will hold their shape on plate, stirring frequently.

3. Remove pan from heat. Stir in lime juice and lime zest, and season with pepper. Garnish each serving with 1 Tbs. cilantro.

PER SERVING: 227 CAL; 11 G PROT; 4.5 G TOTAL FAT (0.5 G SAT FAT); 36 G CARB; 0 MG CHOL; 476 MG SOD; 9 G FIBER; 4 G SUGARS

Beans and Bratwurst

SERVES 6

Browned-till-crisp leeks make this basic sausage and bean stew truly special.
Spice it up with hot mustard and serve with brown rice or potatoes.

1 14-oz. pkg. vegan bratwurst sausages, sliced into ½-inch rounds

3 large leeks, white and pale green parts only, halved and sliced into ½-inch pieces (4 cups)

1 14.5-oz. can diced tomatoes

1 15-oz. can cannellini beans, rinsed and drained

3 Tbs. molasses

1. Coat large nonstick skillet with cooking spray, and heat over medium heat. Add bratwurst rounds, and cook 3 minutes per side, or until browned. Transfer to plate.

2. Coat skillet with cooking spray once more, increase heat to high, and add leeks. Cook 4 minutes, or until leeks brown around edges, stirring halfway through. Add tomatoes and liquid, beans, molasses, ¾ cup water, and bratwurst. Season with salt and pepper. Reduce heat to medium, and simmer 5 minutes, or until heated through and liquid is thickened.

PER SERVING: 262 CAL; 17 G PROT; 7.5 G TOTAL FAT (0 G SAT FAT); 33 G CARB; 0 MG CHOL; 875 MG SOD; 5 G FIBER; 12 G SUGARS

Shopping Savvy: Molasses

The distinctive flavor of molasses is something some cooks can't get enough of but others prefer in moderation. If you like strong molasses flavor in your recipes, choose unsulfured molasses, which has a robust flavor.

Adzuki Beans and Winter Squash

SERVES 4

This classic macrobiotic dish makes an especially comforting meal as the weather gets colder. Red adzuki beans are slightly sweet and are often used in Japanese desserts. They can be found in natural food stores or Asian markets.

1 cup dried adzuki beans, rinsed and picked through

1 4-inch strip kombu

1 lb. butternut or other winter squash, seeded and cubed (2 cups)

¼ tsp. salt

1 Tbs. low-sodium tamari or soy sauce

3 green onions, thinly sliced on diagonal

1. Place adzuki beans in large non metal bowl, and cover with water. Let soak 8 hours, or overnight. Drain.

2. Place kombu in 1 inch of water in large saucepan. Soak 10 minutes, or until soft. Add adzuki beans and enough water to cover. Put lid on pan, and bring beans to a boil. Reduce heat to medium-low and simmer, covered, 25 minutes. Add squash and salt. Simmer, covered, 25 minutes more, or until squash is soft. Stir in tamari, and sprinkle with green onions.

PER SERVING: 196 CAL; 10 G PROT; 1 G TOTAL FAT (0 G SAT FAT); 42 G CARB; 0 MG CHOL; 499 MG SOD; 8 G FIBER; 4 G SUGARS

....

Buy and Try: Kombu

....

Seaweed as a seasoning for more than Asian dishes? You betcha. Kombu, one of the seaweeds used to make dashi broth for miso soup, can be thrown into soups, stews, and bean dishes the same way you would add a bay leaf to help add flavor depth.

Easy Baked Beans

SERVES 8

Baked beans can easily be doctored up to suit a cook's taste,
so feel free to make these with more or less sugar, a spicier salsa or mustard,
and add-ins such as vegan sausage or vegan hot dogs.

1 ½ cups dried red kidney beans, rinsed and picked through

2 medium onions, thinly sliced (3 cups)

1 8-oz. jar medium salsa

⅓ cup packed dark brown sugar

3 Tbs. yellow mustard

1. Soak beans in 6 cups water overnight. Drain; reserve 1 cup soaking liquid.

2. Coat Dutch oven with cooking spray, and heat over low heat. Add onions, cover, and cook 15 minutes, or until browned. Stir in soaking liquid. Simmer 5 minutes, scraping up onion bits stuck to bottom of pot. Stir in salsa, sugar, mustard, and 5 cups water. Cover, and cook 1 ½ hours. Uncover; simmer 1 hour more, or until sauce has thickened.

PER SERVING: 166 CAL; 8 G PROT; 0.5 G TOTAL FAT (0 G SAT FAT); 33 G CARB; 0 MG CHOL; 566 MG SOD; 9 G FIBER; 12 G SUGARS

....

Prep Talk:
Speedy Bean Soaking

....

Instead of soaking beans overnight, simply simmer them 10 minutes, then let stand 30 minutes. Drain and cook as directed.

White Beans with Oregano

SERVES 6

One of the best things about oregano is that the dried herb is as good as, if not better than, fresh, so you can have it on hand to use in recipes. This dish can be also be puréed, then served cold as a dip for vegetables and bread sticks.

2 Tbs. olive oil

1 small onion, chopped (1 cup)

3 cloves garlic, minced (1 Tbs.)

1 Tbs. dried oregano

2 15-oz. cans cannellini beans, rinsed and drained

1. Heat oil in skillet over medium heat. Add onion, and sauté 5 to 7 minutes, or until onion begins to brown. Stir in garlic and oregano, and cook 30 seconds, or until fragrant.

2. Add beans and 1 cup water, and season with salt and pepper. Reduce heat to medium-low, and simmer 15 minutes, or until half of liquid has evaporated but beans are still a little soupy.

PER SERVING: 164 CAL; 6 G PROT; 5 G TOTAL FAT (0.5 G SAT FAT); 23 G CARB; 0 MG CHOL; 317 MG SOD; 6 G FIBER; 1 G SUGARS

Spicy Black-Eyed Pea Salad

SERVES 6

Pile this protein-packed salad on a bed of greens or fold it into flour tortillas and you've got an easy entrée. The dish is a potluck favorite, too, because it travels well and the recipe can easily be doubled or tripled.

2 14-oz. cans black-eyed peas, rinsed and drained

1 medium green bell pepper, chopped (1 cup)

½ cup chopped red onion

1 jalapeño chile, seeded and finely minced (2 Tbs.)

1 clove garlic, minced (1 tsp.)

1 medium avocado, peeled, pitted, and cubed (1 cup)

2 Tbs. fresh lemon juice

¼ cup olive oil

3 Tbs. red wine vinegar

1 Tbs. Szechuan sauce

2 tsp. sugar

1. Toss together black-eyed peas, bell pepper, onion, jalapeño, and garlic in large bowl. Toss avocado with lemon juice in separate bowl. Add avocado to black-eyed pea mixture.

2. Whisk together oil, vinegar, Szechuan sauce, and sugar in bowl used for avocado. Toss black-eyed pea mixture with Szechuan sauce dressing.

PER SERVING: 223 CAL; 5 G PROT; 14 G TOTAL FAT (2 G SAT FAT); 20 G CARB; 0 MG CHOL; 438 MG SOD; 6 G FIBER; 3 G SUGARS

Buy and Try: Szechuan Sauce

Used to flavor stir-fries, Szechuan sauce is a thick, hot, and sweet liquid sold in bottles in most supermarkets. It can add a spicy kick to soups, stews, salads, and marinated tofu or tempeh.

Lentil Lexicon

Type	Taste and texture	Best in
BELUGA LENTILS	FIRM AND CHEWY, BELUGA LENTILS GET THEIR CAVIAR-THEMED NAME BECAUSE THEY GLISTEN ONCE COOKED.	SALADS, BROTHY SOUPS
BLACK LENTILS OR BLACK GRAM (URAD DAL)	SMALL, STRONG-FLAVORED BLACK INDIAN BEANS, THEY ARE ALSO SKINNED AND SPLIT INTO WHITE LENTILS.	BEAN DISHES BECAUSE THEY REMAIN INTACT AFTER COOKING
BROWN LENTILS	THE MOST COMMONLY FOUND LENTIL TYPE HAS A SOFT, SLIGHTLY CHEWY TEXTURE AND EARTHY TASTE.	SOUPS, STEWS, VEGGIE BURGERS, CHILI
FRENCH GREEN LENTILS	THESE DARK, BROWNISH-GREEN LENTILS HAVE A SLIGHTLY PEPPERY TASTE AND STAY FIRM WHEN THEY'RE COOKED.	SALADS, FRENCH AND ITALIAN DISHES
RED LENTILS	A COMMON INGREDIENT IN MIDDLE EASTERN AND EASTERN EUROPEAN CUISINE, THEY'RE TENDER AND MILD AND BREAK DOWN TO A PURÉE-LIKE CONSISTENCY WHEN COOKED.	THICK SOUPS, PÂTÉS, AND SPREADS
WHITE OR IVORY LENTILS	THESE SKINNED AND SPLIT BLACK LENTILS ARE MILD AND SOFT.	SOUPS AND STEWS, INDIAN FLATBREADS
YELLOW LENTILS	USUALLY SOLD SPLIT, YELLOW LENTILS HAVE A SLIGHTLY NUTTY FLAVOR. THEIR TEXTURE IS SIMILAR TO RED LENTILS.	THICK SOUPS, PÂTÉS, AND SPREADS

Indian Lentil Pilaf

SERVES 6

Ginger and garam masala give this zesty rice dish authentic flavor.
If you're not a lentil lover, try the recipe with 2 cups cooked chickpeas.

1 cup dried brown lentils,
rinsed and picked through

2 Tbs. canola oil

1 medium onion, finely chopped
(1 ⅓ cups)

2 large carrots, diced (2 cups)

1 cup basmati rice

3 cloves garlic, minced (1 Tbs.)

1 Tbs. minced fresh ginger

1 ½ tsp. garam masala

1 14.5-oz. can diced tomatoes

1 cup low-sodium vegetable broth

Fresh cilantro, for garnish, optional

1. Bring lentils and 4 cups water to a boil in large pot or Dutch oven. Reduce heat to low, and simmer 15 minutes, or until lentils are firm-tender. Drain, reserving ¾ cup cooking liquid, and transfer lentils to bowl.

2. Wipe out pot; heat oil over medium-high heat. Sauté onion in oil 4 minutes, or until just golden. Add carrots and rice, and cook 3 minutes, or until rice is toasted and fragrant, stirring constantly. Add garlic, ginger, and garam masala, and cook 1 minute more.

3. Stir in tomatoes, broth, and reserved cooking liquid and lentils, and bring to a boil. Cover, reduce heat to low, and cook 20 minutes, or until liquid is absorbed and rice is tender. Season with salt and pepper. Remove from heat, cover, and let stand 5 minutes. Fluff with fork, then spoon pilaf into shallow bowls, and garnish with cilantro, if desired.

PER SERVING: 302 CAL; 13 G PROT; 4 G TOTAL FAT (2 G SAT FAT); 54 G CARB; 0 MG CHOL; 624 MG SOD; 7 G FIBER; 7 G SUGARS

....
Prep Talk: Rinsing Lentils
....

Rinsing and sorting (picking through) lentils washes off any dust or dirt and gets rid of small stones or empty hulls. Place lentils in a large bowl of cold water; skim off anything that floats. Drain. Pick through the lentils with your fingers to remove anything that's not a lentil.

Curried Lentils with Cauliflower

SERVES 2

Once you have all the ingredients together for this recipe, it's a heat-and-serve dish that takes just 5 minutes.

2 tsp. olive oil

¼ cup green onions

2 cloves garlic, minced (2 tsp.)

1 tsp. curry powder

1 tsp. ground cumin

1 medium head cauliflower (1 lb.), cut into 1-inch florets

1 cup diced tomatoes

1 15-oz. can lentils, rinsed and drained

Paprika, for garnish, optional

1. Heat oil in large saucepan over medium heat. Add green onions and garlic, and sauté until fragrant. Reduce heat, and add curry and cumin. Cook 2 minutes, stirring frequently.

2. Add cauliflower and tomatoes, and sauté until cauliflower is tender. Add lentils; cook 1 to 2 minutes to heat through. Add salt to taste, and garnish with sprinkling of paprika, if desired.

PER SERVING: 217 CAL; 13 G PROT; 5.5 G TOTAL FAT (0.5 G SAT FAT); 34 G CARB; 0 MG CHOL; 248 MG SOD; 14 G FIBER; 11 G SUGARS

Prep Talk: How Many Lentils Are in a Can?

One can of lentils is equal to about 1 ½ cups cooked lentils. And ½ cup dry lentils will make about 1 ½ cups cooked lentils.

Moroccan Pumpkin and Lentils

SERVES 8

This hearty North African stew will ward off the first chill of fall with its colorful ingredients and warm, spicy flavors.

2 Tbs. olive oil

1 large onion, diced (1 ½ cups)

1 jalapeño chile, seeded and sliced

1 14.5-oz. can diced tomatoes, drained, or 4 tomatoes, chopped

1 cup dried green lentils, rinsed and picked through

1 Tbs. paprika

¼ tsp. cayenne pepper

1 tsp. cumin

1 small pumpkin (2 lb.), peeled, seeded, and cubed

½ cup tomato purée

¼ cup chopped fresh cilantro, for garnish

1. Heat oil in large saucepan over medium-high heat. Add onion and jalapeño, and sauté 10 minutes, or until onion is translucent and golden. Add tomatoes, lentils, peprika, cayenne, and cumin, and cook 2 to 3 minutes more. Stir in pumpkin, tomato purée, and 2 ½ cups water. Season with salt and pepper.

2. Reduce heat to medium low, and cook 40 minutes, or until pumpkin and lentils are tender, stirring occasionally and adding more water if needed. Season with salt and pepper. Garnish with cilantro, and serve hot.

PER SERVING: 161 CAL; 9 G PROT; 4 G TOTAL FAT (0 G SAT FAT); 25 G CARB; 0 MG CHOL; 287 MG SOD; 9 G FIBER; 7 G SUGARS

soups and stews

"Serve with a salad and some fresh, crusty bread."

There. We said it. That's pretty much what soup and stew recipes in other cookbooks tell you to do every time. So rather than repeat ourselves over and over again, we figured we'd just write it once—here—because the recommendation applies to all the dishes in this chapter.

And oh, what soups and stews they are. Cool, refreshing summer soups like gazpacho and carrot bisque. Light lunch soups like Mexican Rice (p. 220) and Quinoa and Spinach (p. 224). Exotic soups like Vietnamese Pho (p. 232), Moroccan Harira (p. 231), and Soupe au Pistou (p. 225). Satisfying, one-bowl meal soups like Roasted Corn Chowder (p. 222) and Curried White Bean and Kale (p. 229). . . . Flip through the pages and you'll find them hard to resist. Of course, if you prefer cornbread, biscuits, tortillas, Indian flat-bread, or pitas, that's OK too. Heck, you could even serve these recipes with a handful of potato chips or saltines and they'd still shine.

Cold Carrot-Ginger Bisque

SERVES 6

Pick up a quart of carrot juice in the refrigerated section of the grocery store
and you have the base for this satisfying summer soup thickened
with pine nuts and avocado. To keep it completely raw (store-bought carrot juice
has been pasteurized), juice the carrots yourself.

4 cups fresh carrot juice

¾ cup pine nuts

1 medium avocado, peeled, pitted,
and sliced

2 tsp. grated fresh ginger

2 tsp. fresh lime juice

1 clove garlic, minced (1 tsp.)

¼ tsp. ground cumin

Purée all ingredients in blender or
food processor until smooth. Season
with salt and pepper.

PER SERVING: 199 CAL; 4 G PROT; 15 G TOTAL FAT
(1.5 G SAT FAT); 14 G CARB; 0 MG CHOL; 296 MG SOD;
2 G FIBER; 1 G SUGARS

Storage Hint:
Use Glass or Ceramic Container

Carrot juice can stain plastic containers and metal bowls can turn avocado
brown, so store this soup in a glass or
ceramic bowl.

Green-and-Gold Gazpacho

SERVES 6

There are so many nifty things about this cold soup. The first is that it uses up peppery radish leaves so that you don't have to throw them all away. Another is that it's made with yellow tomatoes, which makes it look and taste like a surprise to guests.

1 cup radishes

1 cup radish leaves or watercress

½ cup basil leaves

4 green onions, coarsely chopped

3 large yellow or green zebra tomatoes (1 ½ lb.), cut into quarters

2 Tbs. fresh lime juice

1 Tbs. olive oil

1 Tbs. prepared horseradish

½ tsp. celery salt

¼ tsp. vegan Worcestershire sauce

Lime wedges and radish quarters, for garnish

1. Place radishes, radish leaves, basil, and green onions in bowl of food processor, and pulse until finely chopped and almost smooth. Add tomatoes, lime juice, oil, horseradish, celery salt, and Worcestershire sauce, and pulse until finely chopped. Season with salt and pepper, and thin with water if soup is too thick.

2. Thread lime wedges and radish quarters onto 6 toothpicks.

3. To serve, ladle soup into glasses, and garnish with lime-and-radish skewers.

PER SERVING: 47 CAL; 1 G PROT; 2.5 G TOTAL FAT (0.5 G SAT FAT); 6 G CARB; 0 MG CHOL; 304 MG SOD; 2 G FIBER; 3 G SUGARS

Storage Hint: Picnic Soup

For easy transport and serving on a picnic, pack this soup in a tight-closing bottle or wide-mouthed Thermos, and preassemble skewers of lime wedges and radish quarters to pack in a resealable plastic bag. Because the gazpacho is puréed, guests can sip it from small cups rather than using spoons.

Mexican Rice Soup

SERVES 6

This light soup (traditionally made with chicken and chicken broth) gets its body from diced avocado and tortilla strips added at the table. The heat of the soup warms the avocado and tortilla strips without turning them to mush.

BROTH

1 Tbs. olive oil

1 small onion, finely chopped (¾ cup)

2 cloves garlic, minced (2 tsp.)

3 cups low-sodium vegetable broth

1 Tbs. freshly grated lime zest

1 tsp. dried oregano

SOUP

¼ cup short-grain rice

2 small tomatoes, seeded and diced (1 cup)

⅓ cup fresh or frozen corn kernels

1 8-inch flour tortilla

1 medium avocado, peeled, pitted, and diced (1 cup)

2 green onions, thinly sliced (¼ cup)

¼ cup chopped fresh cilantro

6 lime wedges

Hot sauce, for garnish, optional

1. To make Broth: Heat oil in large saucepan over medium heat. Add onion, and sauté 5 to 7 minutes, or until softened. Stir in garlic, and sauté 1 minute more. Add broth, lime zest, oregano, and 3 cups water; cover, and reduce heat to medium-low. Simmer 10 minutes. Strain broth, discard solids, and return to saucepan.

2. To make Soup: Add rice to broth. Bring to a simmer over medium-low heat, cover, and simmer 15 minutes, or until rice is soft. Stir in tomatoes and corn, and season with salt and pepper. Simmer 10 minutes.

3. Meanwhile, preheat oven to 350°F. Spray flour tortilla with cooking spray, and cut into thin strips. Arrange strips on baking sheet, and bake 5 to 7 minutes, or until tortilla is crisp.

4. Ladle soup into serving bowls. Garnish with avocado, tortilla strips, green onions, cilantro, lime wedges, and hot sauce, if desired.

PER SERVING: 131 CAL; 2 G PROT; 7 G TOTAL FAT (1 G SAT FAT); 16 G CARB; 0 MG CHOL; 321 MG SOD; 3 G FIBER; 3 G SUGARS

"Wild" Mushroom Soup with Sage and Croutons

SERVES 6

Wild mushroom mixes in the store are a collection of cultivated species—not varieties gathered in the woods. The blends do feature mushrooms with more robust flavor, so they're ideal in recipes like this soup where 'shrooms are the stars.

3 Tbs. olive oil, divided

1 medium onion, chopped (1 ⅓ cups)

1 ½ lb. assorted mushrooms

1 0.75-oz. pkg. dried porcini mushrooms (¼ cup), soaked in hot water 30 minutes and drained

2 cloves garlic, minced (2 tsp.)

1 tsp. chopped fresh thyme

¼ tsp. freshly grated lemon zest

2 Tbs. sherry vinegar

3 cups low-sodium vegetable broth

12 sage leaves

6 slices French bread, cut into ¾-inch cubes (3 cups)

1. Heat 1 Tbs. oil in large pot over medium-high heat. Add onion, and sauté 7 minutes. Stir in all mushrooms. Cook 10 minutes, stirring occasionally. Add garlic, thyme, and lemon zest, and cook 1 minute more. Stir in vinegar, and simmer 1 to 2 minutes. Add broth and 2 cups water, and bring to a boil. Reduce heat to medium-low. Simmer, partially covered, 45 minutes. Cool 20 minutes, then purée in blender until smooth.

2. Preheat oven to 350°F. Heat remaining 2 Tbs. oil in pan over medium-high heat. Add sage leaves, and fry 1 to 2 minutes, or until bubbling subsides. Remove sage leaves, and drain.

3. Toss bread cubes with sage oil, and season with salt and pepper. Transfer to baking sheet and bake 15 minutes, or until golden brown. Serve soup garnished with sage leaves and croutons.

PER SERVING: 193 CAL; 7 G PROT; 7.5 G TOTAL FAT (1 G SAT FAT); 25 G CARB; 0 MG CHOL; 213 MG SOD; 4 G FIBER; 5 G SUGARS

Buy and Try: Porcini Mushroom

Porcini mushrooms are true wild mushrooms—buy them dry and add to other mushroom dishes to boost flavor.

SERVING SUGGESTION
This rich, elegant soup calls for a rich, elegant red wine from Bordeaux or Napa.

Roasted Corn Chowder

SERVES 6

Frozen roasted corn gives chowder a flavor usually achieved by a long simmer. A blend of corn and soymilk thickens the soup and speeds the cooking process.

1 Tbs. olive oil

3.5 oz. frozen diced shallots, or 1 cup frozen diced onions

1 orange bell pepper, diced (1 cup)

1 ½ cups frozen O'Brien potatoes

2 14-oz. cans low-sodium vegetable broth

16 oz. frozen roasted corn kernels, divided

4 strips smoky tempeh bacon

¼ cup chopped fresh parsley

2 cups unsweetened plain soymilk

1. Heat oil in large pot over medium-high heat. Add shallots and bell pepper, and cook 5 minutes, or until vegetables are soft. Stir in potatoes, and cook 3 minutes more. Add broth and all but 1 cup corn, and bring to a simmer. Reduce heat to medium-low, cover, and cook 7 minutes.

2. Meanwhile, heat skillet over medium-high heat, and coat with cooking spray. Cook bacon strips 8 minutes, or until crispy. Chop, and toss with parsley.

3. Blend reserved 1 cup corn with soymilk in blender; add to soup. Return chowder to a simmer, then remove from heat. Serve sprinkled with bacon and parsley.

PER SERVING: 207 CAL; 8 G PROT; 5 G TOTAL FAT (‹1 G SAT FAT); 35 G CARB; 0 MG CHOL; 192 MG SOD; 4 G FIBER; 6 G SUGARS

Buy and Try:
Frozen Roasted Corn

Corn kernels are one of the best frozen products out there, but the recently released frozen roasted corn kicks the food into the stratosphere. Stock up if you find it and use in salads, soups (like this one), chili, and anywhere you want bold, grilled flavor.

Sherried Kabocha Soup with Spiced Pepitas

SERVES 6

You may want to double or triple the pepitas in this recipe. They're crunchy and snackable, plus they taste delicious sprinkled over salads. If kabocha squash is unavailable, any other type of winter squash will work in this recipe.

PEPITAS

½ cup hulled raw pepitas (pumpkin seeds)

1 Tbs. olive oil

2 tsp. agave nectar

½ tsp. smoked paprika

½ tsp. salt

2 Tbs. chopped fresh cilantro

SOUP

1 Tbs. olive oil

1 medium onion, thinly sliced (1 cup)

2 cloves garlic, minced (2 tsp.)

2 tsp. smoked paprika

1 bay leaf

2 Tbs. dry sherry

1 ½ lb. kabocha squash, peeled, seeded, and cut into 1-inch pieces

2 cups low-sodium vegetable broth

1. To make Pepitas: Preheat oven to 350°F. Line baking sheet with parchment paper. Toss together pepitas, oil, agave nectar, paprika, and salt in bowl. Spread on prepared baking sheet, and bake 10 to 12 minutes, stirring occasionally. Cool. Break pepitas apart, and toss with cilantro.

2. To make Soup: Heat oil in large pot over medium-high heat. Add onion, sauté 5 to 7 minutes, then stir in garlic, paprika, and bay leaf. Cook 1 minute more. Add sherry, and cook 2 minutes. Add squash, broth, and 1 cup water. Bring to a simmer, cover, and reduce heat to medium-low. Cook 25 minutes, or until squash is tender.

3. Remove bay leaf, and purée soup in food processor until smooth. Season with salt and pepper, if desired. Serve sprinkled with pepitas.

PER SERVING: 157 CAL; 4 G PROT; 10 G TOTAL FAT (1.5 G SAT FAT); 15 G CARB; 0 MG CHOL; 341 MG SOD; 3 G FIBER; 7 G SUGARS

SERVING SUGGESTION

To highlight the hints of sherry in the soup, serve it with a Vinho Verde from Portugal.

Quinoa and Spinach Soup

SERVES 6

This satisfying soup gets its texture from quinoa rather than cream or a thickener. Feel free to throw in 2 cups of your favorite frozen vegetables to add flavor and nutrients.

1 medium red onion, diced (1 ¼ cups)

3 cups low-sodium vegetable broth

¾ cup quinoa, rinsed

1 14.5-oz. can diced tomatoes with basil, garlic, and oregano

10 oz. spinach leaves (12 cups)

1. Coat large pot with cooking spray, and heat over medium heat. Add onion, and sauté 5 minutes, or until soft. Stir in broth and 4 cups water, and bring to a boil. Add quinoa, and reduce heat to medium-low. Cover, and simmer 15 minutes.

2. Stir in tomatoes and liquid and spinach leaves. Simmer 5 minutes, uncovered, or until spinach and quinoa are tender. Season with salt and pepper, if desired, and serve immediately.

PER SERVING: 138 CAL; 6 G PROT; 1.5 G TOTAL FAT (0 G SAT FAT); 26 G CARB; 0 MG CHOL; 591 MG SOD; 4 G FIBER; 7 G SUGARS

Success Secret: Seasoning Plain Canned Tomatoes

If you don't have preseasoned diced tomatoes on hand, doctor up plain diced tomatoes with ½ tsp. each dried basil and oregano and 1 clove minced garlic.

Soupe au Pistou

SERVES 8

Pistou is a fragrant sauce of garlic, basil, and olive oil that's related to Italian pesto. Here, the heat of the soup releases the flavors of the garlic and basil.

SOUP

⅓ cup dried chickpeas, rinsed and picked through

⅓ cup dried pinto beans, rinsed and picked through

1 15-oz. can chopped tomatoes

1 medium onion, chopped (1 cup)

1 clove garlic, minced (1 tsp.)

1 bay leaf

1 sprig thyme

3 medium red potatoes, cut into ½-inch chunks (1 cup)

2 carrots, sliced (1 cup)

1 cup frozen Italian flat green beans

2 oz. vermicelli, optional

PISTOU

8 cups basil leaves

8 cloves garlic, peeled

½ cup olive oil

1. To make Soup: Place chickpeas and pinto beans in large pot, and cover with water. Bring to a boil, cover, and cook 10 minutes. Remove from heat, and let stand 30 minutes. Drain beans, and rinse. Return beans to pot and add tomatoes and juice, onion, garlic, bay leaf, thyme, and 5 cups water. Cover, and bring to a boil. Season with pepper, reduce heat to medium-low, cover, and simmer 30 minutes. Add potatoes and carrots, and simmer, covered, 30 minutes. Stir in flat beans, and cook 10 minutes. Stir in vermicelli, if desired. Cook 3 minutes more. Remove bay leaf.

2. To make Pistou: Pulse basil and garlic in food processor until finely chopped. Add oil, and pulse until combined. Transfer to small bowl. Spoon 2 Tbs. pistou in bottom of each bowl. Spoon soup over top.

PER SERVING: 237 CAL; 6 G PROT; 14.5 G TOTAL FAT (2 G SAT FAT); 22 G CARB; 0 MG CHOL; 375 MG SOD; 6 G FIBER; 5 G SUGARS

Fresh Pea Soup with Tarragon

SERVES 4

Warm or chilled, this bright green soup is the epitome of spring. Tarragon has a strong, slightly anise-y flavor, so a little goes a long way in recipes.

1 Tbs. olive oil

2 medium leeks, white and pale green parts only, thinly sliced (1 ½ cups)

1 clove garlic, minced (1 tsp.)

2 cups low-sodium vegetable broth

3 cups fresh or frozen peas, thawed

1 Tbs. tarragon leaves

3 small radishes, thinly sliced

1. Heat oil in large pot over medium heat. Add leeks, and sauté 7 to 9 minutes, or until soft. Stir in garlic, and cook 1 minute more. Add broth and 1 cup water, and bring to a simmer. Cook 15 minutes, stir in peas, and cook 1 minute more. Remove from heat, and cool 30 minutes.

2. Purée soup in blender with tarragon leaves until smooth and creamy. Season with salt and pepper. Serve warm or chilled, with sliced radishes on top.

PER SERVING: 139 CAL; 6 G PROT; 3.5 G TOTAL FAT (1.5 G SAT FAT); 22 G CARB; 8 MG CHOL; 366 MG SOD; 6 G FIBER; 8 G SUGARS

Success Secret: Smooth Soups

For ultrasmooth soup, strain it after blending to remove pieces of skin. This soup is easier to strain than others, and it's worth the extra time.

Roasted Apple-Potato Soup

SERVES 4

If you hate peeling and chopping vegetables, you'll love this recipe, in which whole potatoes and apples get baked, then mashed into a creamy soup. Don't worry if the apples burst open in the oven while they're baking—just pull off the skin, and scoop the flesh into the bowl with the potatoes.

2 large russet potatoes (2 lb.)

3 large medium-tart apples, such as Gala or Braeburn, unpeeled and cored

2 Tbs. olive oil

1 Tbs. curry powder

2 tsp. onion powder

Shopping Savvy: Russet Potatoes

Large russet (or Idaho) potatoes are perfect for cream soups because the high starch content makes their flesh soft when cooked.

1. Preheat oven to 350°F. Line baking sheet with parchment paper, and prick potatoes all over with fork. Bake 30 minutes. Place apples on same baking sheet and bake 30 to 45 minutes more, or until both apples and potatoes are very soft. Cool 10 to 15 minutes, or until easy to handle. Scoop flesh from potatoes and apples, and mash with hand masher in bowl.

2. Heat oil in large pot over medium heat. Add curry and onion powders, and cook 30 seconds, or until fragrant, stirring constantly. Stir in apple-potato mixture and 4 cups water, and season with salt and pepper. Cover, reduce heat to medium-low, and simmer 30 minutes, stirring occasionally. Adjust seasonings if necessary, and serve hot or cold.

PER SERVING: 292 CAL; 4 G PROT; 7.5 G TOTAL FAT (1 G SAT FAT); 56 G CARB; 0 MG CHOL; 155 MG SOD; 5 G FIBER; 16 G SUGARS

Curried White Bean and Kale Soup

SERVES 6

Greens-and-beans soups usually get Italian seasonings
like thyme, oregano and basil, but this one mixes things up with
smoky paprika and curry powder.

1 Tbs. olive oil

1 small onion, halved and thinly sliced
(1 cup)

3 cups chopped kale

1 small garnet yam or sweet potato,
peeled and diced (1 cup)

1 Tbs. smoked paprika, plus more for
garnish

1 Tbs. curry powder

1 bay leaf

4 cups low-sodium vegetable broth

2 15.5-oz. cans great Northern beans,
rinsed and drained, divided

2 Tbs. red wine vinegar

1. Heat oil in large pot over medium heat. Add onion, and cook 8 minutes, or until lightly caramelized, stirring often.

2. Add kale, and cook 4 to 5 minutes, or until wilted. Stir in yam, paprika, curry powder, and bay leaf; cook 1 minute more, or until fragrant.

3. Add broth, and bring to a simmer. Reduce heat to medium-low, and cook 30 minutes, or until kale and yam are tender. Purée 1 cup beans with ¾ cup water in blender or food processor. Add purée and remaining beans to soup. Simmer 10 minutes, then stir in vinegar. Remove bay leaf and season soup with salt and pepper. Sprinkle each serving with paprika.

PER SERVING: 165 CAL; 9 G PROT; 2.5 G TOTAL FAT (0.5 G SAT FAT); 34 G CARB; 0 MG CHOL; 543 MG SOD; 10 G FIBER; 7 G SUGARS

Chard and Pearl Barley Stew

Pearl barley has been polished to remove the outer hull (the same way white rice has had its hull removed), which makes the grain more tender and easier to cook. Serve this stew with a sprinkling of your favorite vegan cheese.

2 Tbs. olive oil

1 ¼ lb. Swiss chard, leaves and stems chopped separately

2 medium leeks, white and pale green parts only, halved lengthwise and sliced ½-inch thick (2 cups)

3 medium carrots, sliced (1 ½ cups)

2 medium stalks celery, sliced (1 cup)

⅛ tsp. ground nutmeg

3 cups low-sodium vegetable broth

½ cup medium pearl barley

1 cup frozen baby lima beans

1. Heat oil in large pot over medium-high heat. Stir in chard stems, leeks, carrots, celery, and nutmeg. Cook 7 to 9 minutes, or until vegetables release juices but are still brightly colored, stirring often.

2. Add broth, barley, and 1 ½ cups water. Cover, and bring to a boil. Reduce heat and simmer, covered, 45 minutes, stirring halfway through. Add lima beans and chard leaves. Simmer 10 minutes more, or until lima beans are tender.

PER SERVING: 186 CAL; 6 G PROT; 5 G TOTAL FAT (1 G SAT FAT); 31 G CARB; 0 MG CHOL; 278 MG SOD; 8 G FIBER; 6 G SUGARS

Success Secret: Other Grains

Wheat berries, farro, kasha, or brown rice—any grain that needs 30 minutes or more to cook—can be used in place of pearl barley.

Moroccan Harira

SERVES 8

This traditional soup is thickened with a tadouira—a mixture of flour, tomato paste, and cilantro—and served with lemon wedges.

HARIRA

½ cup dried green or brown lentils, rinsed and picked through

1 Tbs. olive oil

1 large onion, chopped (2 cups)

½ cup chopped fresh parsley

½ cup chopped fresh cilantro

½ tsp. ground ginger

1 cinnamon stick

1 15-oz. can chopped tomatoes, drained, liquid reserved

2 cups low-sodium vegetable broth

1 15-oz. can chickpeas, rinsed and drained

4 oz. vermicelli

TADOUIRA

2 Tbs. all-purpose flour

¼ cup chopped fresh cilantro

2 Tbs. fresh lemon juice

1 Tbs. tomato paste

1. To make Harira: Cook lentils in pot of boiling salted water 2 minutes. Drain.

2. Heat oil in large pot over medium heat. Add onion, parsley, cilantro, ginger, and cinnamon; sauté 5 minutes, or until onion is soft. Stir in tomatoes, and sauté 5 minutes more.

3. Stir in broth, chickpeas, lentils, reserved tomato liquid, and 3 cups water. Season with salt and pepper, and bring to a boil. Cover, reduce heat to medium-low, and simmer 45 minutes, or until lentils are tender, stirring occasionally. Remove cinnamon stick,

4. To make Tadouira: Whisk flour with 1 cup water in bowl. Whisk in cilantro, lemon juice, and tomato paste. Stir tadouira and vermicelli into harira, and cook 3 minutes, or until noodles are soft.

PER SERVING: 179 CAL; 7 G PROT; 3 G TOTAL FAT (0.5 G SAT FAT); 33 G CARB; 0 MG CHOL; 537 MG SOD; 6 G FIBER; 5 G SUGARS

Pho *(Vietnamese Noodle Soup)*

SERVES 6

The national soup of Vietnam is a bowl of rice noodles, fresh herbs, and bean sprouts swimming in a fragrant broth. Only the broth is traditionally made with beef. Here, a vegetable broth infused with herbs, spices, and dried shiitake mushrooms creates a soup base that's fragrant and full-bodied. Once the broth is made, this soup only takes a few minutes to assemble.

BROTH

6 cups low-sodium vegetable broth

3 large shallots, sliced (1 cup)

½ cup dried shiitake mushrooms, stems removed

10 cloves garlic, lightly crushed

3 Tbs. low-sodium soy sauce

1 3-inch piece fresh ginger, cut into ¼-inch-thick coins

1 Tbs. light brown sugar

1 Tbs. rice wine vinegar

1 tsp. ground black pepper

2 cinnamon sticks

2 star anise

5 to 6 basil stems, leaves reserved for soup

5 to 6 cilantro stems, leaves reserved for soup

1. To make Broth: Place all ingredients in large pot with 8 cups water. Cover, and bring to a boil. Reduce heat to medium-low, and simmer, covered, 1 hour. Strain broth, and return to pot. Discard solids. Use broth immediately, or refrigerate 3 to 5 days, or freeze up to 6 months.

Success Secret: Straining Broth

Press hard on the cooked vegetables when straining the broth. This releases more juice and flavor.

PHO

1 8-oz. pkg. rice noodles

1 8-oz. pkg. Asian-flavor baked tofu, thinly sliced

2 cups soybean sprouts

2 cups watercress

4 green onions, sliced (½ cup)

¼ cup chopped fresh cilantro

1 cup basil leaves

1 lime, cut into wedges

2. To make Pho: Cook rice noodles according to package directions. Drain, and rinse under cold water. Divide among 6 large soup bowls. Ladle broth over noodles, and top with tofu, sprouts, watercress, and green onions. Serve cilantro, basil, and lime wedges on the side to be stirred into soup.

PER SERVING: 290 CAL; 16 G PROT; 5.5 G TOTAL FAT (1 G SAT FAT); 42 G CARB; 0 MG CHOL; 578 MG SOD; 3 G FIBER; 5 G SUGARS

Storage Hint: Storing Herbs

When storing bunches of fresh herbs, wrap loosely in paper towels and place in a separate closed plastic bags in the refrigerator. This prevents moisture from gathering on the leaves and turning them brown, black, or moldy before you have a chance to use them all.

Curry-Kuri Squash Soup

SERVES 8

The secret to keeping this squash soup creamy and luscious?
A single sweet potato is added to the mix. Tear-shaped kuri squash have a rich,
reddish orange color and nutty flavor—perfect for spicy dishes.

1 medium red kuri squash (3 lb.), seeded and quartered

1 large onion, quartered

2 cloves garlic, halved

2 Tbs. canola or olive oil, divided

1 large sweet potato (1 lb.), pricked with fork

1 Tbs. minced fresh ginger

2 tsp. curry powder

½ cup fresh orange juice

¼ tsp. ground nutmeg

1 Tbs. chopped fresh chives, for garnish

....

Success Secret: Red Kuri Squash

....

No need to peel red kuri squash.
The thin skin can be cooked and eaten
with the flesh, unlike other
winter squash.

1. Heat oven to 350°F. In center of each squash quarter, set 1 onion quarter and 1 garlic half; drizzle with 1 tsp. oil, and season with salt and pepper. Wrap in foil, and place on baking sheet with potato. Bake 1 hour, or until squash and potato are soft. Cool until easy to handle.

2. Heat remaining 2 tsp. oil in large pot over medium heat. Coarsely chop onion quarters, and add to oil with garlic halves. Sauté 4 to 5 minutes. Add ginger and curry, and cook 30 seconds.

3. Scoop squash and sweet potato flesh into pot, cover with 6 cups water, and season with salt and pepper. Cover, and bring to a boil. Reduce heat to medium-low and simmer 30 minutes. Remove from heat, and purée squash mixture in blender or food processor until smooth. Stir in orange juice and nutmeg. Season with salt and pepper, and garnish with pinch of chives.

PER SERVING: 108 CAL; 3 G PROT; 2.5 G TOTAL FAT (0.5 G SAT FAT); 21 G CARB; 0 MG CHOL; 167 MG SOD; 2 G FIBER; 7 G SUGARS

Root Vegetable Chili Soup

SERVES 4

Root vegetables like rutabagas and carrots are great for spicy kitchen experiments because they lend subtle sweetness to dishes. You could also use curry powder in place of the chili powder here—the soup will have an Indian flair.

½ cup fresh or frozen corn, thawed

2 Tbs. canola oil

1 small onion, chopped (1 cup)

2 cloves garlic, minced (2 tsp.)

4 tsp. mild chili powder

2 tsp. ground cumin

2 small rutabagas (1 ½ lb.), peeled and cut into ½-inch cubes

2 medium carrots (½ lb.), cut into ½-inch cubes

1 28-oz. can diced tomatoes

1 small russet potato, peeled and finely diced (1 cup)

2 Anaheim chiles, seeded and chopped (¾ cup)

1 small red bell pepper, chopped (⅔ cup)

1 15-oz. can red kidney beans, rinsed and drained

Chopped green onions, for garnish

1. Heat large pot over medium heat. Add corn, and sauté 2 minutes, or until beginning to brown. Add oil, onion, and garlic, and sauté 3 to 5 minutes, or until onion is soft. Stir in chili powder and cumin, and cook 2 minutes, scraping bottom of pan with spatula.

2. Add rutabagas, carrots, tomatoes and juice, potato, chiles, bell pepper, and 3 cups water. Bring soup to a simmer, and season with salt. Cover, reduce heat to medium low, and cook 1 hour, stirring occasionally.

3. Add beans and cook, uncovered, 45 minutes, or until soup thickens. Serve garnished with green onions.

PER SERVING: 236 CAL; 8 G PROT; 6 G TOTAL FAT (0.5 G SAT FAT); 40 G CARB; 0 MG CHOL; 417 MG SOD; 13 G FIBER; 15 G SUGARS

Success Secret:
Make Soup a Day Ahead

Dishes that call for chili and curry powders get better over time, so make this soup a day ahead.

Italian Eggplant Ragoût with Capers

SERVES 6

Capers are a cook's secret weapon for adding tangy herbal flavor to simple soups and stews. Here, we've gone light on the caper count, but you can always add more to suit your taste. If you're not a caper fan, try substituting ¼ cup chopped olives instead.

2 medium eggplants, halved

2 Tbs. salt

2 Tbs. olive oil

1 large onion, chopped (2 cups)

2 cloves garlic, minced (2 tsp.)

1 15-oz. can diced tomatoes, drained

1 15-oz. can chickpeas, rinsed and drained

2 Tbs. capers, drained

1 tsp. sugar

¼ cup chopped fresh parsley

1. Scoop out center and seeds of eggplant halves. Cut eggplants into ¾-inch dice. Toss with salt in bowl, and let stand 30 minutes. Drain, rinse well, and pat dry.

2. Heat oil in large pot over medium heat. Add onion, and sauté 5 minutes, or until softened. Add garlic, and cook 1 minute more, or until fragrant. Stir in tomatoes, chickpeas, and eggplant. Reduce heat to medium-low, and cook 15 minutes, or until eggplant is tender but not mushy. Stir in capers and sugar, and cook 2 minutes more. Fold in parsley, and season with black pepper.

PER SERVING: 197 CAL; 6 G PROT; 5.5 G TOTAL FAT (1 G SAT FAT); 33 G CARB; 0 MG CHOL; 681 MG SOD; 10 G FIBER; 8 G SUGARS

Prep Talk: Salting Eggplant

Salting the eggplant before cooking it draws out any bitter juices and helps the vegetable hold its shape when cooked.

Italian Wedding Soup

SERVES 6

This quick, brothy soup is just the thing to make on a cold weeknight.

4 Tbs. olive oil, divided

1 medium onion, chopped (1 cup)

2 cloves garlic, minced (2 tsp.), plus 1 whole clove, peeled, divided

¾ cup diced carrot

¾ cup diced celery

1 Tbs. dried oregano

1 Tbs. dried basil

1 Tbs. dried parsley

6 cups low-sodium vegetable broth

¾ cup ditalini pasta

18 small frozen vegan meatballs, thawed or 1 recipe "Meat" Balls (p. 157)

5 oz. spinach leaves

2 Tbs. fresh lemon juice

1. Heat 2 Tbs. olive oil in large pot over medium-high heat. Add onion and minced garlic; sauté 5 minutes, or until beginning to soften. Stir in carrot and celery, and cook 5 minutes more, or until onion is soft and just beginning to brown. Add oregano, basil, and parsley, and cook 1 minute. Stir in broth, and bring to a boil.

2. Reduce heat to medium, add ditalini, and simmer 5 minutes. Add meatballs, reduce heat to medium-low, and simmer 10 minutes.

3. Meanwhile, heat remaining 2 Tbs. oil in skillet over medium heat. Add whole garlic clove, and crush with wooden spoon in oil while heating. Add spinach; cook 3 to 5 minutes, turning constantly so spinach becomes evenly coated and wilted but is still bright green. After meatballs have simmered, add spinach and lemon juice to soup, and season with salt and pepper.

PER SERVING: 234 CAL; 9 G PROT; 11.5 G TOTAL FAT (2 G SAT FAT); 25 G CARB; 0 MG CHOL; 499 MG SOD; 6 G FIBER; 5 G SUGARS

Shopping Savvy: Frozen Meat-Free Meatballs

When buying frozen meat-free meatballs, check the ingredients to make sure they don't contain dairy or egg.

Braised Lebanese Eggplant with Chickpeas

SERVES 6

Slow-cooking eggplant in tomato sauce makes it incredibly
silky and tender, and mint, when simmered into a stew, adds flavor that's
more delicate than its cousin, oregano.

2 Tbs. olive oil

1 large onion, diced (1 ½ cups)

6 medium Japanese eggplant, halved
lengthwise and cut into 2-inch pieces

1 clove garlic, minced (1 tsp.)

½ tsp. ground allspice

¼ tsp. ground cumin

1 cup marinara sauce

1 Tbs. red wine vinegar

1 15-oz. can chickpeas, rinsed and
drained

2 large sprigs mint, plus 2 Tbs.
chopped fresh mint

1. Preheat oven to 325°F. Heat oil in Dutch oven over medium-high heat. Add onion, and sauté 7 minutes, or until soft. Stir in eggplant, and cook 5 minutes or until beginning to brown. Add garlic, allspice, and cumin, and cook 1 minute more.

2. Stir in marinara sauce, vinegar, and ⅔ cup water, and bring to a simmer. Reduce heat to medium, and simmer 5 minutes. Remove from heat, and stir in chickpeas. Season with salt and pepper. Lay mint sprigs on top of eggplant mixture, cover, and transfer pot to oven. Bake 45 to 50 minutes, or until eggplant is tender. Remove mint sprigs, and stir in chopped mint. Serve hot or at room temperature.

PER SERVING: 188 CAL; 7 G PROT; 16.5 G TOTAL FAT
(1 G SAT FAT); 29 G CARB; 0 MG CHOL; 427 MG SOD;
8 G FIBER; 11 G SUGARS

....
Success Secret: Marinara Sauce
....

Choose a marinara sauce that has as few
ingredients as possible so the flavors
don't overwhelm the eggplant, or make
the recipe with Speedy Red Sauce (p. 307).

Vietnamese Hot Pot

SERVES 8

"Hot pot" is a variation on fondue that invites diners to plunge bite-size veggies and other nibbles into a pot of summering broth, then dip the just-cooked foods in a variety of sauces. Once the dipping course is done, rice noodles and bean sprouts are added to the broth to create a second course of comforting soup.

BROTH

4 cups low-sodium vegetable broth

2 stalks lemongrass, chopped

½ cup chopped fresh cilantro

6 ¼-inch coins fresh ginger

4 cloves garlic, peeled

2 Thai chiles

¼ cup low-sodium soy sauce

2 Tbs. packed light brown sugar

1 Tbs. rice wine vinegar

DIPPERS

Broccoli florets, mushrooms, bok choy slices, dumplings, and green beans

SOUP

5 oz. dry rice noodles or rice vermicelli

1 cup bean sprouts

Green onions, mint, cilantro, and peanuts

1. To make Broth: Bring broth and 5 cups water to a boil in electric skillet over medium-high heat. Add lemongrass, cilantro, ginger, garlic, Thai chiles, soy sauce, sugar, and vinegar. Reduce heat to low, and simmer 30 minutes. Remove lemongrass, ginger, garlic, and chiles with slotted spoon, and discard. Place broth in center of table.

2. Let guests dip vegetables, potatoes, and dumplings in simmering broth to cook. Serve with Sweet Chile Mayonnaise (p. 316) and Pineapple Miso Sambal (p. 313).

3. To make Soup: When dippers have been cooked, add rice noodles and sprouts to broth. Simmer 5 minutes, or until noodles are tender. Serve garnished with onions, mint, cilantro, and peanuts.

PER SERVING: 440 CAL; 23 G PROT; 5 G TOTAL FAT (0 G SAT FAT); 78 G CARB; 1 MG CHOL; 734 MG SOD; 11 G FIBER; 12 G SUGARS

Thai Red Curry

SERVES 8

Thai takeout is usually off-limits to vegans because many Thai restaurants use fish sauce to flavor curries and noodle dishes. Serve this over steamed rice.

1 Tbs. olive oil

1 medium onion, diced (1 ½ cups)

3 Tbs. red curry paste

2 Tbs. low-sodium soy sauce

1 clove garlic, minced (1 tsp.)

1 stalk lemongrass, cut into thirds and smashed with back of knife

1 ½-inch piece fresh ginger, smashed

5 kaffir lime leaves, or 2 Tbs. freshly grated lime zest

1 to 2 Thai chiles, sliced

2 medium carrots, sliced

2 zucchini, cut into ¼-inch-thick rounds

1 russet potato, peeled and cut into ½-inch cubes

1 12-oz. can light coconut milk

3 Tbs. packed light brown sugar

1 cup trimmed green beans

1 cup Thai basil leaves or basil leaves, torn

1. Heat oil in large pot over medium heat. Add onion, curry paste, soy sauce, and garlic, and sauté 1 to 2 minutes. Add lemongrass, ginger, kaffir lime leaves, and Thai chile. Sauté 30 seconds.

2. Stir in carrots, zucchini, and potato, and sauté 1 minute. Add coconut milk, sugar, and 1 cup water. Reduce heat to medium-low, cover, and simmer 10 minutes, or until potatoes can be pierced with tip of knife. Add green beans and simmer 5 minutes more. Remove lemongrass, ginger, and kaffir lime leaves, and season with salt and pepper. Sprinkle with basil leaves.

PER SERVING: 132 CAL; 2 G PROT; 5.5 G TOTAL FAT (2.5 G SAT FAT); 19 G CARB; 0 MG CHOL; 404 MG SOD; 3 G FIBER; 10 G SUGARS

SERVING SUGGESTION

Pair this and other spicy Asian foods with a sweet wine, such as Riesling or Gewürztraminer, or a light and fruity red wine.

Mixed Vegetable Masala

SERVES 4

This Indian-style stew gets spicier as it sits, so if you prefer milder flavors,
serve it immediately.

1 1-inch piece fresh ginger, sliced

2 cloves garlic, peeled

1 15-oz. can diced tomatoes

½ tsp. cayenne pepper

2 Tbs. canola or vegetable oil

1 medium onion, chopped (1 cup)

1 small yellow bell pepper, diced (1 cup)

2 medium boiling potatoes, peeled and cubed (1 cup)

2 medium carrots, sliced (1 cup)

1 ½ tsp. garam masala

½ tsp. chili powder

1 small head cauliflower (12 oz.), cut into florets (2 cups)

½ cup light coconut milk

1. Pulse ginger and garlic in food processor until finely chopped. Add tomatoes and juice and cayenne pepper, and pulse until combined. Set aside.

2. Heat oil in large pot over medium heat. Add onion and bell pepper, and sauté 10 minutes, or until softened. Stir in potatoes, carrots, garam masala, and chili powder. Cover, reduce heat to medium-low, and cook 10 minutes, stirring occasionally.

3. Add cauliflower, tomato mixture, and ½ cup water. Simmer 20 minutes. Remove from heat, and stir in coconut milk. Season with black pepper.

PER SERVING: 200 CAL; 4 G PROT; 10 G TOTAL FAT (2 G SAT FAT), 26 G CARB; 0 MG CHOL; 465 MG SOD; 6 G FIBER; 10 G SUGARS

Buy and Try: Garam Masala

Most cooks are familiar with curry powder; garam masala is another Indian spice blend that tends to be sweeter and milder. Swap curry powder for garam masala in recipes.

Miso-Adzuki Stew

SERVES 6

Small, dark red adzuki beans have a sweet, nutty flavor and are often used in Asian desserts. Here, they're flavored with miso and shiitake mushrooms for a satisfying, protein-packed stew.

1 cup dried adzuki beans

2 bunches green onions, white and green parts chopped separately, divided

½ cup dried shiitake mushrooms, stems removed and crumbled

12 oz. red potatoes, quartered

1 ½ to 2 Tbs. yellow or red miso (Japanese soybean paste)

Buy and Try: Miso Paste

Most people wouldn't think of miso in conjunction with good ol' all-American burgers, but the Japanese fermented soybean paste can do so much more than flavor soups in sushi restaurants. The rich, thick, salty stuff can add depth to meatless recipes that need hearty flavor, such as veggie burgers, stews, and chili. White miso has a mild flavor; yellow and red are much more robust. Miso will keep as long as other condiments in the fridge, so buy a tub of white and a tub of yellow or red, and use them according to what flavors you want to achieve in a recipe.

1. Soak adzuki beans in 4 cups cold water 5 hours, or overnight. Drain, and reserve soaking liquid.

2. Coat large pot with cooking spray, and heat over medium-low heat. Add white parts of green onions, sprinkle with salt, and cover. Cook 5 to 7 minutes, or until soft. Add mushrooms and beans. Add enough water to adzuki soaking liquid to make 4 cups, and stir into bean mixture. Cover, and bring to a boil. Reduce heat to medium-low, and simmer 45 minutes, adding a little water if necessary. Stir in potatoes, cover, and cook 15 minutes more, or until potatoes are tender and beans are soft but not mushy.

3. Ladle 1 cup broth from bean mixture into measuring cup. Stir in miso with fork until dissolved. Stir miso mixture into bean mixture, and simmer 2 to 3 minutes more, or until heated through. Sprinkle with green parts of green onions before serving.

PER SERVING: 178 CAL; 8 G PROT; 0.5 G TOTAL FAT (0 G SAT FAT); 37 G CARB; 0 MG CHOL; 252 MG SOD; 6 G FIBER; 3 G SUGARS

Spring Vegetable Stew with Soft Polenta

SERVES 8

"Stew" is almost a misnomer for this light, brothy dish that makes
the most of tender spring vegetables.

1 large carrot, sliced into
¼-inch matchsticks

1 large yellow squash, sliced into
¼-inch matchsticks

1 large zucchini, sliced into
½-inch matchsticks

2 Tbs. olive oil

10 oz. sliced cremini mushrooms,
trimmed

2 large leeks, white and pale green
parts only, sliced into thin rounds

5 cloves garlic, minced (1 ½ Tbs.)

½ cup pitted kalamata olives,
chopped

1 28-oz. can chopped tomatoes

2 14-oz. cans white beans,
rinsed and drained

1 cup polenta or coarse yellow
cornmeal

1. Bring 8 cups salted water to a boil, and fill large bowl with 8 cups ice water. Add carrot to boiling water, and simmer 1 minute. Add squash and zucchini, and cook 1 minute more. Drain, and plunge in bowl of ice water to stop cooking. Drain.

2. Heat oil in large pot over medium heat. Add mushrooms, and sprinkle with salt. Sauté 10 minutes, or until mushrooms begin to brown. Add leeks and garlic, and sauté 5 minutes. Add olives, and sauté 1 minute more. Stir in tomatoes and beans. Reduce heat to medium-low, cover, and simmer 10 to 15 minutes.

3. Whisk together polenta and 4 cups salted water in large saucepan. Bring to a boil over medium-high heat, whisking frequently. Reduce heat to low, and cook 10 to 15 minutes, or until thick and porridgelike, stirring often. Season with salt and pepper. Stir carrots, zucchini, and squash into stew; simmer 2 to 3 minutes, or until heated through. Season with salt and pepper. Serve stew on top of polenta.

PER SERVING: 280 CAL; 10 G PROT; 7.5 G TOTAL FAT
(1.5 G SAT FAT); 44 G CARB; 0 MG CHOL; 896 MG
SOD; 9 G FIBER; 8 G SUGARS

Vegetable Gumbo

SERVES 8

The rich, dark roux of a Louisiana-style gumbo is laced with
carrots, parsnips, okra, and green beans, but feel free to substitute any
vegetables you have on hand. Serve over rice.

½ cup vegetable oil

⅓ cup all-purpose flour

1 small onion, chopped (1 cup)

1 small green bell pepper,
chopped (1 cup)

3 medium stalks celery,
chopped (1 cup)

1 28-oz. can diced tomatoes

2 cups fresh or frozen green beans

3 medium carrots, sliced (2 cups)

1 medium parsnip, diced (1 cup)

1 cup fresh or frozen sliced okra,
optional

1 Tbs. ground cumin

1 Tbs. paprika

1 Tbs. dried oregano

¼ tsp. cayenne pepper

1. Stir together oil and flour in Dutch oven or heavy-bottomed pot until smooth. Cook over high heat 10 minutes, or until roux turns a dark caramel color, stirring constantly.

2. Add onion, bell pepper, and celery, and cook 5 minutes, or until vegetables are softened. Stir in all remaining ingredients and 4 cups water. Season with salt and black pepper. Reduce heat to medium-low, cover, and cook 40 minutes, or until carrots are tender.

PER SERVING: 216 CAL; 3 G PROT; 14.5 G TOTAL FAT (2 G SAT FAT); 21 G CARB; 0 MG CHOL; 309 MG SOD; 6 G FIBER; 8 G SUGARS

Success Secret: Add Sausage

Bump up the protein and boost the flavor of a gumbo by adding sliced vegan sausage or smoked tofu with the vegetables.

Irish Stew

There are as many versions of Irish stew as there are church steeples on the Emerald Isle, so consider this one an animal-friendly addition. This stew tastes even better as leftovers, once the flavors have had a chance to develop. Serve it over mashed potatoes for a deliciously comforting meal.

2 Tbs. olive oil

20 small frozen pearl onions, thawed

2 medium carrots, cut into ½-inch pieces (1½ cups)

2 Tbs. all-purpose flour

8 oz. seitan, cut into 1-inch pieces

4 slices smoky tempeh bacon, cut into ½-inch pieces

2 cloves garlic, minced (2 tsp.)

2 tsp. chopped fresh thyme

2 cups vegan stout beer

3 cups low-sodium vegetable broth

12 oz. butternut squash, seeded and cut into ½-inch cubes (2 cups)

⅔ cup frozen shelled edamame

1. Heat oil in large pot over medium-high heat. Add onions and carrot, and cook 5 minutes. Stir in flour, and cook 2 minutes more. Add seitan, bacon, garlic, and thyme, and cook 2 minutes.

2. Pour in beer, and bring mixture to a boil. Cook 3 minutes, stirring and scraping any bits that may be stuck to bottom. Add broth and squash, and bring to a simmer. Reduce heat to medium-low, and cook 20 minutes. Add edamame and cook 10 minutes more. Season with salt and pepper.

PER SERVING: 308 CAL; 23 G PROT; 8.5 G TOTAL FAT (1 G SAT FAT); 36 G CARB; 0 MG CHOL; 384 MG SOD; 6 G FIBER; 7 G SUGARS

Shopping Savvy: Vegan Stout

Traditional Irish stout is not vegan, so search the Internet for a brand that is in your area.

Chili sin (Without) Carne

SERVES 10

The ultimate American stew is also one of the best veg dishes to please omnivores, because who misses the meat when there's all that spicy, bean-laced goodness going on? If you've never tried corn in your chili, now's the time. This recipe is for one big batch of chili—but then it's hard to make a small batch of chili. Put it on the stove, then invite over some friends for a casual supper— or freeze it in plastic containers for future dinners.

2 Tbs. olive oil

1 medium onion, diced (1 ½ cups)

2 carrots, diced (1 cup)

1 small green bell pepper, diced (1 cup)

4 cloves garlic, minced (4 tsp.)

1 28-oz. can crushed tomatoes

1 15.5-oz. can black beans, rinsed and drained

1 15.5-oz. can kidney beans, rinsed and drained

1 12-oz. pkg. soy crumbles

2 Tbs. chili powder

1 Tbs. plus 1 tsp. ground cumin

1 Tbs. light brown sugar

2 tsp. dried oregano

1 tsp. red pepper flakes

1 10-oz. pkg. frozen corn

1. Heat oil in large pot over medium-high heat. Add onion, and sauté 2 minutes. Add carrots and bell pepper, and cook 2 minutes more. Add garlic, and cook 1 minute, or until fragrant. Stir in 2 cups water and all remaining ingredients except corn, and season with salt and black pepper.

2. Reduce heat to medium, and simmer 20 minutes, stirring occasionally. Fold in corn and ½ cup water, and simmer 10 minutes more.

PER SERVING: 287 CAL; 18 G PROT; 6.5 G TOTAL FAT (1 G SAT FAT); 45 G CARB; 0 MG CHOL; 545 MG SOD; 14 G FIBER; 7 G SUGARS

Slow Cooker Vegetable Vindaloo

Vindaloo is a spicy stew from the Goa region of India. Here, cauliflower and chickpeas replace the lamb or pork traditionally used in the dish. You can also substitute 3 cups of potatoes for half of the cauliflower for a heartier meal. To make the dish on the stove top, bring the ingredients to a simmer, then cook 1 ½ hours over medium-low heat.

1 medium head cauliflower, cut into bite-size florets (6 cups)

2 15.5-oz. cans chickpeas, rinsed and drained

2 large leeks, white and pale green parts only, sliced into 1-inch pieces (1 ½ cups)

1 cup tomato sauce

¼ cup white wine vinegar

2 Tbs. minced fresh ginger

2 Tbs. curry powder

2 cloves garlic, minced (2 tsp.)

2 tsp. ground cumin

1 tsp. ground cinnamon

1 tsp. hot sauce

3 Tbs. chopped fresh cilantro

3 cups cooked basmati rice

1. Combine cauliflower, chickpeas, leeks, tomato sauce, vinegar, ginger, curry powder, garlic, cumin, cinnamon, hot sauce, and ¼ cup water in 4-quart slow cooker. Season with salt and pepper. Cook on high 3 hours, stirring occasionally.

2. Transfer vindaloo to large bowl, and cool 15 minutes. Stir in cilantro, and serve over basmati rice.

PER SERVING: 265 CAL; 10 G PROT; 2 G TOTAL FAT (0.5 G SAT FAT); 53 G CARB; 0 MG CHOL; 478 MG SOD; 9 G FIBER; 4 G SUGARS

Success Secret: Cinnamon

A little ground cinnamon goes a long way toward boosting the flavor of savory dishes. Try it in Indian, Asian, and Mexican recipes.

Southwestern Spinach Stew

SERVES 6

If it always seems like there's never enough time to get dinner on the table, turn to this stew some weeknight. Using seasoned stewed tomatoes, frozen corn mix, and baby spinach means there's no slicing or dicing involved. Serve the stew over rice, or try as a filling for soft tacos.

6 slices vegan turkey

2 14.5-oz. cans Mexican-style stewed tomatoes

¾ cup frozen Mexican-style corn, thawed and drained

10 oz. baby spinach leaves (10 cups)

½ cup shredded vegan cheddar cheese

1. Coat large nonstick skillet with cooking spray, and heat over medium-high heat. Add turkey slices, and cook 2 minutes per side, or until browned. Transfer to plate, and set aside.

2. Add tomatoes and liquid to skillet, and bring to a boil. Simmer 5 minutes, or until liquid is reduced by half. Add corn and cook 2 minutes, or until heated through. Add spinach and cook 1 minute more, stirring constantly, or until spinach is just wilted. Divide tomato-spinach mixture among 6 plates, and top with reserved turkey slices and shredded cheese.

PER SERVING· 108 CAL; 8 G PROT; 2 G TOTAL FAT (0 G SAT FAT); 17 G CARB; 0 MG CHOL; 683 MG SOD; 5 G FIBER; 9 G SUGARS

....
Shopping Savvy: Baby Spinach
....

Before you grab that bag of prewashed leaves, pick it up, shake it, and look at the bottom. Make sure all the leaves look fresh and dry, not damp or discolored.

baked goodies
yeast breads, quick breads, biscuits, and scones

If you've ever impatiently awaited the arrival of the bread basket at a restaurant table or caved and bought a muffin at a coffee shop even though you just had breakfast, then you know just how tempting fresh baked goods can be. Making them at home is supremely satisfying when that perfect combination of ingredients turns into something that's fragrant, tasty, and irresistible.

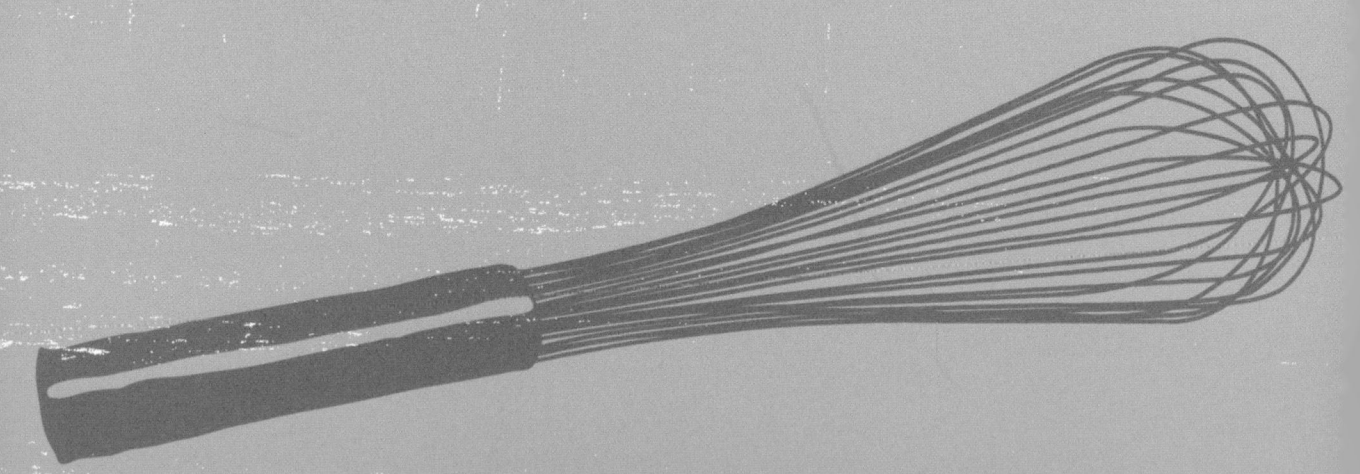

Garlic Bread

SERVES 8

Rather than just spreading some oil and garlic on French bread and baking, this recipe gets a flavor boost from infusing the oil with minced garlic first and adding a pinch of salt.

1 baguette, halved lengthwise

¼ cup olive oil

6 cloves garlic, minced (2 Tbs.)

2 Tbs. finely chopped fresh parsley

¼ tsp. salt

1. Preheat oven to 375°F. Lay baguette, cut-sides up, on sheet of foil several inches longer than bread.

2. Heat oil in small saucepan over low heat. Add garlic, and cook 1 to 2 minutes, or until light golden. Stir in parsley and salt, and remove from heat.

3. Brush garlic mixture on both halves of bread with pastry brush. Press baguette halves back together, and wrap with foil. Bake 15 to 20 minutes, or until warm and fragrant. Cut crosswise with serrated knife into 8 thick pieces. Serve hot.

PER SLICE: 154 CAL; 4 G PROT; 7 G TOTAL FAT (1 G SAT FAT); 18 G CARB; 0 MG CHOL; 242 MG SOD; 1 G FIBER; 1 G SUGARS

Success Secret: Slicing Bread

Use a serrated knife to slice baguettes and quick bread loaves. The knife's teeth saw through the baked good rather than mashing it down the way other knives can.

Classic Rye Bread

MAKES 2 LOAVES

This tangy bread is made with a *petrin* starter, a mixture of flour and yeast that is allowed to develop before the dough is mixed. The starter method helps keep the bread fresher longer.

5 cups white bread flour, divided

1 0.25-oz. pkg. active dry yeast

½ cup olive oil

2 Tbs. caraway seeds

1 Tbs. salt

2 cups rye flour

Buy and Try: Caraway Seeds

Caraway seeds have hints of cumin, parsley, and anise flavors and can be used to jazz up the flavors of sweet and savory recipes in addition to rye bread and Irish soda bread.

1. Combine 2 cups bread flour, yeast, and 3 cups warm water in bowl. Cover, and set in warm place 1 hour.

2. Stir oil, caraway seeds, and salt into yeast mixture. Stir in rye flour and remaining 2 cups bread flour 1 cup at a time. Sprinkle with remaining 1 cup of flour. Knead dough onto floured work surface 15 minutes, adding more flour as needed. Transfer to lightly oiled bowl. Cover with damp towel, and let rise 1 hour, or until doubled in size. Punch down dough, and let rise 1 hour more, or refrigerate overnight, if desired.

3. Coat 2 baking sheets with cooking spray. Shape dough into 2 round loaves, stretching surface until smooth, then drawing excess dough together at bottom. Place on prepared baking sheets, and cover with damp towel. Let rise 30 minutes, or until doubled in size.

4. Preheat oven to 400°F. Bake loaves 45 to 50 minutes, or until well browned on outside.

PER SLICE: 117 CAL; 3 G PROT; 3.5 G TOTAL FAT (0.5 G SAT FAT); 19 G CARB; 0 MG CHOL; 219 MG SOD; 1 G FIBER; 0 G SUGARS

Whole-Wheat Rosemary Focaccia

MAKES 1 LOAF (24 SLICES)

Focaccia is one of the easiest yeast breads to make because there's no shaping or scoring loaves. Just pat the dough on the baking sheet, and you're done.

1 Tbs. sugar

1 0.75-oz. pkg. active dry yeast

2 cups all-purpose flour

1 cup whole-wheat flour

1 ¼ tsp. kosher salt or sea salt, plus more for sprinkling

4 Tbs. olive oil, plus more for brushing

2 Tbs. fresh or dried rosemary

Success Secret: Topping Variations

Try replacing the rosemary topping with vegan Parmesan, prepared pesto, herbes de Provence, or sesame seeds.

1. Stir sugar and yeast into 1 ½ cups warm water. Let stand 5 minutes, or until yeast has dissolved.

2. Combine flours and 1 ¼ tsp. salt in bowl of food processor fitted with metal or dough blade. Add sugar-yeast mixture, and process until soft dough forms. Pour 4 Tbs. oil through feed tube of food processor with motor running. Process 2 minutes more, or until dough begins to pull away from sides of bowl. Transfer to bowl coated with oil, cover with kitchen towel, and let rise 45 minutes in warm spot.

3. Transfer dough to baking sheet coated with cooking spray, and pat into 11- × 13-inch rectangle. Cover with towel, and let rise 1 hour.

4. Set oven rack on lowest level, and preheat oven to 425°F. Poke indentations all over top of bread with fingers. Brush with oil, and sprinkle with salt and rosemary. Bake 30 minutes, or until both top and bottom are golden brown. Cool on baking sheet 15 minutes before slicing.

PER SLICE: 79 CAL; 2 G PROT; 2 G TOTAL FAT (0 G SAT FAT); 12 G CARB; 0 MG CHOL; 121 MG SOD; 1 G FIBER; 1 G SUGARS

Super-Flax Whole-Wheat Boule

MAKES 1 LOAF (16 SLICES)

This dense, crusty loaf calls for flaxseeds in three different forms.

1 cup plus 1 Tbs. flaxseeds, divided, plus more for sprinkling

2 Tbs. sugar, agave nectar, or honey

1 0.25-oz. pkg. active dry yeast

3 cups all-purpose or bread flour

1 ½ cups whole-wheat flour

1 ½ tsp. salt

1. Cover ½ cup flaxseeds with 3 inches water in bowl. Let soak overnight.

2. Combine sugar, yeast, and 2 cups warm water in bowl. Let stand 5 minutes, or until mixture is bubbly.

3. Grind remaining ½ cup plus 1 Tbs. flaxseeds in coffee grinder. Stir together ground flaxseeds, all-purpose flour, whole-wheat flour, and salt in bowl. Drain soaked flaxseeds, and stir into flour mixture with yeast mixture.

4. Knead dough on floured work surface 10 minutes, adding flour as needed to form a smooth dough. Shape into ball, and place in bowl coated with oil. Cover, and let rise in warm place 1 ½ hours, or until doubled in size. Punch down, reshape into ball, and let rise 1 hour more.

5. Preheat oven to 400°F, and coat large baking sheet with cooking spray. Shape dough into tight ball, and place on prepared baking sheet. Brush with water, and sprinkle with flaxseeds. Cut a tic-tac-toe crisscross in top of loaf. Bake 1 hour, or until loaf is dark brown and sounds hollow when tapped.

PER SLICE: 197 CAL; 7 G PROT; 6 G TOTAL FAT (•1 G SAT FAT); 32 G CARB; 0 MG CHOL; 223 MG SOD; 6 G FIBER; 2 G SUGARS

Sunset Sweet Potato Drop Biscuits

MAKES 12 BISCUITS

Mashed sweet potatoes keep these biscuits tender and low in fat, plus they eliminate the need for eggs or dairy. For a more elegant look, roll out the dough and cut with a 2-inch round biscuit cutter.

1 cup mashed cooked sweet potatoes (2 small baked sweet potatoes)

3 Tbs. vegetable oil

1 Tbs. pure maple syrup

1 tsp. apple cider vinegar

½ tsp. salt

1 cup all-purpose or whole-wheat pastry flour

2 tsp. baking powder

1 tsp. ground nutmeg

1. Preheat oven to 400°F. Coat baking sheet with cooking spray.

2. Combine sweet potatoes, oil, maple syrup, vinegar, and salt in large bowl. Sift in flour, baking powder, and nutmeg.

3. Cut dry ingredients into sweet potato mixture with fork until mixture comes together. Stir in 2 to 3 Tbs. water, or enough to get dough to hold together.

4. Drop golf ball–size rounds of dough onto prepared baking sheet. Bake 15 to 17 minutes, or until tops are lightly browned and firm to the touch. Serve warm.

PER BISCUIT: 91 CAL; 1 G PROT; 3.5 G TOTAL FAT (0.5 G SAT FAT); 14 G CARB; 0 MG CHOL; 196 MG SOD; 1 G FIBER; 3 G SUGARS

Prep Talk: Biscuits into Scones

To turn these biscuits into scones, bump up the maple syrup to 4 tablespoons and stir in 1 cup raisins.

Grilled Flatbread

MAKES 8 FLATBREADS

Here's a way to wow cookout guests: throw a few homemade flatbreads onto the grill for hot, fresh bread to serve with the meal. You can vary the flavor by adding minced fresh herbs or cracked black pepper to the dough. Cover the dough and refrigerate after the first rise, then grill or bake the next day.

1 .25-oz. pkg. active dry yeast

2 ¾ cups all-purpose flour, plus more for rolling

¼ cup whole-wheat flour or coarsely ground rye flour

2 tsp. kosher salt

2 tsp. crushed fennel seeds

Olive oil, for brushing

Success Secret: Other Ways to Bake Flatbreads

Flatbreads can also be cooked in a heavy skillet on the stove top, under the broiler, or in a preheated 500°F oven on a baking sheet or pizza stone.

1. Combine yeast and 1 ¼ cups warm water in bowl of electric mixer. Let stand 15 minutes. Using paddle attachment, incorporate flours into yeast mixture. Beat in salt and fennel seeds. Switch to dough hook and knead 5 to 7 minutes. Remove dough and place in lightly oiled bowl, turning to coat. Cover and let rise 1 hour. Punch down, cover and let rise again 45 minutes.

2. Turn dough out onto work surface and divide into 8 equal-size balls. Place balls on floured baking sheet, cover with damp towel, and let stand 20 minutes. Dust work surface with flour, and roll balls into 7-inch-round disks, dusting with flour as needed.

3. Heat gas or stove top grill to high. Lightly brush disks with oil. Place disks, oiled side down, on grill. The breads will begin to rise almost immediately. Cook 4 to 5 minutes per side, until browned.

PER FLATBREAD: 203 CAL; 5 G PROT; 4 G TOTAL FAT (1 G SAT FAT); 36 G CARB; 0 MG CHOL; 484 MG SOD; 2 G FIBER; 0 G SUGARS

Lemon-Raspberry Muffins

MAKES 12 MUFFINS

These may just become your go-to muffin recipe when you get
the urge to bake. Try them with blueberries, diced apple or pear, or dried
cranberries or cherries in place of the raspberries.

1 cup whole-grain spelt flour or
all-purpose flour

½ tsp. baking soda

¼ tsp. baking powder

⅛ tsp. salt

½ cup unsweetened plain soymilk

½ cup brown rice syrup

¼ cup canola oil

½ tsp. organic lemon flavoring, or
1 tsp. freshly grated lemon zest

¾ cup fresh or frozen raspberries

1. Preheat oven to 375°F. Line 12-cup muffin tin with paper liners. Whisk together flour, baking soda, baking powder, and salt in large bowl. Whisk together soymilk, rice syrup, oil, and lemon flavoring in separate bowl.

2. Stir soymilk mixture into flour mixture.

3. Fold in raspberries. Fill cups of prepared muffin tin two-thirds full.

4. Bake 20 to 25 minutes, or until toothpick inserted in center comes out clean. Cool muffins 20 minutes in pan on wire rack. Unmold muffins, and cool completely on wire rack.

PER MUFFIN: 136 CAL; 2 G PROT; 5.5 G TOTAL FAT (0.5 G SAT FAT); 20 G CARB; 0 MG CHOL; 108 MG SOD; 2 G FIBER; 8 G SUGARS

Double-Corn Cornbread

Cream-style corn makes this cornbread amazingly moist and almost buttery. The squares are great for breakfast, too.

1 cup unsweetened plain soymilk

2 tsp. apple cider vinegar

1 cup cream-style corn

½ cup shredded vegan cheddar cheese

⅓ cup canola oil

4 green onions, finely chopped

1 cup yellow cornmeal

½ cup all-purpose flour

2 Tbs. maple sugar or light brown sugar

1 Tbs. salt

2 tsp. baking powder

½ tsp. baking soda

1. Preheat oven to 350°F. Coat 8-inch square baking dish with cooking spray.

2. Combine soymilk and vinegar. Let stand 5 minutes to develop a buttermilk-like consistency. Whisk in corn, cheddar, oil, and onions; set aside.

3. Combine all dry ingredients in large bowl, and make well in the middle. Pour wet mixture into well, and stir until mixed. Pour batter into prepared baking dish, and bake 35 to 40 minutes, or until a toothpick inserted in the middle comes out clean.

PER SERVING: 151 CAL; 3 G PROT; 7.5 G TOTAL FAT (0.5 G SAT FAT); 18 G CARB; 0 MG CHOL; 799 MG SOD; 15 G FIBER; 15 G SUGARS

Shopping Savvy: Cornmeal

Cornmeal is sold according to grind. Finely-ground cornmeal is sometimes labeled corn flour. Coarsely-ground cornmeal gives breads and crusted vegetables a tasty crunch. Medium-grind is a safe choice for most recipes; it's coarse enough to give baked goods that extra crunch, but fine enough to keep batters light and tender.

Chocolate Chip–Banana Muffins

Betcha can't eat just one of these dense, sweet, decadent muffins
that are more like dessert than a breakfast bread.

1 cup all-purpose flour

1 cup whole-wheat pastry flour

1 cup unrefined cane sugar or sugar

1 tsp. baking soda

1 cup unsweetened applesauce

½ cup canola oil

1 tsp. vanilla extract

¼ cup unsweetened plain soymilk

3 small ripe bananas, mashed (1 cup)

6 oz. vegan chocolate chips

½ cup chopped raw walnuts

1. Preheat oven to 350°F. Line 18 muffin-tin cups with paper liners. Whisk together flours, sugar, and baking soda in large bowl. Combine applesauce, oil, and vanilla in separate bowl. Fold applesauce mixture into flour mixture with spatula or wooden spoon. Stir in soymilk and bananas. Fold in chocolate chips and walnuts.

2. Fill cups of prepared muffin tins two-thirds full with batter. Bake 25 to 30 minutes, or until toothpick inserted in center comes out clean. Let stand 10 minutes, then unmold onto wire rack to cool.

PER MUFFIN: 237 CAL; 2 G PROT; 11 G TOTAL FAT (2.5 G SAT FAT); 34 G CARB; 0 MG CHOL; 79 MG SOD; 3 G FIBER; 18 G SUGARS

Buy and Try: Unrefined Cane Sugar

Unrefined cane sugar, sometimes sold as Sucanat, is both an earth-friendly option and a boon in baked goods, where it lends a light, caramel flavor due to the trace of molasses in the final product.

Morning Glory Loaf

MAKES 1 LOAF, 3 MINI LOAVES, OR 12 MUFFINS

Spicy, sweet, and good for you, this loaf is a great way to start the day. We've provided instructions on how to make it into muffins or mini muffins.

2 cups all-purpose flour

2 tsp. ground cinnamon

2 tsp. ground ginger

2 tsp. baking powder

½ tsp. baking soda

¼ tsp. salt

⅔ cup packed light brown sugar

½ cup canola oil

1 8-oz. can crushed pineapple in its own juice, drained, juice reserved

½ cup fresh carrot juice

1 tsp. vanilla extract

1 cup finely grated carrots (2 to 3 medium)

½ cup raisins

½ cup walnuts or pecans, coarsely chopped, optional

1. Preheat oven to 350°F. Coat 9- × 5-inch loaf pan, 3 6- × 3-inch mini loaf pans, or 12-cup muffin tin with cooking spray.

2. Whisk together flour, cinnamon, ginger, baking powder, baking soda, and salt in bowl. Whisk sugar, oil, ¼ cup reserved pineapple juice, carrot juice, and vanilla in separate bowl. Fold sugar mixture into flour mixture. Stir in crushed pineapple, carrots, raisins, and walnuts, if desired.

3. Scoop batter into prepared pan(s). Bake large loaf 50 to 60 minutes, mini loaves 35 to 45 minutes, or muffins 18 to 22 minutes, or until golden brown and toothpick inserted in center comes out clean. Cool in pan 5 minutes. Loosen edges, and turn out onto wire rack to cool completely.

PER MUFFIN: 256 CAL; 3 G PROT; 9.5 G TOTAL FAT (0.5 G SAT FAT); 41 G CARB; 0 MG CHOL; 209 MG SOD; 2 G FIBER; 21 G SUGARS

Blueberry-Apple Tea Bread

SERVES 12

Just calling this quick bread "tea bread" makes you think of a lovely, relaxing afternoon treat. With a cup of steaming tea, it's sublime, but really, it's the kind of quick bread you can treat yourself to anytime.

1 medium Granny Smith apple, peeled, cored, and sliced

1 Tbs. fresh lemon juice

½ cup dried blueberries

2 cups all-purpose flour

⅓ cup oat bran

1 tsp. ground cinnamon

⅛ tsp. ground nutmeg

1 tsp. baking powder

1 tsp. baking soda

½ tsp. sea salt

½ cup unsweetened applesauce

1 cup evaporated cane juice

1 Tbs. vegan egg replacer powder

¾ cup unsweetened plain soymilk

½ Tbs. vanilla extract

½ cup chopped raw walnuts

1. Preheat oven to 350°F. Spray 9- × 5-inch loaf pan with oil.

2. Place apple slices in bowl, and toss with lemon juice. Add blueberries, and set aside.

3. Combine flour with oat bran, cinnamon, nutmeg, baking powder, baking soda, and salt in medium bowl.

4. Blend applesauce with cane juice in separate bowl. Using fork or wire whisk, stir together egg replacer powder with ¼ cup water in liquid measuring cup. Add egg replacer powder mixture, soymilk, and vanilla to applesauce. Fold dry ingredients into wet ingredients, adding apple-blueberry mixture halfway through before ingredients are totally combined, stirring just until blended. Do not overbeat. Pour batter into prepared pan, and sprinkle with walnuts.

5. Bake 40 minutes, or until toothpick inserted in center comes out clean. Cool slightly before serving.

PER SERVING: 223 CAL; 5 G PROT; 4 G TOTAL FAT (0 G SAT FAT); 45 G CARB; 0 MG CHOL; 236 MG SOD; 2 G FIBER; 22 G SUGARS

chapter 12

sweet treats

Once upon a time, if you asked a restaurant for a dessert without eggs or dairy, you'd have ended up with a fruit salad. But times have changed. Now, even classically trained pastry chefs (who live to cook with butter and cream) have added vegan desserts to their repertoire. Bakeries and restaurants boast an impressive selection of sweets that use no animal products whatsoever. Times are good—and they're getting better as bakers experiment with new ways to take the eggs and dairy out of old favorites. And when their creations taste like the treats in this chapter, it prompts the question: who needs eggs and dairy at all?

Thumbprint Cookies

MAKES 36 COOKIES

Kids can pitch in during almost every step of this recipe, from mixing the dough to rolling the cookie balls to leaving their mark (a thumbprint) on each. For drip-free results, fill the cookie centers with jam before baking, as described below, or squeeze jam into thumbprint indentations after the cookies have cooled.

1 ½ cups all-purpose flour

½ cup whole-wheat flour

½ tsp. baking powder

¼ tsp. salt

¾ cup sugar

½ cup nonhydrogenated margarine (1 stick)

⅓ cup vanilla soymilk

1 tsp. vanilla extract

¼ tsp. almond extract

1 cup seedless raspberry jam

1. Whisk together all-purpose flour, whole-wheat flour, baking powder, and salt in large bowl.

2. Beat sugar and margarine with electric mixer until light and fluffy. Gradually beat in soymilk, vanilla extract, and almond extract until combined. Beat in flour mixture until soft dough forms. Wrap dough in plastic wrap, and refrigerate 30 minutes, or overnight.

3. Preheat oven to 325°F. Line 2 baking sheets with parchment paper, or spray with cooking spray. Roll dough into 1 ½-inch balls, and place dough balls 1 inch apart on prepared baking sheets. Press indentation in center of each ball with thumb.

4. Place jam in resealable plastic bag, close, and snip bottom corner with scissors. Squeeze jam into indentations in cookies. Bake 12 to 15 minutes, or until cookies are light brown. Transfer to wire rack, and cool.

PER COOKIE: 76 CAL; 1 G PROT; 1.5 G TOTAL FAT (0.5 G SAT FAT); 15 G CARB; 0 MG CHOL; 38 MG SOD; 1 G FIBER; 10 G SUGARS

Cinnamon Heart Cookies

MAKES 30 COOKIES

Also called palmiers, these quick cookies are made by folding cinnamon and sugar into layers of prepared puff pastry. The crisp, heart-shaped bites are wonderful with coffee or tea and make great Valentine gifts.

¾ cup sugar

2 ½ tsp. ground cinnamon

1 17.3-oz. pkg. prepared puff pastry, thawed

Prep Talk: *Working with Puff Pastry*

Puff pastry is a vegan's best friend when it comes to baking. Where else can you find flaky-good, premade dough that can be used in pies and cookies? The main rule to remember when working with puff pastry: keep it cold. If the dough begins to feel sticky, put it back in the fridge or freezer for 10 minutes, then start working with it again.

1. Preheat oven to 450°F. Line 2 baking sheets with parchment paper. Combine sugar and cinnamon in bowl. Sprinkle work surface with ¼ cup sugar mixture.

2. Open 1 puff pastry sheet, with fold lines parallel to edge of work surface. Spread 2 Tbs. sugar mixture on puff pastry. Roll lightly to press in sugar mixture. Flip, and repeat to coat second side.

3. Fold short ends to first fold line. Fold again so 2 folds meet at middle of dough. Fold 1 half over other to make log. Cut into 15 slices. Dip cut sides in remaining sugar on work surface, and place on prepared baking sheet, cut-side up. Repeat with remaining puff pastry and sugar mixture.

4. Bake 6 minutes, or until sugar begins to caramelize on bottoms. Flip with spatula, and bake 3 to 5 minutes more, or until caramelized on both sides. Cool on wire rack. Store in airtight containers for up to 2 weeks.

PER COOKIE: 111 CAL; 1 G PROT; 6.5 G TOTAL FAT (1 G SAT FAT); 13 G CARB; 0 MG CHOL; 41 MG SOD; 1 G FIBER; 5 G SUGARS

Kourabiedes *(Almond Shortbread Crescents)*

MAKES 36 COOKIES

These crunchy cookies, traditionally served on New Year's Day in Greece, are the perfect accompaniment to a glass of Champagne when the clock strikes midnight on New Year's Eve.

1 ½ cups all-purpose flour

½ cup ground almonds or almond flour

1 tsp. baking powder

½ tsp. salt

1 cup nonhydrogenated margarine, softened (2 sticks)

⅔ cup confectioners' sugar, plus more for dusting

1 Tbs. unsweetened plain soymilk

1 tsp. vanilla extract

½ tsp. almond extract

1 cup chopped almonds

1. Preheat oven to 350°F. Coat 2 baking sheets with cooking spray. Combine flour, ground almonds, baking powder, and salt in bowl.

2. Beat margarine and confectioners' sugar with electric mixer until creamy. Beat in soymilk and vanilla and almond extracts. Add flour mixture; beat until smooth. Stir in chopped almonds.

3. Shape piece of dough into 1-inch ball. Roll into 3-inch log, and bend into crescent. Set on baking sheet. Repeat with remaining dough, setting cookies 1 inch apart. Bake 12 to 15 minutes, or until just beginning to brown on top. Transfer to wire rack, and dust with confectioners' sugar. Cool; roll in confectioners' sugar to completely coat.

PER COOKIE: 37 CAL; 1 G PROT; 0.5 G TOTAL FAT (0 G SAT FAT); 7 G CARB; 0 MG CHOL; 48 MG SOD; 1 G FIBER; 3 G SUGARS

Storage Tip: Use Parchment Paper

To prevent the pretty dusting of confectioners' sugar from shaking off the Kourabiedes, layer them between sheets of parchment or wax paper in the cookie tin.

Snickerdoodles

MAKES 45 COOKIES

For sentimental satisfaction, snickerdoodles can't be beat,
which is probably why you find them in most vegan bakeries these days.
Cornstarch keeps this version tender and chewy.

COOKIE DOUGH

1 ¾ cups all-purpose flour

¼ cup cornstarch

1 tsp. baking powder

½ cup nonhydrogenated margarine,
softened (1 stick)

¾ cup sugar

¼ cup vanilla soymilk

1 tsp. vanilla extract

CINNAMON SUGAR

½ cup sugar

3 Tbs. ground cinnamon

Success Secret: Add More Spice

Try adding ½ teaspoon ground
nutmeg or allspice to the cinnamon
sugar to boost flavor.

1. Preheat oven to 350°F. Coat baking sheet with cooking spray.

2. To make Cookie Dough: Whisk together flour, cornstarch, and baking powder in bowl. Beat margarine in separate bowl with electric mixer until soft. Add sugar, and beat until fluffy. Beat in soymilk and vanilla 30 seconds or until smooth. Add flour mixture, and beat 30 seconds or until smooth.

3. To make Cinnamon Sugar: Combine sugar and cinnamon on large plate.

4. Shape dough into 1-inch balls. Roll each ball in cinnamon sugar, and place 1 ½ inches apart on prepared baking sheet. Bake 10 to 12 minutes, or until cookies look dry on tops and are lightly browned on bottoms. Transfer to wire rack to cool. Store in airtight container.

PER COOKIE: 49 CAL; 1 G PROT; 1.5 G TOTAL FAT
(0.5 G SAT FAT); 9 G CARB; 0 MG CHOL; 29 MG SOD;
1 G FIBER; 4 G SUGARS

Glazed Raisin-Almond Bites

MAKES 54 COOKIES

The secret ingredient here is strong coffee, which gives these cookies their rich flavor. Flaxseeds and prunes keep them moist and chewy.

BITES

2 ¼ cups all-purpose flour

¾ tsp. baking powder

¾ tsp. baking soda

¼ tsp. salt

1 Tbs. flaxseeds

¾ cup cold, strong coffee

½ cup pitted prunes (3 oz.)

¼ cup nonhydrogenated margarine, melted and cooled (1/2 stick)

1 tsp. almond extract or rum extract

1 ⅓ cups sugar

¾ cup golden raisins

½ cup almonds, chopped

GLAZE

2 cups confectioners' sugar

2 Tbs. fresh lemon juice

½ tsp. almond extract

1. To make Bites: Preheat oven to 375°F. Line 2 baking sheets with parchment paper.

2. Whisk together flour, baking powder, baking soda, and salt in bowl. Grind flaxseeds in blender 30 seconds, or until reduced to fine powder. Add ¼ cup coffee, and blend 2 minutes. Add prunes and remaining ½ cup coffee, blend 1 minute, or until combined. Add margarine and almond extract; blend 20 seconds to combine. Blend in sugar, then add to flour mixture. Fold in raisins and almonds.

3. Drop 1-Tbs. dollops of dough 1 ½ inches apart onto prepared baking sheets. Bake 14 minutes. Transfer to wire rack to cool.

4. To make Glaze: Whisk together all ingredients and 1 Tbs. water in bowl until smooth. Drizzle ½ tsp. glaze over each cooled bite.

PER COOKIE: 83 CAL; 1 G PROT; 1.5 G TOTAL FAT (0.5 G SAT FAT); 17 G CARB; 0 MG CHOL; 46 MG SOD; 1 G FIBER; 11 G SUGARS

Peanut Butter–Oatmeal Cookies

MAKES 26 COOKIES

Everybody loves a good peanut butter cookie. And a good
peanut butter cookie laced with oatmeal and chocolate chips—
well, it's hard to go wrong with that combination.

1 ½ cups all-purpose flour

½ cup quick-cooking or
old-fashioned oats

½ tsp. baking soda

½ tsp. salt

1 cup packed light brown sugar

¼ cup nonhydrogenated
vegetable shortening

¼ cup canola oil

¼ cup creamy natural peanut butter

1 Tbs. vegan egg replacer powder

1 tsp. vanilla extract

1 cup vegan chocolate chips

1. Preheat oven to 375°F. Combine flour, oats, baking soda, and salt in medium bowl. Beat sugar, shortening, and oil with electric mixer until smooth and fluffy. Add peanut butter, and beat until well combined. Stir together 5 Tbs. water and egg replacer powder in measuring cup. Beat egg replacer mixture and vanilla into sugar mixture until smooth.

2. Beat flour mixture into wet mixture, then add chocolate chips and mix until combined. Scoop 1-Tbs. dollops of dough 3 inches apart on ungreased baking sheets. Flatten dough balls to ½-inch thickness with fingers.

3. Bake 12 minutes, or until cookies are golden brown and dry on top. Cool on baking sheet 5 minutes, then transfer to wire rack to cool completely.

PER COOKIE: 148 CAL; 2 G PROT; 7 G TOTAL FAT
(2 G SAT FAT); 15 G CARB; 0 MG CHOL; 97 MG SOD;
1 G FIBER; 12 G SUGARS

Shopping Savvy: Peanut Butter

Read the label and look for all-natural, no-sugar-added peanut butter when buying your bread spread. Many popular brands are high in sugar and added fat.

Iced Ginger Gems

MAKES 35 COOKIES

You don't even need an electric mixer to make these drop cookies, which will become a holiday favorite once you try them.

¾ cup sugar

¼ cup nonhydrogenated margarine, softened (½ stick)

¼ cup vegetable oil

¼ cup crystallized ginger, chopped

1 Tbs. molasses

1 Tbs. vanilla extract

2 cups whole-wheat flour

1 tsp. baking soda

½ tsp. salt

1 cup finely chopped raw walnuts

4 ½ Tbs. fresh lime juice

3 cups confectioners' sugar

1. Preheat oven to 375°F. Coat 2 baking sheets with cooking spray. Whisk together sugar, margarine, oil, ginger, molasses, vanilla, and ¼ cup warm water. Combine flour, baking soda, and salt in separate bowl. Stir flour mixture into sugar mixture. Fold in walnuts.

2. Drop spoonfuls of dough 1 inch apart onto prepared baking sheets. Bake 10 to 12 minutes. Cool 3 minutes, then transfer to wire racks to cool completely.

3. Whisk lime juice and confectioners' sugar until smooth. Dip cookies in glaze. Let glaze harden on wire racks, then store cookies in airtight container.

PER COOKIE: 134 CAL; 1 G PROT; 5 G TOTAL FAT (1 G SAT FAT); 22 G CARB; 0 MG CHOL; 78 MG SOD; 1 G FIBER; 15 G SUGARS

Chocolate Shortbread Cookies

MAKES 16 COOKIES

Baby food is the secret ingredient that keeps these cookies rich tasting
and dense without butter or eggs. Brown sugar and a large dose of vanilla extract
help bring out the chocolate flavor.

1 cup all-purpose flour

½ cup packed dark brown sugar

¼ cup unsweetened cocoa powder

½ tsp. baking soda

¼ tsp. salt

1 oz. unsweetened chocolate

3 Tbs. canola oil

5 Tbs. prune-oatmeal baby food

1 tsp. vanilla extract

Success Secret: Timing

When making cookies, set the timer
to go off after the shortest amount
of time recommended in the recipe.
Most cookies taste best slightly
underbaked—and overbaked often
means burnt.

1. Preheat oven to 350°F. Coat baking sheet with cooking spray. Whisk together flour, sugar, cocoa, baking soda, and salt in bowl. Heat chocolate and oil in glass measuring cup in microwave on medium power 30 seconds to 1 minute, or until melted. Stir in baby food and vanilla, then stir into flour mixture. If dough is too crumbly to hold together, add 1 Tbs. more baby food.

2. Roll dough into 1 ½-inch balls and place 1 inch apart on prepared baking sheet. Press with bottom of drinking glass to flatten. Bake 9 to 12 minutes, or until small cracks form on cookie tops. Cool 5 minutes on baking sheet; transfer to wire rack to cool completely.

PER COOKIE: 94 CAL; 1 G PROT; 4 G TOTAL FAT
(1 G SAT FAT); 15 G CARB; 0 MG CHOL; 80 MG SOD;
1 G FIBER; 7 G SUGARS

The Heart-Healthiest Chocolate Chip Cookies in the World

MAKES 30 COOKIES

What started out as a way to incorporate heart-healthy foods into a dessert became a sweet sensation.

2 cups walnuts

3 Tbs. canola oil

1 cup packed light brown sugar

2 tsp. vanilla extract

1 ½ cups oat flour

1 tsp. baking soda

1 tsp. salt

¼ tsp. ground cinnamon

2 cups rolled oats

3 3.5-oz. bars bittersweet vegan chocolate, chopped, or 1 ½ cups vegan chocolate chips (12 oz.)

1. Preheat oven to 350°F. Coat 2 baking sheets with cooking spray.

2. Blend walnuts in food processor 30 seconds, or until ground into a fine meal. Add oil, and blend 2 to 3 minutes, or until mixture has the consistency of natural peanut butter. Transfer to bowl.

3. Bring sugar and ½ cup water to a boil in saucepan. Pour sugar mixture over ground walnut butter, add vanilla, and stir until no lumps remain.

4. Whisk together oat flour, baking soda, salt, and cinnamon in separate bowl. Stir oat flour mixture into walnut mixture. Cool 10 minutes. Fold in oats, then chocolate pieces.

5. Shape dough into 2-inch balls, and place 2 inches apart on prepared baking sheets. Flatten with bottom of drinking glass dipped in water. Bake 8 to 10 minutes, or until cookies begin to brown. Cool 3 minutes on baking sheets, then transfer to wire rack to cool completely.

PER COOKIE: 173 CAL; 3 G PROT; 10 G TOTAL FAT (3 G SAT FAT); 21 G CARB; 0 MG CHOL; 122 MG SOD; 2 G FIBER; 12 G SUGARS

Dark Chocolate Nuggets

MAKES 24 NUGGETS

Studded with dried fruit, nuts, and crisp cereal, these orange-scented chocolate clusters make exceptionally easy, irresistible gifts.

2 oz. coarsely chopped hazelnuts or pistachios (½ cup)

12 oz. bittersweet vegan chocolate, finely chopped, divided

1 cup puffed whole-grain cereal (rice or mixed grains)

½ cup dried cranberries, dried cherries, or chopped dried apricots

1 tsp. freshly grated orange zest, plus julienned orange zest for garnish

Prep Talk: Melting Chocolate

Melting the chocolate in stages may seem a little picky, but it's actually a short-cut method for "tempering" chocolate. (Tempering stabilizes the chocolate and prevents a cloudy appearance.)

1. Line 2 baking sheets with wax paper.

2. Toast hazelnuts in dry skillet over medium-low heat 2 to 3 minutes, or until lightly browned and fragrant, stirring constantly. Transfer to small bowl and cool.

3. Melt 9 oz. chocolate in double boiler. Stir remaining 3 oz. chocolate into melted chocolate, in 2 additions, stirring until all chocolate is melted and smooth. Stir in toasted nuts, cereal, dried fruit, and grated orange zest.

4. Drop chocolate mixture onto prepared baking sheets in tablespoon-size clumps; leave 1 inch between each. Garnish clusters with julienned orange zest. Chill uncovered in refrigerator 10 to 15 minutes, or until set. Transfer clusters to paper candy cups, and store, covered, in refrigerator up to 1 month or in freezer up to 2 months.

PER NUGGET: 97 CAL; 1 G PROT; 7.5 G TOTAL FAT (3 G SAT FAT); 10 G CARB; 0 MG CHOL; 0 MG SOD; 1 G FIBER; 7 G SUGARS

Fudgy Brownies

MAKES 16 BROWNIES

What could be better than warm brownies and a glass of (soy) milk
after a big day at school? Or work, for that matter? Don't be put off
by the banana that goes into the batter here—it keeps the brownies
dense and moist. You won't taste it in the final product.

¾ cup all-purpose flour

¼ cup unsweetened cocoa powder

⅛ tsp. baking powder

⅛ tsp. baking soda

⅛ tsp. salt

¼ cup vegan chocolate chips

¼ cup canola oil

1 small ripe banana, mashed

½ cup sugar

½ cup unsweetened plain soymilk

1 Tbs. ground flaxseed

1 tsp. vanilla extract

1. Preheat oven to 350°F. Coat 9-inch square baking pan with cooking spray. Whisk together flour, cocoa powder, baking powder, baking soda, and salt in large bowl.

2. Heat chocolate and oil in glass measuring cup in microwave on medium power 30 seconds to 1 minute, or until melted. Whisk in banana and sugar. Combine soymilk, flaxseed, and vanilla in measuring cup, then fold into chocolate mixture. Stir chocolate mixture into flour mixture until just combined, then spread in prepared baking pan.

3. Bake 20 to 25 minutes, or until toothpick inserted 2 inches from side of pan comes out dry but middle is still soft. Cool in pan on wire rack, then cut into 16 squares.

PER BROWNIE: 106 CAL; 2 G PROT; 5 G TOTAL FAT
(1 G SAT FAT); 15 G CARB; 0 MG CHOL; 42 MG SOD;
1 G FIBER; 9 G SUGARS

Buy and Try: Ground Flaxseed

Ground flaxseed (sometimes sold as flaxseed meal) can be used to replace eggs in baking. To veganize a baking recipe, substitute 1 Tbs. ground flaxseed plus 3 Tbs. water for each egg.

Chocolate Truffles

Truffle chocolates are usually made with butter and cream. Here, the dairy products are eliminated in favor of chocolate soymilk, which reduces the saturated fat of the final product to a fraction of what it would be. But who's thinking of fat when something's this sweet and luscious?

½ cup chocolate soymilk

1 12-oz. pkg. vegan chocolate chips

½ cup unsweetened cocoa powder

Success Secret: *Jazz Up Your Truffles*

Melt-in-your-mouth truffles don't need much to make them irresistible, but if you want to jazz up this recipe, try stirring in 2 teaspoons of a flavored liqueur, such as Chambord, Frangelico, or Kahlúa.

1. Warm soymilk in small saucepan on medium heat until hot to the touch. Set aside.

2. Melt chocolate chips in large metal bowl set over saucepan of simmering water, stirring until smooth. Stir in warmed soymilk until smooth. Cover, and refrigerate 4 hours, or overnight.

3. Place cocoa powder on plate. Shape chilled chocolate mixture into 1-inch balls, and roll in cocoa.

PER TRUFFLE: 45 CAL; 1 G PROT; 3 G TOTAL FAT (2 G SAT FAT); 6 G CARB; 0 MG CHOL; 19 MG SOD; 1 G FIBER; 4 G SUGARS

Roasted Strawberry Compote with Vanilla Bean

MAKES 3 CUPS

When strawberry season is still a long way away (forget buying those overpriced imports), get your berry fix. Roasting frozen strawberries at a high temperature creates an intensely flavored compote that is equally delicious on morning yogurt or a bowl of ice cream.

5 cups frozen whole strawberries

⅓ cup sugar

¼ tsp. salt

½ vanilla bean

Preheat oven to 475°F. Coat 13- × 9-inch baking dish with cooking spray. Toss together strawberries, sugar, and salt in large bowl. Scrape seeds from vanilla bean with back of knife, and stir into strawberries along with bean. Bake 25 minutes, stirring often. Remove vanilla bean before serving.

PER ½-CUP SERVING: 55 CAL; 1 G PROT; 0 G TOTAL FAT (0 G SAT FAT); 14 G CARB; 0 MG CHOL; 65 MG SOD; 2 G FIBER, 12 G SUGARS

Buy and Try: Fresh Vanilla Beans

Vanilla extract is great in baked goods, but for recipes that need to be infused with flavor while they heat (custards, compotes, etc.), turn to a fresh vanilla bean. Splitting the pods and scraping out the seeds is easy, and the empty pods can be put in a jar of sugar to make vanilla sugar once you're done using them.

Vanilla Pound Cake with Lime Glaze

SERVES 6

This is a fantastic all-purpose cake recipe that can be baked
as cupcakes or layer cakes, though you may have to reduce baking time.

VANILLA POUND CAKE

5 oz. silken tofu, drained

⅔ cup sugar

¼ cup canola oil

¼ cup vanilla soymilk

2 tsp. vanilla extract

1 ½ cups cake flour or pastry flour

1 ½ tsp. baking powder

1 tsp. baking soda

½ tsp. salt

LIME GLAZE

⅓ cup confectioners' sugar

1 Tbs. fresh lime juice

1. To make Vanilla Pound Cake: Preheat oven to 350°F. Coat 9- x 5-inch loaf pan with cooking spray.

2. Blend tofu, sugar, oil, soymilk, and vanilla extract in food processor until smooth.

3. Whisk together flour, baking powder, baking soda, and salt in large bowl. Fold in tofu mixture. Pour into loaf pan, and bake 30 minutes, or until toothpick inserted in center comes out clean.

4. Cool in pan 5 minutes, then unmold and cool on wire rack until just warm.

5. To make Lime Glaze: Whisk together sugar and lime juice in small bowl until smooth. Drizzle over top of cake. Cool cake completely before serving to allow glaze to set.

PER SLICE: 343 CAL; 4 G PROT; 10.5 G TOTAL FAT (1 G SAT FAT); 58 G CARB; 0 MG CHOL; 547 MG SOD; 1 G FIBER; 30 G SUGARS

Prep Talk: Egg Substitutes

Because of their smooth texture and fat content, silken and soft tofu are good choices as egg substitutes in baked goods. To use in other recipes, replace each egg with ¼ cup silken or soft tofu.

Orange Spice Cupcakes

MAKES 12 CUPCAKES

Grated orange zest, fresh orange juice, and a hint of orange liqueur
(Cointreau or Grand Marnier) all go into these cupcakes to give them
orange flavor to the max. For a sparkling garnish, try sprinkling
the cupcakes with crushed hard candies or lemon or orange drops.

CUPCAKES

2 cups all-purpose flour

½ cup sugar

1 ½ tsp. baking soda

½ tsp. salt

½ tsp. pumpkin pie spice

1 cup fresh orange juice

½ cup canola oil or light olive oil

2 Tbs. apple cider vinegar

1 Tbs. freshly grated orange zest

ICING

1 ½ cups confectioners' sugar

3 Tbs. nonhydrogenated margarine,
softened

2 Tbs. fresh orange juice

1 Tbs. orange liqueur, optional

1 Tbs. freshly grated orange zest

1. To make Cupcakes: Preheat oven to 350°F. Line 12-cup muffin tin with paper liners.

2. Whisk together flour, sugar, baking soda, salt, and pumpkin pie spice in bowl. Stir in orange juice, oil, vinegar, and orange zest. Fill liners two-thirds full and bake 30 minutes, or until toothpick inserted in center comes out clean. Cool on wire rack.

3. To make Icing: Beat all ingredients with electric mixer until smooth. Spread on cupcakes.

PER CUPCAKE: 242 CAL; 2 G PROT; 6 G TOTAL FAT (1 G SAT FAT); 45 G CARB; 0 MG CHOL; 299 MG SOD; 1 G FIBER; 30 G SUGARS

Prep Talk: Vinegar

Vinegar and vegan baking go hand in hand, as the acid works in place of eggs to bind batters and interacts with baking soda to make cakes and quick breads rise.

Raw Cashew Cheesecake

SERVES 12

If you're looking for an introduction to the raw food movement,
this cheesecake showcases some of the techniques that make recipes "work."
Soaked cashews are used in place of cream cheese; macadamia nuts,
dates, and coconut are blended together for a crust; and everything's sweetened
with agave nectar, a raw sweetener derived from the agave plant.

2 cups unsalted macadamia nuts

1 ½ cups unsalted raw cashews

½ cup pitted dates

¼ cup dried coconut

6 Tbs. coconut oil, gently warmed

¼ cup fresh lime juice

¼ cup agave nectar

½ vanilla bean

3 cups mixed berries, such as
blueberries and raspberries

1. Place macadamia nuts in large bowl, and cover with cold water. Place cashews in separate bowl, and cover with cold water. Soak nuts 4 hours, then rinse, drain, and set aside.

2. Pulse macadamia nuts and dates in food processor to a sticky crumb-like consistency. Sprinkle coconut on bottom of 8-inch pie pan. Press macadamia nut mixture onto coconut to make crust.

3. Place cashews, coconut oil, lime juice, agave nectar, and 6 Tbs. water in bowl of food processor. Scrape seeds from vanilla bean into food processor bowl, and purée until smooth. Pour mixture onto crust, and freeze 1 to 2 hours, or until firm. Remove from freezer, slice while frozen, and transfer to serving platter. Defrost in fridge 1 hour, or on countertop 30 minutes; top with berries; and serve.

PER SLICE: 359 CAL; 5 G PROT; 28.5 G TOTAL FAT (9.5 G SAT FAT); 24 G CARB; 0 MG CHOL; 7 MG SOD; 4 G FIBER; 14 G SUGARS

Storage Hint:
Wrap Your Cheesecake

Raw desserts like this one take on refrigerator and freezer odors easily, so cover or wrap tightly in plastic wrap before chilling.

Glazed Chocolate-Avocado Cupcakes

MAKES 12 CUPCAKES

Avocado replaces the eggs and most of the oil in a rich, chocolaty batter that turns out supermoist baked goodies. It also kicks up the fiber content even better than whole-wheat flour.

CUPCAKES

1 ½ cups all-purpose flour

¾ cup unsweetened cocoa powder

1 tsp. baking powder

¾ tsp. baking soda

¾ tsp. salt

1 medium avocado, peeled and pitted

1 cup pure maple syrup

¾ cup unsweetened plain soymilk

⅓ cup canola oil

2 tsp. vanilla extract

GLAZE

3.5 oz. soft silken tofu, drained and patted dry

3 Tbs. pure maple syrup

½ tsp. vanilla extract

⅛ tsp. salt

4 oz. semisweet vegan chocolate, melted and cooled

1. To make Cupcakes: Preheat oven to 350°F. Line 12-cup muffin tin with paper liners. Whisk together flour, cocoa powder, baking powder, baking soda, and salt in bowl. Purée avocado in food processor until smooth. Add maple syrup, soymilk, oil, and vanilla, and blend until creamy. Whisk avocado mixture into flour mixture.

2. Spoon batter into prepared muffin tin. Bake 25 minutes, or until toothpick inserted in center comes out with some crumbs attached. Cool.

3. To make Glaze: Blend tofu, maple syrup, vanilla, and salt in food processor until smooth. Add chocolate to tofu mixture and blend until smooth. Transfer to bowl. Dip tops of cupcakes into glaze, pulling straight up from glaze to form peaks.

PER CUPCAKE: 287 CAL; 4 G PROT; 12.5 G TOTAL FAT (3 G SAT FAT); 44 G CARB; 0 MG CHOL; 304 MG SOD; 4 G FIBER; 24 G SUGARS

Chocolate Layer Cake with Peanut Butter Filling

SERVES 16

Here's a cake that's beautifully birthday-worthy. Layers of chocolate cake and a creamy peanut butter filling are topped with a fudgy frosting for bakeshop taste.

CAKE

3 cups all-purpose flour

2 cups beet sugar or cane sugar

6 Tbs. unsweetened cocoa powder

2 tsp. baking soda

1 tsp. salt

¾ cup vegetable oil

2 Tbs. white vinegar

2 tsp. vanilla extract

ICING

1 lb. confectioners' sugar

½ cup unsweetened cocoa powder

½ cup nonhydrogenated vegetable shortening

1 tsp. vanilla extract

FILLING

4 oz. creamy peanut butter

4 oz. firm silken tofu, drained

½ cup confectioners' sugar

1 ½ tsp. vanilla extract

1. To make Cake: Preheat oven to 350°F. Coat 2 8-inch round cake pans with cooking spray and dust with flour. Sift flour, sugar, cocoa powder, baking soda, and salt into bowl. Whisk together oil, vinegar, vanilla, and 2 cups water in separate bowl. Fold oil mixture into flour mixture. Pour into prepared pans, and bake 40 minutes, or until toothpick inserted in center comes out clean. Cool in pan, then unmold.

2. To make Icing: Sift confectioners' sugar and cocoa into bowl. Add margarine; beat 1 minute with electric mixer on low speed. Add ⅔ cup boiling water and vanilla. Beat until smooth. Cool 20 minutes.

3. To make Filling: Purée peanut butter and tofu in blender until smooth. Blend in confectioners' sugar 1 Tbs. at a time, then blend in vanilla. Refrigerate until firm enough to spread.

4. To assemble: Place one cake layer on plate; top with filling, then second cake layer. Frost with icing. Refrigerate until ready to serve.

PER SLICE: 526 CAL; 6 G PROT; 22 G TOTAL FAT (4.5 G SAT FAT); 78 G CARB; 0 MG CHOL; 354 MG SOD; 3 G FIBER; 55 G SUGARs

Carrot Cake

SERVES 15

What we love about this recipe: there are no hard-to-find ingredients required to make it. What we hate: there are never enough slices in just one cake.

CAKE

1 medium ripe banana, frozen and thawed

⅔ cup sugar

⅓ cup vegetable oil

2 medium carrots, grated (1 ½ cups)

1 ½ cups all-purpose flour

1 Tbs. baking powder

½ tsp. salt

1 tsp. ground cinnamon

½ tsp. ground nutmeg

½ cup raisins

½ cup chopped raw walnuts

ICING

1 ½ cups confectioners' sugar

1 Tbs. nonhydrogenated margarine

½ tsp. vanilla extract

1. To make Cake: Preheat oven to 350°F. Coat 9-inch cake pan with cooking spray. Mash banana in large bowl. Whisk in sugar, oil, and carrots. Whisk together flour, baking powder, salt, cinnamon, and nutmeg in separate bowl. Stir flour mixture into banana mixture. Fold in raisins and walnuts.

2. Pour batter into prepared baking pan. Bake 25 to 30 minutes, or until toothpick inserted in center comes out clean. Cool 10 minutes in pan. Transfer to wire rack, and cool.

3. To make Icing: Whisk together all ingredients in bowl. Drizzle icing over cake.

PER SLICE: 222 CAL; 2 G PROT; 8 G TOTAL FAT (1 G SAT FAT); 37 G CARB; 0 MG CHOL; 205 MG SOD; 1 G FIBER; 26 G SUGARS

Success Secret: Finely or Coarsely Grated Carrots?

Finely grated carrots will yield a carrot cake that's dense and moist—the vegetables "melt" into the cake. Coarsely grated carrots will make a chewier cake with more texture.

Triple Nut Chocolate Tart

This rich, elegant holiday tart screams for a scoop of vanilla soy ice cream on top. The press-and-go crust is slightly sweet, with a hint of crunch from cornmeal. It works well in other pie and tart recipes, too.

CRUST

1 cup cake flour or pastry flour

½ cup yellow cornmeal

2 Tbs. sugar

¼ tsp. salt

½ cup nonhydrogenated margarine (1 stick)

1 tsp. vanilla extract

FILLING

3 cups mixed walnuts, pecans, and almonds (1 cup each), coarsely chopped

¼ cup nonhydrogenated margarine (½ stick)

5 oz. vegan bittersweet chocolate, chopped or chips

2 Tbs. cake or pastry flour

¼ tsp. salt

½ cup pure maple syrup

2 tsp. vanilla extract

1. To make Crust: Combine flour, cornmeal, sugar, and salt in bowl. Rub margarine into flour mixture with fingers until mixture is crumbly. Sprinkle in vanilla, and stir. Add 1 to 2 Tbs. cold water until dough clumps together loosely. Press dough into pie pan or tart pan until sides and bottom are covered. Chill in freezer 30 minutes.

2. To make Filling: Preheat oven to 375°F. Spread nuts on baking sheet, and bake 10 to 12 minutes, until lightly browned.

3. Melt margarine and chocolate in saucepan over low heat, stirring until smooth. Sprinkle in flour and salt, and stir until smooth. Stir in maple syrup and vanilla. Stir in nuts.

4. Spread nut mixture in piecrust. Bake 25 minutes, or until crust is golden and filling is firm. Cool on wire rack at least 20 minutes before serving.

PER SLICE: 459 CAL; 7 G PROT; 33.5 G TOTAL FAT (8 G SAT FAT); 38 G CARB; 0 MG CHOL; 225 MG SOD; 4 G FIBER; 16 G SUGARS

Cranberry-Cherry Lattice Pie

SERVES 8

Because cranberries are naturally high in pectin, the fruit fiber that sets jams and jellies, there's no need to add a thickener to this filling. If you prefer a sweeter dessert, use refrigerated sugar cookie dough to craft the crust and lattice top.

3 cups fresh cranberries, divided

1 ½ cups sugar, plus more for sprinkling, divided

1 tsp. freshly grated orange zest

1 cup dried sweet cherries

⅓ cup fresh orange juice

Refrigerated pastry for 2-crust pie (plain or whole wheat), or double recipe Perfect Every Time Piecrust (p. 292)

1. Preheat oven to 375°F. Line baking sheet with foil, and coat 9-inch pie pan with cooking spray.

2. Place 1 ½ cups cranberries, ½ cup sugar, orange zest, and cherries in food processor, and pulse until berries are coarsely chopped. Transfer to bowl, and stir in remaining 1 ½ cups cranberries, remaining 1 cup sugar, and orange juice.

3. Roll 1 piecrust into 10-inch disk. Press into prepared pan. Spoon in cranberry mixture, and brush edges with water.

4. Roll second piecrust into 10-inch disk. Cut dough into 1-inch-wide strips using knife or fluted pastry wheel. Lay strips in lattice pattern over top of pie, pressing edges to seal. Trim off any excess from strips. Sprinkle lattice with sugar, and bake on prepared baking sheet 55 minutes, or until filling is bubbly and crust is golden. Cool on wire rack.

PER SLICE: 356 CAL; 7 G PROT; 1.5 G TOTAL FAT (0 G SAT FAT); 79 G CARB; 0 MG CHOL; 155 MG SOD; 5 G FIBER; 53 G SUGARS

Perfect Every Time Piecrust

MAKES 1 9-INCH CRUST

This recipe is just what its name says: a piecrust that's perfect, every time.
It can be used for any type of pie or quiche and keeps up to 5 days in the fridge.
Using the food processor (on pulse) prevents overworking the dough
so that it doesn't become tough once baked.

1 ½ cups all-purpose flour

1 Tbs. sugar

½ tsp. salt

½ cup cold nonhydrogenated vegetable shortening, cut into small pieces

Success Secret: Chill Piecrust

Chill the piecrust dough well before
rolling out—overnight is best.
This gives the dough a chance to rest
so that it won't shrink when baked.

1. Pulse flour, sugar, and salt in food processor several times to combine. Add butter, and pulse 5 times, or until mixture resembles coarse sand.

2. Add ¼ cup water to flour mixture in food processor. Pulse until dough just comes together, adding 1 or 2 Tbs. more water, if necessary. Transfer to large piece of plastic wrap or wax paper and press into flat disk. Wrap tightly, and chill 1 hour, or overnight. Roll out to desired size on well-floured work surface and bake according to recipe.

PER SERVING: 117 CAL; 0 G PROT; 13 G TOTAL FAT
(6 G SAT FAT); 2 G CARB; 0 MG CHOL; 145 MG SOD;
0 G FIBER; 2 G SUGARS

Apple-Cinnamon Tarte Tatin

SERVES 8

"Tarte tatin" is the French term for an upside-down apple pie where
the apples cook in sugar on the bottom of the pan and become soft and
coated in a sweet, rich caramel.

¾ cup sugar

8 medium sweet-tart apples (4 lb.),
such as Braeburn, peeled, cored, and
cut into 12 wedges each

2 Tbs. fresh lemon juice

1 tsp. ground cinnamon

Refrigerated pastry for 1-crust pie, or
1 Perfect Every Time Piecrust (p. 292)

Success Secret:
Cool Before Unmolding

If you don't plan on serving this pie
immediately, cool it in the skillet,
then warm it for 10 minutes in a 350°F
oven before unmolding. This will
keep the crust from getting soggy.

1. Preheat oven to 350°F. Spread sugar in even layer over bottom of 10-inch cast-iron or ovenproof skillet (not nonstick), and heat over medium-low heat. Cook 12 to 15 minutes, or until sugar has caramelized to a pale amber color, stirring often with wooden spoon. Remove from heat.

2. Toss apple wedges with lemon juice and cinnamon in bowl. Arrange apple wedges flat-side down in concentric circles in skillet over caramel.

3. Roll crust into 10-inch disk. Place dough over apples, folding edges inward to make a rim but covering apples completely. Make 2 to 3 small slits in dough to let steam escape while baking. Bake 1 hour 45 minutes to 2 hours, or until crust is golden brown.

4. Cool 15 minutes on wire rack. Run knife around edges, then place large cake plate over skillet, and invert tart onto cake plate. Transfer any apples remaining in skillet into tart and smooth with knife.

PER SLICE: 287 CAL; 2 G PROT; 7.5 G TOTAL FAT
(3 G SAT FAT); 57 G CARB; 0 MG CHOL; 100 MG SOD;
3 G FIBER; 39 G SUGARS

Tofu Custard Tart with Fresh Fruit

SERVES 8

Once you've discovered how easy it is to use tofu as a custard in this dessert, you'll want to make it all the time. Fresh vanilla bean masks the "soy" flavor of the tofu, so all you get is the smooth, creamy texture. This version is topped with fresh mango and kiwi, but choose any favorite fruit that's in season.

2 12-oz. pkgs. lite silken firm tofu, drained

1 cup confectioners' sugar

1 vanilla bean

1 6-oz. prepared graham cracker crust

1 small mango, peeled, pitted, halved, and thinly sliced

1 kiwi, peeled and thinly sliced

1. Place tofu and confectioners' sugar in bowl of food processor. Purée 3 minutes, or until smooth, scraping down sides often.

2. Cut vanilla bean in half lengthwise, and scrape seeds into tofu mixture with back of small knife. Pulse in food processor 30 seconds, or until blended.

3. Spread tofu mixture in graham cracker crust. Arrange mango and kiwi slices in concentric circles on top of tart. Chill 2 hours to set.

PER SLICE: 218 CAL; 7 G PROT; 6 G TOTAL FAT
(1 G SAT FAT); 35 G CARB; 0 MG CHOL; 188 MG SOD;
1 G FIBER; 25 G SUGARS

Success Secret: Slicing Mango

For perfect mango slices, peel the fruit, then stand it upright on a cutting board with the narrowest side facing you. Slice away the flesh on each side of the large pit in the center so that you have two lobes. Cut the lobes into thin slices, then cut away any remaining flesh and slice.

Creamy Cardamom Rice Pudding

SERVES 6

If you like chai, you'll love this comforting cardamom-flavored dessert that uses the spices that flavor chai drinks.

5 cups vanilla soymilk

⅓ cup basmati or Jasmine rice

¼ tsp. salt

½ cup packed light brown sugar

⅓ cup golden raisins

⅓ cup chopped almonds, plus more for garnish, optional

1 tsp. vanilla extract

1 tsp. ground cinnamon

½ tsp. ground cardamom

1. Bring soymilk, rice, and salt to a boil in saucepan. Reduce heat to medium-low, and simmer 15 to 20 minutes, or until rice is tender, stirring frequently.

2. Stir in sugar, raisins, almonds, vanilla, cinnamon, and cardamom. Cook 5 minutes, until thickened.

3. Remove from heat, and divide among 6 dishes. Serve warm or cold, garnished with chopped almonds, if desired.

PER SERVING: 258 CAL; 7 G PROT; 6 G TOTAL FAT (1 G SAT FAT); 45 G CARB; 0 MG CHOL; 182 MG SOD; 2 G FIBER; 29 G SUGARS

Buy and Try: Cardamom

Ground cardamom ranks right up there with cinnamon for its ability to transform simple dishes into spectacular taste sensations. In addition to using it to flavor rice pudding, try stirring it into sweetened yogurt, or add it to curries to tame the heat of the other spices.

Three-Cherry Crumble

SERVES 8

Take cherry flavor to the max with this healthy crumble.
The filling is sweetened with cherry juice and dried cherries, while the topping
is made with whole-wheat pastry flour. (Note: If you want to use tart cherries
in this recipe, add ½ cup brown rice syrup to the filling ingredients.)

THREE-CHERRY FILLING

3 cups fresh or frozen pitted cherries

1 cup cherry juice, pomegranate juice,
or cranberry juice

½ cup dried cherries

¼ cup cornstarch

SESAME SEED TOPPING

1 ½ cups whole-wheat pastry flour

¼ cup sesame seeds

½ cup vegetable oil

½ cup brown rice syrup

½ tsp. vanilla extract

1. Preheat oven to 375°F.

2. To make Three-Cherry Filling: Combine fresh cherries, cherry juice, and dried cherries in large nonreactive saucepan. Bring to a boil, reduce heat to medium low, and simmer 5 minutes. Remove from heat, and stir in cornstarch. Spoon into 9-inch square baking dish.

3. To make Sesame Seed Topping: Stir together flour and sesame seeds in large bowl. Whisk together oil, rice syrup, and vanilla in small bowl. Stir oil mixture into flour mixture until it clumps together.

4. Crumble topping over cherry filling. Bake 45 minutes, or until topping is golden brown. Let stand 10 minutes before serving.

PER SERVING: 375 CAL; 4 G PROT; 15 G TOTAL FAT
(2 G SAT FAT); 54 G CARB; 0 MG CHOL; 47 MG SOD;
5 G FIBER; 25 G SUGARS

Buy and Try: Frozen Cherries

Because cherry season is short and fresh fruit is so expensive, we flip for the frozen kind—and recommend keeping a bag in the freezer. The sweet gems can be added to cakes, muffins, pies, and crumbles.

Tropsicles

Coconut milk and banana give these ice pops a creamy consistency without dairy.

2 cups pineapple chunks

1 large ripe banana, sliced

¾ cup light coconut milk

¼ to ½ cup agave nectar

Purée all ingredients in blender 1 to 2 minutes, or until mixture is smooth. Ladle into ice pop molds, and freeze at least 4 hours. Run molds under warm water to unmold.

PER POP: 102 CAL; 1 G PROT; 2 G TOTAL FAT
(1 G SAT FAT); 22 G CARB; 0 MG CHOL; 2 MG SOD;
1 G FIBER; 19 G SUGARS

Peaches-and-Cream Pops

MAKES 8 POPS

This is a wonderful recipe to try when peaches are in season and you have a couple that have gotten too soft to eat on their own.

2 large peaches, peeled and sliced, or
2 cups frozen sliced peaches, thawed

1 cup vanilla soymilk

⅓ to ⅔ cup agave nectar

Purée all ingredients in blender 1 to 2 minutes, or until mixture is smooth. Ladle into ice pop molds, and freeze at least 4 hours. Run molds under warm water to unmold.

PER POP: 90 CAL; 1 G PROT; 0.5 G TOTAL FAT
(0 G SAT FAT); 21 G CARB; 0 MG CHOL; 12 MG SOD;
1 G FIBER; 20 G SUGARS

Prep Talk: Peeling Peaches

To peel peaches, dunk them in a pot of boiling water 30 seconds, then cool. The peel will come right off.

Pomegranate-Pineapple Granita

For a light, bright dessert after a heavy meal, turn to this slightly tart granita,
which will satisfy your sweet tooth without making you feel stuffed.
The frozen cubes blended to create the granita can be made ahead and stored
in the freezer for 1 week, so it's a nice option for dinner parties, too.

2 cups fresh or canned
pineapple chunks

2 ⅔ cups unsweetened
pomegranate juice

¼ cup pure maple syrup or
agave nectar

¾ tsp. ground cinnamon, optional

Speedy Substitution:
Any Juice Will Do

This recipe will work with any fruit juice,
so feel free to try it with whatever you
have on hand.

1. Purée all ingredients in blender
until smooth. Pour into 2 or 3 plastic
ice cube trays. Freeze at least 4 hours
or overnight, until firmly frozen.

2. Twist cubes out of trays and into
bowl of food processor. Blend 30 seconds, or until smooth, evenly colored,
and snowy. Scoop into individual
bowls, and serve immediately.

PER SERVING: 94 CAL; 1 G PROT; 1 G TOTAL FAT
(0 G SAT FAT); 24 G CARB; 0 MG CHOL; 11 MG SOD;
1 G FIBER; 21 G SUGARS

Peanut Butter–Coconut Ice Cream

SERVES 6

A heavy-duty blender (such as a Vita-Mix) makes quick work of this frozen treat, but a regular blender will get the job done if you just keep turning it off and pushing down the frozen cubes. Or you can simply blend all the ingredients, chill, and process in an ice cream maker.

1 13.5-oz. can light coconut milk (1 ½ cups)

½ cup pure maple syrup

½ cup crunchy peanut butter

1 tsp. vanilla extract

1 cup French vanilla soy creamer, divided

1. Purée coconut milk, maple syrup, peanut butter, and vanilla in blender until smooth. Pour mixture into 2 ice cube trays, and freeze solid.

2. Place half of ice cream cubes and ½ cup soy creamer in blender, and process until smooth and creamy. Repeat with second tray of cubes and remaining ½ cup soy creamer.

PER SERVING: 305 CAL; 6 G PROT; 18.5 G TOTAL FAT (5 G SAT FAT); 32 G CARB; 0 MG CHOL; 107 MG SOD; 1 G FIBER; 26 G SUGARS

Storage Hint: Plastic Bags

Not serving the ice cream right away? Transfer frozen cubes to resealable plastic bags and you can store them up to a month before blending.

Strawberry Swirl Ice Cream

SERVES 6

Thanks to the chilling effect of frozen strawberries,
this recipe freezes faster than other homemade ice creams.
The strawberry jam makes a beautiful swirl of sweetness.

1 10-oz. bag frozen strawberries

6 oz. silken tofu, drained

½ cup plain soy creamer

½ cup agave nectar or
pure maple syrup

1 Tbs. vanilla extract

1 Tbs. freshly grated lemon zest

¼ cup all-fruit strawberry jam

1. Purée strawberries and tofu in blender or food processor until smooth. Add soy creamer, agave nectar, vanilla, and lemon zest; purée until smooth.

2. Freeze in ice cream maker according to manufacturer's instructions. When ice cream is ready, swirl in strawberry jam while machine paddles are still going, then serve, or transfer to tub to freeze.

PER SERVING: 169 CAL; 2 G PROT; 2 G TOTAL FAT
(0 G SAT FAT); 34 G CARB; 0 MG CHOL; 20 MG SOD;
1 G FIBER; 30 G SUGARS

Buy and Try: Ice Cream Maker

Even though you may not make ice cream as often as you turn on a food processor, no one has ever regretted the purchase of an ice cream maker. There's really no substitution for the chilling and churning it does to make smooth, creamy frozen treats.

Super Chocolate Vegan Gelato

SERVES 6

To get the rich texture of Italian gelato, this ice cream base is thickened with cornstarch, like a pudding.

2 cups plain soy creamer

½ cup packed dark brown sugar

3 Tbs. unsweetened cocoa powder

3 Tbs. cornstarch

½ tsp. salt

4 oz. semisweet vegan chocolate, finely chopped

2 tsp. vanilla extract

1. Combine soy creamer, sugar, cocoa powder, cornstarch, and salt in small saucepan, and bring to a simmer over medium heat. Cook 3 to 4 minutes, or until slightly thickened, whisking constantly. Remove from heat, and stir in chocolate and vanilla until chocolate is melted.

2. Cover, and chill 4 hours, or overnight.

3. Freeze in ice cream maker according to manufacturer's instructions.

PER SERVING: 266 CAL; 1 G PROT; 11.5 G TOTAL FAT (3.5 G SAT FAT); 41 G CARB; 0 MG CHOL; 132 MG SOD, 2 G FIBER; 28 G SUGARS

Açai Sorbet

In its pure state, açai pulp is sour and slightly bitter, but once a little sweetener is added, the flavor resembles concentrated blueberries with a hint of chocolate. Most people buy açai to boost their antioxidant intake, but it's worth trying for its taste as well.

4 pure açai pulp smoothie packs
(4 oz. each), thawed

¾ cup agave nectar

2 Tbs. fresh lemon juice

Success Secret:
Save Your Orange Rinds

Fill hollowed-out oranges and lemons with sorbet for a bright, beautiful serving option.

Whisk together all ingredients in bowl. Transfer to 9-inch square metal baking pan, and place in freezer. Stir with fork every half hour, scraping frozen bits from sides, to keep from freezing into a block. Scoop into bowls, and serve, or store in airtight container up to 1 week.

PER SERVING: 132 CAL; 1 G PROT; 2.5 G TOTAL FAT (0.5 G SAT FAT); 27 G CARB; 0 MG CHOL; 5 MG SOD; 2 G FIBER; 24 G SUGARS

Tulip Cones

A silicone baking mat is a must for these edible ice cream "bowls"
that make a pretty presentation for homemade frozen treats.
Limit the number you make at once to three so that you have plenty of
time to handle and shape them before they harden.

½ cup all-purpose flour

¼ cup confectioners' sugar

¼ cup nonhydrogenated margarine,
melted (½ stick)

2 Tbs. unsweetened plain soymilk,
plus more if needed

⅛ tsp. vanilla extract

Success Secret:
Soften Cones in Oven

If baked cone circles become too
hard to shape, pop them in the oven
30 seconds to soften them up.

1. Sift together flour and confectioners' sugar in bowl. Stir in margarine, then add soymilk and vanilla. Add 2 to 3 Tbs. more soymilk if mixture is too thick. Cover, and refrigerate overnight.

2. Preheat oven to 350°F. Line baking sheet with silicone baking mat. Set out 3 cereal bowls. Dollop 2 Tbs. batter on baking mat, and spread into 6-inch circle with back of spoon (batter should be about ⅛ inch thick). Make 2 more batter circles on baking mat. Bake 10 to 12 minutes, or until circles are evenly browned.

3. Cool circles 30 seconds to 1 minute, or until disks are firm enough to lift off mat but still pliable. Lift first circle from mat and press into bowl so that it forms cup. Repeat with remaining disks. If disks become too hard to bend, place in oven 1 to 2 minutes to soften. When cones are firm, transfer to wire rack to cool. Repeat with remaining batter.

PER CONE: 95 CAL; 1 G PROT; 5.5 G TOTAL FAT
(2.5 G SAT FAT); 10 G CARB; 0 MG CHOL; 61 MG SOD;
1 G FIBER; 4 G SUGARS

Roasted Maple Pecans

SERVES 6

You can nibble on these crunchy sweet pecans as is or sprinkle them on just about any dessert you can think of. Try them on baked apples or with fresh pears or as a topping for frozen desserts. The nuts will keep in an airtight container at room temperature for up to 3 weeks.

1 cup pecans, coarsely chopped

2 Tbs. maple syrup

2 Tbs. evaporated cane sugar or maple sugar

½ tsp. cinnamon

1. Preheat oven to 350°F.

2. Combine all ingredients in small bowl, and toss to coat. Spread pecans on parchment- or foil-covered baking sheet. Bake 20 to 30 minutes, stirring every 10 minutes, or until sugar is caramelized. Set pan on wire rack, and let cool 10 minutes. Break apart any nuts that have stuck together, and serve.

PER CONE: 153 CAL; 2 G PROT; 13 G TOTAL FAT (1 G SAT FAT); 10 G CARB; 0 MG CHOL; 1 MG SOD; 2 G FIBER; 7 G SUGARS

sauces, dips, spreads, jams, and marinades

Condiments that complement. The chapter is a catchall for recipes that do one thing (jams) and recipes that can do a lot of things (dips, vinaigrettes, sauces, marinades). But it's also a chapter to flip through for inspiration. Skim through dips, such as Sweet Chile Mayonnaise (p. 316), and you may just find a killer sandwich spread. Even the marinades come with mix-and-match instructions for possible uses. So what's the one thing this hodgepodge collection of recipes has in common? They all bring out the best in the foods they're served with.

Speedy Red Sauce

MAKES 5 ½ CUPS

This all-purpose pasta sauce can be used on spaghetti as well as in our Ultimate Vegan Lasagna (p. 104). Puréed roasted red peppers help thicken it quickly. You can also serve a bowl of it warm as a dip for fresh bread.

1 12-oz. jar roasted red bell peppers, rinsed and drained

1 Tbs. olive oil

2 small onions, diced (2 cups)

2 Tbs. dried basil, or 3 Tbs. finely chopped fresh basil

3 cloves garlic, minced (1 Tbs.)

1 28-oz. can fire-roasted crushed tomatoes

1. Purée roasted red peppers in food processor or blender until smooth.

2. Heat oil in saucepan over medium heat. Add onions, and sauté 5 minutes, or until golden. Add basil and garlic, and sauté 1 minute more. Stir in tomatoes and red pepper purée. Season with salt and pepper, if desired. Simmer 10 minutes, or until slightly thickened.

PER 1/2-CUP SERVING: 53 CAL; 2 G PROT; 1 G TOTAL FAT (1 G SAT FAT); 10 G CARB; 0 MG CHOL; 352 MG SOD; 2 G FIBER; 5 G SUGARS

Holiday Gravy

Browning the vegetables before making the gravy stock is what sets this rich sauce apart. Double the recipe if you've got a gravy-loving crowd for the holidays.

3 Tbs. olive oil, divided

2 medium onions, sliced

2 large carrots, cut into chunks

4 oz. button mushrooms, halved

3 cloves garlic, lightly crushed

1 tsp. salt

½ tsp. ground black pepper

½ cup dry white wine

4 sun-dried tomatoes, quartered

2 sprigs marjoram

1 sprig thyme

2 Tbs. all-purpose flour

1. Heat 2 Tbs. oil in saucepan over medium-low heat. Add onions, carrots, mushrooms, garlic, salt, and pepper. Cover, and cook 30 minutes. Uncover pan, increase heat to medium, and cook 10 minutes more, or until vegetables are browned. Add wine; simmer 2 to 3 minutes. Stir in sun-dried tomatoes, marjoram, thyme, and 2 ½ cups water. Reduce heat to medium-low, cover, and simmer 30 minutes. Strain into large measuring cup.

2. Heat remaining 1 Tbs. oil in saucepan over medium heat. Stir in flour, and cook 5 minutes, or until flour begins to turn golden. Whisk in vegetable liquid. Cook 3 to 5 minutes, or until gravy thickens, whisking constantly.

PER 2-TBS. SERVING: 29 CAL; 0 G PROT; 3 G TOTAL FAT (0 G SAT FAT); 1 G CARB; 0 MG CHOL; 142 MG SOD; 0 G FIBER; 0 G SUGARS

Arugula Pesto

MAKES 1 1/4 CUPS

This peppery twist on pesto is lighter than the classic version made
with pine nuts and Parmesan. Serve it surrounded by thin toasted
rounds of French bread and pita wedges, or pour it over
a block of low-fat vegan cream cheese, and accompany with crackers.

½ cup hulled unsalted
sunflower seeds

4 cups arugula or watercress
(from 2 large bunches), tough stems
removed

6 Tbs. olive oil

2 Tbs. fresh lemon juice

2 cloves garlic, peeled

Toast sunflower seeds in dry skillet
3 minutes, or until lightly browned.
Transfer to food processor. Add arugula, oil, lemon juice, and garlic, and
process until smooth. Season with
salt and pepper.

PER ¼-CUP SERVING: 60 CAL; 1 G PROT; 6 G TOTAL
FAT (1 G SAT FAT); 1 G CARB; 0 MG CHOL; 1 MG SOD;
0 G FIBER; 0 G SUGARS

....

Storage Hint: Use Olive Oil

....

To store this and other homemade pestos in the refrigerator,
transfer to a tightly closing container and pour a film of olive oil over top
to preserve its green color. It will keep several weeks.

Coffee Barbecue Sauce

Coffee has long been a secret ingredient in prize-winning barbecue sauces. Try this sauce as a dip for vegetarian chicken strips, brush it over grilled tofu, or stir an 8-ounce package of shredded seitan into it for barbecue sandwiches.

1 Tbs. canola oil

1 medium onion, chopped (1 cup)

1 Tbs. ground cumin

1 Tbs. chili powder

2 cloves garlic, minced (2 tsp.)

1 tsp. paprika

¾ cup ketchup

½ cup strong coffee

½ cup cider vinegar

¼ cup molasses

2 Tbs. Dijon mustard

Heat oil in saucepan over medium heat. Sauté onion 5 minutes, or until soft. Add cumin, chili powder, garlic, and paprika, and cook 30 seconds, or until fragrant. Stir in remaining ingredients and 1 cup water. Cover, reduce heat to medium-low, and simmer 30 minutes, or until slightly thickened. Strain into bowl, and discard solids. Refrigerate overnight to let flavors develop.

PER ¼-CUP SERVING: 108 CAL; 1 G PROT; 3 G TOTAL FAT (1 G SAT FAT); 20 G CARB; 0 MG CHOL; 481 MG SOD; 1 G FIBER; 14 G SUGARS

Shopping Savvy: Organic Ketchup

If there's one conventional supermarket item we want to encourage you to buy organic, it's ketchup. Name brands have now come out with organic lines that do not cost that much more than "regular" ketchup. And your purchase sends the large companies the message that cleaning up their growing act is worth it.

Onion Confit

MAKES 2 CUPS

Cooking chopped onions slowly over low heat caramelizes their
natural sugars and turns the pungent vegetables into a rich, ultra-
versatile spread that will keep for up to a week in the fridge.
Try slathering it on bread with vegan cheese and toasting for an
open-face sandwich, spread it on pizza dough, stir it into sour cream for
a homemade dip, or thin it with vegetable broth for easy onion soup.

3 Tbs. olive oil

8 large red or yellow onions, chopped,
or 3 10-oz. bags frozen diced onions
(8 cups)

1 tsp. salt

1 cup vegan lager beer

1 sprig thyme, or ½ tsp. dried thyme

2 Tbs. Dijon mustard

Heat oil in large pot over medium-low heat. Add onions and salt, cover, and cook 45 minutes (frozen onions may take longer) or until browned, stirring occasionally. Stir in beer, 1 cup water, and thyme, scraping up bits stuck to pot. Partially cover, and simmer 15 minutes, or until liquid has evaporated. Stir in mustard; season with pepper, if desired.

PER ¼-CUP SERVING: 128 CAL; 2 G PROT; 5 G TOTAL FAT (0.75 G SAT FAT); 17 G CARB; 0 MG CHOL; 388 MG SOD; 2.5 G FIBER; 7 G SUGARS

Double Cranberry Chutney

The simple flavors of this sauce will satisfy the traditionalists at your holiday table, while the chunky, chewy consistency will win over any foodies in the group.

2 Tbs. fresh orange juice

1 Tbs. fresh lemon juice

1 tsp. cornstarch

½ tsp. powdered mustard

4 cups fresh or frozen cranberries (2 12-oz. pkgs.)

1 cup sugar

¾ cup ruby port

½ cup dried cranberries

3 Tbs. finely diced crystallized ginger

2 Tbs. freshly grated orange zest

1 Tbs. freshly grated lemon zest

⅛ tsp. ground cloves

1. Whisk together orange juice, lemon juice, cornstarch, and mustard in small bowl. Set aside.

2. Combine cranberries, sugar, port, dried cranberries, ginger, orange zest, lemon zest, cloves, and pinch of salt in medium saucepan. Bring to a boil, stirring to dissolve sugar.

3. Stir cornstarch mixture into saucepan. Reduce heat to medium-low, and simmer 10 to 15 minutes, or until sauce is thick and berries have burst. Cool, and serve chilled or at room temperature.

PER ¼-CUP SERVING: 90 CAL; 0 G PROT; 0 G TOTAL FAT (0 G SAT FAT); 23 G CARB; 0 MG CHOL; 11 MG SOD; 2 G FIBER; 19 G SUGARS

Pineapple-Miso Sambal

MAKES 1 ¼ CUPS

Hot, sour, salty, and sweet are the four taste combinations going on in this fresh fruit sauce that can be served with Vietnamese Hot Pot (p. 240).

1 cup fresh pineapple chunks

¼ cup fresh cilantro leaves

3 Tbs. chile-garlic sauce

3 Tbs. minced fresh ginger

3 Tbs. white miso
(Japanese soybean paste)

3 Tbs. rice wine vinegar

2 Tbs. light brown sugar

1 tsp. toasted sesame oil

Pulse all ingredients in blender or food processor until mixed, leaving pineapple in small chunks.

PER 2-TBS. SERVING: 40 CAL; 1 G PROT; 0.5 G TOTAL FAT (0 G SAT FAT); 8 G CARB; 0 MG CHOL; 206 MG SOD; 0 G FIBER, 5 G SUGARS

Shopping Savvy:
Fresh Pineapple

When buying fresh pineapple, take a whiff of the fruit to make sure it smells sweet and fragrant. Or pull a leaf off—if it comes away easily, the fruit is ripe.

Maple-Mustard Sauce

MAKES ½ CUP

Here's another one for the kid files: a vegan alternative to honey-mustard sauce.

½ cup brown mustard

1 Tbs. pure maple syrup

Whisk together ingredients. Store up to 1 week in the fridge.

PER ¼-CUP SERVING: 86 CAL; 0 G PROT; 0 G TOTAL FAT (0 G SAT FAT); 7 G CARB; 0 MG CHOL; 601 MG SOD; 0 G FIBER; 6 G SUGARS

Raspberry-Sesame Vinaigrette

MAKES ³/₄ CUP

Try this tangy sweet sauce with Perfect Steamed Artichokes à la Française (p. 31),
or use it to jazz up a basic tossed salad.

¼ cup raspberry vinegar

¼ cup toasted sesame oil

2 Tbs. Dijon mustard

2 Tbs. vegetable oil

4 tsp. seedless raspberry jam

Combine all ingredients and 1 Tbs.
water in jar with lid, and season with
salt and pepper. Close jar, and shake
until combined.

PER 1-TBS. SERVING: 72 CAL; 0 G PROT; 7 G TOTAL FAT
(1 G SAT FAT); 3 G CARB; 0 MG CHOL; 85 MG SOD;
0 G FIBER; 2 G SUGARS

....

Success Secret: Toasted Sesame Seeds

....

Add a little crunch to the sauce with 1 Tbs. toasted sesame seeds.

Tarragon Mayonnaise

MAKES ³/₄ CUP

Serve this tarragon-spiked sauce as a dip for Perfect Steamed Artichokes à la Française (p. 31), spread on sandwiches, or spoon into a bowl as a dip for fresh veggies.

½ cup vegan mayonnaise

2 Tbs. fresh lemon juice

2 tsp. dried tarragon

Combine all ingredients in bowl, and
season with salt and pepper to taste.
Let stand 30 minutes.

PER 3-TBS. SERVING: 101 CAL; 2 G PROT; 9.5 G TOTAL
FAT (1 G SAT FAT); 2 G CARB; 0 MG CHOL; 305 MG
SOD; ‹1 G FIBER; ‹1 G SUGARS

TARRAGON MAYONNAISE

RASPBERRY-SESAME
VINAIGRETTE

JALAPEÑO-ORANGE
DIPPING SAUCE

Sweet Chile Mayonnaise

MAKES 1 1/4 CUPS

Stir together a surprising dip or spread with hot and sweet Thai red chili sauce, vegan mayo, and sesame seeds for crunch. Use as a dip for Vietnamese Hot Pot (p. 240), spread on sandwiches, or thin with a little water to use as a salad dressing.

1 cup vegan mayonnaise

¼ cup vegetarian sweet Thai red chili sauce

2 tsp. toasted sesame seeds

Whisk together all ingredients. Refrigerate until ready to use.

PER 2-TBS. SERVING: 97 CAL; 2 G PROT; 8 G TOTAL FAT (1 G SAT FAT); 5 G CARB; 0 MG CHOL; 278 MG SOD; 0 G FIBER; 2 G SUGARS

Jalapeño-Orange Dipping Sauce

MAKES 3/4 CUP

Believe it or not, artichokes stand up well to the bold flavors in this spicy sauce. So do tossed salads.

½ cup fresh orange 2 tsp. juice agave nectar, optional

2 tsp. cornstarch

2 jalapeño chiles in escabeche sauce, drained and sliced, plus 2 Tbs. escabeche sauce

¼ cup chopped fresh chives

2 Tbs. olive oil

Bring orange juice and agave nectar, if using, to a boil in saucepan. Whisk together cornstarch and ¼ cup water in bowl. Add cornstarch mixture to orange juice mixture, and cook 1 minute, or until thickened, whisking constantly. Remove from heat, and stir in jalapeños and escabeche sauce. Stir chives and oil into sauce.

PER 3-TBS. SERVING: 82 CAL; 1 G PROT; 7 G TOTAL FAT (1 G SAT FAT); 5 G CARB; 0 MG CHOL; 353 MG SOD; 1 G FIBER; 3 G SUGARS

Orange-Hazelnut Vinaigrette

MAKES 1 ½ CUPS

Try this on a salad of arugula, pear, and hazelnuts with
a sprinkling of chopped chives.

½ cup apple cider vinegar

¼ cup fresh orange juice

¼ cup hazelnut oil

1 ½ tsp. freshly grated orange zest

½ cup olive oil

Whisk together vinegar, orange juice, hazelnut oil, and orange zest in bowl. Slowly pour in oil while whisking. Season with salt and pepper to taste.

PER 1-TBS. SERVING: 62 CAL; 0 G PROT; 7 G TOTAL FAT (0.5 G SAT FAT); 0 G CARD, 0 MG CHOL; 49 MG SOD; 0 G FIBER; 0 G SUGARS

Maple Vinaigrette

MAKES 1 ½ CUPS

This sauce avoids refined sugars (a pitfall of bottled dressings),
relying instead on maple syrup. Plus, it makes a great dip.

⅓ cup olive oil

2 Tbs. balsamic vinegar

1 Tbs. pure maple syrup

2 to 2 ½ tsp. Dijon mustard

2 tsp. chopped fresh basil

1 tsp. fresh lemon juice

½ tsp. salt

Whisk all ingredients together. Store in airtight container up to 3 days.

PER 1-TBS. SERVING: 91 CAL; 0 G PROT; 9 G TOTAL FAT (1 G SAT FAT); 2 G CARB; 0 MG CHOL; 26 MG SOD; 0 G FIBER; 2 G SUGARS

Tzatziki Sauce

Serve this all-purpose Mediterranean sauce with Greek-Style Lentil Burgers (p. 62).

2 cups plain soy yogurt

1 medium cucumber, peeled, seeded, shredded and drained

2 cloves garlic, minced (about 2 tsp.)

1 tsp. lemon zest

1 tsp. chopped fresh mint

1 tsp. chopped fresh parsley

Combine all ingredients in small bowl.

PER ½-CUP SERVING: 45 CAL; 2 G PROTEIN; 0 G TOTAL FAT (0 G SAT FAT); 7 G CARB; 0 MG CHOL; 98 MG SOD; ½ G FIBER; 4 G SUGARS

Homemade Salsa

Why buy salsa when homemade is so easy to put together? This quick dip rivals store-bought fresh salsas—and costs a lot less.

1 14.5-oz. can petite diced tomatoes with mild green chiles

1 bunch green onions, finely chopped (½ cup)

¼ cup chopped fresh cilantro

2 Tbs. fresh lime juice

½ tsp. sugar

Combine all ingredients in small bowl. Season with salt and pepper to taste. Cover and chill 2 hours, or overnight.

PER ¼-CUP SERVING: 22 CAL; 1 G PROT; 0 G TOTAL FAT (0 G SAT FAT); 6 G CARB; 0 MG CHOL; 280 MG SOD; 1 G FIBER; 3 G SUGARS

Mango Salsa

MAKES 3 CUPS

Smoked paprika comes from Spain, not Hungary, and lends
rich flavor to this sweet and spicy salsa. Serve with corn chips, or try as a
sauce on grilled tofu steaks.

2 mangoes, peeled, pitted, and diced

1 large yellow bell pepper, finely chopped (1 cup)

1 small red onion, finely chopped (1 cup)

¼ cup chopped fresh cilantro

2 Tbs. fresh lime juice

1 red jalapeño chile, finely chopped

½ tsp. smoked paprika

Toss together all ingredients in small bowl. Season with salt and additional paprika, if desired.

PER ¼-CUP SERVING: 25 CAL; 1 G PROT; 0 G TOTAL FAT (0 G SAT FAT); 6 G CARB; 0 MG CHOL, 98 MG SOD; 1 G FIBER; 5 G SUGARS

Shopping Savvy: Mangoes

Don't necessarily look for color as an indication of ripeness in mangoes—just as different apples have different colored skin, mango varieties can vary as well. Choose plump, firm, fragrant fruits that have rounded "shoulders" by the stem end, indicating the mango was picked when it was mature. Mangoes will ripen on the counter and are ready to eat when they give a bit under pressure.

Ginger-Pear Jam

Commercial pectin helps thicken jams to give them a more spreadable consistency. The pectin here is optional, though the jam will be thinner without it. But a little liquid isn't a bad thing if you don't mind licking your fingers!

4 lb. ripe but firm pears, such as Bosc, peeled

4 cups sugar

¼ cup fresh lemon juice

2 tsp. grated fresh ginger

1 Tbs. pectin, optional

Shopping Savvy: Imperfect Fruit Is Perfect for Jam

Fruit for jam doesn't have to be perfect. If you shop at a farmers' market or roadside stand, ask the grower if he or she will sell you bruised or damaged fruit at a lower price. Then just cut away the bruised areas as you're cutting up the fruit.

1. Grate pears using largest holes on hand grater. Combine grated pears with sugar, lemon juice, and ginger in large stainless steel pot.

2. Bring pear mixture to a boil. Reduce heat to medium-low, and cook 30 to 45 minutes, or until jam has thickened. Stir pectin into ¼ cup jam liquid, if desired, and add back to jam. Cook 3 minutes more, or until jam is thick.

3. Meanwhile, sterilize jars and lids: Submerge jars in large pot filled halfway with simmering water, and lids in small pot of simmering water. Keep jars and lids in hot water until ready to use.

4. Remove jars one at a time from hot water, and fill with jam, leaving ¼ inch headspace. Seal with lids. Place canning rack or cake rack in bottom of large pot, and return sealed jars to pot, adding extra water to cover jars by 1 inch, if necessary. Bring water to a boil, and boil 10 minutes. Remove jars from water, and cool.

PER 2-TBS. SERVING: 103 CAL; 1 G PROT; 0 G TOTAL FAT (0 G SAT FAT); 27 G CARB, 0 MG CHOL; 1 MG SOD; 1 G FIBER; 24 G SUGARS

GINGER-PEAR JAM

EASY KIWI JAM

Easy Kiwi Jam

Kiwifruits may taste like they come from the tropics, but they are actually a late-fall crop grown in temperate climates. This is a fun jam to make when the weather turns cooler and you're looking for homemade gift ideas for the holidays.

4 lb. peeled kiwis

4 cups sugar

¼ cup fresh lemon juice

Prep Talk

To easily "peel" kiwis for jam, halve the fruit, then scoop flesh from kiwifruit halves with a spoon. Discard skins.

1. Mash kiwi flesh in large pot until smooth. Stir in sugar and lemon juice.

2. Bring mixture to a boil. Reduce heat to medium-low, and simmer 15 minutes, or until thickened, stirring occasionally.

3. Meanwhile, sterilize jars and lids: Submerge jars in large pot filled half-way with simmering water, and lids in small pot of simmering water. Keep jars and lids in hot water until ready to use.

4. Remove jars one at a time from hot water, and fill with jam, leaving ¼ inch headspace. Seal with lids. Place canning rack or cake rack in bottom of large pot, and return sealed jars to pot, adding extra water to cover jars by 1 inch, if necessary. Bring water to a boil, and boil 10 minutes. Remove jars from water, and cool.

PER 2-TBS. SERVING: 77 CAL; 1 G PROT; 0 G TOTAL FAT (0 G SAT FAT); 20 G CARB; 0 MG CHOL; 1 MG SOD; 1 G FIBER; 18 G SUGARS

Fantastic Fig Spread

MAKES 5 8-OZ. JARS

Dried figs naturally thicken and sweeten this chunky jam, which means
you don't need to add pectin and can use less sugar. This spread can also be
served with cheese or used as a chutney alongside a spicy main dish.

2 ½ cups sugar

2 lb. fresh figs, stems trimmed
and quartered

12 oz. dried figs,
stems trimmed and sliced

3 Tbs. fresh lemon juice

1 Tbs. freshly grated lemon zest

1. Combine all ingredients in large stainless steel pot. Bring to a boil over medium-high heat, and simmer 1 minute. Remove from heat, cover, and cool overnight.

2. Stir jam, and bring to a boil over medium-high heat. Reduce heat to medium, and cook 25 to 30 minutes, or until jam is thick, stirring often.

3. Meanwhile, sterilize jars and lids: Submerge jars in large pot filled halfway with simmering water, and lids in small pot of simmering water. Keep jars and lids in hot water until ready to use.

4. Remove jars one at a time from hot water, and fill with jam, leaving ¼ inch headspace. Seal with lids. Place canning rack or cake rack in bottom of large pot, and return sealed jars to pot, adding extra water to cover jars by 1 inch, if necessary. Bring water to a boil, and boil 10 minutes. Remove jars from water, and cool.

PER 2-TBS. SERVING: 88 CAL; 1 G PROT; 0 G TOTAL FAT
(0 G SAT FAT); 22 G CARB; 0 MG CHOL; 1 MG SOD;
1 G FIBER; 18 G SUGARS

Tangy Tomato Jam

MAKES 4 CUPS

This chutney-like condiment can be served on its own, as a dip, as a topping for vegan cream cheese, or as a sandwich spread. It's a great way to preserve slightly overripe tomatoes. The jam will keep in the refrigerator up to 1 month.

2 ½ lb. beefsteak tomatoes (4 tomatoes)

2 Granny Smith apples, grated (2 cups)

1 ⅓ cups sugar

2 Tbs. fresh lemon juice

2 tsp. freshly grated lemon zest

1 ½ tsp. minced jalapeño chile

1. Bring large pot of water to a boil. Cut an X on ends of tomatoes with knife, and drop into boiling water for 10 seconds. Remove, and cool in bowl of ice water. Peel and quarter tomatoes.

2. Combine tomatoes, apples, sugar, lemon juice, lemon zest, and jalapeño in large nonreactive saucepan. Bring to a rapid boil, and cook 30 minutes, stirring occasionally and smashing tomatoes until broken down. Skim off any foam.

3. Reduce heat to medium-low, and simmer 20 minutes more, or until jam thickens. Transfer to 8-oz. jars or serving bowl. Serve warm or chilled.

PER 2-TBS. SERVING: 44 CAL; 1 G PROT; 0 G TOTAL FAT (0 G SAT FAT); 11 G CARB; 0 MG CHOL; 2 MG SOD; 1 G FIBER; 10 G SUGARS

Korean BBQ Marinade

MAKES 1 CUP

For a different style of barbecue, try this version of bulgogi, a traditional Korean dish that features a sweet soy marinade. Marinate 1 to 1 ½ pounds of sliced tofu, tempeh, seitan, or portobello mushroom caps for 30 minutes to 3 hours in this BBQ marinade, then sear over high heat.

½ cup low-sodium soy sauce

⅓ cup sugar

¼ cup sherry, sake, or mirin (Japanese rice wine)

6 cloves garlic, minced (2 Tbs.)

1 Tbs. toasted sesame oil

Whisk together soy sauce, sugar, sherry, garlic, oil, and ½ cup cold water in saucepan. Simmer over medium heat 5 to 6 minutes, or until sugar is dissolved. Season with pepper before using.

PER ¼-CUP SERVING: 156 CAL; 2 G PROT; 2.5 G TOTAL FAT (0.5 G SAT FAT); 25 G CARB; 0 MG CHOL, 781 MG SOD; 1 G FIBER; 21 G SUGARS

Mediterranean Marinade

MAKES 1 CUP

Marinate vegetables for 30 minutes to 8 hours in this tangy mixture. Grill or sear until vegetables are softened and golden.

⅓ cup red wine vinegar

Juice and zest of 1 lemon

4 cloves garlic, minced (4 tsp.)

1 Tbs. chopped fresh oregano

½ cup olive oil

Blend vinegar, 3 Tbs. lemon juice, 1 Tbs. lemon zest, garlic, and oregano in blender. Blend in oil while blender is running. Season with salt and pepper.

PER ¼-CUP SERVING: 255 CAL; 1 G PROT; 27 G TOTAL FAT (3.5 G SAT FAT); 4 G CARB; 0 MG CHOL; 148 MG SOD; 1 G FIBER; 1 G SUGARS

Sweet-and-Sour Sherry Vinegar Marinade

MAKES ³/4 CUP

You'll have enough of this marinade to flavor a pound of cubed tofu, tempeh, seitan, or vegetables. This recipe works best for steaming or sautéing.

¼ cup sugar

½ cup fresh grapefruit juice

2 Tbs. freshly grated grapefruit zest

3 Tbs. sherry vinegar

⅓ cup canola or grapeseed oil

Bring sugar and 1 ½ Tbs. water to a boil in saucepan over medium-high heat 10 to 12 minutes, or until sugar caramelizes and browns. Remove from heat, and add grapefruit juice and zest. Return to burner and boil 1 minute, swirling pan occasionally. Stir in vinegar and oil. Cool.

PER 2-TBS. SERVING: 154 CAL; 0 G PROT; 12.5 G TOTAL FAT (1 G SAT FAT); 12 G CARB; 0 MG CHOL; 1 MG SOD; 0 G FIBER; 8 G SUGARS

South-of-the-Border Marinade

MAKES 1 ½ CUPS

For fiesta-worthy vegetarian fajitas, soak sliced green onions and red bell peppers in this marinade with 1 ½ pounds tempeh, tofu, or seitan for 30 minutes to 2 hours.

1 1.13-oz. pkg. taco seasoning

2 Tbs. fresh lime juice

2 Tbs. vegetable oil

1 tsp. freshly grated lime zest

¼ tsp. chipotle hot sauce

Whisk all ingredients with 1 ½ cups water in bowl. Season with salt, pepper, and additional hot sauce, if desired.

PER ¼-CUP SERVING: 60 CAL; 1 G PROT; 5 G TOTAL FAT (0.5 G SAT FAT); 4 G CARB; 0 MG CHOL; 331 MG SOD; 1 G FIBER; ‹1 G SUGARS

sources

Good, Clean Food

AMAZON

www.amazon.com

Plug "vegan" into the search field of the Web site and a whole universe of dried goods, snacks, and pantry products awaits you.

BARNIVORE

www.barnivore.com

Is your booze vegan-friendly? This online tool lets you plug in your favorite beers, wines, and spirits to find out which ones are free of animal products.

BOB'S RED MILL

www.bobsredmill.com

Find any grain- or gluten-free product from amaranth to xanthan gum at this Oregon-based company's Web site.

EDEN ORGANIC

www.edenfoods.com

Eden Organic offers more than 250 organic ingredients and snacks that can be ordered online.

FOOD FIGHT

foodfightgrocery.com

Can't find a favorite vegan product? Get thee to the online store for this Portland, Oregon-based vegan shopper's paradise.

FRONTIER NATURAL PRODUCTS CO-OP

www.frontiercoop.com

While these spices and seasonings are available in most natural supermarkets, this Web site allows you to order such hard-to-find items as gumbo file or green peppercorns.

HAPPYCOW

www.happycow.net

Locate a vegan-friendly restaurant no matter where you are in the world with this user-based collection of eateries.

KALUSTYAN'S SPICES AND SWEETS

www.kalustyans.com

Don't live in an ethnic shopping mecca? Don't worry. Kalustyan's Spices and Sweets in New York City is now open for business online, offering an enormous selection of Middle Eastern and Indian ingredients.

LOCAL HARVEST

www.localharvest.org

Log on to this site to find a comprehensive directory of farmers' markets, family farms, and other sources of sustainably grown food around the country.

MEXGROCER.COM

www.mexgrocer.com

If you feel like hosting a fiesta but can't find all the ingredients, get the goods at this Mexican grocery source.

PANGEA: THE VEGAN STORE

www.veganstore.com

The one-stop online shop offers everything from vegan candy and cheese to books, fashion, body care, and vitamins.

VEGANESSENTIALS

www.veganessentials.com

Find your favorite vegan ingredients—and discover some new tasty treats—at this vegan superstore.

VEGETARIANVITAMIN.COM
www.vegetarianvitamin.com
Avoid the pitfalls of potentially non-veg vitamins and supplements with one click. This online resource offers a wide range of products and brands and all are veg.

VEGGUIDE.ORG
www.vegguide.org
No matter where hunger hits, this community-maintained guide to veg restaurants around the world will lead you to someplace good to eat.

Vegan Nutrition, Community, and Education

ANIMALFREEZONE
www.animalfreezone.co.uk
This British Web site is like an all-veg Wikipedia with definitions, answers to common questions, and regularly updated entries and articles.

NATURAL GOURMET INSTITUTE
www.naturalgourmetinstitute.com
With a plant-based curriculum that focuses on healthful vegan and vegetarian cuisine, this accredited cooking school in New York City is an excellent starting place for up-and-coming vegan chefs.

PEOPLE FOR THE ETHICAL TREATMENT OF ANIMALS (PETA)
www.peta.org
From animal welfare news to advice on cruelty-free living, PETA, the largest animal rights organization in the world, puts information in your hands so you can make educated lifestyle choices.

PHYSICIANS COMMITTEE FOR RESPONSIBLE MEDICINE (PCRM)
www.pcrm.org
PCRM is a nonprofit organization of physicians and laypersons working together to promote the health benefits of a vegan diet and advocate higher ethical standards and effectiveness in research.

USDA NATIONAL NUTRIENT DATABASE
www.nal.usda.gov/fnic/foodcomp/ search/
Want to know exactly how many calories a bowl of rice has versus a bowl of quinoa? Can't decide if spinach or kale is the best source of iron? Get nutritional values on this Web site maintained by the United States Department of Agriculture.

THE VEGETARIAN RESOURCE GROUP
www.vrg.org
Got a veg question? Log on to this educational Web site for answers on everything from how to eat right when you're pregnant to where to find vegan marshmallows.

VEGETARIAN NUTRITION DIETETIC PRACTICE GROUP
www.vegetariannutrition.net
The veg branch of the American Dietetic Association (ADA) provides information and support for nutrition professionals and registered dietitians.

Tools That Rule: Kitchen Must-Haves

Lots of cookbooks provide a compendium of kitchen gadgets that often read more like wish lists than cooking essentials. We've limited ourselves to items you might or might not have but we really, truly, couldn't live without in a vegan kitchen.

BAMBOO STEAMER
These simple, stackable bamboo baskets let you steam everything from Asian dumplings to fresh vegetables, and you won't burn your fingers trying to get the cooked items out.

CAST-IRON SKILLET
The original non-stick pan. Seasoned and cared for properly, it will last a lifetime (or several).

DIGITAL KITCHEN TIMER
Why do you need a timer that isn't attached to the stove or microwave? So that you can walk away from the kitchen when something's simmering or roasting and not worry about forgetting to come back in time.

DUTCH OVEN
Yet another cast-iron tool that's virtually indestructible. With a 7-quart Dutch oven, you can boil pasta, make a big batch of chili, or can your own jams and preserves—just to name a few uses.

FOOD PROCESSOR
This kitchen workhorse slices prep time to a fraction of what it would be if you were chopping, mashing, or puréeing by hand.

IMMERSION BLENDER
Inexpensive and easy to store, this handheld blender can be dipped straight into the pot or saucepan, which means less time, effort, and mess. We like models that come with a chopping attachment that's perfect for small batches of fresh herbs and nuts.

MICROPLANE CLASSIC SERIES ZESTER/GRATER
When this gadget hit the market a decade ago, celebrity chefs hawked it like they were infomercial hosts. And with good reason: it's the best tool ever created for grating citrus zest, Parmesan, fresh nutmeg, and fresh ginger.

SILICONE BAKING MATS
So long stuck-on cookies and baked goods! These long-lasting baking mats let you bake cookies, scones, and even meringues without worrying they'll stick to the pan—and without cooking spray.

VITA-MIX HIGH PERFORMANCE BLENDER
Yes, it may be a bit pricier than other blenders, but a Vita-Mix doesn't just blend. It purées fruits, juices vegetables, and pulverizes nuts with high-speed power that can't compare to other kitchen appliances. Raw food chefs swear by their Vita-Mixes to make their delectable creations.

index

Pages in italics refer to photographs.

DO IT YOURSELF
ASTROLOGY

Lyn Birkbeck has been a professional astrological consultant
since 1979. His interest in astrology began at a time when
his life had reached crisis point, and it is in part his own experience
that has inspired and enabled him to help others to enrich and
transform their lives through astrological analysis.
As well as giving personal consultations, Lyn is featured frequently
on radio and television and in the press.

DO IT YOURSELF ASTROLOGY

A User-Friendly Guide to Your Personality

LYN BIRKBECK

CASTLE BOOKS

This edition published in 2008 by
Castle Books ®
A division of BOOK SALES, INC.
114 Northfield Avenue
Edison, NJ 08837

This book is reprinted by arrangement with
Element
An imprint of HarperCollins Publishers
77-85 Fulham Palace Road
Hammersmith, London W6 8JB

First published in Great Britain in 1996 by
Element Books Limited

Published in the USA in 1996 by
Element Books, Inc.
160 North Washington Street
Boston, MA 02114

Published in Australia in 1996 by
Element Books and distributed by
Penguin Australia Limited
487 Maroondah Highway, Ringwood, Victoria 3134

Reprinted January and March 1998 February and July 1997
Reprinted 1999 (twice), Reprinted 2003

British Library Cataloguing in Publication data available

ISBN-13: 978-0-7858-2421-3
ISBN-10: 0-7858-2421-9

Library of Congress Cataloging-in-Publication Data

Birkbeck, Lyn.
    Do it yourself astrology : a user-friendly guide to your personality / Lyn Birkbeck.
    p. cm.
  ISBN: 0-7858-2421-9
1. Astrology and psychology. I. Title.

BF1729.P8b57 1996
133.5—dc20   96-41399
                                                                       CIP

Printed in the United States of America

To Tali, innocent and transparent —
'I know you, you have just begun.'

To all those who further and assist
astrological understanding.

To my mother —
and her Jupiter in Cancer.

CONTENTS

Introduction

HOW YOU AND THIS WORLD WORK

**The outside world is created by what is inside all of us.
Your outside world is created by what is inside you. Change what is on the
inside and you change what is on the outside.**

Your outside world is a reflection of what is inside you, that is, how you think and feel and act. A negative thought or feeling or action creates a negative outer effect – a problem – which itself becomes a thought or feeling, or a physical condition. This makes it into a vicious circle that is hard to break. But if we look at the situation from a different angle or a higher point of view – as if seen from above, from an aeroplane, or from the Planets! – we can then begin to approach life with a new idea or action. In so doing, a negative personality trait may be transformed into a positive one, and, consequently, a more creative and problem-free lifestyle may evolve.

By the same token, positively transforming yourself helps positively to transform the world – for you are a part of this world. Conversely, the negative condition of the outside world in general offers no relief to any negative condition of your own. On the contrary, it should be seen as a challenge to transform it! Even though it might be relieving temporarily to blame it, this does absolutely nothing towards finding a lasting solution.

Everything on this Earth that was made by a human being began inside, with either a seed, an idea, or a feeling. What we have made the world into, and what we can change it into, can and has been done in exactly the same way – beginning, most importantly, with YOU.

DO IT YOURSELF ASTROLOGY is an astrological guide to discovering who that YOU is, solving its problems, and transforming it by giving it a more positive sense of itself – YOUR self.

HOW THIS BOOK WORKS

This book looks at the essential parts of your personality and the various positive and negative traits that characterize them. These are astrologically determined, not just by the Sign in which the Sun was placed when you were born (your Sun-Sign), but also by the Sign positions of the Moon, Mercury, Venus, Mars, Jupiter and Saturn. The Sign positions of the Sun, the Moon and what are called the Inner Planets, are to be found in the easy-to-read Tables (no sums or symbols) that begin with simple instructions on page 18.

In addition, *Do It Yourself Astrology* also includes the Sign positions for the Outer Planets – that is, Uranus, Neptune and Pluto. Knowing how the Outer Planets figure in your life is inspiring and intriguing for they reveal how you are a part of a greater, spiritual whole; they operate as agents of Change and Transformation, for both yourself, the generation you were born into, and for the Human Race itself.

Finally, to deepen and sharpen your self-awareness even more, the book contains a section on Rising Signs and how to calculate them. In many respects, knowing your Rising Sign is one of the greatest astrological keys to understanding your identity and how it interacts with the world around you.

The section on the Outer Planets begins on page 305, and the one on Rising Signs on page 331. But first let us return to the main body of the book, the Sun, Moon and Inner Planets through the Signs of the Zodiac.

After you have looked up the Sign positions for the Sun, Moon and Inner Planets for your date of birth (or anyone else's), you may then, after consulting the Index on page 329, turn to the relevant double-page spread for each of these Planet-Sign positions.

Note: For the sake of convenience the Sun and Moon are also referred to as Planets.

Whilst doing the above, I recommend that you enter these Planet-Sign positions and their Keyphrases on the SUN M.A.P.S. LIFE PLAN form. This can be found subsequent to the example form on page 371. This form (which gets its acronym-type name from the original title of this book *Sun, Moon and Planet Signs*) also has spaces for further astrological information, such as the Outer Planets, Ascendant (Rising Sign), Elements, Planetary Dignities, etc, Houses and Compatibility, all of which you will encounter later on. Make sure to photocopy the blank form before it gets filled in!

On each double page spread concerning the Sun, Moon and Inner Planets, then, this is what you will find:

LEFT-HAND PAGE

The top left-hand corner gives a picture representing the Planet in question; the top right-hand corner gives a picture representing the Sign in which that Planet is placed. These pictures have been drawn specially to illustrate the symbolic qualities of the Planets and Signs.

The main body of the text, headed 'ESSENCE', contains a description of the essential meaning of the Planet-Sign position. It aims to reveal to you the heart or root of that part of your being that is symbolized by that Planet-Sign combination. It is through contacting such a dynamic and fundamental part of you that all your comparatively minor characteristics and apparent difficulties may be drawn into perspective – just as the extremities of your body draw life from your heart, or as a tree is supported and sustained by its roots. In short, by going to the root you find meaning and sustenance; and by coming from the heart you find truth and vitality. Reading ESSENCE, you will find, speaks for itself.

Between the word 'ESSENCE' and the text are smaller subheadings. The upper one gives the general Keyphrase for that Planet-Sign combination. This is always compiled simply by coupling the Keyword of the Planet and the Keyword of the Sign with the word 'through' or 'in', for example, Moon in Sagittarius = Security (Moon) through Seeking (Sagittarius). (See Index for Sun, Moon and Planets through the Signs for all Keywords.) The lower ones give two other phrases, epithets or sayings. These serve as personal mottoes or handles, giving a readily remembered direction or sentiment with regard to that attribute of your personality.

Two sections at the bottom of the page, headed 'LIKES' and 'DISLIKES'. Your Likes and Dislikes are highly indicative of your fundamental being, and thereby reveal much about you – or about whoever you are looking at. This can be appreciated through realizing that the oldest part of the brain (the limbic system) is the part that says simply 'Like it' or 'Don't like it', which, if you think about it, is how we got by in the first place!

So, as a rule, you may go for the Likes as they indicate your natural flow of urges and needs. However, although your Dislikes are usually best avoided, in some cases it might be worth re-evaluating what you think of as dislikable – unless it is obviously negative. This is because what once may have seemed bad for you may now actually be beneficial to you.

RIGHT-HAND PAGE

This page, which is headed in the same way as the left-hand page, is the 'TRANSFORMER'. It comprises four sections which flow into one another: 'POSITIVE' traits and 'NEGATIVE' traits (of the Planet-Sign position in question), 'PROBLEM' (problems arising from negative traits) and 'SOLUTION' (solutions to those problems).

If, on perusing the POSITIVE traits, you reckon to be in possession of some (or all!) of them, then well and good. You can also take it a step further by seeing how one positive trait fits into the whole perspective given by the others, thereby making it even more positive!

Secondly, you may simply observe how the NEGATIVE traits are revealing mirror-opposites or negative expressions of the POSITIVE traits. This can be very helpful in understanding how a bright side exists to every dark side – and vice versa – both in yourself and in others.

But the main use and purpose of the TRANSFORMER is PROBLEM-SOLVING. This is done, not merely by sitting on a problem and hoping it will go away, but by transforming the NEGATIVE traits behind the PROBLEM into POSITIVE traits. So, by following the ARROWS along the relevant channels you can see how a PROBLEM springs from NEGATIVE traits; and by continuing to follow the arrows see how a given SOLUTION to a PROBLEM effectively TRANSFORMS the original NEGATIVE traits into POSITIVE ones.

As you begin to apply the TRANSFORMER to yourself, or to someone else, it may be productive to look first at the PROBLEM section and note which problems you identify with. You may then trace the arrows backwards to the originating cause, or NEGATIVE trait.

On reading the SOLUTION, you will possibly have to ponder its meaning and significance – after all, as a rule, nothing worthwhile is achieved without some effort. On the other hand, reading a SOLUTION may cause something just to fall into place in your mind, or may simply confirm and agree with an idea that had already occurred to you.

Furthermore, you will see that the solutions often take the form of questions, quips or suggestions aimed at provoking greater clarity and shedding light on problems. Overall, the solutions are intended to prompt or stimulate you into looking at life, yourself and others in a more creative and positive fashion.

The TRANSFORMER has many uses. Apart from helping you gain a deeper understanding of how you and others tick, it also illustrates graphically the cyclical patterns and geometrical symmetry of life, which is what astrology is truly about.

Finally, in the bottom left-hand corner you will see the astrological glyph for the Planet, and in the bottom right-hand corner, the glyph for the Sign.

TAKING IT FURTHER

Here we go a little further into the complexities of the vastness of Astrology, which will enable you to get even more out of this book. It is suggested that you look initially at your seven Inner Planet-Sign combinations, and then if you feel up to it, to take it further ...

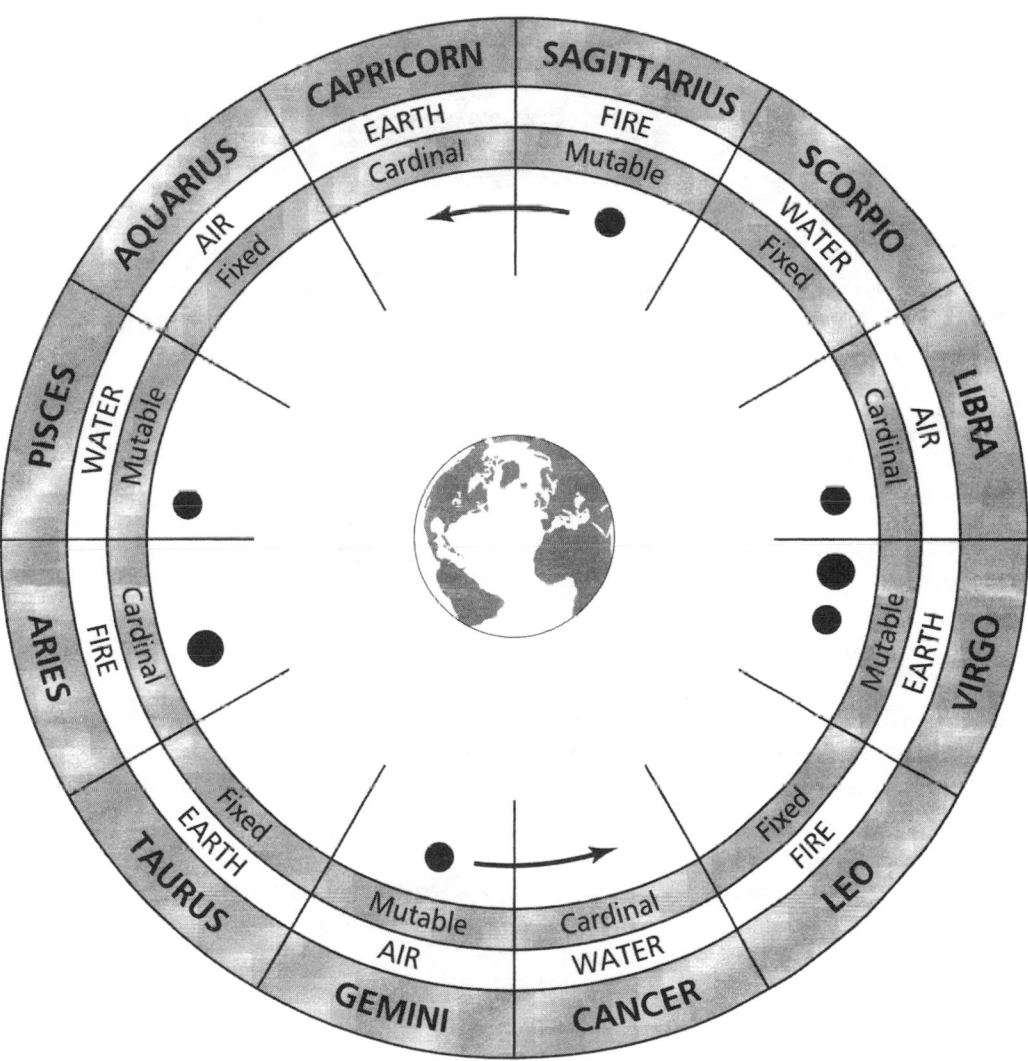

Figure 1

Look at Figure 1 on page 5 to see how the Sun, Moon and Planets, the Zodiac and the Earth are related in physical reality. The Sun, Moon and Planets are seen from the point of view of the Earth to travel progressively through the Signs of the Zodiac in an anti-clockwise direction (although every so often they appear to wander backwards; the word 'planet' means 'wanderer'). Interestingly, however, the Earth's own *faster* anti-clockwise rotation creates the illusion of the Planets revolving around us in a *clock*wise direction.

So, at any given moment, most particularly at the time of birth in question, each Planet will be positioned in a certain Zodiacal Sign. These positions are given in the Planet-Sign Tables.

Each Sign belongs to a specific ELEMENT (FIRE, AIR, WATER or EARTH) and MODE (CARDINAL, FIXED and MUTABLE). Figure 1 shows which belongs to which.

If you wish, you may now pencil on to Figure 1 your Sun, Moon and Planet-Sign positions.

THE ELEMENTS

The Four Elements describe your most basic personality traits. Their symbolic meanings are as follows:

FIRE
Intuition, Creativity, Initiative, Adventure, Vision
'Fire with enthusiasm'

EARTH
Sensation, Practicality, Objectivity, Material Stability
'Down to earth'

AIR
Thinking, Concepts, Ideals, Principles, Impartiality
'Air your views'

WATER
Feeling, Receptivity, Empathy, Instinct, Security
'Going with the flow'

Now by using Figure 1 you may ascertain the Planetary Weight of each Element in your Chart, which means to say how much each Element is *emphasized* in your Chart. This is simply done by applying the following points system to the Sun, Moon and Inner Planets, as if each 'weighs' a certain number of points:

SUN and MOON = 4 points each
MERCURY, VENUS and MARS = 3 points each
JUPITER and SATURN = 2 points each

The example given in Figure 1 illustrates how this is worked out.

SUN in VIRGO (EARTH Sign) = 4 points in EARTH
MOON in ARIES (FIRE Sign) = 4 points in FIRE

MERCURY in VIRGO (EARTH Sign) = 3 points in EARTH
VENUS in LIBRA (AIR Sign) = 3 points in AIR
MARS in VIRGO (EARTH Sign) = 3 points in EARTH
JUPITER in LIBRA (AIR Sign) = 2 points in AIR
SATURN in SAGITTARIUS (FIRE Sign) = 2 points in FIRE

In this example the total scores for Element Distribution or Emphasis are:

FIRE = 4 + 2 = 6
EARTH = 4 + 3 + 3 = 10
AIR = 3 + 2 = 5
WATER = 0

Now, considering that there is an overall total of 21 points, we can interpret the Elemental weighting as follows:

3 points or less – that Element is UNDER-EMPHASIZED

12 points or more – that Element is OVER-EMPHASIZED

4–11 points – there is a BALANCED amount of that Element

Working towards correcting any particular Element that is UNDER- or OVER-EMPHASIZED, possibly in the ways suggested below, will effectively lead to a

BALANCED expression of that Element. As a general guideline, if you have an under-emphasis but there is a Planet or two in the Sign(s) of that Element, then make a conscious effort to stress the positive traits of that Planet-Sign position(s). Alternatively, with an over-emphasis, in order to compensate, look to the positive expression of any Planets in the opposing Element. As a rule, FIRE is opposite to WATER, and AIR is opposite to EARTH. This 'art of compensation' is very important – elementary, in fact! Through using a little common sense or imagination you will find that other Elements will also compensate for those that are under- or over-emphasized.

BORDERLINERS Avoid applying the above Point Rating too rigidly. If you are barely the Balanced side of under- or over-emphasis, then consider the over- or under- descriptions. Conversely, if you are close to the Balanced score, it could well be that you are actually Balanced – sometimes!

POSITIVE POTENTIAL You may find that a Balanced expression of an Element is what you have but that in reality it is not the case. This is because it has been compromised by a strong under- or over-emphasis of another Element or two. Or there could be some other reason (displayed elsewhere in your Chart) that has made you unable to make this potential real. But that potential is still there! Again, it is down to that Cosmic Law of Compensation or Balance.

RISING SIGN and OUTER PLANETS When you have determined your Rising Sign and Outer Planet positions, which are given later on in the book, you may add FOUR points for your Rising Sign's Element (make sure it is correct though) and ONE point for each of the three Outer Planets. This raises the grand total of points to 28, but the Point Ratings above have taken this into account and still may be used in the same way, as long as you bear in mind those Borderliners.

Having worked out the point score for each of the Elements in your own or someone else's Chart, you can use the descriptions given below to discover what it actually means. As you do so, note down the number of Element points and then tot them up in the spaces provided on your SUN M.A.P.S. LIFE PLAN.

Under-emphasized, Over-emphasized or Balanced?

FIRE

UNDER-EMPHASIZED You suffer from a basic lack of life energy. It is therefore hard for you to whip up or maintain enough enthusiasm for, or take the initiative in, a particular project or relationship. On a physical level you may periodically have to endure digestive problems as you lack what is called internal fire. If this is the case, make sure you eat more regularly, and drink fresh ginger tea to organically introduce that much-needed internal fire. On the psychological side, endeavour to create a positive attitude, give yourself manageable challenges and achievable goals, and surround yourself with people who are naturally fiery and therefore able and willing to encourage and motivate you. Vigorous physical exercise can also do much to generate that raw fire energy. If you develop the positive traits of the Sun and Mars in your Chart, you will find this also does much to rectify an under-emphasis of Fire.

OVER-EMPHASIZED This can be described somewhat crudely as more energy than sense (or sensibility). At least, an over-enthusiastic approach is often what you can be accused of. You go hell-for-leather into projects and relationships and are in danger of burning out yourself or others, or both. Unfortunately, by the very nature of having too much energy and optimism, you won't appreciate this until it is almost too late, or actually too late. More than anything, you need to pace yourself, or get, or rather allow, someone or something else to do this for you. Equally, you require a project that will consume your prodigious energy and enthusiasm. But this should include a spiritual dimension through working towards some kind of vision that serves the greater whole. Otherwise your tendency to be self-important and self-serving can find you high and dry – that is, alone and emotionally bereft. These egoistic and ultimately destructive drives may be ameliorated by emphasizing the positive traits of your Moon and Saturn, and of any Planets in Water Signs – something which you may have learnt to do already.

BALANCED You believe in action as the way of achieving goals and resolving problems. Your directness may at first be startling to others, but in the end it works out for the best for it means that everyone knows where they stand. Temper and anger in you should be readily expressed, but they subside as soon as the excess energy has been discharged. You are a live-wire without being over the top. Parties and enterprises benefit from your steady flow of joy and enthusiasm.

EARTH

UNDER-EMPHASIZED You have the typical problem of not being grounded, not being in your body and in the material here and now. Consequently, what many people take for granted – having to eat properly and regularly, make money and have practical concerns more or less under control and in order – does not come naturally or easily to you. Others could accuse you of living in a dreamworld and of leaning on them for material guidance and support. As well as resolving any obvious case of being materially dependent on others, it is important that you find a way of being more earthed: because your life energy is not filling your body it can become devitalized in some way – skin tone and digestive problems are common expressions of this, in addition to a lack of physical energy itself. Perversely, you can be very *pre*occupied with your body state, because your life energy has not fully *occupied* your body. The Earthiest of the Planets, Saturn, is your most important route to rectifying your possibly spaced-out situation. So study the Sign position (and House when you have determined it later) of this Planet and endeavour to establish what your actual purpose on Planet Earth is. I think that in your case there is a basic reluctance to live in the material world – which includes your physical body – for some reason or other. But that, or rather THIS is where you are – so reappraise what it means and work up an enthusiasm for it and a commitment to it. Simply learn or be willing to BE HERE NOW.

OVER-EMPHASIZED This is at first probably not perceived as a problem because you function only too well in the type of world in which we live, one that itself has an over-emphasis of Earth – the material world. And so you perform efficiently in the world of business and areas where logic, concrete results and physical prowess are the main criteria. Problems arise, however, when some change outside of your material control arises. Most significantly, such a change would be one that occurred in your working life or whatever you have invested money in. You then find it hard to adjust and look at life from a viewpoint that takes into account more than just the price and physical nature of things. On a more emotional level, difficulties would be those of not being able to recognize the needs and values of someone you were more dependent upon than you realized before disaster struck. In more day-to-day terms your disinclination to acknowledge more than the physically obvious could amount to significant others finding your philosophy restricting to the point of being boring or coarse. And so when these eventualities occur, look to the positive expression of the more visionary and unusual qualities of such Planets as Jupiter, Uranus and Neptune.

BALANCED You are reliable and consistent, more often than not delivering what you promise. You have a good sense of the physical, which can show as a healing or sensual touch, but without it being the sole means of making contact with others, which would amount to being gross. As a rule you manage to keep material affairs in order, yet you do not attach too much importance to money and material status. In a world that stresses the material side at the expense of the spiritual, you might feel inadequate at times – but this would be a misapprehension. Your material values are sound.

AIR

UNDER-EMPHASIZED Stopping to ponder the implications of any particular issue is not something you are naturally inclined to do. It is difficult for you to detach yourself physically or emotionally and survey the situation in an objective and impartial fashion. As a result of failing to see your particular role in any given process – or to see the process in things at all – you tend to not know what you have got yourself involved in until problems and differences of opinion inevitably arise. You then find it hard to see your own contribution to this. And as new or foreign ideas are hard for you to accept, this can create a suffocating deadlock. Sooner or later though, you will have to work out why you mistrust an intellectual approach to sorting matters out – for that is precisely what is required. If you have not discovered it already, using the positive traits of your Mercury will help here, as will the positive transformation of negative Moon traits.

OVER-EMPHASIZED   You are inclined to live life as a theory rather than a reality. You work things out in your head interminably because basically you fear involvement on a material or emotional level where you mistakenly believe you will get trapped with no further choice in the matter. Issues are constantly kept in the air, which in extreme cases can lead to finding yourself in a very unreal space. Another trouble with living in your head is that you are able to tuck pressing issues to the back of it – your head, that is – where they can grow into a crisis that forces you to decide and act in the very way that you feared you'd have to. You need to use your undeniable intellectual abilities to appreciate that life is lived, and therefore made sense of, in the physical and emotional here and now. Failing to appreciate this puts a strain on your nervous system, giving rise to even more problems that you see as 'head' issues. And so a vicious circle can ensue. It is all very well to think before you act – but make sure you do act before you blow a fuse! Endeavouring to emphasize your positive Saturn traits, and positively transform your negative Mercury traits, does much to deliver you from the hell that can dwell in your head. As the Hindu book of wisdom, the Bhagavad Gita, says: 'The mind is the slayer of the real.'

BALANCED   You have a healthy sense of how everything and everyone need to have room to breathe. This means that you are able to see how things and people interrelate, yet at the same time have their own definition. You are therefore a good communicator or arbitrator. You entertain a wide and varied range of interests and this enables you to fit in with many different walks of life. Humour is probably a strong point too – although a bit dry if there is little Water in your Chart. If anyone wants to gain an objective and impartial perspective, you are the one they should come to.

WATER

UNDER-EMPHASIZED   You have difficulty relating and responding on an emotional level. This does not necessarily mean that you do not actually feel anything, it is just that what you do feel is rather raw and fearful. As a result you are liable to keep any and all feelings to yourself. This can eventually reach a point where you find it hard to accept what you regard as the chaotic and irrational nature of emotions. You then either avoid emotional situations and people, or you are unconsciously attracted to those that express their feelings very, even too, freely. You then become very dependent upon such persons to carry your own unexpressed feelings for you. On top of all this, you can get a reputation for lacking empathy and compassion. This does not mean you are necessarily insensitive – but you could well be – rather, you are disconnected from the part of you that itself connects directly with others on a feeling level. In fact, you could be very sensitive, simply because your feelings were never recognized as a child, with the result that your most commonly felt feelings are resentment or anger. Dealing with the denied feelings that exist beneath these surface ones is a priority: continued denial (eventually of the surface feelings as well) can lead to attracting more and more emotionally painful situations that are in aid of getting you to open up and let it FLOW. Apart from actual therapy, using imagination and visualization (of still and moving Water itself) will help a great deal, as too will endeavouring to express how you feel to someone you trust not to judge you. As recognizing the problem is the problem, study your Moon and Venus Signs with all the above in mind – so that it becomes a feeling. On a physical level, you do not flush toxins out of your body very efficiently – so seek out a way of doing this, perhaps by consulting your local health shop.

OVER-EMPHASIZED   This is like being a bucket of water without the bucket! You need something – a relationship or a home and family – that gives you a strong sense of containment. Any threat of such security having to be relinquished or taken away is, or should be, looked at very seriously. You are also impressionable and easily influenced, and can wind up 'at sea' quite easily if you do not have a firm and definite course in mind. Imagination and sensitivity can get the better of you – but then that is the price you pay for having a strong imagination and pronounced sensitivity in the first place. And so you can do well in the arts or caring professions. In fact such activities are essential to your well-being. Failing to embark on one or more of these positive 'voyages' can mean that you emotionally exhaust yourself and those around you. You can be all 'soul' – but a soul needs a body. In other words, unless your feelings are tempered with discipline and a sense of commitment, you can wind up in a sort of drunken, tripped-out or even hysterical state. Unless you have discovered it already, studying and absorbing your positive Saturn traits or any placement in Earth Signs will sort out this dilemma.

BALANCED   You make a good emotional role model for those who have trouble just 'being themselves'. Your response to others is usually rich and heartfelt, and so a warm and buoyant flow is created. You emanate the feeling that feelings themselves are very real. Your empathetic nature can enable you to determine exactly what the state of a given individual is – even in their physical absence. Make sure that you also extend the nurturing to yourself at regular intervals. But in the long run, you find that it is your concern for the well-being of others that balances your own emotions.

KEYWORDS

To understand and get the most out of what follows, and to help you in 'taking it further', you need to make use of Keywords as they are the most effective bridge between symbolic and literal meaning. Keywords for the Sun, Moon and all Planets are given in CAPITALS on the Introduction page for each Planet. The main Keyword for each Sign (and Planet) is given in the Index on page 329. All Keywords used in this book are given in the Glossary on page 375. Feel free to use the Keywords flexibly, allowing your intuition and common sense to arrive at a fruitful meaning. Also, be open to conceiving of new Keywords of your own which are analogous or correspond to the overall meaning of the Planet, Sign, House or Aspect in question. You will notice that I do this myself every so often, giving you some idea of this intuitive process which is actually the backbone of Astrology. It is called The Law of Correspondence, or 'As Above – So Below'.

COMPATIBILITY

By using Figure 1 in the way described below, you may determine both your Internal Compatibility – that is, how the various dimensions of your personality coexist – and your External Compatibility, or how you get on with others and what kind of people or experiences you will attract or be attracted to. It will also be seen how your External Compatibility has a lot to do with your Internal Compatibility.

Internal Compatibility

First of all it is important to understand that the seven dimensions of your being – as symbolized by the Sun, Moon and Inner Planets – really go to make up ONE WHOLE BEING. Internal Compatibility shows how these parts interact to comprise that whole. Like this ...

1) A Planet in the same Sign as another is *CONJUNCT* or UNITED with it in such a way as to greatly emphasize

in your personality the quality of that Sign. Also, the quality of the one Planet will bind together with the other Planet in such a way as to make them operate together – with ease and/or difficulty, depending on the nature of the two Planets involved. For example, if you had both the Sun and Mercury in Virgo, the ANALYTICAL quality of Virgo would be intensified, and the manner of your LIVING (Sun) would be inextricably BOUND UP with your way of THINKING (Mercury).

In any case, by reading those two Planet-Sign positions one after the other, you will get a clearer idea of how they can be positively united in their expression.

If there should be more than two Planets placed in the same Sign, then that Sign's qualities are even more emphasized, and the group of Planets would give rise to quite an intense personality complex.

2) Planets placed in the same MODE but not the same Sign will be CHALLENGING or in CONFLICT with each other. However, this can work one of two ways. Firstly, when the Planets are in Signs that are in OPPOSITION to each other, you will probably express the one which you feel most at home with, and PROJECT the characteristics of the other Planet on to someone else. Yet really you are actually trying to incorporate both into your being and are forcing the other Planet's qualities into AWARENESS through seeing it embodied in another being. For example, with Sun in Virgo (Mutable) and Mars in Pisces (also Mutable), you would probably express the Sun in that ANALYTICAL and CRITICAL way of Virgo, but encounter others who FORCE (Mars) you to ACCEPT (Pisces) things more.

In the second case, when Planets are in Signs at right-angles or SQUARE to one another, you will feel the CONFLICT as something more internal and self-generated. For example, Sun in Virgo (Mutable) Square to Saturn in Sagittarius (Mutable) could mean that the Virgo Sun ANALYTICAL nature and the IMPORTANCE (Sun) of WORK (Virgo) would be CHALLENGED by the TEST in SEEKING or BELIEF that Saturn in Sagittarius poses. In other words, you would have to have a JOB (Virgo) that you BELIEVED IN (Sagittarius) to satisfy both the Sun in Virgo and Saturn in Sagittarius, or there would be a conflict between the two.

3) Planets in the same ELEMENT but different Signs are TRINE to one another, and will FLOW and HARMONIZE together. Again, for example: Moon in Aries (Fire Sign) and Saturn in Sagittarius (another Fire Sign) would suggest that the restless NEED to look for NEW FRONTIERS that is characteristic of Moon in Aries would greatly assist the NECESSITY OF SEEKING something in which you BELIEVED, symbolized by the Saturn in Sagittarius.

To a lesser extent, Planets placed in compatible Elements (Fire and Air, or Water and Earth) will be SEXTILE and also harmonize with one another, but more conscious effort is needed. For example, that NEED to find NEW FRONTIERS of Moon in Aries (Fire) could be helped by the BROAD sweep of CONTACTS created by Jupiter in Gemini (Air).

It is very important to appreciate that although, or rather because, 1) and 2) above are harder to deal with, they are more dynamic and have more power of expression – for the simple reason that they cannot coexist unless something is done about it!

And, although 3) is easier, such Planet-Sign interaction does not necessarily provoke or stimulate you into making anything out of it.

The above is only a sketchy outline of how what are called ASPECTS work in Astrology – that is, how one Planet Aspects another from Sign to Sign. These Aspects have been indicated above in ITALIC CAPITALS; namely, CONJUNCT, OPPOSITION, SQUARE, TRINE and SEXTILE. By studying your Planet-Sign positions and how they interact, you will be more and more able to understand your Internal Compatibility. In the simplest terms, you will find that the more consciously and positively you express any Planet-Sign combination, then the more easily it will support, harmonize and co-operate with any other Planet-Sign combination in your chart.

External Compatibility

Relationships are really just the externalization of ourselves. We are attracted to certain people because they reflect or stimulate parts of our being. Through growing to know, like and love another we come to know, like and love ourselves. Similarly, the parts of us we do not like or know much will attract relationships that include dislike, fascination and even hate, yet at times mixed up with loving feelings – again reflecting and projecting those parts within us.

So again, by using Figure 1 you can see what you attract and are attracted to, and why. Like this ...

1) Someone with a Planet in the same Sign (Conjunct) or the Opposite Sign (Opposition) as a Planet of yours will strongly affect you according to the qualities of the two Planets in question, (and, to a lesser extent, you will be affected by someone with a Planet at right-angles or Square to one of yours). For example, if you had Sun in Virgo and you were involved with someone with Saturn in Virgo or Pisces, your EGO (Sun) would feel TESTED (Saturn) by them, and their sense of AUTHORITY (Saturn) would be ILLUMINATED (Sun) by you. Your Ego could feel either CONSOLIDATED or RESTRICTED, and their sense of Authority could feel either VITALIZED or OUTSHONE by your Sun.

2) A Planet in the same ELEMENT (Trine) as a Planet of someone else would be in harmony – again, according to the nature of the Planets involved. For example, the SENSITIVE DESIRE of Mars in Pisces (Water) would be COMFORTABLE (Trine) with the SYMPATHETIC LOVING of Venus in Cancer (Water). Additionally, Planet-to-Planet contacts between Signs of compatible Elements (Fire to Air, or Water to Earth) are quite harmonious with some conscious effort.

Note: As with Internal Compatibility, 1) is more dynamic and would elicit a more magnetic attraction.

Obviously there are many, many combinations here, and the whole subject of Astrological Compatibility (or Synastry, as it is called) is pretty complex. However, the following is a general guide, along with the more important Planet-to-Planet contacts and their meanings.

● Any Planet to Sun: The Sun-person will feel that they are a strong or even ruling influence, whereas the other person's Planet will feel VITALIZED and STRENGTHENED by the Sun-person – or DOMINATED by them.

Sun to Sun: EGO conflict or support, challenge or harmony.

Moon to Sun: A very good interchange when in similar Elements. In the same Sign it is very powerful, with the Sun WARMING the Moon FEELINGS or,

alternatively, making those Feelings uncomfortably EXPOSED. Conversely, the Moon REFLECTS or SECURES the Ego-expression of the Sun. In all cases it is preferable if the Sun belongs to the male, and the Moon to the female.

● Any Planet to Moon: The Moon-person feels very EMOTIONAL about the quality of the Planet it is contacting in the other person. The other person feels that the Moon-person NURTURES and REFLECTS back that Planet's qualities.

Moon to Moon: EMOTIONAL/DOMESTIC harmony or conflict. Feeling comfortably or uncomfortably familiar with each other.

Venus to Moon: This contact creates an affectionate and sympathetic feeling for each other.

Saturn to Moon: This has been called a Fated contact, because the Moon person's FEELINGS are strongly affected through being either CONSOLIDATED or INHIBITED (or both) by the Saturn-person's AUTHORITY or FEAR (of FEELING). And the Saturn-person's FEARS can feel assuaged by the NURTURING of the Moon-person, or feel rather INADEQUATE and RIGID by comparison.

● Any Planet to Mercury: The Mercury-person will give VOICE and MENTAL awareness in response to the nature of the Planet-person in question. VERBAL/MENTAL harmony or conflict. The other Planet-person will stimulate the Mercury-person's THOUGHT PROCESSES.

● Any Planet to Venus: The Venus-person will bestow LOVE and HARMONY upon the other Planet-person – or will INDULGE them. The Venus person will feel very ATTRACTED to the quality of the Planet in the other person. Venus-Mars contacts are very SENSUAL.

● Any Planet to Mars: The Mars-person will STIMULATE – SEXUALLY, AGGRESSIVELY or just ENERGETICALLY – the Planet of the other person. In the case of the RECEPTIVE Moon, for example, the Mars person could be experienced as EXCITING but THREATENING. The Mars-person's manner of ASSERTION is affected according to the nature of the other Planet. The INHIBITION or AUTHORITY of Saturn for instance, can be particularly irresistible to DESIROUS or IMPULSIVE Mars – and ultimately

Saturn could well DISCIPLINE or RESTRICT the Mars person.

● Any Planet to Jupiter: The Jupiter-person encourages the other Planet-person with their ENTHUSIASM and FAITH, or alternatively, the Jupiter-person can be experienced as too OPTIMISTIC and OVERBEARING. If Saturn, for instance, came into same-Sign or opposing-Sign contact with Jupiter, it would LIMIT its ENTHUSIASM, make it more aware of CONCRETE REALITY. Conversely, Jupiter could lend some FAITH and OPPORTUNITY to the DOUBTS of Saturn.

● Any Planet to Saturn: These contacts are very important because DOUBTS and FEARS are a stumbling block in relationships, and it is through love and understanding that such fears can be lessened or eliminated – and this is why Saturn will be attracted to the Planet in someone else which the Saturn-person is not too good at expressing. So any Planet contacting Saturn will be TESTED – but through passing that test it is hoped that the Saturn-person will become more confident and less REPRESSED.

Through carefully observing the Planets and the people with whom you are closely involved, your skill in relating – and 'astrologizing' – will steadily increase. This area of inquiry may be taken further still when you familiarize yourself with the Rising and Setting Signs, and the Outer Planets, as covered later on in this book.

PLANETS IN THE SIGNS OF THEIR DIGNITY OR DETRIMENT, EXALTATION OR FALL

When you see this symbol on the left-hand page immediately above LIKES and DISLIKES, it means that this Planet is in the Sign of its Dignity (or the Sign that it is said to Rule). This indicates that the Planet's nature is expressed well in that Sign. Example: Moon in Cancer.

When you see this symbol on the left-hand page immediately above LIKES and DISLIKES, it means that this Planet is in the Sign of its Detriment (or the Sign opposite to the one it Rules). This indicates that the Planet's nature is difficult to express in that Sign, and therefore has to be worked on. Example: Moon in Capricorn.

When you see this symbol on the left-hand page immediately above LIKES and DISLIKES, it means that this Planet is in the Sign of its Exaltation. This indicates that the Planet's nature can potentially be expressed in its highest, most spiritual, way. Example: Mercury in Aquarius.

When you see this symbol on the left-hand page immediately above LIKES and DISLIKES, it means that this Planet is in the Sign of its Fall. This indicates that in order to express positively that Planet's nature, the old way of expressing it has to 'die' in order to be reborn. Example: Moon in Scorpio.

	DIGNITY	DETRIMENT	EXALTATION	FALL
SUN	LEO	AQU	ARI	LIB
MOON	CAN	CAP	TAU	SCO
MERCURY	GEM + VIR	SAG + PIS	AQU	LEO
VENUS	TAU + LIB	SCO + ARI	PIS	VIR
MARS	ARI + SCO	LIB + TAU	CAP	CAN
JUPITER	SAG + PIS	GEM + VIR	CAN	CAP
SATURN	CAP + AQU	CAN + LEO	LIB	ARI

RULING PLANETS Throughout this book you will find that it is useful to know which Planet Rules each Sign. A Planet is said to Rule the Sign whose Quality is similar to its own Energy. Simply by looking under the DIGNITY Column above, you will discover which Sign a Planet rules over – for example, the Sun over Leo. However, when you come to the Outer Planets later on in the book, note that they make preferable Rulers, as follows:

URANUS rules AQUARIUS, rather than Saturn as given above.

NEPTUNE rules PISCES, rather than Jupiter as given above.

PLUTO rules SCORPIO, rather than Mars as given above.

The reason for this is that when these Outer Planets were discovered (long after the Inner Planets) they were seen to be far more suitable Rulers for these Signs than the previous ones.

NOTE YOUR PLANETARY DIGNITIES, DETRIMENTS, EXALTATIONS AND FALLS ON YOUR SUN M.A.P.S. SIGNS LIFE PLAN!

THE SUN, MOON AND INNER PLANETS

Tables for the Sun, Moon and Inner Planet-Sign Positions

for all Birth Dates from
1 January 1900 to 31 December 2000

HOW TO READ THE TABLES

Sign-Name Abbreviations

Aries	ARI	Libra	LIB
Taurus	TAU	Scorpio	SCO
Gemini	GEM	Sagittarius	SAG
Cancer	CAN	Capricorn	CAP
Leo	LEO	Aquarius	AQU
Virgo	VIR	Pisces	PIS

EXAMPLE BIRTH TIME AND DATE:

22 JULY 1945 at 4.10pm British Summer Time (BST).

1) All the tables are in Greenwich Mean Time (GMT), so convert Birth Time to that, if necessary. In our example, then, we subtract one hour to give 3.10pm (BST is one hour ahead of GMT).

2) All times given in the tables are in 24-hour clock time, so our example becomes 15.10 GMT.

3) Turn to the page of the year in question. For our example (1945) this will be page 64.

4) First of all we find the Sign positions for SUN, MERCURY, VENUS, MARS, JUPITER and SATURN, which are given in the panels on the top half of the page. Each of the tables for these planets gives the MONTH (mth), DAY (dy) and TIME (time) when the relevant planet changed or entered a Sign. Using our example of 22 JULY 1945 at 15.10 GMT, we look at the SUN table and see that this time and day fell between 21 JUNE 18.52 when the SUN entered the Sign of CANcer, and 23 JULY 05.45 when the SUN left CANcer and entered LEO. At our example time and day, then, the SUN was in CANcer. If, however, our example was for the same time but a day later (i.e. 15.10 on 23 JULY), then the SUN would have been in LEO. Note: If you were born at the exact time that a planet entered a new Sign, then that would be that planet's Sign position.

Using the tables for MERCURY, VENUS, MARS, JUPITER and SATURN in the same way as for the SUN will give for our example (22 JULY 15.10) the following Sign positions: MERCURY in LEO, VENUS in GEMini, MARS in TAUrus, JUPITER in VIRgo, and SATURN in CANcer.

5) Now we will find the Sign position for the MOON which is given in the panel on the bottom half of the page. This is set out differently because, compared with the other planets, the Moon moves so quickly through the Signs.

First go to the MONTH column. Example: JULY (jul). Then go the DAY (dy) of the month in question (example: 22nd) and there will be given the Moon's Sign position, OR, when it is a day that the Moon entered a new Sign, a time is given in GMT/24-hour clock for when that Sign change occurred (in the case of our example, 16.28). If you were born BEFORE that changeover time, then the Sign Position of the Moon will be given immediately ABOVE that changeover time (i.e. the previous day) or at the bottom of the previous column. If you were born AFTER or EXACTLY ON that changeover time, then the position of the MOON will be given immediately BELOW that changeover time (i.e. the following day) or at the top of the next column.

In our example, then, the MOON was placed in SAGittarius.

Note: In a few cases, when the MOON has changed Signs twice within 48 hours, because of the space available, both the time of the changeover and the new Sign that the MOON has just entered are given on the same line. An example of this is 13 February 1957, where it is written: 00.19 > LEO – meaning that the MOON moved from CANcer to LEO at 00.19 GMT. On the following day the time given for the Sign change is read in the usual way, i.e. looking to the Sign name above or below the line. In this example of 13 Feb 1957, then, on the following day of 14 Feb the time given is 23.17, meaning that the MOON moved from LEO to VIRgo at 23.17 GMT.

6) With all the above concerning Moon Sign positions, for 1 January birthdays, you may have to refer to 31 December of the previous year for the Sign position. Likewise, for 31 December birthdays, you may have to refer to 1 January of the following year.

7) Now turn to the Index on page 329 to find the relevant pages for your seven Planet-Sign positions.

SUN

mth	dy	time → sign
JAN	1	00.00 → CAP
JAN	20	11.35 → AQU
FEB	19	02.01 → PIS
MAR	21	01.38 → ARI
APR	20	13.27 → TAU
MAY	21	13.18 → GEM
JUN	21	21.41 → CAN
JUL	23	08.36 → LEO
AUG	23	15.20 → VIR
SEP	23	12.21 → LIB
OCT	23	20.55 → SCO
NOV	22	17.49 → SAG
DEC	22	06.42 → CAP

MERCURY

mth	dy	time → sign
JAN	1	00.00 → SAG
JAN	9	02.13 → CAP
JAN	28	17.11 → AQU
FEB	15	00.05 → PIS
MAR	3	21.23 → ARI
MAR	29	23.09 → PIS
APR	17	01.05 → ARI
MAY	11	00.16 → TAU
MAY	26	10.51 → GEM
JUN	9	09.23 → CAN
JUN	27	09.14 → LEO
SEP	3	00.39 → VIR
SEP	18	23.19 → LIB
OCT	7	08.22 → SCO
OCT	30	06.27 → SAG
NOV	18	20.38 → SCO
DEC	12	15.04 → SAG

VENUS

mth	dy	time → sign
JAN	1	00.00 → AQU
JAN	20	01.40 → PIS
FEB	13	14.08 → ARI
MAR	10	18.09 → TAU
APR	6	04.15 → GEM
MAY	5	15.47 → CAN
SEP	8	20.55 → LEO
OCT	8	13.37 → VIR
NOV	3	21.34 → LIB
NOV	28	21.56 → SCO
DEC	23	07.48 → SAG

MARS

mth	dy	time → sign
JAN	1	00.00 → CAP
JAN	21	18.56 → AQU
FEB	28	22.15 → PIS
APR	8	03.54 → ARI
MAY	17	09.09 → TAU
JUN	27	09.21 → GEM
AUG	10	01.13 → CAN
SEP	26	18.04 → LEO
NOV	23	08.46 → VIR

SATURN

mth	dy	time → sign
JAN	1	00.00 → SAG
JAN	21	08.21 → CAP
JUL	18	17.43 → SAG
OCT	17	05.20 → CAP

JUPITER

mth	dy	time → sign
JAN	1	00.00 → SAG

MOON

dy	jan	feb	mar	apr	may	jun	jul	aug	sep	oct	nov	dec	dy
1	CAP	07.46	PIS	05.02	GEM	15.44	10.42	LIB	13.49	05.57	23.07	08.22	1
2	21.26	PIS	18.02	TAU	22.24	LEO	VIR	19.10	SAG	CAP	PIS	ARI	2
3	AQU	07.37	ARI	07.14	CAN	LEO	22.59	SCO	22.27	12.04	PIS	10.01	3
4	22.08	ARI	18.25	GEM	CAN	02.35	LIB	SCO	CAP	AQU	00.27	TAU	4
5	PIS	09.49	TAU	13.18	07.01	VIR	LIB	06.02	CAP	14.22	ARI	11.27	5
6	23.44	TAU	22.05	CAN	LEO	15.00	11.13	SAG	02.53	PIS	00.25	GEM	6
7	ARI	15.08	GEM	23.11	18.36	LIB	SCO	13.15	AQU	14.06	TAU	14.04	7
8	ARI	GEM	GEM	LEO	VIR	LIB	21.05	CAP	03.47	ARI	00.50	CAN	8
9	03.26	23.51	05.46	LEO	VIR	02.45	SAG	16.33	PIS	13.16	GEM	19.19	9
10	TAU	CAN	CAN	11.27	07.10	SCO	SAG	AQU	03.00	TAU	03.22	LEO	10
11	09.36	CAN	16.39	VIR	LIB	12.06	03.28	17.11	ARI	14.02	CAN	LEO	11
12	GEM	10.48	LEO	VIR	18.42	SAG	CAP	PIS	02.45	GEM	09.49	04.03	12
13	18.07	LEO	LEO	00.01	SCO	18.31	06.41	17.09	TAU	18.02	LEO	VIR	13
14	CAN	23.00	05.04	LIB	SCO	CAP	AQU	ARI	04.58	CAN	09.48	15.49	14
15	CAN	VIR	VIR	11.37	04.08	22.37	08.13	18.25	GEM	CAN	VIR	LIB	15
16	04.31	VIR	17.39	SCO	SAG	AQU	PIS	TAU	10.40	01.53	VIR	LIB	16
17	LEO	11.37	LIB	21.39	11.20	AQU	09.38	22.14	CAN	LEO	08.09	04.34	17
18	16.27	LIB	LIB	SAG	CAP	01.27	ARI	GEM	19.39	12.52	LIB	SCO	18
19	VIR	23.45	05.35	SAG	16.31	PIS	12.17	GEM	LEO	VIR	20.48	15.56	19
20	VIR	SCO	SCO	05.37	AQU	03.57	TAU	04.56	LEO	VIR	SCO	SAG	20
21	05.07	SCO	16.03	CAP	20.02	ARI	16.49	CAN	06.53	01.25	SCO	SAG	21
22	LIB	09.54	SAG	11.06	PIS	06.54	GEM	14.03	VIR	LIB	08.09	00.33	22
23	16.55	SAG	23.57	AQU	22.22	TAU	23.20	LEO	19.19	SAG	14.05	CAP	23
24	SCO	16.33	CAP	14.00	ARI	10.52	CAN	LEO	LIB	SCO	17.27	06.35	24
25	SCO	CAP	CAP	PIS	ARI	GEM	CAN	00.57	LIB	SCO	CAP	AQU	25
26	01.50	19.16	04.26	15.00	00.21	16.28	07.49	VIR	08.06	01.50	CAP	10.47	26
27	SAG	AQU	AQU	ARI	TAU	CAN	LEO	13.13	SCO	SAG	00.30	PIS	27
28	06.48	19.05	05.42	15.34	03.06	CAN	18.18	LIB	20.10	AQU	14.02	ARI	28
29	CAP		PIS	TAU	GEM	00.19	VIR	LIB	SAG	CAP	05.24	ARI	29
30	08.13		05.13	17.30	07.55	LEO	VIR	02.03	SAG	19.02	PIS	16.55	30
31	AQU		ARI		CAN		06.30	SCO		AQU		TAU	31

SUN

mth	dy	time → sign
JAN	1	00.00 → CAP
JAN	20	17.18 → AQU
FEB	19	07.47 → PIS
MAR	21	07.25 → ARI
APR	20	19.16 → TAU
MAY	21	19.06 → GEM
JUN	22	03.28 → CAN
JUL	23	14.25 → LEO
AUG	23	21.09 → VIR
SEP	23	18.10 → LIB
OCT	24	02.46 → SCO
NOV	22	23.41 → SAG
DEC	22	12.37 → CAP

MERCURY

mth	dy	time → sign
JAN	1	00.00 → SAG
JAN	2	12.28 → CAP
JAN	21	06.30 → AQU
FEB	7	10.36 → PIS
APR	15	17.11 → ARI
MAY	3	13.58 → TAU
MAY	17	20.09 → GEM
JUN	1	23.35 → CAN
AUG	10	04.46 → LEO
AUG	25	22.24 → VIR
SEP	11	06.22 → LIB
OCT	1	04.35 → SCO
DEC	6	23.39 → SAG
DEC	26	09.32 → CAP

VENUS

mth	dy	time → sign
JAN	1	00.00 → SAG
JAN	16	11.27 → CAP
FEB	9	13.07 → AQU
MAR	5	14.52 → PIS
MAR	29	18.03 → ARI
APR	22	23.33 → TAU
MAY	17	07.34 → GEM
JUN	10	17.37 → CAN
JUL	5	05.21 → LEO
JUL	29	19.13 → VIR
AUG	23	12.34 → LIB
SEP	17	11.29 → SCO
OCT	12	19.14 → SAG
NOV	7	19.26 → CAP
DEC	5	13.32 → AQU

MARS

mth	dy	time → sign
JAN	1	00.00 → VIR
MAR	1	19.21 → LEO
MAY	11	06.12 → VIR
JUL	13	19.55 → LIB
AUG	31	18.18 → SCO
OCT	14	12.39 → SAG
NOV	24	04.48 → CAP

SATURN

mth	dy	time → sign
JAN	1	00.00 → CAP

JUPITER

mth	dy	time → sign
JAN	1	00.00 → SAG
JAN	19	08.26 → CAP

MOON

dy	jan	feb	mar	apr	may	jun	jul	aug	sep	oct	nov	dec	dy
1	19.54	CAN	19.31	VIR	LIB	11.46	05.32	AQU	ARI	23.29	CAN	LEO	1
2	GEM	13.12	LEO	21.58	16.45	SAG	CAP	01.58	14.17	GEM	13.10	03.12	2
3	23.35	LEO	LEO	LIB	SCO	22.43	13.34	PIS	TAU	GEM	LEO	VIR	3
4	CAN	21.34	04.39	LIB	SCO	CAP	AQU	05.17	16.33	01.55	VIR	12.25	4
5	CAN	VIR	VIR	10.37	05.27	CAP	19.23	ARI	GEM	CAN	VIR	LIB	5
6	04.58	VIR	15.37	SCO	SAG	07.31	PIS	08.08	20.11	06.52	VIR	LIB	6
7	LEO	08.19	LIB	23.31	16.55	AQU	23.37	TAU	CAN	LEO	06.16	00.38	7
8	13.03	LIB	LIB	SAG	CAP	13.55	ARI	11.08	CAN	14.27	LIB	SCO	8
9	VIR	22.57	04.12	SAG	CAP	PIS	ARI	GEM	01.27	VIR	18.30	13.45	9
10	VIR	SCO	SCO	11.03	01.59	18.03	02.46	14.38	LEO	VIR	SCO	SAG	10
11	00.06	SCO	17.04	CAP	AQU	ARI	TAU	CAN	08.33	00.26	SCO	SAG	11
12	LIB	09.26	SAG	19.27	07.55	20.10	05.10	19.05	VIR	LIB	07.33	02.05	12
13	12.54	SAG	SAG	AQU	PIS	TAU	GEM	LEO	17.53	12.18	SAG	CAP	13
14	SCO	19.10	03.56	23.57	10.44	21.11	07.32	LEO	LIB	SCO	20.10	12.42	14
15	SCO	CAP	CAP	PIS	ARI	GEM	CAN	01.18	LIB	SCO	CAP	AQU	15
16	00.42	CAP	10.56	PIS	11.16	22.23	10.54	VIR	05.31	01.23	CAP	21.13	16
17	SAG	00.51	AQU	01.06	TAU	CAN	LEO	10.14	SCO	SAG	07.04	PIS	17
18	09.30	AQU	13.52	ARI	11.07	CAN	16.44	LIB	18.33	14.01	AQU	PIS	18
19	CAP	03.06	PIS	00.35	GEM	01.24	VIR	21.58	SAG	CAP	15.04	03.10	19
20	14.47	PIS	14.06	TAU	12.03	LEO	VIR	SCO	SAG	CAP	PIS	ARI	20
21	AQU	03.44	ARI	00.18	CAN	07.40	01.55	SCO	06.44	00.18	19.32	06.23	21
22	17.41	ARI	13.41	GEM	15.49	VIR	LIB	10.54	CAP	AQU	ARI	TAU	22
23	PIS	04.42	TAU	02.12	LEO	17.42	14.00	SAG	15.45	06.46	20.52	07.23	23
24	19.45	TAU	14.37	CAN	23.18	LIB	SCO	22.18	AQU	PIS	TAU	GEM	24
25	ARI	07.22	GEM	07.28	VIR	LIB	SCO	CAP	20.43	09.26	20.24	07.23	25
26	22.16	GEM	18.15	LEO	VIR	06.14	02.45	CAP	PIS	ARI	GEM	CAN	26
27	TAU	12.22	CAN	16.20	10.18	SCO	SAG	06.13	22.29	09.34	20.02	08.19	27
28	TAU	CAN	CAN	VIR	LIB	18.51	13.33	AQU	ARI	TAU	CAN	LEO	28
29	01.53		01.00	VIR	23.07	SAG	CAP	10.36	22.47	09.01	21.43	12.04	29
30	GEM		LEO	03.54	SCO	SAG	21.09	PIS	TAU	GEM	LEO	VIR	30
31	06.51		10.29		SCO		AQU	12.44		GEM		19.57	31

SUN

mth	dy	time → sign
JAN	1	00.00 → CAP
JAN	20	23.14 → AQU
FEB	19	13.40 → PIS
MAR	21	13.16 → ARI
APR	21	01.05 → TAU
MAY	22	00.54 → GEM
JUN	22	09.17 → CAN
JUL	23	20.13 → LEO
AUG	24	02.53 → VIR
SEP	23	23.58 → LIB
OCT	24	08.36 → SCO
NOV	23	05.37 → SAG
DEC	22	18.39 → CAP

MERCURY

mth	dy	time → sign
JAN	1	00.00 → CAP
JAN	13	19.38 → AQU
FEB	1	15.58 → PIS
FEB	18	07.12 → AQU
MAR	19	03.04 → PIS
APR	9	12.09 → ARI
APR	25	08.41 → TAU
MAY	9	12.11 → GEM
MAY	29	08.28 → CAN
JUN	26	06.28 → GEM
JUL	13	09.31 → CAN
AUG	2	21.23 → LEO
AUG	17	16.34 → VIR
SEP	4	02.33 → LIB
SEP	28	07.22 → SCO
OCT	15	23.36 → LIB
NOV	10	15.08 → SCO
NOV	30	01.33 → SAG
DEC	19	03.01 → CAP

VENUS

mth	dy	time → sign
JAN	1	00.00 → AQU
JAN	11	17.49 → PIS
FEB	6	22.56 → AQU
APR	4	19.34 → PIS
MAY	7	07.05 → ARI
JUN	3	23.57 → TAU
JUN	30	06.28 → GEM
JUL	25	18.58 → CAN
AUG	19	18.25 → LEO
SEP	13	07.18 → VIR
OCT	7	12.04 → LIB
OCT	31	11.55 → SCO
NOV	24	09.06 → SAG
DEC	18	05.35 → CAP

MARS

mth	dy	time → sign
JAN	1	00.00 → CAP
JAN	1	23.49 → AQU
FEB	8	23.48 → PIS
MAR	19	04.34 → ARI
APR	27	10.47 → TAU
JUN	7	11.26 → GEM
JUL	20	17.38 → CAN
SEP	4	14.48 → LEO
OCT	23	22.55 → VIR
DEC	20	03.36 → LIB

SATURN

mth	dy	time → sign
JAN	1	00.00 → CAP

JUPITER

mth	dy	time → sign
JAN	1	00.00 → CAP
FEB	6	19.22 → AQU

MOON

dy	jan	feb	mar	apr	may	jun	jul	aug	sep	oct	nov	dec	dy
1	LIB	SCO	12.27	CAP	AQU	03.35	TAU	02.34	14.12	03.19	SCO	SAG	1
2	LIB	04.17	SAG	20.20	13.16	ARI	17.14	CAN	VIR	LIB	05.26	00.33	2
3	07.30	SAG	SAG	AQU	PIS	06.46	GEM	03.06	18.42	11.07	SAG	CAP	3
4	SCO	16.38	01.04	AQU	18.30	TAU	17.07	LEO	LIB	SCO	17.44	13.16	4
5	20.36	CAP	CAP	04.03	ARI	07.10	CAN	04.43	LIB	21.40	CAP	AQU	5
6	SAG	CAP	11.22	PIS	20.23	GEM	16.54	VIR	02.25	SAG	CAP	AQU	6
7	SAG	02.27	AQU	08.11	TAU	06.26	LEO	09.15	SCO	SAG	06.22	01.01	7
8	08.47	AQU	18.16	ARI	20.21	CAN	18.43	LIB	13.25	10.06	AQU	PIS	8
9	CAP	09.29	PIS	09.50	GEM	06.39	VIR	17.43	SAG	CAP	17.16	10.03	9
10	18.48	PIS	22.21	TAU	20.15	LEO	VIR	SCO	SAG	22.19	PIS	ARI	10
11	AQU	14.30	ARI	10.37	CAN	09.44	00.16	SCO	02.01	AQU	PIS	15.11	11
12	AQU	ARI	ARI	GEM	21.54	VIR	LIB	05.26	CAP	AQU	00.44	TAU	12
13	02.40	18.26	00.55	12.04	LEO	16.45	09.56	SAG	13.44	08.07	ARI	16.38	13
14	PIS	TAU	TAU	CAN	LEO	LIB	SCO	18.10	AQU	PIS	04.24	GEM	14
15	08.44	21.43	03.13	15.18	02.36	LIB	22.17	CAP	22.53	14.30	TAU	15.55	15
16	ARI	GEM	GEM	LEO	VIR	03.22	SAG	CAP	PIS	ARI	05.19	CAN	16
17	13.06	GEM	06.04	20.57	10.42	SCO	SAG	05.38	PIS	17.56	GEM	15.13	17
18	TAU	00.37	CAN	VIR	LIB	15.58	11.04	AQU	05.14	TAU	05.14	LEO	18
19	15.49	CAN	09.54	VIR	21.33	SAG	CAP	14.51	ARI	19.40	CAN	16.40	19
20	GEM	03.37	LEO	05.05	SCO	SAG	22.38	PIS	09.31	GEM	06.05	VIR	20
21	17.21	LEO	15.12	LIB	SCO	04.46	AQU	21.57	TAU	21.10	LEO	21.46	21
22	CAN	07.44	VIR	15.28	09.58	CAP	AQU	ARI	12.39	CAN	09.24	LIB	22
23	18.56	VIR	22.31	SCO	SAG	16.37	08.24	ARI	GEM	23.39	VIR	LIB	23
24	LEO	14.18	LIB	SCO	22.47	AQU	PIS	03.20	15.23	LEO	15.49	06.39	24
25	22.16	LIB	LIB	03.36	CAP	AQU	16.15	TAU	CAN	LEO	LIB	SCO	25
26	VIR	LIB	08.20	SAG	CAP	02.50	ARI	07.13	18.16	03.53	LIB	18.09	26
27	VIR	00.05	SCO	16.26	10.50	PIS	21.57	GEM	LEO	VIR	01.01	SAG	27
28	04.57	SCO	20.24	CAP	AQU	10.39	TAU	09.50	21.58	10.14	SCO	SAG	28
29	LIB		SAG	CAP	20.50	ARI	TAU	CAN	VIR	LIB	12.12	06.44	29
30	15.28		SAG	04.16	PIS	15.26	01.16	11.45	VIR	18.46	SAG	CAP	30
31	SCO		09.12		PIS		GEM	LEO		SCO		19.20	31

SUN

mth	dy	time → sign
JAN	1	00.00 → CAP
JAN	21	05.12 → AQU
FEB	19	19.44 → PIS
MAR	21	19.15 → ARI
APR	21	06.56 → TAU
MAY	22	06.45 → GEM
JUN	22	15.07 → CAN
JUL	24	01.58 → LEO
AUG	24	08.42 → VIR
SEP	24	05.45 → LIB
OCT	24	14.24 → SCO
NOV	23	11.22 → SAG
DEC	23	00.24 → CAP

MERCURY

mth	dy	time → sign
JAN	1	00.00 → CAP
JAN	6	19.34 → AQU
MAR	14	21.53 → PIS
APR	2	00.26 → ARI
APR	16	21.51 → TAU
MAY	2	13.39 → GEM
JUL	10	13.08 → CAN
JUL	25	12.13 → LEO
AUG	9	17.51 → VIR
AUG	29	05.35 → LIB
NOV	4	04.54 → SCO
NOV	22	19.22 → SAG
DEC	12	00.11 → CAP

VENUS

mth	dy	time → sign
JAN	1	00.00 → CAP
JAN	11	02.20 → AQU
FEB	4	00.49 → PIS
FEB	28	03.03 → ARI
MAR	24	11.54 → TAU
APR	18	06.43 → GEM
MAY	13	16.23 → CAN
JUN	9	03.07 → LEO
JUL	7	20.37 → VIR
AUG	17	21.53 → LIB
SEP	6	02.33 → VIR
NOV	8	14.41 → LIB
DEC	9	14.42 → SCO

MARS

mth	dy	time → sign
JAN	1	00.00 → LIB
APR	19	20.48 → VIR
MAY	30	17.23 → LIB
AUG	6	16.34 → SCO
SEP	22	13.54 → SAG
NOV	3	05.35 → CAP
DEC	12	09.49 → AQU

SATURN

mth	dy	time → sign
JAN	1	00.00 → CAP
JAN	19	22.01 → AQU

JUPITER

mth	dy	time → sign
JAN	1	00.00 → AQU
FEB	20	08.48 → PIS

MOON

dy	jan	feb	mar	apr	may	jun	jul	aug	sep	oct	nov	dec	dy
1	AQU	22.52	04.45	22.50	08.02	18.45	05.19	SCO	CAP	AQU	PIS	18.14	1
2	AQU	ARI	ARI	GEM	CAN	VIR	LIB	03.21	CAP	AQU	00.36	TAU	2
3	07.12	ARI	12.00	GEM	10.02	23.18	11.58	SAG	09.45	05.24	ARI	22.56	3
4	PIS	06.36	TAU	02.00	LEO	LIB	SCO	14.49	AQU	PIS	08.36	GEM	4
5	17.14	TAU	17.16	CAN	13.08	LIB	21.31	CAP	22.07	16.11	TAU	GEM	5
6	ARI	11.27	GEM	04.39	VIR	06.28	SAG	CAP	PIS	ARI	13.39	00.55	6
7	ARI	GEM	20.34	LEO	17.52	SCO	SAG	03.21	PIS	ARI	GEM	CAN	7
8	00.09	13.25	CAN	07.27	LIB	15.46	08.56	AQU	09.12	00.34	CAN	01.58	8
9	TAU	CAN	22.23	VIR	LIB	SAG	CAP	15.50	ARI	TAU	CAN	LEO	9
10	03.19	13.33	LEO	11.11	00.26	21.21	PIS	18.22	ARI	06.41	19.24	03.47	10
11	GEM	LEO	23.47	LIB	SCO	02.47	AQU	PIS	TAU	GEM	LEO	VIR	11
12	03.28	13.41	VIR	16.45	09.02	CAP	AQU	03.23	TAU	11.00	22.16	07.21	12
13	CAN	VIR	VIR	SCO	SAG	15.06	09.59	ARI	01.11	CAN	VIR	LIB	13
14	02.27	15.53	02.18	SCO	19.46	AQU	PIS	12.52	GEM	14.03	VIR	12.56	14
15	LEO	LIB	LIB	00.56	CAP	AQU	21.36	TAU	05.27	LEO	01.55	SCO	15
16	02.32	21.43	07.26	SAG	CAP	03.42	ARI	19.15	CAN	16.24	LIB	20.19	16
17	VIR	SCO	SCO	11.49	08.05	PIS	ARI	GEM	07.30	VIR	06.41	SAG	17
18	05.47	SCO	16.01	CAP	AQU	14.43	06.28	22.12	LEO	18.49	SCO	SAG	18
19	LIB	07.29	SAG	CAP	20.21	ARI	TAU	CAN	08.20	LIB	13.06	05.34	19
20	13.14	SAG	SAG	00.15	PIS	22.17	11.26	22.37	VIR	22.23	SAG	CAP	20
21	SCO	19.46	03.33	AQU	PIS	TAU	GEM	LEO	09.28	SCO	21.50	16.48	21
22	SCO	CAP	CAP	12.01	06.22	TAU	12.47	22.13	LIB	SCO	CAP	AQU	22
23	00.15	CAP	16.06	PIS	ARI	01.46	CAN	VIR	12.33	04.15	CAP	AQU	23
24	SAG	08.20	AQU	21.07	12.40	GEM	12.06	23.00	SCO	SAG	09.09	05.35	24
25	12.55	AQU	AQU	ARI	TAU	02.12	LEO	LIB	18.53	13.14	AQU	PIS	25
26	CAP	19.31	03.24	ARI	15.27	CAN	11.33	LIB	SAG	CAP	21.55	18.08	26
27	CAP	PIS	PIS	02.55	GEM	01.35	VIR	02.46	SAG	CAP	PIS	ARI	27
28	01.27	PIS	12.13	TAU	16.10	LEO	13.13	SCO	04.45	00.58	PIS	ARI	28
29	AQU		ARI	06.07	CAN	02.04	LIB	10.21	CAP	AQU	09.42	03.57	29
30	12.55		18.29	GEM	16.42	VIR	18.27	SAG	16.59	13.35	ARI	TAU	30
31	PIS		TAU		LEO		SCO	21.14		PIS		09.33	31

SUN

mth	dy	time → sign
JAN	1	00.00 → CAP
JAN	21	10.56 → AQU
FEB	20	01.23 → PIS
MAR	21	00.56 → ARI
APR	20	12.42 → TAU
MAY	21	12.29 → GEM
JUN	21	20.54 → CAN
JUL	23	07.52 → LEO
AUG	23	14.37 → VIR
SEP	23	11.43 → LIB
OCT	23	20.19 → SCO
NOV	22	17.18 → SAG
DEC	22	06.17 → CAP

SATURN

mth	dy	time → sign
JAN	1	00.00 → AQU

MERCURY

mth	dy	time → sign
JAN	1	00.00 → CAP
JAN	2	09.22 → AQU
JAN	14	03.48 → CAP
FEB	15	10.59 → AQU
MAR	7	08.07 → PIS
MAR	23	23.34 → ARI
APR	7	19.16 → TAU
JUN	14	06.23 → GEM
JUL	1	22.12 → CAN
JUL	16	00.26 → LEO
AUG	1	13.22 → VIR
AUG	28	08.17 → LIB
SEP	7	20.25 → VIR
OCT	9	01.54 → LIB
OCT	26	20.16 → SCO
NOV	14	13.48 → SAG
DEC	4	14.14 → CAP

VENUS

mth	dy	time → sign
JAN	1	00.00 → SCO
JAN	5	03.45 → SAG
JAN	30	09.28 → CAP
FEB	24	03.05 → AQU
MAR	19	16.03 → PIS
APR	13	03.27 → ARI
MAY	7	14.54 → TAU
JUN	1	02.28 → GEM
JUN	25	13.26 → CAN
JUL	19	23.03 → LEO
AUG	13	06.54 → VIR
SEP	6	13.55 → LIB
SEP	30	21.01 → SCO
OCT	25	05.38 → SAG
NOV	18	16.40 → CAP
DEC	13	09.05 → AQU

MARS

mth	dy	time → sign
JAN	1	00.00 → AQU
JAN	19	15.38 → PIS
FEB	27	03.04 → ARI
APR	6	18.19 → TAU
MAY	18	03.33 → GEM
JUN	30	14.51 → CAN
AUG	15	03.31 → LEO
OCT	1	13.51 → VIR
NOV	20	06.20 → LIB

JUPITER

mth	dy	time → sign
JAN	1	00.00 → PIS
MAR	1	03.15 → ARI
AUG	8	20.26 → TAU
AUG	31	13.52 → ARI

MOON

dy	jan	feb	mar	apr	may	jun	jul	aug	sep	oct	nov	dec	dy
1	GEM	LEO	09.16	21.04	10.36	CAP	AQU	02.59	TAU	21.50	LEO	21.33	1
2	11.25	21.45	VIR	SCO	SAG	11.13	06.58	ARI	07.59	CAN	12.40	LIB	2
3	CAN	VIR	08.53	SCO	16.58	AQU	PIS	15.13	GEM	CAN	VIR	LIB	3
4	11.18	22.01	LIB	00.41	CAP	23.15	19.55	TAU	14.47	02.38	14.27	00.01	4
5	LEO	LIB	10.24	SAG	CAP	PIS	ARI	TAU	CAN	LEO	LIB	SCO	5
6	11.22	LIB	SCO	07.57	02.50	PIS	ARI	00.30	17.53	04.36	15.20	02.38	6
7	VIR	01.08	15.18	CAP	AQU	12.02	07.29	GEM	LEO	VIR	SCO	SAG	7
8	13.25	SCO	SAG	18.49	15.17	ARI	TAU	05.44	18.18	04.45	16.54	06.46	8
9	LIB	07.49	SAG	AQU	PIS	22.50	15.32	CAN	VIR	LIB	SAG	CAP	9
10	18.20	SAG	00.03	AQU	PIS	TAU	GEM	07.30	17.44	04.43	20.56	13.53	10
11	SCO	17.41	CAP	07.38	03.51	TAU	19.41	LEO	LIB	SCO	CAP	AQU	11
12	SCO	CAP	11.47	PIS	ARI	06.06	CAN	07.25	18.05	06.25	CAP	AQU	12
13	02.03	CAP	AQU	20.04	14.12	GEM	21.10	VIR	SCO	SAG	04.47	00.30	13
14	SAG	05.36	AQU	ARI	TAU	10.10	LEO	07.25	21.05	11.31	AQU	PIS	14
15	11.58	AQU	00.43	ARI	21.30	CAN	21.48	LIB	SAG	CAP	16.14	13.19	15
16	CAP	18.27	PIS	06.31	GEM	12.26	VIR	09.12	SAG	20.39	PIS	ARI	16
17	23.32	PIS	13.13	TAU	GEM	LEO	23.14	SCO	03.45	AQU	PIS	ARI	17
18	AQU	PIS	ARI	14.31	02.21	14.26	LIB	13.50	CAP	AQU	05.14	01.33	18
19	AQU	07.10	ARI	GEM	CAN	VIR	LIB	SAG	13.55	08.50	ARI	TAU	19
20	12.18	ARI	00.09	20.22	05.50	17.11	02.34	21.37	AQU	PIS	17.06	10.57	20
21	PIS	18.31	TAU	CAN	LEO	LIB	SCO	CAP	AQU	21.51	TAU	GEM	21
22	PIS	TAU	08.52	CAN	08.49	21.09	08.10	CAP	02.20	ARI	TAU	17.08	22
23	01.10	TAU	GEM	00.27	VIR	SCO	SAG	08.02	PIS	ARI	02.25	CAN	23
24	ARI	03.05	14.55	LEO	11.48	SCO	16.01	AQU	15.20	09.44	GEM	21.04	24
25	12.09	GEM	CAN	03.10	LIB	02.31	CAP	20.16	ARI	TAU	09.17	LEO	25
26	TAU	08.00	18.16	VIR	15.08	SAG	CAP	PIS	ARI	19.38	CAN	LEO	26
27	19.26	CAN	LEO	05.05	SCO	09.39	02.01	PIS	03.33	GEM	14.26	00.01	27
28	GEM	09.36	19.31	LIB	19.29	CAP	AQU	09.17	TAU	GEM	LEO	VIR	28
29	22.32	LEO	VIR	07.06	SAG	19.07	13.58	ARI	13.59	03.24	18.27	02.56	29
30	CAN		19.54	SCO	SAG	AQU	PIS	21.44	GEM	CAN	VIR	LIB	30
31	22.38		LIB		01.53		PIS	TAU		09.04		06.12	31

SUN

mth	dy	time → sign
JAN	1	00.00 → CAP
JAN	20	16.55 → AQU
FEB	19	07.23 → PIS
MAR	21	06.56 → ARI
APR	20	18.47 → TAU
MAY	21	18.33 → GEM
JUN	22	02.53 → CAN
JUL	23	13.45 → LEO
AUG	23	20.27 → VIR
SEP	23	17.32 → LIB
OCT	24	02.08 → SCO
NOV	22	23.07 → SAG
DEC	22	12.04 → CAP

MERCURY

mth	dy	time → sign
JAN	1	00.00 → CAP
FEB	9	05.38 → AQU
FEB	27	22.08 → PIS
MAR	15	19.36 → ARI
APR	1	18.19 → TAU
APR	28	12.45 → ARI
MAY	15	20.06 → TAU
JUN	8	18.01 → GEM
JUN	23	09.54 → CAN
JUL	7	22.09 → LEO
JUL	27	06.51 → VIR
OCT	1	23.19 → LIB
OCT	19	07.45 → SCO
NOV	7	16.24 → SAG
DEC	2	04.44 → CAP
DEC	10	00.57 → SAG

VENUS

mth	dy	time → sign
JAN	1	00.00 → AQU
JAN	7	14.42 → PIS
FEB	3	04.43 → ARI
MAR	6	05.26 → TAU
MAY	9	10.37 → ARI
MAY	28	11.18 → TAU
JUL	8	12.02 → GEM
AUG	6	08.18 → CAN
SEP	1	20.16 → LEO
SEP	27	04.02 → VIR
OCT	21	18.34 → LIB
NOV	14	22.43 → SCO
DEC	8	21.33 → SAG

MARS

mth	dy	time → sign
JAN	1	00.00 → LIB
JAN	13	19.35 → SCO
AUG	21	19.46 → SAG
OCT	8	00.12 → CAP
NOV	18	04.12 → AQU
DEC	27	13.44 → PIS

SATURN

mth	dy	time → sign
JAN	1	00.00 → AQU
APR	13	08.23 → PIS
AUG	17	00.22 → AQU

JUPITER

mth	dy	time → sign
JAN	1	00.00 → ARI
MAR	7	18.11 → TAU
JUL	21	00.12 → GEM
DEC	4	22.20 → TAU

MOON

dy	jan	feb	mar	apr	may	jun	jul	aug	sep	oct	nov	dec	dy
1	SCO	CAP	CAP	05.03	00.03	TAU	23.17	LEO	03.32	SCO	00.37	AQU	1
2	10.08	CAP	12.05	PIS	ARI	06.55	CAN	17.09	LIB	13.35	CAP	21.26	2
3	SAG	06.08	AQU	17.52	12.52	GEM	CAN	VIR	04.12	SAG	05.19	PIS	3
4	15.20	AQU	23.12	ARI	TAU	15.57	05.27	19.20	SCO	16.20	AQU	PIS	4
5	CAP	16.39	PIS	ARI	TAU	CAN	LEO	LIB	06.04	CAP	14.05	08.24	5
6	22.43	PIS	PIS	06.44	00.21	22.59	09.53	21.28	SAG	22.36	PIS	ARI	6
7	AQU	PIS	11.46	TAU	GEM	LEO	VIR	SCO	10.13	AQU	PIS	21.06	7
8	AQU	05.03	ARI	18.35	10.01	LEO	13.16	SCO	CAP	AQU	01.48	TAU	8
9	08.57	ARI	ARI	GEM	CAN	04.17	LIB	00.24	17.02	08.09	ARI	TAU	9
10	PIS	18.00	00.42	GEM	17.34	VIR	16.04	SAG	AQU	PIS	14.32	09.24	10
11	21.29	TAU	TAU	04.28	LEO	07.53	SCO	04.45	AQU	19.49	TAU	GEM	11
12	ARI	TAU	12.35	CAN	22.40	LIB	18.46	CAP	02.20	ARI	TAU	20.14	12
13	ARI	05.17	GEM	11.30	VIR	10.01	SAG	11.00	PIS	ARI	02.54	CAN	13
14	10.11	GEM	21.48	LEO	VIR	SCO	22.12	13.35	13.35	08.25	GEM	CAN	14
15	TAU	13.05	CAN	15.13	01.12	11.29	CAP	19.34	ARI	TAU	14.14	05.19	15
16	20.25	CAN	CAN	VIR	LIB	SAG	CAP	PIS	ARI	20.59	CAN	LEO	16
17	GEM	17.00	03.19	16.04	01.50	13.46	03.29	PIS	02.05	GEM	23.50	12.30	17
18	GEM	LEO	LEO	LIB	SCO	CAP	AQU	06.30	TAU	GEM	LEO	VIR	18
19	02.56	18.05	05.18	15.30	02.05	18.33	11.36	ARI	14.40	LEO	17.25	19
20	CAN	VIR	VIR	SCO	SAG	AQU	PIS	19.02	GEM	CAN	06.47	LIB	20
21	06.13	18.03	05.03	15.28	03.56	AQU	22.39	TAU	GEM	17.33	VIR	20.01	21
22	LEO	LIB	LIB	SAG	CAP	02.57	ARI	TAU	01.37	LEO	10.29	SCO	22
23	07.46	18.42	04.26	18.03	09.12	PIS	ARI	07.18	CAN	23.03	LIB	21.00	23
24	VIR	SCO	SCO	CAP	AQU	14.33	11.16	GEM	09.17	VIR	11.19	SAG	24
25	09.09	21.31	05.25	CAP	18.34	ARI	TAU	17.12	LEO	VIR	SCO	21.53	25
26	LIB	SAG	SAG	00.41	PIS	ARI	23.01	CAN	13.07	00.55	10.47	CAP	26
27	11.35	SAG	09.40	AQU	PIS	03.16	GEM	23.31	VIR	LIB	SAG	CAP	27
28	SCO	03.19	CAP	11.15	06.53	TAU	GEM	LEO	13.54	00.24>SCO	11.03	00.31	28
29	15.44		17.47	PIS	ARI	14.37	08.00	LEO	LIB	23.33	CAP	AQU	29
30	SAG		AQU	PIS	19.41	GEM	CAN	02.32	13.22	SAG	14.11	06.30	30
31	21.51		AQU		TAU		13.47	VIR		SAG		PIS	31

SUN

mth	dy	time → sign
JAN	1	00.00 → CAP
JAN	20	22.40 → AQU
FEB	19	13.18 → PIS
MAR	21	12.52 → ARI
APR	21	00.39 → TAU
MAY	22	00.25 → GEM
JUN	22	08.42 → CAN
JUL	23	19.36 → LEO
AUG	24	02.14 → VIR
SEP	23	23.16 → LIB
OCT	24	07.55 → SCO
NOV	23	04.51 → SAG
DEC	22	17.51 → CAP

MERCURY

mth	dy	time → sign
JAN	1	00.00 → SAG
JAN	12	20.59 → CAP
FEB	12	12.04 → AQU
FEB	20	03.33 → PIS
MAR	8	02.10 → ARI
MAY	15	03.08 → TAU
MAY	31	22.49 → GEM
JUN	14	19.23 → CAN
JUN	30	21.27 → LEO
SEP	7	21.52 → VIR
SEP	24	03.26 → LIB
OCT	11	23.32 → SCO
NOV	1	19.33 → SAG
DEC	6	22.07 → SCO
DEC	12	23.47 → SAG

VENUS

mth	dy	time → sign
JAN	1	00.00 → SAG
JAN	1	18.20 → CAP
JAN	25	15.10 → AQU
FEB	18	13.17 → PIS
MAR	14	13.43 → ARI
APR	7	17.59 → TAU
MAY	2	03.13 → GEM
MAY	26	18.19 → CAN
JUN	20	16.32 → LEO
JUL	16	01.19 → VIR
AUG	11	03.21 → LIB
SEP	7	15.35 → SCO
OCT	9	10.34 → SAG
DEC	15	11.40 → SCO
DEC	25	23.59 → SAG

MARS

mth	dy	time → sign
JAN	1	00.00 → PIS
FEB	4	23.39 → ARI
MAR	17	11.44 → TAU
APR	28	17.16 → GEM
JUN	11	19.31 → CAN
JUL	27	14.02 → LEO
SEP	12	12.41 → VIR
OCT	30	04.29 → LIB
DEC	17	12.17 → SCO

SATURN

mth	dy	time → sign
JAN	1	00.00 → AQU
JAN	8	12.38 → PIS

JUPITER

mth	dy	time → sign
JAN	1	00.00 → TAU
MAR	9	21.32 → GEM
JUL	30	23.27 → CAN

MOON

dy	jan	feb	mar	apr	may	jun	jul	aug	sep	oct	nov	dec	dy
1	16.16	TAU	TAU	05.20	LEO	19.38	05.43	15.58	AQU	20.56	TAU	GEM	1
2	ARI	TAU	09.31	CAN	LEO	LIB	SCO	CAP	06.28	ARI	TAU	20.01	2
3	ARI	01.17	GEM	15.31	07.03	21.35	06.53	17.57	PIS	ARI	00.56	CAN	3
4	04.33	GEM	21.19	LEO	VIR	SCO	SAG	AQU	13.04	06.20	GEM	CAN	4
5	TAU	12.21	CAN	21.53	10.53	21.15	07.06	21.36	ARI	TAU	13.43	08.37	5
6	16.58	CAN	CAN	VIR	LIB	SAG	CAP	PIS	22.21	17.52	CAN	LEO	6
7	GEM	20.32	06.16	VIR	11.23	20.40	08.11	PIS	TAU	GEM	CAN	19.30	7
8	GEM	LEO	LEO	00.25	SCO	CAP	AQU	04.07	TAU	GEM	02.13	VIR	8
9	03.38	LEO	11.34	LIB	10.24	21.55	11.52	ARI	10.05	LEO	06.38	VIR	9
10	CAN	01.50	VIR	00.29	SAG	AQU	PIS	13.55	GEM	CAN	12.10	03.00	10
11	11.57	VIR	13.53	SCO	10.12	AQU	19.12	TAU	22.39	VIR	18.27	LIB	11
12	LEO	05.07	LIB	00.08	CAP	02.40	ARI	TAU	CAN	LEO	18.00	06.31	12
13	18.11	LIB	14.48	SAG	12.45	PIS	ARI	02.03	CAN	LIB	LIB	SCO	13
14	VIR	07.34	SCO	01.23	AQU	11.20	05.55	GEM	09.37	03.02	19.54	06.55	14
15	22.48	SCO	16.01	CAP	19.06	ARI	TAU	14.23	LEO	VIR	SCO	SAG	15
16	LIB	10.08	SAG	05.39	PIS	22.55	18.25	CAN	17.18	07.34	19.29	06.02	16
17	LIB	SAG	18.54	AQU	PIS	TAU	GEM	CAN	VIR	LIB	SAG	CAP	17
18	02.08	13.32	CAP	13.10	04.54	TAU	GEM	00.50	21.39	09.00	18.58	06.03	18
19	SCO	CAP	CAP	PIS	ARI	11.35	06.37	LEO	LIB	SCO	CAP	AQU	19
20	04.36	18.17	00.06	23.15	16.49	GEM	CAN	08.31	23.53	09.14	20.23	08.48	20
21	SAG	AQU	AQU	ARI	TAU	23.51	17.09	VIR	SCO	SAG	AQU	PIS	21
22	06.59	AQU	07.38	ARI	TAU	CAN	LEO	13.40	SCO	10.14	AQU	15.17	22
23	CAP	00.52	PIS	10.56	05.27	CAN	LEO	LIB	01.35	CAP	00.59	ARI	23
24	10.26	PIS	17.10	TAU	GEM	10.49	01.29	17.10	SAG	13.24	PIS	ARI	24
25	AQU	09.45	ARI	23.28	17.54	LEO	VIR	SCO	04.02	AQU	08.53	01.15	25
26	16.12	ARI	ARI	GEM	CAN	19.50	07.38	19.55	CAP	19.11	ARI	TAU	26
27	PIS	20.58	04.27	GEM	CAN	VIR	LIB	SAG	07.58	PIS	19.17	13.23	27
28	PIS	TAU	TAU	12.02	05.14	VIR	11.46	22.38	AQU	PIS	TAU	GEM	28
29	01.06		16.58	CAN	LEO	02.13	SCO	CAP	13.34	03.18	TAU	GEM	29
30	ARI		GEM	23.09	14.10	LIB	14.17	CAP	PIS	ARI	07.15	02.11	30
31	12.45		GEM		VIR		SAG	01.56		13.18		CAN	31

SUN

mth	dy	time	→ sign
JAN	1	00.00	→ CAP
JAN	21	04.33	→ AQU
FEB	19	18.56	→ PIS
MAR	21	18.35	→ ARI
APR	21	06.14	→ TAU
MAY	22	06.04	→ GEM
JUN	22	14.23	→ CAN
JUL	24	01.17	→ LEO
AUG	24	08.04	→ VIR
SEP	24	05.07	→ LIB
OCT	24	13.52	→ SCO
NOV	23	10.53	→ SAG
DEC	22	23.53	→ CAP

MERCURY

mth	dy	time	→ sign
JAN	1	00.00	→ SAG
JAN	7	00.57	→ CAP
JAN	26	05.00	→ AQU
FEB	12	08.39	→ PIS
MAR	3	20.52	→ ARI
MAR	14	05.02	→ PIS
APR	18	10.44	→ ARI
MAY	8	15.23	→ TAU
MAY	23	10.38	→ GEM
JUN	6	16.43	→ CAN
JUN	27	08.07	→ LEO
JUL	26	14.36	→ CAN
AUG	12	16.22	→ LEO
AUG	31	06.54	→ VIR
SEP	16	06.52	→ LIB
OCT	5	04.36	→ SCO
DEC	11	03.37	→ SAG
DEC	31	03.58	→ CAP

VENUS

mth	dy	time	→ sign
JAN	1	00.00	→ SAG
FEB	6	16.27	→ CAP
MAR	6	20.44	→ AQU
APR	2	01.25	→ PIS
APR	27	12.27	→ ARI
MAY	22	15.14	→ TAU
JUN	16	13.16	→ GEM
JUL	11	06.43	→ CAN
AUG	4	19.08	→ LEO
AUG	29	02.31	→ VIR
SEP	22	05.52	→ LIB
OCT	16	06.58	→ SCO
NOV	9	07.07	→ SAG
DEC	3	07.25	→ CAP
DEC	27	08.52	→ AQU

MARS

mth	dy	time	→ sign
JAN	1	00.00	→ SCO
FEB	5	09.38	→ SAG
APR	1	18.21	→ CAP
OCT	13	14.22	→ AQU
NOV	29	04.43	→ PIS

SATURN

mth	dy	time	→ sign
JAN	1	00.00	→ PIS

JUPITER

mth	dy	time	→ sign
JAN	1	00.00	→ CAN
AUG	18	23.01	→ LEO

MOON

dy	jan	feb	mar	apr	may	jun	jul	aug	sep	oct	nov	dec	dy
1	14.29	VIR	21.31	SCO	20.59	AQU	21.14	TAU	17.22	14.05	VIR	LIB	1
2	LEO	15.10	LIB	11.59	CAP	09.10	ARI	21.56	CAN	LEO	19.43	11.35	2
3	LEO	LIB	LIB	SAG	23.07	PIS	ARI	GEM	CAN	LEO	LIB	SCO	3
4	01.18	20.55	02.26	14.24	AQU	14.46	04.56	GEM	06.20	01.49	LIB	14.28	4
5	VIR	SCO	SCO	CAP	AQU	ARI	TAU	10.27	LEO	VIR	01.23	SAG	5
6	09.41	SCO	06.04	17.35	03.12	23.12	15.41	CAN	10.39	SCO	LIB	15.18	6
7	LIB	00.34	SAG	AQU	PIS	TAU	GEM	23.26	VIR	LIB	04.25	CAP	7
8	14.55	SAG	09.03	21.47	09.20	TAU	LEO	VIR	16.38	SAG	06.24	15.53	8
9	SCO	02.35	CAP	PIS	ARI	09.55	04.16	LEO	03.07	SCO	06.24	AQU	9
10	17.07	CAP	11.50	PIS	17.29	GEM	CAN	11.16	LIB	20.47	CAP	17.44	10
11	SAG	03.50	AQU	03.16	TAU	22.16	17.18	VIR	10.01	SAG	08.38	PIS	11
12	17.21	AQU	14.56	ARI	TAU	CAN	LEO	21.07	SCO	00.07	11.52	21.48	12
13	CAP	05.41	PIS	10.35	03.41	CAN	LEO	LIB	15.07	CAP	PIS	ARI	13
14	17.20	PIS	19.20	TAU	GEM	11.21	05.29	LIB	SAG	CAP	PIS	ARI	14
15	AQU	09.38	ARI	20.24	15.50	LEO	VIR	04.35	18.46	03.13	16.24	04.24	15
16	18.55	ARI	ARI	GEM	CAN	23.35	15.34	SCO	CAP	AQU	ARI	TAU	16
17	PIS	16.58	02.10	GEM	CAN	VIR	LIB	09.31	21.12	06.20	22.31	13.25	17
18	23.42	TAU	TAU	08.34	04.52	VIR	22.34	SAG	AQU	PIS	TAU	GEM	18
19	ARI	TAU	12.10	CAN	LEO	09.05	SCO	12.05	23.02	09.57	TAU	GEM	19
20	ARI	03.46	GEM	21.25	16.37	LIB	SCO	CAP	PIS	ARI	06.43	00.31	20
21	08.21	GEM	GEM	LEO	VIR	14.43	02.11	13.00	PIS	15.00	GEM	CAN	21
22	TAU	16.30	00.36	LEO	VIR	SCO	SAG	AQU	01.25	TAU	17.24	13.09	22
23	20.04	CAN	CAN	08.17	00.54	16.42	03.06	13.33	ARI	22.38	CAN	LEO	23
24	GEM	CAN	13.07	VIR	LIB	SAG	CAP	PIS	05.55	GEM	CAN	LEO	24
25	GEM	04.41	LEO	15.22	05.03	16.30	02.46	15.28	TAU	GEM	06.04	02.06	25
26	08.56	LEO	23.10	LIB	SCO	CAP	AQU	ARI	13.49	09.25	LEO	VIR	26
27	CAN	14.28	VIR	18.47	06.05	16.00	03.00	20.26	GEM	CAN	18.50	13.27	27
28	21.00	VIR	VIR	SCO	SAG	AQU	PIS	TAU	GEM	22.14	VIR	LIB	28
29	LEO		05.46	20.02	05.54	17.07	05.37	01.09	CAN	LEO	VIR	21.26	29
30	LEO		LIB	SAG	CAP	PIS	ARI	05.19	CAN	LEO	05.09	SCO	30
31	07.12		09.33		06.26		11.53	GEM		10.28		SCO	31

SUN

mth	dy	time	→ sign
JAN	1	00.00	→ CAP
JAN	21	10.26	→ AQU
FEB	20	00.54	→ PIS
MAR	21	00.28	→ ARI
APR	20	12.13	→ TAU
MAY	21	11.59	→ GEM
JUN	21	20.19	→ CAN
JUL	23	07.16	→ LEO
AUG	23	13.58	→ VIR
SEP	23	10.58	→ LIB
OCT	23	19.39	→ SCO
NOV	22	16.35	→ SAG
DEC	22	05.34	→ CAP

MERCURY

mth	dy	time	→ sign
JAN	1	00.00	→ CAP
JAN	18	17.25	→ AQU
FEB	5	04.24	→ PIS
APR	12	22.46	→ ARI
APR	29	19.03	→ TAU
MAY	13	20.52	→ GEM
MAY	30	04.35	→ CAN
AUG	6	23.47	→ LEO
AUG	22	01.34	→ VIR
SEP	7	18.14	→ LIB
SEP	28	19.38	→ SCO
NOV	1	22.44	→ LIB
NOV	11	17.55	→ SCO
DEC	3	17.54	→ SAG
DEC	22	22.31	→ CAP

VENUS

mth	dy	time	→ sign
JAN	1	00.00	→ AQU
JAN	20	13.52	→ PIS
FEB	14	02.55	→ ARI
MAR	10	08.07	→ TAU
APR	5	20.58	→ GEM
MAY	5	17.42	→ CAN
SEP	8	22.32	→ LEO
OCT	8	06.15	→ VIR
NOV	3	11.28	→ LIB
NOV	28	10.43	→ SCO
DEC	22	20.03	→ SAG

MARS

mth	dy	time	→ sign
JAN	1	00.00	→ PIS
JAN	11	04.47	→ ARI
FEB	23	03.22	→ TAU
APR	7	04.12	→ GEM
MAY	22	14.14	→ CAN
JUL	8	03.48	→ LEO
AUG	24	06.53	→ VIR
OCT	10	06.14	→ LIB
NOV	25	14.15	→ SCO

SATURN

mth	dy	time	→ sign
JAN	1	00.00	→ PIS
MAR	19	14.10	→ ARI

JUPITER

mth	dy	time	→ sign
JAN	1	00.00	→ LEO
SEP	12	10.19	→ VIR

MOON

dy	jan	feb	mar	apr	may	jun	jul	aug	sep	oct	nov	dec	dy
1	01.28	13.32	AQU	ARI	TAU	CAN	LEO	22.56	SCO	SAG	AQU	PIS	1
2	SAG	AQU	00.05	13.04	03.44	CAN	LEO	LIB	SCO	13.12	AQU	10.26	2
3	02.25	12.50	PIS	TAU	GEM	07.59	03.58	LIB	00.52	CAP	02.10	ARI	3
4	CAP	PIS	00.20	18.26	12.23	LEO	VIR	09.53	SAG	17.16	PIS	13.37	4
5	01.58	13.31	ARI	GEM	CAN	20.42	16.19	SCO	06.40	AQU	03.58	TAU	5
6	AQU	ARI	02.50	GEM	CAN	VIR	LIB	17.47	CAP	18.49	ARI	18.01	6
7	02.03	17.24	TAU	03.43	00.01	VIR	LIB	SAG	09.06	PIS	05.43	GEM	7
8	PIS	TAU	09.13	CAN	08.33	02.23	21.57	AQU	19.01	TAU	GEM	8
9	04.24	TAU	GEM	15.58	12.46	LIB	SCO	CAP	09.04	ARI	09.00	00.33	9
10	ARI	01.23	19.39	LEO	VIR	17.30	08.49	22.53	PIS	19.42	GEM	CAN	10
11	10.05	GEM	CAN	LEO	VIR	SCO	SAG	AQU	08.21	TAU	15.18	09.52	11
12	TAU	12.48	CAN	04.41	00.01	22.52	11.40	22.09	ARI	22.54	CAN	LEO	12
13	19.10	CAN	08.28	VIR	LIB	SAG	CAP	PIS	09.11	GEM	CAN	21.38	13
14	GEM	CAN	LEO	15.33	08.12	SAG	12.07	21.49	TAU	GEM	01.07	VIR	14
15	GEM	01.46	21.09	LIB	SCO	01.25	AQU	ARI	13.27	LEO	VIR	15
16	06.45	LEO	VIR	23.44	13.26	CAP	11.58	23.55	GEM	CAN	13.23	10.12	16
17	CAN	14.28	VIR	SCO	SAG	02.35	PIS	TAU	21.57	16.51	VIR	LIB	17
18	19.33	VIR	08.04	SCO	16.44	AQU	13.02	TAU	CAN	LEO	VIR	21.12	18
19	LEO	VIR	LIB	05.41	CAP	03.51	ARI	05.48	CAN	LEO	01.44	SCO	19
20	LEO	01.48	16.52	SAG	19.14	PIS	16.46	GEM	09.42	LIB	05.32	SCO	20
21	08.23	LIB	SCO	10.10	AQU	06.27	TAU	15.26	LEO	VIR	12.04	05.02	21
22	VIR	11.14	23.45	CAP	21.49	ARI	23.48	CAN	22.34	17.43	SCO	SAG	22
23	20.03	SCO	SAG	13.40	PIS	11.09	GEM	CAN	VIR	LIB	19.39	09.38	23
24	LIB	18.15	SAG	AQU	PIS	TAU	GEM	03.32	VIR	LIB	SAG	CAP	24
25	LIB	SAG	04.48	16.25	01.03	18.16	09.44	LEO	10.46	03.59	SAG	12.01	25
26	05.17	22.28	CAP	PIS	ARI	GEM	CAN	16.23	LIB	SCO	00.54	AQU	26
27	SCO	CAP	07.57	18.57	05.30	GEM	21.38	VIR	21.30	12.12	CAP	13.38	27
28	11.08	CAP	AQU	ARI	TAU	03.44	LEO	VIR	SCO	SAG	04.40	PIS	28
29	SAG	00.04	09.33	22.16	11.48	CAN	LEO	04.47	SCO	18.34	AQU	15.48	29
30	13.33		PIS	TAU	GEM	15.14	10.24	LIB	06.28	CAP	07.39	ARI	30
31	CAP		10.41		20.37		VIR	15.55		23.12		19.24	31

27

SUN

mth	dy	time	→ sign
JAN	1	00.00	→ CAP
JAN	20	16.13	→ AQU
FEB	19	06.38	→ PIS
MAR	21	06.12	→ ARI
APR	20	17.58	→ TAU
MAY	21	17.47	→ GEM
JUN	22	02.06	→ CAN
JUL	23	13.03	→ LEO
AUG	23	19.44	→ VIR
SEP	23	16.46	→ LIB
OCT	24	01.23	→ SCO
NOV	22	22.22	→ SAG
DEC	22	11.23	→ CAP

MERCURY

mth	dy	time	→ sign
JAN	1	00.00	→ CAP
JAN	10	09.01	→ AQU
MAR	17	11.32	→ PIS
APR	6	01.25	→ ARI
APR	21	10.00	→ TAU
MAY	5	21.47	→ GEM
JUL	13	06.04	→ CAN
JUL	30	00.36	→ LEO
AUG	13	21.32	→ VIR
SEP	1	00.07	→ LIB
NOV	7	18.06	→ SCO
NOV	26	14.57	→ SAG
DEC	15	16.32	→ CAP

VENUS

mth	dy	time	→ sign
JAN	1	00.00	→ SAG
JAN	15	23.22	→ CAP
FEB	9	00.41	→ AQU
MAR	5	02.12	→ PIS
MAR	29	05.14	→ ARI
APR	22	10.37	→ TAU
MAY	16	18.31	→ GEM
JUN	10	04.36	→ CAN
JUL	4	16.32	→ LEO
JUL	29	06.40	→ VIR
AUG	23	00.37	→ LIB
SEP	17	00.23	→ SCO
OCT	12	09.29	→ SAG
NOV	7	12.11	→ CAP
DEC	5	13.03	→ AQU

MARS

mth	dy	time	→ sign
JAN	1	00.00	→ SCO
JAN	10	03.49	→ SAG
FEB	24	02.01	→ CAP
APR	9	20.34	→ AQU
MAY	25	22.47	→ PIS
JUL	21	08.26	→ ARI
SEP	26	21.29	→ PIS
NOV	20	20.37	→ ARI

SATURN

mth	dy	time	→ sign
JAN	1	00.00	→ ARI

JUPITER

mth	dy	time	→ sign
JAN	1	00.00	→ VIR
OCT	11	23.50	→ LIB

MOON

dy	jan	feb	mar	apr	may	jun	jul	aug	sep	oct	nov	dec	dy
1	TAU	14.32	CAN	LEO	20.11	SCO	SAG	06.22	17.18	03.14	16.57	08.17	1
2	TAU	CAN	CAN	00.51	LIB	SCO	17.04	AQU	ARI	TAU	CAN	LEO	2
3	00.54	CAN	06.41	VIR	LIB	01.32	CAP	07.42	17.26	04.04	23.10	16.50	3
4	GEM	00.50	LEO	13.31	08.04	SAG	21.14	PIS	TAU	GEM	LEO	VIR	4
5	08.24	LEO	18.48	LIB	SCO	08.54	AQU	08.22	19.55	08.09	LEO	VIR	5
6	CAN	12.35	VIR	LIB	18.16	CAP	23.41	ARI	GEM	CAN	09.04	04.30	6
7	18.01	VIR	VIR	01.33	SAG	14.04	PIS	10.05	GEM	15.58	VIR	LIB	7
8	LEO	VIR	07.23	SCO	02.26	17.40	PIS	13.55	01.35	LEO	21.19	17.17	8
9	LEO	01.10	LIB	12.17	CAP	PIS	01.45	GEM	CAN	LEO	LIB	SCO	9
10	05.33	LIB	19.40	SAG	CAP	PIS	ARI	GEM	10.11	02.42	LIB	SCO	10
11	VIR	13.30	SCO	20.57	08.26	20.21	04.29	20.08	LEO	VIR	10.04	05.01	11
12	18.11	SCO	SCO	CAP	AQU	TAU	CAN	TAU	20.54	VIR	15.01	SCO	SAG	12
13	LIB	23.48	06.37	CAP	12.14	22.50	08.30	CAN	VIR	LIB	21.57	14.31	13
14	LIB	SAG	SAG	02.44	PIS	TAU	GEM	04.29	VIR	LIB	SAG	CAP	14
15	06.02	SAG	14.46	AQU	14.13	TAU	14.07	LEO	09.00	03.46	SAG	21.39	15
16	SCO	06.27	CAP	05.26	ARI	01.53	CAN	14.42	LIB	SCO	08.09	AQU	16
17	15.01	CAP	19.09	PIS	15.24	GEM	21.41	VIR	21.49	16.02	CAP	AQU	17
18	SAG	09.08	AQU	05.51	TAU	06.28	LEO	VIR	SCO	SAG	16.05	02.48	18
19	20.09	AQU	20.08	ARI	17.13	CAN	LEO	02.36	SCO	SAG	AQU	PIS	19
20	CAP	09.00	PIS	05.43	GEM	13.32	07.32	LIB	10.11	02.37	21.20	06.25	20
21	22.00	PIS	19.17	TAU	21.15	LEO	VIR	15.24	SAG	CAP	PIS	ARI	21
22	AQU	08.08	ARI	07.02	CAN	23.29	19.26	SCO	20.13	10.13	PIS	08.57	22
23	22.09	ARI	18.50	GEM	CAN	VIR	LIB	SCO	CAP	AQU	00.02	TAU	23
24	PIS	08.44	TAU	11.34	04.36	VIR	LIB	03.16	CAP	14.09	ARI	11.04	24
25	22.36	TAU	20.55	CAN	LEO	11.36	08.01	SAG	02.22	PIS	00.57	GEM	25
26	ARI	12.33	GEM	20.02	15.14	LIB	SCO	12.01	AQU	15.02	TAU	13.45	26
27	ARI	GEM	GEM	LEO	VIR	23.51	19.00	CAP	04.32	ARI	01.31	CAN	27
28	01.02	20.08	02.55	LEO	VIR	SCO	SAG	16.37	PIS	14.27	GEM	18.17	28
29	TAU		CAN	07.33	03.39	SCO	SAG	AQU	04.07	TAU	03.26	LEO	29
30	06.22		12.43	VIR	LIB	10.03	02.32	17.45	ARI	14.27	CAN	LEO	30
31	GEM		LEO		15.37		CAP	PIS		GEM		01.49	31

SUN

mth	dy	time → sign
JAN	1	00.00 → CAP
JAN	20	21.57 → AQU
FEB	19	12.26 → PIS
MAR	21	12.05 → ARI
APR	20	23.46 → TAU
MAY	21	23.32 → GEM
JUN	22	07.49 → CAN
JUL	23	18.45 → LEO
AUG	24	01.29 → VIR
SEP	23	22.32 → LIB
OCT	24	07.11 → SCO
NOV	23	04.12 → SAG
DEC	22	17.14 → CAP

MERCURY

mth	dy	time → sign
JAN	1	00.00 → CAP
JAN	3	21.29 → AQU
JAN	31	02.44 → CAP
FEB	15	13.13 → AQU
MAR	11	21.34 → PIS
MAR	29	06.54 → ARI
APR	13	00.28 → TAU
APR	30	14.55 → GEM
JUN	1	23.39 → TAU
JUN	12	00.16 → GEM
JUL	7	03.28 → CAN
JUL	21	12.39 → LEO
AUG	6	04.37 → VIR
AUG	27	06.44 → LIB
SEP	28	13.21 → VIR
OCT	12	04.36 → LIB
OCT	31	18.11 → SCO
NOV	19	08.12 → SAG
DEC	8	18.24 → CAP

VENUS

mth	dy	time → sign
JAN	1	00.00 → AQU
JAN	15	20.54 → PIS
JAN	29	09.13 → AQU
APR	5	09.53 → PIS
MAY	7	02.29 → ARI
JUN	3	14.56 → TAU
JUN	29	19.33 → GEM
JUL	25	07.04 → CAN
AUG	19	05.56 → LEO
SEP	12	18.27 → VIR
OCT	6	23.11 → LIB
OCT	30	22.51 → SCO
NOV	23	20.13 → SAG
DEC	17	16.39 → CAP

MARS

mth	dy	time → sign
JAN	1	00.00 → ARI
JAN	23	01.45 → TAU
MAR	14	07.26 → GEM
MAY	1	20.34 → CAN
JUN	19	03.33 → LEO
AUG	6	00.49 → VIR
SEP	22	00.11 → LIB
NOV	6	13.28 → SCO
DEC	20	12.23 → SAG

SATURN

mth	dy	time → sign
JAN	1	00.00 → ARI
MAY	17	07.13 → TAU
DEC	14	23.02 → ARI

JUPITER

mth	dy	time → sign
JAN	1	00.00 → LIB
NOV	11	17.24 → SCO

MOON

dy	jan	feb	mar	apr	may	jun	jul	aug	sep	oct	nov	dec	dy
1	VIR	09.33	SCO	SAG	16.46	PIS	18.48	GEM	LEO	VIR	08.12	03.15	1
2	12.37	SCO	SCO	00.56	AQU	09.37	TAU	06.11	22.56	14.28	SCO	SAG	2
3	LIB	22.05	06.10	CAP	22.50	ARI	20.38	CAN	VIR	LIB	21.06	15.57	3
4	LIB	SAG	SAG	09.32	PIS	11.19	GEM	09.40	VIR	LIB	SAG	CAP	4
5	01.19	SAG	17.12	AQU	PIS	TAU	22.09	LEO	07.22	01.45	SAG	CAP	5
6	SCO	08.03	CAP	14.01	01.24	11.40	CAN	14.58	LIB	SCO	10.01	03.17	6
7	13.20	CAP	CAP	PIS	ARI	GEM	CAN	VIR	18.29	14.37	CAP	AQU	7
8	SAG	14.14	00.23	15.05	01.33	12.16	00.43	23.13	SCO	SAG	21.19	12.20	8
9	22.40	AQU	AQU	ARI	TAU	CAN	LEO	LIB	SCO	SAG	AQU	PIS	9
10	CAP	17.13	03.33	14.32	01.03	14.51	05.54	LIB	07.22	03.25	AQU	18.22	10
11	CAP	PIS	PIS	TAU	GEM	LEO	VIR	10.34	SAG	CAP	05.26	ARI	11
12	04.53	18.40	04.10	14.26	01.50	20.52	14.41	SCO	19.39	13.51	PIS	21.13	12
13	AQU	ARI	ARI	GEM	CAN	VIR	LIB	23.27	CAP	AQU	09.43	TAU	13
14	08.50	20.19	04.15	16.33	05.32	VIR	LIB	SAG	CAP	20.22	ARI	21.39	14
15	PIS	TAU	TAU	CAN	LEO	06.42	02.35	SAG	04.53	PIS	10.47	GEM	15
16	11.46	23.19	05.39	21.56	12.58	LIB	SCO	11.05	AQU	23.06	TAU	21.11	16
17	ARI	GEM	GEM	LEO	VIR	19.08	15.25	CAP	10.12	ARI	10.12	CAN	17
18	14.38	GEM	09.31	LEO	23.46	SCO	SAG	19.31	PIS	23.27	GEM	21.48	18
19	TAU	04.03	CAN	06.35	LIB	SCO	SAG	AQU	12.30	TAU	09.53	LEO	19
20	17.58	CAN	16.03	VIR	LIB	07.56	02.41	AQU	ARI	23.18	CAN	LEO	20
21	GEM	10.28	LEO	17.44	12.27	SAG	CAP	00.40	13.29	GEM	11.45	01.25	21
22	22.02	LEO	LEO	LIB	SCO	19.14	11.06	PIS	TAU	GEM	LEO	VIR	22
23	CAN	18.41	00.57	LIB	SCO	CAP	AQU	03.42	14.49	00.26	17.08	09.10	23
24	CAN	VIR	VIR	06.19	01.17	CAP	16.57	ARI	GEM	CAN	VIR	LIB	24
25	03.24	VIR	11.46	SCO	SAG	04.15	PIS	06.02	17.37	04.08	VIR	20.36	25
26	LEO	04.58	LIB	19.14	12.57	AQU	21.08	TAU	CAN	LEO	02.17	SCO	26
27	10.52	LIB	LIB	SAG	CAP	10.59	ARI	08.43	22.26	10.54	LIB	SCO	27
28	VIR	17.16	00.07	SAG	22.33	PIS	ARI	GEM	LEO	VIR	14.12	09.41	28
29	21.05		SCO	07.12	AQU	15.44	00.27	12.14	LEO	20.30	SCO	SAG	29
30	LIB		13.06	CAP	AQU	ARI	TAU	CAN	05.22	LIB	SCO	22.14	30
31	LIB		SAG		05.31		03.20	16.48		LIB		CAP	31

SUN

mth	dy	time	→ sign
JAN	1	00.00	→ CAP
JAN	21	03.54	→ AQU
FEB	19	18.22	→ PIS
MAR	21	17.54	→ ARI
APR	21	05.37	→ TAU
MAY	22	05.19	→ GEM
JUN	22	13.35	→ CAN
JUL	24	00.29	→ LEO
AUG	24	07.15	→ VIR
SEP	24	04.19	→ LIB
OCT	24	12.56	→ SCO
NOV	23	09.56	→ SAG
DEC	22	22.55	→ CAP

MERCURY

mth	dy	time	→ sign
JAN	1	00.00	→ CAP
FEB	13	04.05	→ AQU
MAR	4	21.12	→ PIS
MAR	21	03.30	→ ARI
APR	5	09.00	→ TAU
JUN	13	01.27	→ GEM
JUN	28	23.57	→ CAN
JUL	13	03.20	→ LEO
JUL	30	13.43	→ VIR
OCT	6	20.49	→ LIB
OCT	24	06.34	→ SCO
NOV	12	04.58	→ SAG
DEC	3	01.44	→ CAP
DEC	27	16.35	→ SAG

VENUS

mth	dy	time	→ sign
JAN	1	00.00	→ CAP
JAN	10	13.26	→ AQU
FEB	3	12.05	→ PIS
FEB	27	14.27	→ ARI
MAR	23	23.25	→ TAU
APR	17	18.53	→ GEM
MAY	13	05.44	→ CAN
JUN	8	18.46	→ LEO
JUL	7	19.05	→ VIR
NOV	9	00.55	→ LIB
DEC	9	09.24	→ SCO

MARS

mth	dy	time	→ sign
JAN	1	00.00	→ SAG
JAN	31	21.23	→ CAP
MAR	14	00.14	→ AQU
APR	23	08.20	→ PIS
JUN	2	21.37	→ ARI
JUL	15	16.21	→ TAU
SEP	5	15.28	→ GEM
NOV	30	04.01	→ TAU

SATURN

mth	dy	time	→ sign
JAN	1	00.00	→ ARI
JAN	20	09.02	→ TAU

JUPITER

mth	dy	time	→ sign
JAN	1	00.00	→ SCO
DEC	10	11.48	→ SAG

MOON

dy	jan	feb	mar	apr	may	jun	jul	aug	sep	oct	nov	dec	dy
1	CAP	PIS	PIS	00.14	GEM	LEO	VIR	06.44	SAG	CAP	06.12	ARI	1
2	09.02	PIS	12.49	TAU	11.06	LEO	13.59	14.37	10.56	10.56	PIS	ARI	2
3	AQU	05.57	ARI	01.49	CAN	00.14	LIB	18.21	CAP	AQU	13.49	04.43	3
4	17.50	ARI	16.21	GEM	13.09	VIR	23.27	SAG	CAP	20.59	ARI	TAU	4
5	PIS	10.36	TAU		LEO	07.07	SCO	SAG	02.35	PIS	17.54	06.18	5
6	PIS	TAU	19.23	CAN	17.49	LIB	SCO	07.10	AQU	PIS	TAU	GEM	6
7	00.33	14.03	GEM	07.15	VIR	17.21	11.39	CAP	12.17	03.56	19.29	05.55	7
8	ARI	GEM	22.24	LEO	VIR	SCO	SAG	19.02	PIS	ARI	GEM	CAN	8
9	05.01	16.28	CAN	12.23	01.26	SCO	SAG	AQU	19.31	08.12	20.11	05.39	9
10	TAU	CAN	CAN	VIR	LIB	05.37	00.32	AQU	ARI	TAU	CAN	LEO	10
11	07.17	18.33	01.45	19.36	11.35	SAG	CAP	05.00	ARI	10.55	21.38	07.27	11
12	GEM	LEO	LEO	LIB	SCO	18.27	12.34	PIS	00.49	GEM	LEO	VIR	12
13	08.03	21.39	06.04	LIB	23.33	CAP	AQU	13.02	TAU	13.12	LEO	12.35	13
14	CAN	VIR	VIR	05.06	SAG	CAP	23.04	ARI	04.47	CAN	01.05	LIB	14
15	08.48	VIR	12.19	SCO	SAG	06.44	PIS	19.12	GEM	15.54	VIR	21.09	15
16	LEO	03.22	LIB	16.46	12.20	AQU	PIS	TAU	07.47	LEO	07.04	SCO	16
17	11.30	LIB	21.21	SAG	CAP	17.27	07.35	23.23	CAN	19.41	LIB	SCO	17
18	VIR	12.39	SCO	SAG	CAP	PIS	ARI	GEM	10.18	VIR	15.28	08.08	18
19	17.47	SCO	SCO	05.34	00.40	PIS	13.34	GEM	LEO	VIR	SCO	SAG	19
20	LIB	SCO	09.05	CAP	AQU	01.32	TAU	01.42	13.05	01.05	SCO	20.24	20
21	LIB	00.53	SAG	17.33	10.53	ARI	16.42	CAN	VIR	LIB	01.54	CAP	21
22	04.06	SAG	21.53	AQU	PIS	06.14	GEM	02.54	17.21	08.36	SAG	CAP	22
23	SCO	13.37	CAP	AQU	17.41	TAU	17.30	LEO	LIB	SCO	13.55	09.05	23
24	16.54	CAP	CAP	02.41	ARI	07.46	CAN	04.26	LIB	18.34	CAP	AQU	24
25	SAG	CAP	09.13	PIS	20.48	GEM	17.24	VIR	00.17	SAG	CAP	21.18	25
26	SAG	00.17	AQU	08.03	TAU	07.20	LEO	08.06	SCO	SAG	02.40	PIS	26
27	05.30	AQU	17.14	ARI	21.12	CAN	18.26	LIB	10.21	06.37	AQU	PIS	27
28	CAP	07.51	PIS	10.13	GEM	06.54	VIR	15.16	SAG	CAP	14.32	07.36	28
29	15.57		21.52	TAU	20.37	LEO	22.32	SCO	22.39	19.14	PIS	ARI	29
30	AQU		ARI	10.39	CAN	08.34	LIB	SCO	CAP	AQU	23.35	14.31	30
31	23.55		ARI		21.03		LIB	02.01		AQU		TAU	31

SUN

mth	dy	time → sign
JAN	1	00.00 → CAP
JAN	21	09.27 → AQU
FEB	19	23.54 → PIS
MAR	20	23.28 → ARI
APR	20	11.12 → TAU
MAY	21	10.56 → GEM
JUN	21	19.17 → CAN
JUL	23	06.16 → LEO
AUG	23	13.03 → VIR
SEP	23	10.09 → LIB
OCT	23	18.52 → SCO
NOV	22	15.48 → SAG
DEC	22	04.46 → CAP

MERCURY

mth	dy	time → sign
JAN	1	00.00 → SAG
JAN	15	07.16 → CAP
FEB	7	02.24 → AQU
FEB	25	06.35 → PIS
MAR	12	01.26 → ARI
MAY	16	19.52 → TAU
JUN	5	05.14 → GEM
JUN	19	09.00 → CAN
JUL	4	09.04 → LEO
JUL	26	08.13 → VIR
AUG	21	03.21 → LEO
SEP	10	17.09 → VIR
SEP	28	07.27 → LIB
OCT	15	18.56 → SCO
NOV	4	14.48 → SAG

VENUS

mth	dy	time → sign
JAN	1	00.00 → SCO
JAN	4	18.36 → SAG
JAN	29	22.47 → CAP
FEB	23	15.29 → AQU
MAR	19	03.47 → PIS
APR	12	14.50 → ARI
MAY	7	01.54 → TAU
MAY	31	13.19 → GEM
JUN	25	00.14 → CAN
JUL	19	09.47 → LEO
AUG	12	17.42 → VIR
SEP	6	00.53 → LIB
SEP	30	08.24 → SCO
OCT	24	17.27 → SAG
NOV	18	05.03 → CAP
DEC	12	22.25 → AQU

MARS

mth	dy	time → sign
JAN	1	00.00 → TAU
JAN	30	21.13 → GEM
APR	5	11.43 → CAN
MAY	28	08.03 → LEO
JUL	17	02.34 → VIR
SEP	2	17.15 → LIB
OCT	18	02.43 → SCO
NOV	30	07.50 → SAG

SATURN

mth	dy	time → sign
JAN	1	00.00 → TAU
JUL	7	06.23 → GEM
NOV	30	18.26 → TAU

JUPITER

mth	dy	time → sign
JAN	1	00.00 → SAG

MOON

dy	jan	feb	mar	apr	may	jun	jul	aug	sep	oct	nov	dec	dy
1	17.28	CAN	LEO	01.40	SCO	16.17	10.57	PIS	09.20	GEM	11.46	VIR	1
2	GEM	03.47	14.14	LIB	22.30	CAP	AQU	17.40	TAU	GEM	LEO	23.26	2
3	17.25	LEO	VIR	06.15	SAG	CAP	23.40	ARI	16.45	03.09	14.34	LIB	3
4	CAN	03.23	15.53	SCO	SAG	04.19	PIS	ARI	GEM	CAN	VIR	LIB	4
5	16.17	VIR	LIB	13.47	08.42	AQU	PIS	03.37	21.06	06.11	17.32	04.22	5
6	LEO	05.12	20.25	SAG	CAP	16.55	11.30	TAU	CAN	LEO	LIB	SCO	6
7	16.23	LIB	SCO	SAG	20.50	PIS	ARI	10.10	22.43	07.55	21.17	10.48	7
8	VIR	10.53	SCO	00.24	AQU	PIS	20.33	GEM	LEO	VIR	SCO	SAG	8
9	19.42	SCO	04.43	CAP	AQU	04.03	TAU	12.57	22.51	09.24	SCO	19.10	9
10	LIB	20.35	SAG	12.47	09.08	ARI	TAU	CAN	VIR	LIB	02.44	CAP	10
11	LIB	SAG	16.12	AQU	PIS	11.46	01.34	13.00	23.18	12.04	SAG	CAP	11
12	03.07	SAG	CAP	AQU	19.20	TAU	GEM	LEO	LIB	SCO	10.48	05.51	12
13	SCO	08.52	CAP	00.42	ARI	15.33	02.55	12.14	LIB	17.18	CAP	AQU	13
14	13.57	CAP	04.50	PIS	ARI	GEM	CAN	VIR	01.54	SAG	21.45	18.26	14
15	SAG	21.33	AQU	10.15	02.04	16.24	02.16	12.48	SCO	SAG	AQU	PIS	15
16	SAG	AQU	16.28	ARI	TAU	CAN	LEO	LIB	07.58	01.56	AQU	PIS	16
17	02.28	AQU	PIS	16.51	05.33	16.16	01.49	16.28	SAG	CAP	10.24	07.00	17
18	CAP	09.13	PIS	TAU	GEM	LEO	VIR	SCO	17.42	13.30	PIS	ARI	18
19	15.07	PIS	01.59	21.03	07.04	17.09	03.37	23.59	CAP	AQU	22.17	16.57	19
20	AQU	19.17	ARI	GEM	CAN	VIR	LIB	SAG	CAP	AQU	ARI	TAU	20
21	AQU	ARI	09.16	23.53	08.18	20.33	08.52	SAG	05.51	02.08	ARI	22.51	21
22	03.06	ARI	TAU	CAN	LEO	LIB	SCO	10.43	AQU	PIS	07.13	GEM	22
23	PIS	03.26	14.37	CAN	10.40	LIB	17.34	CAP	18.25	13.29	TAU	GEM	23
24	13.41	TAU	GEM	02.22	VIR	02.58	SAG	23.07	PIS	ARI	12.40	01.11	24
25	ARI	09.15	18.22	LEO	15.00	SCO	SAG	AQU	PIS	22.15	GEM	CAN	25
26	21.52	GEM	CAN	05.17	LIB	11.58	04.41	AQU	05.44	TAU	15.36	01.43	26
27	TAU	12.30	20.54	VIR	21.27	SAG	CAP	11.40	ARI	TAU	CAN	LEO	27
28	TAU	CAN	LEO	09.15	SCO	22.49	17.01	PIS	15.04	04.22	17.34	02.27	28
29	02.42	13.42	22.58	LIB	SCO	CAP	AQU	23.21	TAU	GEM	LEO	VIR	29
30	GEM		VIR	14.47	05.54	CAP	AQU	ARI	22.12	08.36	19.55	04.55	30
31	04.15		VIR		SAG		05.40	ARI		CAN		LIB	31

SUN

mth	dy	time	→	sign
JAN	1	00.00	→	CAP
JAN	20	15.21	→	AQU
FEB	19	05.45	→	PIS
MAR	21	05.18	→	ARI
APR	20	17.05	→	TAU
MAY	21	16.52	→	GEM
JUN	22	01.11	→	CAN
JUL	23	12.04	→	LEO
AUG	23	18.47	→	VIR
SEP	23	15.51	→	LIB
OCT	24	00.36	→	SCO
NOV	22	21.37	→	SAG
DEC	22	10.35	→	CAP

MERCURY

mth	dy	time	→	sign
JAN	1	00.00	→	SAG
JAN	10	05.22	→	CAP
JAN	30	01.47	→	AQU
FEB	16	10.44	→	PIS
MAR	4	22.35	→	ARI
APR	7	15.04	→	PIS
APR	14	02.48	→	ARI
MAY	12	06.16	→	TAU
MAY	28	00.30	→	GEM
JUN	10	21.33	→	CAN
JUN	28	05.37	→	LEO
SEP	4	10.55	→	VIR
SEP	20	10.03	→	LIB
OCT	8	14.54	→	SCO
OCT	30	18.09	→	SAG
NOV	23	12.26	→	SCO
DEC	13	08.52	→	SAG

VENUS

mth	dy	time	→	sign
JAN	1	00.00	→	AQU
JAN	7	05.29	→	PIS
FEB	2	23.24	→	ARI
MAR	6	17.09	→	TAU
MAY	2	05.15	→	ARI
MAY	31	09.47	→	TAU
JUL	8	09.16	→	GEM
AUG	5	23.32	→	CAN
SEP	1	09.22	→	LEO
SEP	26	16.05	→	VIR
OCT	21	06.04	→	LIB
NOV	14	09.57	→	SCO
DEC	8	08.37	→	SAG

MARS

mth	dy	time	→	sign
JAN	1	00.00	→	SAG
JAN	10	13.36	→	CAP
FEB	19	08.09	→	AQU
MAR	30	05.45	→	PIS
MAY	8	03.13	→	ARI
JUN	17	00.36	→	TAU
JUL	29	10.41	→	GEM
SEP	15	17.27	→	CAN

SATURN

mth	dy	time	→	sign
JAN	1	00.00	→	TAU
MAR	26	13.18	→	GEM

JUPITER

mth	dy	time	→	sign
JAN	1	00.00	→	SAG
JAN	2	19.59	→	CAP

MOON

dy	jan	feb	mar	apr	may	jun	jul	aug	sep	oct	nov	dec	dy
1	09.49	SAG	13.52	AQU	PIS	11.45	04.47	21.25	VIR	18.31	SAG	CAP	1
2	SCO	07.59	CAP	20.39	16.39	TAU	GEM	LEO	07.47	SCO	10.08	02.42	2
3	17.01	CAP	CAP	PIS	ARI	19.42	09.29	21.44	LIB	20.08	CAP	AQU	3
4	SAG	19.25	01.21	PIS	ARI	GEM	CAN	VIR	08.21	SAG	17.44	13.00	4
5	SAG	AQU	AQU	09.22	03.35	GEM	11.40	22.13	SCO	SAG	AQU	PIS	5
6	02.10	AQU	14.10	ARI	TAU	00.40	LEO	LIB	11.32	01.10	AQU	PIS	6
7	CAP	08.03	PIS	20.32	11.49	CAN	13.00	LIB	SAG	CAP	05.01	01.45	7
8	13.07	PIS	PIS	TAU	GEM	03.51	VIR	00.22	18.07	10.09	PIS	ARI	8
9	AQU	20.59	02.57	TAU	17.43	LEO	14.59	SCO	CAP	AQU	18.02	14.12	9
10	AQU	ARI	ARI	05.31	CAN	06.31	LIB	05.03	CAP	22.07	ARI	TAU	10
11	01.38	ARI	14.35	GEM	21.57	VIR	18.26	SAG	03.56	PIS	ARI	TAU	11
12	PIS	08.47	TAU	12.09	LEO	09.27	SCO	12.24	AQU	PIS	06.17	00.09	12
13	14.36	TAU	TAU	CAN	LEO	LIB	23.37	CAP	15.57	11.08	TAU	GEM	13
14	ARI	17.38	00.01	16.30	01.10	13.00	SAG	22.09	PIS	ARI	16.24	07.12	14
15	ARI	GEM	GEM	LEO	VIR	SCO	SAG	AQU	PIS	23.30	GEM	CAN	15
16	01.46	22.29	06.21	18.53	03.44	17.31	06.39	AQU	04.55	TAU	GEM	12.09	16
17	TAU	CAN	CAN	VIR	LIB	SAG	CAP	09.52	ARI	TAU	00.17	LEO	17
18	09.07	23.47	09.27	20.02	06.14	23.41	15.48	PIS	17.34	10.13	CAN	16.00	18
19	GEM	LEO	LEO	LIB	SCO	CAP	AQU	22.46	TAU	GEM	06.18	VIR	19
20	12.14	23.08	10.08	21.14	09.38	CAP	AQU	ARI	TAU	18.45	LEO	19.19	20
21	CAN	VIR	VIR	SCO	SAG	08.21	03.12	ARI	04.35	CAN	10.40	LIB	21
22	12.26	22.37	09.54	SCO	15.13	AQU	PIS	11.30	GEM	CAN	VIR	22.21	22
23	LEO	LIB	LIB	00.03	CAP	19.45	16.07	TAU	12.45	00.45	13.30	SCO	23
24	11.48	LIB	10.37	SAG	CAP	PIS	ARI	22.03	CAN	LEO	LIB	SCO	24
25	VIR	00.11	SCO	05.56	00.01	PIS	ARI	GEM	17.26	04.06	15.13	01.28	25
26	12.26	SCO	13.59	CAP	AQU	08.38	04.29	GEM	LEO	VIR	SCO	SAG	26
27	LIB	05.11	SAG	15.33	11.47	ARI	TAU	04.54	19.02	05.17	16.54	05.36	27
28	15.50	SAG	21.09	AQU	PIS	20.22	13.57	CAN	VIR	LIB	SAG	CAP	28
29	SCO		CAP	AQU	PIS	TAU	GEM	07.55	18.47	05.30	20.12	12.01	29
30	22.30		CAP	3.54	00.36	TAU	19.23	LEO	LIB	SCO	CAP	AQU	30
31	SAG		07.53		ARI		CAN	08.16		06.29		21.38	31

SUN		
mth	dy	time → sign
JAN	1	00.00 → CAP
JAN	20	21.14 → AQU
FEB	19	11.39 → PIS
MAR	21	11.11 → ARI
APR	20	22.55 → TAU
MAY	21	22.38 → GEM
JUN	22	06.57 → CAN
JUL	23	17.47 → LEO
AUG	24	00.33 → VIR
SEP	23	21.35 → LIB
OCT	24	06.17 → SCO
NOV	23	03.22 → SAG
DEC	22	16.25 → CAP

MERCURY		
mth	dy	time → sign
JAN	1	00.00 → SAG
JAN	3	19.22 → CAP
JAN	22	15.53 → AQU
FEB	8	19.11 → PIS
APR	16	16.04 → ARI
MAY	5	00.58 → TAU
MAY	19	10.06 → GEM
JUN	3	05.53 → CAN
AUG	11	06.33 → LEO
AUG	27	10.48 → VIR
SEP	12	15.47 → LIB
OCT	2	05.52 → SCO
DEC	8	04.53 → SAG
DEC	27	17.42 → CAP

VENUS		
mth	dy	time → sign
JAN	1	00.00 → SAG
JAN	1	05.26 → CAP
JAN	25	02.12 → AQU
FEB	18	00.05 → PIS
MAR	14	00.33 → ARI
APR	7	04.48 → TAU
MAY	1	14.12 → GEM
MAY	26	05.36 → CAN
JUN	20	04.26 → LEO
JUL	15	14.11 → VIR
AUG	10	18.13 → LIB
SEP	7	10.59 → SCO
OCT	10	01.50 → SAG
DEC	5	23.23 → SCO
DEC	30	23.16 → SAG

MARS		
mth	dy	time → sign
JAN	1	00.00 → CAN
MAY	1	20.25 → LEO
JUN	26	04.40 → VIR
AUG	14	14.00 → LIB
SEP	29	10.25 → SCO
NOV	11	10.38 → SAG
DEC	22	03.54 → CAP

SATURN		
mth	dy	time → sign
JAN	1	00.00 → GEM
AUG	24	17.38 → CAN
DEC	7	06.34 → GEM

JUPITER		
mth	dy	time → sign
JAN	1	00.00 → CAP
JAN	21	15.26 → AQU

MOON														
dy	jan	feb	mar	apr	may	jun	jul	aug	sep	oct	nov	dec	dy
1	PIS	ARI	14.07	GEM	CAN	VIR	LIB	SAG	08.03	PIS	ARI	22.53	1
2	PIS	06.54	TAU	18.59	08.53	23.51	08.19	20.14	AQU	PIS	04.08	GEM	2
3	09.58	TAU	TAU	CAN	LEO	LIB	SCO	CAP	16.26	09.38	TAU	GEM	3
4	ARI	18.20	02.14	CAN	14.02	LIB	10.25	CAP	PIS	ARI	16.44	10.19	4
5	22.43	GEM	GEM	02.06	VIR	01.30	SAG	01.27	PIS	21.58	GEM	CAN	5
6	TAU	GEM	11.34	LEO	16.13	SCO	12.53	AQU	03.00	TAU	GEM	20.13	6
7	TAU	02.16	CAN	05.37	LIB	02.12	CAP	09.03	ARI	TAU	04.33	LEO	7
8	09.13	CAN	17.03	VIR	16.20	SAG	17.10	PIS	15.15	10.40	CAN	LEO	8
9	GEM	06.26	LEO	06.12	SCO	03.40	AQU	19.25	TAU	GEM	14.36	04.03	9
10	16.12	LEO	19.02	LIB	16.04	CAP	AQU	ARI	TAU	22.26	LEO	VIR	10
11	CAN	08.00	VIR	05.27	SAG	07.46	00.33	ARI	03.55	CAN	21.42	09.09	11
12	20.13	VIR	18.57	SCO	17.30	AQU	PIS	07.46	GEM	CAN	VIR	LIB	12
13	LEO	08.37	LIB	05.23	CAP	15.44	11.14	TAU	14.56	07.36	VIR	11.23	13
14	22.40	LIB	18.39	SAG	22.29	PIS	ARI	20.06	CAN	LEO	01.10	SCO	14
15	VIR	09.55	SCO	07.58	AQU	PIS	23.49	GEM	22.41	13.02	LIB	11.40	15
16	VIR	SCO	20.01	CAP	AQU	03.11	TAU	GEM	LEO	VIR	01.36	SAG	16
17	00.53	13.03	SAG	14.31	07.40	ARI	TAU	06.11	LEO	14.49	SCO	11.46	17
18	LIB	SAG	SAG	AQU	PIS	16.01	11.47	CAN	02.42	LIB	00.42	CAP	18
19	03.44	18.38	00.23	AQU	19.54	TAU	GEM	12.52	VIR	14.21	SAG	13.47	19
20	SCO	CAP	CAP	00.52	ARI	TAU	21.12	LEO	03.52	SCO	00.42	AQU	20
21	07.40	CAP	08.15	PIS	ARI	03.44	CAN	16.30	LIB	13.40	CAP	19.25	21
22	SAG	02.41	AQU	13.30	08.51	GEM	CAN	VIR	03.53	SAG	03.42	PIS	22
23	12.59	AQU	19.01	ARI	TAU	13.07	03.42	18.18	SCO	14.55	AQU	PIS	23
24	CAP	13.01	PIS	ARI	20.37	CAN	LEO	LIB	04.36	CAP	10.53	05.02	24
25	20.13	PIS	PIS	02.28	GEM	20.14	08.00	19.43	SAG	19.39	PIS	ARI	25
26	AQU	PIS	07.30	TAU	GEM	LEO	VIR	SCO	07.34	AQU	21.44	17.19	26
27	AQU	01.09	ARI	14.29	06.28	LEO	11.05	21.59	CAP	AQU	ARI	TAU	27
28	05.54	ARI	20.27	GEM	CAN	01.35	LIB	SAG	13.36	04.13	ARI	TAU	28
29	PIS		TAU	GEM	14.22	VIR	13.45	SAG	AQU	PIS	10.22	05.53	29
30	17.57		TAU	00.50	LEO	05.32	SCO	01.57	22.33	15.35	TAU	GEM	30
31	ARI		08.42		20.13		16.35	CAP		ARI		17.01	31

33

SUN

mth	dy	time	→ sign
JAN	1	00.00	→ CAP
JAN	21	03.02	→ AQU
FEB	19	17.25	→ PIS
MAR	21	16.53	→ ARI
APR	21	04.29	→ TAU
MAY	22	04.11	→ GEM
JUN	22	12.29	→ CAN
JUL	23	23.28	→ LEO
AUG	24	06.14	→ VIR
SEP	24	03.24	→ LIB
OCT	24	12.11	→ SCO
NOV	23	09.17	→ SAG
DEC	22	22.18	→ CAP

MERCURY

mth	dy	time	→ sign
JAN	1	00.00	→ CAP
JAN	15	04.26	→ AQU
FEB	2	10.35	→ PIS
FEB	23	15.04	→ AQU
MAR	19	08.44	→ PIS
APR	10	19.22	→ ARI
APR	26	21.43	→ TAU
MAY	10	23.49	→ GEM
MAY	29	10.34	→ CAN
AUG	4	09.04	→ LEO
AUG	19	04.38	→ VIR
SEP	5	09.04	→ LIB
SEP	28	08.11	→ SCO
OCT	21	01.15	→ LIB
NOV	11	14.09	→ SCO
DEC	1	09.18	→ SAG
DEC	20	11.16	→ CAP

VENUS

mth	dy	time	→ sign
JAN	1	00.00	→ SAG
FEB	6	15.56	→ CAP
MAR	6	13.14	→ AQU
APR	1	15.17	→ PIS
APR	27	00.56	→ ARI
MAY	22	02.54	→ TAU
JUN	16	00.22	→ GEM
JUL	10	17.33	→ CAN
AUG	4	05.47	→ LEO
AUG	28	13.07	→ VIR
SEP	21	16.31	→ LIB
OCT	15	17.42	→ SCO
NOV	8	18.07	→ SAG
DEC	2	18.35	→ CAP
DEC	26	20.23	→ AQU

MARS

mth	dy	time	→ sign
JAN	1	00.00	→ CAP
JAN	30	06.14	→ AQU
MAR	9	12.48	→ PIS
APR	16	20.35	→ ARI
MAY	26	03.19	→ TAU
JUL	6	06.12	→ GEM
AUG	19	09.19	→ CAN
OCT	7	20.37	→ LEO

SATURN

mth	dy	time	→ sign
JAN	1	00.00	→ GEM
MAY	11	21.36	→ CAN

JUPITER

mth	dy	time	→ sign
JAN	1	00.00	→ AQU
FEB	4	00.33	→ PIS

MOON

dy	jan	feb	mar	apr	may	jun	jul	aug	sep	oct	nov	dec	dy
1	CAN	16.10	01.03	14.49	00.37	11.49	01.14	ARI	GEM	CAN	LEO	17.09	1
2	CAN	VIR	VIR	SCO	SAG	AQU	PIS	02.40	GEM	CAN	01.30	LIB	2
3	02.12	20.32	04.15	15.05	00.39	16.32	08.24	TAU	11.12	07.13	VIR	20.33	3
4	LEO	LIB	LIB	SAG	CAP	PIS	ARI	14.43	CAN	LEO	07.29	SCO	4
5	09.28	23.48	06.05	16.47	03.23	PIS	19.01	GEM	22.24	16.05	LIB	20.47	5
6	VIR	SCO	SCO	CAP	AQU	01.06	TAU	GEM	LEO	VIR	09.37	SAG	6
7	14.53	SCO	07.58	21.03	09.41	ARI	TAU	03.11	LEO	21.09	SCO	19.52	7
8	LIB	02.33	SAG	AQU	PIS	12.30	07.30	CAN	06.42	LIB	09.36	CAP	8
9	18.25	SAG	10.59	AQU	19.10	TAU	GEM	14.08	VIR	23.20	SAG	20.01	9
10	SCO	05.25	CAP	04.08	ARI	TAU	19.56	LEO	12.00	SCO	09.33	AQU	10
11	20.25	CAP	15.40	PIS	ARI	01.06	CAN	22.42	LIB	SCO	CAP	22.57	11
12	SAG	09.09	AQU	13.31	06.40	GEM	CAN	VIR	15.14	00.21	11.22	PIS	12
13	21.52	AQU	22.16	ARI	TAU	13.38	07.06	VIR	SCO	SAG	AQU	PIS	13
14	CAP	14.40	PIS	ARI	19.09	CAN	LEO	04.55	17.41	01.56	16.05	05.30	14
15	CAP	PIS	PIS	00.38	GEM	CAN	16.22	LIB	SAG	CAP	PIS	ARI	15
16	00.17	22.46	06.55	TAU	GEM	01.12	VIR	09.17	20.20	05.15	23.40	15.14	16
17	AQU	ARI	ARI	12.57	07.47	LEO	23.21	SCO	CAP	AQU	ARI	TAU	17
18	05.14	ARI	17.38	GEM	CAN	10.53	LIB	12.18	23.49	10.38	ARI	TAU	18
19	PIS	09.37	TAU	GEM	19.31	VIR	LIB	SAG	AQU	PIS	09.29	03.02	19
20	13.42	TAU	TAU	01.36	LEO	17.39	03.50	14.38	AQU	17.57	TAU	GEM	20
21	ARI	22.05	05.58	CAN	LEO	LIB	SCO	CAP	04.32	ARI	20.56	15.44	21
22	ARI	GEM	GEM	12.53	04.47	21.03	06.06	17.03	PIS	ARI	GEM	CAN	22
23	01.13	GEM	18.22	LEO	VIR	SCO	SAG	AQU	10.55	03.08	GEM	CAN	23
24	TAU	09.57	CAN	20.53	10.16	21.45	07.03	20.35	ARI	TAU	09.34	04.23	24
25	13.48	CAN	CAN	VIR	LIB	SAG	CAP	PIS	19.35	14.15	CAN	LEO	25
26	GEM	19.11	04.38	VIR	12.02	21.22	08.10	PIS	TAU	GEM	22.23	15.51	26
27	GEM	LEO	LEO	00.47	SCO	CAP	AQU	02.21	TAU	GEM	LEO	VIR	27
28	01.08	LEO	11.13	LIB	11.27	21.54	11.04	ARI	06.42	02.53	LEO	VIR	28
29	CAN		VIR	01.23	SAG	AQU	PIS	11.08	GEM	CAN	09.33	00.41	29
30	09.55		14.10	SCO	10.39	AQU	17.06	TAU	19.20	15.26	VIR	LIB	30
31	LEO		LIB		CAP		ARI	22.38		LEO		05.55	31

SUN

mth	dy	time → sign
JAN	1	00.00 → CAP
JAN	21	08.57 → AQU
FEB	19	23.19 → PIS
MAR	20	22.44 → ARI
APR	20	10.25 → TAU
MAY	21	10.04 → GEM
JUN	21	18.22 → CAN
JUL	23	05.24 → LEO
AUG	23	12.09 → VIR
SEP	23	09.15 → LIB
OCT	23	17.58 → SCO
NOV	22	14.56 → SAG
DEC	22	03.57 → CAP

MERCURY

mth	dy	time → sign
JAN	1	00.00 → CAP
JAN	8	01.25 → AQU
MAR	15	00.05 → PIS
APR	2	10.57 → ARI
APR	17	11.02 → TAU
MAY	2	16.14 → GEM
JUL	10	18.19 → CAN
JUL	26	01.43 → LEO
AUG	10	04.04 → VIR
AUG	29	04.53 → LIB
NOV	4	12.26 → SCO
NOV	23	03.40 → SAG
DEC	12	07.14 → CAP

VENUS

mth	dy	time → sign
JAN	1	00.00 → AQU
JAN	20	01.44 → PIS
FEB	13	15.26 → ARI
MAR	9	21.49 → TAU
APR	5	13.32 → GEM
MAY	5	20.37 → CAN
SEP	8	22.29 → LEO
OCT	7	22.11 → VIR
NOV	3	00.57 → LIB
NOV	27	23.03 → SCO
DEC	22	07.53 → SAG

MARS

mth	dy	time → sign
JAN	1	00.00 → LEO
MAY	28	18.34 → VIR
JUL	23	05.12 → LIB
SEP	8	17.55 → SCO
OCT	22	02.51 → SAG
DEC	1	17.23 → CAP

SATURN

mth	dy	time → sign
JAN	1	00.00 → CAN
OCT	17	15.26 → LEO
DEC	7	19.03 → CAN

JUPITER

mth	dy	time → sign
JAN	1	00.00 → PIS
FEB	12	07.01 → ARI
JUN	26	01.24 → TAU
OCT	26	14.41 → ARI

MOON

dy	jan	feb	mar	apr	may	jun	jul	aug	sep	oct	nov	dec	dy
1	SCO	CAP	03.18	17.48	07.49	GEM	CAN	01.18	LIB	12.28	CAP	09.29	1
2	07.43	18.09	AQU	ARI	TAU	11.46	06.57	01.24	SAG	00.50	PIS		2
3	SAG	AQU	05.27	ARI	17.12	CAN	LEO	11.54	SCO	16.23	AQU	13.34	3
4	07.25	19.16	PIS	00.11	GEM	CAN	19.32	LIB	07.05	CAP	04.04	ARI	4
5	CAP	PIS	08.56	TAU	GEM	00.47	VIR	19.56	SAG	19.28	PIS	19.35	5
6	06.58	22.45	ARI	09.19	04.53	LEO	VIR	SCO	10.44	AQU	07.59	TAU	6
7	AQU	ARI	15.08	GEM	CAN	13.15	06.06	SCO	CAP	22.00	ARI	TAU	7
8	08.21	ARI	TAU	21.11	17.51	VIR	LIB	00.56	12.39	PIS	13.07	03.40	8
9	PIS	05.50	TAU	CAN	LEO	22.59	13.16	SAG	AQU	PIS	TAU	GEM	9
10	13.07	TAU	00.46	CAN	LIB	SCO	03.08	13.42	00.40	20.19	14.00	10
11	ARI	16.30	GEM	10.01	05.45	LIB	16.43	CAP	PIS	ARI	GEM	CAN	11
12	21.43	GEM	13.03	LEO	VIR	04.40	SAG	03.28	15.17	04.45	GEM	CAN	12
13	TAU	GEM	CAN	21.07	14.15	SCO	17.20	AQU	ARI	TAU	06.19	02.18	13
14	TAU	05.13	CAN	VIR	LIB	06.40	CAP	03.29	19.09	11.38	CAN	LEO	14
15	09.18	CAN	01.41	VIR	18.42	SAG	16.46	PIS	TAU	GEM	18.44	15.19	15
16	GEM	17.38	LEO	04.40	SCO	06.33	AQU	05.02	TAU	21.58	LEO	VIR	16
17	22.07	LEO	12.12	LIB	20.09	CAP	16.55	ARI	02.38	CAN	LEO	VIR	17
18	CAN	LEO	VIR	08.48	SAG	06.16	PIS	09.45	GEM	CAN	07.33	02.50	18
19	CAN	04.08	19.37	SCO	20.30	AQU	19.32	TAU	13.45	10.40	VIR	LIB	19
20	10.33	VIR	LIB	10.52	CAP	07.39	ARI	18.27	CAN	LEO	18.03	10.52	20
21	LEO	12.13	LIB	SAG	21.33	PIS	ARI	GEM	CAN	23.04	LIB	SCO	21
22	21.32	LIB	00.26	12.34	AQU	11.55	01.46	GEM	02.41	VIR	LIB	14.58	22
23	VIR	18.09	SCO	CAP	AQU	ARI	TAU	06.21	LEO	VIR	0.48	SAG	23
24	VIR	SCO	03.48	15.07	00.35	19.26	11.36	CAN	14.47	08.45	SCO	16.07	24
25	06.26	22.20	SAG	AQU	PIS	TAU	GEM	19.24	VIR	LIB	04.12	CAP	25
26	LIB	SAG	06.43	19.05	06.03	TAU	23.53	LEO	VIR	15.09	SAG	16.05	26
27	12.43	SAG	CAP	PIS	ARI	05.43	CAN	LEO	00.22	SCO	05.45	AQU	27
28	SCO	01.13	09.47	PIS	13.54	GEM	CAN	07.30	LIB	19.07	CAP	16.41	28
29	16.18	CAP	AQU	00.35	TAU	17.55	12.56	VIR	07.21	SAG	07.06	PIS	29
30	SAG		13.18	ARI	23.53	CAN	LEO	17.34	SCO	22.00	AQU	19.25	30
31	17.43		PIS		GEM		LEO	LIB		CAP		ARI	31

35

SUN

mth	dy	time → sign
JAN	1	00.00 → CAP
JAN	20	14.39 → AQU
FEB	19	05.04 → PIS
MAR	21	04.37 → ARI
APR	20	16.14 → TAU
MAY	21	16.02 → GEM
JUN	22	00.11 → CAN
JUL	23	11.08 → LEO
AUG	23	17.52 → VIR
SEP	23	15.01 → LIB
OCT	23	23.44 → SCO
NOV	22	20.47 → SAG
DEC	22	09.48 → CAP

MERCURY

mth	dy	time → sign
JAN	1	00.00 → CAP
JAN	1	17.05 → AQU
JAN	18	04.28 → CAP
FEB	15	03.21 → AQU
MAR	8	15.36 → PIS
MAR	25	11.35 → ARI
APR	9	05.45 → TAU
JUN	14	18.11 → GEM
JUL	3	10.27 → CAN
JUL	17	13.28 → LEO
AUG	2	19.31 → VIR
AUG	26	22.52 → LIB
SEP	14	12.12 → VIR
OCT	10	04.45 → LIB
OCT	28	05.23 → SCO
NOV	15	21.26 → SAG
DEC	5	16.56 → CAP

VENUS

mth	dy	time → sign
JAN	1	00.00 → SAG
JAN	15	10.44 → CAP
FEB	8	11.51 → AQU
MAR	4	13.12 → PIS
MAR	28	16.01 → ARI
APR	21	21.15 → TAU
MAY	16	05.08 → GEM
JUN	9	15.13 → CAN
JUL	4	03.20 → LEO
JUL	28	17.50 → VIR
AUG	22	12.19 → LIB
SEP	16	13.03 → SCO
OCT	11	23.35 → SAG
NOV	7	05.04 → CAP
DEC	5	13.12 → AQU

MARS

mth	dy	time → sign
JAN	1	00.00 → CAP
JAN	9	12.46 → AQU
FEB	16	13.24 → PIS
MAR	26	17.49 → ARI
MAY	4	22.23 → TAU
JUN	14	20.45 → GEM
JUL	28	04.07 → CAN
SEP	12	10.45 → LEO
NOV	2	11.11 → VIR

SATURN

mth	dy	time → sign
JAN	1	00.00 → CAN
JUN	24	13.38 → LEO

JUPITER

mth	dy	time → sign
JAN	1	00.00 → ARI
FEB	12	15.44 → TAU
JUN	29	23.39 → GEM

MOON

dy	jan	feb	mar	apr	may	jun	jul	aug	sep	oct	nov	dec	dy
1	ARI	GEM	GEM	04.39	01.19	LIB	22.14	CAP	PIS	ARI	GEM	CAN	1
2	01.04	GEM	08.52	LEO	VIR	06.34	SAG	12.50	22.20	09.25	GEM	22.32	2
3	TAU	02.31	CAN	17.32	12.52	SCO	SAG	AQU	ARI	TAU	04.09	LEO	3
4	09.39	CAN	21.36	VIR	LIB	12.27	01.25	12.20	23.06	12.14	CAN	LEO	4
5	GEM	15.16	LEO	VIR	21.39	SAG	CAP	PIS	TAU	GEM	13.42	10.07	5
6	20.35	LEO	LEO	04.54	SCO	15.45	02.25	12.18	TAU	19.06	LEO	VIR	6
7	CAN	LEO	10.29	LIB	SCO	CAP	AQU	ARI	03.19	CAN	LEO	22.42	7
8	CAN	04.09	VIR	13.54	03.44	17.45	02.53	14.36	GEM	CAN	01.56	LIB	8
9	09.03	VIR	22.01	SCO	SAG	AQU	PIS	TAU	11.40	05.50	VIR	LIB	9
10	LEO	16.04	LIB	20.50	08.00	19.42	04.25	20.24	CAN	LEO	14.26	09.52	10
11	22.01	LIB	LIB	SAG	CAP	PIS	ARI	GEM	23.13	LIB	SCO	11
12	VIR	LIB	07.40	SAG	11.18	22.31	08.13	GEM	LEO	VIR	LIB	18.10	12
13	VIR	02.06	SCO	02.08	AQU	ARI	TAU	05.39	LEO	VIR	01.13	SAG	13
14	10.04	SCO	15.18	CAP	14.11	ARI	14.47	CAN	12.02	06.58	SCO	23.35	14
15	LIB	09.23	SAG	05.56	PIS	02.48	GEM	17.19	VIR	LIB	09.36	CAP	15
16	19.32	SAG	20.38	AQU	17.04	TAU	GEM	LEO	VIR	17.53	SAG	CAP	16
17	SCO	13.24	CAP	08.25	ARI	09.02	00.01	LEO	00.33	SCO	15.55	02.59	17
18	SCO	CAP	23.33	PIS	20.38	GEM	CAN	06.02	LIB	SCO	CAP	AQU	18
19	01.17	14.32	AQU	10.10	TAU	17.33	11.17	VIR	11.55	03.00	20.38	05.31	19
20	SAG	AQU	AQU	ARI	TAU	CAN	LEO	18.42	SCO	SAG	AQU	PIS	20
21	03.28	14.06	00.31	12.30	01.53	CAN	23.51	LIB	21.32	10.14	AQU	08.06	21
22	CAP	PIS	PIS	TAU	GEM	04.27	VIR	LIB	SAG	CAP	00.04	ARI	22
23	03.19	14.00	00.53	17.04	09.49	LEO	VIR	06.16	SAG	15.17	PIS	11.26	23
24	AQU	ARI	ARI	GEM	CAN	16.59	12.33	SCO	04.37	AQU	02.35	TAU	24
25	02.41	16.19	02.35	GEM	20.42	VIR	LIB	15.28	CAP	18.03	ARI	16.03	25
26	PIS	TAU	TAU	01.07	LEO	VIR	23.40	SAG	08.33	PIS	04.55	GEM	26
27	03.33	22.34	07.28	CAN	LEO	05.26	SCO	21.15	AQU	19.08	TAU	22.29	27
28	ARI	GEM	GEM	12.31	09.21	LIB	SCO	CAP	09.39	ARI	08.13	CAN	28
29	07.34		16.28	LEO	VIR	15.37	07.38	23.27	PIS	19.59	GEM	CAN	29
30	TAU		CAN	LEO	21.20	SCO	SAG	AQU	09.15	TAU	13.48	07.15	30
31	15.26		CAN		LIB		11.48	23.11		22.26		LEO	31

SUN

mth	dy	time	→ sign
JAN	1	00.00	→ CAP
JAN	20	20.26	→ AQU
FEB	19	10.55	→ PIS
MAR	21	10.27	→ ARI
APR	20	22.05	→ TAU
MAY	21	21.44	→ GEM
JUN	22	06.02	→ CAN
JUL	23	16.51	→ LEO
AUG	23	23.35	→ VIR
SEP	23	20.46	→ LIB
OCT	24	05.35	→ SCO
NOV	23	02.36	→ SAG
DEC	22	15.44	→ CAP

MERCURY

mth	dy	time	→ sign
JAN	1	00.00	→ CAP
FEB	10	09.26	→ AQU
MAR	1	07.54	→ PIS
MAR	17	07.24	→ ARI
APR	2	13.16	→ TAU
JUN	10	01.22	→ GEM
JUN	24	23.52	→ CAN
JUL	9	08.39	→ LEO
JUL	28	01.28	→ VIR
OCT	3	08.59	→ LIB
OCT	20	16.49	→ SCO
NOV	8	22.03	→ SAG
DEC	1	16.19	→ CAP
DEC	15	13.04	→ SAG

VENUS

mth	dy	time	→ sign
JAN	1	00.00	→ AQU
APR	5	20.14	→ PIS
MAY	6	20.56	→ ARI
JUN	3	05.26	→ TAU
JUN	29	08.15	→ GEM
JUL	24	18.44	→ CAN
AUG	18	17.06	→ LEO
SEP	12	05.23	→ VIR
OCT	6	10.04	→ LIB
OCT	30	09.45	→ SCO
NOV	23	07.04	→ SAG
DEC	17	03.30	→ CAP

MARS

mth	dy	time	→ sign
JAN	1	00.00	→ VIR
JAN	11	08.48	→ LIB
FEB	25	19.13	→ VIR
JUN	23	19.10	→ LIB
AUG	17	04.27	→ SCO
OCT	1	07.42	→ SAG
NOV	11	10.22	→ CAP
DEC	20	09.00	→ AQU

SATURN

mth	dy	time	→ sign
JAN	1	00.00	→ LEO

JUPITER

mth	dy	time	→ sign
JAN	1	00.00	→ GEM
JUL	13	06.07	→ CAN

MOON

dy	jan	feb	mar	apr	may	jun	jul	aug	sep	oct	nov	dec	dy
1	18.23	LIB	LIB	02.47	CAP	09.53	ARI	05.48	CAN	16.46	LIB	SCO	1
2	VIR	LIB	09.32	SAG	CAP	PIS	20.44	GEM	00.53	VIR	23.31	18.20	2
3	VIR	02.52	SCO	11.59	00.12	12.37	TAU	11.21	LEO	VIR	SCO	SAG	3
4	06.56	SCO	20.47	CAP	AQU	ARI	TAU	CAN	10.56	04.43	SCO	SAG	4
5	LIB	13.15	SAG	17.56	04.07	14.30	00.04	18.49	VIR	LIB	11.52	04.41	5
6	18.50	SAG	SAG	AQU	PIS	TAU	GEM	LEO	22.35	17.28	SAG	CAP	6
7	SCO	19.57	05.05	20.22	05.41	16.36	04.42	LEO	LIB	SCO	22.50	12.52	7
8	SCO	CAP	CAP	PIS	ARI	GEM	CAN	04.17	LIB	SCO	CAP	AQU	8
9	03.58	22.46	09.23	20.19	06.05	20.14	11.20	VIR	11.19	06.04	CAP	18.47	9
10	SAG	AQU	AQU	ARI	TAU	CAN	LEO	15.45	SCO	SAG	07.25	PIS	10
11	09.27	22.57	10.12	19.40	07.06	CAN	20.33	LIB	23.50	17.06	AQU	22.33	11
12	CAP	PIS	PIS	TAU	GEM	02.35	VIR	LIB	SAG	CAP	12.52	ARI	12
13	11.55	22.31	09.15	20.37	10.31	LEO	VIR	04.27	SAG	CAP	PIS	ARI	13
14	AQU	ARI	ARI	GEM	CAN	12.10	08.09	SCO	10.02	00.54	15.11	00.35	14
15	12.53	23.31	08.48	GEM	17.31	VIR	LIB	16.22	CAP	AQU	ARI	TAU	15
16	PIS	TAU	TAU	00.57	LEO	VIR	20.41	SAG	16.15	04.42	15.26	01.49	16
17	14.03	TAU	10.57	CAN	LEO	00.10	SCO	SAG	AQU	PIS	TAU	GEM	17
18	ARI	03.29	GEM	19.19	04.00	LIB	SCO	01.17	18.27	05.14	15.20	03.35	18
19	16.48	GEM	16.58	LEO	VIR	12.30	07.49	CAP	PIS	ARI	GEM	CAN	19
20	TAU	10.50	CAN	20.46	16.25	SCO	SAG	06.11	18.07	04.20	16.46	07.25	20
21	21.52	CAN	CAN	VIR	LIB	23.04	15.46	AQU	ARI	TAU	CAN	LEO	21
22	GEM	20.53	02.37	VIR	LIB	SAG	CAP	07.48	17.27	04.10	21.23	14.33	22
23	GEM	LEO	LEO	09.25	04.38	SAG	20.19	PIS	TAU	GEM	LEO	VIR	23
24	05.17	LEO	14.30	LIB	SCO	06.51	AQU	07.56	18.31	06.40	LEO	VIR	24
25	CAN	08.33	VIR	21.37	15.08	CAP	22.32	ARI	GEM	CAN	05.50	01.10	25
26	14.45	VIR	VIR	SCO	SAG	12.01	PIS	08.35	22.45	12.54	VIR	LIB	26
27	LEO	21.01	03.07	SCO	23.27	AQU	23.59	TAU	CAN	LEO	17.25	13.49	27
28	LEO	LIB	LIB	08.30	CAP	15.26	ARI	11.19	CAN	22.42	LIB	SCO	28
29	01.59		LIB	SAG	CAP	PIS	ARI	GEM	06.25	VIR	LIB	SCO	29
30	VIR		15.28	17.33	05.38	18.04	02.06	16.50	LEO	VIR	06.13	02.03	30
31	14.26		SCO		AQU		TAU	CAN		10.45		SAG	31

37

SUN

mth	dy	time	→ sign
JAN	1	00.00	→ CAP
JAN	21	02.23	→ AQU
FEB	19	16.46	→ PIS
MAR	21	16.19	→ ARI
APR	21	03.57	→ TAU
MAY	22	03.39	→ GEM
JUN	22	11.55	→ CAN
JUL	23	22.46	→ LEO
AUG	24	05.26	→ VIR
SEP	24	02.37	→ LIB
OCT	24	11.22	→ SCO
NOV	23	08.25	→ SAG
DEC	22	21.26	→ CAP

MERCURY

mth	dy	time	→ sign
JAN	1	00.00	→ SAG
JAN	13	18.15	→ CAP
FEB	3	19.29	→ AQU
FEB	21	14.11	→ PIS
MAR	9	10.42	→ ARI
MAY	16	02.27	→ TAU
JUN	2	11.08	→ GEM
JUN	16	08.44	→ CAN
JUL	2	02.04	→ LEO
SEP	9	03.43	→ VIR
SEP	25	14.17	→ LIB
OCT	13	07.26	→ SCO
NOV	2	19.09	→ SAG

VENUS

mth	dy	time	→ sign
JAN	1	00.00	→ CAP
JAN	10	00.26	→ AQU
FEB	2	23.05	→ PIS
FEB	27	01.43	→ ARI
MAR	23	11.06	→ TAU
APR	17	07.03	→ GEM
MAY	12	19.02	→ CAN
JUN	8	10.33	→ LEO
JUL	7	18.16	→ VIR
NOV	9	08.05	→ LIB
DEC	9	03.26	→ SCO

MARS

mth	dy	time	→ sign
JAN	1	00.00	→ AQU
JAN	27	11.11	→ PIS
MAR	6	18.34	→ ARI
APR	15	05.19	→ TAU
MAY	26	09.29	→ GEM
JUL	8	17.13	→ CAN
AUG	23	06.26	→ LEO
OCT	10	03.48	→ VIR
NOV	30	12.00	→ LIB

SATURN

mth	dy	time	→ sign
JAN	1	00.00	→ LEO
AUG	12	13.43	→ VIR

JUPITER

mth	dy	time	→ sign
JAN	1	00.00	→ CAN
AUG	2	08.49	→ LEO

MOON

dy	jan	feb	mar	apr	may	jun	jul	aug	sep	oct	nov	dec	dy
1	12.01	AQU	17.14	ARI	15.00	CAN	19.06	LIB	19.58	16.28	AQU	PIS	1
2	CAP	07.38	PIS	04.40	GEM	04.26	VIR	23.08	SAG	CAP	19.19	09.02	2
3	19.15	PIS	18.28	TAU	15.50	LEO	VIR	SCO	SAG	CAP	PIS	ARI	3
4	AQU	10.02	ARI	04.56	CAN	10.18	03.34	SCO	08.21	03.05	23.30	11.33	4
5	AQU	ARI	19.14	GEM	19.38	VIR	LIB	11.57	CAP	AQU	ARI	TAU	5
6	00.18	12.22	TAU	07.22	LEO	19.58	15.18	SAG	17.54	09.44	ARI	11.36	6
7	PIS	TAU	21.00	CAN	LEO	LIB	SCO	23.52	AQU	PIS	00.31	GEM	7
8	04.00	15.31	GEM	12.48	03.01	LIB	SCO	CAP	23.45	12.44	TAU	10.54	8
9	ARI	GEM	GEM	LEO	VIR	08.15	04.13	CAP	PIS	ARI	00.03	CAN	9
10	07.01	19.46	01.09	21.07	13.32	SCO	SAG	08.56	PIS	13.32	GEM	11.28	10
11	TAU	CAN	CAN	VIR	LIB	21.12	15.56	AQU	02.48	TAU	00.03	LEO	11
12	09.49	CAN	07.18	VIR	LIB	SAG	CAP	14.59	ARI	13.59	CAN	15.06	12
13	GEM	01.17	LEO	07.43	01.57	SAG	CAP	PIS	04.35	GEM	02.14	VIR	13
14	12.56	LEO	15.26	LIB	SCO	09.04	01.14	18.59	TAU	15.39	LEO	22.47	14
15	CAN	08.32	VIR	19.54	14.54	CAP	AQU	ARI	06.35	CAN	07.41	LIB	15
16	17.16	VIR	VIR	SCO	SAG	18.58	08.06	22.05	GEM	19.32	VIR	LIB	16
17	LEO	18.06	01.29	SCO	SAG	AQU	PIS	TAU	09.39	LEO	16.32	10.01	17
18	23.57	LIB	LIB	08.52	03.06	AQU	13.06	TAU	CAN	LEO	LIB	SCO	18
19	VIR	LIB	13.24	SAG	CAP	02.31	ARI	01.03	14.08	01.58	LIB	22.59	19
20	VIR	06.04	SCO	21.14	13.23	PIS	16.43	GEM	LEO	VIR	03.58	SAG	20
21	09.43	SCO	SCO	CAP	AQU	07.38	TAU	04.14	20.15	10.51	SCO	SAG	21
22	LIB	18.57	02.23	CAP	20.45	ARI	19.19	CAN	VIR	LIB	16.47	11.49	22
23	22.00	SAG	SAG	07.08	PIS	10.29	GEM	08.00	VIR	21.52	SAG	CAP	23
24	SCO	SAG	14.25	AQU	PIS	TAU	21.25	LEO	04.24	SCO	SAG	23.20	24
25	SCO	06.08	CAP	13.17	00.47	11.42	CAN	13.08	LIB	SCO	05.45	AQU	25
26	10.35	CAP	23.11	PIS	ARI	GEM	CAN	VIR	14.59	10.30	CAP	AQU	26
27	SAG	13.36	AQU	15.40	02.02	12.28	00.01	20.41	SCO	SAG	17.37	08.55	27
28	20.54	AQU	AQU	ARI	TAU	CAN	LEO	LIB	SCO	23.34	AQU	PIS	28
29	CAP		03.45	15.36	01.53	14.24	04.28	LIB	03.36	CAP	AQU	16.06	29
30	03.44		PIS	TAU	GEM	LEO	VIR	07.15	SAG	CAP	03.03	ARI	30
31	AQU		04.57		02.05		12.06	SCO		11.08		20.28	31

SUN

mth	dy	time → sign
JAN	1	00.00 → CAP
JAN	21	08.05 → AQU
FEB	19	22.31 → PIS
MAR	20	21.59 → ARI
APR	20	09.36 → TAU
MAY	21	09.22 → GEM
JUN	21	17.42 → CAN
JUL	23	04.35 → LEO
AUG	23	11.23 → VIR
SEP	23	08.28 → LIB
OCT	23	17.15 → SCO
NOV	22	14.12 → SAG
DEC	22	03.15 → CAP

SATURN

mth	dy	time → sign
JAN	1	00.00 → VIR

MERCURY

mth	dy	time → sign
JAN	1	00.00 → SAG
JAN	8	05.52 → CAP
JAN	27	13.52 → AQU
FEB	13	18.42 → PIS
MAR	2	19.27 → ARI
MAR	19	16.26 → PIS
APR	17	18.07 → ARI
MAY	8	23.56 → TAU
MAY	24	00.35 → GEM
JUN	7	03.02 → CAN
JUN	26	12.32 → LEO
AUG	2	22.11 → CAN
AUG	10	09.15 → LEO
AUG	31	18.29 → VIR
SEP	16	17.15 → LIB
OCT	5	09.27 → SCO
OCT	30	12.42 → SAG
NOV	10	19.45 → SCO
DEC	11	04.36 → SAG
DEC	31	11.24 → CAP

VENUS

mth	dy	time → sign
JAN	1	00.00 → SCO
JAN	4	09.19 → SAG
JAN	29	11.55 → CAP
FEB	23	03.44 → AQU
MAR	18	15.31 → PIS
APR	12	02.11 → ARI
MAY	6	12.56 → TAU
MAY	31	00.05 → GEM
JUN	24	10.53 → CAN
JUL	18	20.28 → LEO
AUG	12	04.31 → VIR
SEP	5	11.54 → LIB
SEP	29	19.47 › SCO
OCT	24	05.13 → SAG
NOV	17	17.26 → CAP
DEC	12	11.43 → AQU

MARS

mth	dy	time → sign
JAN	1	00.00 → LIB
JAN	31	23.28 → SCO
APR	23	20.17 → LIB
JUL	10	18.11 → SCO
SEP	4	20.18 → SAG
OCT	18	13.33 → CAP
NOV	27	13.48 → AQU

JUPITER

mth	dy	time → sign
JAN	1	00.00 → LEO
AUG	27	05.38 → VIR

MOON

dy	jan	feb	mar	apr	may	jun	jul	aug	sep	oct	nov	dec	dy
1	TAU	07.54	17.22	VIR	LIB	SAG	CAP	19.18	ARI	TAU	CAN	22.45	1
2	22.13	CAN	LEO	09.59	01.37	SAG	CAP	PIS	16.19	02.32	13.37	VIR	2
3	GEM	09.05	20.40	LIB	SCO	08.05	02.30	PIS	TAU	GEM	LEO	VIR	3
4	22.19	LEO	VIR	18.33	12.59	CAP	AQU	04.10	20.58	05.29	17.03	03.50	4
5	CAN	11.18	VIR	SCO	SAG	20.38	13.37	ARI	GEM	CAN	VIR	LIB	5
6	22.30	VIR	01.53	SCO	SAG	AQU	PIS	10.56	GEM	08.14	22.23	11.51	6
7	LEO	16.19	LIB	05.42	01.39	AQU	22.38	TAU	00.04	LEO	LIB	SCO	7
8	LEO	LIB	10.10	SAG	CAP	07.43	ARI	15.15	CAN	11.23	LIB	22.09	8
9	00.46	LIB	SCO	18.25	14.09	PIS	ARI	GEM	02.02	VIR	05.49	SAG	9
10	VIR	01.13	21.35	CAP	AQU	15.57	04.45	17.11	LEO	15.44	SCO	SAG	10
11	06.47	SCO	SAG	CAP	AQU	ARI	TAU	CAN	03.54	LIB	15.26	09.59	11
12	LIB	13.21	SAG	06.32	00.32	20.35	07.40	17.41	VIR	22.14	SAG	CAP	12
13	16.57	SAG	10.25	AQU	PIS	TAU	GEM	LEO	07.10	SCO	SAG	22.39	13
14	SCO	SAG	CAP	15.50	07.23	21.57	08.03	18.27	LIB	SCO	03.03	AQU	14
15	SCO	02.14	21.58	PIS	ARI	GEM	CAN	VIR	13.19	07.30	CAP	AQU	15
16	05.43	CAP	AQU	21.29	10.35	21.26	07.32	21.28	SCO	SAG	15.44	11.03	16
17	SAG	13.20	AQU	ARI	TAU	CAN	LEO	LIB	22.58	19.16	AQU	PIS	17
18	18.34	AQU	06.25	ARI	11.13	21.01	08.12	LIB	SAG	CAP	AQU	21.30	18
19	CAP	21.39	PIS	00.08	GEM	LEO	VIR	04.12	SAG	CAP	03.39	ARI	19
20	CAP	PIS	11.43	TAU	11.01	22.44	12.02	SCO	11.09	07.52	PIS	ARI	20
21	05.39	PIS	ARI	01.14	CAN	VIR	LIB	14.45	CAP	AQU	12.45	04.22	21
22	AQU	03.36	14.58	GEM	11.49	VIR	20.03	SAG	23.33	18.57	ARI	TAU	22
23	14.34	ARI	TAU	02.22	LEO	04.05	SCO	SAG	AQU	PIS	18.02	07.15	23
24	PIS	08.05	17.25	CAN	15.10	LIB	SCO	03.22	AQU	PIS	TAU	GEM	24
25	21.32	TAU	GEM	04.48	VIR	13.19	07.31	CAP	09.57	02.52	20.00	07.13	25
26	ARI	11.42	20.02	LEO	21.50	SCO	SAG	15.36	PIS	ARI	GEM	CAN	26
27	ARI	GEM	CAN	09.21	LIB	SCO	20.22	AQU	17.35	07.33	20.12	06.16	27
28	02.43	14.40	23.20	VIR	LIB	01.15	CAP	AQU	ARI	TAU	CAN	LEO	28
29	TAU	CAN	LEO	16.18	07.32	SAG	CAP	01.55	22.49	09.59	20.32	06.37	29
30	06.05		LEO	LIB	SCO	14.06	08.37	PIS	TAU	GEM	LEO	VIR	30
31	GEM		03.48		19.20		AQU	10.03		11.34		10.06	31

39

SUN

mth	dy	time → sign
JAN	1	00.00 → CAP
JAN	20	13.57 → AQU
FEB	19	04.22 → PIS
MAR	21	03.51 → ARI
APR	20	15.34 → TAU
MAY	21	15.17 → GEM
JUN	21	23.38 → CAN
JUL	23	10.30 → LEO
AUG	23	17.17 → VIR
SEP	23	14.23 → LIB
OCT	23	23.01 → SCO
NOV	22	20.04 → SAG
DEC	22	09.07 → CAP

MERCURY

mth	dy	time → sign
JAN	1	00.00 → CAP
JAN	19	02.26 → AQU
FEB	5	10.14 → PIS
APR	14	02.14 → ARI
MAY	1	07.03 → TAU
MAY	15	10.07 → GEM
MAY	31	05.12 → CAN
AUG	8	07.41 → LEO
AUG	23	13.54 → VIR
SEP	9	02.35 → LIB
SEP	29	16.01 → SCO
DEC	5	00.25 → SAG
DEC	24	06.44 → CAP

VENUS

mth	dy	time → sign
JAN	1	00.00 → AQU
JAN	6	20.33 → PIS
FEB	2	18.34 → ARI
MAR	7	09.16 → TAU
APR	25	23.44 → ARI
JUN	2	04.21 → TAU
JUL	8	05.55 → GEM
AUG	5	14.42 → CAN
AUG	31	22.25 → LEO
SEP	26	04.08 → VIR
OCT	20	17.33 → LIB
NOV	13	21.12 → SCO
DEC	7	19.49 → SAG
DEC	31	16.31 → CAP

MARS

mth	dy	time → sign
JAN	1	00.00 → AQU
JAN	5	07.42 → PIS
FEB	13	05.23 → ARI
MAR	25	06.16 → TAU
MAY	6	01.36 → GEM
JUN	18	20.48 → CAN
AUG	3	11.14 → LEO
SEP	19	11.49 → VIR
NOV	6	16.22 → LIB
DEC	26	11.36 → SCO

SATURN

mth	dy	time → sign
JAN	1	00.00 → VIR
OCT	7	17.35 → LIB

JUPITER

mth	dy	time → sign
JAN	1	00.00 → VIR
SEP	25	23.28 → LIB

MOON

dy	jan	feb	mar	apr	may	jun	jul	aug	sep	oct	nov	dec	dy
1	LIB	10.04	SAG	CAP	21.46	ARI	TAU	03.18	13.06	LIB	16.08	08.32	1
2	17.27	SAG	SAG	01.22	PIS	ARI	15.23	CAN	VIR	LIB	SAG	CAP	2
3	SCO	22.14	05.03	AQU	PIS	01.03	GEM	03.11	13.05	01.37	23.38	18.41	3
4	SCO	CAP	CAP	13.28	08.14	TAU	16.55	LEO	LIB	SCO	CAP	AQU	4
5	03.58	CAP	17.46	PIS	ARI	05.17	CAN	02.18	15.24	06.22	CAP	AQU	5
6	SAG	10.59	AQU	23.31	15.32	GEM	16.33	VIR	SCO	SAG	10.17	07.03	6
7	16.10	AQU	AQU	ARI	TAU	06.46	LEO	02.51	21.20	14.45	AQU	PIS	7
8	CAP	23.03	05.44	ARI	19.51	CAN	16.26	LIB	SAG	22.51	PIS	19.37	8
9	CAP	PIS	PIS	07.00	GEM	07.18	VIR	06.33	SAG	CAP	PIS	ARI	9
10	04.50	PIS	15.58	TAU	22.19	LEO	18.28	SCO	06.58	02.12	ARI	ARI	10
11	AQU	09.51	ARI	12.16	CAN	08.41	LIB	13.59	CAP	AQU	10.52	05.46	11
12	17.10	ARI	ARI	GEM	CAN	VIR	23.43	SAG	19.01	14.51	ARI	TAU	12
13	PIS	18.45	00.14	15.58	00.16	12.10	SCO	SAG	AQU	PIS	20.19	12.07	13
14	PIS	TAU	TAU	CAN	LEO	LIB	SCO	00.30	AQU	PIS	TAU	GEM	14
15	04.15	TAU	06.29	18.47	02.51	18.10	08.05	CAP	07.39	02.34	TAU	15.12	15
16	ARI	00.54	GEM	LEO	VIR	SCO	SAG	12.42	PIS	ARI	02.41	CAN	16
17	12.40	GEM	10.36	21.21	06.46	SCO	18.43	AQU	19.29	12.08	GEM	16.34	17
18	TAU	03.58	CAN	VIR	LIB	02.28	CAP	AQU	ARI	TAU	06.41	LEO	18
19	17.23	CAN	12.52	VIR	12.21	SAG	CAP	01.20	ARI	19.21	CAN	18.02	19
20	GEM	04.34	LEO	00.24	SCO	12.39	06.43	PIS	05.41	GEM	09.32	VIR	20
21	18.35	LEO	14.07	LIB	19.53	CAP	AQU	13.30	TAU	GEM	LEO	20.52	21
22	CAN	04.20	VIR	04.54	SAG	CAP	19.23	ARI	13.41	00.32	12.17	LIB	22
23	17.45	VIR	15.49	SCO	SAG	00.24	PIS	ARI	GEM	CAN	VIR	LIB	23
24	LEO	05.21	LIB	11.45	05.34	AQU	PIS	00.07	19.06	04.08	15.31	01.33	24
25	17.04	LIB	19.33	SAG	CAP	13.04	07.42	TAU	CAN	LEO	LIB	SCO	25
26	VIR	09.28	SCO	21.27	17.17	PIS	ARI	07.58	21.57	06.40	19.37	08.02	26
27	18.46	SCO	SCO	CAP	AQU	PIS	17.58	GEM	LEO	VIR	SCO	SAG	27
28	LIB	17.36	02.34	CAP	AQU	01.02	TAU	12.17	23.01	08.49	SCO	16.16	28
29	LIB		SAG	09.26	05.50	ARI	TAU	CAN	VIR	LIB	01.03	CAP	29
30	00.25		12.58	AQU	PIS	10.14	00.37	13.31	23.41	11.33	SAG	CAP	30
31	SCO		CAP		17.05		GEM	LEO		SCO		02.31	31

SUN

mth	dy	time → sign
JAN	1	00.00 → CAP
JAN	20	19.46 → AQU
FEB	19	10.17 → PIS
MAR	21	09.47 → ARI
APR	20	21.29 → TAU
MAY	21	21.13 → GEM
JUN	22	05.27 → CAN
JUL	23	16.23 → LEO
AUG	23	23.04 → VIR
SEP	23	20.12 → LIB
OCT	24	04.54 → SCO
NOV	23	01.59 → SAG
DEC	22	14.57 → CAP

MERCURY

mth	dy	time → sign
JAN	1	00.00 → CAP
JAN	11	16.56 → AQU
FEB	1	17.44 → PIS
FEB	9	04.25 → AQU
MAR	18	06.33 → PIS
APR	7	10.22 → ARI
APR	22	23.17 → TAU
MAY	7	07.03 → GEM
JUN	1	03.06 → CAN
JUN	10	22.13 → GEM
JUL	13	20.02 → CAN
JUL	31	13.27 → LEO
AUG	15	08.58 → VIR
SEP	2	04.23 → LIB
OCT	1	09.14 → SCO
OCT	5	01.48 → LIB
NOV	8	22.32 → SCO
NOV	27	23.07 → SAG
DEC	17	00.28 → CAP

VENUS

mth	dy	time → sign
JAN	1	00.00 → CAP
JAN	24	13.13 → AQU
FEB	17	11.08 → PIS
MAR	13	11.32 → ARI
APR	6	15.51 → TAU
MAY	1	01.25 → GEM
MAY	25	17.04 → CAN
JUN	19	16.33 → LEO
JUL	15	03.22 → VIR
AUG	10	09.33 → LIB
SEP	7	07.14 → SCO
OCT	10	22.33 → SAG
NOV	28	21.49 → SCO

MARS

mth	dy	time → sign
JAN	1	00.00 → SCO
FEB	18	16.28 → SAG
SEP	13	13.13 → CAP
OCT	30	18.55 → AQU
DEC	11	13.23 → PIS

SATURN

mth	dy	time → sign
JAN	1	00.00 → LIB

JUPITER

mth	dy	time → sign
JAN	1	00.00 → LIB
OCT	26	19.28 → SCO

MOON

dy	jan	feb	mar	apr	may	jun	jul	aug	sep	oct	nov	dec	dy
1	AQU	10.35	ARI	20.29	09.12	22.48	07.04	20.35	CAP	AQU	07.04	03.00	1
2	14.44	ARI	ARI	GEM	CAN	VIR	LIB	SAG	18.12	11.40	ARI	TAU	2
3	PIS	22.41	04.52	GEM	14.05	VIR	10.29	SAG	AQU	PIS	19.40	13.34	3
4	PIS	TAU	TAU	03.46	LEO	01.43	SCO	03.22	AQU	PIS	TAU	GEM	4
5	03.42	TAU	14.49	CAN	17.19	LIB	15.05	CAP	05.41	00.36	TAU	21.34	5
6	ARI	07.42	GEM	08.13	VIR	04.42	SAG	12.19	PIS	ARI	06.33	CAN	6
7	14.58	GEM	21.19	LEO	19.21	SCO	21.12	AQU	18.29	13.20	GEM	CAN	7
8	TAU	12.30	CAN	10.09	LIB	08.18	CAP	23.23	ARI	TAU	15.23	03.33	8
9	22.27	CAN	CAN	VIR	21.00	SAG	CAP	PIS	ARI	TAU	CAN	LEO	9
10	GEM	13.39	00.09	10.36	SCO	13.30	05.27	PIS	07.24	00.44	22.05	08.09	10
11	GEM	LEO	LEO	LIB	23.32	CAP	AQU	12.05	TAU	GEM	LEO	VIR	11
12	01.47	12.58	00.22>VIR	11.07	SAG	21.25	16.16	ARI	18.50	09.52	LEO	11.39	12
13	CAN	VIR	23.44	SCO	SAG	AQU	PIS	ARI	GEM	CAN	02.36	LIB	13
14	02.21	12.34	LIB	13.25	04.25	AQU	PIS	00.57	GEM	16.01	VIR	14.14	14
15	LEO	LIB	LIB	SAG	CAP	08.25	04.59	TAU	03.13	LEO	05.01	SCO	15
16	02.13	14.23	00.13	19.01	12.46	PIS	ARI	11.42	CAN	19.04	LIB	16.28	16
17	VIR	SCO	SCO	CAP	AQU	21.12	17.28	GEM	07.48	VIR	05.59	SAG	17
18	03.21	19.31	03.33	CAP	AQU	ARI	TAU	18.40	LEO	19.43	SCO	19.34	18
19	LIB	SAG	SAG	04.28	00.21	ARI	TAU	CAN	09.08	LIB	06.52	CAP	19
20	07.02	SAG	10.41	AQU	PIS	09.09	03.10	21.45	VIR	19.26	SAG	CAP	20
21	SCO	04.05	CAP	16.44	13.13	TAU	GEM	LEO	08.43	SCO	09.31	01.08	21
22	13.33	CAP	21.18	PIS	ARI	18.02	08.56	22.16	LIB	20.05	CAP	AQU	22
23	SAG	15.12	AQU	PIS	ARI	GEM	CAN	VIR	08.27	SAG	15.36	10.14	23
24	22.28	AQU	AQU	05.37	00.46	23.27	11.26	22.05	SCO	23.33	AQU	PIS	24
25	CAP	AQU	09.56	ARI	TAU	CAN	LEO	LIB	10.11	CAP	AQU	22.22	25
26	CAP	03.45	PIS	17.08	09.29	CAN	12.21	23.02	SAG	CAP	01.39	ARI	26
27	09.16	PIS	22.49	TAU	GEM	02.28	VIR	SCO	15.15	07.00	PIS	ARI	27
28	AQU	16.41	ARI	TAU	15.26	LEO	13.26	SCO	CAP	AQU	14.20	11.13	28
29	21.34		ARI	02.19	CAN	04.36	LIB	02.26	CAP	18.07	ARI	TAU	29
30	PIS		10.38	GEM	19.34	VIR	15.59	SAG	00.02	PIS	ARI	22.02	30
31	PIS		TAU		LEO		SCO	08.53		PIS		GEM	31

SUN

mth	dy	time → sign
JAN	1	00.00 → CAP
JAN	21	01.33 → AQU
FEB	19	16.02 → PIS
MAR	21	15.29 → ARI
APR	21	03.03 → TAU
MAY	22	02.45 → GEM
JUN	22	11.05 → CAN
JUL	23	22.02 → LEO
AUG	24	04.52 → VIR
SEP	24	02.04 → LIB
OCT	24	10.54 → SCO
NOV	23	07.51 → SAG
DEC	22	20.52 → CAP

MERCURY

mth	dy	time → sign
JAN	1	00.00 → CAP
JAN	4	23.42 → AQU
FEB	6	15.34 → CAP
FEB	13	23.23 → AQU
MAR	13	02.38 → PIS
MAR	30	18.11 → ARI
APR	14	12.56 → TAU
MAY	1	05.18 → GEM
JUL	8	12.44 → CAN
JUL	23	02.07 → LEO
AUG	7	13.34 → VIR
AUG	27	22.27 → LIB
OCT	4	11.53 → VIR
OCT	11	22.24 → LIB
NOV	2	02.47 → SCO
NOV	20	16.24 → SAG
DEC	10	00.17 → CAP

VENUS

mth	dy	time → sign
JAN	1	00.00 → SCO
JAN	2	07.28 → SAG
FEB	6	14.33 → CAP
MAR	6	05.38 → AQU
APR	1	05.13 → PIS
APR	26	13.36 → ARI
MAY	21	14.52 → TAU
JUN	15	11.46 → GEM
JUL	10	04.38 → CAN
AUG	3	16.42 → LEO
AUG	27	23.56 → VIR
SEP	21	03.29 → LIB
OCT	15	04.46 → SCO
NOV	8	05.24 → SAG
DEC	2	06.05 → CAP
DEC	26	08.05 → AQU

MARS

mth	dy	time → sign
JAN	1	00.00 → PIS
JAN	21	10.23 → ARI
MAR	4	00.42 → TAU
APR	16	02.43 → GEM
MAY	30	21.28 → CAN
JUL	16	01.12 → LEO
SEP	1	00.50 → VIR
OCT	18	04.12 → LIB
DEC	4	02.22 → SCO

SATURN

mth	dy	time → sign
JAN	1	00.00 → LIB
DEC	20	04.09 → SCO

JUPITER

mth	dy	time → sign
JAN	1	00.00 → SCO
NOV	24	17.20 → SAG

MOON

dy	jan	feb	mar	apr	may	jun	jul	aug	sep	oct	nov	dec	dy
1	GEM	LEO	LEO	LIB	SCO	CAP	AQU	08.11	TAU	GEM	05.00	VIR	1
2	05.39	22.12	08.41	19.26	05.59	21.04	13.28	ARI	16.50	12.00	LEO	VIR	2
3	CAN	VIR	VIR	SCO	SAG	AQU	PIS	20.22	GEM	CAN	12.07	00.24	3
4	10.34	23.38	09.00	19.33	07.14	23.51	TAU	GEM	21.14	VIR	LIB	4
5	LEO	LIB	LIB	SAG	CAP	04.43	ARI	TAU	03.59	LEO	15.24	02.14	5
6	13.59	LIB	09.16	22.19	12.05	PIS	ARI	08.47	CAN	LEO	LIB	SCO	6
7	VIR	01.37	SCO	CAP	AQU	16.02	12.25	GEM	11.54	02.41	15.37	01.57	7
8	16.59	SCO	11.05	CAP	21.06	ARI	TAU	19.08	LEO	VIR	SCO	SAG	8
9	LIB	04.59	SAG	04.48	PIS	ARI	TAU	CAN	16.16	04.35	14.37	01.31	9
10	20.04	SAG	15.34	AQU	PIS	04.56	00.37	CAN	VIR	LIB	SAG	CAP	10
11	SCO	10.08	CAP	14.51	09.12	TAU	GEM	02.19	18.03	04.25	14.37	03.10	11
12	23.34	CAP	23.02	PIS	ARI	17.03	10.34	LEO	LIB	SCO	CAP	AQU	12
13	SAG	17.18	AQU	PIS	22.14	GEM	CAN	06.44	18.47	04.08	17.39	08.35	13
14	SAG	AQU	AQU	03.08	TAU	GEM	07.53	VIR	SCO	SAG	AQU	PIS	14
15	03.56	AQU	09.08	ARI	TAU	03.10	LEO	09.27	20.05	05.43	AQU	18.08	15
16	CAP	02.43	PIS	16.07	10.27	CAN	23.10	LIB	SAG	CAP	00.46	ARI	16
17	10.05	PIS	21.06	TAU	GEM	11.11	VIR	11.38	23.14	10.29	PIS	ARI	17
18	AQU	14.20	ARI	TAU	21.03	LEO	VIR	SCO	CAP	AQU	11.25	06.21	18
19	18.57	ARI	ARI	04.33	CAN	17.22	03.05	14.12	CAP	18.43	ARI	TAU	19
20	PIS	ARI	10.00	GEM	CAN	VIR	LIB	SAG	04.53	PIS	23.53	19.03	20
21	PIS	03.15	TAU	15.28	05.40	21.44	06.08	17.49	AQU	PIS	TAU	GEM	21
22	06.37	TAU	22.33	CAN	LEO	LIB	SCO	CAP	13.03	05.33	TAU	GEM	22
23	ARI	15.31	GEM	23.50	11.54	LIB	08.43	23.03	PIS	ARI	12.32	06.40	23
24	19.34	GEM	GEM	LEO	VIR	00.20	SAG	AQU	23.23	17.48	GEM	CAN	24
25	TAU	GEM	09.05	LEO	15.25	SCO	11.32	AQU	ARI	TAU	GEM	16.40	25
26	TAU	00.57	CAN	04.56	LIB	01.46	CAP	06.25	ARI	TAU	00.28	LEO	26
27	07.07	CAN	16.13	VIR	16.35	SAG	15.42	PIS	11.22	06.29	CAN	LEO	27
28	GEM	06.30	LEO	06.48	SCO	03.20	AQU	16.15	TAU	GEM	11.01	00.51	28
29	15.19		19.36	LIB	16.37	CAP	22.23	ARI	TAU	18.39	LEO	VIR	29
30	CAN		VIR	06.32	SAG	06.44	PIS	ARI	00.06	CAN	19.19	06.51	30
31	19.57		20.06		17.27		PIS	04.12		CAN		LIB	31

SUN

mth	dy	time → sign
JAN	1	00.00 → CAP
JAN	21	07.29 → AQU
FEB	19	21.53 → PIS
MAR	20	21.20 → ARI
APR	20	08.56 → TAU
MAY	21	08.40 → GEM
JUN	21	16.57 → CAN
JUL	23	03.56 → LEO
AUG	23	10.49 → VIR
SEP	23	07.59 → LIB
OCT	23	16.44 → SCO
NOV	22	13.44 → SAG
DEC	22	02.47 → CAP

MERCURY

mth	dy	time → sign
JAN	1	00.00 → CAP
FEB	14	03.16 → AQU
MAR	5	05.51 → PIS
MAR	21	15.39 → ARI
APR	5	16.23 → TAU
JUN	13	01.44 → GEM
JUN	29	13.22 → CAN
JUL	13	15.35 → LEO
JUL	30	16.48 → VIR
OCT	7	04.14 → LIB
OCT	24	15.59 → SCO
NOV	12	12.05 → SAG
DEC	2	23.41 → CAP
DEC	31	15.55 → SAG

VENUS

mth	dy	time → sign
JAN	1	00.00 → AQU
JAN	19	13.43 → PIS
FEB	13	04.13 → ARI
MAR	9	11.52 → TAU
APR	5	06.48 → GEM
MAY	6	01.49 → CAN
SEP	8	21.45 → LEO
OCT	7	14.17 → VIR
NOV	2	14.46 → LIB
NOV	27	11.46 → SCO
DEC	21	19.57 → SAG

MARS

mth	dy	time → sign
JAN	1	00.00 → SCO
JAN	19	19.20 → SAG
MAR	6	19.13 → CAP
APR	24	15.50 → AQU
JUN	24	16.21 → PIS
AUG	24	15.44 → AQU
OCT	19	18.49 → PIS
DEC	19	11.18 → ARI

SATURN

mth	dy	time → sign
JAN	1	00.00 → SCO
APR	6	08.33 → LIB
SEP	13	22.19 → SCO

JUPITER

mth	dy	time → sign
JAN	1	00.00 → SAG
DEC	18	06.13 → CAP

MOON

dy	jan	feb	mar	apr	may	jun	jul	aug	sep	oct	nov	dec	dy
1	10.23	21.03	CAP	PIS	ARI	14.47	09.28	LEO	02.38	SCO	00.39	AQU	1
2	SCO	CAP	07.11	PIS	20.37	GEM	CAN	13.05	LIB	15.54	CAP	13.38	2
3	11.48	23.43	AQU	03.45	TAU	GEM	21.11	VIR	06.54	SAG	02.53	PIS	3
4	SAG	AQU	12.44	ARI	TAU	03.27	LEO	20.20	SCO	18.02	AQU	20.10	4
5	12.22	AQU	PIS	14.11	08.48	CAN	LEO	LIB	10.00	CAP	07.34	ARI	5
6	CAP	04.12	20.26	TAU	GEM	15.29	07.15	LIB	SAG	21.19	PIS	ARI	6
7	13.54	PIS	ARI	TAU	21.30	LEO	VIR	01.24	12.41	AQU	14.39	05.33	7
8	AQU	11.36	ARI	02.13	CAN	LEO	14.55	SCO	CAP	AQU	ARI	TAU	8
9	18.13	ARI	06.35	GEM	CAN	01.41	LIB	04.32	15.33	02.06	23.44	16.52	9
10	PIS	22.09	TAU	14.53	09.30	VIR	19.36	SAG	AQU	PIS	TAU	GEM	10
11	PIS	TAU	18.43	CAN	LEO	08.41	SCO	06.20	19.17	08.31	TAU	GEM	11
12	02.22	TAU	GEM	CAN	18.57	LIB	21.32	CAP	PIS	ARI	10.34	05.21	12
13	ARI	10.35	GEM	02.15	VIR	11.57	SAG	07.52	PIS	16.50	GEM	CAN	13
14	13.48	GEM	07.08	LEO	VIR	SCO	21.49	AQU	00.42	TAU	22.57	18.13	14
15	TAU	22.34	CAN	10.21	00.28	12.17	CAP	10.28	ARI	TAU	CAN	LEO	15
16	TAU	CAN	17.31	VIR	LIB	SAG	22.11	PIS	08.39	03.23	CAN	LEO	16
17	02.28	CAN	LEO	14.27	02.10	11.28	AQU	15.32	TAU	GEM	11.51	06.07	17
18	GEM	08.09	LEO	LIB	SCO	CAP	AQU	ARI	19.24	15.48	LEO	VIR	18
19	14.05	LEO	00.27	15.24	01.33	11.42	00.30	23.54	GEM	CAN	23.11	15.15	19
20	CAN	14.45	VIR	SCO	SAG	AQU	PIS	TAU	GEM	CAN	VIR	LIB	20
21	23.33	VIR	04.00	15.04	00.48	14.52	06.12	TAU	07.54	04.21	VIR	20.26	21
22	LEO	18.57	LIB	SAG	CAP	PIS	ARI	11.14	CAN	LEO	06.51	SCO	22
23	LEO	LIB	05.27	15.33	02.04	21.56	15.36	GEM	19.52	14.33	LIB	21.55	23
24	06.49	21.47	SCO	CAP	AQU	ARI	TAU	23.48	LEO	VIR	10.17	SAG	24
25	VIR	SCO	06.29	18.30	06.49	ARI	TAU	CAN	LEO	20.49	SCO	21.18	25
26	12.14	SCO	SAG	AQU	PIS	08.27	03.36	CAN	05.06	LIB	10.38	CAP	26
27	LIB	00.16	08.37	AQU	15.16	TAU	GEM	11.19	VIR	23.26	SAG	20.41	27
28	16.09	SAG	CAP	00.39	ARI	20.51	16.11	LEO	10.53	SCO	09.57	AQU	28
29	SCO	03.12	12.47	PIS	ARI	GEM	CAN	20.19	LIB	SCO	CAP	22.06	29
30	18.52		AQU	09.39	02.23	GEM	CAN	VIR	14.00	00.03	10.25	PIS	30
31	SAG		19.13		TAU		03.38	VIR		SAG		PIS	31

SUN

mth	dy	time → sign
JAN	1	00.00 → CAP
JAN	20	13.22 → AQU
FEB	19	03.43 → PIS
MAR	21	03.13 → ARI
APR	20	14.51 → TAU
MAY	21	14.35 → GEM
JUN	21	22.52 → CAN
JUL	23	09.47 → LEO
AUG	23	16.33 → VIR
SEP	23	13.44 → LIB
OCT	23	22.31 → SCO
NOV	22	19.37 → SAG
DEC	22	08.36 → CAP

MERCURY

mth	dy	time → sign
JAN	1	00.00 → SAG
JAN	14	07.12 → CAP
FEB	7	08.12 → AQU
FEB	25	16.53 → PIS
MAR	13	12.36 → ARI
APR	1	15.24 → TAU
APR	15	23.15 → ARI
MAY	17	01.32 → TAU
JUN	6	15.25 → GEM
JUN	20	23.07 → CAN
JUL	5	17.55 → LEO
JUL	26	11.46 → VIR
AUG	27	06.26 → LEO
SEP	11	05.09 → VIR
SEP	29	18.05 → LIB
OCT	17	03.52 → SCO
NOV	5	18.55 → SAG

VENUS

mth	dy	time → sign
JAN	1	00.00 → SAG
JAN	14	22.26 → CAP
FEB	7	23.13 → AQU
MAR	4	00.21 → PIS
MAR	28	03.03 → ARI
APR	21	08.17 → TAU
MAY	15	16.04 → GEM
JUN	9	02.16 → CAN
JUL	3	14.33 → LEO
JUL	28	05.25 → VIR
AUG	22	00.29 → LIB
SEP	16	02.07 → SCO
OCT	11	14.10 → SAG
NOV	6	22.35 → CAP
DEC	5	15.11 → AQU

MARS

mth	dy	time → sign
JAN	1	00.00 → ARI
FEB	5	10.02 → TAU
MAR	24	00.33 → GEM
MAY	9	22.52 → CAN
JUN	26	09.19 → LEO
AUG	12	21.12 → VIR
SEP	28	19.18 → LIB
NOV	13	14.16 → SCO
DEC	28	00.23 → SAG

SATURN

mth	dy	time → sign
JAN	1	00.00 → SCO

JUPITER

mth	dy	time → sign
JAN	1	00.00 → CAP

MOON

dy	jan	feb	mar	apr	may	jun	jul	aug	sep	oct	nov	dec	dy
1	02.57	TAU	13.26	CAN	LEO	12.30	03.33	17.46	AQU	15.06	TAU	GEM	1
2	ARI	05.32	22.32	18.38	LIB	SCO	CAP	04.02	PIS	ARI	09.44	03.19	2
3	11.31	GEM	GEM	LEO	VIR	18.21	06.55	17.40	PIS	18.20	GEM	CAN	3
4	TAU	18.11	01.38	LEO	VIR	SCO	SAG	AQU	05.02	TAU	19.06	15.13	4
5	22.52	CAN	CAN	09.55	03.26	20.33	07.24	17.23	ARI	TAU	CAN	LEO	5
6	GEM	CAN	14.22	VIR	LIB	SAG	CAP	PIS	08.27	00.35	CAN	LEO	6
7	GEM	06.50	LEO	18.05	08.22	20.45	06.49	18.46	TAU	GEM	07.16	04.14	7
8	11.32	LEO	LEO	LIB	SCO	CAP	AQU	ARI	15.39	10.33	LEO	VIR	8
9	CAN	18.01	01.24	23.04	10.27	20.54	07.06	23.24	GEM	CAN	20.07	15.52	9
10	CAN	VIR	VIR	SCO	SAG	AQU	PIS	TAU	GEM	23.09	VIR	LIB	10
11	00.14	VIR	09.44	SCO	11.30	22.40	09.53	TAU	02.35	LEO	VIR	LIB	11
12	LEO	03.06	LIB	02.05	CAP	PIS	ARI	07.57	CAN	LEO	06.52	00.03	12
13	11.55	LIB	15.37	SAG	13.08	PIS	16.05	GEM	15.30	11.43	LIB	SCO	13
14	VIR	09.54	SCO	04.32	AQU	03.03	TAU	19.39	LEO	VIR	14.05	04.23	14
15	21.33	SCO	19.51	CAP	16.23	ARI	TAU	CAN	LEO	21.57	SCO	SAG	15
16	LIB	14.28	SAG	07.23	PIS	10.15	01.37	CAN	03.56	LIB	18.13	05.59	16
17	LIB	SAG	23.07	AQU	21.34	TAU	GEM	08.41	VIR	LIB	SAG	CAP	17
18	04.11	17.02	CAP	11.02	ARI	19.57	13.33	LEO	14.18	05.12	20.38	06.35	18
19	SCO	CAP	CAP	PIS	ARI	GEM	CAN	21.13	LIB	SCO	CAP	AQU	19
20	07.34	18.21	01.51	15.45	04.41	GEM	CAN	VIR	22.18	10.11	22.48	07.51	20
21	SAG	AQU	AQU	ARI	TAU	07.36	02.32	VIR	SCO	SAG	AQU	PIS	21
22	08.22	19.36	04.33	22.00	13.50	CAN	LEO	08.05	SCO	13.57	AQU	10.57	22
23	CAP	PIS	PIS	TAU	GEM	20.30	15.17	LIB	04.18	CAP	01.37	ARI	23
24	08.09	22.21	08.04	TAU	GEM	LEO	VIR	16.44	SAG	17.12	PIS	16.25	24
25	AQU	ARI	ARI	06.33	01.07	LEO	VIR	SCO	08.37	AQU	05.31	TAU	25
26	08.45	ARI	13.34	GEM	CAN	09.21	02.30	22.50	CAP	20.14	ARI	TAU	26
27	PIS	04.04	TAU	17.45	13.59	VIR	LIB	SAG	11.29	PIS	10.46	00.18	27
28	11.59	TAU	22.08	CAN	LEO	20.16	15.17	SAG	AQU	23.24	TAU	GEM	28
29	ARI		GEM	CAN	LEO	LIB	10.56	02.19	13.19	ARI	17.50	10.26	29
30	18.58		GEM	06.36	02.35	LIB	15.56	CAP	PIS	ARI	GEM	CAN	30
31	TAU		09.42		VIR		SAG	03.41		03.29		22.26	31

SUN

mth	dy	time → sign
JAN	1	00.00 → CAP
JAN	20	19.11 → AQU
FEB	19	09.35 → PIS
MAR	21	09.03 → ARI
APR	20	20.36 → TAU
MAY	21	20.13 → GEM
JUN	22	04.30 → CAN
JUL	23	15.27 → LEO
AUG	23	22.14 → VIR
SEP	23	19.26 → LIB
OCT	24	04.19 → SCO
NOV	23	01.26 → SAG
DEC	22	14.35 → CAP

MERCURY

mth	dy	time → sign
JAN	1	00.00 → SAG
JAN	11	07.29 → CAP
JAN	31	10.03 → AQU
FEB	17	21.33 → PIS
MAR	6	02.57 → ARI
MAY	13	10.55 → TAU
MAY	29	13.51 → GEM
JUN	12	10.06 → CAN
JUN	29	05.01 → LEO
SEP	5	20.35 → VIR
SEP	21	20.57 → LIB
OCT	9	21.55 → SCO
OCT	31	11.01 → SAG
NOV	28	05.06 → SCO
DEC	13	20.36 → SAG

VENUS

mth	dy	time → sign
JAN	1	00.00 → AQU
APR	6	03.56 → PIS
MAY	6	15.11 → ARI
JUN	2	19.59 → TAU
JUN	28	21.09 → GEM
JUL	24	06.42 → CAN
AUG	18	04.34 → LEO
SEP	11	16.36 → VIR
OCT	5	21.08 → LIB
OCT	29	20.50 → SCO
NOV	22	18.13 → SAG
DEC	16	14.46 → CAP

MARS

mth	dy	time → sign
JAN	1	00.00 → SAG
FEB	9	03.23 → CAP
MAR	23	04.26 → AQU
MAY	3	17.20 → PIS
JUN	15	00.36 → ARI
AUG	1	09.19 → TAU

SATURN

mth	dy	time → sign
JAN	1	00.00 → SCO
DEC	2	22.49 → SAG

JUPITER

mth	dy	time → sign
JAN	1	00.00 → CAP
JAN	6	01.19 → AQU

MOON

dy	jan	feb	mar	apr	may	jun	jul	aug	sep	oct	nov	dec	dy
1	LEO	VIR	12.03	SCO	23.32	AQU	20.14	TAU	01.48	LEO	VIR	22.39	1
2	LEO	06.11	LIB	12.08	CAP	11.53	ARI	11.24	CAN	LEO	03.22	SCO	2
3	11.26	LIB	22.28	SAG	CAP	PIS	23.59	GEM	13.01	07.49	LIB	SCO	3
4	VIR	16.39	SCO	18.04	03.31	14.45	TAU	20.08	LEO	VIR	14.37	07.32	4
5	23.44	SCO	SCO	CAP	AQU	ARI	TAU	CAN	LEO	20.28	SCO	SAG	5
6	LIB	SCO	06.40	22.01	06.32	18.28	05.57	CAN	01.40	LIB	23.51	13.52	6
7	LIB	00.02	SAG	AQU	PIS	TAU	GEM	07.12	VIR	LIB	SAG	CAP	7
8	09.19	SAG	12.06	AQU	08.55	23.43	14.16	LEO	14.23	07.59	SAG	18.22	8
9	SCO	03.49	CAP	00.03	ARI	GEM	CAN	19.39	LIB	SCO	07.11	AQU	9
10	15.02	CAP	14.40	PIS	11.33	GEM	CAN	VIR	LIB	17.54	CAP	21.44	10
11	SAG	04.37	AQU	01.02	TAU	07.16	00.50	VIR	02.15	SAG	12.42	PIS	11
12	17.09	AQU	15.03	ARI	15.46	CAN	LEO	08.26	SCO	SAG	AQU	PIS	12
13	CAP	03.57	PIS	02.31	GEM	17.28	13.07	LIB	12.22	01.47	16.22	00.33	13
14	17.07	PIS	14.52	TAU	22.52	LEO	VIR	20.18	SAG	CAP	PIS	ARI	14
15	AQU	03.47	ARI	06.20	CAN	LEO	VIR	SCO	19.37	07.02	18.28	03.23	15
16	16.48	ARI	16.06	GEM	CAN	05.48	01.52	SCO	CAP	AQU	ARI	TAU	16
17	PIS	06.08	TAU	13.55	09.20	VIR	LIB	05.39	23.23	09.30	19.54	06.59	17
18	18.03	TAU	20.42	CAN	LEO	18.18	13.08	SAG	AQU	PIS	TAU	GEM	18
19	ARI	12.22	GEM	CAN	21.54	LIB	SCO	11.24	AQU	09.56	22.10	12.20	19
20	22.16	GEM	GEM	01.07	VIR	LIB	21.10	CAP	00.06>PIS	ARI	GEM	CAN	20
21	TAU	22.28	05.30	LEO	VIR	04.41	SAG	13.31	23.20	10.01	GEM	20.17	21
22	TAU	CAN	CAN	13.59	10.04	SCO	SAG	AQU	ARI	TAU	02.54	LEO	22
23	05.55	CAN	17.35	VIR	LIB	11.34	01.28	13.14	23.12	11.50	CAN	LEO	23
24	GEM	11.00	LEO	VIR	19.42	SAG	CAP	PIS	TAU	GEM	11.10	07.02	24
25	16.30	LEO	LEO	01.52	SCO	15.18	02.48	12.30	TAU	17.08	LEO	VIR	25
26	CAN	23.59	06.36	LIB	SCO	CAP	AQU	ARI	01.50	CAN	22.36	19.31	26
27	CAN	VIR	VIR	11.19	02.14	17.02	02.46	13.24	GEM	CAN	VIR	LIB	27
28	04.52	VIR	18.27	SCO	SAG	AQU	PIS	TAU	08.35	02.31	VIR	LIB	28
29	LEO		LIB	18.19	06.24	18.14	03.13	17.39	CAN	LEO	11.14	07.28	29
30	17.49		LIB	SAG	CAP	PIS	ARI	GEM	19.10	14.43	LIB	SCO	30
31	VIR		04.17		09.19		05.46	GEM		VIR		16.50	31

SUN

mth	dy	time	→ sign
JAN	1	00.00	→ CAP
JAN	21	01.11	→ AQU
FEB	19	15.34	→ PIS
MAR	21	14.57	→ ARI
APR	21	02.32	→ TAU
MAY	22	02.06	→ GEM
JUN	22	10.22	→ CAN
JUL	23	21.15	→ LEO
AUG	24	04.05	→ VIR
SEP	24	01.15	→ LIB
OCT	24	10.07	→ SCO
NOV	23	07.11	→ SAG
DEC	22	20.20	→ CAP

MERCURY

mth	dy	time	→ sign
JAN	1	00.00	→ SAG
JAN	5	01.55	→ CAP
JAN	24	01.11	→ AQU
FEB	10	04.27	→ PIS
APR	17	12.24	→ ARI
MAY	6	11.28	→ TAU
MAY	21	00.07	→ GEM
JUN	4	13.38	→ CAN
JUN	28	19.34	→ LEO
JUL	14	04.08	→ LEO
AUG	12	03.46	→ LEO
AUG	28	23.07	→ VIR
SEP	14	01.34	→ LIB
OCT	3	08.38	→ SCO
DEC	9	09.24	→ SAG
DEC	29	01.46	→ CAP

VENUS

mth	dy	time	→ sign
JAN	1	00.00	→ CAP
JAN	9	11.44	→ AQU
FEB	2	10.36	→ PIS
FEB	26	13.18	→ ARI
MAR	22	22.57	→ TAU
APR	16	19.23	→ GEM
MAY	12	08.34	→ CAN
JUN	8	02.52	→ LEO
JUL	7	18.55	→ VIR
NOV	9	13.28	→ LIB
DEC	8	21.28	→ SCO

MARS

mth	dy	time	→ sign
JAN	1	00.00	→ TAU
FEB	22	00.32	→ GEM
APR	17	01.20	→ CAN
JUN	6	11.21	→ LEO
JUL	25	07.33	→ VIR
SEP	10	14.07	→ LIB
OCT	26	00.01	→ SCO
DEC	8	11.13	→ SAG

SATURN

mth	dy	time	→ sign
JAN	1	00.00	→ SAG

JUPITER

mth	dy	time	→ sign
JAN	1	00.00	→ AQU
JAN	18	11.59	→ PIS
JUN	6	10.01	→ ARI
SEP	11	03.55	→ PIS

MOON

dy	jan	feb	mar	apr	may	jun	jul	aug	sep	oct	nov	dec	dy
1	SAG	12.22	AQU	10.30	TAU	09.50	00.48	VIR	00.36	SAG	22.26	10.37	1
2	22.51	AQU	AQU	ARI	20.52	CAN	LEO	04.44	SCO	SAG	AQU	PIS	2
3	CAP	13.07	00.05>PIS	09.36	GEM	15.37	09.27	LIB	13.10	07.13	AQU	14.20	3
4	CAP	PIS	23.19	TAU	23.51	LEO	VIR	17.16	SAG	CAP	03.56	ARI	4
5	02.10	13.19	ARI	10.25	CAN	LEO	20.47	SCO	23.28	15.07	PIS	15.47	5
6	AQU	ARI	23.07	GEM	CAN	00.54	LIB	SCO	CAP	AQU	05.53	TAU	6
7	04.05	14.50	TAU	14.42	06.39	VIR	LIB	05.14	CAP	18.50	ARI	16.10	7
8	PIS	TAU	TAU	CAN	LEO	12.48	09.17	SAG	05.50	PIS	05.37	GEM	8
9	05.59	18.54	01.29	23.00	17.03	LIB	SCO	14.23	AQU	19.15	TAU	17.11	9
10	ARI	GEM	GEM	LEO	VIR	LIB	20.37	CAP	08.16	ARI	05.03	CAN	10
11	08.56	GEM	07.29	LEO	VIR	01.16	SAG	19.46	PIS	18.17	GEM	20.31	11
12	TAU	01.51	CAN	10.19	05.27	SCO	SAG	08.18	AQU	TAU	06.15	LEO	12
13	13.30	CAN	16.52	VIR	LIB	12.16	05.06	22.04	ARI	18.12	CAN	03.25	13
14	GEM	11.11	LEO	22.53	17.52	SAG	CAP	PIS	08.03	GEM	10.48	VIR	14
15	19.59	LEO	LEO	LIB	SCO	20.51	10.31	22.57	TAU	20.50	LEO	VIR	15
16	CAN	22.15	04.22	LIB	SCO	CAP	AQU	ARI	09.29	CAN	19.14	13.55	16
17	CAN	VIR	VIR	11.20	04.58	CAP	13.43	ARI	GEM	CAN	VIR	LIB	17
18	04.31	VIR	16.48	SCO	SAG	03.05	PIS	00.12	13.49	03.07	VIR	LIB	18
19	LEO	10.31	LIB	22.49	14.11	AQU	15.58	TAU	CAN	LEO	06.41	02.31	19
20	15.10	LIB	LIB	SAG	CAP	07.25	ARI	03.08	21.13	12.43	LIB	SCO	20
21	VIR	23.08	05.21	SAG	21.16	PIS	18.24	GEM	LEO	VIR	19.26	14.59	21
22	VIR	SCO	SCO	08.35	AQU	10.29	TAU	08.19	LEO	VIR	SCO	SAG	22
23	03.27	SCO	17.06	CAP	AQU	ARI	21.46	CAN	07.01	00.28	SCO	SAG	23
24	LIB	10.35	SAG	15.43	02.01	12.54	GEM	15.39	VIR	LIB	07.53	01.38	24
25	15.54	SAG	SAG	AQU	PIS	TAU	GEM	LEO	18.30	13.08	SAG	CAP	25
26	SCO	18.56	02.39	19.37	04.37	15.26	02.31	LEO	LIB	SCO	19.01	09.54	26
27	SCO	CAP	CAP	PIS	ARI	GEM	CAN	00.55	LIB	SCO	CAP	AQU	27
28	02.21	23.14	08.39	20.43	05.50	19.04	09.00	VIR	07.05	01.48	CAP	16.00	28
29	SAG		AQU	ARI	TAU	CAN	LEO	12.02	SCO	SAG	04.06	PIS	29
30	09.12		10.53	20.28	07.02	CAN	17.42	LIB	19.54	13.22	AQU	20.19	30
31	CAP		PIS		GEM		VIR	LIB		CAP		ARI	31

SUN

mth	dy	time → sign
JAN	1	00.00 → CAP
JAN	21	06.58 → AQU
FEB	19	21.17 → PIS
MAR	20	20.44 → ARI
APR	20	08.18 → TAU
MAY	21	07.52 → GEM
JUN	21	16.07 → CAN
JUL	23	03.02 → LEO
AUG	23	09.54 → VIR
SEP	23	07.09 → LIB
OCT	23	15.55 → SCO
NOV	22	13.02 → SAG
DEC	22	02.05 → CAP

SATURN

mth	dy	time → sign
JAN	1	00.00 → SAG

MERCURY

mth	dy	time → sign
JAN	1	00.00 → CAP
JAN	16	13.33 → AQU
FEB	3	10.20 → PIS
FEB	29	06.00 → AQU
MAR	18	02.46 → PIS
APR	11	01.55 → ARI
APR	27	10.38 → TAU
MAY	11	12.08 → GEM
MAY	28	23.05 → CAN
AUG	4	20.02 → LEO
AUG	19	16.59 → VIR
SEP	5	16.22 → LIB
SEP	27	18.13 → SCO
OCT	24	21.46 → LIB
NOV	11	09.05 → SCO
DEC	1	16.58 → SAG
DEC	20	19.35 → CAP

VENUS

mth	dy	time → sign
JAN	1	00.00 → SCO
JAN	4	00.02 → SAG
JAN	29	01.11 → CAP
FEB	22	16.15 → AQU
MAR	18	03.26 → PIS
APR	11	13.35 → ARI
MAY	6	00.01 → TAU
MAY	30	11.00 → GEM
JUN	23	21.44 → CAN
JUL	18	07.16 → LEO
AUG	11	15.27 → VIR
SEP	4	23.03 → LIB
SEP	29	07.28 → SCO
OCT	23	17.13 → SAG
NOV	17	06.06 → CAP
DEC	12	01.22 → AQU

MARS

mth	dy	time → sign
JAN	1	00.00 → SAG
JAN	19	02.22 → CAP
FEB	28	06.21 → AQU
APR	7	14.39 → PIS
MAY	16	21.35 → ARI
JUN	26	09.15 → TAU
AUG	9	04.01 → GEM
OCT	3	03.40 → CAN
DEC	20	05.35 → GEM

JUPITER

mth	dy	time → sign
JAN	1	00.00 → PIS
JAN	23	02.43 → ARI
JUN	4	04.38 → TAU

MOON

dy	jan	feb	mar	apr	may	jun	jul	aug	sep	oct	nov	dec	dy
1	23.15	GEM	CAN	11.53	03.36	SCO	SAG	AQU	17.26	03.59	14.40	01.28	1
2	TAU	11.21	22.38	VIR	LIB	10.38	05.23	AQU	ARI	TAU	CAN	LEO	2
3	TAU	CAN	LEO	21.47	15.38	SAG	CAP	05.34	20.07	05.09	17.14	05.16	3
4	01.20	15.53	LEO	LIB	SCO	23.00	15.32	PIS	TAU	GEM	LEO	VIR	4
5	GEM	LEO	05.51	LIB	SCO	CAP	AQU	10.33	22.43	07.21	22.41	12.52	5
6	03.28	22.09	VIR	09.27	04.32	CAP	23.23	ARI	GEM	CAN	VIR	LIB	6
7	CAN	VIR	15.04	SCO	SAG	09.42	PIS	14.18	GEM	11.18	VIR	23.46	7
8	06.52	VIR	LIB	22.20	17.09	AQU	PIS	TAU	01.51	LEO	07.05	SCO	8
9	LEO	07.03	LIB	SAG	CAP	17.55	05.04	17.22	CAN	17.13	LIB	SCO	9
10	12.53	LIB	02.31	SAG	CAP	PIS	ARI	GEM	05.49	VIR	17.53	12.29	10
11	VIR	18.41	SCO	10.56	03.58	23.14	08.49	20.03	LEO	VIR	SCO	SAG	11
12	22.18	SCO	15.24	CAP	AQU	ARI	TAU	CAN	11.01	01.14	SCO	SAG	12
13	LIB	SCO	SAG	21.07	11.35	ARI	11.00	22.57	VIR	LIB	06.20	01.29	13
14	LIB	07.32	SAG	AQU	PIS	01.45	GEM	LEO	18.12	11.29	SAG	CAP	14
15	10.26	SAG	03.33	AQU	15.30	TAU	12.20	LEO	LIB	SCO	19.25	13.36	15
16	SCO	18.54	CAP	03.19	ARI	02.25	CAN	03.07	LIB	23.44	CAP	AQU	16
17	23.06	CAP	12.31	PIS	16.25	GEM	14.06	VIR	04.04	SAG	CAP	23.49	17
18	SAG	CAP	AQU	05.40	TAU	02.34	LEO	09.53	SCO	SAG	07.40	PIS	18
19	SAG	02.47	17.20	ARI	15.56	CAN	17.53	LIB	16.23	12.50	AQU	PIS	19
20	09.49	AQU	PIS	05.36	GEM	04.02	VIR	19.57	SAG	CAP	17.19	07.15	20
21	CAP	07.05	18.54	TAU	15.57	LEO	VIR	SCO	SAG	CAP	PIS	ARI	21
22	17.27	PIS	ARI	05.09	CAN	08.27	01.02	SCO	05.16	00.33	23.14	11.25	22
23	AQU	09.09	19.06	GEM	18.17	VIR	LIB	08.29	CAP	AQU	ARI	TAU	23
24	22.24	ARI	TAU	06.14	LEO	16.43	11.46	SAG	16.01	08.50	ARI	12.40	24
25	PIS	10.42	19.53	CAN	LEO	LIB	SCO	20.59	AQU	PIS	01.30	GEM	25
26	PIS	TAU	GEM	10.11	00.07	LIB	SCO	CAP	23.01	13.04	TAU	12.17	26
27	01.48	13.07	22.42	LEO	VIR	04.15	00.34	CAP	PIS	ARI	01.23	CAN	27
28	ARI	GEM	CAN	17.28	09.36	SCO	SAG	06.57	PIS	14.16	GEM	12.07	28
29	04.42	17.04	CAN	VIR	LIB	17.13	12.47	AQU	02.31	TAU	00.43	LEO	29
30	TAU		04.04	VIR	21.40	SAG	CAP	13.31	ARI	14.11	CAN	14.12	30
31	07.47		LEO		SCO		22.33	PIS		GEM		VIR	31

SUN

mth	dy	time → sign
JAN	1	00.00 → CAP
JAN	20	12.44 → AQU
FEB	19	03.09 → PIS
MAR	21	02.33 → ARI
APR	20	14.11 → TAU
MAY	21	13.49 → GEM
JUN	21	22.03 → CAN
JUL	23	08.54 → LEO
AUG	23	15.43 → VIR
SEP	23	12.53 → LIB
OCT	23	21.42 → SCO
NOV	22	18.47 → SAG
DEC	22	07.54 → CAP

MERCURY

mth	dy	time → sign
JAN	1	00.00 → CAP
JAN	8	08.06 → AQU
MAR	16	01.07 → PIS
APR	3	21.22 → ARI
APR	19	00.22 → TAU
MAY	3	21.33 → GEM
JUL	11	21.06 → CAN
JUL	27	15.13 → LEO
AUG	11	14.45 → VIR
AUG	30	06.03 → LIB
NOV	5	19.28 → SCO
NOV	24	12.04 → SAG
DEC	13	14.44 → CAP

VENUS

mth	dy	time → sign
JAN	1	00.00 → AQU
JAN	6	12.02 → PIS
FEB	2	14.36 → ARI
MAR	8	07.33 → TAU
APR	20	02.05 → ARI
JUN	3	09.44 → TAU
JUL	8	02.02 → GEM
AUG	5	05.39 → CAN
AUG	31	11.22 → LEO
SEP	25	16.15 → VIR
OCT	20	05.12 → LIB
NOV	13	08.36 → SCO
DEC	7	07.05 → SAG
DEC	31	03.46 → CAP

MARS

mth	dy	time → sign
JAN	1	00.00 → GEM
MAR	10	23.29 → CAN
MAY	13	02.33 → LEO
JUL	4	10.20 → VIR
AUG	21	21.41 → LIB
OCT	6	12.17 → SCO
NOV	18	13.13 → SAG
DEC	29	10.40 → CAP

SATURN

mth	dy	time → sign
JAN	1	00.00 → SAG
MAR	15	13.59 → CAP
MAY	5	04.28 → SAG
NOV	30	04.03 → CAP

JUPITER

mth	dy	time → sign
JAN	1	00.00 → TAU
JUN	12	12.12 → GEM

MOON

dy	jan	feb	mar	apr	may	jun	jul	aug	sep	oct	nov	dec	dy
1	20.08	SCO	SCO	07.03	03.19	PIS	19.31	GEM	LEO	VIR	SCO	SAG	1
2	LIB	SCO	10.03	CAP	AQU	05.58	TAU	08.15	18.27	06.09	SCO	23.25	2
3	LIB	01.59	SAG	19.18	13.51	ARI	22.14	CAN	VIR	LIB	04.47	CAP	3
4	06.10	SAG	22.55	AQU	PIS	10.34	GEM	08.11	20.51	11.40	SAG	CAP	4
5	SCO	15.00	CAP	AQU	20.51	TAU	22.21	LEO	LIB	SCO	15.57	11.57	5
6	18.50	CAP	CAP	04.52	ARI	11.57	CAN	08.22	LIB	20.18	CAP	AQU	6
7	SAG	CAP	10.44	PIS	ARI	GEM	21.37	VIR	02.20	SAG	CAP	AQU	7
8	SAG	02.34	AQU	10.58	00.18	11.35	LEO	10.56	SCO	SAG	04.33	0.27	8
9	07.51	AQU	19.44	ARI	TAU	CAN	22.10	LIB	11.38	07.49	AQU	PIS	9
10	CAP	11.43	PIS	14.17	01.22	11.24	VIR	17.22	SAG	CAP	16.30	10.57	10
11	19.33	PIS	PIS	TAU	GEM	LEO	VIR	SCO	23.45	20.25	PIS	ARI	11
12	AQU	18.41	01.51	16.12	01.44	13.20	01.54	SCO	CAP	AQU	PIS	17.50	12
13	AQU	ARI	ARI	GEM	CAN	VIR	LIB	03.44	CAP	AQU	01.43	TAU	13
14	05.21	ARI	06.05	18.04	03.03	18.38	09.44	SAG	12.17	07.40	ARI	20.49	14
15	PIS	00.02	TAU	CAN	LEO	LIB	SCO	16.21	AQU	PIS	07.19	GEM	15
16	13.07	TAU	09.23	20.50	06.33	LIB	21.00	CAP	23.07	16.02	TAU	21.05	16
17	ARI	04.01	GEM	LEO	VIR	03.32	SAG	CAP	PIS	ARI	09.53	CAN	17
18	18.37	GEM	12.24	LEO	12.52	SCO	SAG	04.50	PIS	21.29	GEM	20.34	18
19	TAU	06.45	CAN	01.05	LIB	15.02	09.48	AQU	07.30	TAU	10.53	LEO	19
20	21.43	CAN	15.27	VIR	21.54	SAG	CAP	15.46	ARI	TAU	CAN	21.22	20
21	GEM	08.41	LEO	07.13	SCO	SAG	22.20	PIS	13.45	00.54	11.58	VIR	21
22	22.52	LEO	19.05	LIB	SCO	03.45	AQU	PIS	TAU	GEM	LEO	VIR	22
23	CAN	10.58	VIR	15.34	09.04	CAP	AQU	00.47	18.25	03.24	14.32	01.03	23
24	23.16	VIR	VIR	SCO	SAG	16.24	09.39	ARI	GEM	CAN	VIR	LIB	24
25	LEO	15.15	00.11	SCO	21.34	AQU	PIS	07.55	21.52	05.55	19.23	08.12	25
26	LEO	LIB	LIB	02.16	CAP	AQU	19.13	TAU	CAN	LEO	LIB	SCO	26
27	00.47	22.54	07.49	SAG	CAP	03.58	ARI	13.03	CAN	09.08	LIB	18.12	27
28	VIR	SCO	SCO	14.43	10.17	PIS	ARI	GEM	00.28	VIR	02.40	SAG	28
29	05.19		18.26	CAP	AQU	13.20	02.25	16.04	LEO	13.39	SCO	SAG	29
30	LIB		SAG	CAP	21.37	ARI	TAU	CAN	02.52	LIB	12.08	05.56	30
31	13.57		SAG		PIS		06.43	17.26		20.02		CAP	31

48

SUN

mth	dy	time → sign
JAN	1	00.00 → CAP
JAN	20	18.31 → AQU
FEB	19	09.00 → PIS
MAR	21	08.30 → ARI
APR	20	20.03 → TAU
MAY	21	19.42 → GEM
JUN	22	03.53 → CAN
JUL	23	14.48 → LEO
AUG	23	21.26 → VIR
SEP	23	18.36 → LIB
OCT	24	03.22 → SCO
NOV	23	00.35 → SAG
DEC	22	13.37 → CAP

SATURN

mth	dy	time → sign
JAN	1	00.00 → CAP

MERCURY

mth	dy	time → sign
JAN	1	00.00 → CAP
JAN	2	10.25 → AQU
JAN	23	00.32 → CAP
FEB	15	15.09 → AQU
MAR	9	22.37 → PIS
MAR	26	23.36 → ARI
APR	10	17.05 → TAU
MAY	1	05.33 → GEM
MAY	17	11.06 → TAU
JUN	14	20.09 → GEM
JUL	4	22.11 → CAN
JUL	19	02.44 → LEO
AUG	4	02.36 → VIR
AUG	26	18.04 → LIB
SEP	20	02.13 → VIR
OCT	11	04.42 → LIB
OCT	29	14.35 → SCO
NOV	17	05.35 → SAG
DEC	6	20.57 → CAP

VENUS

mth	dy	time → sign
JAN	1	00.00 → CAP
JAN	24	00.24 → AQU
FEB	16	22.14 → PIS
MAR	12	22.33 → ARI
APR	6	02.57 → TAU
APR	30	12.37 → GEM
MAY	25	04.36 → CAN
JUN	19	04.39 → LEO
JUL	14	16.32 → VIR
AUG	10	00.54 → LIB
SEP	7	04.06 → SCO
OCT	12	02.45 → SAG
NOV	22	07.43 → SCO

MARS

mth	dy	time → sign
JAN	1	00.00 → CAP
FEB	6	18.26 → AQU
MAR	17	05.57 → PIS
APR	24	17.22 → ARI
JUN	3	03.14 → TAU
JUL	14	12.54 → GEM
AUG	28	11.28 → CAN
OCT	20	14.45 → LEO

JUPITER

mth	dy	time → sign
JAN	1	00.00 → GEM
JUN	26	22.33 → CAN

MOON

dy	jan	feb	mar	apr	may	jun	jul	aug	sep	oct	nov	dec	dy
1	18.25	PIS	PIS	TAU	GEM	LEO	VIR	SCO	20.33	15.09	PIS	ARI	1
2	AQU	PIS	06.07	TAU	13.55	LEO	09.47	SCO	CAP	AQU	23.36	18.33	2
3	AQU	00.23	ARI	03.42	CAN	00.37	LIB	04.22	CAP	AQU	ARI	TAU	3
4	07.03	ARI	15.19	GEM	16.32	VIR	14.53	SAG	08.27	03.48	ARI	TAU	4
5	PIS	09.49	TAU	08.11	LEO	04.04	SCO	14.34	AQU	PIS	09.33	01.32	5
6	18.27	TAU	22.16	CAN	19.13	LIB	22.49	CAP	21.05	15.52	TAU	GEM	6
7	ARI	16.08	GEM	11.09	VIR	09.30	SAG	CAP	PIS	ARI	16.58	05.31	7
8	ARI	GEM	GEM	LEO	22.30	SCO	SAG	02.24	PIS	ARI	GEM	CAN	8
9	02.55	18.55	02.34	13.11	LIB	16.56	08.47	AQU	09.21	02.14	22.05	07.55	9
10	TAU	CAN	CAN	VIR	LIB	SAG	CAP	15.03	ARI	TAU	CAN	LEO	10
11	07.34	19.00	04.25	15.17	03.07	SAG	20.23	PIS	20.19	10.29	CAN	10.04	11
12	GEM	LEO	LEO	LIB	18.44	02.20	AQU	PIS	TAU	GEM	01.47	VIR	12
13	08.35	18.14	04.54	18.45	09.39	CAP	AQU	03.33	TAU	16.29	LEO	13.05	13
14	CAN	VIR	VIR	SCO	SAG	13.39	08.57	ARI	05.01	CAN	04.42	LIB	14
15	07.37	18.50	05.43	SCO	18.41	AQU	PIS	14.38	GEM	20.19	VIR	17.19	15
16	LEO	LIB	LIB	00.49	CAP	AQU	21.25	TAU	10.43	LEO	07.25	SCO	16
17	06.57	22.45	08.46	SAG	CAP	02.12	ARI	22.44	CAN	22.26	LIB	22.55	17
18	VIR	SCO	SCO	10.07	06.03	PIS	ARI	GEM	13.18	VIR	10.36	SAG	18
19	08.44	SCO	15.24	CAP	AQU	14.15	07.54	GEM	LEO	23.43	SCO	SAG	19
20	LIB	06.49	SAG	21.58	18.33	ARI	TAU	03.02	13.45	LIB	15.00	06.11	20
21	14.25	SAG	SAG	AQU	PIS	23.25	14.38	CAN	VIR	LIB	SAG	CAP	21
22	SCO	18.13	01.40	AQU	PIS	TAU	GEM	03.58	13.43	01.32	21.42	15.43	22
23	23.56	CAP	CAP	10.23	05.55	TAU	17.22	LEO	LIB	SCO	CAP	AQU	23
24	SAG	CAP	14.05	PIS	ARI	05.00	CAN	03.13	15.07	05.23	CAP	AQU	24
25	SAG	06.57	AQU	21.10	14.15	GEM	17.16	VIR	SCO	SAG	07.23	03.35	25
26	11.53	AQU	AQU	ARI	TAU	06.57	LEO	02.58	19.34	12.27	AQU	PIS	26
27	CAP	19.13	02.24	ARI	19.09	CAN	16.34	LIB	SAG	CAP	19.32	16.29	27
28	CAP	PIS	PIS	05.08	GEM	07.06	VIR	05.11	SAG	22.54	PIS	ARI	28
29	00.35		13.00	TAU	21.26	LEO	17.18	SCO	03.48	AQU	PIS	ARI	29
30	AQU		ARI	10.26	CAN	07.28	LIB	11.04	CAP	AQU	08.06	03.51	30
31	12.59		21.24		22.47		21.06	SAG		11.23		TAU	31

SUN

mth	dy	time	→	sign
JAN	1	00.00	→	CAP
JAN	21	00.18	→	AQU
FEB	19	14.40	→	PIS
MAR	21	14.06	→	ARI
APR	21	01.40	→	TAU
MAY	22	01.15	→	GEM
JUN	22	09.28	→	CAN
JUL	23	20.21	→	LEO
AUG	24	03.10	→	VIR
SEP	24	00.23	→	LIB
OCT	24	09.15	→	SCO
NOV	23	06.25	→	SAG
DEC	22	19.30	→	CAP

MERCURY

mth	dy	time	→	sign
JAN	1	00.00	→	CAP
FEB	11	12.27	→	AQU
MAR	2	17.28	→	PIS
MAR	18	19.31	→	ARI
APR	3	13.38	→	TAU
JUN	11	07.26	→	GEM
JUN	26	13.49	→	CAN
JUL	10	19.56	→	LEO
JUL	28	23.24	→	VIR
OCT	4	18.27	→	LIB
OCT	22	02.08	→	SCO
NOV	10	04.27	→	SAG
DEC	2	00.00	→	CAP
DEC	20	07.59	→	SAG

VENUS

mth	dy	time	→	sign
JAN	1	00.00	→	SCO
JAN	3	20.02	→	SAG
FEB	6	12.25	→	CAP
MAR	5	21.45	→	AQU
MAR	31	19.04	→	PIS
APR	26	02.10	→	ARI
MAY	21	02.38	→	TAU
JUN	14	23.04	→	GEM
JUL	9	15.35	→	CAN
AUG	3	03.29	→	LEO
AUG	27	10.42	→	VIR
SEP	20	14.15	→	LIB
OCT	14	15.45	→	SCO
NOV	7	16.32	→	SAG
DEC	1	17.29	→	CAP
DEC	25	19.44	→	AQU

MARS

mth	dy	time	→	sign
JAN	1	00.00	→	LEO
FEB	16	14.21	→	CAN
MAR	30	03.43	→	LEO
JUN	10	14.55	→	VIR
AUG	1	16.32	→	LIB
SEP	17	08.51	→	SCO
OCT	30	12.41	→	SAG
DEC	10	03.11	→	CAP

SATURN

mth	dy	time	→	sign
JAN	1	00.00	→	CAP

JUPITER

mth	dy	time	→	sign
JAN	1	00.00	→	CAN
JUL	17	07.46	→	LEO

MOON

dy	jan	feb	mar	apr	may	jun	jul	aug	sep	oct	nov	dec	dy
1	11.34	CAN	14.25	VIR	11.26	SAG	18.56	PIS	20.59	15.03	CAN	LEO	1
2	GEM	03.24	LEO	00.49	SCO	03.07	AQU	PIS	TAU	GEM	13.39	00.16	2
3	15.21	LEO	14.21	LIB	13.14	CAP	AQU	01.10	TAU	GEM	LEO	VIR	3
4	CAN	02.56	VIR	00.50	SAG	10.23	05.10	ARI	08.43	00.38	18.08	03.44	4
5	16.32	VIR	13.32	SCO	17.35	AQU	PIS	14.05	GEM	CAN	VIR	LIB	5
6	LEO	02.54	LIB	02.52	CAP	21.01	17.40	TAU	17.15	06.49	20.03	05.43	6
7	17.06	LIB	14.03	SAG	CAP	PIS	ARI	TAU	CAN	LEO	LIB	SCO	7
8	VIR	05.04	SCO	08.20	01.37	PIS	ARI	01.01	21.47	09.34	20.21	07.04	8
9	18.48	SCO	17.30	CAP	AQU	09.44	06.14	GEM	LEO	VIR	SCO	SAG	9
10	LIB	10.21	SAG	17.40	13.02	ARI	TAU	08.10	23.04	09.50	20.39	09.18	10
11	22.40	SAG	SAG	AQU	PIS	21.54	16.14	CAN	VIR	LIB	SAG	CAP	11
12	SCO	18.39	00.39	AQU	PIS	TAU	GEM	11.31	22.43	09.17	22.52	14.10	12
13	SCO	CAP	CAP	05.49	01.57	TAU	22.30	LEO	LIB	SCO	CAP	AQU	13
14	04.50	CAP	11.03	PIS	ARI	07.21	CAN	12.25	22.40	09.51	CAP	22.50	14
15	SAG	05.14	AQU	18.48	13.54	GEM	CAN	VIR	SCO	SAG	04.40	PIS	15
16	13.02	AQU	23.26	ARI	TAU	13.38	01.41	12.45	SCO	13.18	AQU	PIS	16
17	CAP	17.23	PIS	ARI	23.26	CAN	LEO	LIB	00.39	CAP	14.32	10.49	17
18	23.04	PIS	PIS	06.50	GEM	17.36	03.21	14.10	SAG	20.39	PIS	ARI	18
19	AQU	PIS	12.24	TAU	GEM	LEO	VIR	SCO	05.48	AQU	PIS	23.45	19
20	AQU	06.21	ARI	16.56	06.26	20.32	05.06	17.47	CAP	AQU	03.08	TAU	20
21	10.55	ARI	ARI	GEM	CAN	VIR	LIB	SAG	14.18	07.32	ARI	TAU	21
22	PIS	18.54	00.44	GEM	11.27	23.23	07.56	23.58	AQU	PIS	16.00	10.59	22
23	23.55	TAU	TAU	00.42	LEO	LIB	SCO	CAP	AQU	20.21	TAU	GEM	23
24	ARI	TAU	11.19	CAN	15.07	LIB	12.18	CAP	01.28	ARI	TAU	19.21	24
25	ARI	05.13	GEM	06.04	VIR	02.34	SAG	08.38	PIS	ARI	03.12	CAN	25
26	12.10	GEM	19.04	LEO	17.51	SCO	18.21	AQU	14.09	09.12	GEM	CAN	26
27	TAU	11.47	CAN	09.10	LIB	06.26	CAP	19.27	ARI	TAU	12.09	01.16	27
28	21.18	CAN	23.29	VIR	20.08	SAG	CAP	PIS	ARI	20.48	CAN	LEO	28
29	GEM		LEO	10.35	SCO	11.35	02.24	PIS	03.07	GEM	19.06	05.41	29
30	GEM		LEO	LIB	22.48	CAP	AQU	07.56	TAU	GEM	LEO	VIR	30
31	02.09		00.58		SAG		12.45	ARI		06.26		09.17	31

SUN

mth	dy	time	→ sign
JAN	1	00.00	→ CAP
JAN	21	06.05	→ AQU
FEB	19	20.28	→ PIS
MAR	20	19.54	→ ARI
APR	20	07.27	→ TAU
MAY	21	07.06	→ GEM
JUN	21	15.21	→ CAN
JUL	23	02.18	→ LEO
AUG	23	09.06	→ VIR
SEP	23	06.16	→ LIB
OCT	23	15.02	→ SCO
NOV	22	12.10	→ SAG
DEC	22	01.17	→ CAP

MERCURY

mth	dy	time	→ sign
JAN	1	00.00	→ SAG
JAN	14	12.45	→ CAP
FEB	5	02.36	→ AQU
FEB	23	00.52	→ PIS
MAR	9	20.21	→ ARI
MAY	15	22.47	→ TAU
JUN	2	23.02	→ GEM
JUN	16	22.30	→ CAN
JUL	2	08.16	→ LEO
JUL	27	20.38	→ VIR
AUG	10	07.31	→ LEO
SEP	9	07.18	→ VIR
SEP	26	01.15	→ LIB
OCT	13	15.42	→ SCO
NOV	2	20.28	→ SAG

VENUS

mth	dy	time	→ sign
JAN	1	00.00	→ AQU
JAN	19	01.54	→ PIS
FEB	12	16.58	→ ARI
MAR	9	02.07	→ TAU
APR	5	00.18	→ GEM
MAY	6	09.04	→ CAN
JUL	13	10.32	→ GEM
JUL	28	12.36	→ CAN
SEP	8	19.42	→ LEO
OCT	7	05.46	→ VIR
NOV	2	04.04	→ LIB
NOV	27	00.06	→ SCO
DEC	21	07.45	→ SAG

MARS

mth	dy	time	→ sign
JAN	1	00.00	→ CAP
JAN	18	00.37	→ AQU
FEB	25	02.36	→ PIS
APR	3	07.02	→ ARI
MAY	12	10.51	→ TAU
JUN	22	09.11	→ GEM
AUG	4	19.52	→ CAN
SEP	20	19.48	→ LEO
NOV	13	21.22	→ VIR

SATURN

mth	dy	time	→ sign
JAN	1	00.00	→ CAP
FEB	24	02.22	→ AQU
AUG	13	11.12	→ CAP
NOV	20	02.25	→ AQU

JUPITER

mth	dy	time	→ sign
JAN	1	00.00	→ LEO
AUG	11	07.36	→ VIR

MOON

dy	jan	feb	mar	apr	may	jun	jul	aug	sep	oct	nov	dec	dy
1	LIB	SAG	07.05	AQU	22.46	TAU	GEM	15.57	VIR	18.44	SAG	16.47	1
2	12.23	SAG	CAP	05.05	ARI	TAU	GEM	LEO	08.32	SCO	04.54	AQU	2
3	SCO	01.39	14.00	PIS	ARI	06.32	00.07	21.15	LIB	19.05	CAP	22.08	3
4	15.15	CAP	AQU	16.54	11.46	GEM	CAN	VIR	10.08	SAG	08.06	PIS	4
5	SAG	07.49	23.14	ARI	TAU	17.21	08.18	VIR	SCO	21.00	AQU	PIS	5
6	18.37	AQU	PIS	ARI	TAU	CAN	LEO	00.56	12.00	CAP	15.06	07.35	6
7	CAP	16.15	PIS	05.47	00.20	CAN	14.33	LIB	SAG	CAP	PIS	ARI	7
8	23.45	PIS	10.35	TAU	GEM	02.14	VIR	03.49	15.11	01.44	PIS	19.41	8
9	AQU	PIS	ARI	18.27	11.34	09.06	19.12	SCO	CAP	AQU	01.24	TAU	9
10	AQU	03.15	23.17	GEM	CAN	09.06	LIB	06.32	20.17	09.27	ARI	TAU	10
11	07.47	ARI	TAU	GEM	20.48	VIR	22.29	SAG	AQU	PIS	13.33	08.24	11
12	PIS	16.06	TAU	05.46	LEO	13.41	SCO	09.38	AQU	19.36	TAU	GEM	12
13	19.07	TAU	12.03	CAN	LEO	LIB	SCO	CAP	03.31	ARI	TAU	20.28	13
14	ARI	TAU	GEM	14.23	03.13	16.00	00.38	13.54	PIS	ARI	02.13	CAN	14
15	ARI	04.27	22.46	LEO	VIR	SCO	SAG	AQU	13.01	07.24	GEM	CAN	15
16	08.05	GEM	CAN	19.24	06.32	16.45	02.37	20.13	ARI	TAU	14.32	07.12	16
17	TAU	14.02	CAN	VIR	LIB	SAG	CAP	PIS	ARI	20.04	CAN	LEO	17
18	19.47	CAN	05.54	21.01	07.16	17.31	05.44	PIS	00.34	GEM	CAN	16.09	18
19	GEM	19.47	LEO	LIB	SCO	CAP	AQU	05.18	TAU	GEM	01.35	VIR	19
20	GEM	LEO	09.18	20.34	06.48	20.12	11.34	ARI	13.14	08.26	LEO	22.33	20
21	04.22	22.25	VIR	SCO	SAG	AQU	PIS	16.56	GEM	CAN	10.08	LIB	21
22	CAN	VIR	09.55	19.57	07.12	AQU	20.53	TAU	GEM	18.56	VIR	LIB	22
23	09.40	23.23	LIB	SAG	CAP	02.25	ARI	TAU	01.13	15.08	LIB	01.53	23
24	LEO	LIB	09.35	21.15	10.31	PIS	ARI	05.33	CAN	LIB	LIB	SCO	24
25	12.47	LIB	SCO	CAP	AQU	12.34	08.54	GEM	10.32	02.02	16.38	02.42	25
26	VIR	00.21	10.06	CAP	17.58	ARI	TAU	16.50	LEO	VIR	SCO	SAG	26
27	15.02	SCO	SAG	02.04	PIS	ARI	21.27	CAN	16.08	05.15	15.58	02.31	27
28	LIB	02.38	13.06	AQU	PIS	01.08	GEM	CAN	VIR	LIB	SAG	CAP	28
29	17.43	SAG	CAP	10.56	05.09	TAU	GEM	01.03	18.22	05.30	15.16	03.23	29
30	SCO		19.30	PIS	ARI	13.35	08.07	LEO	LIB	SCO	CAP	AQU	30
31	21.08		AQU		18.05		CAN	05.58		04.40		07.16	31

SUN

mth	dy	time → sign
JAN	1	00.00 → CAP
JAN	20	11.53 → AQU
FEB	19	02.17 → PIS
MAR	21	01.42 → ARI
APR	20	13.18 → TAU
MAY	21	12.59 → GEM
JUN	21	21.12 → CAN
JUL	23	08.05 → LEO
AUG	23	14.52 → VIR
SEP	23	12.01 → LIB
OCT	23	20.48 → SCO
NOV	22	17.57 → SAG
DEC	22	06.58 → CAP

MERCURY

mth	dy	time → sign
JAN	1	00.00 → SAG
JAN	8	10.26 → CAP
JAN	27	22.39 → AQU
FEB	14	05.06 → PIS
MAR	3	10.49 → ARI
MAR	25	21.52 → PIS
APR	17	15.27 → ARI
MAY	10	07.42 → TAU
MAY	25	14.26 → GEM
JUN	8	14.12 → CAN
JUN	27	01.11 → LEO
SEP	2	05.44 → VIR
SEP	18	03.48 → LIB
OCT	6	15.04 → SCO
OCT	30	04.28 → SAG
NOV	16	02.07 → SCO
DEC	12	03.43 → SAG

VENUS

mth	dy	time → sign
JAN	1	00.00 → SAG
JAN	14	09.54 → CAP
FEB	7	10.30 → AQU
MAR	3	11.22 → PIS
MAR	27	13.58 → ARI
APR	20	19.03 → TAU
MAY	15	02.47 → GEM
JUN	8	13.01 → CAN
JUL	3	01.29 → LEO
JUL	27	16.47 → VIR
AUG	21	12.23 → LIB
SEP	15	14.58 → SCO
OCT	11	04.32 → SAG
NOV	6	16.05 → CAP
DEC	5	18.00 → AQU

MARS

mth	dy	time → sign
JAN	1	00.00 → VIR
JUL	6	22.07 → LIB
AUG	26	06.30 → SCO
OCT	9	11.38 → SAG
NOV	19	07.12 → CAP
DEC	28	03.48 → AQU

SATURN

mth	dy	time → sign
JAN	1	00.00 → AQU

JUPITER

mth	dy	time → sign
JAN	1	00.00 → VIR
SEP	10	05.23 → LIB

MOON

dy	jan	feb	mar	apr	may	jun	jul	aug	sep	oct	nov	dec	dy
1	PIS	10.40	TAU	GEM	23.06	VIR	LIB	SAG	07.00	PIS	13.53	06.45	1
2	15.13	TAU	03.50	LEO	23.15	10.57	SCO	21.40	AQU	22.51	TAU	GEM	2
3	ARI	23.06	07.18	CAN	LEO	LIB	SCO	CAP	09.46	ARI	TAU	18.53	3
4	ARI	GEM	GEM	15.17	08.41	LIB	12.32	22.22	PIS	ARI	00.05	CAN	4
5	02.32	GEM	19.43	LEO	VIR	02.25	SAG	AQU	14.15	06.18	GEM	CAN	5
6	TAU	11.13	CAN	23.33	14.17	SCO	12.18	AQU	ARI	TAU	12.05	07.49	6
7	15.19	CAN	CAN	VIR	LIB	02.32	CAP	00.11	21.35	16.18	CAN	LEO	7
8	GEM	21.18	06.14	VIR	16.08	SAG	12.05	PIS	TAU	GEM	CAN	20.00	8
9	GEM	LEO	LEO	04.00	SCO	01.33	AQU	04.40	TAU	GEM	00.59	VIR	9
10	03.15	LEO	13.42	LIB	15.43	CAP	14.01	ARI	08.00	04.29	LEO	VIR	10
11	CAN	04.33	VIR	05.32	SAG	01.41	PIS	12.45	GEM	CAN	12.24	05.18	11
12	13.26	VIR	18.03	SCO	15.15	AQU	19.33	TAU	20.26	17.02	VIR	LIB	12
13	LEO	09.59	LIB	05.52	CAP	04.49	ARI	23.57	CAN	LEO	20.13	10.27	13
14	21.43	LIB	20.28	SAG	16.47	PIS	ARI	GEM	CAN	LEO	LIB	SCO	14
15	VIR	13.46	SCO	06.53	AQU	11.50	04.49	GEM	08.30	03.24	23.52	11.48	15
16	VIR	SCO	22.18	CAP	21.34	ARI	TAU	12.35	LEO	VIR	SCO	SAG	16
17	04.03	16.42	SAG	10.02	PIS	22.12	16.46	CAN	18.16	10.07	SCO	11.08	17
18	LIB	SAG	SAG	AQU	PIS	TAU	GEM	CAN	VIR	LIB	00.36	CAP	18
19	08.26	19.24	00.47	15.54	05.45	TAU	GEM	00.22	VIR	13.27	SAG	10.37	19
20	SCO	CAP	CAP	PIS	ARI	10.25	05.25	LEO	00.51	SCO	00.23	AQU	20
21	10.54	22.29	04.39	PIS	16.26	GEM	CAN	10.07	LIB	14.54	CAP	12.15	21
22	SAG	AQU	AQU	00.14	TAU	23.06	17.19	VIR	05.01	SAG	01.21	PIS	22
23	12.17	AQU	10.16	ARI	TAU	CAN	LEO	17.29	SCO	16.13	AQU	17.15	23
24	CAP	02.57	PIS	10.31	04.31	CAN	LEO	LIB	07.49	CAP	04.52	ARI	24
25	13.56	PIS	17.49	TAU	GEM	11.17	03.35	22.44	SAG	18.48	PIS	ARI	25
26	AQU	09.42	ARI	22.18	17.12	LEO	VIR	SCO	10.23	AQU	11.13	01.42	26
27	17.33	ARI	ARI	GEM	CAN	22.01	11.44	SCO	CAP	23.17	ARI	TAU	27
28	PIS	19.20	03.32	GEM	CAN	VIR	LIB	02.21	13.29	PIS	20.04	12.43	28
29	PIS		TAU	10.58	05.33	VIR	17.21	SAG	AQU	PIS	TAU	GEM	29
30	00.23		15.13	CAN	LEO	06.11	SCO	04.52	17.27	05.40	TAU	GEM	30
31	ARI		GEM		16.06		20.27	CAP		ARI		01.07	31

SUN

mth	dy	time → sign
JAN	1	00.00 → CAP
JAN	20	17.37 → AQU
FEB	19	08.02 → PIS
MAR	21	07.27 → ARI
APR	20	19.00 → TAU
MAY	21	18.35 → GEM
JUN	22	02.48 → CAN
JUL	23	13.42 → LEO
AUG	23	20.32 → VIR
SEP	23	17.45 → LIB
OCT	24	02.36 → SCO
NOV	22	23.44 → SAG
DEC	22	12.49 → CAP

MERCURY

mth	dy	time → sign
JAN	1	18.40 → CAP
JAN	20	11.44 → AQU
FEB	6	17.24 → PIS
APR	15	04.13 → ARI
MAY	2	18.45 → TAU
MAY	16	23.43 → GEM
JUN	1	08.22 → CAN
AUG	9	13.49 → LEO
AUG	25	02.18 → VIR
SEP	10	11.29 → LIB
SEP	30	14.46 → SCO
DEC	6	06.42 → SAG
DEC	25	14.59 → CAP

VENUS

mth	dy	time → sign
JAN	1	00.00 → AQU
APR	6	09.22 → PIS
MAY	6	08.54 → ARI
JUN	2	10.11 → TAU
JUN	28	09.38 → GEM
JUL	23	18.22 → CAN
AUG	17	15.45 → LEO
SEP	11	03.32 → VIR
OCT	5	07.56 → LIB
OCT	29	07.37 → SCO
NOV	22	04.59 → SAG
DEC	16	01.39 → CAP

MARS

mth	dy	time → sign
JAN	1	00.00 → AQU
FEB	4	04.13 → PIS
MAR	14	09.09 → ARI
APR	22	15.40 → TAU
JUN	2	16.28 → GEM
JUL	15	21.36 → CAN
AUG	30	13.38 → LEO
OCT	18	04.52 → VIR
DEC	11	09.38 → LIB

SATURN

mth	dy	time → sign
JAN	1	00.00 → AQU

JUPITER

mth	dy	time → sign
JAN	1	00.00 → LIB
OCT	11	04.45 → SCO

MOON

dy	jan	feb	mar	apr	may	jun	jul	aug	sep	oct	nov	dec	dy
1	CAN	08.00	VIR	13.35	01.02	11.55	PIS	13.25	GEM	CAN	08.36	04.39	1
2	13.56	VIR	VIR	SCO	SAG	AQU	PIS	TAU	15.40	11.44	VIR	LIB	2
3	LEO	17.59	00.02	17.37	02.53	14.06	00.39	21.48	CAN	LEO	19.41	13.06	3
4	LEO	LIB	LIB	SAG	CAP	PIS	ARI	GEM	CAN	LEO	LIB	SCO	4
5	02.09	LIB	06.59	20.45	05.06	18.31	06.47	GEM	04.32	00.31	LIB	17.52	5
6	VIR	01.31	SCO	CAP	AQU	ARI	TAU	09.13	LEO	VIR	03.32	SAG	6
7	12.21	SCO	11.58	23.43	08.26	ARI	15.55	CAN	17.16	11.21	SCO	20.09	7
8	LIB	06.14	SAG	AQU	PIS	01.17	GEM	22.08	VIR	LIB	08.34	CAP	8
9	19.11	SAG	15.22	AQU	13.09	TAU	GEM	LEO	VIR	19.31	SAG	21.34	9
10	SCO	08.23	CAP	02.52	ARI	10.14	03.21	LEO	04.23	SCO	11.57	AQU	10
11	22.18	CAP	17.36	PIS	19.24	GEM	CAN	10.59	LIB	SCO	CAP	23.31	11
12	SAG	08.57	AQU	06.40	TAU	21.14	16.07	VIR	13.19	01.32	14.52	PIS	12
13	22.37	AQU	19.25	ARI	TAU	CAN	LEO	22.34	SCO	SAG	AQU	PIS	13
14	CAP	09.27	PIS	11.55	03.38	CAN	LEO	LIB	20.03	06.04	17.56	02.51	14
15	21.56	PIS	22.00	TAU	GEM	09.53	05.07	LIB	SAG	CAP	PIS	ARI	15
16	AQU	11.39	ARI	19.41	14.17	LEO	VIR	07.51	SAG	09.32	21.26	07.56	16
17	22.17	ARI	ARI	GEM	CAN	22.51	16.47	SCO	00.36	AQU	ARI	TAU	17
18	PIS	17.03	02.46	GEM	CAN	VIR	LIB	14.12	CAP	12.10	ARI	14.58	18
19	PIS	TAU	TAU	06.26	02.55	VIR	LIB	SAG	03.06	PIS	01.46	GEM	19
20	01.28	TAU	10.51	CAN	LEO	09.59	01.31	17.27	AQU	14.28	TAU	GEM	20
21	ARI	02.16	GEM	19.10	15.35	LIB	SCO	CAP	04.14	ARI	07.47	00.11	21
22	08.26	GEM	22.13	LEO	VIR	17.25	06.28	18.18	PIS	17.34	GEM	CAN	22
23	TAU	14.22	CAN	LEO	VIR	SCO	SAG	AQU	05.13	TAU	16.25	11.37	23
24	18.54	CAN	CAN	07.21	01.43	20.49	08.03	18.08	ARI	22.58	CAN	LEO	24
25	GEM	CAN	11.03	VIR	LIB	SAG	CAP	PIS	07.47	GEM	CAN	LEO	25
26	GEM	03.13	LEO	16.32	07.52	21.24	07.43	18.44	TAU	GEM	03.54	00.32	26
27	07.24	LEO	22.44	LIB	SCO	CAP	AQU	ARI	13.34	07.46	LEO	VIR	27
28	CAN	14.46	VIR	22.07	10.28	21.02	07.21	21.55	GEM	CAN	16.52	12.59	28
29	20.12		VIR	SCO	SAG	AQU	PIS	TAU	23.14	19.42	VIR	LIB	29
30	LEO		07.37	SCO	11.12	21.38	08.45	TAU	CAN	LEO	VIR	22.41	30
31	LEO		LIB		CAP		ARI	04.55		LEO		SCO	31

SUN

mth	dy	time	→ sign
JAN	1	00.00	→ CAP
JAN	20	23.25	→ AQU
FEB	19	13.52	→ PIS
MAR	21	13.17	→ ARI
APR	21	00.50	→ TAU
MAY	22	00.24	→ GEM
JUN	22	08.38	→ CAN
JUL	23	19.32	→ LEO
AUG	24	02.24	→ VIR
SEP	23	23.38	→ LIB
OCT	24	08.28	→ SCO
NOV	23	05.35	→ SAG
DEC	22	18.34	→ CAP

MERCURY

mth	dy	time	→ sign
JAN	1	00.00	→ CAP
JAN	13	01.17	→ AQU
FEB	1	11.17	→ PIS
FEB	15	03.04	→ AQU
MAR	18	21.53	→ PIS
APR	8	18.37	→ ARI
APR	24	12.29	→ TAU
MAY	8	17.22	→ GEM
MAY	29	19.26	→ CAN
JUN	20	17.56	→ GEM
JUL	13	22.21	→ CAN
AUG	2	01.45	→ LEO
AUG	16	20.38	→ VIR
SEP	3	09.34	→ LIB
SEP	28	15.56	→ SCO
OCT	12	18.03	→ LIB
NOV	10	01.24	→ SCO
NOV	29	07.05	→ SAG
DEC	18	08.29	→ CAP

VENUS

mth	dy	time	→ sign
JAN	1	00.00	→ CAP
JAN	8	22.42	→ AQU
FEB	1	21.37	→ PIS
FEB	26	00.31	→ ARI
MAR	22	10.29	→ TAU
APR	16	07.38	→ GEM
MAY	11	22.02	→ CAN
JUN	7	19.12	→ LEO
JUL	7	20.34	→ VIR
NOV	9	16.34	→ LIB
DEC	8	14.37	→ SCO

MARS

mth	dy	time	→ sign
JAN	1	00.00	→ LIB
JUL	29	17.33	→ SCO
SEP	16	12.56	→ SAG
OCT	28	18.21	→ CAP
DEC	7	04.32	→ AQU

SATURN

mth	dy	time	→ sign
JAN	1	00.00	→ AQU
FEB	14	14.24	→ PIS

JUPITER

mth	dy	time	→ sign
JAN	1	00.00	→ SCO
NOV	9	02.49	→ SAG

MOON

dy	jan	feb	mar	apr	may	jun	jul	aug	sep	oct	nov	dec	dy
1	SCO	CAP	CAP	PIS	ARI	GEM	CAN	09.07	LIB	SCO	CAP	AQU	1
2	04.24	18.28	05.17	15.34	02.03	20.44	14.13	VIR	16.22	08.41	CAP	14.03	2
3	SAG	AQU	AQU	ARI	TAU	CAN	LEO	21.55	SCO	SAG	PIS	16.55	3
4	06.44	17.47	05.13	16.18	05.26	CAN	LEO	LIB	SCO	17.02	AQU	16.55	4
5	CAP	PIS	PIS	TAU	GEM	06.19	02.08	LIB	02.48	CAP	08.20	ARI	5
6	07.03	17.49	04.40	19.35	11.50	LEO	VIR	09.57	SAG	22.20	PIS	19.03	6
7	AQU	ARI	ARI	GEM	CAN	18.25	14.52	SCO	10.08	AQU	09.56	TAU	7
8	07.17	20.24	05.43	GEM	21.56	VIR	LIB	19.25	CAP	AQU	ARI	21.38	8
9	PIS	TAU	TAU	02.49	LEO	VIR	LIB	SAG	13.44	00.27	10.29	GEM	9
10	09.02	TAU	10.14	CAN	LEO	06.57	02.17	SAG	AQU	PIS	TAU	GEM	10
11	ARI	02.35	GEM	13.55	10.26	LIB	SCO	01.10	14.15	00.20>ARI	11.52	01.54	11
12	13.24	GEM	18.52	LEO	VIR	17.35	10.27	CAP	PIS	23.54	GEM	CAN	12
13	TAU	12.24	CAN	LEO	22.48	SCO	SAG	03.20	13.21	TAU	15.55	09.08	13
14	20.43	CAN	CAN	02.47	LIB	SCO	15.03	AQU	ARI	TAU	CAN	LEO	14
15	GEM	CAN	06.48	VIR	LIB	00.58	CAP	03.20	13.11	01.17	23.51	19.33	15
16	GEM	00.35	LEO	15.01	08.55	SAG	16.54	PIS	TAU	GEM	LEO	VIR	16
17	06.37	LEO	19.51	LIB	SCO	05.21	AQU	02.55	15.48	06.21	LEO	VIR	17
18	CAN	13.36	VIR	LIB	16.13	CAP	17.30	ARI	GEM	11.10	07.58		18
19	18.28	VIR	VIR	01.09	SAG	07.56	PIS	04.08	22.27	15.35	VIR	LIB	19
20	LEO	VIR	08.08	SCO	21.20	AQU	18.36	TAU	CAN	LEO	23.53	20.03	20
21	LEO	02.02	LIB	09.06	CAP	09.56	ARI	08.25	CAN	LEO	LIB	SCO	21
22	07.19	LIB	18.44	SAG	CAP	PIS	21.21	GEM	08.51	03.44	LIB	SCO	22
23	VIR	13.04	SCO	15.13	01.09	12.23	TAU	16.17	LEO	VIR	11.36	05.44	23
24	19.59	SCO	SCO	CAP	AQU	ARI	TAU	CAN	21.18	16.31	SCO	SAG	24
25	LIB	21.40	03.24	19.43	04.13	15.54	02.42	CAN	VIR	LIB	21.08	12.27	25
26	LIB	SAG	SAG	AQU	PIS	TAU	GEM	03.00	VIR	LIB	SAG	CAP	26
27	06.46	SAG	09.49	22.40	06.59	21.06	10.43	LEO	10.05	04.15	SAG	16.46	27
28	SCO	03.04	CAP	PIS	ARI	GEM	CAN	15.20	LIB	SCO	04.28	AQU	28
29	14.11		13.41	PIS	09.59	GEM	21.04	VIR	22.06	14.17	CAP	19.42	29
30	SAG		AQU	00.26	TAU	04.26	LEO	VIR	SCO	SAG	10.00	PIS	30
31	17.47		15.14		14.11		LEO	04.08		22.31		22.15	31

SUN

mth	dy	time → sign
JAN	1	00.00 → CAP
JAN	21	05.14 → AQU
FEB	19	19.33 → PIS
MAR	20	18.56 → ARI
APR	20	06.31 → TAU
MAY	21	06.06 → GEM
JUN	21	14.21 → CAN
JUL	23	01.18 → LEO
AUG	23	08.13 → VIR
SEP	23	05.26 → LIB
OCT	23	14.19 → SCO
NOV	22	11.26 → SAG
DEC	22	00.27 → CAP

MERCURY

mth	dy	time → sign
JAN	1	00.00 → CAP
JAN	6	03.32 → AQU
MAR	13	06.40 → PIS
MAR	31	05.07 → ARI
APR	15	01.45 → TAU
MAY	1	01.30 → GEM
JUL	8	20.49 → CAN
JUL	23	15.39 → LEO
AUG	7	22.59 → VIR
AUG	27	17.42 → LIB
NOV	2	11.00 → SCO
NOV	21	00.39 → SAG
DEC	10	06.43 → CAP

VENUS

mth	dy	time → sign
JAN	1	00.00 → SCO
JAN	3	14.15 → SAG
JAN	28	14.00 → CAP
FEB	22	04.15 → AQU
MAR	17	14.53 → PIS
APR	11	00.43 → ARI
MAY	5	10.56 → TAU
MAY	29	21.39 → GEM
JUN	23	08.17 → CAN
JUL	17	17.51 → LEO
AUG	11	02.11 → VIR
SEP	4	10.03 → LIB
SEP	28	18.36 → SCO
OCT	23	05.01 → SAG
NOV	16	18.36 → CAP
DEC	11	14.53 → AQU

MARS

mth	dy	time → sign
JAN	1	00.00 → AQU
JAN	14	13.57 → PIS
FEB	22	04.02 → ARI
APR	1	21.38 → TAU
MAY	13	09.14 → GEM
JUN	25	21.53 → CAN
AUG	10	09.41 → LEO
SEP	26	14.51 → VIR
NOV	14	14.55 → LIB

SATURN

mth	dy	time → sign
JAN	1	00.00 → PIS

JUPITER

mth	dy	time → sign
JAN	1	00.00 → SAG
DEC	2	08.26 → CAP

MOON

dy	jan	feb	mar	apr	may	jun	jul	aug	sep	oct	nov	dec	dy
1	ARI	10.38	22.25	LEO	VIR	14.13	09.28	CAP	PIS	ARI	GEM	CAN	1
2	ARI	GEM	CAN	LEO	18.43	SCO	SAG	09.25	22.43	08.26	20.00	09.44	2
3	01.12	16.58	CAN	00.07	LIB	SCO	18.34	AQU	ARI	TAU	CAN	LEO	3
4	TAU	CAN	07.21	VIR	LIB	01.37	CAP	12.36	23.04	08.37	CAN	16.31	4
5	05.04	CAN	LEO	12.33	07.16	SAG	CAP	PIS	TAU	GEM	00.37	VIR	5
6	GEM	01.24	18.18	LIB	SCO	11.07	00.56	14.21	TAU	11.27	LEO	VIR	6
7	10.27	LEO	VIR	LIB	18.55	CAP	AQU	ARI	00.55	CAN	09.01	02.55	7
8	CAN	11.48	VIR	01.06	SAG	18.17	05.10	16.11	GEM	17.45	VIR	LIB	8
9	18.03	VIR	06.26	SCO	SAG	AQU	PIS	TAU	05.16	LEO	20.15	15.28	9
10	LEO	23.44	LIB	13.03	04.56	23.27	08.10	19.12	CAN	LEO	LIB	SCO	10
11	LEO	LIB	19.06	SAG	CAP	PIS	ARI	GEM	12.13	03.01	LIB	SCO	11
12	04.04	LIB	SCO	23.27	12.47	PIS	10.46	23.52	LEO	VIR	08.52	04.07	12
13	VIR	12.24	SCO	CAP	AQU	02.47	TAU	CAN	21.21	14.19	SCO	SAG	13
14	16.10	SCO	07.06	CAP	17.52	ARI	13.39	CAN	VIR	LIB	21.36	15.26	14
15	LIB	23.57	SAG	06.49	PIS	04.48	GEM	06.20	VIR	LIB	SAG	CAP	15
16	LIB	SAG	16.51	AQU	20.14	TAU	17.28	LEO	08.12	02.47	SAG	CAP	16
17	04.38	SAG	CAP	10.38	ARI	06.29	CAN	14.44	LIB	SCO	09.20	00.42	17
18	SCO	08.21	22.52	PIS	20.47	GEM	22.58	VIR	20.33	15.38	CAP	AQU	18
19	15.11	CAP	AQU	11.20	TAU	09.08	LEO	VIR	SCO	SAG	19.13	07.43	19
20	SAG	12.49	AQU	ARI	21.12	CAN	LEO	01.18	SCO	SAG	AQU	PIS	20
21	22.17	AQU	00.59	10.37	GEM	14.06	06.56	LIB	09.24	03.37	AQU	12.26	21
22	CAP	13.55	PIS	TAU	23.20	LEO	VIR	13.36	SAG	CAP	02.04	ARI	22
23	CAP	PIS	00.31>ARI	10.37	CAN	22.15	17.30	SCO	20.53	13.00	PIS	15.07	23
24	02.02	13.35	23.37	GEM	CAN	VIR	LIB	SCO	CAP	AQU	05.38	TAU	24
25	AQU	ARI	TAU	13.22	04.43	VIR	LIB	02.09	CAP	18.29	ARI	16.24	25
26	03.33	13.51	TAU	CAN	LEO	09.25	05.54	SAG	04.53	PIS	06.29	GEM	26
27	PIS	TAU	00.31	20.03	13.48	LIB	SCO	12.35	AQU	20.09	TAU	17.36	27
28	04.36	16.32	GEM	LEO	VIR	21.53	17.57	CAP	08.39	ARI	06.11	CAN	28
29	ARI	GEM	04.52	LEO	VIR	SCO	SAG	19.13	PIS	19.34	GEM	20.15	29
30	06.35		CAN	06.22	01.39	SCO	SAG	AQU	09.10	TAU	06.40	LEO	30
31	TAU		13.04		LIB		03.24	22.06		18.49		LEO	31

55

SUN

mth	dy	time	→ sign
JAN	1	00.00	→ CAP
JAN	20	11.04	→ AQU
FEB	19	01.21	→ PIS
MAR	21	00.45	→ ARI
APR	20	12.17	→ TAU
MAY	21	11.57	→ GEM
JUN	21	20.12	→ CAN
JUL	23	07.09	→ LEO
AUG	23	13.58	→ VIR
SEP	23	11.13	→ LIB
OCT	23	20.07	→ SCO
NOV	22	17.18	→ SAG
DEC	22	06.23	→ CAP

MERCURY

mth	dy	time	→ sign
JAN	1	16.43	→ AQU
JAN	9	21.28	→ CAP
FEB	14	00.26	→ AQU
MAR	6	14.07	→ PIS
MAR	23	03.41	→ ARI
APR	7	01.09	→ TAU
JUN	13	22.28	→ GEM
JUL	1	02.25	→ CAN
JUL	15	04.11	→ LEO
JUL	31	21.07	→ VIR
OCT	8	10.13	→ LIB
OCT	26	01.14	→ SCO
NOV	13	19.25	→ SAG
DEC	3	23.55	→ CAP

VENUS

mth	dy	time	→ sign
JAN	1	00.00	→ AQU
JAN	6	03.19	→ PIS
FEB	2	10.39	→ ARI
MAR	9	13.19	→ TAU
APR	14	04.17	→ ARI
JUN	4	06.41	→ TAU
JUL	7	21.13	→ GEM
AUG	4	20.15	→ CAN
AUG	31	00.08	→ LEO
SEP	25	04.03	→ VIR
OCT	19	16.34	→ LIB
NOV	12	19.43	→ SCO
DEC	6	18.08	→ SAG
DEC	30	14.43	→ CAP

MARS

mth	dy	time	→ sign
JAN	1	00.00	→ LIB
JAN	5	20.29	→ SCO
MAR	13	03.06	→ SAG
MAY	14	22.59	→ SCO
AUG	8	22.18	→ SAG
SEP	30	09.08	→ CAP
NOV	11	18.39	→ AQU
DEC	21	17.46	→ PIS

SATURN

mth	dy	time	→ sign
JAN	1	00.00	→ PIS
APR	25	06.45	→ ARI
OCT	18	03.53	→ PIS

JUPITER

mth	dy	time	→ sign
JAN	1	00.00	→ CAP
DEC	20	04.24	→ AQU

MOON

dy	jan	feb	mar	apr	may	jun	jul	aug	sep	oct	nov	dec	dy
1	01.45	LIB	15.23	SAG	CAP	08.58	ARI	09.29	21.22	08.27	LIB	SCO	1
2	VIR	07.10	SCO	SAG	18.08	PIS	ARI	GEM	LEO	VIR	07.48	02.05	2
3	10.54	SCO	SCO	00.16	AQU	14.22	00.34	11.34	LEO	15.31	SCO	SAG	3
4	LIB	19.57	04.08	CAP	AQU	ARI	TAU	CAN	01.34	LIB	19.46	15.06	4
5	22.58	SAG	SAG	10.37	01.57	16.37	02.16	13.35	VIR	LIB	SAG	CAP	5
6	SCO	SAG	16.23	AQU	PIS	TAU	GEM	LEO	07.47	00.54	SAG	CAP	6
7	SCO	07.34	CAP	16.59	05.47	16.46	02.53	16.54	LIB	SCO	08.50	03.40	7
8	11.44	CAP	CAP	PIS	ARI	GEM	CAN	VIR	16.59	12.44	CAP	AQU	8
9	SAG	16.02	01.36	19.26	06.34	16.32	03.59	22.58	SCO	SAG	21.19	14.21	9
10	22.53	AQU	AQU	ARI	TAU	CAN	LEO	LIB	SCO	SAG	AQU	PIS	10
11	CAP	21.10	06.50	19.39	05.56	17.44	07.16	LIB	04.57	01.46	AQU	21.56	11
12	CAP	PIS	PIS	TAU	GEM	LEO	VIR	08.37	SAG	CAP	07.07	ARI	12
13	07.25	PIS	09.00	19.34	06.01	22.01	14.04	SCO	17.52	13.37	PIS	ARI	13
14	AQU	00.18	ARI	GEM	CAN	VIR	LIB	20.59	CAP	AQU	12.59	01.50	14
15	13.29	ARI	09.54	21.05	08.27	VIR	LIB	SAG	CAP	22.03	ARI	TAU	15
16	PIS	02.34	TAU	CAN	LEO	06.08	00.36	SAG	04.51	PIS	15.12	02.42	16
17	17.48	TAU	11.19	CAN	14.19	LIB	SCO	09.37	AQU	PIS	TAU	GEM	17
18	ARI	05.22	GEM	01.11	VIR	17.31	13.20	CAP	12.19	02.33	15.10	02.04	18
19	21.07	GEM	14.25	LEO	23.35	SCO	SAG	20.05	PIS	ARI	GEM	CAN	19
20	TAU	09.05	CAN	08.17	LIB	SCO	SAG	AQU	16.31	04.09	14.47	01.48	20
21	23.55	CAN	19.35	VIR	LIB	06.25	01.50	AQU	ARI	TAU	CAN	LEO	21
22	GEM	13.51	LEO	17.51	11.18	SAG	CAP	03.28	18.49	04.40	15.55	03.57	22
23	GEM	LEO	LEO	LIB	SCO	18.58	12.20	PIS	TAU	GEM	LEO	VIR	23
24	02.39	20.05	02.44	LIB	SCO	CAP	AQU	08.23	20.46	05.47	19.55	09.53	24
25	CAN	VIR	VIR	05.21	00.11	CAP	20.21	ARI	GEM	CAN	VIR	LIB	25
26	06.08	VIR	11.47	SCO	SAG	05.54	PIS	11.57	23.24	08.42	VIR	19.45	26
27	LEO	04.26	LIB	18.06	12.53	AQU	PIS	TAU	CAN	LEO	03.22	SCO	27
28	11.30	LIB	22.51	SAG	CAP	14.37	02.15	15.01	CAN	14.01	LIB	SCO	28
29	VIR		SCO	SAG	CAP	PIS	ARI	GEM	03.14	VIR	13.46	08.12	29
30	19.49		SCO	06.54	00.15	20.50	06.31	18.03	LEO	21.47	SCO	SAG	30
31	LIB		11.32		AQU		TAU	CAN		LIB		21.17	31

SUN

mth	dy	time → sign
JAN	1	00.00 → CAP
JAN	20	16.57 → AQU
FEB	19	07.20 → PIS
MAR	21	06.43 → ARI
APR	20	18.17 → TAU
MAY	21	17.50 → GEM
JUN	22	02.04 → CAN
JUL	23	12.56 → LEO
AUG	23	19.46 → VIR
SEP	23	17.00 → LIB
OCT	24	01.56 → SCO
NOV	22	23.06 → SAG
DEC	22	12.14 → CAP

MERCURY

mth	dy	time → sign
JAN	1	00.00 → CAP
JAN	6	21.39 → SAG
JAN	12	22.30 → CAP
FEB	8	13.18 → AQU
FEB	27	03.01 → PIS
MAR	15	00.03 → ARI
APR	1	13.26 → TAU
APR	23	13.56 → ARI
MAY	16	17.46 → TAU
JUN	8	00.32 → GEM
JUN	22	13.09 → CAN
JUL	7	03.21 → LEO
JUL	26	22.56 → VIR
SEP	3	02.59 → LEO
SEP	10	15.38 → VIR
OCT	1	04.19 → LIB
OCT	18	12.43 → SCO
NOV	6	23.33 → SAG

VENUS

mth	dy	time → sign
JAN	1	00.00 → CAP
JAN	23	11.17 → AQU
FEB	16	09.01 → PIS
MAR	12	09.20 → ARI
APR	5	13.48 → TAU
APR	29	23.35 → GEM
MAY	24	15.58 → CAN
JUN	18	16.37 → LEO
JUL	14	05.45 → VIR
AUG	9	16.29 → LIB
SEP	7	01.36 → SCO
OCT	13	18.48 → SAG
NOV	15	16.07 → SCO

MARS

mth	dy	time → sign
JAN	1	00.00 → PIS
JAN	30	12.50 → ARI
MAR	12	07.48 → TAU
APR	23	18.45 → GEM
JUN	7	01.28 → CAN
JUL	22	22.23 → LEO
SEP	7	20.23 → VIR
OCT	25	06.20 → LIB
DEC	11	23.13 → SCO

SATURN

mth	dy	time → sign
JAN	1	00.00 → PIS
JAN	14	10.22 → ARI

JUPITER

mth	dy	time → sign
JAN	1	00.00 → AQU
MAY	14	07.23 → PIS
JUL	30	03.13 → AQU
DEC	29	18.25 → PIS

MOON

dy	jan	feb	mar	apr	may	jun	jul	aug	sep	oct	nov	dec	dy
1	CAP	AQU	09.13	ARI	15.45	CAN	12.24	LIB	00.28	CAP	AQU	PIS	1
2	CAP	01.59	PIS	04.44	GEM	02.09	VIR	06.49	SAG	CAP	05.09	00.02	2
3	09.32	PIS	16.16	TAU	16.50	LEO	16.09	SCO	12.30	08.58	PIS	ARI	3
4	AQU	09.54	ARI	07.33	CAN	04.21	LIB	17.02	CAP	AQU	14.35	07.01	4
5	20.07	ARI	21.29	GEM	18.42	VIR	23.47	SAG	CAP	20.27	ARI	TAU	5
6	PIS	15.58	TAU	10.07	LEO	09.35	SCO	SAG	01.11	PIS	20.42	10.19	6
7	PIS	TAU	TAU	CAN	22.19	LIB	SCO	05.33	AQU	PIS	TAU	GEM	7
8	04.30	20.08	01.33	13.07	VIR	18.03	10.45	CAP	12.28	05.22	TAU	11.08	8
9	ARI	GEM	GEM	LEO	VIR	SCO	SAG	18.15	PIS	ARI	00.03	CAN	9
10	10.06	22.22	04.46	16.51	04.06	SCO	23.25	AQU	21.40	11.43	GEM	11.17	10
11	TAU	CAN	CAN	VIR	LIB	04.57	CAP	AQU	ARI	TAU	01.57	LEO	11
12	12.51	23.33	07.23	22.02	12.16	SAG	CAP	05.45	ARI	16.10	CAN	12.38	12
13	GEM	LEO	LEO	LIB	SCO	17.21	12.05	PIS	04.55	GEM	03.50	VIR	13
14	13.21	LEO	10.05	LIB	22.40	CAP	AQU	15.34	TAU	19.31	LEO	16.27	14
15	CAN	00.57	VIR	05.23	SAG	CAP	23.53	ARI	10.23	CAN	06.38	LIB	15
16	13.09	VIR	14.08	SCO	SAG	06.07	PIS	23.25	GEM	22.19	VIR	23.13	16
17	LEO	04.28	LIB	15.19	10.51	AQU	PIS	TAU	14.09	LEO	11.03	SCO	17
18	14.12	LIB	20.53	SAG	CAP	18.02	10.02	TAU	CAN	LEO	LIB	SCO	18
19	VIR	11.37	SCO	SAG	23.37	PIS	ARI	04.51	16.26	01.09	LIB	08.32	19
20	18.27	SCO	SCO	03.31	AQU	PIS	17.31	GEM	LEO	VIR	SCO	SAG	20
21	LIB	22.33	07.01	CAP	AQU	03.42	TAU	07.40	18.02	04.43	SCO	19.39	21
22	LIB	SAG	SAG	16.11	11.06	ARI	21.44	CAN	VIR	LIB	01.56	CAP	22
23	02.56	SAG	19.32	AQU	PIS	09.50	GEM	08.27	20.19	10.00	SAG	CAP	23
24	SCO	11.28	CAP	AQU	19.35	TAU	22.55	LEO	LIB	SCO	12.37	07.59	24
25	14.51	CAP	CAP	02.54	ARI	12.25	CAN	08.43	LIB	17.54	CAP	AQU	25
26	SAG	23.36	07.56	PIS	ARI	GEM	22.26	VIR	00.57	SAG	CAP	20.41	26
27	SAG	AQU	AQU	10.08	00.17	12.27	LEO	10.26	SCO	SAG	00.58	PIS	27
28	03.58	AQU	17.52	ARI	TAU	CAN	22.18	LIB	09.03	CAP	04.39	PIS	28
29	CAP		PIS	14.02	01.52	11.45	VIR	15.26	SAG	CAP	13.30	08.14	29
30	16.00		PIS	TAU	GEM	LEO	VIR	SCO	20.20	17.08	PIS	ARI	30
31	AQU		00.33		01.55		00.35	SCO		AQU		16.48	31

SUN

mth	dy	time → sign
JAN	1	00.00 → CAP
JAN	20	22.51 → AQU
FEB	19	13.09 → PIS
MAR	21	12.28 → ARI
APR	20	23.55 → TAU
MAY	21	23.27 → GEM
JUN	22	07.39 → CAN
JUL	23	18.37 → LEO
AUG	24	01.31 → VIR
SEP	23	22.49 → LIB
OCT	24	07.44 → SCO
NOV	23	04.59 → SAG
DEC	22	18.06 → CAP

MERCURY

mth	dy	time → sign
JAN	1	00.00 → SAG
JAN	12	07.57 → CAP
FEB	1	17.57 → AQU
FEB	19	08.10 → PIS
MAR	7	09.14 → ARI
MAY	14	13.43 → TAU
MAY	31	02.44 → GEM
JUN	13	23.01 → CAN
JUN	30	06.41 → LEO
SEP	7	04.58 → VIR
SEP	23	07.48 → LIB
OCT	11	05.20 → SCO
NOV	1	07.03 → SAG
DEC	3	07.22 → SCO
DEC	13	19.16 → SAG

VENUS

mth	dy	time → sign
JAN	1	00.00 → SCO
JAN	4	21.48 → SAG
FEB	6	09.20 → CAP
MAR	5	13.29 → AQU
MAR	31	08.34 → PIS
APR	25	14.28 → ARI
MAY	20	14.13 → TAU
JUN	14	10.11 → GEM
JUL	9	02.25 → CAN
AUG	2	14.11 → LEO
AUG	26	21.24 → VIR
SEP	20	01.02 → LIB
OCT	14	02.41 → SCO
NOV	7	03.41 → SAG
DEC	1	04.52 → CAP
DEC	25	07.25 → AQU

MARS

mth	dy	time → sign
JAN	1	00.00 → SCO
JAN	29	09.52 → SAG
MAR	21	07.25 → CAP
MAY	25	00.23 → AQU
JUL	21	19.31 → CAP
SEP	24	01.17 → AQU
NOV	19	15.56 → PIS

SATURN

mth	dy	time → sign
JAN	1	00.00 → ARI
JUL	6	05.39 → TAU
SEP	22	05.11 → ARI

JUPITER

mth	dy	time → sign
JAN	1	00.00 → PIS
MAY	11	14.16 → ARI
OCT	30	00.49 → PIS
DEC	20	17.10 → ARI

MOON

dy	jan	feb	mar	apr	may	jun	jul	aug	sep	oct	nov	dec	dy
1	TAU	09.22	CAN	04.39	LIB	07.15	CAP	AQU	ARI	TAU	13.41	LEO	1
2	21.19	CAN	19.31	VIR	17.36	SAG	CAP	04.41	ARI	TAU	CAN	LEO	2
3	GEM	09.06	LEO	05.48	SCO	15.50	PIS	10.47	01.38	18.01	02.23		3
4	22.20	LEO	19.17	LIB	23.11	CAP	AQU	17.22	TAU	GEM	LEO	VIR	4
5	CAN	08.02	VIR	08.20	SAG	CAP	22.17	ARI	20.02	08.16	20.57	05.22	5
6	21.32	VIR	19.25	SCO	SAG	02.40	PIS	ARI	GEM	CAN	VIR	LIB	6
7	LEO	08.29	LIB	13.47	07.34	AQU	PIS	04.47	GEM	12.10	23.03	08.57	7
8	21.08	LIB	21.59	SAG	15.04	CAP	10.50	TAU	01.52	LEO	LIB	SCO	8
9	VIR	12.22	SCO	SCO	22.47	18.41	ARI	13.06	CAN	13.44	LIB	13.32	9
10	23.10	SCO	SCO	CAP	PIS	PIS	21.27	GEM	04.12	VIR	01.14	SAG	10
11	LIB	20.24	04.23	CAP	AQU	03.10	TAU	17.20	LEO	14.15	SCO	19.51	11
12	LIB	SAG	SAG	10.33	07.09	ARI	TAU	CAN	04.09	LIB	04.41	CAP	12
13	04.54	SAG	14.35	AQU	PIS	12.43	04.20	18.09	VIR	15.18	SAG	CAP	13
14	SCO	07.41	CAP	23.04	18.41	TAU	GEM	LEO	03.39	SCO	10.42	04.42	14
15	14.10	CAP	CAP	PIS	ARI	18.32	07.16	17.19	LIB	18.36	CAP	AQU	15
16	SAG	20.22	03.01	PIS	ARI	GEM	CAN	VIR	04.43	SAG	20.00	16.14	16
17	SAG	AQU	AQU	10.13	03.28	21.06	07.31	17.03	SCO	SAG	AQU	PIS	17
18	01.44	AQU	15.31	ARI	TAU	CAN	LEO	LIB	09.02	01.22	AQU	PIS	18
19	CAP	08.52	PIS	18.57	09.06	21.58	07.07	19.20	SAG	CAP	08.00	05.03	19
20	14.15	PIS	PIS	TAU	GEM	LEO	VIR	SCO	17.11	11.40	PIS	ARI	20
21	AQU	20.23	02.41	TAU	12.23	22.56	08.10	SCO	CAP	AQU	20.36	16.32	21
22	AQU	ARI	ARI	01.16	CAN	VIR	LIB	01.14	CAP	AQU	ARI	TAU	22
23	02.51	ARI	11.58	GEM	14.33	VIR	12.04	SAG	04.24	00.05	ARI	TAU	23
24	PIS	06.19	TAU	05.43	LEO	01.31	SCO	10.33	AQU	PIS	07.23	00.37	24
25	14.42	TAU	19.15	CAN	16.51	LIB	19.10	CAP	17.00	12.28	TAU	GEM	25
26	ARI	13.47	GEM	08.55	VIR	06.25	SAG	22.09	PIS	ARI	15.09	05.03	26
27	ARI	GEM	GEM	LEO	20.06	SCO	SAG	AQU	PIS	23.09	GEM	CAN	27
28	00.29	18.07	00.19	11.26	LIB	13.39	04.51	AQU	05.22	TAU	20.11	07.05	28
29	TAU		CAN	VIR	LIB	SAG	CAP	10.42	ARI	TAU	CAN	LEO	29
30	06.50		03.15	14.02	00.47	22.53	16.15	PIS	16.29	07.31	23.34	08.29	30
31	GEM		LEO		SCO		AQU	23.15		GEM		VIR	31

SUN

mth	dy	time → sign
JAN	1	00.00 → CAP
JAN	21	04.42 → AQU
FEB	19	19.04 → PIS
MAR	20	18.25 → ARI
APR	20	05.51 → TAU
MAY	21	05.23 → GEM
JUN	21	13.37 → CAN
JUL	23	00.34 → LEO
AUG	23	07.28 → VIR
SEP	23	04.46 → LIB
OCT	23	13.39 → SCO
NOV	22	10.48 → SAG
DEC	21	23.54 → CAP

MERCURY

mth	dy	time → sign
JAN	1	00.00 → SAG
JAN	6	07.57 → CAP
JAN	25	10.15 → AQU
FEB	11	14.01 → PIS
MAR	4	10.11 → ARI
MAR	8	01.26 → PIS
APR	17	04.56 → ARI
MAY	6	21.15 → TAU
MAY	21	13.58 → GEM
JUN	4	22.29 → CAN
JUN	26	14.32 → LEO
JUL	21	01.39 → CAN
AUG	11	17.06 → LEO
AUG	29	11.11 → VIR
SEP	14	11.34 → LIB
OCT	3	12.16 → SCO
DEC	9	12.45 → SAG
DEC	29	09.37 → CAP

VENUS

mth	dy	time → sign
JAN	1	00.00 → AQU
JAN	18	14.02 → PIS
FEB	12	05.51 → ARI
MAR	8	16.25 → TAU
APR	4	18.11 → GEM
MAY	6	18.46 → CAN
JUL	5	16.17 → GEM
AUG	1	02.20 → CAN
SEP	8	16.59 → LEO
OCT	6	21.14 → VIR
NOV	1	17.23 → LIB
NOV	26	12.33 → SCO
DEC	20	19.36 → SAG

MARS

mth	dy	time → sign
JAN	1	00.00 → PIS
JAN	4	00.25 → ARI
FEB	17	01.59 → TAU
APR	1	18.41 → GEM
MAY	17	14.45 → CAN
JUL	3	10.35 → LEO
AUG	19	15.58 → VIR
OCT	5	14.31 → LIB
NOV	20	17.22 → SCO

SATURN

mth	dy	time → sign
JAN	1	00.00 → ARI
MAR	20	09.35 → TAU

JUPITER

mth	dy	time → sign
JAN	1	00.00 → ARI
MAY	16	07.37 → TAU

MOON

dy	jan	feb	mar	apr	may	jun	jul	aug	sep	oct	nov	dec	dy
1	10.44	SCO	SAG	07.13	01.56	ARI	TAU	CAN	12.57	LIB	10.21	CAP	1
2	LIB	01.37	15.02	AQU	PIS	10.46	05.15	CAN	VIR	23.12	SAG	CAP	2
3	14.36	SAG	CAP	19.16	14.52	TAU	GEM	01.21	12.55	SCO	12.23	03.12	3
4	SCO	09.27	CAP	PIS	ARI	20.49	12.10	LEO	23.54	CAP	AQU	11.35	4
5	20.12	CAP	01.07	PIS	ARI	GEM	CAN	02.50	13.16	SAG	18.03	11.35	5
6	SAG	19.23	AQU	08.10	03.12	GEM	16.12	VIR	SCO	SAG	AQU	PIS	6
7	SAG	AQU	13.07	ARI	TAU	04.05	LEO	03.52	15.36	03.28	AQU	23.26	7
8	03.33	AQU	PIS	20.38	13.34	CAN	18.44	LIB	SAG	CAP	03.45	ARI	8
9	CAP	06.58	PIS	TAU	GEM	09.00	VIR	05.46	20.46	10.45	PIS	ARI	9
10	12.42	PIS	02.01	TAU	21.33	LEO	21.07	SCO	CAP	AQU	16.13	12.27	10
11	AQU	19.49	ARI	07.32	CAN	12.41	LIB	09.27	CAP	ARI	TAU	11
12	AQU	ARI	14.44	GEM	CAN	VIR	LIB	SAG	04.51	PIS	ARI	TAU	12
13	00.05	ARI	TAU	16.05	03.22	15.43	00.07	15.15	AQU	PIS	05.13	00.08	13
14	PIS	08.38	TAU	CAN	LEO	LIB	SCO	CAP	15.25	09.50	TAU	GEM	14
15	12.57	TAU	01.53	21.44	07.17	18.32	04.05	23.08	PIS	ARI	17.00	09.21	15
16	ARI	19.10	GEM	LEO	VIR	SCO	SAG	AQU	PIS	22.47	GEM	CAN	16
17	ARI	GEM	09.57	LEO	09.40	21.34	09.17	AQU	03.43	TAU	GEM	16.16	17
18	01.15	GEM	CAN	00.35	LIB	SAG	CAP	09.11	ARI	TAU	02.52	LEO	18
19	TAU	01.46	14.15	VIR	11.12	SAG	16.22	PIS	16.44	10.59	CAN	21.35	19
20	10.32	CAN	LEO	01.23	SCO	01.44	AQU	21.15	TAU	GEM	10.38	VIR	20
21	GEM	04.19	15.20	LIB	13.00	CAP	AQU	ARI	TAU	21.18	LEO	VIR	21
22	15.35	LEO	VIR	01.33	SAG	08.15	01.58	ARI	05.05	CAN	16.11	01.37	22
23	CAN	04.11	14.47	SCO	16.35	AQU	PIS	10.17	GEM	CAN	VIR	LIB	23
24	17.10	VIR	LIB	02.47	CAP	17.56	14.01	TAU	14.57	04.51	19.25	04.30	24
25	LEO	03.29	14.33	SAG	23.19	PIS	ARI	22.13	CAN	LEO	LIB	SCO	25
26	17.12	LIB	SCO	06.50	AQU	PIS	ARI	GEM	21.09	09.09	20.44	06.36	26
27	VIR	04.13	16.31	CAP	AQU	06.13	02.56	GEM	LEO	VIR	SCO	SAG	27
28	17.43	SCO	SAG	14.39	09.39	ARI	TAU	06.53	23.41	10.37	21.18	08.58	28
29	LIB	07.54	21.59	AQU	PIS	18.52	14.04	CAN	VIR	LIB	SAG	CAP	29
30	20.17		CAP	AQU	22.18	TAU	GEM	11.31	23.46	10.25	22.50	13.09	30
31	SCO		CAP		ARI		21.32	LEO		SCO		AQU	31

SUN

mth	dy	time	→ sign
JAN	1	00.00	→ CAP
JAN	20	10.33	→ AQU
FEB	19	00.56	→ PIS
MAR	21	00.23	→ ARI
APR	20	11.50	→ TAU
MAY	21	11.23	→ GEM
JUN	21	19.35	→ CAN
JUL	23	06.26	→ LEO
AUG	23	13.17	→ VIR
SEP	23	10.33	→ LIB
OCT	23	19.28	→ SCO
NOV	22	16.38	→ SAG
DEC	22	05.42	→ CAP

MERCURY

mth	dy	time	→ sign
JAN	1	00.00	→ CAP
JAN	16	22.37	→ AQU
FEB	3	13.08	→ PIS
MAR	7	02.22	→ AQU
MAR	16	12.28	→ PIS
APR	12	07.19	→ ARI
APR	28	23.09	→ TAU
MAY	13	00.51	→ GEM
MAY	29	17.33	→ CAN
AUG	6	05.57	→ LEO
AUG	21	05.18	→ VIR
SEP	6	23.58	→ LIB
SEP	28	09.22	→ SCO
OCT	29	20.34	→ LIB
NOV	11	20.11	→ SCO
DEC	3	00.11	→ SAG
DEC	22	03.54	→ CAP

VENUS

mth	dy	time	→ sign
JAN	1	00.00	→ SAG
JAN	13	21.32	→ CAP
FEB	6	21.49	→ AQU
MAR	2	22.33	→ PIS
MAR	27	00.58	→ ARI
APR	20	05.53	→ TAU
MAY	14	13.37	→ GEM
JUN	7	23.53	→ CAN
JUL	2	12.35	→ LEO
JUL	27	04.12	→ VIR
AUG	21	00.29	→ LIB
SEP	15	04.01	→ SCO
OCT	10	19.23	→ SAG
NOV	6	10.17	→ CAP
DEC	5	23.05	→ AQU

MARS

mth	dy	time	→ sign
JAN	1	00.00	→ SCO
JAN	4	19.38	→ SAG
FEB	17	23.34	→ CAP
APR	2	11.32	→ AQU
MAY	16	05.15	→ PIS
JUL	2	05.24	→ ARI

SATURN

mth	dy	time	→ sign
JAN	1	00.00	→ TAU

JUPITER

mth	dy	time	→ sign
JAN	1	00.00	→ TAU
MAY	26	12.14	→ GEM

MOON

dy	jan	feb	mar	apr	may	jun	jul	aug	sep	oct	nov	dec	dy
1	20.35	ARI	ARI	08.06	01.56	LEO	11.17	22.49	CAP	AQU	ARI	TAU	1
2	PIS	ARI	12.23	GEM	CAN	00.38	LIB	SAG	11.39	00.18	ARI	22.01	2
3	PIS	04.41	TAU	19.45	11.34	VIR	14.33	SAG	AQU	PIS	03.18	GEM	3
4	07.35	TAU	TAU	CAN	LEO	05.17	SCO	01.17	17.52	09.37	TAU	GEM	4
5	ARI	17.09	01.12	CAN	18.06	LIB	16.13	CAP	PIS	ARI	15.54	10.23	5
6	20.28	GEM	GEM	04.26	VIR	07.14	SAG	PIS	20.52	GEM	CAN	6
7	TAU	GEM	12.04	LEO	21.12	SCO	17.21	AQU	02.29	TAU	GEM	21.43	7
8	TAU	02.58	CAN	09.22	LIB	07.23	CAP	ARI	13.32	04.26	CAN	LEO	8
9	08.27	CAN	19.19	VIR	21.34	SAG	19.36	PIS	13.32	09.23	CAN	07.12	9
10	GEM	09.07	LEO	10.54	SCO	07.31	AQU	18.14	TAU	GEM	15.46	07.12	10
11	17.34	LEO	22.51	LIB	20.47	CAP	AQU	ARI	TAU	21.54	LEO	VIR	11
12	CAN	12.22	VIR	10.31	SAG	09.42	00.43	02.04	GEM	CAN	LEO	13.46	12
13	23.39	VIR	23.51	SCO	21.03	AQU	PIS	05.32	GEM	CAN	00.29	LIB	13
14	LEO	14.07	LIB	10.07	CAP	15.33	09.34	14.09	14.09	08.29	VIR	16.53	14
15	LEO	LIB	LIB	SAG	CAP	PIS	ARI	18.09	CAN	LEO	05.23	SCO	15
16	03.46	15.52	00.03	11.38	00.15	PIS	21.30	GEM	23.36	15.36	LIB	17.10	16
17	VIR	SCO	SCO	CAP	AQU	01.32	TAU	GEM	LEO	VIR	06.40	SAG	17
18	07.00	18.37	01.08	16.32	07.36	ARI	TAU	05.37	LEO	18.54	SCO	16.26	18
19	LIB	SAG	SAG	AQU	PIS	14.09	10.08	CAN	05.29	LIB	05.53	CAP	19
20	10.04	22.55	04.25	AQU	18.34	TAU	GEM	14.15	VIR	19.25	SAG	16.53	20
21	SCO	CAP	CAP	01.07	ARI	TAU	21.15	LEO	08.17	SCO	05.11	AQU	21
22	13.18	CAP	10.34	PIS	ARI	02.44	CAN	19.53	LIB	19.00	CAP	20.33	22
23	SAG	05.01	AQU	12.36	07.26	GEM	CAN	VIR	09.23	SAG	06.46	PIS	23
24	17.01	AQU	19.30	ARI	TAU	13.51	05.48	23.21	SCO	19.40	AQU	PIS	24
25	CAP	13.18	PIS	ARI	20.11	CAN	LEO	LIB	10.24	CAP	12.09	04.24	25
26	22.06	PIS	PIS	01.22	GEM	22.55	12.03	LIB	SAG	23.02	PIS	ARI	26
27	AQU	23.54	06.39	TAU	GEM	LEO	VIR	01.48	12.44	AQU	21.26	15.43	27
28	AQU	ARI	ARI	14.13	07.36	LEO	16.41	SCO	CAP	AQU	ARI	TAU	28
29	05.34		19.13	GEM	CAN	06.03	LIB	04.13	17.17	05.51	ARI	TAU	29
30	PIS		TAU	GEM	17.16	VIR	20.09	SAG	AQU	PIS	09.18	04.27	30
31	16.02		TAU		LEO		SCO	07.18		15.38		GEM	31

SUN

mth	dy	time → sign
JAN	1	00.00 → CAP
JAN	20	16.25 → AQU
FEB	19	06.46 → PIS
MAR	21	06.12 → ARI
APR	20	17.39 → TAU
MAY	21	17.08 → GEM
JUN	22	01.17 → CAN
JUL	23	12.07 → LEO
AUG	23	18.59 → VIR
SEP	23	16.16 → LIB
OCT	24	01.15 → SCO
NOV	22	22.32 → SAG
DEC	22	11.39 → CAP

MERCURY

mth	dy	time → sign
JAN	1	00.00 → CAP
JAN	9	15.26 → AQU
MAR	17	00.10 → PIS
APR	5	07.06 → ARI
APR	20	13.42 → TAU
MAY	5	04.38 → GEM
JUL	12	20.24 → CAN
JUL	29	04.24 → LEO
AUG	13	01.46 → VIR
AUG	31	08.27 → LIB
NOV	7	01.44 → SCO
NOV	25	20.27 → SAG
DEC	14	22.22 → CAP

VENUS

mth	dy	time → sign
JAN	1	00.00 → AQU
APR	6	13.13 → PIS
MAY	6	02.25 → ARI
JUN	2	00.26 → TAU
JUN	27	22.19 → GEM
JUL	23	06.10 → CAN
AUG	17	03.05 → LEO
SEP	10	14.38 → VIR
OCT	4	18.57 → LIB
OCT	28	18.41 → SCO
NOV	21	16.09 → SAG
DEC	15	12.53 → CAP

MARS

mth	dy	time → sign
JAN	1	00.00 → ARI
JAN	11	22.27 → TAU
MAR	7	08.03 → GEM
APR	26	06.18 → CAN
JUN	14	03.54 → LEO
AUG	1	08.24 → VIR
SEP	17	10.13 → LIB
NOV	1	22.36 → SCO
DEC	15	16.52 → SAG

SATURN

mth	dy	time → sign
JAN	1	00.00 → TAU
MAY	8	19.32 → GEM

JUPITER

mth	dy	time → sign
JAN	1	00.00 → GEM
JUN	10	10.31 → CAN

MOON

dy	jan	feb	mar	apr	may	jun	jul	aug	sep	oct	nov	dec	dy
1	16.41	LEO	LEO	LIB	SCO	CAP	AQU	ARI	20.40	17.03	LEO	VIR	1
2	CAN	18.57	03.07	19.55	06.04	15.58	03.46	ARI	GEM	CAN	LEO	18.55	2
3	CAN	VIR	VIR	SCO	SAG	AQU	PIS	01.48	GEM	CAN	01.19	LIB	3
4	03.31	VIR	08.23	21.04	06.04	19.14	09.12	TAU	09.01	05.36	VIR	LIB	4
5	LEO	01.19	LIB	SAG	CAP	PIS	ARI	12.54	CAN	LEO	09.22	00.07	5
6	12.42	LIB	11.51	22.42	07.57	PIS	18.22	GEM	21.15	16.13	LIB	SCO	6
7	VIR	05.56	SCO	CAP	AQU	02.12	TAU	GEM	LEO	VIR	13.27	01.34	7
8	19.48	SCO	09.07	CAP	12.44	ARI	TAU	01.31	LEO	23.34	SCO	SAG	8
9	LIB	09.07	SAG	01.56	PIS	12.16	GEM	06.11	CAN	LIB	14.48	01.06	9
10	LIB	SAG	17.09	AQU	20.32	TAU	13.39	VIR		LIB	SAG	CAP	10
11	00.25	11.19	CAP	07.18	ARI	TAU	18.51	LEO	15.05	03.46	15.18	00.57	11
12	SCO	CAP	20.30	PIS	ARI	00.13	CAN	LIB	SCO	CAP	AQU	AQU	12
13	02.33	13.28	AQU	14.49	06.37	GEM	CAN	00.10	20.18	06.11	16.49	02.57	13
14	SAG	AQU	AQU	ARI	TAU	12.50	07.08	VIR	SCO	SAG	AQU	PIS	14
15	03.07	16.51	01.09	ARI	18.15	CAN	LEO	08.31	23.57	08.14	20.29	08.04	15
16	CAP	PIS	PIS	00.19	GEM	CAN	18.08	LIB	SAG	CAP	PIS	ARI	16
17	03.52	22.47	07.42	TAU	GEM	01.18	VIR	14.38	SAG	11.01	PIS	16.18	17
18	AQU	ARI	ARI	11.37	06.49	LEO	VIR	SCO	02.49	AQU	02.30	TAU	18
19	06.44	ARI	16.39	GEM	CAN	12.34	03.02	18.36	CAP	15.05	ARI	TAU	19
20	PIS	07.57	TAU	GEM	19.21	VIR	LIB	SAG	05.27	PIS	10.37	02.48	20
21	13.08	TAU	TAU	00.11	LEO	21.04	09.02	20.46	AQU	20.36	TAU	GEM	21
22	ARI	19.48	04.02	CAN	LEO	LIB	SCO	CAP	08.34	ARI	20.35	14.47	22
23	23.18	GEM	GEM	12.21	06.07	LIB	11.58	22.08	PIS	ARI	GEM	CAN	23
24	TAU	GEM	16.33	LEO	VIR	01.51	SAG	AQU	12.57	03.52	GEM	CAN	24
25	TAU	08.15	CAN	22.03	13.22	SCO	12.38	23.55	ARI	TAU	08.18	03.35	25
26	11.43	CAN	CAN	VIR	LIB	03.09	CAP	PIS	19.35	13.19	CAN	LEO	26
27	GEM	19.07	04.06	VIR	16.32	SAG	12.37	PIS	TAU	GEM	21.09	16.10	27
28	GEM	LEO	LEO	03.50	SCO	02.32	AQU	03.38	TAU	GEM	LEO	VIR	28
29	00.03		12.36	LIB	16.39	CAP	13.49	ARI	05.05	LEO	VIR	VIR	29
30	CAN		VIR	05.59	SAG	02.00	PIS	10.29	GEM	CAN	09.30	02.45	30
31	10.38		17.36		15.43		17.55	TAU		13.48		LIB	31

SUN

mth	dy	time → sign
JAN	1	00.00 → CAP
JAN	20	22.19 → AQU
FEB	19	12.40 → PIS
MAR	21	12.03 → ARI
APR	20	23.31 → TAU
MAY	21	23.03 → GEM
JUN	22	07.12 → CAN
JUL	23	18.04 → LEO
AUG	24	00.55 → VIR
SEP	23	22.12 → LIB
OCT	24	07.08 → SCO
NOV	23	04.21 → SAG
DEC	22	17.29 → CAP

SATURN

mth	dy	time → sign
JAN	1	00.00 → GEM

MERCURY

mth	dy	time → sign
JAN	1	00.00 → CAP
JAN	3	08.27 → AQU
JAN	27	23.43 → CAP
FEB	15	19.00 → AQU
MAR	11	04.59 → PIS
MAR	28	11.19 → ARI
APR	12	04.57 → TAU
APR	30	15.56 → GEM
MAY	26	10.22 → TAU
JUN	14	00.46 → GEM
JUL	6	09.05 → CAN
JUL	20	16.08 → LEO
AUG	5	10.33 → VIR
AUG	27	00.36 → LIB
SEP	25	09.56 → VIR
OCT	11	23.26 → LIB
OCT	30	23.37 → SCO
NOV	18	13.39 → SAG
DEC	8	01.47 → CAP

VENUS

mth	dy	time → sign
JAN	1	00.00 → CAP
JAN	8	10.03 → AQU
FEB	1	09.02 → PIS
FEB	25	12.04 → ARI
MAR	21	22.25 → TAU
APR	15	20.12 → GEM
MAY	11	11.56 → CAN
JUN	7	12.09 → LEO
JUL	7	23.56 → VIR
NOV	9	18.25 → LIB
DEC	8	07.44 → SCO

MARS

mth	dy	time → sign
JAN	1	00.00 → SAG
JAN	26	19.18 → CAP
MAR	8	12.44 → AQU
APR	17	10.25 → PIS
MAY	27	09.29 → ARI
JUL	7	23.08 → TAU
AUG	23	23.51 → GEM

JUPITER

mth	dy	time → sign
JAN	1	00.00 → CAN
JUN	30	21.33 → LEO

MOON

dy	jan	feb	mar	apr	may	jun	jul	aug	sep	oct	nov	dec	dy
1	09.39	23.15	07.19	18.27	04.39	TAU	17.13	LEO	18.33	10.04	SAG	13.01	1
2	SCO	CAP	CAP	PIS	ARI	00.29	CAN	LIB	LIB	SCO	03.37	AQU	2
3	12.33	23.10	08.56	21.17	09.57	GEM	CAN	LIB	00.45	17.03	CAP	15.36	3
4	SAG	AQU	AQU	ARI	TAU	10.45	05.39	VIR	04.20	SAG	07.09	PIS	4
5	12.35	23.07	09.54	ARI	17.16	CAN	LEO	12.51	SCO	22.11	AQU	19.00	5
6	CAP	PIS	PIS	01.37	GEM	23.03	18.45	LIB	11.38	CAP	10.16	ARI	6
7	11.42	PIS	11.41	TAU	GEM	LEO	VIR	22.40	SAG	CAP	PIS	23.30	7
8	AQU	01.00	ARI	08.41	03.17	LEO	VIR	SCO	16.13	01.39	13.10	TAU	8
9	12.03	ARI	15.53	GEM	CAN	12.03	06.44	SCO	CAP	AQU	ARI	TAU	9
10	PIS	06.17	TAU	19.03	15.39	VIR	LIB	05.08	18.18	03.44	16.32	05.32	10
11	15.21	TAU	23.39	CAN	LEO	23.22	15.40	SAG	AQU	PIS	TAU	GEM	11
12	ARI	15.25	GEM	CAN	04.21	LIB	SCO	08.09	18.46	05.12	21.31	13.46	12
13	22.22	GEM	GEM	07.39	LIB	06.59	20.37	CAP	PIS	ARI	GEM	CAN	13
14	TAU	GEM	10.51	LEO	VIR	SCO	SAG	08.36	19.09	07.26	GEM	CAN	14
15	TAU	03.25	CAN	19.59	14.44	SCO	22.07	AQU	ARI	TAU	05.22	00.37	15
16	08.39	CAN	23.41	VIR	LIB	10.36	CAP	08.06	21.14	12.07	CAN	LEO	16
17	GEM	16.18	LEO	VIR	21.19	SAG	21.46	PIS	TAU	GEM	16.27	13.22	17
18	20.53	LEO	LEO	05.41	SCO	11.29	AQU	08.32	TAU	20.28	LEO	VIR	18
19	CAN	LEO	11.43	LIB	SCO	CAP	21.30	ARI	02.42	CAN	LEO	VIR	19
20	CAN	04.20	VIR	12.04	00.33	11.33	PIS	11.39	GEM	CAN	05.21	01.55	20
21	09.44	VIR	21.21	SCO	SAG	AQU	23.08	TAU	12.10	08.12	VIR	LIB	21
22	LEO	14.30	LIB	15.56	02.00	12.36	ARI	18.34	CAN	LEO	17.19	11.46	22
23	22.03	LIB	LIB	SAG	CAP	PIS	ARI	GEM	CAN	21.10	LIB	SCO	23
24	VIR	22.25	04.23	18.39	03.23	15.52	03.53	GEM	00.34	LIB	LIB	17.44	24
25	VIR	SCO	SCO	CAP	AQU	ARI	TAU	05.07	LEO	VIR	02.09	SAG	25
26	08.47	SCO	09.23	21.21	05.58	21.52	12.04	CAN	13.30	08.38	SCO	20.25	26
27	LIB	03.59	SAG	AQU	PIS	TAU	GEM	17.49	VIR	LIB	07.35	CAP	27
28	16.51	SAG	13.05	AQU	10.16	TAU	23.04	LEO	VIR	17.14	SAG	21.21	28
29	SCO		CAP	00.36	ARI	06.27	CAN	LEO	00.56	SCO	10.43	AQU	29
30	21.34		15.57	PIS	16.25	GEM	CAN	06.47	LIB	23.14	CAP	22.17	30
31	SAG		AQU		TAU		11.43	VIR		SAG		PIS	31

SUN

mth	dy	time → sign
JAN	1	00.00 → CAP
JAN	21	04.07 → AQU
FEB	19	18.27 → PIS
MAR	20	17.49 → ARI
APR	20	05.18 → TAU
MAY	21	04.51 → GEM
JUN	21	13.02 → CAN
JUL	22	23.56 → LEO
AUG	23	06.46 → VIR
SEP	23	04.02 → LIB
OCT	23	12.56 → SCO
NOV	22	10.08 → SAG
DEC	21	23.15 → CAP

MERCURY

mth	dy	time → sign
JAN	1	00.00 → CAP
FEB	12	14.17 → AQU
MAR	3	02.45 → PIS
MAR	19	07.43 → ARI
APR	3	17.29 → TAU
JUN	11	11.46 → GEM
JUN	27	03.39 → CAN
JUL	11	07.41 → LEO
JUL	28	23.44 → VIR
OCT	5	03.17 → LIB
OCT	22	11.33 → SCO
NOV	10	11.09 → SAG
DEC	1	15.31 → CAP
DEC	23	23.21 → SAG

VENUS

mth	dy	time → sign
JAN	1	00.00 → SCO
JAN	3	04.43 → SAG
JAN	28	03.11 → CAP
FEB	21	16.40 → AQU
MAR	17	02.46 → PIS
APR	10	12.09 → ARI
MAY	4	22.04 → TAU
MAY	29	08.39 → GEM
JUN	22	19.12 → CAN
JUL	17	04.47 → LEO
AUG	10	13.13 → VIR
SEP	3	21.17 → LIB
SEP	28	06.12 → SCO
OCT	22	17.07 → SAG
NOV	16	07.26 → CAP
DEC	11	04.47 → AQU

MARS

mth	dy	time → sign
JAN	1	00.00 → GEM
MAR	28	09.44 → CAN
MAY	22	14.16 → LEO
JUL	12	02.57 → VIR
AUG	29	00.27 → LIB
OCT	13	12.15 → SCO
NOV	25	16.10 → SAG

SATURN

mth	dy	time → sign
JAN	1	00.00 → GEM
JUN	20	07.55 → CAN

JUPITER

mth	dy	time → sign
JAN	1	00.00 → LEO
JUL	26	01.12 → VIR

MOON

dy	jan	feb	mar	apr	may	jun	jul	aug	sep	oct	nov	dec	dy
1	PIS	TAU	00.06	CAN	23.04	LIB	SCO	14.42	AQU	14.30	TAU	15.17	1
2	00.34	17.17	GEM	02.54	VIR	LIB	23.38	CAP	04.14	ARI	01.28	CAN	2
3	ARI	GEM	08.38	LEO	VIR	06.32	SAG	17.10	PIS	13.46	GEM	21.53	3
4	04.58	GEM	CAN	15.49	11.39	SCO	SAG	AQU	03.27	TAU	05.04	LEO	4
5	TAU	02.40	20.19	VIR	LIB	14.27	04.42	17.35	ARI	14.59	CAN	LEO	5
6	11.44	CAN	LEO	VIR	22.18	SAG	CAP	PIS	03.28	GEM	12.44	08.04	6
7	GEM	14.20	LEO	04.22	SCO	19.41	07.14	17.43	TAU	19.56	LEO	VIR	7
8	20.48	LEO	09.18	LIB	SCO	CAP	AQU	ARI	06.13	CAN	23.59	20.28	8
9	CAN	LEO	VIR	15.12	06.27	23.12	08.39	19.19	GEM	CAN	VIR	LIB	9
10	CAN	03.08	21.55	SCO	SAG	AQU	PIS	TAU	12.47	05.03	VIR	LIB	10
11	07.57	VIR	LIB	SCO	12.33	AQU	10.18	23.38	CAN	LEO	12.45	08.42	11
12	LEO	15.54	LIB	00.02	CAP	01.58	ARI	GEM	22.50	LIB	17.04	SCO	12
13	20.38	LIB	09.12	SAG	17.10	PIS	13.16	GEM	LEO	VIR	LIB	18.50	13
14	VIR	LIB	SCO	06.56	AQU	04.41	TAU	07.03	LEO	VIR	00.48	SAG	14
15	VIR	03.24	18.31	CAP	20.35	ARI	18.11	CAN	11.00	05.55	SCO	SAG	15
16	09.29	SCO	SAG	11.46	PIS	07.52	GEM	17.08	VIR	LIB	11.02	02.22	16
17	LIB	12.15	SAG	AQU	23.03	TAU	GEM	LEO	23.48	18.03	SAG	CAP	17
18	20.27	SAG	01.13	14.28	ARI	12.11	01.21	LEO	LIB	SCO	19.20	07.44	18
19	SCO	17.33	CAP	PIS	ARI	GEM	CAN	05.00	LIB	SCO	CAP	AQU	19
20	SCO	CAP	04.55	15.35	01.15	18.28	10.51	VIR	12.11	04.50	CAP	11.39	20
21	03.53	19.27	AQU	ARI	TAU	CAN	LEO	17.45	SCO	SAG	01.47	PIS	21
22	SAG	AQU	05.59	16.29	04.26	CAN	22.24	LIB	23.16	13.48	AQU	14.42	22
23	07.26	19.09	PIS	TAU	GEM	03.24	VIR	LIB	SAG	CAP	06.18	ARI	23
24	CAP	PIS	05.42	18.59	10.04	LEO	VIR	06.13	SAG	20.19	PIS	17.24	24
25	08.09	18.31	ARI	GEM	CAN	14.58	11.08	SCO	07.55	AQU	08.57	TAU	25
26	AQU	ARI	06.01	GEM	19.04	VIR	LIB	16.52	CAP	23.53	ARI	20.26	26
27	07.48	19.36	TAU	00.49	LEO	VIR	23.16	SAG	13.10	PIS	10.22	GEM	27
28	PIS	TAU	08.58	CAN	LEO	03.40	SCO	SAG	AQU	PIS	TAU	GEM	28
29	08.15	TAU	GEM	10.36	06.58	LIB	SCO	00.12	14.58	00.54	11.55	00.44	29
30	ARI		15.59	LEO	VIR	15.10	08.50	CAP	PIS	ARI	GEM	CAN	30
31	11.07		CAN		19.37		SAG	03.44		00.45		07.19	31

SUN

mth	dy	time → sign
JAN	1	00.00 → CAP
JAN	20	09.54 → AQU
FEB	19	00.14 → PIS
MAR	20	23.37 → ARI
APR	20	11.07 → TAU
MAY	21	10.40 → GEM
JUN	21	18.52 → CAN
JUL	23	05.45 → LEO
AUG	23	12.35 → VIR
SEP	23	09.50 → LIB
OCT	23	18.44 → SCO
NOV	22	15.55 → SAG
DEC	22	05.03 → CAP

MERCURY

mth	dy	time → sign
JAN	1	00.00 → SAG
JAN	14	03.04 → CAP
FEB	5	09.20 → AQU
FEB	23	11.26 → PIS
MAR	11	06.45 → ARI
MAY	16	15.21 → TAU
JUN	4	10.30 → GEM
JUN	18	12.27 → CAN
JUL	3	15.39 → LEO
JUL	26	14.48 → VIR
AUG	17	08.35 → LEO
SEP	10	07.20 → VIR
SEP	27	12.08 → LIB
OCT	15	00.13 → SCO
NOV	3	23.06 → SAG

VENUS

mth	dy	time → sign
JAN	1	00.00 → AQU
JAN	5	19.18 → PIS
FEB	2	08.07 → ARI
MAR	11	11.17 → TAU
APR	7	19.15 → ARI
JUN	4	22.57 → TAU
JUL	7	16.20 → GEM
AUG	4	10.59 → CAN
AUG	30	13.05 → LEO
SEP	24	16.06 → VIR
OCT	19	04.09 → LIB
NOV	12	07.05 → SCO
DEC	6	05.22 → SAG
DEC	30	01.56 → CAP

MARS

mth	dy	time → sign
JAN	1	00.00 → SAG
JAN	5	19.34 → CAP
FEB	14	09.53 → AQU
MAR	25	03.41 → PIS
MAY	2	20.28 → ARI
JUN	11	11.57 → TAU
JUL	23	08.48 → GEM
SEP	7	20.54 → CAN
NOV	11	21.03 → LEO
DEC	26	15.14 → CAN

SATURN

mth	dy	time → sign
JAN	1	00.00 → CAN

JUPITER

mth	dy	time → sign
JAN	1	00.00 → VIR
AUG	25	06.26 → LIB

MOON

dy	jan	feb	mar	apr	may	jun	jul	aug	sep	oct	nov	dec	dy
1	LEO	12.46	LIB	SCO	19.40	AQU	PIS	TAU	CAN	LEO	10.08	04.43	1
2	16.49	LIB	LIB	03.08	CAP	15.25	00.28	11.23	CAN	17.34	LIB	SCO	2
3	VIR	LIB	08.32	SAG	CAP	PIS	ARI	GEM	03.19	VIR	22.28	17.30	3
4	VIR	01.22	SCO	13.51	04.06	18.51	03.04	15.23	LEO	VIR	SCO	SAG	4
5	04.44	SCO	20.45	CAP	AQU	ARI	TAU	CAN	11.36	04.16	SCO	SAG	5
6	LIB	12.57	SAG	21.28	09.21	20.23	05.20	20.52	VIR	LIB	11.18	05.23	6
7	17.13	SAG	SAG	AQU	PIS	TAU	GEM	LEO	21.48	16.24	SAG	CAP	7
8	SCO	21.28	06.37	AQU	11.25	21.15	08.10	LEO	LIB	SCO	23.35	15.34	8
9	SCO	CAP	CAP	01.10	ARI	GEM	CAN	04.24	LIB	SCO	CAP	AQU	9
10	03.55	CAP	12.40	PIS	11.24	23.02	12.43	VIR	09.48	05.17	CAP	23.20	10
11	SAG	02.12	AQU	01.38	TAU	CAN	LEO	14.21	SCO	SAG	09.59	PIS	11
12	11.28	AQU	14.50	ARI	11.12	CAN	19.58	LIB	22.37	17.33	AQU	PIS	12
13	CAP	03.52	PIS	00.40	GEM	03.20	VIR	LIB	SAG	CAP	17.05	04.15	13
14	15.57	PIS	14.32	TAU	12.51	LEO	VIR	02.24	SAG	CAP	PIS	ARI	14
15	AQU	04.12	ARI	00.31	CAN	11.07	06.13	SCO	10.11	03.07	20.24	06.30	15
16	18.27	ARI	13.54	GEM	17.57	VIR	LIB	14.56	CAP	AQU	ARI	TAU	16
17	PIS	05.05	TAU	03.13	LEO	22.06	18.28	SAG	18.19	08.34	20.48	07.03	17
18	20.21	TAU	15.04	CAN	LEO	LIB	SCO	SAG	AQU	PIS	TAU	GEM	18
19	ARI	08.01	GEM	09.52	02.56	LIB	SCO	01.31	22.19	10.09	20.02	07.27	19
20	22.48	GEM	19.31	LEO	VIR	10.36	06.36	CAP	PIS	ARI	GEM	CAN	20
21	TAU	13.42	CAN	20.03	14.43	SCO	SAG	08.32	23.11	09.30	20.14	09.30	21
22	TAU	CAN	CAN	VIR	LIB	22.27	16.28	AQU	ARI	TAU	CAN	LEO	22
23	02.35	21.58	03.32	VIR	LIB	SAG	CAP	12.05	22.53	08.49	23.12	14.44	23
24	GEM	LEO	LEO	08.15	03.21	SAG	23.16	PIS	TAU	GEM	LEO	VIR	24
25	08.05	LEO	14.11	LIB	SCO	08.14	AQU	13.30	23.32	10.11	LEO	23.45	25
26	CAN	08.13	VIR	20.52	15.11	CAP	AQU	ARI	GEM	CAN	05.59	LIB	26
27	15.33	VIR	VIR	SCO	SAG	15.36	03.26	14.34	GEM	14.55	VIR	LIB	27
28	LEO	19.57	02.15	SCO	SAG	AQU	PIS	TAU	02.38	LEO	16.18	11.43	28
29	LEO		LIB	08.56	01.24	20.51	06.07	16.47	CAN	23.12	LIB	SCO	29
30	01.09		14.50	SAG	CAP	PIS	ARI	GEM	08.47	VIR	LIB	SCO	30
31	VIR		SCO		09.35		08.28	21.00		VIR		00.32	31

SUN

mth	dy	time → sign
JAN	1	00.00 → CAP
JAN	20	15.45 → AQU
FEB	19	06.08 → PIS
MAR	21	05.32 → ARI
APR	20	17.02 → TAU
MAY	21	16.34 → GEM
JUN	22	00.44 → CAN
JUL	23	11.37 → LEO
AUG	23	18.26 → VIR
SEP	23	15.41 → LIB
OCT	24	00.35 → SCO
NOV	22	21.46 → SAG
DEC	22	10.54 → CAP

MERCURY

mth	dy	time → sign
JAN	1	00.00 → SAG
JAN	9	14.10 → CAP
JAN	29	07.22 → AQU
FEB	15	15.43 → PIS
MAR	4	09.27 → ARI
APR	1	18.16 → PIS
APR	16	14.54 → ARI
MAY	11	14.29 → TAU
MAY	27	04.13 → GEM
JUN	10	02.00 → CAN
JUN	27	19.07 → LEO
SEP	3	16.29 → VIR
SEP	19	14.34 → LIB
OCT	7	21.21 → SCO
OCT	30	11.23 → SAG
NOV	20	20.16 → SCO
DEC	13	00.03 → SAG

VENUS

mth	dy	time → sign
JAN	1	00.00 → CAP
JAN	22	22.29 → AQU
FEB	15	20.12 → PIS
MAR	11	20.32 → ARI
APR	5	01.01 → TAU
APR	29	10.59 → GEM
MAY	24	03.40 → CAN
JUN	18	05.00 → LEO
JUL	13	19.22 → VIR
AUG	9	08.35 → LIB
SEP	7	00.16 → SCO
OCT	16	10.45 → SAG
NOV	8	08.56 → SCO

MARS

mth	dy	time → sign
JAN	1	00.00 → CAN
APR	22	19.40 → LEO
JUN	20	08.38 → VIR
AUG	9	13.17 → LIB
SEP	24	16.31 → SCO
NOV	6	18.18 → SAG
DEC	17	10.52 → CAP

SATURN

mth	dy	time → sign
JAN	1	00.00 → CAN
AUG	2	14.31 → LEO

JUPITER

mth	dy	time → sign
JAN	1	00.00 → LIB
SEP	25	10.28 → SCO

MOON

dy	jan	feb	mar	apr	may	jun	jul	aug	sep	oct	nov	dec	dy
1	SAG	05.23	AQU	09.16	TAU	06.29	LEO	12.05	SCO	SAG	10.36	04.30	1
2	12.11	AQU	20.25	ARI	20.03	CAN	20.45	LIB	17.31	14.29	AQU	PIS	2
3	CAP	11.32	PIS	09.56	GEM	07.39	VIR	21.23	SAG	CAP	20.32	12.05	3
4	21.38	PIS	23.23	TAU	20.23	LEO	VIR	SCO	SAG	CAP	PIS	ARI	4
5	AQU	15.38	ARI	10.25	CAN	11.57	03.21	SCO	06.24	02.27	PIS	15.48	5
6	AQU	ARI	ARI	GEM	23.04	VIR	LIB	09.36	CAP	AQU	03.29	TAU	6
7	04.47	18.47	01.08	12.21	LEO	19.57	13.41	SAG	17.41	11.09	ARI	16.30	7
8	PIS	TAU	TAU	CAN	LEO	LIB	SCO	22.23	AQU	PIS	04.49	GEM	8
9	09.56	21.45	03.12	16.37	04.57	LIB	SCO	CAP	AQU	16.05	TAU	15.50	9
10	ARI	GEM	GEM	LEO	VIR	07.04	02.20	CAP	01.46	ARI	05.07	CAN	10
11	13.25	GEM	06.29	23.20	13.53	SCO	SAG	09.23	PIS	18.20	GEM	15.46	11
12	TAU	00.59	CAN	VIR	LIB	19.50	15.05	AQU	06.49	TAU	05.15	LEO	12
13	15.42	CAN	11.14	VIR	LIB	SAG	CAP	17.41	ARI	19.37	CAN	18.09	13
14	GEM	04.50	LEO	08.13	01.08	SAG	CAP	PIS	10.03	GEM	06.53	VIR	14
15	17.32	LEO	17.32	LIB	SCO	08.39	02.17	23.37	TAU	21.23	LEO	VIR	15
16	CAN	10.03	VIR	19.03	13.46	CAP	AQU	ARI	12.45	CAN	11.05	00.07	16
17	20.04	VIR	VIR	SCO	SAG	20.16	11.15	ARI	GEM	CAN	VIR	LIB	17
18	LEO	17.36	01.40	SCO	SAG	AQU	PIS	03.59	15.42	00.35	18.12	09.43	18
19	LEO	LIB	LIB	07.30	02.42	AQU	17.59	TAU	CAN	LEO	LIB	SCO	19
20	00.40	LIB	12.04	SAG	CAP	05.43	ARI	07.22	19.13	05.35	LIB	21.48	20
21	VIR	04.05	SCO	20.29	14.31	PIS	22.35	GEM	LEO	VIR	03.58	SAG	21
22	08.31	SCO	SCO	CAP	AQU	12.19	TAU	10.06	23.38	12.33	SCO	SAG	22
23	LIB	16.41	00.30	CAP	23.39	ARI	TAU	CAN	VIR	LIB	15.44	10.50	23
24	19.40	SAG	SAG	07.56	PIS	15.56	01.18	12.38	VIR	21.41	SAG	CAP	24
25	SCO	SAG	13.18	AQU	PIS	TAU	GEM	LEO	05.40	SCO	SAG	23.29	25
26	SCO	05.01	CAP	15.54	05.05	17.07	02.44	15.54	LIB	SCO	04.40	AQU	26
27	08.27	CAP	23.51	PIS	ARI	GEM	CAN	VIR	14.12	09.03	CAP	AQU	27
28	SAG	14.34	AQU	19.45	07.03	17.10	03.57	21.15	SCO	SAG	17.30	10.43	28
29	20.18		AQU	ARI	TAU	CAN	LEO	LIB	SCO	21.59	AQU	PIS	29
30	CAP		06.26	20.31	06.54	17.47	06.32	LIB	01.32	CAP	AQU	19.31	30
31	CAP		PIS		GEM		VIR	05.49		CAP		ARI	31

SUN

mth	dy	time	→ sign
JAN	1	00.00	→ CAP
JAN	20	21.31	→ AQU
FEB	19	11.52	→ PIS
MAR	21	11.13	→ ARI
APR	20	22.39	→ TAU
MAY	21	22.09	→ GEM
JUN	22	06.19	→ CAN
JUL	23	17.14	→ LEO
AUG	24	00.09	→ VIR
SEP	23	21.29	→ LIB
OCT	24	06.26	→ SCO
NOV	23	03.38	→ SAG
DEC	22	16.43	→ CAP

MERCURY

mth	dy	time	→ sign
JAN	1	00.00	→ SAG
JAN	3	01.46	→ CAP
JAN	21	21.06	→ AQU
FEB	8	01.32	→ PIS
APR	16	04.31	→ ARI
MAY	4	06.03	→ TAU
MAY	18	13.33	→ GEM
JUN	2	13.40	→ CAN
AUG	10	17.40	→ LEO
AUG	26	14.50	→ VIR
SEP	11	20.54	→ LIB
OCT	1	15.26	→ SCO
DEC	7	12.32	→ SAG
DEC	26	23.18	→ CAP

VENUS

mth	dy	time	→ sign
JAN	1	00.00	→ SCO
JAN	5	16.45	→ SAG
FEB	6	05.41	→ CAP
MAR	5	05.09	→ AQU
MAR	30	22.15	→ PIS
APR	25	03.03	→ ARI
MAY	20	02.06	→ TAU
JUN	13	21.35	→ GEM
JUL	8	13.30	→ CAN
AUG	2	01.06	→ LEO
AUG	26	08.17	→ VIR
SEP	19	12.01	→ LIB
OCT	13	13.49	→ SCO
NOV	6	14.59	→ SAG
NOV	30	16.23	→ CAP
DEC	24	19.13	→ AQU

MARS

mth	dy	time	→ sign
JAN	1	00.00	→ CAP
JAN	25	11.41	→ AQU
MAR	4	16.47	→ PIS
APR	11	23.19	→ ARI
MAY	21	03.44	→ TAU
JUL	1	03.34	→ GEM
AUG	13	21.21	→ CAN
OCT	1	02.38	→ LEO
DEC	1	11.41	→ VIR

SATURN

mth	dy	time	→ sign
JAN	1	00.00	→ LEO

JUPITER

mth	dy	time	→ sign
JAN	1	00.00	→ SCO
OCT	24	03.10	→ SAG

MOON

dy	jan	feb	mar	apr	may	jun	jul	aug	sep	oct	nov	dec	dy
1	ARI	GEM	20.59	LEO	19.24	SCO	SAG	07.50	PIS	ARI	GEM	CAN	1
2	01.06	13.38	CAN	08.30	LIB	18.54	13.03	AQU	02.15	TAU	17.32	02.30	2
3	TAU	CAN	23.00	VIR	LIB	SAG	CAP	19.49	ARI	07.44	CAN	LEO	3
4	03.26	14.01	LEO	12.39	02.35	SAG	CAP	PIS	20.10	GEM	20.03	04.23	4
5	GEM	LEO	LEO	LIB	SCO	06.51	01.50	PIS	TAU	GEM	LEO	VIR	5
6	03.28	14.42	00.46	18.56	12.09	CAP	AQU	06.20	TAU	11.47	22.55	08.14	6
7	CAN	VIR	VIR	SCO	SAG	19.38	14.03	ARI	02.18	CAN	VIR	LIB	7
8	02.53	17.39	03.51	SCO	23.55	AQU	PIS	14.43	GEM	14.41	VIR	14.24	8
9	LEO	LIB	LIB	04.12	CAP	AQU	PIS	TAU	06.12	LEO	02.42	SCO	9
10	03.45	LIB	09.51	SAG	CAP	07.47	00.34	20.17	CAN	16.57	LIB	22.49	10
11	VIR	00.28	SCO	16.08	12.41	PIS	ARI	GEM	08.03	VIR	08.02	SAG	11
12	07.54	SCO	19.34	CAP	AQU	17.34	08.12	22.49	LEO	19.31	SCO	SAG	12
13	LIB	11.15	SAG	CAP	AQU	ARI	TAU	CAN	08.51	LIB	15.33	09.14	13
14	16.15	SAG	SAG	04.51	00.20	23.45	12.16	23.06	VIR	23.45	SAG	CAP	14
15	SCO	SAG	08.00	AQU	PIS	TAU	GEM	LEO	10.16	SCO	SAG	21.16	15
16	SCO	00.12	CAP	15.47	08.56	TAU	13.14	22.49	LIB	SCO	01.37	AQU	16
17	04.03	CAP	20.35	PIS	ARI	02.23	CAN	VIR	06.53	CAP	AQU	17
18	SAG	12.38	AQU	23.25	13.51	GEM	12.34	VIR	SCO	SAG	13.45	09.59	18
19	17.10	AQU	AQU	ARI	TAU	02.32	LEO	00.04	21.49	17.14	AQU	PIS	19
20	CAP	22.57	06.57	ARI	15.51	CAN	12.19	LIB	SAG	CAP	AQU	21.37	20
21	CAP	PIS	PIS	03.56	GEM	02.06	VIR	04.44	SAG	CAP	02.16	ARI	21
22	05.37	PIS	14.23	TAU	16.27	LEO	14.33	SCO	08.58	05.39	PIS	ARI	22
23	AQU	06.57	ARI	06.27	CAN	03.01	LIB	13.34	CAP	AQU	12.53	06.11	23
24	16.23	ARI	19.29	GEM	17.18	VIR	20.41	SAG	21.38	17.45	ARI	TAU	24
25	PIS	13.08	TAU	08.22	LEO	06.51	SCO	SAG	AQU	PIS	20.06	10.47	25
26	PIS	TAU	23.16	CAN	19.50	LIB	SCO	01.31	AQU	PIS	TAU	GEM	26
27	01.10	17.47	GEM	10.44	VIR	14.17	06.40	CAP	09.24	03.31	23.55	12.03	27
28	ARI	GEM	GEM	LEO	VIR	SCO	SAG	14.18	PIS	ARI	GEM	CAN	28
29	07.45		02.26	14.15	00.54	SCO	19.01	AQU	18.58	10.16	GEM	11.41	29
30	TAU		CAN	VIR	LIB	00.46	CAP	AQU	ARI	TAU	01.31	LEO	30
31	11.52		05.22		08.42		CAP	02.03		14.36		11.47	31

SUN

mth	dy	time → sign
JAN	1	00.00 → CAP
JAN	21	03.17 → AQU
FEB	19	17.36 → PIS
MAR	20	16.57 → ARI
APR	20	04.25 → TAU
MAY	21	03.57 → GEM
JUN	21	12.11 → CAN
JUL	22	23.08 → LEO
AUG	23	06.03 → VIR
SEP	23	03.22 → LIB
OCT	23	12.17 → SCO
NOV	22	09.29 → SAG
DEC	21	22.33 → CAP

MERCURY

mth	dy	time → sign
JAN	1	00.00 → CAP
JAN	14	10.06 → AQU
FEB	2	00.47 → PIS
FEB	20	11.05 → AQU
MAR	18	08.14 → PIS
APR	9	02.26 → ARI
APR	25	01.38 → TAU
MAY	9	04.38 → GEM
MAY	28	10.50 → CAN
JUN	28	17.57 → GEM
JUL	11	20.56 → CAN
AUG	2	13.54 → LEO
AUG	17	08.44 → VIR
SEP	3	15.47 → LIB
SEP	27	07.19 → SCO
OCT	17	03.33 → LIB
NOV	10	02.19 → SCO
NOV	29	15.09 → SAG
DEC	18	16.47 → CAP

VENUS

mth	dy	time → sign
JAN	1	00.00 → AQU
JAN	18	02.14 → PIS
FEB	11	18.51 → ARI
MAR	8	07.00 → TAU
APR	4	12.40 → GEM
MAY	7	08.26 → CAN
JUN	29	07.58 → GEM
AUG	3	02.14 → CAN
SEP	8	13.40 → LEO
OCT	6	12.25 → VIR
NOV	1	06.42 → LIB
NOV	26	00.55 → SCO
DEC	20	07.28 → SAG

MARS

mth	dy	time → sign
JAN	1	00.00 → VIR
FEB	12	10.19 → LEO
MAY	18	20.51 → VIR
JUL	17	05.38 → LIB
SEP	3	13.52 → SCO
OCT	17	05.39 → SAG
NOV	26	21.57 → CAP

SATURN

mth	dy	time → sign
JAN	1	00.00 → LEO
SEP	19	04.23 → VIR

JUPITER

mth	dy	time → sign
JAN	1	00.00 → SAG
NOV	15	10.27 → CAP

MOON

dy	jan	feb	mar	apr	may	jun	jul	aug	sep	oct	nov	dec	dy
1	VIR	02.26	17.41	CAP	AQU	15.55	10.40	GEM	LEO	VIR	SCO	SAG	1
2	14.10	SCO	SAG	23.17	19.44	ARI	TAU	07.20	18.20	04.30	18.10	09.16	2
3	LIB	10.26	SAG	AQU	PIS	ARI	17.48	CAN	VIR	LIB	SAG	CAP	3
4	19.51	SAG	03.50	AQU	PIS	01.43	GEM	08.13	17.35	04.58	23.39	17.32	4
5	SCO	21.30	CAP	11.56	07.28	TAU	21.07	LEO	LIB	SCO	CAP	AQU	5
6	SCO	CAP	16.14	PIS	ARI	08.06	CAN	07.32	18.34	07.55	CAP	AQU	6
7	04.40	CAP	AQU	23.28	16.48	GEM	21.53	VIR	SCO	SAG	08.41	04.46	7
8	SAG	09.59	AQU	ARI	TAU	11.28	LEO	07.30	22.52	14.31	AQU	PIS	8
9	15.41	AQU	04.53	ARI	23.20	CAN	22.03	LIB	SAG	CAP	20.34	17.30	9
10	CAP	22.36	PIS	08.58	GEM	13.11	VIR	09.56	SAG	CAP	PIS	ARI	10
11	CAP	PIS	16.33	TAU	GEM	LEO	23.31	SCO	06.56	00.42	PIS	ARI	11
12	03.54	PIS	ARI	16.20	03.38	14.49	LIB	15.49	CAP	AQU	09.12	05.09	12
13	AQU	10.36	ARI	GEM	CAN	VIR	LIB	SAG	17.58	13.03	ARI	TAU	13
14	16.35	ARI	02.40	21.41	06.39	17.33	03.28	SAG	AQU	PIS	20.24	13.44	14
15	PIS	21.08	TAU	CAN	LEO	LIB	SCO	00.51	AQU	PIS	TAU	GEM	15
16	PIS	TAU	10.45	CAN	09.14	22.03	10.11	CAP	06.26	01.36	TAU	19.01	16
17	04.44	TAU	GEM	01.16	VIR	SCO	SAG	12.02	PIS	ARI	05.02	CAN	17
18	ARI	04.56	16.14	LEO	12.07	SCO	19.13	AQU	19.02	12.54	GEM	22.03	18
19	14.42	GEM	CAN	03.30	LIB	04.28	CAP	AQU	ARI	TAU	11.11	LEO	19
20	TAU	09.09	18.58	VIR	15.56	SAG	CAP	00.23	ARI	22.15	CAN	LEO	20
21	21.01	CAN	LEO	05.16	SCO	12.51	06.02	PIS	06.45	GEM	15.32	00.19	21
22	GEM	10.07	19.42	LIB	21.22	CAP	AQU	13.05	TAU	GEM	LEO	VIR	22
23	23.23	LEO	VIR	07.49	SAG	23.15	18.13	ARI	16.40	05.21	18.48	02.59	23
24	CAN	09.22	20.01	SCO	SAG	AQU	PIS	ARI	GEM	CAN	VIR	LIB	24
25	23.00	VIR	LIB	12.31	05.08	AQU	PIS	01.03	23.46	10.10	21.33	06.39	25
26	LEO	09.05	21.49	SAG	CAP	11.23	06.57	TAU	CAN	LEO	LIB	SCO	26
27	21.56	LIB	SCO	20.21	15.31	PIS	ARI	10.40	CAN	12.53	LIB	11.29	27
28	VIR	11.24	SCO	CAP	AQU	23.56	18.34	GEM	03.35	VIR	00.19	SAG	28
29	22.29	SCO	02.46	CAP	AQU	ARI	TAU	16.34	LEO	14.16	SCO	17.47	29
30	LIB		SAG	07.16	03.46	ARI	TAU	CAN	LEO	LIB	03.52	CAP	30
31	LIB		11.34		PIS		03.01	18.41		15.31		CAP	31

SUN

mth	dy	time	→ sign
JAN	1	00.00	→ CAP
JAN	20	09.09	→ AQU
FEB	18	23.27	→ PIS
MAR	20	22.48	→ ARI
APR	20	10.18	→ TAU
MAY	21	09.50	→ GEM
JUN	21	18.03	→ CAN
JUL	23	04.57	→ LEO
AUG	23	11.48	→ VIR
SEP	23	09.06	→ LIB
OCT	23	18.03	→ SCO
NOV	22	15.16	→ SAG
DEC	22	04.23	→ CAP

MERCURY

mth	dy	time	→ sign
JAN	1	00.00	→ CAP
JAN	6	08.53	→ AQU
MAR	14	09.52	→ PIS
APR	1	16.02	→ ARI
APR	16	14.55	→ TAU
MAY	2	02.19	→ GEM
JUL	10	03.19	→ CAN
JUL	25	05.20	→ LEO
AUG	9	09.04	→ VIR
AUG	28	15.48	→ LIB
NOV	3	18.58	→ SCO
NOV	22	09.07	→ SAG
DEC	11	13.37	→ CAP

VENUS

mth	dy	time	→ sign
JAN	1	00.00	→ SAG
JAN	13	09.01	→ CAP
FEB	6	09.06	→ AQU
MAR	2	09.38	→ PIS
MAR	26	11.54	→ ARI
APR	19	16.44	→ TAU
MAY	14	00.26	→ GEM
JUN	7	10.47	→ CAN
JUL	1	23.41	→ LEO
JUL	26	15.44	→ VIR
AUG	20	12.39	→ LIB
SEP	14	17.12	→ SCO
OCT	10	10.18	→ SAG
NOV	6	04.53	→ CAP
DEC	6	06.06	→ AQU

MARS

mth	dy	time	→ sign
JAN	1	00.00	→ CAP
JAN	4	17.50	→ AQU
FEB	11	18.16	→ PIS
MAR	21	22.02	→ ARI
APR	30	02.33	→ TAU
JUN	10	00.49	→ GEM
JUL	23	05.54	→ CAN
SEP	7	04.55	→ LEO
OCT	27	00.58	→ VIR
DEC	26	05.20	→ LIB

SATURN

mth	dy	time	→ sign
JAN	1	00.00	→ VIR
APR	3	03.44	→ LEO
MAY	29	12.49	→ VIR

JUPITER

mth	dy	time	→ sign
JAN	1	00.00	→ CAP
APR	12	19.24	→ AQU
JUN	27	18.37	→ CAP
NOV	30	20.18	→ AQU

MOON

dy	jan	feb	mar	apr	may	jun	jul	aug	sep	oct	nov	dec	dy
1	02.07	PIS	15.35	TAU	GEM	00.35	VIR	SCO	12.05	01.13	PIS	ARI	1
2	AQU	09.04	ARI	22.03	12.43	LEO	13.22	SCO	CAP	AQU	05.34	01.22	2
3	12.58	ARI	ARI	GEM	CAN	04.53	LIB	01.25	19.37	11.19	ARI	TAU	3
4	PIS	21.57	04.33	GEM	19.11	VIR	16.22	SAG	AQU	PIS	18.37	13.28	4
5	PIS	TAU	TAU	07.10	LEO	07.57	SCO	06.35	AQU	23.27	TAU	GEM	5
6	01.40	TAU	16.05	CAN	23.11	LIB	19.45	CAP	05.26	ARI	TAU	23.31	6
7	ARI	08.40	GEM	12.59	VIR	10.13	SAG	13.34	PIS	ARI	06.55	CAN	7
8	14.03	GEM	GEM	LEO	VIR	SCO	SAG	AQU	17.13	12.26	GEM	CAN	8
9	TAU	15.22	00.21	15.32	01.07	12.23	00.02	22.45	ARI	TAU	17.35	07.27	9
10	23.31	CAN	CAN	VIR	LIB	SAG	CAP	PIS	ARI	TAU	CAN	LEO	10
11	GEM	18.00	04.33	15.48	01.54	15.40	06.09	PIS	06.12	01.02	CAN	13.31	11
12	GEM	LEO	LEO	LIB	SCO	CAP	AQU	10.20	TAU	GEM	02.00	VIR	12
13	04.57	18.05	05.24	15.27	02.57	21.26	15.01	ARI	18.47	11.51	LEO	17.45	13
14	CAN	VIR	VIR	SCO	SAG	AQU	PIS	23.18	GEM	CAN	07.42	LIB	14
15	07.08	17.44	04.40	16.23	05.57	AQU	PIS	TAU	GEM	19.35	VIR	20.13	15
16	LEO	LIB	LIB	SAG	CAP	06.38	02.43	TAU	04.51	LEO	10.35	SCO	16
17	07.52	18.53	04.25	20.16	12.19	PIS	ARI	11.23	CAN	23.42	LIB	21.32	17
18	VIR	SCO	SCO	CAP	AQU	18.45	15.35	GEM	11.04	LIB	11.18	SAG	18
19	09.03	22.49	06.30	CAP	22.26	ARI	TAU	20.15	LEO	VIR	SCO	23.00	19
20	LIB	SAG	SAG	03.59	PIS	ARI	TAU	CAN	13.34	00.48	11.15	CAP	20
21	11.59	SAG	12.04	AQU	PIS	07.30	02.57	CAN	VIR	LIB	SAG	CAP	21
22	SCO	05.50	CAP	15.08	11.02	TAU	GEM	01.07	13.41	00.18	12.19	02.24	22
23	17.09	CAP	21.10	PIS	ARI	18.20	10.52	LEO	LIB	SCO	CAP	AQU	23
24	SAG	15.26	AQU	PIS	23.42	GEM	CAN	02.55	13.20	00.08	16.24	09.20	24
25	SAG	AQU	AQU	04.01	TAU	GEM	15.19	VIR	SCO	SAG	AQU	PIS	25
26	00.21	AQU	08.50	ARI	TAU	02.01	LEO	03.24	14.21	02.10	AQU	20.05	26
27	CAP	02.54	PIS	16.41	10.27	CAN	17.35	LIB	SAG	CAP	00.35	ARI	27
28	09.26	PIS	21.41	TAU	GEM	07.00	VIR	04.19	18.07	07.50	PIS	ARI	28
29	AQU		ARI	TAU	18.38	LEO	19.20	SCO	CAP	AQU	12.18	08.58	29
30	20.26		ARI	03.48	CAN	10.27	LIB	07.00	CAP	17.21	ARI	TAU	30
31	PIS		10.29		CAN		21.44	SAG		PIS		21.13	31

SUN

mth	dy	time → sign
JAN	1	00.00 → CAP
JAN	20	15.00 → AQU
FEB	19	05.17 → PIS
MAR	21	04.34 → ARI
APR	20	15.59 → TAU
MAY	21	15.27 → GEM
JUN	21	23.36 → CAN
JUL	23	10.30 → LEO
AUG	23	17.20 → VIR
SEP	23	14.44 → LIB
OCT	23	23.45 → SCO
NOV	22	21.02 → SAG
DEC	22	10.14 → CAP

MERCURY

mth	dy	time → sign
JAN	1	12.40 → AQU
JAN	15	07.34 → CAP
FEB	14	19.12 → AQU
MAR	7	22.05 → PIS
MAR	24	15.52 → ARI
APR	8	11.13 → TAU
JUN	14	14.33 → GEM
JUL	2	14.57 → CAN
JUL	16	17.08 → LEO
AUG	2	02.44 → VIR
AUG	27	14.17 → LIB
SEP	10	19.15 → VIR
OCT	9	14.40 → LIB
OCT	27	10.36 → SCO
NOV	15	03.10 → SAG
DEC	5	01.57 → CAP

VENUS

mth	dy	time → sign
JAN	1	00.00 → AQU
APR	6	15.13 → PIS
MAY	5	19.19 → ARI
JUN	1	14.19 → TAU
JUN	27	10.45 → GEM
JUL	22	17.50 → CAN
AUG	16	14.18 → LEO
SEP	10	01.37 → VIR
OCT	4	05.51 → LIB
OCT	28	05.33 → SCO
NOV	21	03.03 → SAG
DEC	14	23.54 → CAP

MARS

mth	dy	time → sign
JAN	1	00.00 → LIB
MAR	28	11.09 → VIR
JUN	11	20.18 → LIB
AUG	10	16.42 → SCO
SEP	25	19.45 → SAG
NOV	6	06.40 → CAP
DEC	15	08.47 → AQU

SATURN

mth	dy	time → sign
JAN	1	00.00 → VIR
NOV	20	15.45 → LIB

JUPITER

mth	dy	time → sign
JAN	1	00.00 → AQU
APR	15	08.51 → PIS
SEP	15	02.25 → AQU
DEC	1	19.48 → PIS

MOON

dy	jan	feb	mar	apr	may	jun	jul	aug	sep	oct	nov	dec	dy
1	GEM	22.34	08.30	VIR	11.37	21.27	09.19	PIS	02.19	GEM	CAN	21.53	1
2	GEM	LEO	LEO	00.40	SCO	CAP	AQU	07.03	TAU	GEM	05.38	VIR	2
3	06.56	LEO	12.25	LIB	10.50	23.18	13.51	ARI	14.45	10.59	LEO	VIR	3
4	CAN	02.37	VIR	00.34	SAG	AQU	PIS	18.06	GEM	CAN	14.21	04.29	4
5	13.58	VIR	14.00	SCO	11.08	AQU	22.25	TAU	GEM	21.40	VIR	LIB	5
6	LEO	05.19	LIB	00.37	CAP	04.57	ARI	TAU	02.54	LEO	19.10	07.19	6
7	19.06	LIB	14.55	SAG	14.22	PIS	ARI	06.44	CAN	LEO	LIB	SCO	7
8	VIR	07.50	SCO	02.29	AQU	14.44	10.13	GEM	04.54	VIR	20.29	07.17	8
9	23.08	SCO	16.37	CAP	21.34	ARI	TAU	18.27	LEO	VIR	SCO	SAG	9
10	LIB	10.51	SAG	07.25	PIS	ARI	23.02	CAN	18.55	19.51	19.51	06.16	10
11	LIB	SAG	20.07	AQU	PIS	03.12	GEM	CAN	VIR	LIB	SAG	CAP	11
12	02.28	14.45	CAP	15.38	08.18	TAU	GEM	03.36	22.28	09.31	19.25	06.34	12
13	SCO	CAP	CAP	PIS	ARI	16.05	10.33	LEO	LIB	SCO	CAP	AQU	13
14	05.16	19.57	01.52	PIS	20.59	GEM	CAN	10.03	LIB	09.44	21.14	10.10	14
15	SAG	AQU	AQU	02.32	TAU	GEM	19.52	VIR	00.27	SAG	AQU	PIS	15
16	08.06	AQU	09.59	ARI	TAU	03.45	LEO	14.31	SCO	10.55	AQU	17.58	16
17	CAP	03.11	PIS	15.00	09.52	CAN	LEO	LIB	02.12	CAP	02.38	ARI	17
18	12.07	PIS	20.21	TAU	GEM	13.37	03.05	17.49	SAG	14.27	PIS	ARI	18
19	AQU	13.01	ARI	TAU	21.50	LEO	VIR	SCO	04.49	AQU	11.39	05.09	19
20	18.41	ARI	ARI	03.54	CAN	21.31	08.34	20.36	CAP	20.53	ARI	TAU	20
21	PIS	ARI	08.32	GEM	CAN	VIR	LIB	SAG	08.59	PIS	23.08	17.49	21
22	PIS	01.12	TAU	16.02	08.06	VIR	12.27	23.23	AQU	PIS	TAU	GEM	22
23	04.37	TAU	21.28	CAN	LEO	03.09	SCO	CAP	15.09	05.59	TAU	GEM	23
24	ARI	14.03	GEM	CAN	15.50	LIB	14.55	CAP	PIS	ARI	11.38	06.18	24
25	17.08	GEM	GEM	01.51	VIR	06.19	SAG	02.53	23.32	17.03	GEM	CAN	25
26	TAU	GEM	09.17	LEO	20.26	SCO	16.39	AQU	ARI	TAU	GEM	17.45	26
27	TAU	01.03	CAN	08.30	LIB	07.26	CAP	08.02	ARI	TAU	00.13	LEO	27
28	05.43	CAN	18.04	VIR	22.01	SAG	18.55	PIS	10.08	CAN	05.22	LEO	28
29	GEM		LEO	11.25	SCO	07.48	AQU	15.44	TAU	GEM	12.02	03.41	29
30	15.50		23.01	LIB	21.43	CAP	23.19	ARI	22.26	18.03	LEO	VIR	30
31	CAN		VIR		SAG		PIS	ARI		CAN		11.20	31

SUN

mth	dy	time → sign
JAN	1	00.00 → CAP
JAN	20	20.52 → AQU
FEB	19	11.11 → PIS
MAR	21	10.26 → ARI
APR	20	20.48 → TAU
MAY	21	21.15 → GEM
JUN	22	05.25 → CAN
JUL	23	16.21 → LEO
AUG	23	23.16 → VIR
SEP	23	20.37 → LIB
OCT	24	05.36 → SCO
NOV	23	02.51 → SAG
DEC	22	16.00 → CAP

MERCURY

mth	dy	time → sign
JAN	1	00.00 → CAP
FEB	9	17.50 → AQU
FEB	28	13.04 → PIS
MAR	16	11.53 → ARI
APR	2	03.27 → TAU
MAY	1	21.25 → ARI
MAY	15	01.40 → TAU
JUN	9	08.43 → GEM
JUN	24	03.13 → CAN
JUL	8	13.40 → LEO
JUL	27	15.24 → VIR
OCT	2	14.25 → LIB
OCT	19	21.53 → SCO
NOV	8	04.59 → SAG
DEC	1	20.41 → CAP
DEC	12	12.40 → SAG

VENUS

mth	dy	time → sign
JAN	1	00.00 → CAP
JAN	7	21.11 → AQU
JAN	31	20.14 → PIS
FEB	24	23.27 → ARI
MAR	21	10.06 → TAU
APR	15	08.33 → GEM
MAY	11	01.42 → CAN
JUN	7	05.11 → LEO
JUL	8	04.54 → VIR
NOV	9	18.48 → LIB
DEC	8	00.20 → SCO

MARS

mth	dy	time → sign
JAN	1	00.00 → AQU
JAN	22	13.08 → PIS
MAR	1	22.13 → ARI
APR	10	09.37 → TAU
MAY	21	15.23 → GEM
JUL	3	23.42 → CAN
AUG	18	10.48 → LEO
OCT	5	00.20 → VIR
NOV	24	06.14 → LIB

SATURN

mth	dy	time → sign
JAN	1	00.00 → LIB
MAR	7	12.13 → VIR
AUG	13	16.36 → LIB

JUPITER

mth	dy	time → sign
JAN	1	00.00 → PIS
APR	21	14.42 → ARI

MOON

dy	jan	feb	mar	apr	may	jun	jul	aug	sep	oct	nov	dec	dy
1	LIB	01.16	SAG	AQU	PIS	02.33	GEM	CAN	VIR	LIB	05.20	CAP	1
2	15.58	SAG	09.29	22.44	11.26	TAU	GEM	03.07	VIR	18.23	SAG	15.45	2
3	SCO	02.52	CAP	PIS	ARI	14.03	08.27	LEO	05.32	SCO	06.40	AQU	3
4	17.38	CAP	12.11	PIS	20.46	GEM	CAN	14.18	LIB	21.48	CAP	18.08	4
5	SAG	04.04	AQU	05.16	TAU	GEM	21.00	VIR	11.49	SAG	08.43	PIS	5
6	17.32	AQU	15.45	ARI	TAU	02.31	LEO	23.34	SCO	SAG	AQU	23.18	6
7	CAP	06.29	PIS	13.52	07.51	CAN	LEO	LIB	16.11	00.30	12.23	ARI	7
8	17.35	PIS	21.16	TAU	GEM	15.12	08.36	LIB	19.06	CAP	PIS	ARI	8
9	AQU	11.43	ARI	TAU	20.13	LEO	VIR	06.24	SAG	03.20	17.52	07.04	9
10	19.56	ARI	ARI	00.41	CAN	LEO	18.04	SCO	CAP	AQU	ARI	TAU	10
11	PIS	20.33	05.33	GEM	CAN	02.46	LIB	10.31	21.11	06.46	ARI	16.54	11
12	PIS	TAU	TAU	13.04	08.49	VIR	LIB	SAG	AQU	PIS	01.07	GEM	12
13	02.05	TAU	16.36	CAN	LEO	11.31	00.20	12.18	23.21	11.20	TAU	GEM	13
14	ARI	08.18	GEM	CAN	19.44	LIB	SCO	CAP	PIS	ARI	10.15	04.22	14
15	12.11	GEM	GEM	01.18	VIR	16.17	03.03	12.53	PIS	17.37	GEM	CAN	15
16	TAU	20.51	05.06	LEO	VIR	SCO	SAG	AQU	02.47	TAU	21.27	17.05	16
17	TAU	CAN	CAN	11.07	03.05	17.26	03.14	13.52	ARI	TAU	CAN	LEO	17
18	00.36	CAN	16.44	VIR	LIB	SAG	CAP	PIS	08.41	02.22	CAN	LEO	18
19	GEM	08.01	LEO	17.13	06.23	16.38	02.41	16.58	TAU	GEM	10.12	05.52	19
20	13.06	LEO	LEO	LIB	SCO	CAP	AQU	ARI	17.47	13.42	LEO	VIR	20
21	CAN	16.43	01.40	19.56	06.44	16.04	03.29	23.26	GEM	CAN	22.35	16.41	21
22	CAN	VIR	VIR	SCO	SAG	AQU	PIS	TAU	GEM	CAN	VIR	LIB	22
23	00.12	23.01	07.21	20.40	06.07	17.49	07.21	TAU	05.34	02.25	VIR	23.38	23
24	LEO	LIB	LIB	SAG	CAP	PIS	ARI	09.27	CAN	LEO	08.09	SCO	24
25	09.26	LIB	10.36	21.20	06.41	23.13	15.07	GEM	18.08	14.01	LIB	SCO	25
26	VIR	03.31	SCO	CAP	AQU	ARI	TAU	21.44	LEO	VIR	13.32	02.27	26
27	16.46	SCO	12.40	23.32	10.05	ARI	TAU	CAN	LEO	22.25	SCO	SAG	27
28	LIB	06.49	SAG	AQU	PIS	08.17	02.07	CAN	05.05	LIB	15.20	02.24	28
29	22.04		14.51	AQU	16.53	TAU	GEM	10.11	VIR	LIB	SAG	CAP	29
30	SCO		CAP	04.13	ARI	19.51	14.42	LEO	13.08	03.09	15.22	01.36	30
31	SCO		18.02		ARI		CAN	21.00		SCO		AQU	31

SUN

mth	dy	time → sign
JAN	1	00.00 → CAP
JAN	21	02.38 → AQU
FEB	19	16.57 → PIS
MAR	20	16.13 → ARI
APR	20	03.37 → TAU
MAY	21	03.04 → GEM
JUN	21	11.12 → CAN
JUL	22	22.07 → LEO
AUG	23	05.03 → VIR
SEP	23	02.24 → LIB
OCT	23	11.23 → SCO
NOV	22	08.36 → SAG
DEC	21	21.43 → CAP

MERCURY

mth	dy	time → sign
JAN	1	00.00 → SAG
JAN	13	06.44 → CAP
FEB	3	01.38 → AQU
FEB	20	18.54 → PIS
MAR	7	17.11 → ARI
MAY	14	14.43 → TAU
MAY	31	15.26 → GEM
JUN	14	12.23 → CAN
JUN	30	10.27 → LEO
SEP	7	12.02 → VIR
SEP	23	18.45 → LIB
OCT	11	13.05 → SCO
NOV	1	05.34 → SAG

VENUS

mth	dy	time → sign
JAN	1	00.00 → SCO
JAN	2	18.44 → SAG
JAN	27	15.58 → CAP
FEB	21	04.42 → AQU
MAR	16	14.18 → PIS
APR	9	23.17 → ARI
MAY	4	08.55 → TAU
MAY	28	19.19 → GEM
JUN	22	05.46 → CAN
JUL	16	15.23 → LEO
AUG	9	23.58 → VIR
SEP	3	08.17 → LIB
SEP	27	17.36 → SCO
OCT	22	05.02 → SAG
NOV	15	20.03 → CAP
DEC	10	18.31 → AQU

MARS

mth	dy	time → sign
JAN	1	00.00 → LIB
JAN	20	01.41 → SCO
AUG	27	18.51 → SAG
OCT	12	04.38 → CAP
NOV	21	19.42 → AQU
DEC	30	21.27 → PIS

SATURN

mth	dy	time → sign
JAN	1	00.00 → LIB

JUPITER

mth	dy	time → sign
JAN	1	00.00 → ARI
APR	28	20.52 → TAU

MOON

dy	jan	feb	mar	apr	may	jun	jul	aug	sep	oct	nov	dec	dy
1	02.11	19.51	TAU	07.39	04.12	VIR	LIB	SAG	09.03	PIS	06.58	GEM	1
2	PIS	TAU	12.36	CAN	LEO	12.26	05.25	22.27	AQU	19.34	TAU	GEM	2
3	05.42	TAU	GEM	20.11	16.57	LIB	SCO	CAP	09.00	ARI	11.02	03.08	3
4	ARI	04.55	23.40	LEO	VIR	20.19	10.27	22.41	PIS	21.05	GEM	CAN	4
5	12.43	GEM	CAN	LEO	VIR	SCO	SAG	AQU	08.57	TAU	18.12	13.23	5
6	TAU	16.44	CAN	08.40	03.39	SCO	12.02	22.05	ARI	TAU	CAN	LEO	6
7	22.42	CAN	12.30	VIR	LIB	00.21	CAP	PIS	10.48	01.15	CAN	LEO	7
8	GEM	CAN	LEO	18.56	10.49	SAG	11.54	22.33	TAU	GEM	04.56	01.57	8
9	GEM	05.36	LEO	LIB	SCO	01.46	AQU	ARI	16.06	09.16	LEO	VIR	9
10	10.34	LEO	00.51	LIB	14.50	CAP	11.59	ARI	GEM	CAN	17.47	14.35	10
11	CAN	18.02	VIR	02.13	SAG	02.26	PIS	01.46	GEM	20.50	VIR	LIB	11
12	23.19	VIR	11.16	SCO	17.09	AQU	13.56	TAU	01.24	LEO	VIR	LIB	12
13	LEO	VIR	LIB	07.08	CAP	04.00	ARI	08.36	CAN	LEO	05.57	00.39	13
14	LEO	05.00	19.20	SAG	19.14	PIS	18.45	GEM	13.38	09.51	LIB	SCO	14
15	12.00	LIB	SCO	10.41	AQU	07.29	TAU	18.52	LEO	VIR	15.18	07.00	15
16	VIR	13.45	SCO	CAP	22.05	ARI	TAU	CAN	LEO	21.44	SCO	SAG	16
17	23.19	SCO	01.15	13.43	PIS	13.11	02.37	CAN	02.41	LIB	21.33	10.17	17
18	LIB	19.42	SAG	AQU	PIS	TAU	GEM	07.19	VIR	LIB	SAG	CAP	18
19	LIB	SAG	05.19	16.40	02.07	21.03	13.05	LEO	14.41	07.11	SAG	12.02	19
20	07.44	22.49	CAP	PIS	ARI	GEM	CAN	20.23	LIB	SCO	01.40	AQU	20
21	SCO	CAP	07.55	19.56	07.29	GEM	CAN	VIR	LIB	14.12	CAP	13.45	21
22	12.23	23.48	AQU	ARI	TAU	07.04	01.20	VIR	00.43	SAG	04.52	PIS	22
23	SAG	AQU	09.39	ARI	14.37	CAN	LEO	08.42	SCO	19.28	AQU	16.30	23
24	13.39	AQU	PIS	00.15	GEM	19.02	14.24	LIB	08.33	CAP	07.55	ARI	24
25	CAP	00.01	11.34	TAU	GEM	LEO	VIR	19.11	SAG	23.28	PIS	20.46	25
26	13.06	PIS	ARI	06.40	00.06	LEO	VIR	SCO	14.06	AQU	11.09	TAU	26
27	AQU	01.11	15.05	GEM	CAN	08.06	02.54	SCO	CAP	AQU	ARI	TAU	27
28	12.45	ARI	TAU	16.06	11.59	VIR	LIB	02.53	17.24	02.23	14.54	02.48	28
29	PIS	05.02	21.36	CAN	LEO	20.18	13.04	SAG	AQU	PIS	TAU	GEM	29
30	14.33		GEM	CAN	LEO	LIB	SCO	07.24	18.52	04.34	19.53	10.53	30
31	ARI		GEM		00.57		19.37	CAP		ARI		CAN	31

SUN

mth	dy	time → sign
JAN	1	00.00 → CAP
JAN	20	08.21 → AQU
FEB	18	22.42 → PIS
MAR	20	22.00 → ARI
APR	20	09.25 → TAU
MAY	21	08.53 → GEM
JUN	21	17.00 → CAN
JUL	23	03.52 → LEO
AUG	23	10.44 → VIR
SEP	23	08.06 → LIB
OCT	23	17.06 → SCO
NOV	22	14.22 → SAG
DEC	22	03.32 → CAP

MERCURY

mth	dy	time → sign
JAN	1	00.00 → SAG
JAN	6	13.24 → CAP
JAN	25	19.11 → AQU
FEB	11	23.57 → PIS
MAR	2	19.22 → ARI
MAR	15	21.01 → PIS
APR	17	16.47 → ARI
MAY	8	06.22 → TAU
MAY	23	03.58 → GEM
JUN	6	08.22 → CAN
JUN	26	11.00 → LEO
JUL	28	13.40 → CAN
AUG	11	14.04 → LEO
AUG	30	22.59 → VIR
SEP	15	21.44 → LIB
OCT	4	16.40 → SCO
OCT	31	15.51 → SAG
NOV	6	22.18 → SCO
DEC	10	14.48 → SAG
DEC	30	17.14 → CAP

VENUS

mth	dy	time → sign
JAN	1	00.00 → AQU
JAN	5	11.11 → PIS
FEB	2	05.54 → ARI
MAR	14	18.58 → TAU
MAR	31	04.50 → ARI
JUN	5	10.33 → TAU
JUL	7	10.29 → GEM
AUG	4	01.08 → CAN
AUG	30	01.35 → LEO
SEP	24	03.48 → VIR
OCT	18	15.29 → LIB
NOV	11	18.12 → SCO
DEC	5	16.24 → SAG
DEC	29	12.54 → CAP

MARS

mth	dy	time → sign
JAN	1	00.00 → PIS
FEB	8	01.12 → ARI
MAR	20	06.51 → TAU
MAY	1	06.12 → GEM
JUN	14	03.46 → CAN
JUL	29	19.25 → LEO
SEP	14	17.58 → VIR
NOV	1	14.14 → LIB
DEC	20	11.23 → SCO

SATURN

mth	dy	time → sign
JAN	1	00.00 → LIB
OCT	22	15.26 → SCO

JUPITER

mth	dy	time → sign
JAN	1	00.00 → TAU
MAY	9	15.24 → GEM

MOON

dy	jan	feb	mar	apr	may	jun	jul	aug	sep	oct	nov	dec	dy
1	21.17	VIR	VIR	05.19	SAG	14.44	00.08	10.57	GEM	18.53	VIR	LIB	1
2	LEO	VIR	11.41	SCO	SAG	AQU	PIS	TAU	03.30	LEO	VIR	21.30	2
3	LEO	05.31	LIB	14.58	03.55	18.12	02.22	15.10	CAN	LEO	01.51	SCO	3
4	09.41	LIB	23.31	SAG	CAP	PIS	ARI	GEM	13.05	06.40	LIB	SCO	4
5	VIR	17.21	SCO	22.29	09.12	21.01	05.22	21.59	LEO	VIR	14.12	08.09	5
6	22.36	SCO	SCO	CAP	AQU	ARI	TAU	CAN	LEO	19.28	SCO	SAG	6
7	LIB	SCO	09.20	CAP	12.46	23.41	09.42	CAN	00.47	LIB	SCO	16.33	7
8	LIB	02.20	SAG	03.29	PIS	TAU	GEM	07.16	VIR	LIB	01.06	CAP	8
9	09.44	SAG	16.10	AQU	14.49	TAU	15.54	LEO	13.29	07.56	SAG	22.59	9
10	SCO	07.32	CAP	05.49	ARI	03.03	CAN	18.33	LIB	SCO	10.18	AQU	10
11	17.14	CAP	19.37	PIS	16.12	GEM	CAN	VIR	LIB	19.19	CAP	AQU	11
12	SAG	09.16	AQU	06.19	TAU	08.17	00.28	VIR	02.05	SAG	17.31	03.46	12
13	20.55	AQU	20.17	ARI	18.29	CAN	LEO	07.08	SCO	SAG	AQU	PIS	13
14	CAP	08.58	PIS	06.31	GEM	16.29	11.28	LIB	13.32	04.51	22.17	07.06	14
15	21.57	PIS	19.39	TAU	23.16	LEO	VIR	19.43	SAG	CAP	PIS	ARI	15
16	AQU	08.30	ARI	08.29	CAN	LEO	VIR	SCO	22.21	11.34	PIS	09.22	16
17	22.07	ARI	19.44	GEM	CAN	03.36	00.04	SCO	CAP	AQU	00.35	TAU	17
18	PIS	09.51	TAU	13.53	07.47	VIR	LIB	06.30	CAP	14.55	ARI	11.29	18
19	23.08	TAU	22.35	CAN	LEO	16.16	12.17	SAG	03.30	PIS	01.15	GEM	19
20	ARI	14.29	GEM	23.29	19.31	LIB	SCO	13.53	AQU	15.29	TAU	14.40	20
21	ARI	GEM	GEM	LEO	VIR	LIB	21.59	CAP	05.06	ARI	01.54	CAN	21
22	02.20	22.47	05.29	LEO	VIR	03.57	SAG	17.29	PIS	14.47	GEM	20.22	22
23	TAU	CAN	CAN	11.53	08.16	SCO	SAG	AQU	04.30	TAU	04.31	LEO	23
24	08.21	CAN	16.14	VIR	LIB	12.47	04.06	18.12	ARI	15.04	CAN	LEO	24
25	GEM	10.05	LEO	VIR	19.32	SAG	CAP	PIS	03.44	GEM	10.40	05.24	25
26	17.07	LEO	LEO	00.40	SCO	18.29	07.03	17.46	TAU	18.24	LEO	VIR	26
27	CAN	22.51	05.04	LIB	SCO	CAP	AQU	ARI	05.01	CAN	20.41	17.11	27
28	CAN	VIR	VIR	11.52	04.08	21.51	08.07	18.10	GEM	CAN	VIR	LIB	28
29	04.06		17.51	SCO	SAG	AQU	08.56	TAU	09.56	01.55	VIR	LIB	29
30	LEO		LIB	20.52	10.17	AQU	PIS	21.07	CAN	LEO	09.06	05.43	30
31	16.35		LIB		CAP		ARI	GEM		13.04		SCO	31

SUN

mth	dy	time → sign
JAN	1	00.00 → CAP
JAN	20	14.11 → AQU
FEB	19	04.32 → PIS
MAR	21	03.53 → ARI
APR	20	15.19 → TAU
MAY	21	14.47 → GEM
JUN	21	22.54 → CAN
JUL	23	09.45 → LEO
AUG	23	16.36 → VIR
SEP	23	13.55 → LIB
OCT	23	22.56 → SCO
NOV	22	20.14 → SAG
DEC	22	09.25 → CAP

MERCURY

mth	dy	time → sign
JAN	1	00.00 → CAP
JAN	18	07.43 → AQU
FEB	4	18.03 → PIS
APR	13	11.34 → ARI
APR	30	11.26 → TAU
MAY	14	13.57 → GEM
MAY	30	16.13 → CAN
AUG	7	14.43 → LEO
AUG	22	17.42 → VIR
SEP	8	08.05 → LIB
SEP	29	04.06 → SCO
NOV	4	12.37 → LIB
NOV	11	10.23 → SCO
DEC	4	07.03 → SAG
DEC	23	12.10 → CAP

VENUS

mth	dy	time → sign
JAN	1	00.00 → CAP
JAN	22	09.22 → AQU
FEB	15	07.01 → PIS
MAR	11	07.22 → ARI
APR	4	11.55 → TAU
APR	28	22.03 → GEM
MAY	23	15.04 → CAN
JUN	17	17.04 → LEO
JUL	13	08.43 → VIR
AUG	9	00.34 → LIB
SEP	6	23.28 → SCO
OCT	23	22.07 → SAG
OCT	27	10.42 → SCO

MARS

mth	dy	time → sign
JAN	1	00.00 → SCO
FEB	9	19.11 → SAG
APR	12	16.24 → CAP
JUL	3	07.25 → SAG
AUG	24	13.27 → CAP
OCT	21	12.03 → AQU
DEC	4	07.42 → PIS

SATURN

mth	dy	time → sign
JAN	1	00.00 → SCO

JUPITER

mth	dy	time → sign
JAN	1	00.00 → GEM
MAY	24	04.36 → CAN

MOON

dy	jan	feb	mar	apr	may	jun	jul	aug	sep	oct	nov	dec	dy
1	16.39	CAP	CAP	PIS	ARI	GEM	CAN	VIR	22.48	18.41	CAP	AQU	1
2	SAG	15.38	02.07	15.40	01.42	12.46	02.16	VIR	SCO	SAG	CAP	14.38	2
3	SAG	AQU	AQU	ARI	TAU	CAN	LEO	03.14	SCO	SAG	00.22	PIS	3
4	00.45	18.03	04.32	14.43	01.06	16.34	08.56	LIB	11.32	07.04	AQU	19.34	4
5	CAP	PIS	PIS	TAU	GEM	LEO	VIR	15.03	SAG	CAP	07.34	ARI	5
6	06.09	19.14	04.40	14.40	02.30	LEO	18.53	SCO	23.10	16.45	PIS	21.23	6
7	AQU	ARI	ARI	GEM	CAN	00.06	LIB	SCO	CAP	AQU	10.42	TAU	7
8	09.43	20.47	04.32	17.29	VIR	VIR	LIB	03.32	CAP	22.17	ARI	21.16	8
9	PIS	TAU	TAU	CAN	LEO	10.59	07.04	SAG	07.31	PIS	10.48	GEM	9
10	12.27	23.54	06.06	CAN	16.23	LIB	SCO	14.20	AQU	23.58	TAU	21.06	10
11	ARI	GEM	GEM	00.05	VIR	23.30	19.19	CAP	11.55	ARI	09.50	CAN	11
12	15.10	GEM	10.37	LEO	VIR	SCO	SAG	21.54	PIS	23.32	GEM	22.48	12
13	TAU	05.10	CAN	10.03	04.03	SCO	SAG	AQU	13.22	TAU	09.59	LEO	13
14	18.29	CAN	18.17	VIR	LIB	11.37	05.40	AQU	ARI	23.10	CAN	LEO	14
15	GEM	12.34	LEO	21.57	16.42	SAG	CAP	02.17	13.45	GEM	13.03	03.54	15
16	23.01	LEO	LEO	LIB	SCO	22.05	13.19	PIS	TAU	GEM	LEO	VIR	16
17	CAN	22.00	04.22	LIB	SCO	CAP	AQU	04.37	14.55	00.50	19.52	12.51	17
18	CAN	VIR	VIR	10.32	04.53	CAP	18.33	ARI	GEM	CAN	VIR	LIB	18
19	05.24	VIR	15.57	SCO	SAG	06.26	PIS	06.26	18.13	05.41	VIR	LIB	19
20	LEO	09.14	LIB	22.55	15.49	AQU	22.07	TAU	CAN	LEO	06.02	00.43	20
21	14.14	LIB	LIB	SAG	CAP	12.37	ARI	08.56	CAN	13.45	LIB	SCO	21
22	VIR	21.43	04.26	SAG	CAP	PIS	ARI	GEM	00.04	VIR	18.13	13.34	22
23	VIR	SCO	SCO	10.11	00.48	16.43	00.52	12.50	LEO	VIR	SCO	SAG	23
24	01.30	SCO	16.56	CAP	AQU	ARI	TAU	CAN	08.11	00.12	SCO	SAG	24
25	LIB	10.00	SAG	19.02	07.08	19.09	03.30	18.22	VIR	LIB	07.01	01.40	25
26	14.03	SAG	SAG	AQU	PIS	TAU	GEM	LEO	18.11	12.11	SAG	CAP	26
27	SCO	19.58	03.55	AQU	10.31	20.41	06.41	LEO	LIB	SCO	19.24	12.00	27
28	SCO	CAP	CAP	00.22	ARI	GEM	CAN	01.45	LIB	SCO	CAP	AQU	28
29	01.42		11.37	PIS	11.33	22.34	11.10	VIR	05.52	00.59	CAP	20.09	29
30	SAG		AQU	02.08	TAU	CAN	LEO	11.12	SCO	SAG	06.19	PIS	30
31	10.26		15.16		11.41		17.50	LIB		13.36		PIS	31

SUN

mth	dy	time → sign
JAN	1	00.00 → CAP
JAN	20	20.02 → AQU
FEB	19	10.19 → PIS
MAR	21	09.35 → ARI
APR	20	20.58 → TAU
MAY	21	20.24 → GEM
JUN	22	04.31 → CAN
JUL	23	15.25 → LEO
AUG	23	22.19 → VIR
SEP	23	19.41 → LIB
OCT	24	04.43 → SCO
NOV	23	02.01 → SAG
DEC	22	15.11 → CAP

MERCURY

mth	dy	time → sign
JAN	1	00.00 → CAP
JAN	10	23.05 → AQU
MAR	17	20.49 → PIS
APR	6	16.14 → ARI
APR	22	02.57 → TAU
MAY	6	13.05 → GEM
JUL	13	14.44 → CAN
JUL	30	17.21 → LEO
AUG	14	13.08 → VIR
SEP	1	12.06 → LIB
NOV	8	06.57 → SCO
NOV	27	04.33 → SAG
DEC	16	06.07 → CAP

VENUS

mth	dy	time → sign
JAN	1	00.00 → SCO
JAN	6	06.48 → SAG
FEB	6	01.15 → CAP
MAR	4	20.21 → AQU
MAR	30	11.30 → PIS
APR	24	15.13 → ARI
MAY	19	13.35 → TAU
JUN	13	08.38 → GEM
JUL	8	00.15 → CAN
AUG	1	11.43 → LEO
AUG	25	18.52 → VIR
SEP	18	22.41 → LIB
OCT	13	00.39 → SCO
NOV	6	02.02 → SAG
NOV	30	03.42 → CAP
DEC	24	06.53 → AQU

MARS

mth	dy	time → sign
JAN	1	00.00 → PIS
JAN	15	04.26 → ARI
FEB	26	10.21 → TAU
APR	10	23.12 → GEM
MAY	26	00.50 → CAN
JUL	11	09.28 → LEO
AUG	27	10.13 → VIR
OCT	13	11.17 → LIB
NOV	29	01.30 → SCO

SATURN

mth	dy	time → sign
JAN	1	00.00 → SCO

JUPITER

mth	dy	time → sign
JAN	1	00.00 → CAN
JUN	13	00.07 → LEO
NOV	17	03.45 → VIR

MOON

dy	jan	feb	mar	apr	may	jun	jul	aug	sep	oct	nov	dec	dy
1	01.56	14.02	GEM	08.20	VIR	20.54	15.33	CAP	15.23	05.46	19.23	05.46	1
2	ARI	GEM	22.40	LEO	VIR	SCO	SAG	22.52	PIS	ARI	GEM	CAN	2
3	05.24	16.36	CAN	14.31	04.26	SCO	SAG	AQU	21.24	08.52	20.11	06.07	3
4	TAU	CAN	CAN	VIR	LIB	09.23	04.29	AQU	ARI	TAU	CAN	LEO	4
5	07.04	19.28	02.48	22.33	15.04	SAG	CAP	08.04	ARI	10.59	22.20	08.50	5
6	GEM	LEO	LEO	LIB	SCO	22.21	16.18	PIS	01.36	GEM	LEO	VIR	6
7	08.00	23.43	08.09	LIB	SCO	CAP	AQU	15.00	TAU	13.23	LEO	14.48	7
8	CAN	VIR	VIR	08.38	03.19	CAP	AQU	ARI	04.58	CAN	02.36	LIB	8
9	09.41	VIR	15.20	SCO	SAG	10.30	02.08	20.03	GEM	16.41	VIR	23.59	9
10	LEO	06.33	LIB	20.41	16.19	AQU	PIS	TAU	08.01	LEO	09.15	SCO	10
11	13.43	LIB	LIB	SAG	CAP	20.32	09.33	23.33	CAN	21.11	LIB	SCO	11
12	VIR	16.38	01.04	SAG	CAP	PIS	ARI	GEM	11.02	VIR	18.12	11.33	12
13	21.15	SCO	SCO	09.40	04.29	PIS	14.20	GEM	LEO	VIR	SCO	SAG	13
14	LIB	SCO	13.13	CAP	AQU	03.24	TAU	01.50	14.33	03.13	SCO	SAG	14
15	LIB	05.07	SAG	21.20	13.53	ARI	16.43	CAN	VIR	LIB	05.17	00.23	15
16	08.14	SAG	SAG	AQU	PIS	06.50	GEM	03.33	19.35	11.23	SAG	CAP	16
17	SCO	17.33	02.01	AQU	19.21	TAU	17.30	LEO	LIB	SCO	17.59	13.19	17
18	21.01	CAP	CAP	05.28	ARI	07.36	CAN	05.57	LIB	22.07	CAP	AQU	18
19	SAG	CAP	12.47	PIS	21.12	GEM	18.03	VIR	03.18	SAG	CAP	AQU	19
20	SAG	03.33	AQU	09.29	TAU	07.15	LEO	10.33	SCO	SAG	06.58	01.02	20
21	09.09	AQU	19.45	ARI	20.56	CAN	20.06	LIB	14.11	10.52	AQU	PIS	21
22	CAP	10.09	PIS	10.29	GEM	07.36	VIR	18.37	SAG	CAP	18.10	10.05	22
23	18.58	PIS	23.09	TAU	20.33	LEO	VIR	SCO	SAG	23.33	PIS	ARI	23
24	AQU	14.06	ARI	10.24	CAN	10.26	01.16	SCO	03.01	AQU	PIS	15.33	24
25	AQU	ARI	ARI	GEM	21.52	VIR	LIB	06.03	CAP	AQU	01.47	TAU	25
26	02.11	16.46	00.31	11.09	LEO	16.55	10.19	SAG	15.07	09.37	ARI	17.33	26
27	PIS	TAU	TAU	CAN	LEO	LIB	SCO	18.57	AQU	PIS	05.27	GEM	27
28	07.19	19.24	01.42	14.09	02.16	LIB	22.24	CAP	AQU	15.46	TAU	17.17	28
29	ARI		GEM	LEO	VIR	03.04	SAG	CAP	00.12	ARI	06.11	CAN	29
30	11.06		04.05	19.58	10.08	SCO	SAG	06.35	PIS	18.30	GEM	16.36	30
31	TAU		CAN		LIB		11.18	AQU		TAU		LEO	31

SUN

mth	dy	time → sign
JAN	1	00.00 → CAP
JAN	21	01.48 → AQU
FEB	19	16.05 → PIS
MAR	20	15.20 → ARI
APR	20	02.43 → TAU
MAY	21	02.12 → GEM
JUN	21	10.24 → CAN
JUL	22	21.20 → LEO
AUG	23	04.15 → VIR
SEP	23	01.35 → LIB
OCT	23	10.34 → SCO
NOV	22	07.50 → SAG
DEC	21	20.59 → CAP

MERCURY

mth	dy	time → sign
JAN	1	00.00 → CAP
JAN	4	09.15 → AQU
FEB	2	12.18 → CAP
FEB	15	06.34 → AQU
MAR	11	10.28 → PIS
MAR	28	22.41 → ARI
APR	12	17.10 → TAU
APR	29	22.42 → GEM
JUL	6	19.02 → CAN
JUL	21	05.35 → LEO
AUG	5	19.06 → VIR
AUG	26	13.29 → LIB
SEP	29	21.25 → VIR
OCT	11	07.28 → LIB
OCT	31	08.19 → SCO
NOV	18	21.42 → SAG
DEC	8	07.11 → CAP

VENUS

mth	dy	time → sign
JAN	1	00.00 → AQU
JAN	17	14.22 → PIS
FEB	11	07.47 → ARI
MAR	7	21.32 → TAU
APR	4	07.23 → GEM
MAY	8	02.17 → CAN
JUN	23	12.10 → GEM
AUG	4	09.48 → CAN
SEP	8	09.23 → LEO
OCT	6	03.12 → VIR
OCT	31	19.40 → LIB
NOV	25	13.01 → SCO
DEC	19	19.07 → SAG

MARS

mth	dy	time → sign
JAN	1	00.00 → SCO
JAN	14	02.26 → SAG
FEB	28	20.12 → CAP
APR	14	23.32 → AQU
JUN	3	07.53 → PIS
DEC	6	11.24 → ARI

SATURN

mth	dy	time → sign
JAN	1	00.00 → SCO
JAN	12	18.44 → SAG
MAY	14	03.40 → SCO
OCT	10	15.24 → SAG

JUPITER

mth	dy	time → sign
JAN	1	00.00 → VIR
JAN	18	02.12 → LEO
JUL	7	19.14 → VIR
DEC	13	02.20 → LIB

MOON

dy	jan	feb	mar	apr	may	jun	jul	aug	sep	oct	nov	dec	dy
1	17.31	LIB	SCO	SAG	CAP	PIS	ARI	11.15	23.14	08.24	22.24	12.59	1
2	VIR	13.34	SCO	04.37	01.27	PIS	22.26	GEM	LEO	VIR	SCO	SAG	2
3	21.44	SCO	08.09	CAP	AQU	07.04	TAU	13.32	23.20	10.01	LIB	22.36	3
4	LIB	SCO	SAG	17.24	13.15	ARI	TAU	CAN	VIR	LIB	04.56	CAP	4
5	LIB	00.13	20.32	AQU	PIS	13.22	02.26	13.27	VIR	13.19	SAG	CAP	5
6	06.00	SAG	CAP	AQU	22.05	TAU	GEM	LEO	00.04	SCO	14.24	10.15	6
7	SCO	13.08	CAP	04.37	ARI	16.09	03.20	12.50	LIB	19.46	CAP	AQU	7
8	17.32	CAP	09.19	PIS	ARI	GEM	CAN	VIR	03.26	SAG	CAP	22.57	8
9	SAG	CAP	AQU	12.46	03.24	16.42	02.42	13.50	SCO	SAG	02.19	PIS	9
10	SAG	01.52	20.11	ARI	TAU	CAN	LEO	LIB	10.46	05.48	AQU	PIS	10
11	06.34	AQU	PIS	18.03	06.00	16.45	02.34	18.20	SAG	CAP	14.51	10.37	11
12	CAP	12.52	PIS	TAU	GEM	LEO	VIR	SCO	21.46	18.09	PIS	ARI	12
13	19.19	PIS	04.26	21.29	07.21	18.03	04.54	SCO	CAP	AQU	PIS	19.15	13
14	AQU	21.48	ARI	GEM	CAN	VIR	LIB	03.00	CAP	AQU	01.36	TAU	14
15	AQU	ARI	10.32	GEM	08.52	21.58	10.56	SAG	10.28	06.25	ARI	TAU	15
16	06.47	ARI	TAU	00.15	LEO	LIB	SCO	14.47	AQU	PIS	09.12	00.06	16
17	PIS	04.48	15.11	CAN	11.40	LIB	20.38	CAP	22.34	16.35	TAU	GEM	17
18	16.17	TAU	GEM	03.00	VIR	05.03	SAG	CAP	PIS	ARI	13.45	01.52	18
19	ARI	09.50	18.47	LEO	16.25	SCO	SAG	03.38	PIS	ARI	GEM	CAN	19
20	23.11	GEM	CAN	06.17	LIB	14.55	08.40	AQU	08.47	00.07	16.17	02.11	20
21	TAU	12.50	21.31	VIR	23.26	SAG	CAP	15.47	ARI	TAU	CAN	LEO	21
22	TAU	CAN	LEO	10.36	SCO	SAG	21.28	PIS	17.01	05.28	18.10	02.56	22
23	03.05	14.10	23.53	LIB	SCO	02.43	AQU	PIS	TAU	GEM	LEO	VIR	23
24	GEM	LEO	VIR	16.44	08.46	CAP	AQU	02.29	23.25	09.23	20.32	05.39	24
25	04.20	15.05	VIR	SCO	SAG	15.26	09.50	ARI	GEM	CAN	VIR	LIB	25
26	CAN	VIR	03.00	SCO	20.11	AQU	PIS	11.23	GEM	12.27	VIR	11.09	26
27	04.06	17.20	LIB	01.25	CAP	AQU	20.54	TAU	04.00	LEO	00.11	SCO	27
28	LEO	LIB	08.18	SAG	CAP	03.54	ARI	17.59	CAN	15.09	LIB	19.20	28
29	04.17	22.45	SCO	12.44	08.52	PIS	ARI	GEM	06.49	VIR	05.34	SAG	29
30	VIR		16.56	CAP	AQU	14.43	05.40	21.51	LEO	18.10	SCO	SAG	30
31	06.56		SAG		21.09		TAU	CAN		LIB		05.37	31

SUN

mth	dy	time → sign
JAN	1	00.00 → CAP
JAN	20	07.39 → AQU
FEB	18	21.58 → PIS
MAR	20	21.16 → ARI
APR	20	08.41 → TAU
MAY	21	08.10 → GEM
JUN	21	16.20 → CAN
JUL	23	03.16 → LEO
AUG	23	10.07 → VIR
SEP	23	07.26 → LIB
OCT	23	16.24 → SCO
NOV	22	13.39 → SAG
DEC	22	02.49 → CAP

MERCURY

mth	dy	time → sign
JAN	1	00.00 → CAP
FEB	12	14.30 → AQU
MAR	4	11.34 → PIS
MAR	20	19.48 → ARI
APR	4	23.38 → TAU
JUN	12	13.40 → GEM
JUN	28	17.08 → CAN
JUL	12	19.41 → LEO
JUL	30	01.44 → VIR
OCT	6	11.09 → LIB
OCT	23	20.50 → SCO
NOV	11	18.00 → SAG
DEC	2	11.19 → CAP
DEC	28	17.30 → SAG

VENUS

mth	dy	time → sign
JAN	1	00.00 → SAG
JAN	12	20.23 → CAP
FEB	5	20.16 → AQU
MAR	1	20.39 → PIS
MAR	25	22.46 → ARI
APR	19	03.29 → TAU
MAY	13	11.08 → GEM
JUN	6	21.34 → CAN
JUL	1	10.42 → LEO
JUL	26	03.10 → VIR
AUG	20	00.44 → LIB
SEP	14	06.20 → SCO
OCT	10	01.16 → SAG
NOV	5	23.46 → CAP
DEC	6	15.26 → AQU

MARS

mth	dy	time → sign
JAN	1	00.00 → ARI
JAN	28	14.23 → TAU
MAR	17	21.32 → GEM
MAY	4	15.26 → CAN
JUN	21	12.11 → LEO
AUG	8	05.29 → VIR
SEP	24	04.31 → LIB
NOV	8	21.05 → SCO
DEC	23	01.25 → SAG

SATURN

mth	dy	time → sign
JAN	1	00.00 → SAG

JUPITER

mth	dy	time → sign
JAN	1	00.00 → LIB
FEB	19	15.23 → VIR
AUG	7	02.13 → LIB

MOON

dy	jan	feb	mar	apr	may	jun	jul	aug	sep	oct	nov	dec	dy
1	CAP	12.20	PIS	23.11	13.47	CAN	13.23	LIB	SAG	CAP	09.18	05.56	1
2	17.24	PIS	PIS	TAU	GEM	04.45	VIR	01.00	21.05	14.04	PIS	ARI	2
3	AQU	PIS	06.31	TAU	19.08	LEO	15.16	SCO	CAP	AQU	22.00	17.48	3
4	AQU	00.42	ARI	07.30	CAN	06.59	LIB	06.47	CAP	AQU	ARI	TAU	4
5	06.04	ARI	17.20	GEM	22.53	VIR	19.10	SAG	07.50	02.17	ARI	TAU	5
6	PIS	11.37	TAU	13.37	LEO	09.45	SCO	15.23	AQU	PIS	09.38	03.00	6
7	18.23	TAU	TAU	CAN	LEO	01.37	SCO	CAP	20.04	14.57	TAU	GEM	7
8	ARI	19.34	02.03	17.24	01.37	13.41	01.20	CAP	PIS	ARI	19.09	09.16	8
9	ARI	GEM	GEM	LEO	VIR	SCO	SAG	02.01	PIS	ARI	GEM	CAN	9
10	04.26	23.39	07.45	19.13	03.57	19.09	09.34	AQU	08.45	02.48	GEM	13.23	10
11	TAU	CAN	CAN	VIR	LIB	SAG	CAP	14.02	ARI	TAU	02.24	LEO	11
12	10.44	CAN	10.12	20.08	06.48	SAG	19.43	PIS	20.57	13.01	CAN	16.28	12
13	GEM	00.19>LEO	LEO	LIB	SCO	02.36	AQU	PIS	TAU	GEM	07.36	VIR	13
14	13.05	23.17	10.20	21.45	11.13	CAP	AQU	02.46	TAU	20.55	LEO	19.23	14
15	CAN	VIR	VIR	SCO	SAG	12.23	07.32	ARI	07.26	CAN	11.07	LIB	15
16	12.50	22.50	09.59	SCO	18.13	AQU	PIS	15.00	GEM	CAN	VIR	22.34	16
17	LEO	LIB	LIB	01.43	CAP	AQU	20.14	TAU	14.49	01.59	13.25	SCO	17
18	12.03	LIB	11.16	SAG	CAP	00.16	ARI	TAU	CAN	LEO	LIB	SCO	18
19	VIR	01.06	SCO	09.08	04.12	PIS	ARI	00.51	18.31	04.23	15.17	02.30	19
20	12.55	SCO	15.55	CAP	AQU	12.46	07.58	GEM	LEO	VIR	SCO	SAG	20
21	LIB	07.23	SAG	19.53	16.20	ARI	TAU	06.48	19.11	05.03	17.52	07.47	21
22	17.02	SAG	SAG	AQU	PIS	23.38	16.34	CAN	VIR	LIB	SAG	CAP	22
23	SCO	17.27	00.34	AQU	PIS	TAU	GEM	08.51	18.33	05.31	22.29	15.19	23
24	SCO	CAP	CAP	08.23	04.34	TAU	21.05	LEO	LIB	SCO	CAP	AQU	24
25	00.52	CAP	12.17	PIS	ARI	07.07	CAN	08.26	18.40	07.33	CAP	AQU	25
26	SAG	05.42	AQU	20.22	14.43	GEM	22.16	VIR	SCO	SAG	06.16	01.41	26
27	11.32	AQU	AQU	ARI	TAU	11.00	LEO	07.41	21.27	12.41	AQU	PIS	27
28	CAP	18.25	01.00	ARI	21.47	CAN	21.59	LIB	SAG	CAP	17.16	14.13	28
29	23.42		PIS	06.18	GEM	12.31	VIR	08.45	SAG	21.32	PIS	ARI	29
30	AQU		12.55	TAU	GEM	LEO	22.20	SCO	03.59	AQU	PIS	ARI	30
31	AQU		ARI		02.05		13.07	LIB		AQU		02.37	31

SUN

mth	dy	time → sign
JAN	1	00.00 → CAP
JAN	20	13.29 → AQU
FEB	19	03.48 → PIS
MAR	21	03.06 → ARI
APR	20	14.27 → TAU
MAY	21	13.51 → GEM
JUN	21	21.57 → CAN
JUL	23	08.50 → LEO
AUG	23	15.46 → VIR
SEP	23	13.09 → LIB
OCT	23	22.12 → SCO
NOV	22	19.29 → SAG
DEC	22	08.40 → CAP

MERCURY

mth	dy	time → sign
JAN	1	00.00 → SAG
JAN	14	10.03 → CAP
FEB	6	15.23 → AQU
FEB	24	21.44 → PIS
MAR	12	17.31 → ARI
APR	2	19.17 → TAU
APR	10	13.41 → ARI
MAY	17	01.53 → TAU
JUN	5	20.59 → GEM
JUN	20	02.20 → CAN
JUL	4	23.46 → LEO
JUL	26	10.08 → VIR
AUG	23	14.36 → LEO
SEP	11	01.08 → VIR
SEP	28	22.46 → LIB
OCT	16	08.52 → SCO
NOV	5	02.36 → SAG

VENUS

mth	dy	time → sign
JAN	1	00.00 → AQU
APR	6	16.00 → PIS
MAY	5	11.59 → ARI
JUN	1	04.07 → TAU
JUN	26	23.08 → GEM
JUL	22	05.26 → CAN
AUG	16	01.28 → LEO
SEP	9	12.36 → VIR
OCT	3	16.44 → LIB
OCT	27	16.26 → SCO
NOV	20	13.59 → SAG
DEC	14	10.55 → CAP

MARS

mth	dy	time → sign
JAN	1	00.00 → SAG
FEB	3	18.45 → CAP
MAR	17	07.17 → AQU
APR	27	02.32 → PIS
JUN	7	06.21 → ARI
JUL	21	07.11 → TAU
SEP	21	05.24 → GEM
OCT	29	00.01 → TAU

SATURN

mth	dy	time → sign
JAN	1	00.00 → SAG

JUPITER

mth	dy	time → sign
JAN	1	00.00 → LIB
JAN	13	12.42 → SCO
MAR	20	19.18 → LIB
SEP	7	08.48 → SCO

MOON

dy	jan	feb	mar	apr	may	jun	jul	aug	sep	oct	nov	dec	dy
1	TAU	04.40	CAN	06.01	LIB	02.53	CAP	12.11	ARI	TAU	08.09	LEO	1
2	12.23	CAN	18.27	VIR	16.14	SAG	19.44	PIS	19.24	14.50	CAN	LEO	2
3	GEM	07.37	LEO	05.54	SCO	05.23	AQU	23.14	TAU	GEM	17.02	05.18	3
4	18.22	LEO	19.15	LIB	16.43	CAP	AQU	ARI	TAU	GEM	LEO	VIR	4
5	CAN	08.11	VIR	05.16	SAG	10.35	03.57	ARI	08.07	02.00	22.45	09.31	5
6	21.23	VIR	18.35	SCO	19.23	AQU	PIS	12.04	GEM	CAN	VIR	LIB	6
7	LEO	08.23	LIB	06.07	CAP	19.24	15.18	TAU	18.22	09.50	VIR	11.28	7
8	22.59	LIB	18.35	SAG	CAP	PIS	ARI	TAU	CAN	LEO	01.16	SCO	8
9	VIR	10.03	SCO	10.00	01.29	PIS	ARI	00.16	CAN	13.49	LIB	12.02	9
10	VIR	SCO	20.56	CAP	AQU	07.20	04.09	GEM	00.41	VIR	01.30	SAG	10
11	00.52	14.11	SAG	17.41	11.27	ARI	TAU	09.25	LEO	14.44	SCO	12.46	11
12	LIB	SAG	SAG	AQU	PIS	20.12	15.46	CAN	03.19	LIB	01.03	CAP	12
13	04.02	20.55	02.36	AQU	23.58	TAU	GEM	14.43	VIR	14.11	SAG	15.38	13
14	SCO	CAP	CAP	04.38	TAU	TAU	GEM	LEO	03.44	SCO	01.54	AQU	14
15	08.49	CAP	11.28	PIS	ARI	07.31	00.15	17.07	LIB	14.09	CAP	22.12	15
16	SAG	05.51	AQU	17.23	12.50	GEM	CAN	VIR	03.49	SAG	05.53	PIS	16
17	15.13	AQU	22.41	ARI	TAU	16.04	05.31	18.17	SCO	16.23	AQU	PIS	17
18	CAP	16.39	PIS	ARI	TAU	CAN	LEO	LIB	05.16	CAP	13.56	08.45	18
19	23.22	PIS	PIS	06.16	00.14	22.04	08.41	19.50	SAG	22.04	PIS	ARI	19
20	AQU	PIS	11.17	TAU	GEM	LEO	VIR	SCO	09.13	AQU	PIS	21.38	20
21	AQU	05.02	ARI	18.03	09.23	LEO	11.11	22.48	CAP	AQU	01.28	TAU	21
22	09.41	ARI	ARI	GEM	CAN	02.22	LIB	SAG	16.03	07.19	ARI	TAU	22
23	PIS	18.05	00.16	GEM	16.14	VIR	13.57	SAG	AQU	PIS	14.30	10.09	23
24	22.03	TAU	TAU	03.46	LEO	05.41	SCO	03.38	AQU	19.10	TAU	GEM	24
25	ARI	TAU	12.20	CAN	21.00	LIB	17.25	CAP	01.33	ARI	TAU	20.33	25
26	ARI	05.52	GEM	10.44	VIR	08.30	SAG	10.28	PIS	ARI	03.00	CAN	26
27	10.56	GEM	21.53	LEO	23.55	SCO	21.53	AQU	13.07	08.07	GEM	CAN	27
28	TAU	14.17	CAN	14.40	LIB	11.11	CAP	19.25	ARI	TAU	13.51	04.33	28
29	21.47		CAN	VIR	LIB	SAG	CAP	PIS	ARI	20.49	CAN	LEO	29
30	GEM		03.45	16.06	01.33	14.32	03.52	PIS	01.58	GEM	22.41	10.41	30
31	GEM		LEO		SCO		AQU	06.35		GEM		VIR	31

SUN

mth	dy	time → sign
JAN	1	00.00 → CAP
JAN	20	19.19 → AQU
FEB	19	09.38 → PIS
MAR	21	08.55 → ARI
APR	20	20.17 → TAU
MAY	21	19.42 → GEM
JUN	22	03.50 → CAN
JUL	23	14.45 → LEO
AUG	23	21.43 → VIR
SEP	23	19.09 → LIB
OCT	24	04.11 → SCO
NOV	23	01.27 → SAG
DEC	22	14.35 → CAP

MERCURY

mth	dy	time → sign
JAN	1	00.00 → SAG
JAN	10	16.48 → CAP
JAN	30	15.42 → AQU
FEB	17	02.15 → PIS
MAR	5	11.53 → ARI
MAY	12	19.48 → TAU
MAY	28	17.35 → GEM
JUN	11	14.11 → CAN
JUN	28	16.31 → LEO
SEP	5	02.28 → VIR
OCT	21	01.20 → LIB
OCT	9	04.02 → SCO
OCT	31	01.16 → SAG
NOV	25	11.53 → SCO
DEC	13	15.42 → SAG

VENUS

mth	dy	time → sign
JAN	1	00.00 → CAP
JAN	7	08.17 → AQU
JAN	31	07.28 → PIS
FEB	24	10.53 → ARI
MAR	20	21.55 → TAU
APR	14	21.08 → GEM
MAY	10	15.45 → CAN
JUN	6	22.43 → LEO
JUL	8	12.08 → VIR
SEP	20	03.04 → LEO
SEP	25	08.06 → VIR
NOV	9	18.10 → LIB
DEC	7	16.42 → SCO

MARS

mth	dy	time → sign
JAN	1	00.00 → TAU
FEB	10	13.57 → GEM
APR	10	09.37 → CAN
JUN	1	02.24 → LEO
JUL	20	11.13 → VIR
SEP	5	22.42 → LIB
OCT	21	09.45 → SCO
DEC	3	18.09 → SAG

SATURN

mth	dy	time → sign
JAN	1	00.00 → SAG
JAN	5	13.24 → CAP

JUPITER

mth	dy	time → sign
JAN	1	00.00 → SCO
FEB	10	13.35 → SAG
APR	24	14.17 → SCO
OCT	5	14.45 → SAG

MOON

dy	jan	feb	mar	apr	may	jun	jul	aug	sep	oct	nov	dec	dy
1	15.21	SCO	08.33	22.42	11.58	ARI	TAU	07.23	LEO	22.08	SCO	20.11	1
2	LIB	03.11	SAG	AQU	PIS	16.37	12.05	CAN	08.31	LIB	10.02	CAP	2
3	18.42	SAG	12.05	AQU	22.19	TAU	GEM	17.09	VIR	23.54	SAG	20.35	3
4	SCO	06.29	CAP	06.23	ARI	TAU	GEM	LEO	12.56	SCO	10.05	AQU	4
5	20.55	CAP	17.16	PIS	ARI	05.35	00.03	LEO	LIB	SCO	CAP	AQU	5
6	SAG	10.40	AQU	16.33	10.39	GEM	CAN	00.29	15.53	00.54	12.14	00.16	6
7	22.50	AQU	AQU	ARI	TAU	17.44	10.08	VIR	SCO	SAG	AQU	PIS	7
8	CAP	16.50	00.25	ARI	23.34	CAN	LEO	05.56	18.20	02.38	17.35	07.59	8
9	CAP	PIS	PIS	04.32	GEM	CAN	18.15	LIB	SAG	CAP	PIS	ARI	9
10	01.52	PIS	09.54	TAU	GEM	04.19	VIR	09.59	21.04	06.12	PIS	18.56	10
11	AQU	01.55	ARI	17.25	11.57	LEO	VIR	SCO	CAP	AQU	02.10	TAU	11
12	07.39	ARI	21.37	GEM	CAN	12.50	00.26	12.58	CAP	12.06	ARI	TAU	12
13	PIS	13.47	TAU	GEM	22.40	VIR	LIB	SAG	00.43	PIS	13.04	07.22	13
14	17.10	TAU	TAU	05.48	LEO	18.42	04.33	15.18	AQU	20.20	TAU	GEM	14
15	ARI	TAU	10.30	CAN	LEO	LIB	SCO	CAP	05.54	ARI	TAU	20.00	15
16	ARI	02.39	GEM	15.55	06.38	21.38	06.42	17.53	PIS	ARI	01.16	CAN	16
17	05.33	GEM	22.28	LEO	VIR	SCO	SAG	AQU	13.16	06.40	GEM	CAN	17
18	TAU	13.50	CAN	22.27	11.06	22.14	07.42	21.59	ARI	TAU	13.56	07.58	18
19	18.16	CAN	CAN	VIR	LIB	SAG	CAP	PIS	23.12	18.40	CAN	LEO	19
20	GEM	20.38	07.22	VIR	12.22	22.01	09.05	PIS	TAU	GEM	CAN	18.29	20
21	GEM	LEO	LEO	01.19	SCO	CAP	AQU	04.51	TAU	GEM	02.04	VIR	21
22	04.47	LEO	12.28	LIB	11.51	23.00	12.42	ARI	11.16	07.22	LEO	VIR	22
23	CAN	02.06	VIR	01.34	SAG	AQU	PIS	14.58	GEM	CAN	12.08	02.29	23
24	12.12	VIR	14.27	SCO	11.22	AQU	19.53	TAU	23.49	19.03	VIR	LIB	24
25	LEO	04.29	LIB	00.59	CAP	03.09	ARI	TAU	CAN	LEO	18.42	07.00	25
26	17.12	LIB	14.53	SAG	13.09	PIS	ARI	03.18	CAN	LEO	LIB	SCO	26
27	VIR	06.14	SCO	01.32	AQU	11.28	06.43	GEM	10.36	03.48	21.21	08.15	27
28	20.54	SCO	15.31	CAP	18.42	ARI	TAU	15.33	LEO	VIR	SCO	SAG	28
29	LIB		SAG	04.55	PIS	23.11	19.23	CAN	18.04	08.42	21.12	07.38	29
30	LIB		17.49	AQU	PIS	TAU	GEM	CAN	VIR	LIB	SAG	CAP	30
31	00.05		CAP		04.18		GEM	01.33		10.14		07.15	31

SUN

mth	dy	time	→ sign
JAN	1	00.00	→ CAP
JAN	21	01.10	→ AQU
FEB	19	15.26	→ PIS
MAR	20	14.42	→ ARI
APR	20	02.06	→ TAU
MAY	21	01.33	→ GEM
JUN	21	09.42	→ CAN
JUL	22	20.37	→ LEO
AUG	23	03.34	→ VIR
SEP	23	00.59	→ LIB
OCT	23	10.02	→ SCO
NOV	22	07.19	→ SAG
DEC	21	20.26	→ CAP

MERCURY

mth	dy	time	→ sign
JAN	1	00.00	→ SAG
JAN	4	08.24	→ CAP
JAN	23	06.16	→ AQU
FEB	9	10.12	→ PIS
APR	16	02.22	→ ARI
MAY	4	16.45	→ TAU
MAY	19	03.27	→ GEM
JUN	2	20.31	→ CAN
JUL	1	01.12	→ LEO
JUL	6	01.23	→ CAN
AUG	10	17.49	→ LEO
AUG	27	03.11	→ VIR
SEP	12	06.29	→ LIB
OCT	1	17.17	→ SCO
DEC	7	17.30	→ SAG
DEC	27	07.21	→ CAP

VENUS

mth	dy	time	→ sign
JAN	1	00.00	→ SCO
JAN	2	08.43	→ SAG
JAN	27	04.46	→ CAP
FEB	20	16.45	→ AQU
MAR	16	01.53	→ PIS
APR	9	10.32	→ ARI
MAY	3	19.56	→ TAU
MAY	28	06.11	→ GEM
JUN	21	16.34	→ CAN
JUL	16	02.11	→ LEO
AUG	9	10.54	→ VIR
SEP	2	19.29	→ LIB
SEP	27	05.12	→ SCO
OCT	21	17.12	→ SAG
NOV	15	08.57	→ CAP
DEC	10	08.35	→ AQU

MARS

mth	dy	time	→ sign
JAN	1	00.00	→ SAG
JAN	14	04.54	→ CAP
FEB	23	04.12	→ AQU
APR	2	06.24	→ PIS
MAY	11	07.23	→ ARI
JUN	20	09.05	→ TAU
AUG	2	04.25	→ GEM
SEP	21	04.11	→ CAN

SATURN

mth	dy	time	→ sign
JAN	1	00.00	→ CAP

JUPITER

mth	dy	time	→ sign
JAN	1	00.00	→ SAG
MAR	1	13.01	→ CAP
JUN	10	01.46	→ SAG
OCT	26	03.11	→ CAP

MOON

dy	jan	feb	mar	apr	may	jun	jul	aug	sep	oct	nov	dec	dy
1	AQU	00.39	18.18	GEM	CAN	16.38	08.46	SCO	CAP	22.12	ARI	TAU	1
2	09.19	ARI	TAU	01.46	21.59	VIR	LIB	02.04	12.35	PIS	15.27	GEM	2
3	PIS	09.16	TAU	01.46	LEO	VIR	15.08	SAG	AQU	PIS	TAU	GEM	3
4	15.21	TAU	05.08	CAN	LEO	01.31	SCO	03.25	13.51	01.46	23.46	17.52	4
5	ARI	20.58	GEM	14.01	08.59	LIB	17.42	CAP	PIS	ARI	GEM	CAN	5
6	ARI	GEM	17.37	LEO	VIR	06.20	SAG	03.21	16.26	07.09	GEM	CAN	6
7	01.22	GEM	CAN	LEO	16.30	SCO	17.34	AQU	ARI	TAU	10.26	06.21	7
8	TAU	09.37	CAN	00.02	LIB	07.31	CAP	03.42	21.46	15.16	CAN	LEO	8
9	13.45	CAN	05.25	VIR	20.07	SAG	16.43	PIS	TAU	GEM	22.59	19.12	9
10	GEM	21.08	LEO	06.35	SCO	06.48	AQU	06.21	TAU	GEM	LEO	VIR	10
11	GEM	LEO	14.45	LIB	20.55	CAP	17.19	ARI	06.31	02.18	LEO	VIR	11
12	02.23	LEO	VIR	10.01	SAG	06.23	PIS	12.36	GEM	CAN	11.24	06.10	12
13	CAN	06.35	21.19	SCO	20.50	AQU	21.07	TAU	18.10	14.55	VIR	LIB	13
14	13.59	VIR	LIB	11.37	CAP	08.17	ARI	22.29	CAN	LEO	21.07	13.12	14
15	LEO	13.55	LIB	SAG	21.51	PIS	ARI	GEM	CAN	LEO	LIB	SCO	15
16	LEO	LIB	01.37	13.01	AQU	13.42	04.48	GEM	06.46	02.40	LIB	16.07	16
17	00.03	19.24	SCO	CAP	AQU	ARI	TAU	10.43	LEO	VIR	02.53	SAG	17
18	VIR	SCO	04.37	15.32	01.23	22.33	15.40	CAN	18.07	11.32	SCO	16.16	18
19	08.12	23.12	SAG	AQU	PIS	TAU	GEM	23.17	VIR	LIB	05.17	CAP	19
20	LIB	SAG	07.12	19.55	07.55	TAU	GEM	LEO	VIR	17.06	SAG	15.49	20
21	13.59	SAG	CAP	PIS	ARI	09.46	04.09	LEO	02.58	SCO	06.02	AQU	21
22	SCO	01.39	10.10	PIS	17.00	GEM	CAN	10.41	LIB	20.16	CAP	16.45	22
23	17.02	CAP	AQU	02.23	TAU	22.10	16.46	VIR	09.18	SAG	07.04	PIS	23
24	SAG	03.42	14.02	ARI	TAU	CAN	LEO	20.09	SCO	22.28	AQU	20.34	24
25	17.59	AQU	PIS	10.50	03.55	CAN	LEO	LIB	13.42	CAP	09.49	ARI	25
26	CAP	06.04	19.29	TAU	GEM	10.51	04.31	LIB	SAG	CAP	PIS	ARI	26
27	18.19	PIS	ARI	21.16	16.06	LEO	VIR	03.23	16.54	00.57	14.51	03.30	27
28	AQU	10.38	ARI	GEM	CAN	22.53	14.33	SCO	CAP	AQU	ARI	TAU	28
29	19.56	ARI	03.12	09.22	CAN	VIR	LIB	08.19	19.32	04.26	22.00	13.01	29
30	PIS		TAU	CAN	04.50	VIR	21.55	SAG	AQU	PIS	TAU	GEM	30
31	PIS		13.32		LEO		SCO	11.09		09.11		GEM	31

SUN

mth	dy	time	→ sign
JAN	1	00.00	→ CAP
JAN	20	07.01	→ AQU
FEB	18	21.17	→ PIS
MAR	20	20.32	→ ARI
APR	20	07.55	→ TAU
MAY	21	07.23	→ GEM
JUN	21	15.30	→ CAN
JUL	23	02.24	→ LEO
AUG	23	09.19	→ VIR
SEP	23	06.43	→ LIB
OCT	23	15.46	→ SCO
NOV	22	13.08	→ SAG
DEC	22	02.19	→ CAP

MERCURY

mth	dy	time	→ sign
JAN	1	00.00	→ CAP
JAN	14	18.59	→ AQU
FEB	1	21.39	→ PIS
FEB	24	20.23	→ AQU
MAR	18	10.16	→ PIS
APR	10	09.23	→ ARI
APR	26	14.34	→ TAU
MAY	10	16.34	→ GEM
MAY	28	17.23	→ CAN
AUG	4	01.17	→ LEO
AUG	18	20.52	→ VIR
SEP	4	22.32	→ LIB
SEP	27	12.16	→ SCO
OCT	22	02.29	→ LIB
NOV	10	23.53	→ SCO
NOV	30	22.55	→ SAG
DEC	20	01.04	→ CAP

VENUS

mth	dy	time	→ sign
JAN	1	00.00	→ AQU
JAN	5	03.31	→ PIS
FEB	2	04.44	→ ARI
JUN	5	19.25	→ TAU
JUL	7	04.32	→ GEM
AUG	3	15.28	→ CAN
AUG	29	14.18	→ LEO
SEP	23	15.43	→ VIR
OCT	18	19.58	→ LIB
NOV	11	05.33	→ SCO
DEC	5	03.40	→ SAG
DEC	29	00.07	→ CAP

MARS

mth	dy	time	→ sign
JAN	1	00.00	→ CAN
FEB	5	00.28	→ GEM
FEB	7	05.18	→ CAN
MAY	6	01.15	→ LEO
JUN	28	23.51	→ VIR
AUG	17	00.42	→ LIB
OCT	1	20.12	→ SCO
NOV	13	21.55	→ SAG
DEC	24	17.50	→ CAP

SATURN

mth	dy	time	→ sign
JAN	1	00.00	→ CAP

JUPITER

mth	dy	time	→ sign
JAN	1	00.00	→ CAP
MAR	15	08.11	→ AQU
AUG	12	08.47	→ CAP
NOV	4	02.43	→ AQU

MOON

dy	jan	feb	mar	apr	may	jun	jul	aug	sep	oct	nov	dec	dy
1	00.23	LEO	14.13	LIB	SCO	CAP	AQU	ARI	05.52	CAN	LEO	VIR	1
2	CAN	07.48	VIR	16.36	05.25	17.45	02.52	16.19	GEM	CAN	06.17	03.08	2
3	12.54	VIR	VIR	SCO	SAG	AQU	PIS	TAU	15.00	09.43	VIR	LIB	3
4	LEO	19.27	01.21	22.34	08.40	19.50	04.13	23.04	CAN	LEO	18.42	13.30	4
5	LEO	LIB	LIB	SAG	CAP	PIS	ARI	GEM	CAN	22.45	LIB	SCO	5
6	01.48	LIB	10.24	SAG	11.24	23.23	10.01	GEM	03.01	VIR	LIB	20.24	6
7	VIR	04.51	SCO	02.52	AQU	ARI	TAU	08.56	LEO	VIR	04.40	SAG	7
8	13.31	SCO	17.04	CAP	14.23	ARI	17.27	CAN	16.05	11.04	SCO	SAG	8
9	LIB	11.01	SAG	06.03	PIS	04.38	GEM	20.59	VIR	LIB	11.51	00.31	9
10	22.09	SAG	21.19	AQU	17.56	TAU	GEM	LEO	VIR	21.19	SAG	CAP	10
11	SCO	13.50	CAP	08.31	ARI	11.40	03.13	LEO	04.33	SCO	16.59	03.11	11
12	SCO	CAP	23.29	PIS	22.25	GEM	CAN	10.00	LIB	SCO	CAP	AQU	12
13	02.40	14.13	AQU	10.55	TAU	20.50	14.56	VIR	15.23	05.21	20.59	05.41	13
14	SAG	AQU	AQU	ARI	TAU	CAN	LEO	22.45	SCO	SAG	AQU	PIS	14
15	03.41	13.53	00.26	14.16	04.34	CAN	LEO	LIB	23.54	11.24	AQU	08.45	15
16	CAP	PIS	PIS	TAU	GEM	08.16	03.55	LIB	SAG	CAP	00.18	ARI	16
17	02.55	14.41	01.32	19.55	13.17	LEO	VIR	09.45	SAG	15.37	PIS	12.39	17
18	AQU	ARI	ARI	GEM	CAN	21.13	16.39	SCO	05.42	AQU	03.10	TAU	18
19	02.32	18.21	04.25	GEM	CAN	VIR	LIB	17.45	CAP	18.10	ARI	17.46	19
20	PIS	TAU	TAU	04.50	00.45	VIR	LIB	SAG	08.43	PIS	06.03	GEM	20
21	04.26	TAU	10.32	CAN	LEO	09.32	03.04	22.07	AQU	19.35	TAU	GEM	21
22	ARI	01.51	GEM	16.43	13.38	LIB	SCO	CAP	09.36	ARI	09.59	00.50	22
23	09.51	GEM	20.23	LEO	VIR	18.51	09.42	23.25	PIS	21.07	GEM	CAN	23
24	TAU	12.49	CAN	LEO	VIR	SCO	SAG	AQU	09.40	TAU	16.20	10.26	24
25	18.50	CAN	CAN	05.31	01.18	SCO	12.28	23.02	ARI	TAU	CAN	LEO	25
26	GEM	CAN	08.48	VIR	LIB	00.05	CAP	PIS	10.42	00.24	CAN	22.29	26
27	GEM	01.34	LEO	16.34	09.34	SAG	12.41	22.49	TAU	02.01	02.01	VIR	27
28	06.23	LEO	21.30	LIB	SCO	02.00	AQU	ARI	14.32	07.03	LEO	VIR	28
29	CAN		VIR	LIB	14.11	CAP	12.13	ARI	GEM	CAN	14.25	11.26	29
30	19.05		VIR	00.27	SAG	02.18	PIS	00.37	22.19	17.30	VIR	LIB	30
31	LEO		08.21		16.20		12.56	TAU		LEO		22.42	31

SUN

mth	dy	time → sign
JAN	1	00.00 → CAP
JAN	20	12.58 → AQU
FEB	19	03.15 → PIS
MAR	21	02.29 → ARI
APR	20	13.51 → TAU
MAY	21	13.16 → GEM
JUN	21	21.24 → CAN
JUL	23	08.18 → LEO
AUG	23	15.11 → VIR
SEP	23	12.35 → LIB
OCT	23	21.40 → SCO
NOV	22	19.02 → SAG
DEC	22	08.16 → CAP

MERCURY

mth	dy	time → sign
JAN	1	00.00 → CAP
JAN	7	15.08 → AQU
MAR	15	11.43 → PIS
APR	3	02.33 → ARI
APR	18	04.10 → TAU
MAY	3	06.05 → GEM
JUL	11	07.36 → CAN
JUL	26	18.50 → LEO
AUG	10	19.29 → VIR
AUG	29	15.48 → LIB
NOV	5	02.20 → SCO
NOV	23	17.31 → SAG
DEC	12	20.51 → CAP

VENUS

mth	dy	time → sign
JAN	1	00.00 → CAP
JAN	21	20.31 → AQU
FEB	14	18.09 → PIS
MAR	10	18.28 → ARI
APR	3	23.05 → TAU
APR	28	09.22 → GEM
MAY	23	02.47 → CAN
JUN	17	05.31 → LEO
JUL	12	22.33 → VIR
AUG	8	17.14 → LIB
SEP	7	00.11 → SCO

MARS

mth	dy	time → sign
JAN	1	00.00 → CAP
FEB	1	23.17 → AQU
MAR	12	07.59 → PIS
APR	19	16.52 → ARI
MAY	28	23.44 → TAU
JUL	9	03.42 → GEM
AUG	22	11.32 → CAN
OCT	11	23.45 → LEO

SATURN

mth	dy	time → sign
JAN	1	00.00 → CAP
JAN	3	19.15 → AQU

JUPITER

mth	dy	time → sign
JAN	1	00.00 → AQU
MAR	25	22.15 → PIS

MOON

dy	jan	feb	mar	apr	may	jun	jul	aug	sep	oct	nov	dec	dy
1	SCO	21.09	06.38	20.42	06.12	17.40	06.19	LEO	03.02	SCO	SAG	14.26	1
2	SCO	CAP	CAP	PIS	ARI	GEM	CAN	07.57	LIB	SCO	01.17	AQU	2
3	06.22	22.57	09.53	20.41	06.49	21.56	13.55	VIR	15.47	CAP	09.40	19.53	3
4	SAG	AQU	AQU	ARI	TAU	CAN	LEO	20.17	SCO	SAG	09.02	PIS	4
5	10.24	22.53	10.16	20.25	08.16	CAN	LEO	LIB	SCO	19.35	AQU	23.17	5
6	CAP	PIS	PIS	TAU	GEM	05.22	00.22	LIB	03.26	CAP	13.53	ARI	6
7	12.00	22.50	09.33	22.00	12.28	LEO	VIR	08.56	SAG	CAP	PIS	ARI	7
8	AQU	ARI	ARI	GEM	CAN	16.12	12.48	SCO	12.20	02.20	15.45	00.59	8
9	12.53	ARI	09.40	GEM	20.35	VIR	LIB	19.48	CAP	AQU	ARI	TAU	9
10	PIS	00.35	TAU	03.12	LEO	VIR	LIB	SAG	17.26	05.29	15.45	02.07	10
11	14.34	TAU	12.35	CAN	LEO	04.51	01.05	SAG	AQU	PIS	TAU	GEM	11
12	ARI	05.18	GEM	12.36	08.11	LIB	SCO	03.17	19.02	05.40	15.43	04.20	12
13	18.02	GEM	19.25	LEO	VIR	16.45	11.00	CAP	PIS	ARI	GEM	CAN	13
14	TAU	13.20	CAN	LEO	21.01	SCO	SAG	07.07	18.33	04.43	17.49	09.20	14
15	23.42	CAN	CAN	00.57	LIB	SCO	17.33	AQU	ARI	TAU	CAN	LEO	15
16	GEM	CAN	05.56	VIR	LIB	02.01	CAP	08.17	18.02	04.50	23.40	17.59	16
17	GEM	00.03	LEO	13.53	08.43	SAG	21.07	PIS	TAU	GEM	LEO	VIR	17
18	07.39	LEO	18.33	LIB	SCO	08.30	AQU	08.25	19.29	08.05	LEO	VIR	18
19	CAN	12.26	VIR	LIB	18.02	CAP	23.00	ARI	GEM	CAN	09.33	05.41	19
20	17.50	VIR	VIR	01.37	SAG	12.49	PIS	09.20	GEM	15.30	VIR	LIB	20
21	LEO	VIR	07.28	SCO	SAG	AQU	PIS	TAU	00.26	LEO	21.58	18.18	21
22	LEO	01.20	LIB	11.27	01.08	15.59	00.34	12.28	CAN	LEO	LIB	SCO	22
23	05.53	LIB	19.28	SAG	CAP	PIS	ARI	GEM	09.07	02.31	LIB	SCO	23
24	VIR	13.36	SCO	19.20	06.31	18.43	02.57	18.34	LEO	VIR	10.33	05.33	24
25	18.53	SCO	SCO	CAP	AQU	ARI	TAU	CAN	20.31	15.11	SCO	SAG	25
26	LIB	23.47	05.48	CAP	10.29	21.34	06.57	CAN	VIR	LIB	21.43	14.19	26
27	LIB	SAG	SAG	01.08	PIS	TAU	GEM	03.30	VIR	LIB	SAG	CAP	27
28	06.53	SAG	13.47	AQU	13.15	TAU	13.00	LEO	09.08	03.48	SAG	20.42	28
29	SCO		CAP	04.40	ARI	01.09	CAN	14.36	LIB	SCO	07.00	AQU	29
30	15.59		18.43	PIS	15.17	GEM	21.20	VIR	21.49	15.19	CAP	AQU	30
31	SAG		AQU		TAU		LEO	VIR		SAG		01.20	31

SUN

mth	dy	time → sign
JAN	1	00.00 → CAP
JAN	20	18.54 → AQU
FEB	19	09.09 → PIS
MAR	21	08.20 → ARI
APR	20	19.36 → TAU
MAY	21	18.58 → GEM
JUN	22	03.04 → CAN
JUL	23	13.59 → LEO
AUG	23	20.58 → VIR
SEP	23	18.23 → LIB
OCT	24	03.29 → SCO
NOV	23	00.50 → SAG
DEC	22	14.02 → CAP

MERCURY

mth	dy	time → sign
JAN	1	00.00 → CAP
JAN	2	01.11 → AQU
JAN	20	04.59 → CAP
FEB	15	10.09 → AQU
MAR	9	05.26 → PIS
MAR	26	03.52 → ARI
APR	9	22.04 → TAU
MAY	3	04.17 → GEM
MAY	10	20.39 → TAU
JUN	14	23.20 → GEM
JUL	4	03.00 → CAN
JUL	18	06.19 → LEO
AUG	3	09.20 → VIR
AUG	26	20.33 → LIB
SEP	16	20.29 → VIR
OCT	10	16.44 → LIB
OCT	28	19.54 → SCO
NOV	16	11.07 → SAG
DEC	6	05.17 → CAP

VENUS

mth	dy	time → sign
JAN	1	00.00 → SCO
JAN	6	17.35 → SAG
FEB	5	20.35 → CAP
MAR	4	11.42 → AQU
MAR	30	01.00 → PIS
APR	24	03.39 → ARI
MAY	19	01.21 → TAU
JUN	12	19.57 → GEM
JUL	7	11.18 → CAN
JUL	31	22.39 → LEO
AUG	25	05.49 → VIR
SEP	18	09.43 → LIB
OCT	12	11.50 → SCO
NOV	5	13.25 → SAG
NOV	29	15.21 → CAP
DEC	23	18.53 → AQU

MARS

mth	dy	time → sign
JAN	1	00.00 → LEO
JUN	3	06.30 → VIR
JUL	27	04.15 → LIB
SEP	12	09.11 → SCO
OCT	25	17.32 → SAG
DEC	5	09.03 → CAP

SATURN

mth	dy	time → sign
JAN	1	00.00 → AQU

JUPITER

mth	dy	time → sign
JAN	1	00.00 → PIS
APR	4	03.19 → ARI

MOON

dy	jan	feb	mar	apr	may	jun	jul	aug	sep	oct	nov	dec	dy
1	PIS	TAU	21.39	CAN	LEO	00.09	SCO	SAG	AQU	PIS	00.42>TAU	GEM	1
2	04.48	16.03	GEM	14.45	06.13	LIB	SCO	03.12	AQU	13.48	23.48	10.45	2
3	ARI	GEM	GEM	LE0	VIR	12.38	08.11	CAP	01.37	ARI	GEM	CAN	3
4	07.33	20.40	02.08	LEO	17.42	SCO	SAG	11.25	PIS	13.50	GEM	12.20	4
5	TAU	CAN	CAN	00.20	LIB	SCO	19.03	AQU	03.52	TAU	00.08	LEO	5
6	10.14	CAN	09.15	VIR	LIB	01.01	CAP	ARI	13.58	CAN	17.26	6
7	GEM	03.06	LEO	11.49	06.16	SAG	CAP	PIS	05.02	GEM	03.24	VIR	7
8	13.41	LEO	18.34	LIB	SCO	12.07	03.36	20.07	TAU	16.01	LEO	VIR	8
9	CAN	11.36	VIR	LIB	18.42	CAP	AQU	ARI	06.46	CAN	10.14	02.21	9
10	19.01	VIR	VIR	00.14	SAG	21.22	09.53	22.37	GEM	20.54	VIR	LIB	10
11	LEO	22.18	05.35	SCO	SAG	AQU	PIS	TAU	10.08	LEO	20.07	14.04	11
12	LEO	LIB	LIB	12.48	06.13	AQU	14.16	TAU	CAN	LEO	LIB	SCO	12
13	03.07	LIB	17.51	SAG	CAP	04.20	ARI	01.16	15.30	04.34	LIB	SCO	13
14	VIR	10.38	SCO	SAG	15.51	PIS	17.15	GEM	LEO	VIR	07.57	02.53	14
15	14.05	SCO	SCO	00.27	AQU	08.46	TAU	04.39	22.47	14.24	SCO	SAG	15
16	LIB	22.57	06.27	CAP	22.32	ARI	19.27	CAN	VIR	LIB	20.40	15.21	16
17	LIB	SAG	SAG	09.34	PIS	10.54	GEM	09.17	VIR	LIB	SAG	CAP	17
18	02.35	SAG	17.35	AQU	PIS	TAU	21.45	LEO	08.00	01.52	SAG	CAP	18
19	SCO	09.00	CAP	14.53	01.47	11.44	CAN	15.40	LIB	SCO	09.23	02.29	19
20	14.20	CAP	CAP	PIS	ARI	GEM	CAN	VIR	19.10	14.32	CAP	AQU	20
21	SAG	15.23	01.21	16.30	02.21	12.46	01.15	VIR	SCO	SAG	20.51	11.28	21
22	23.23	AQU	AQU	ARI	TAU	CAN	LEO	00.25	SCO	SAG	AQU	PIS	22
23	CAP	18.17	05.04	15.51	01.53	15.44	07.06	LIB	07.50	03.21	AQU	17.41	23
24	CAP	PIS	PIS	TAU	GEM	LEO	VIR	11.39	SAG	CAP	05.32	ARI	24
25	05.14	19.05	05.37	15.06	02.29	21.56	16.02	SCO	20.15	14.20	PIS	20.57	25
26	AQU	ARI	ARI	GEM	CAN	VIR	LIB	SCO	CAP	AQU	10.25	TAU	26
27	08.35	19.38	04.57	16.27	05.58	VIR	LIB	00.15	CAP	21.36	ARI	21.58	27
28	PIS	TAU	TAU	CAN	LEO	07.41	03.38	SAG	06.03	PIS	11.49	GEM	28
29	10.44		05.13	21.25	13.22	LIB	SCO	11.57	AQU	PIS	TAU	22.07	29
30	ARI		GEM	LEO	VIR	19.48	16.08	CAP	11.46	00.40	11.14	CAN	30
31	12.55		08.14		VIR		SAG	20.37		ARI		23.09	31

SUN

mth	dy	time → sign
JAN	1	00.00 → CAP
JAN	21	00.41 → AQU
FEB	19	14.57 → PIS
MAR	20	14.10 → ARI
APR	20	01.27 → TAU
MAY	21	00.50 → GEM
JUN	21	08.57 → CAN
JUL	22	19.53 → LEO
AUG	23	02.51 → VIR
SEP	23	00.17 → LIB
OCT	23	09.21 → SCO
NOV	22	06.39 → SAG
DEC	21	19.50 → CAP

MERCURY

mth	dy	time → sign
JAN	1	00.00 → CAP
FEB	10	21.30 → AQU
FEB	29	22.50 → PIS
MAR	16	23.55 → ARI
APR	2	00.58 → TAU
JUN	9	15.45 → GEM
JUN	24	17.17 → CAN
JUL	9	00.39 → LEO
JUL	27	11.35 → VIR
OCT	3	00.12 → LIB
OCT	20	07.11 → SCO
NOV	8	11.02 → SAG
NOV	30	19.30 → CAP
DEC	16	14.31 → SAG

VENUS

mth	dy	time → sign
JAN	1	00.00 → AQU
JAN	17	02.53 → PIS
FEB	10	21.10 → ARI
MAR	7	12.38 → TAU
APR	4	03.03 → GEM
MAY	9	03.15 → CAN
JUN	17	18.17 → GEM
AUG	5	08.52 → CAN
SEP	8	04.53 → LEO
OCT	5	18.10 → VIR
OCT	31	08.54 → LIB
NOV	25	01.25 → SCO
DEC	19	07.02 → SAG

MARS

mth	dy	time → sign
JAN	1	00.00 → CAP
JAN	13	06.14 → AQU
FEB	20	07.33 → PIS
MAR	29	11.24 → ARI
MAY	7	14.41 → TAU
JUN	17	11.43 → GEM
JUL	30	18.23 → CAN
SEP	15	05.22 → LEO
NOV	6	03.20 → VIR

SATURN

mth	dy	time → sign
JAN	1	00.00 → AQU
MAR	24	04.17 → PIS
SEP	16	21.04 → AQU
DEC	16	05.39 → PIS

JUPITER

mth	dy	time → sign
JAN	1	00.00 → ARI
APR	12	06.53 → TAU

MOON

dy	jan	feb	mar	apr	may	jun	jul	aug	sep	oct	nov	dec	dy
1	LEO	19.25	LIB	09.41	05.42	AQU	PIS	TAU	00.13	LEO	00.24	SCO	1
2	LEO	LIB	13.54	SAG	CAP	11.01	00.52	15.28	CAN	12.42	LIB	SCO	2
3	02.48	LIB	SCO	22.36	18.06	PIS	ARI	GEM	02.36	VIR	08.25	01.24	3
4	VIR	05.12	SCO	CAP	AQU	18.03	05.42	17.13	LEO	17.44	SCO	SAG	4
5	10.10	SCO	01.47	CAP	AQU	ARI	TAU	CAN	05.12	LIB	18.43	13.53	5
6	LIB	17.35	SAG	10.24	03.43	21.20	07.43	18.11	VIR	LIB	SAG	CAP	6
7	21.04	SAG	14.35	AQU	PIS	TAU	GEM	LEO	09.19	00.57	SAG	CAP	7
8	SCO	SAG	CAP	18.47	09.15	21.50	07.57	19.50	LIB	SCO	07.06	02.57	8
9	SCO	06.11	CAP	PIS	ARI	GEM	CAN	VIR	16.20	11.02	CAP	AQU	9
10	09.49	CAP	01.35	23.08	11.09	21.16	08.01	23.51	SCO	SAG	20.08	15.00	10
11	SAG	16.39	AQU	ARI	TAU	CAN	LEO	LIB	SCO	23.32	AQU	PIS	11
12	22.14	AQU	09.05	ARI	11.01	21.35	09.44	LIB	02.47	CAP	AQU	PIS	12
13	CAP	AQU	PIS	00.37	GEM	LEO	VIR	07.31	SAG	CAP	07.28	00.12	13
14	CAP	00.09	13.15	TAU	10.53	LEO	14.41	SCO	15.30	12.15	PIS	ARI	14
15	08.48	PIS	ARI	01.06	CAN	00.27	LIB	18.44	CAP	AQU	15.10	05.32	15
16	AQU	05.10	15.30	GEM	12.31	VIR	23.32	SAG	CAP	22.33	ARI	TAU	16
17	17.04	ARI	TAU	02.23	LEO	06.54	SCO	SAG	03.47	PIS	18.57	07.21	17
18	PIS	08.45	17.26	CAN	17.02	LIB	SCO	07.38	AQU	PIS	TAU	GEM	18
19	23.10	TAU	GEM	05.40	VIR	16.49	11.28	CAP	13.22	05.05	19.58	07.02	19
20	ARI	11.48	20.11	LEO	VIR	SCO	SAG	19.39	PIS	ARI	GEM	CAN	20
21	ARI	GEM	CAN	11.17	00.41	SCO	SAG	AQU	19.44	08.24	20.04	06.31	21
22	03.23	14.49	CAN	VIR	LIB	05.03	00.27	AQU	ARI	TAU	CAN	LEO	22
23	TAU	CAN	00.15	19.08	10.58	SAG	CAP	05.13	23.46	10.03	20.59	07.41	23
24	06.05	18.11	LEO	LIB	SCO	18.02	12.30	PIS	TAU	GEM	LEO	VIR	24
25	GEM	LEO	05.42	LIB	23.03	CAP	AQU	12.15	TAU	11.37	LEO	12.04	25
26	07.51	22.30	VIR	05.01	SAG	CAP	22.36	ARI	02.46	CAN	00.02	LIB	26
27	CAN	VIR	12.48	SCO	SAG	06.22	PIS	17.24	GEM	14.14	VIR	20.11	27
28	09.45	VIR	LIB	16.46	12.00	AQU	PIS	TAU	05.39	LEO	05.54	SCO	28
29	LEO	04.46	22.03	SAG	CAP	16.56	06.25	21.16	CAN	18.25	LIB	SCO	29
30	13.09		SCO	SAG	CAP	PIS	ARI	GEM	08.52	VIR	14.31	07.20	30
31	VIR		SCO		00.32		12.00	GEM		VIR		SAG	31

SUN

mth	dy	time	→ sign
JAN	1	00.00	→ CAP
JAN	20	06.29	→ AQU
FEB	18	20.48	→ PIS
MAR	20	20.05	→ ARI
APR	20	07.26	→ TAU
MAY	21	06.50	→ GEM
JUN	21	14.56	→ CAN
JUL	23	01.48	→ LEO
AUG	23	08.43	→ VIR
SEP	23	06.06	→ LIB
OCT	23	15.10	→ SCO
NOV	22	12.30	→ SAG
DEC	22	01.40	→ CAP

MERCURY

mth	dy	time	→ sign
JAN	1	00.00	→ SAG
JAN	13	03.12	→ CAP
FEB	3	09.02	→ AQU
FEB	21	05.40	→ PIS
MAR	9	02.19	→ ARI
MAY	15	13.19	→ TAU
JUN	2	03.47	→ GEM
JUN	16	02.04	→ CAN
JUL	1	15.55	→ LEO
JUL	31	08.08	→ VIR
AUG	3	04.57	→ LEO
SEP	8	17.14	→ VIR
SEP	25	05.49	→ LIB
OCT	12	21.15	→ SCO
NOV	2	06.04	→ SAG

VENUS

mth	dy	time	→ sign
JAN	1	00.00	→ SAG
JAN	12	08.01	→ CAP
FEB	5	07.42	→ AQU
MAR	1	07.55	→ PIS
MAR	25	09.54	→ ARI
APR	18	14.31	→ TAU
MAY	12	22.08	→ GEM
JUN	6	08.39	→ CAN
JUN	30	21.59	→ LEO
JUL	25	14.52	→ VIR
AUG	19	13.06	→ LIB
SEP	13	19.50	→ SCO
OCT	9	16.46	→ SAG
NOV	5	19.36	→ CAP
DEC	7	04.37	→ AQU

MARS

mth	dy	time	→ sign
JAN	1	00.00	→ VIR
JUN	29	01.12	→ LIB
AUG	20	12.16	→ SCO
OCT	4	06.46	→ SAG
NOV	14	07.19	→ CAP
DEC	23	05.36	→ AQU

SATURN

mth	dy	time	→ sign
JAN	1	00.00	→ PIS

JUPITER

mth	dy	time	→ sign
JAN	1	00.00	→ TAU
APR	22	14.33	→ GEM
SEP	21	04.39	→ CAN
NOV	17	03.08	→ GEM

MOON

dy	jan	feb	mar	apr	may	jun	jul	aug	sep	oct	nov	dec	dy
1	20.06	AQU	AQU	02.19	TAU	07.05	LEO	03.54	SCO	18.29	AQU	PIS	1
2	CAP	AQU	09.38	ARI	20.26	CAN	17.11	LIB	00.00	CAP	AQU	23.22	2
3	CAP	02.56	PIS	08.29	GEM	07.47	VIR	08.20	SAG	CAP	03.23	ARI	3
4	09.04	PIS	18.45	TAU	22.39	LEO	19.43	SCO	10.51	06.48	PIS	ARI	4
5	AQU	12.43	ARI	12.55	CAN	09.33	LIB	16.49	CAP	AQU	14.21	08.11	5
6	21.06	ARI	ARI	GEM	CAN	VIR	LIB	SAG	23.34	19.14	ARI	TAU	6
7	PIS	20.24	01.49	16.24	00.50	13.29	01.38	SAG	AQU	PIS	22.29	13.27	7
8	PIS	TAU	TAU	CAN	LEO	LIB	SCO	04.22	AQU	PIS	TAU	GEM	8
9	07.08	TAU	07.14	19.23	03.47	20.04	10.53	CAP	11.56	05.54	TAU	15.57	9
10	ARI	01.36	GEM	LEO	VIR	SCO	SAG	17.09	PIS	ARI	03.54	CAN	10
11	14.10	GEM	11.03	22.14	08.04	SCO	22.29	AQU	22.50	14.16	GEM	17.08	11
12	TAU	04.14	CAN	VIR	LIB	05.10	CAP	AQU	ARI	TAU	07.29	LEO	12
13	17.48	CAN	13.23	VIR	14.10	SAG	CAP	05.37	ARI	20.40	CAN	18.35	13
14	GEM	04.54	LEO	01.38	SCO	16.20	11.08	PIS	07.56	GEM	10.13	VIR	14
15	18.35	LEO	14.55	LIB	22.32	CAP	AQU	16.57	TAU	GEM	LEO	21.33	15
16	CAN	05.05	VIR	06.42	SAG	CAP	23.45	ARI	15.06	01.27	12.54	LIB	16
17	17.57	VIR	17.04	SCO	SAG	04.51	PIS	ARI	GEM	CAN	VIR	LIB	17
18	LEO	06.45	LIB	14.31	09.20	AQU	PIS	02.27	20.01	04.51	16.10	02.40	18
19	17.55	LIB	21.32	SAG	CAP	17.29	11.13	TAU	CAN	LEO	LIB	SCO	19
20	VIR	11.45	SCO	SAG	21.50	PIS	ARI	09.20	22.35	07.13	20.37	10.01	20
21	20.28	SCO	SCO	01.24	AQU	PIS	20.14	GEM	LEO	VIR	SCO	SAG	21
22	LIB	20.57	05.37	CAP	AQU	04.29	TAU	13.04	23.30	09.21	SCO	19.27	22
23	LIB	SAG	SAG	14.04	10.14	ARI	TAU	CAN	VIR	LIB	02.56	CAP	23
24	03.01	SAG	17.07	AQU	PIS	12.16	01.48	14.01	VIR	12.31	SAG	CAP	24
25	SCO	09.17	CAP	AQU	20.19	TAU	GEM	LEO	00.15	SCO	11.45	06.44	25
26	13.32	CAP	CAP	02.02	ARI	16.18	03.53	13.36	LIB	18.09	CAP	AQU	26
27	SAG	22.14	05.59	PIS	ARI	GEM	CAN	VIR	02.47	SAG	23.03	19.17	27
28	SAG	AQU	AQU	11.12	02.48	17.20	03.37	13.52	SCO	SAG	AQU	PIS	28
29	02.21		17.32	ARI	TAU	CAN	LEO	LIB	08.42	03.05	AQU	PIS	29
30	CAP		PIS	17.03	05.58	16.59	02.55	16.54	SAG	CAP	11.40	07.40	30
31	15.17		PIS		GEM		VIR	SCO		14.49		ARI	31

SUN

mth	dy	time → sign
JAN	1	00.00 → CAP
JAN	20	12.24 → AQU
FEB	19	02.39 → PIS
MAR	21	01.54 → ARI
APR	20	13.12 → TAU
MAY	21	12.33 → GEM
JUN	21	20.33 → CAN
JUL	23	07.25 → LEO
AUG	23	14.18 → VIR
SEP	23	11.45 → LIB
OCT	23	20.57 → SCO
NOV	22	18.15 → SAG
DEC	22	07.28 → CAP

SATURN

mth	dy	time → sign
JAN	1	00.00 → PIS

MERCURY

mth	dy	time → sign
JAN	1	00.00 → SAG
JAN	7	18.27 → CAP
JAN	27	04.10 → AQU
FEB	13	10.19 → PIS
MAR	3	02.58 → ARI
MAR	22	02.34 → PIS
APR	17	21.34 → ARI
MAY	9	14.49 → TAU
MAY	24	17.59 → GEM
JUN	7	19.11 → CAN
JUN	26	19.07 → LEO
SEP	1	10.35 → VIR
SEP	17	08.17 → LIB
OCT	5	22.06 → SCO
OCT	30	07.38 → SAG
NOV	13	03.26 → SCO
DEC	11	15.29 → SAG

VENUS

mth	dy	time → sign
JAN	1	00.00 → AQU
FEB	6	12.45 → CAP
FEB	25	10.55 → AQU
APR	6	15.55 → PIS
MAY	5	04.33 → ARI
MAY	31	18.02 → TAU
JUN	26	11.43 → GEM
JUL	21	17.11 → CAN
AUG	15	12.47 → LEO
SEP	8	23.43 → VIR
OCT	3	03.41 → LIB
OCT	27	03.24 → SCO
NOV	20	01.05 → SAG
DEC	13	22.09 → CAP

MARS

mth	dy	time → sign
JAN	1	00.00 → AQU
JAN	30	07.12 → PIS
MAR	9	12.46 → ARI
APR	17	20.35 → TAU
MAY	28	22.14 → GEM
JUL	11	03.11 → CAN
AUG	25	15.55 → LEO
OCT	12	18.39 → VIR
DEC	4	00.56 → LIB

JUPITER

mth	dy	time → sign
JAN	1	00.00 → GEM
MAY	5	14.41 → CAN
SEP	27	13.34 → LEO

MOON

dy	jan	feb	mar	apr	may	jun	jul	aug	sep	oct	nov	dec	dy
1	17.46	GEM	22.48	LEO	19.31	SCO	23.51	AQU	22.27	16.47	GEM	CAN	1
2	TAU	13.41	CAN	10.31	LIB	09.38	CAP	AQU	ARI	TAU	17.43	05.02	2
3	TAU	CAN	CAN	VIR	21.23	SAG	CAP	03.36	ARI	TAU	CAN	LEO	3
4	00.06	14.14	00.57	10.40	SCO	16.10	09.14	PIS	10.59	03.43	23.36	08.48	4
5	GEM	LEO	LEO	LIB	SCO	CAP	AQU	16.15	TAU	GEM	LEO	VIR	5
6	02.40	13.11	00.36>VIR	11.30	00.52	CAP	20.39	ARI	21.52	12.12	LEO	11.43	6
7	CAN	VIR	23.48	SCO	SAG	01.21	PIS	ARI	GEM	CAN	03.10	LIB	7
8	02.50	12.50	LIB	14.54	07.12	AQU	PIS	04.38	GEM	17.25	VIR	14.18	8
9	LEO	LIB	LIB	SAG	CAP	12.57	09.16	TAU	05.26	LEO	04.54	SCO	9
10	02.34	15.15	00.47	22.02	16.52	PIS	ARI	14.38	CAN	19.27	LIB	17.13	10
11	VIR	SCO	SCO	CAP	AQU	PIS	21.03	GEM	09.01	VIR	05.53	SAG	11
12	03.53	21.33	05.18	CAP	AQU	01.26	TAU	20.41	LEO	19.29	SCO	21.30	12
13	LIB	SAG	SAG	08.42	04.55	ARI	TAU	CAN	09.25	LIB	07.37	CAP	13
14	08.08	SAG	13.55	AQU	PIS	12.29	05.51	22.50	VIR	19.21	SAG	CAP	14
15	SCO	07.26	CAP	21.13	17.15	TAU	GEM	LEO	08.33	SCO	11.37	04.19	15
16	15.39	CAP	CAP	PIS	ARI	20.26	10.44	22.35	LIB	20.59	CAP	AQU	16
17	SAG	19.25	01.35	PIS	ARI	GEM	CAN	VIR	08.34	SAG	19.03	14.17	17
18	SAG	AQU	AQU	09.27	03.49	GEM	12.27	22.05	SCO	SAG	AQU	PIS	18
19	01.45	AQU	14.18	ARI	TAU	01.05	LEO	LIB	11.21	01.55	AQU	PIS	19
20	CAP	08.05	PIS	20.00	11.40	CAN	12.47	23.24	SAG	CAP	05.53	02.39	20
21	13.26	PIS	PIS	TAU	GEM	03.29	VIR	SCO	17.53	10.41	PIS	ARI	21
22	AQU	20.30	02.33	TAU	17.00	LEO	13.38	SCO	CAP	AQU	18.31	15.07	22
23	AQU	ARI	ARI	04.27	CAN	05.08	LIB	03.51	CAP	22.20	ARI	TAU	23
24	01.58	ARI	13.32	GEM	20.37	VIR	16.32	SAG	03.48	PIS	ARI	TAU	24
25	PIS	07.53	TAU	10.48	LEO	07.23	SCO	11.37	AQU	PIS	06.37	01.13	25
26	14.33	TAU	22.41	CAN	23.22	LIB	22.04	CAP	15.48	11.03	TAU	GEM	26
27	ARI	17.03	GEM	15.09	VIR	11.04	SAG	21.56	PIS	ARI	16.31	07.58	27
28	ARI	GEM	GEM	LEO	VIR	SCO	SAG	AQU	PIS	23.05	GEM	CAN	28
29	01.43		05.23	17.50	02.00	16.31	06.04	AQU	04.29	TAU	23.50	11.57	29
30	TAU		CAN	VIR	LIB	SAG	CAP	09.48	ARI	TAU	CAN	LEO	30
31	09.43		09.12		05.11		16.02	PIS		09.28		14.33	31

SUN

mth	dy	time → sign
JAN	1	00.00 → CAP
JAN	20	18.10 → AQU
FEB	19	08.26 → PIS
MAR	21	07.36 → ARI
APR	20	18.54 → TAU
MAY	21	18.14 → GEM
JUN	22	02.25 → CAN
JUL	23	13.16 → LEO
AUG	23	20.11 → VIR
SEP	23	17.38 → LIB
OCT	24	02.47 → SCO
NOV	23	00.04 → SAG
DEC	22	13.19 → CAP

MERCURY

mth	dy	time → sign
JAN	1	00.56 → CAP
JAN	19	17.09 → AQU
FEB	6	00.37 → PIS
APR	14	14.35 → ARI
MAY	1	23.26 → TAU
MAY	16	03.23 → GEM
MAY	31	18.06 → CAN
AUG	8	22.05 → LEO
AUG	24	06.16 → VIR
SEP	9	16.54 → LIB
SEP	30	01.46 → SCO
DEC	5	13.44 → SAG
DEC	24	20.36 → CAP

VENUS

mth	dy	time → sign
JAN	1	00.00 → CAP
JAN	6	19.37 → AQU
JAN	30	18.54 → PIS
FEB	23	22.30 → ARI
MAR	20	09.58 → TAU
APR	14	09.57 → GEM
MAY	10	06.01 → CAN
JUN	6	16.48 → LEO
JUL	8	22.14 → VIR
SEP	9	11.57 → LEO
OCT	1	18.09 → VIR
NOV	9	16.35 → LIB
DEC	7	08.48 → SCO

MARS

mth	dy	time → sign
JAN	1	00.00 → LIB
FEB	12	12.13 → SCO
MAR	31	06.19 → LIB
JUL	19	22.47 → SCO
SEP	10	01.41 → SAG
OCT	23	02.26 → CAP
DEC	1	20.22 → AQU

SATURN

mth	dy	time → sign
JAN	1	00.00 → PIS
MAR	3	21.13 → ARI

JUPITER

mth	dy	time → sign
JAN	1	00.00 → LEO
JAN	16	03.32 → CAN
MAY	23	08.28 → LEO
OCT	19	10.57 → VIR

MOON

dy	jan	feb	mar	apr	may	jun	jul	aug	sep	oct	nov	dec	dy
1	VIR	01.44	SCO	00.11	AQU	20.07	16.43	GEM	14.08	03.38	15.26	02.10	1
2	17.04	SCO	11.53	CAP	AQU	ARI	TAU	22.32	LEO	VIR	SCO	SAG	2
3	LIB	05.55	SAG	07.49	00.47	ARI	TAU	CAN	17.07	04.34	14.51	02.25	3
4	20.16	SAG	17.35	AQU	PIS	09.04	04.39	CAN	VIR	LIB	SAG	CAP	4
5	SCO	12.10	CAP	18.29	13.10	TAU	GEM	04.26	18.03	04.14	15.44	04.57	5
6	SCO	CAP	CAP	PIS	ARI	20.52	13.47	LEO	LIB	SCO	CAP	AQU	6
7	00.28	20.17	02.03	PIS	ARI	GEM	CAN	07.36	18.44	04.32	19.45	11.19	7
8	SAG	AQU	AQU	06.57	02.09	GEM	19.58	VIR	20.40	SAG	AQU	PIS	8
9	05.53	AQU	12.41	ARI	TAU	06.18	LEO	09.34	20.40	SAG	AQU	21.43	9
10	CAP	06.19	PIS	19.56	14.08	CAN	LEO	LIB	SAG	CAP	03.42	ARI	10
11	13.05	PIS	PIS	TAU	GEM	13.19	00.07	11.44	SAG	12.45	PIS	ARI	11
12	AQU	18.17	00.53	08.15	GEM	LEO	VIR	14.52	00.43	AQU	14.58	10.32	12
13	22.45	ARI	ARI	GEM	00.11	18.24	03.20	14.52	CAP	21.38	ARI	TAU	13
14	PIS	ARI	13.54	GEM	CAN	VIR	LIB	SAG	07.08	PIS	ARI	23.18	14
15	PIS	07.19	TAU	18.37	07.49	21.58	06.17	19.18	AQU	PIS	03.52	GEM	15
16	10.48	TAU	TAU	CAN	LEO	LIB	SCO	CAP	15.53	08.58	TAU	GEM	16
17	ARI	19.16	02.19	CAN	12.52	LIB	09.22	CAP	PIS	ARI	16.40	10.23	17
18	23.39	GEM	GEM	01.54	VIR	00.25	SAG	01.17	PIS	21.41	GEM	CAN	18
19	TAU	GEM	12.10	LEO	15.31	SCO	12.59	AQU	02.46	TAU	GEM	19.21	19
20	TAU	03.48	CAN	05.42	LIB	02.20	CAP	09.18	ARI	TAU	04.13	LEO	20
21	10.38	CAN	18.04	VIR	16.30	SAG	17.59	PIS	15.20	10.38	CAN	LEO	21
22	GEM	08.04	LEO	06.41	SCO	04.46	AQU	19.47	TAU	GEM	13.47	02.21	22
23	17.51	LEO	20.08	LIB	17.06	CAP	AQU	ARI	TAU	22.27	LEO	VIR	23
24	CAN	09.04	VIR	06.19	SAG	09.11	01.28	ARI	CAN	CAN	20.46	07.27	24
25	21.20	VIR	19.50	SCO	18.58	AQU	PIS	08.21	GEM	CAN	VIR	LIB	25
26	LEO	08.44	LIB	06.27	CAP	16.49	12.00	TAU	15.45	07.40	VIR	10.36	26
27	22.36	LIB	19.10	SAG	23.44	PIS	ARI	21.08	CAN	LEO	00.48	SCO	27
28	VIR	09.09	SCO	08.54	AQU	PIS	ARI	GEM	23.41	13.19	LIB	12.09	28
29	23.33		20.08	CAP	AQU	03.52	00.40	GEM	LEO	VIR	02.13	SAG	29
30	LIB		SAG	14.57	08.18	ARI	TAU	07.34	LEO	15.31	SCO	13.11	30
31	LIB		SAG		PIS		13.00	CAN		LIB		CAP	31

SUN

mth	dy	time → sign
JAN	1	00.00 → CAP
JAN	20	23.52 → AQU
FEB	19	14.12 → PIS
MAR	20	13.22 → ARI
APR	20	00.45 → TAU
MAY	21	00.07 → GEM
JUN	21	08.13 → CAN
JUL	22	19.05 → LEO
AUG	23	02.03 → VIR
SEP	22	23.27 → LIB
OCT	23	08.32 → SCO
NOV	22	05.45 → SAG
DEC	21	19.02 → CAP

MERCURY

mth	dy	time → sign
JAN	1	00.00 → CAP
JAN	12	07.17 → AQU
FEB	1	12.58 → PIS
FEB	11	18.54 → AQU
MAR	17	14.42 → PIS
APR	7	01.01 → ARI
APR	22	16.18 → TAU
MAY	6	22.52 → GEM
MAY	29	22.44 → CAN
JUN	13	22.37 → GEM
JUL	13	01.30 → CAN
JUL	31	06.13 → LEO
AUG	15	00.54 → VIR
SEP	1	16.59 → LIB
SEP	28	14.43 → SCO
OCT	7	22.45 → LIB
NOV	8	11.04 → SCO
NOV	27	12.47 → SAG
DEC	16	14.14 → CAP

VENUS

mth	dy	time → sign
JAN	1	22.37 → SAG
JAN	26	17.35 → CAP
FEB	20	04.57 → AQU
MAR	15	13.32 → PIS
APR	8	21.45 → ARI
MAY	3	06.55 → TAU
MAY	27	17.06 → GEM
JUN	21	03.21 → CAN
JUL	15	12.57 → LEO
AUG	8	21.47 → VIR
SEP	2	06.37 → LIB
SEP	26	16.46 → SCO
OCT	21	05.19 → SAG
NOV	14	21.48 → CAP
DEC	9	22.42 → AQU

MARS

mth	dy	time → sign
JAN	1	00.00 → AQU
JAN	9	09.43 → PIS
FEB	17	03.12 → ARI
MAR	27	23.35 → TAU
MAY	8	14.20 → GEM
JUN	21	05.23 → CAN
AUG	5	17.00 → LEO
SEP	21	18.42 → VIR
NOV	9	06.23 → LIB
DEC	29	22.19 → SCO

SATURN

mth	dy	time → sign
JAN	1	00.00 → ARI

JUPITER

mth	dy	time → sign
JAN	1	00.00 → VIR
FEB	27	03.22 → LEO
JUN	15	14.34 → VIR
NOV	15	22.58 → LIB

MOON

dy	jan	feb	mar	apr	may	jun	jul	aug	sep	oct	nov	dec	dy
1	15.24	PIS	ARI	TAU	GEM	LEO	VIR	02.11	13.22	AQU	16.51	08.58	1
2	AQU	14.39	ARI	06.40	01.50	LEO	16.10	SCO	CAP	AQU	ARI	TAU	2
3	20.35	ARI	10.27	GEM	CAN	03.52	LIB	05.11	16.19	03.21	ARI	21.06	3
4	PIS	ARI	TAU	19.13	12.54	VIR	20.20	SAG	AQU	PIS	03.01	GEM	4
5	PIS	02.15	23.17	CAN	LEO	09.49	SCO	06.57	20.27	10.35	TAU	GEM	5
6	05.45	TAU	GEM	CAN	20.58	LIB	22.05	CAP	PIS	ARI	14.48	09.43	6
7	ARI	15.09	GEM	05.28	VIR	12.30	SAG	08.37	PIS	20.07	GEM	CAN	7
8	18.02	GEM	11.21	LEO	VIR	SCO	22.24	AQU	02.49	TAU	GEM	22.02	8
9	TAU	GEM	CAN	12.04	01.21	12.42	CAP	11.45	ARI	TAU	03.26	LEO	9
10	TAU	02.34	20.27	VIR	LIB	SAG	23.03	PIS	12.06	07.43	CAN	LEO	10
11	06.54	CAN	LEO	15.01	02.30	12.05	AQU	17.53	TAU	GEM	15.45	08.59	11
12	GEM	10.50	LEO	LIB	SCO	CAP	AQU	ARI	23.54	20.23	LEO	VIR	12
13	17.54	LEO	01.51	15.32	01.53	12.46	02.03	ARI	GEM	CAN	LEO	17.08	13
14	CAN	16.02	VIR	SCO	SAG	AQU	PIS	03.36	GEM	CAN	01.55	LIB	14
15	CAN	VIR	04.23	15.23	01.30	16.42	08.51	TAU	12.28	08.08	VIR	21.31	15
16	02.09	19.21	LIB	SAG	CAP	PIS	ARI	15.51	CAN	LEO	08.26	SCO	16
17	LEO	LIB	05.33	16.23	03.22	PIS	19.30	GEM	23.25	16.58	LIB	22.27	17
18	08.11	22.00	SCO	CAP	AQU	00.50	TAU	GEM	LEO	VIR	11.06	SAG	18
19	VIR	SCO	06.54	19.57	08.53	ARI	TAU	04.15	LEO	22.05	SCO	21.32	19
20	12.47	SCO	SAG	AQU	PIS	12.25	08.13	CAN	07.15	LIB	11.04	CAP	20
21	LIB	00.48	09.34	AQU	18.14	TAU	GEM	14.40	VIR	LIB	SAG	20.59	21
22	16.28	SAG	CAP	02.45	ARI	TAU	20.31	LEO	12.00	00.05	10.20	AQU	22
23	SCO	04.12	14.16	PIS	ARI	01.22	CAN	22.21	LIB	SCO	CAP	23.01	23
24	19.23	CAP	AQU	12.32	06.15	GEM	CAN	VIR	14.39	00.32	11.02	PIS	24
25	SAG	08.37	21.15	ARI	TAU	13.43	06.55	VIR	SCO	SAG	AQU	PIS	25
26	21.57	AQU	PIS	ARI	19.12	CAN	LEO	03.45	16.30	01.13	14.52	05.02	26
27	CAP	14.42	PIS	00.22	GEM	CAN	15.10	LIB	SAG	CAP	PIS	ARI	27
28	CAP	PIS	06.32	TAU	GEM	00.30	VIR	07.38	18.44	03.43	22.26	14.57	28
29	01.06	23.14	ARI	13.11	07.43	LEO	21.32	SCO	CAP	AQU	ARI	TAU	29
30	AQU		17.55	GEM	CAN	09.26	LIB	10.40	22.11	08.54	ARI	TAU	30
31	06.16		TAU		18.53		LIB	SAG		PIS		03.11	31

SUN

mth	dy	time → sign
JAN	1	00.00 → CAP
JAN	20	05.33 → AQU
FEB	18	19.53 → PIS
MAR	20	19.08 → ARI
APR	20	06.24 → TAU
MAY	21	05.56 → GEM
JUN	21	13.55 → CAN
JUL	23	00.44 → LEO
AUG	23	07.43 → VIR
SEP	23	05.09 → LIB
OCT	23	14.13 → SCO
NOV	22	11.31 → SAG
DEC	22	00.48 → CAP

MERCURY

mth	dy	time → sign
JAN	1	00.00 → CAP
JAN	4	12.21 → AQU
MAR	12	15.23 → PIS
MAR	30	09.56 → ARI
APR	14	05.55 → TAU
APR	30	15.15 → GEM
JUL	8	03.58 → CAN
JUL	22	19.14 → LEO
AUG	7	04.27 → VIR
AUG	27	06.50 → LIB
OCT	7	02.55 → VIR
OCT	9	16.55 → LIB
NOV	1	16.52 → SCO
NOV	20	06.00 → SAG
DEC	9	13.22 → CAP

VENUS

mth	dy	time → sign
JAN	1	00.00 → AQU
JAN	4	20.06 → PIS
FEB	2	04.44 → ARI
JUN	6	01.43 → TAU
JUL	6	22.02 → GEM
AUG	3	05.34 → CAN
AUG	29	02.49 → LEO
SEP	23	03.22 → VIR
OCT	17	14.13 → LIB
NOV	10	16.46 → SCO
DEC	4	14.41 → SAG
DEC	28	11.08 → CAP

MARS

mth	dy	time → sign
JAN	1	00.00 → SCO
FEB	25	06.10 → SAG
SEP	21	06.22 → CAP
NOV	4	18.43 → AQU
DEC	15	14.33 → PIS

SATURN

mth	dy	time → sign
JAN	1	00.00 → ARI
APR	29	22.35 → TAU

JUPITER

mth	dy	time → sign
JAN	1	00.00 → LIB
MAR	30	21.50 → VIR
JUL	15	13.39 → LIB
DEC	16	15.43 → SCO

MOON

dy	jan	feb	mar	apr	may	jun	jul	aug	sep	oct	nov	dec	dy
1	GEM	10.29	LEO	20.03	09.49	21.07	06.49	19.55	TAU	GEM	11.35	08.14	1
2	15.53	LEO	LEO	LIB	SCO	CAP	AQU	ARI	19.23	14.52	LEO	VIR	2
3	CAN	20.40	04.07	LIB	11.19	21.03	07.26	ARI	GEM	CAN	LEO	19.17	3
4	CAN	VIR	VIR	00.22	SAG	AQU	PIS	02.02	GEM	CAN	00.00	LIB	4
5	03.54	VIR	11.34	SCO	11.57	23.13	11.16	TAU	06.57	03.25	VIR	LIB	5
6	LEO	05.00	LIB	02.57	CAP	PIS	ARI	11.49	CAN	LEO	09.59	02.30	6
7	14.42	LIB	16.56	SAG	13.28	PIS	18.53	GEM	19.36	15.21	LIB	SCO	7
8	VIR	11.18	SCO	05.04	AQU	04.36	TAU	23.57	LEO	VIR	16.18	05.42	8
9	23.32	SCO	20.48	CAP	17.04	ARI	TAU	CAN	LEO	VIR	SCO	SAG	9
10	LIB	15.23	SAG	07.46	PIS	13.06	05.31	CAN	07.20	00.48	19.30	06.20	10
11	LIB	SAG	23.40	AQU	23.09	TAU	GEM	12.38	VIR	LIB	SAG	CAP	11
12	05.32	17.28	CAP	11.41	ARI	23.48	17.47	LEO	17.01	07.19	21.08	06.27	12
13	SCO	CAP	CAP	PIS	ARI	GEM	CAN	LEO	LIB	SCO	CAP	AQU	13
14	08.19	18.30	02.09	17.13	07.28	CAN	CAN	00.32	LIB	11.33	22.53	07.56	14
15	SAG	AQU	AQU	ARI	TAU	11.52	06.29	VIR	00.25	SAG	AQU	PIS	15
16	08.39	20.03	05.04	ARI	17.41	CAN	LEO	10.51	SCO	14.35	AQU	11.56	16
17	CAP	PIS	PIS	00.43	GEM	CAN	18.42	LIB	05.42	CAP	01.52	ARI	17
18	08.17	23.48	09.27	TAU	GEM	00.35	VIR	18.54	SAG	17.21	PIS	18.35	18
19	AQU	ARI	ARI	10.28	05.30	LEO	VIR	SCO	09.14	AQU	06.32	TAU	19
20	09.21	ARI	16.20	GEM	CAN	12.53	05.20	SCO	CAP	20.26	ARI	TAU	20
21	PIS	07.02	TAU	22.17	18.12	VIR	LIB	00.12	11.31	PIS	12.52	03.28	21
22	13.43	TAU	TAU	CAN	LEO	23.03	13.04	SAG	AQU	PIS	TAU	GEM	22
23	ARI	17.41	02.12	CAN	LEO	LIB	SCO	02.49	13.22	00.17	20.59	14.08	23
24	22.13	GEM	GEM	10.51	06.07	LIB	17.10	CAP	PIS	ARI	GEM	CAN	24
25	TAU	GEM	14.18	LEO	VIR	05.31	SAG	03.36	15.55	05.32	GEM	CAN	25
26	TAU	06.11	CAN	21.57	15.07	SCO	18.09	AQU	ARI	TAU	07.10	02.21	26
27	09.53	CAN	CAN	VIR	LIB	08.00	CAP	04.03	20.29	13.00	CAN	LEO	27
28	GEM	18.12	02.37	VIR	20.05	SAG	17.35	PIS	TAU	GEM	19.22	15.20	28
29	22.36		LEO	05.43	SCO	07.44	AQU	05.57	TAU	23.13	LEO	VIR	29
30	CAN		12.54	LIB	21.30	CAP	17.30	04.05	CAN	LEO	VIR	30
31	CAN		VIR		SAG		PIS	10.50		CAN		03.18	31

SUN

mth	dy	time → sign
JAN	1	00.00 → CAP
JAN	20	11.26 → AQU
FEB	19	01.42 → PIS
MAR	21	00.52 → ARI
APR	20	12.15 → TAU
MAY	21	11.32 → GEM
JUN	21	19.43 → CAN
JUL	23	06.33 → LEO
AUG	23	13.34 → VIR
SEP	23	10.53 → LIB
OCT	23	20.08 → SCO
NOV	22	17.23 → SAG
DEC	22	06.32 → CAP

MERCURY

mth	dy	time → sign
JAN	1	00.00 → CAP
JAN	4	04.23 → AQU
JAN	4	11.53 → CAP
FEB	13	13.06 → AQU
MAR	5	20.13 → PIS
MAR	22	07.59 → ARI
APR	6	07.44 → TAU
JUN	13	12.46 → GEM
JUN	30	06.21 → CAN
JUL	14	08.09 → LEO
JUL	31	05.23 → VIR
OCT	7	18.04 → LIB
OCT	25	06.11 → SCO
NOV	13	01.17 → SAG
DEC	3	10.15 → CAP

VENUS

mth	dy	time → sign
JAN	1	00.00 → CAP
JAN	21	07.22 → AQU
FEB	14	05.03 → PIS
MAR	10	05.23 → ARI
APR	3	10.07 → TAU
APR	27	20.34 → GEM
MAY	22	14.16 → CAN
JUN	16	17.49 → LEO
JUL	12	12.17 → VIR
AUG	8	10.00 → LIB
SEP	7	01.55 → SCO

MARS

mth	dy	time → sign
JAN	1	00.00 → PIS
JAN	24	21.22 → ARI
MAR	7	01.35 → TAU
APR	18	18.46 → GEM
JUN	2	06.51 → CAN
JUL	18	06.44 → LEO
SEP	3	04.50 → VIR
OCT	20	10.49 → LIB
DEC	6	16.27 → SCO

SATURN

mth	dy	time → sign
JAN	1	00.00 → TAU

JUPITER

mth	dy	time → sign
JAN	1	00.00 → SCO
APR	30	06.29 → LIB
AUG	15	17.45 → SCO

MOON

dy	jan	feb	mar	apr	may	jun	jul	aug	sep	oct	nov	dec	dy
1	LIB	01.50	SAG	AQU	PIS	TAU	GEM	10.44	VIR	LIB	02.24	CAP	1
2	12.03	SAG	12.54	AQU	09.32	TAU	17.21	LEO	18.25	11.35	SAG	18.45	2
3	SCO	04.21	CAP	00.01	ARI	02.10	CAN	23.34	LIB	SCO	08.32	AQU	3
4	16.33	CAP	14.34	PIS	13.05	GEM	CAN	VIR	LIB	20.31	CAP	21.55	4
5	SAG	04.19	AQU	01.32	TAU	10.25	04.26	VIR	05.54	SAG	13.11	PIS	5
6	17.30	AQU	14.49	ARI	18.17	CAN	LEO	12.32	SCO	SAG	AQU	PIS	6
7	CAP	03.37	PIS	04.02	GEM	21.17	17.11	LIB	14.58	03.10	16.33	01.03	7
8	16.47	PIS	15.16	TAU	GEM	LEO	VIR	23.57	SAG	CAP	PIS	ARI	8
9	AQU	04.17	ARI	09.02	LEO	02.17	VIR	SCO	20.51	07.26	18.52	04.24	9
10	16.37	ARI	17.43	GEM	CAN	10.02	06.02	SCO	CAP	AQU	ARI	TAU	10
11	PIS	07.59	TAU	17.33	13.22	VIR	LIB	08.07	23.34	09.30	20.50	08.33	11
12	18.48	TAU	23.37	CAN	LEO	22.28	16.41	SAG	AQU	PIS	TAU	GEM	12
13	ARI	15.29	GEM	CAN	07.10	LIB	SCO	12.25	23.57	10.12	23.48	14.32	13
14	ARI	GEM	GEM	05.15	VIR	LIB	23.26	CAP	PIS	ARI	GEM	CAN	14
15	00.20	GEM	09.18	LEO	VIR	08.01	SAG	13.31	23.35	11.00	GEM	23.21	15
16	TAU	02.17	CAN	18.07	14.02	SCO	SAG	AQU	ARI	TAU	05.23	LEO	16
17	09.07	CAN	21.39	VIR	LIB	13.39	02.19	13.01	ARI	13.43	CAN	LEO	17
18	GEM	14.53	LEO	VIR	22.49	SAG	CAP	PIS	00.21	GEM	14.36	11.04	18
19	20.13	LEO	LEO	05.35	SCO	16.04	02.44	12.50	TAU	19.59	LEO	VIR	19
20	CAN	LEO	10.30	LIB	SCO	CAP	AQU	ARI	04.02	CAN	LEO	VIR	20
21	CAN	03.42	VIR	14.15	04.11	17.00	02.36	14.46	GEM	CAN	02.50	00.01	21
22	08.40	VIR	21.56	SCO	SAG	AQU	PIS	TAU	11.41	06.12	VIR	LIB	22
23	LEO	15.30	LIB	20.15	07.13	18.11	03.42	20.03	CAN	15.39	15.39	11.27	23
24	21.33	LIB	LIB	SAG	CAP	PIS	ARI	GEM	22.54	18.57	LIB	SCO	24
25	VIR	LIB	07.10	SAG	09.26	20.52	07.18	GEM	LEO	VIR	LIB	19.27	25
26	VIR	01.23	SCO	00.26	AQU	ARI	TAU	04.58	LEO	VIR	02.25	SAG	26
27	09.42	SCO	14.07	CAP	11.59	ARI	13.53	CAN	11.53	07.37	SCO	SAG	27
28	LIB	08.38	SAG	03.43	PIS	01.35	GEM	16.38	VIR	LIB	10.02	00.01	28
29	19.34		19.00	AQU	15.27	TAU	23.14	LEO	VIR	18.15	SAG	CAP	29
30	SCO		CAP	06.37	ARI	08.24	CAN	LEO	00.33	SCO	15.05	02.24	30
31	SCO		22.08		20.03		CAN	05.36		SCO		AQU	31

SUN

mth	dy	time → sign
JAN	1	00.00 → CAP
JAN	20	17.11 → AQU
FEB	19	07.23 → PIS
MAR	21	06.38 → ARI
APR	20	17.50 → TAU
MAY	21	17.15 → GEM
JUN	22	01.14 → CAN
JUL	23	12.16 → LEO
AUG	23	19.15 → VIR
SEP	23	16.49 → LIB
OCT	24	01.58 → SCO
NOV	22	23.11 → SAG
DEC	22	12.27 → CAP

MERCURY

mth	dy	time → sign
JAN	1	00.00 → CAP
JAN	2	23.32 → SAG
JAN	14	02.17 → CAP
FEB	7	20.53 → AQU
FEB	26	07.52 → PIS
MAR	14	04.47 → ARI
APR	1	14.17 → TAU
APR	18	21.52 → ARI
MAY	17	03.33 → TAU
JUN	7	06.45 → GEM
JUN	21	16.28 → CAN
JUL	6	08.53 → LEO
JUL	26	17.03 → VIR
AUG	29	20.45 → LEO
SEP	11	06.42 → VIR
SEP	30	09.12 → LIB
OCT	17	17.49 → SCO
NOV	6	06.52 → SAG

VENUS

mth	dy	time → sign
JAN	1	00.00 → SCO
JAN	7	01.01 → SAG
FEB	5	14.54 → CAP
MAR	4	02.24 → AQU
MAR	29	14.04 → PIS
APR	23	15.47 → ARI
MAY	18	12.48 → TAU
JUN	12	06.56 → GEM
JUL	6	22.02 → CAN
JUL	31	09.12 → LEO
AUG	24	16.22 → VIR
SEP	17	20.26 → LIB
OCT	11	22.48 → SCO
NOV	5	00.33 → SAG
NOV	29	02.41 → CAP
DEC	23	06.34 → AQU

MARS

mth	dy	time → sign
JAN	1	00.00 → SCO
JAN	23	01.26 → SAG
MAR	12	10.23 → CAP
MAY	3	20.49 → AQU
NOV	6	12.33 → PIS
DEC	26	18.22 → ARI

SATURN

mth	dy	time → sign
JAN	1	00.00 → TAU
JUN	18	16.22 → GEM

JUPITER

mth	dy	time → sign
JAN	1	00.00 → SCO
JAN	14	08.56 → SAG
JUN	5	02.32 → SCO
SEP	11	15.39 → SAG

MOON

dy	jan	feb	mar	apr	may	jun	jul	aug	sep	oct	nov	dec	dy
1	04.08	15.49	TAU	16.51	09.34	VIR	LIB	08.49	CAP	19.36	ARI	16.25	1
2	PIS	TAU	TAU	CAN	LEO	17.26	13.46	SAG	07.04	PIS	05.55	GEM	2
3	06.26	20.34	03.01	CAN	21.03	LIB	SCO	16.32	AQU	19.40	TAU	17.51	3
4	ARI	GEM	GEM	02.05	VIR	LIB	23.59	CAP	08.51	ARI	05.27	CAN	4
5	10.00	GEM	09.47	LEO	VIR	05.36	SAG	20.47	PIS	18.42	GEM	22.17	5
6	TAU	04.07	CAN	14.16	09.59	SCO	SAG	AQU	08.43	TAU	07.15	LEO	6
7	15.08	CAN	19.55	VIR	LIB	15.28	07.03	22.34	ARI	18.53	CAN	LEO	7
8	GEM	14.06	LEO	VIR	22.03	SAG	CAP	PIS	08.37	GEM	12.56	06.40	8
9	22.09	LEO	LEO	03.17	SCO	22.45	11.26	23.27	TAU	22.10	LEO	VIR	9
10	CAN	LEO	08.10	LIB	SCO	CAP	AQU	ARI	10.25	CAN	22.44	18.19	10
11	CAN	01.58	VIR	15.28	08.08	CAP	14.14	ARI	GEM	CAN	VIR	LIB	11
12	07.24	VIR	21.06	SCO	SAG	04.03	PIS	00.55	15.21	05.30	VIR	LIB	12
13	LEO	14.50	LIB	SCO	16.09	AQU	16.32	TAU	CAN	LEO	11.05	07.01	13
14	18.57	LIB	LIB	02.03	CAP	08.01	ARI	04.10	23.38	16.16	LIB	SCO	14
15	VIR	LIB	09.31	SAG	22.19	PIS	19.10	GEM	LEO	VIR	23.49	18.37	15
16	VIR	03.22	SCO	10.38	AQU	11.06	TAU	09.50	LEO	VIR	SCO	SAG	16
17	07.53	SCO	20.23	CAP	AQU	ARI	22.47	CAN	10.29	04.47	SCO	SAG	17
18	LIB	13.45	SAG	16.46	02.39	13.39	GEM	17.57	VIR	LIB	11.30	04.07	18
19	20.04	SAG	SAG	AQU	PIS	TAU	GEM	LEO	22.47	17.31	SAG	CAP	19
20	SCO	20.37	04.37	20.07	05.11	16.24	03.56	LEO	LIB	SCO	21.36	11.32	20
21	SCO	CAP	CAP	PIS	ARI	GEM	CAN	04.19	LIB	SCO	CAP	AQU	21
22	05.15	23.43	09.28	21.08	06.31	20.30	11.16	VIR	11.33	05.31	CAP	17.10	22
23	SAG	AQU	AQU	ARI	TAU	CAN	LEO	16.22	SCO	SAG	05.52	PIS	23
24	10.32	AQU	11.07	21.06	08.01	CAN	21.09	LIB	23.43	16.05	AQU	21.09	24
25	CAP	00.05>PIS	PIS	TAU	GEM	03.12	VIR	LIB	SAG	CAP	11.48	ARI	25
26	12.36	23.30	10.45	21.58	11.26	LEO	VIR	05.09	SAG	CAP	PIS	23.45	26
27	AQU	ARI	ARI	GEM	CAN	13.06	09.12	SCO	09.53	00.11	15.03	TAU	27
28	13.02	23.54	10.16	GEM	18.16	VIR	LIB	16.56	CAP	AQU	ARI	TAU	28
29	PIS		TAU	01.43	LEO	VIR	21.50	SAG	16.39	04.56	16.08	01.38	29
30	13.36		11.43	CAN	LEO	01.22	SCO	SAG	AQU	PIS	TAU	GEM	30
31	ARI		GEM		04.48		SCO	01.54		06.26		04.01	31

SUN

mth	dy	time → sign
JAN	1	00.00 → CAP
JAN	20	23.04 → AQU
FEB	19	13.13 → PIS
MAR	20	12.27 → ARI
APR	19	23.38 → TAU
MAY	20	22.56 → GEM
JUN	21	07.07 → CAN
JUL	22	18.03 → LEO
AUG	23	01.08 → VIR
SEP	22	22.37 → LIB
OCT	23	07.42 → SCO
NOV	22	05.04 → SAG
DEC	21	18.17 → CAP

MERCURY

mth	dy	time → sign
JAN	1	00.00 → SAG
JAN	11	18.13 → CAP
JAN	31	23.47 → AQU
FEB	18	12.55 → PIS
MAR	5	16.56 → ARI
MAY	12	23.42 → TAU
MAY	29	06.46 → GEM
JUN	12	02.52 → CAN
JUN	28	16.52 → LEO
SEP	5	11.38 → VIR
SEP	21	12.15 → LIB
OCT	9	11.11 → SCO
OCT	30	19.23 → SAG
NOV	29	07.08 → SCO
DEC	12	23.18 → SAG

VENUS

mth	dy	time → sign
JAN	1	00.00 → AQU
JAN	16	15.10 → PIS
FEB	10	10.07 → ARI
MAR	7	03.24 → TAU
APR	3	22.48 → GEM
MAY	10	13.53 → CAN
JUN	11	20.08 → GEM
AUG	6	01.21 → CAN
SEP	7	23.27 → LEO
OCT	5	08.38 → VIR
OCT	30	21.43 → LIB
NOV	24	13.23 → SCO
DEC	18	18.37 → SAG

MARS

mth	dy	time → sign
JAN	1	00.00 → ARI
FEB	10	14.11 → TAU
MAR	27	04.37 → GEM
MAY	12	13.23 → CAN
JUN	28	16.14 → LEO
AUG	15	00.44 → VIR
SEP	30	23.33 → LIB
NOV	15	22.12 → SCO
DEC	30	16.24 → SAG

SATURN

mth	dy	time → sign
JAN	1	00.00 → GEM
JAN	10	03.28 → TAU
FEB	21	14.33 → GEM

JUPITER

mth	dy	time → sign
JAN	1	00.00 → SAG
FEB	6	19.23 → CAP
JUL	24	16.32 → SAG
SEP	25	18.28 → CAP

MOON

dy	jan	feb	mar	apr	may	jun	jul	aug	sep	oct	nov	dec	dy
1	CAN	00.56	19.00	SCO	SAG	12.15	01.18	14.57	GEM	12.25	VIR	LIB	1
2	08.22	VIR	LIB	SCO	20.29	AQU	PIS	TAU	02.11	LEO	10.27	03.42	2
3	LEO	11.06	LIB	02.27	CAP	19.52	06.22	17.33	CAN	19.31	LIB	SCO	3
4	15.50	LIB	07.00	SAG	CAP	PIS	ARI	GEM	06.54	VIR	21.46	16.22	4
5	VIR	23.18	SCO	14.20	06.35	PIS	09.25	20.18	LEO	VIR	SCO	SAG	5
6	VIR	SCO	19.36	CAP	AQU	00.27	TAU	CAN	13.15	04.35	SCO	SAG	6
7	02.33	SCO	SAG	23.37	13.28	ARI	11.05	23.56	VIR	LIB	10.16	05.06	7
8	LIB	11.38	SAG	AQU	PIS	02.14	GEM	LEO	21.36	15.27	SAG	CAP	8
9	15.03	SAG	06.49	AQU	16.35	TAU	12.29	LEO	LIB	SCO	23.11	16.53	9
10	SCO	21.50	CAP	04.58	ARI	02.24	CAN	05.23	LIB	SCO	CAP	AQU	10
11	SCO	CAP	14.42	PIS	16.47	GEM	15.05	VIR	08.15	03.52	CAP	AQU	11
12	02.57	CAP	AQU	06.32	TAU	02.45	LEO	13.27	SCO	SAG	11.02	02.32	12
13	SAG	04.36	18.39	ARI	15.57	CAN	20.16	LIB	20.42	16.44	AQU	PIS	13
14	12.26	AQU	PIS	05.54	GEM	05.10	VIR	LIB	SAG	CAP	19.56	08.59	14
15	CAP	08.11	19.37	TAU	16.16	LEO	VIR	00.19	SAG	CAP	PIS	ARI	15
16	19.04	PIS	ARI	05.16	CAN	11.03	04.49	SCO	09.07	03.51	PIS	11.59	16
17	AQU	09.51	19.27	GEM	19.38	VIR	LIB	12.49	CAP	AQU	00.44	TAU	17
18	23.28	ARI	TAU	06.46	LEO	20.39	16.15	SAG	19.04	11.12	ARI	12.24	18
19	PIS	11.11	20.12	CAN	LEO	LIB	SCO	SAG	AQU	PIS	01.53	GEM	19
20	PIS	TAU	GEM	11.47	02.56	LIB	SCO	00.38	AQU	14.22	TAU	11.57	20
21	02.35	13.35	23.26	LEO	VIR	08.43	04.46	CAP	01.09	ARI	01.05	CAN	21
22	ARI	GEM	CAN	20.24	13.36	SCO	SAG	PIS	14.37	GEM	12.34	LEO	22
23	05.17	17.52	CAN	VIR	LIB	21.14	16.10	AQU	03.44	TAU	00.31	16.03	23
24	TAU	CAN	05.46	VIR	LIB	SAG	CAP	15.28	ARI	14.02	CAN	VIR	24
25	08.14	CAN	LEO	07.34	02.01	SAG	CAP	PIS	04.27	GEM	02.12	VIR	25
26	GEM	00.15	14.47	LIB	SCO	08.36	01.07	18.40	TAU	14.44	LEO	23.21	26
27	12.01	LEO	VIR	19.56	14.33	CAP	AQU	ARI	05.14	CAN	07.24	LIB	27
28	CAN	08.39	VIR	SCO	SAG	18.02	07.29	20.43	GEM	18.14	VIR	LIB	28
29	17.21	VIR	01.42	SCO	SAG	AQU	PIS	TAU	07.39	LEO	16.15	10.10	29
30	LEO		LIB	08.31	02.13	AQU	11.50	22.56	CAN	LEO	LIB	SCO	30
31	LEO		13.48		CAP		ARI	GEM		00.59		22.51	31

91

SUN

mth	dy	time → sign
JAN	1	00.00 → CAP
JAN	20	04.54 → AQU
FEB	18	19.02 → PIS
MAR	20	18.16 → ARI
APR	20	05.30 → TAU
MAY	21	04.55 → GEM
JUN	21	13.03 → CAN
JUL	22	23.56 → LEO
AUG	23	06.58 → VIR
SEP	23	04.21 → LIB
OCT	23	13.34 → SCO
NOV	22	10.54 → SAG
DEC	22	00.04 → CAP

MERCURY

mth	dy	time → sign
JAN	1	00.00 → SAG
JAN	4	14.47 → CAP
JAN	23	15.23 → AQU
FEB	9	19.33 → PIS
APR	16	21.18 → ARI
MAY	6	02.59 → TAU
MAY	20	17.26 → GEM
JUN	4	04.42 → CAN
JUN	27	06.46 → LEO
JUL	16	08.01 → CAN
AUG	11	12.21 → LEO
AUG	28	15.22 → VIR
SEP	13	16.11 → LIB
OCT	2	20.12 → SCO
DEC	8	21.29 → SAG
DEC	28	15.15 → CAP

VENUS

mth	dy	time → sign
JAN	1	00.00 → SAG
JAN	11	19.12 → CAP
FEB	4	18.43 → AQU
FEB	28	18.42 → PIS
MAR	24	20.34 → ARI
APR	18	01.05 → TAU
MAY	12	08.44 → GEM
JUN	5	19.20 → CAN
JUN	30	08.54 → LEO
JUL	25	02.13 → VIR
AUG	19	01.17 → LIB
SEP	13	09.05 → SCO
OCT	9	08.03 → SAG
NOV	5	15.39 → CAP
DEC	7	21.33 → AQU

MARS

mth	dy	time → sign
JAN	1	00.00 → SAG
FEB	12	05.43 → CAP
MAR	26	20.46 → AQU
MAY	8	04.25 → PIS
JUN	20	20.54 → ARI
AUG	12	14.42 → TAU
OCT	29	22.42 → ARI
DEC	24	08.26 → TAU

SATURN

mth	dy	time → sign
JAN	1	00.00 → GEM
AUG	1	22.40 → CAN

JUPITER

mth	dy	time → sign
JAN	1	00.00 → CAP
FEB	23	09.38 → AQU

MOON

dy	jan	feb	mar	apr	may	jun	jul	aug	sep	oct	nov	dec	dy
1	SAG	CAP	14.22	PIS	ARI	GEM	21.55	VIR	05.17	SAG	CAP	AQU	1
2	SAG	05.55	AQU	12.48	01.01	11.21	LEO	13.12	SCO	SAG	08.58	04.32	2
3	11.30	AQU	22.31	ARI	TAU	CAN	23.31	LIB	15.24	12.02	AQU	PIS	3
4	CAP	14.22	PIS	14.58	01.16	11.49	VIR	20.35	SAG	CAP	20.26	13.50	4
5	22.47	PIS	PIS	TAU	GEM	LEO	VIR	SCO	SAG	CAP	PIS	ARI	5
6	AQU	20.29	03.37	16.12	01.35	14.51	04.23	SCO	04.01	00.48	PIS	19.08	6
7	AQU	ARI	ARI	GEM	CAN	VIR	LIB	07.37	CAP	AQU	04.19	TAU	7
8	08.03	ARI	06.51	18.04	03.36	21.16	13.05	SAG	16.30	11.23	ARI	20.58	8
9	PIS	00.53	TAU	CAN	LEO	LIB	SCO	20.30	AQU	PIS	08.25	GEM	9
10	14.57	TAU	09.31	21.31	08.13	LIB	SCO	CAP	AQU	18.29	TAU	20.52	10
11	ARI	04.10	GEM	LEO	VIR	06.52	00.48	CAP	02.40	ARI	09.59	CAN	11
12	19.24	GEM	12.29	LEO	15.31	SCO	SAG	08.52	PIS	22.36	GEM	20.44	12
13	TAU	06.44	CAN	02.46	LIB	18.43	13.45	AQU	09.56	TAU	10.46	LEO	13
14	21.41	CAN	16.07	VIR	LIB	SAG	CAP	19.14	ARI	TAU	CAN	22.20	14
15	GEM	09.12	LEO	09.50	01.09	SAG	CAP	PIS	14.59	01.09	12.20	VIR	15
16	22.39	LEO	20.42	LIB	SCO	07.37	02.15	PIS	TAU	GEM	LEO	VIR	16
17	CAN	12.31	VIR	18.51	12.41	CAP	AQU	03.15	18.48	03.28	15.41	02.53	17
18	23.40	VIR	VIR	SCO	SAG	20.19	13.07	ARI	GEM	CAN	VIR	LIB	18
19	LEO	17.58	02.48	SCO	SAG	AQU	PIS	09.14	22.01	06.25	21.15	10.44	19
20	LEO	LIB	LIB	06.02	01.30	AQU	21.43	TAU	CAN	LEO	LIB	SCO	20
21	02.23	LIB	11.15	SAG	CAP	07.29	ARI	13.26	CAN	10.19	LIB	21.20	21
22	VIR	02.35	SCO	18.49	14.17	PIS	ARI	GEM	00.56	VIR	05.06	SAG	22
23	08.16	SCO	22.26	CAP	AQU	15.48	03.41	16.08	LEO	15.28	SCO	SAG	23
24	LIB	14.14	SAG	CAP	AQU	ARI	TAU	CAN	03.58	LIB	15.11	09.41	24
25	17.52	SAG	SAG	07.21	01.05	20.37	06.58	17.49	VIR	22.28	SAG	CAP	25
26	SCO	SAG	11.16	AQU	PIS	TAU	GEM	LEO	08.00	SCO	SAG	22.43	26
27	SCO	03.04	CAP	17.09	08.14	22.18	08.10	19.33	LIB	SCO	03.13	AQU	27
28	06.10	CAP	23.12	PIS	ARI	GEM	CAN	VIR	14.18	07.57	CAP	AQU	28
29	SAG		AQU	22.53	11.28	22.08	08.29	22.52	SCO	SAG	16.17	11.10	29
30	18.54		AQU	ARI	TAU	CAN	LEO	LIB	23.47	19.57	AQU	PIS	30
31	CAP		07.55		11.53		09.34	LIB		CAP		21.34	31

SUN, MOON AND INNER PLANET TABLES

1974

SUN

mth	dy	time → sign
JAN	1	00.00 → CAP
JAN	20	10.42 → AQU
FEB	19	00.57 → PIS
MAR	21	00.04 → ARI
APR	20	11.19 → TAU
MAY	21	10.34 → GEM
JUN	21	18.36 → CAN
JUL	23	05.35 → LEO
AUG	23	12.23 → VIR
SEP	23	09.58 → LIB
OCT	23	19.12 → SCO
NOV	22	16.34 → SAG
DEC	22	05.56 → CAP

MERCURY

mth	dy	time → sign
JAN	1	00.00 → CAP
JAN	16	03.52 → AQU
FEB	2	22.42 → PIS
MAR	2	17.48 → AQU
MAR	17	20.11 → PIS
APR	11	15.20 → ARI
APR	28	03.16 → TAU
MAY	12	04.55 → GEM
MAY	29	08.06 → CAN
AUG	5	11.41 → LEO
AUG	20	09.01 → VIR
SEP	6	05.48 → LIB
SEP	28	00.21 → SCO
OCT	26	23.22 → LIB
NOV	11	16.05 → SCO
DEC	2	06.17 → SAG
DEC	21	09.17 → CAP

VENUS

mth	dy	time → sign
JAN	1	00.00 → AQU
JAN	29	19.48 → CAP
FEB	28	14.25 → AQU
APR	6	14.13 → PIS
MAY	4	20.23 → ARI
MAY	31	07.16 → TAU
JUN	25	23.41 → GEM
JUL	21	04.38 → CAN
AUG	14	23.47 → LEO
SEP	8	10.24 → VIR
OCT	2	14.27 → LIB
OCT	26	14.11 → SCO
NOV	19	11.57 → SAG
DEC	13	09.12 → CAP

MARS

mth	dy	time → sign
JAN	1	00.00 → TAU
FEB	27	10.25 → GEM
APR	20	08.23 → CAN
JUN	9	00.54 → LEO
JUL	27	14.21 → VIR
SEP	12	19.15 → LIB
OCT	28	07.25 → SCO
DEC	10	22.17 → SAG

SATURN

mth	dy	time → sign
JAN	1	00.00 → CAN
JAN	7	20.19 → GEM
APR	18	22.22 → CAN

JUPITER

mth	dy	time → sign
JAN	1	00.00 → AQU
MAR	8	11.14 → PIS

MOON

dy	jan	feb	mar	apr	may	jun	jul	aug	sep	oct	nov	dec	dy
1	ARI	16.53	GEM	11.40	VIR	11.10	01.20	CAP	01.29	ARI	18.23	06.22	1
2	ARI	GEM	GEM	LEO	23.39	SCO	SAG	06.46	PIS	ARI	GEM	CAN	2
3	04.38	19.05	02.59	13.56	LIB	19.21	12.19	AQU	12.58	04.39	23.01	08.31	3
4	TAU	CAN	CAN	VIR	LIB	SAG	CAP	19.26	ARI	TAU	CAN	LEO	4
5	08.00	19.11	04.49	16.22	04.43	SAG	CAP	PIS	22.50	12.00	CAN	10.40	5
6	GEM	LEO	LEO	LIB	SCO	05.48	00.41	PIS	TAU	GEM	02.30	VIR	6
7	08.28	18.52	05.33	20.25	12.05	CAP	AQU	07.15	TAU	17.30	LEO	13.42	7
8	CAN	VIR	VIR	SCO	SAG	18.02	13.25	ARI	06.36	CAN	05.18	LIB	8
9	07.42	20.10	06.52	SCO	22.15	AQU	PIS	17.13	GEM	21.03	VIR	18.13	9
10	LEO	LIB	LIB	03.27	CAP	AQU	PIS	TAU	11.39	LEO	07.58	SCO	10
11	07.41	LIB	10.40	SAG	CAP	06.43	01.10	TAU	CAN	22.56	LIB	SCO	11
12	VIR	00.58	SCO	13.56	10.34	PIS	ARI	00.15	13.54	VIR	11.23	00.34	12
13	10.21	SCO	18.20	CAP	AQU	17.52	10.21	GEM	LEO	VIR	SCO	SAG	13
14	LIB	10.01	SAG	CAP	23.33	ARI	TAU	03.49	14.12	00.11	16.39	09.04	14
15	16.54	SAG	SAG	02.34	PIS	ARI	15.54	CAN	VIR	LIB	SAG	CAP	15
16	SCO	22.16	05.41	AQU	PIS	01.46	GEM	04.26	14.17	02.23	SAG	19.48	16
17	SCO	CAP	CAP	14.44	09.19	TAU	17.56	LEO	LIB	SCO	00.42	AQU	17
18	03.12	CAP	18.38	PIS	ARI	05.59	CAN	03.42	16.14	07.14	CAP	AQU	18
19	SAG	11.21	AQU	PIS	16.10	GEM	17.43	VIR	SCO	SAG	11.39	08.12	19
20	15.47	AQU	AQU	00.20	TAU	07.21	LEO	03.45	21.46	15.44	AQU	PIS	20
21	CAP	23.15	06.33	ARI	19.54	CAN	17.10	LIB	SAG	CAP	AQU	20.35	21
22	CAP	PIS	PIS	06.53	GEM	07.30	VIR	06.37	SAG	CAP	00.11	ARI	22
23	04.50	PIS	16.02	TAU	21.46	LEO	18.19	SCO	07.22	03.20	PIS	ARI	23
24	AQU	09.12	ARI	11.11	CAN	08.11	LIB	13.34	CAP	AQU	11.59	06.44	24
25	17.00	ARI	23.09	GEM	23.12	VIR	22.45	SAG	19.38	15.57	ARI	TAU	25
26	PIS	17.11	TAU	14.17	LEO	10.57	SCO	SAG	AQU	PIS	21.05	13.15	26
27	PIS	TAU	TAU	CAN	LEO	LIB	SCO	00.15	AQU	PIS	TAU	GEM	27
28	03.32	23.10	04.33	17.03	01.25	16.40	07.00	CAP	08.14	03.13	TAU	16.15	28
29	ARI		GEM	LEO	VIR	SCO	SAG	12.52	PIS	ARI	02.58	CAN	29
30	11.41		08.40	20.00	05.16	SCO	18.11	AQU	19.25	12.00	GEM	17.05	30
31	TAU		CAN		LIB		CAP	AQU		TAU		LEO	31

93

SUN

mth	dy	time → sign
JAN	1	00.00 → CAP
JAN	20	16.32 → AQU
FEB	19	06.51 → PIS
MAR	21	05.54 → ARI
APR	20	17.07 → TAU
MAY	21	16.27 → GEM
JUN	22	00.26 → CAN
JUL	23	11.27 → LEO
AUG	23	18.24 → VIR
SEP	23	15.50 → LIB
OCT	24	01.06 → SCO
NOV	22	22.37 → SAG
DEC	22	11.42 → CAP

MERCURY

mth	dy	time → sign
JAN	1	00.00 → CAP
JAN	8	21.54 → AQU
MAR	16	11.50 → PIS
APR	4	12.22 → ARI
APR	19	17.20 → TAU
MAY	4	11.55 → GEM
JUL	12	08.52 → CAN
JUL	28	08.05 → LEO
AUG	12	06.14 → VIR
AUG	30	17.20 → LIB
NOV	6	08.54 → SCO
NOV	25	01.44 → SAG
DEC	14	04.11 → CAP

VENUS

mth	dy	time → sign
JAN	1	00.00 → CAP
JAN	6	06.41 → AQU
JAN	30	06.05 → PIS
FEB	23	09.51 → ARI
MAR	19	21.42 → TAU
APR	13	22.23 → GEM
MAY	9	20.12 → CAN
JUN	6	10.57 → LEO
JUL	9	11.06 → VIR
SEP	2	15.36 → LEO
OCT	4	05.19 → VIR
NOV	9	13.54 → LIB
DEC	7	00.26 → SCO

MARS

mth	dy	time → sign
JAN	1	00.00 → SAG
JAN	21	18.32 → CAP
MAR	3	05.44 → AQU
APR	11	19.25 → PIS
MAY	21	08.14 → ARI
JUL	1	03.45 → TAU
AUG	14	20.36 → GEM
OCT	17	08.32 → CAN
NOV	25	18.21 → GEM

SATURN

mth	dy	time → sign
JAN	1	00.00 → CAN
SEP	17	04.44 → LEO

JUPITER

mth	dy	time → sign
JAN	1	00.00 → PIS
MAR	18	16.22 → ARI

MOON

dy	jan	feb	mar	apr	may	jun	jul	aug	sep	oct	nov	dec	dy
1	17.32	LIB	14.33	SAG	CAP	01.32	ARI	TAU	CAN	LEO	LIB	SCO	1
2	VIR	05.53	SCO	11.08	05.34	PIS	ARI	04.02	23.08	10.03	20.07	07.33	2
3	19.21	SCO	19.05	CAP	AQU	14.01	09.54	GEM	LEO	VIR	SCO	SAG	3
4	LIB	12.10	SAG	21.45	17.34	ARI	TAU	10.17	23.29	09.39	21.10	10.58	4
5	23.39	SAG	SAG	AQU	PIS	ARI	18.58	CAN	VIR	LIB	SAG	CAP	5
6	SCO	21.42	03.39	AQU	PIS	01.19	GEM	12.44	22.38	09.09	SAG	17.12	6
7	SCO	CAP	CAP	10.17	06.03	TAU	GEM	LEO	LIB	SCO	00.45	AQU	7
8	06.39	CAP	15.09	PIS	ARI	09.49	00.23	12.53	22.46	10.35	CAP	AQU	8
9	SAG	09.16	AQU	22.44	17.03	GEM	CAN	VIR	SCO	SAG	07.59	02.52	9
10	15.58	AQU	AQU	ARI	TAU	15.21	02.50	12.51	SCO	15.29	AQU	PIS	10
11	CAP	21.45	03.49	ARI	TAU	CAN	LEO	LIB	01.41	CAP	18.42	15.06	11
12	CAP	PIS	PIS	09.53	01.44	18.45	03.55	14.30	SAG	CAP	PIS	ARI	12
13	03.03	PIS	16.18	TAU	GEM	LEO	VIR	SCO	08.11	00.10	PIS	ARI	13
14	AQU	10.22	ARI	19.14	08.08	21.11	05.21	18.59	CAP	AQU	07.17	03.39	14
15	15.23	ARI	ARI	GEM	CAN	VIR	LIB	SAG	17.51	11.40	ARI	TAU	15
16	PIS	22.09	03.52	GEM	12.38	23.41	08.23	SAG	AQU	PIS	19.38	14.12	16
17	PIS	TAU	TAU	02.27	LEO	LIB	SCO	02.25	AQU	PIS	TAU	GEM	17
18	04.03	TAU	13.43	CAN	15.45	LIB	13.32	CAP	05.32	00.20	TAU	21.49	18
19	ARI	07.35	GEM	07.14	VIR	02.59	SAG	12.09	PIS	ARI	06.14	CAN	19
20	15.21	GEM	20.48	LEO	18.05	SCO	20.46	AQU	18.07	12.43	GEM	CAN	20
21	TAU	13.18	CAN	09.42	LIB	07.34	CAP	23.32	ARI	TAU	14.36	02.54	21
22	23.23	CAN	CAN	VIR	20.25	SAG	CAP	PIS	ARI	23.51	CAN	LEO	22
23	GEM	15.13	00.31	10.41	SCO	13.56	05.56	PIS	06.43	GEM	20.48	06.28	23
24	GEM	LEO	LEO	LIB	23.51	CAP	AQU	12.02	TAU	GEM	LEO	VIR	24
25	03.20	14.37	01.21	11.39	SAG	22.33	16.58	ARI	18.13	08.57	LEO	09.27	25
26	CAN	VIR	VIR	SCO	SAG	AQU	PIS	ARI	GEM	CAN	01.04	LIB	26
27	04.00	13.38	00.51	14.20	05.31	AQU	PIS	00.45	GEM	15.20	VIR	12.28	27
28	LEO	LIB	LIB	SAG	CAP	09.33	05.27	TAU	03.07	LEO	03.48	SCO	28
29	03.14		01.08	20.08	14.09	PIS	ARI	11.53	CAN	18.47	LIB	15.53	29
30	VIR		SCO	CAP	AQU	22.02	17.53	GEM	08.20	VIR	05.36	SAG	30
31	03.13		04.09		AQU		TAU	19.35		19.55		20.16	31

SUN

mth	dy	time → sign
JAN	1	00.00 → CAP
JAN	20	22.22 → AQU
FEB	19	12.40 → PIS
MAR	20	11.51 → ARI
APR	19	23.03 → TAU
MAY	20	22.25 → GEM
JUN	21	06.28 → CAN
JUL	22	17.13 → LEO
AUG	23	00.18 → VIR
SEP	22	21.48 → LIB
OCT	23	06.53 → SCO
NOV	22	04.22 → SAG
DEC	21	17.32 → CAP

MERCURY

mth	dy	time → sign
JAN	1	00.00 → CAP
JAN	2	20.21 → AQU
JAN	25	01.36 → CAP
FEB	15	19.03 → AQU
MAR	9	12.04 → PIS
MAR	26	15.36 → ARI
APR	10	09.34 → TAU
APR	29	23.11 → GEM
MAY	19	19.25 → TAU
JUN	13	19.20 → GEM
JUL	4	14.13 → CAN
JUL	18	19.35 → LEO
AUG	3	16.43 → VIR
AUG	25	20.52 → LIB
SEP	21	07.15 → VIR
OCT	10	14.48 → LIB
OCT	29	04.55 → SCO
NOV	16	19.02 → SAG
DEC	6	09.25 → CAP

VENUS

mth	dy	time → sign
JAN	1	12.14 → SAG
JAN	26	06.13 → CAP
FEB	19	16.52 → AQU
MAR	15	00.59 → PIS
APR	8	08.52 → ARI
MAY	2	17.49 → TAU
MAY	27	03.47 → GEM
JUN	20	13.56 → CAN
JUL	14	23.34 → LEO
AUG	8	08.36 → VIR
SEP	1	17.44 → LIB
SEP	26	04.17 → SCO
OCT	20	17.24 → SAG
NOV	14	10.40 → CAP
DEC	9	12.50 → AQU

MARS

mth	dy	time → sign
JAN	1	00.00 → GEM
MAR	18	13.20 → CAN
MAY	16	11.33 → LEO
JUL	6	23.22 → VIR
AUG	24	05.43 → LIB
OCT	8	20.10 → SCO
NOV	20	23.50 → SAG

SATURN

mth	dy	time → sign
JAN	1	00.00 → LEO
JAN	14	13.30 → CAN
JUN	5	05.28 → LEO

JUPITER

mth	dy	time → sign
JAN	1	00.00 → ARI
MAR	26	10.33 → TAU
AUG	23	10.37 → GEM
OCT	16	20.34 → TAU

MOON

dy	jan	feb	mar	apr	may	jun	jul	aug	sep	oct	nov	dec	dy
1	CAP	19.47	PIS	09.34	04.05	CAN	15.46	LIB	SAG	CAP	PIS	ARI	1
2	CAP	PIS	14.22	TAU	GEM	04.37	VIR	03.55	16.29	03.49	PIS	23.41	2
3	02.33	PIS	ARI	22.15	14.53	LEO	19.34	SCO	CAP	AQU	04.46	TAU	3
4	AQU	07.17	ARI	GEM	CAN	10.21	LIB	07.03	22.20	12.10	ARI	TAU	4
5	11.35	ARI	03.18	GEM	23.09	VIR	22.33	SAG	AQU	PIS	17.23	12.38	5
6	PIS	20.13	TAU	09.06	LEO	14.00	SCO	10.54	AQU	22.50	TAU	GEM	6
7	23.21	TAU	15.56	CAN	LEO	LIB	SCO	CAP	06.11	ARI	TAU	GEM	7
8	ARI	TAU	GEM	16.36	04.21	15.58	SCO	15.57	PIS	ARI	06.21	00.21	8
9	ARI	08.16	GEM	LEO	VIR	SCO	SAG	AQU	16.18	11.11	GEM	CAN	9
10	12.10	GEM	01.59	20.16	06.39	17.06	03.49	23.00	ARI	TAU	18.28	10.12	10
11	TAU	16.59	CAN	VIR	LIB	SAG	CAP	PIS	ARI	TAU	CAN	LEO	11
12	23.19	CAN	07.55	20.54	07.03	18.45	07.53	PIS	04.30	00.14	CAN	17.55	12
13	GEM	21.32	LEO	LIB	SCO	CAP	AQU	08.49	TAU	GEM	04.36	VIR	13
14	GEM	LEO	09.59	20.14	07.04	22.31	14.36	ARI	17.32	12.24	LEO	23.13	14
15	07.00	22.59	VIR	SCO	SAG	AQU	PIS	21.05	GEM	CAN	11.46	LIB	15
16	CAN	VIR	09.44	20.15	08.31	AQU	PIS	TAU	GEM	21.49	VIR	LIB	16
17	11.15	23.14	LIB	SAG	CAP	05.43	00.40	TAU	05.07	LEO	15.34	02.01	17
18	LEO	LIB	09.18	22.43	13.02	PIS	ARI	09.54	CAN	LEO	LIB	SCO	18
19	13.25	LIB	SCO	CAP	AQU	16.32	13.11	GEM	13.10	03.25	16.31	02.54	19
20	VIR	00.14	10.34	CAP	21.27	ARI	TAU	20.34	LEO	VIR	SCO	SAG	20
21	15.10	SCO	SAG	04.47	PIS	ARI	TAU	17.16	05.26	VIR	16.03	03.12	21
22	LIB	03.18	14.48	AQU	PIS	05.21	01.40	CAN	VIR	LIB	SAG	CAP	22
23	17.48	SAG	CAP	14.28	09.07	TAU	GEM	03.30	18.28	05.17	16.03	04.48	23
24	SCO	08.54	22.19	PIS	ARI	17.37	11.39	LEO	LIB	SCO	CAP	AQU	24
25	21.51	CAP	AQU	PIS	22.07	GEM	CAN	07.03	18.34	04.49	18.30	09.36	25
26	SAG	16.48	AQU	02.37	TAU	GEM	18.19	VIR	SCO	SAG	AQU	PIS	26
27	SAG	AQU	08.34	ARI	TAU	03.29	LEO	08.42	19.21	05.55	AQU	18.32	27
28	03.24	AQU	PIS	15.37	10.22	CAN	22.23	LIB	SAG	CAP	00.47	ARI	28
29	CAP	02.42	20.37	TAU	GEM	10.39	VIR	10.05	22.13	10.05	PIS	ARI	29
30	10.34		ARI	TAU	20.39	LEO	VIR	SCO	CAP	AQU	11.01	06.43	30
31	AQU		ARI		CAN		01.13	12.28		17.53		TAU	31

SUN

mth	dy	time → sign
JAN	1	00.00 → CAP
JAN	20	04.11 → AQU
FEB	18	18.30 → PIS
MAR	20	17.41 → ARI
APR	20	04.57 → TAU
MAY	21	04.18 → GEM
JUN	21	12.17 → CAN
JUL	22	23.04 → LEO
AUG	23	06.03 → VIR
SEP	23	03.25 → LIB
OCT	23	12.44 → SCO
NOV	22	10.04 → SAG
DEC	21	23.27 → CAP

MERCURY

mth	dy	time → sign
JAN	1	00.00 → CAP
FEB	10	23.53 → AQU
MAR	2	08.12 → PIS
MAR	18	11.53 → ARI
APR	3	02.46 → TAU
JUN	10	21.06 → GEM
JUN	26	07.03 → CAN
JUL	10	12.00 → LEO
JUL	28	10.18 → VIR
OCT	4	09.19 → LIB
OCT	21	16.22 → SCO
NOV	9	17.20 → SAG
DEC	1	06.42 → CAP
DEC	21	07.18 → SAG

VENUS

mth	dy	time → sign
JAN	1	00.00 → AQU
JAN	4	13.08 → PIS
FEB	2	05.48 → ARI
JUN	6	06.12 → TAU
JUL	6	15.09 → GEM
AUG	2	19.16 → CAN
AUG	28	15.10 → LEO
SEP	22	15.07 → VIR
OCT	17	01.36 → LIB
NOV	10	03.55 → SCO
DEC	4	01.44 → SAG
DEC	27	22.12 → CAP

MARS

mth	dy	time → sign
JAN	1	00.41 → CAP
FEB	9	11.44 → AQU
MAR	20	02.09 → PIS
APR	27	15.35 → ARI
JUN	6	03.16 → TAU
JUL	17	15.13 → GEM
SEP	1	00.22 → CAN
OCT	26	18.47 → LEO

SATURN

mth	dy	time → sign
JAN	1	00.00 → LEO
NOV	17	02.28 → VIR

JUPITER

mth	dy	time → sign
JAN	1	00.00 → TAU
APR	3	15.24 → GEM
AUG	20	12.30 → CAN
DEC	30	23.32 → GEM

MOON

dy	jan	feb	mar	apr	may	jun	jul	aug	sep	oct	nov	dec	dy
1	19.43	CAN	CAN	01.25	LIB	02.54	CAP	01.23	ARI	20.33	CAN	LEO	1
2	GEM	CAN	09.25	VIR	16.23	SAG	12.56	PIS	00.52	GEM	CAN	23.05	2
3	GEM	00.11	LEO	04.39	SCO	02.07	AQU	06.54	TAU	09.09	LEO	05.03	VIR	3
4	07.12	LEO	15.19	LIB	15.59	CAP	15.31	ARI	12.27	CAN	LEO	VIR	4
5	CAN	06.17	VIR	05.40	SAG	02.44	PIS	16.18	GEM	CAN	15.16	07.17	5
6	16.20	VIR	18.34	SCO	15.54	AQU	22.03	TAU	GEM	20.58	VIR	LIB	6
7	LEO	10.36	LIB	06.09	CAP	06.35	ARI	TAU	01.03	LEO	21.51	11.33	7
8	23.23	LIB	20.37	SAG	18.00	PIS	ARI	04.29	CAN	LEO	LIB	SCO	8
9	VIR	14.04	SCO	07.40	AQU	14.34	08.33	GEM	12.14	05.58	LIB	12.22	9
10	VIR	SCO	22.42	CAP	23.29	ARI	TAU	17.04	LEO	VIR	00.42	SAG	10
11	04.48	17.11	SAG	11.24	PIS	ARI	21.15	CAN	20.34	11.29	SCO	11.26	11
12	LIB	SAG	SAG	AQU	PIS	01.56	GEM	CAN	VIR	LIB	01.03	CAP	12
13	08.44	20.14	01.40	17.49	08.29	TAU	GEM	03.57	VIR	14.11	SAG	10.59	13
14	SCO	CAP	CAP	PIS	ARI	14.50	09.50	LEO	02.07	SCO	00.50	AQU	14
15	11.18	23.45	06.00	PIS	20.04	GEM	CAN	12.26	LIB	15.27	CAP	13.09	15
16	SAG	AQU	AQU	02.52	TAU	GEM	20.51	VIR	05.45	SAG	02.00	PIS	16
17	13.02	AQU	12.06	ARI	TAU	03.28	LEO	18.49	SCO	16.51	AQU	19.11	17
18	CAP	04.45	PIS	14.02	08.50	CAN	LEO	LIB	08.28	CAP	05.58	ARI	18
19	15.12	PIS	20.23	TAU	GEM	14.53	05.58	23.35	SAG	19.36	PIS	ARI	19
20	AQU	12.22	ARI	TAU	21.35	LEO	VIR	SCO	11.04	AQU	13.13	04.54	20
21	19.30	ARI	ARI	02.37	CAN	LEO	13.09	SCO	CAP	AQU	ARI	TAU	21
22	PIS	23.06	07.05	GEM	CAN	00.29	LIB	03.03	14.12	00.26	23.09	16.51	22
23	PIS	TAU	TAU	15.25	09.13	VIR	18.13	SAG	AQU	PIS	TAU	GEM	23
24	03.19	TAU	19.39	CAN	LEO	07.35	SCO	05.30	18.30	07.34	TAU	GEM	24
25	ARI	11.50	GEM	CAN	18.31	LIB	21.04	CAP	PIS	ARI	10.48	05.30	25
26	14.41	GEM	GEM	02.43	VIR	11.42	SAG	07.41	PIS	16.53	GEM	CAN	26
27	TAU	GEM	08.16	LEO	VIR	SCO	22.15	AQU	00.40	TAU	23.20	17.52	27
28	TAU	00.02	CAN	10.52	00.28	13.02	CAP	10.46	ARI	TAU	CAN	LEO	28
29	03.37		18.40	VIR	LIB	SAG	23.04	PIS	09.21	04.08	CAN	LEO	29
30	GEM		LEO	15.13	02.56	12.48	AQU	16.11	TAU	GEM	11.53	05.13	30
31	15.20		LEO		SCO		AQU	ARI		16.40		VIR	31

SUN

mth	dy	time → sign
JAN	1	00.00 → CAP
JAN	20	10.08 → AQU
FEB	19	00.26 → PIS
MAR	20	23.36 → ARI
APR	20	10.53 → TAU
MAY	21	10.04 → GEM
JUN	21	18.05 → CAN
JUL	23	05.05 → LEO
AUG	23	11.53 → VIR
SEP	23	09.23 → LIB
OCT	23	18.37 → SCO
NOV	22	16.02 → SAG
DEC	22	05.22 → CAP

MERCURY

mth	dy	time → sign
JAN	1	00.00 → SAG
JAN	13	20.10 → CAP
FEB	4	15.55 → AQU
FEB	22	16.14 → PIS
MAR	10	12.10 → ARI
MAY	16	08.23 → TAU
JUN	3	15.26 → GEM
JUN	17	15.47 → CAN
JUL	2	22.28 → LEO
JUL	27	06.07 → VIR
AUG	13	07.04 → LEO
SEP	9	19.23 → VIR
SEP	26	16.44 → LIB
OCT	14	05.30 → SCO
NOV	3	07.48 → SAG

VENUS

mth	dy	time → sign
JAN	1	00.00 → CAP
JAN	20	18.33 → AQU
FEB	13	16.03 → PIS
MAR	9	16.26 → ARI
APR	2	21.10 → TAU
APR	27	07.54 → GEM
MAY	22	02.03 → CAN
JUN	16	06.16 → LEO
JUL	12	02.16 → VIR
AUG	8	03.08 → LIB
SEP	7	05.04 → SCO

MARS

mth	dy	time → sign
JAN	1	00.00 → LEO
JAN	26	02.17 → CAN
APR	10	18.40 → LEO
JUN	14	02.26 → VIR
AUG	4	09.13 → LIB
SEP	19	20.55 → SCO
NOV	2	01.23 → SAG
DEC	12	17.33 → CAP

SATURN

mth	dy	time → sign
JAN	1	00.00 → VIR
JAN	5	00.58 → LEO
JUL	26	11.46 → VIR

JUPITER

mth	dy	time → sign
JAN	1	00.00 → GEM
APR	12	00.27 → CAN
SEP	5	08.16 → LEO

MOON

dy	jan	feb	mar	apr	may	jun	jul	aug	sep	oct	nov	dec	dy
1	14.31	SCO	13.02	CAP	09.00	ARI	19.37	CAN	20.46	14.17	SCO	20.44	1
2	LIB	07.13	SAG	00.05	PIS	03.50	GEM	CAN	VIR	LIB	10.03	CAP	2
3	20.35	SAG	15.58	AQU	14.27	TAU	GEM	02.10	VIR	21.48	SAG	21.35	3
4	SCO	08.50	CAP	03.20	ARI	13.53	07.33	LEO	07.15	SCO	12.40	AQU	4
5	22.03	CAP	17.50	PIS	21.52	GEM	CAN	14.29	GEM	SCO	CAP	23.36	5
6	SAG	09.04	AQU	07.51	TAU	GEM	20.13	VIR	15.38	03.06	15.04	PIS	6
7	22.55	AQU	19.45	ARI	TAU	01.30	LEO	VIR	SCO	SAG	AQU	PIS	7
8	CAP	09.47	PIS	14.21	07.18	CAN	LEO	01.30	21.39	06.52	18.06	03.39	8
9	22.05	PIS	23.08	TAU	GEM	14.07	08.44	LIB	SAG	CAP	PIS	ARI	9
10	AQU	12.56	ARI	23.27	18.41	LEO	VIR	10.11	SAG	09.42	22.11	09.50	10
11	22.50	ARI	ARI	GEM	CAN	LEO	19.48	SCO	01.20	AQU	ARI	TAU	11
12	PIS	19.50	05.18	GEM	CAN	02.35	LIB	15.43	CAP	12.12	ARI	17.54	12
13	PIS	TAU	TAU	10.59	07.17	VIR	LIB	SAG	03.08	PIS	03.35	GEM	13
14	03.05	TAU	14.48	CAN	LEO	12.55	03.47	18.03	AQU	15.06	TAU	GEM	14
15	ARI	06.24	GEM	23.30	19.15	LIB	SCO	CAP	04.09	ARI	10.45	03.50	15
16	11.30	GEM	GEM	LEO	VIR	19.28	07.50	18.15	PIS	19.22	GEM	CAN	16
17	TAU	18.56	02.49	LEO	VIR	SCO	SAG	AQU	05.50	TAU	20.16	15.37	17
18	23.06	CAN	CAN	10.44	04.24	22.01	08.33	18.04	ARI	TAU	CAN	LEO	18
19	GEM	CAN	15.12	VIR	LIB	SAG	CAP	PIS	09.43	02.05	CAN	LEO	19
20	GEM	07.09	LEO	18.53	09.39	21.52	07.41	19.29	TAU	GEM	08.09	04.34	20
21	11.50	LEO	LEO	LIB	SCO	CAP	AQU	ARI	16.56	11.52	LEO	VIR	21
22	CAN	17.39	01.49	23.39	11.31	21.07	07.26	ARI	GEM	CAN	20.57	16.40	22
23	CAN	VIR	VIR	SCO	SAG	AQU	PIS	00.06	GEM	CAN	VIR	LIB	23
24	00.02	VIR	09.41	SCO	11.41	21.57	09.46	TAU	CAN	00.04	VIR	LIB	24
25	LEO	02.03	LIB	02.00	CAP	PIS	ARI	08.31	CAN	LEO	08.07	01.32	25
26	10.56	LIB	15.01	SAG	12.10	PIS	15.50	GEM	16.01	12.32	LIB	SCO	26
27	VIR	08.28	SCO	03.27	AQU	01.53	TAU	19.59	LEO	VIR	15.38	06.07	27
28	20.08	SCO	18.37	CAP	14.37	ARI	TAU	CAN	LEO	22.51	SCO	SAG	28
29	LIB		SAG	05.28	PIS	09.21	01.31	CAN	04.11	LIB	19.23	07.15	29
30	LIB		21.23	AQU	19.52	TAU	GEM	08.40	VIR	LIB	SAG	CAP	30
31	03.03		CAP		ARI		13.28	LEO		05.52		06.53	31

SUN

mth	dy	time → sign
JAN	1	00.00 → CAP
JAN	20	16.04 → AQU
FEB	19	06.12 → PIS
MAR	21	05.22 → ARI
APR	20	16.38 → TAU
MAY	21	15.54 → GEM
JUN	21	23.58 → CAN
JUL	23	10.48 → LEO
AUG	23	17.42 → VIR
SEP	23	15.17 → LIB
OCT	24	00.25 → SCO
NOV	22	21.53 → SAG
DEC	22	11.15 → CAP

MERCURY

mth	dy	time → sign
JAN	1	00.00 → SAG
JAN	8	22.36 → CAP
JAN	28	12.52 → AQU
FEB	14	20.38 → PIS
MAR	3	21.35 → ARI
MAR	28	10.40 → PIS
APR	17	12.47 → ARI
MAY	10	22.03 → TAU
MAY	26	07.48 → GEM
JUN	9	06.32 → CAN
JUN	27	09.54 → LEO
SEP	2	21.39 → VIR
SEP	18	18.54 → LIB
OCT	7	03.55 → SCO
OCT	30	07.02 → SAG
NOV	18	03.08 → SCO
DEC	12	13.34 → SAG

VENUS

mth	dy	time → sign
JAN	1	00.00 → SCO
JAN	7	06.33 → SAG
FEB	5	09.16 → CAP
MAR	3	17.15 → AQU
MAR	29	03.17 → PIS
APR	23	04.05 → ARI
MAY	18	00.29 → TAU
JUN	11	18.15 → GEM
JUL	6	09.07 → CAN
JUL	30	20.05 → LEO
AUG	24	03.14 → VIR
SEP	17	07.21 → LIB
OCT	11	09.44 → SCO
NOV	4	11.50 → SAG
NOV	28	14.22 → CAP
DEC	22	18.25 → AQU

MARS

mth	dy	time → sign
JAN	1	00.00 → CAP
JAN	20	17.12 → AQU
FEB	27	20.22 → PIS
APR	7	01.08 → ARI
MAY	16	04.31 → TAU
JUN	26	01.51 → GEM
AUG	8	13.25 → CAN
SEP	24	21.28 → LEO
NOV	19	21.33 → VIR

SATURN

mth	dy	time → sign
JAN	1	00.00 → VIR

JUPITER

mth	dy	time → sign
JAN	1	00.00 → LEO
FEB	28	23.22 → CAN
APR	20	08.30 → LEO
SEP	29	10.13 → VIR

MOON

dy	jan	feb	mar	apr	may	jun	jul	aug	sep	oct	nov	dec	dy
1	AQU	ARI	ARI	GEM	CAN	22.41	19.08	SCO	11.33	AQU	10.09	TAU	1
2	07.08	22.03	07.09	GEM	CAN	VIR	LIB	22.05	CAP	AQU	ARI	23.02	2
3	PIS	TAU	TAU	06.24	01.56	VIR	LIB	SAG	13.59	00.23	11.16	GEM	3
4	09.41	TAU	12.58	CAN	LEO	11.12	05.57	SAG	AQU	PIS	TAU	GEM	4
5	ARI	05.33	GEM	17.58	14.41	LIB	SCO	02.23	14.03	00.28	13.26	04.01	5
6	15.17	GEM	22.34	LEO	VIR	21.05	12.55	CAP	PIS	ARI	GEM	CAN	6
7	TAU	16.06	CAN	LEO	VIR	SCO	SAG	03.28	13.29	00.45	18.24	12.09	7
8	23.42	CAN	CAN	06.52	02.47	SCO	16.07	AQU	ARI	TAU	CAN	LEO	8
9	GEM	CAN	10.47	VIR	LIB	03.14	CAP	03.05	14.12	03.07	CAN	23.33	9
10	GEM	04.25	LEO	18.45	12.10	SAG	16.59	PIS	TAU	GEM	03.14	VIR	10
11	10.14	LEO	23.42	LIB	SCO	06.23	AQU	03.10	17.54	09.09	LEO	VIR	11
12	CAN	17.18	VIR	LIB	18.25	CAP	17.23	ARI	GEM	CAN	15.20	12.29	12
13	22.16	VIR	VIR	04.16	SAG	08.06	PIS	05.21	GEM	19.12	VIR	LIB	13
14	LEO	VIR	11.41	SCO	22.25	AQU	18.57	TAU	01.27	LEO	VIR	LIB	14
15	LEO	05.37	LIB	11.18	CAP	09.56	ARI	10.41	CAN	LEO	04.16	00.08	15
16	11.10	LIB	21.49	SAG	CAP	PIS	22.43	GEM	12.25	07.51	LIB	SCO	16
17	VIR	16.12	SCO	16.23	01.26	12.52	TAU	19.17	LEO	VIR	15.29	08.36	17
18	23.40	SCO	SCO	CAP	AQU	ARI	TAU	CAN	LEO	20.44	SCO	SAG	18
19	LIB	23.51	05.38	22.02	04.18	17.18	04.59	CAN	01.15	LIB	23.56	13.54	19
20	LIB	SAG	SAG	AQU	PIS	TAU	GEM	06.28	VIR	LIB	SAG	CAP	20
21	09.51	SAG	10.56	22.41	07.30	23.23	13.40	LEO	14.11	08.02	SAG	17.13	21
22	SCO	04.00	CAP	PIS	ARI	GEM	CAN	19.11	LIB	SCO	06.01	AQU	22
23	16.08	CAP	13.52	PIS	11.20	GEM	CAN	VIR	LIB	17.09	CAP	19.50	23
24	SAG	05.12	AQU	00.51	TAU	07.24	00.30	VIR	01.54	SAG	10.37	PIS	24
25	18.27	AQU	15.04	ARI	16.28	CAN	LEO	08.13	SCO	SAG	AQU	22.40	25
26	CAP	04.52	PIS	03.27	GEM	17.47	13.01	LIB	11.36	00.11	14.17	ARI	26
27	18.12	PIS	15.47	TAU	23.51	LEO	VIR	20.12	SAG	CAP	PIS	ARI	27
28	AQU	04.54	ARI	07.49	CAN	LEO	VIR	SCO	18.40	05.16	17.17	02.08	28
29	17.25		17.36	GEM	CAN	06.14	02.06	SCO	CAP	AQU	ARI	TAU	29
30	PIS		TAU	15.11	10.08	VIR	LIB	05.39	22.49	08.29	19.54	06.32	30
31	18.11		22.08		LEO		13.46	SAG		PIS		GEM	31

SUN

mth	dy	time → sign
JAN	1	00.00 → CAP
JAN	20	21.44 → AQU
FEB	19	12.06 → PIS
MAR	20	11.13 → ARI
APR	19	22.24 → TAU
MAY	20	21.42 → GEM
JUN	21	05.44 → CAN
JUL	22	16.42 → LEO
AUG	22	23.46 → VIR
SEP	22	21.09 → LIB
OCT	23	06.12 → SCO
NOV	22	03.42 → SAG
DEC	21	16.53 → CAP

MERCURY

mth	dy	time → sign
JAN	1	00.00 → SAG
JAN	2	08.01 → CAP
JAN	21	02.17 → AQU
FEB	7	08.07 → PIS
APR	14	15.55 → ARI
MAY	2	10.58 → TAU
MAY	16	17.07 → GEM
MAY	31	22.09 → CAN
AUG	9	03.30 → LEO
AUG	24	18.44 → VIR
SEP	10	02.02 → LIB
SEP	30	01.16 → SCO
DEC	5	19.42 → SAG
DEC	25	04.47 → CAP

VENUS

mth	dy	time → sign
JAN	1	00.00 → AQU
JAN	16	03.34 → PIS
FEB	9	23.40 → ARI
MAR	6	18.54 → TAU
APR	3	19.43 → GEM
MAY	12	20.52 → CAN
JUN	5	05.42 → GEM
AUG	6	14.22 → CAN
SEP	7	17.59 → LEO
OCT	4	23.05 → VIR
OCT	30	10.33 → LIB
NOV	24	01.38 → SCO
DEC	18	06.23 → SAG

MARS

mth	dy	time → sign
JAN	1	00.00 → VIR
MAR	11	20.34 → LEO
MAY	4	02.20 → VIR
JUL	10	17.48 → LIB
AUG	29	05.40 → SCO
OCT	12	06.22 → SAG
NOV	22	01.32 → CAP
DEC	30	22.46 → AQU

SATURN

mth	dy	time → sign
JAN	1	00.00 → VIR
SEP	21	10.37 → LIB

JUPITER

mth	dy	time → sign
JAN	1	00.00 → VIR
OCT	27	10.30 → LIB

MOON

dy	jan	feb	mar	apr	may	jun	jul	aug	sep	oct	nov	dec	dy
1	12.29	LEO	VIR	LIB	22.22	CAP	AQU	ARI	01.50	CAN	12.18	07.13	1
2	CAN	15.21	VIR	05.21	SAG	19.29	05.48	16.55	GEM	19.57	VIR	LIB	2
3	20.47	VIR	10.40	SCO	SAG	AQU	PIS	TAU	06.39	LEO	VIR	20.00	3
4	LEO	VIR	LIB	16.35	07.14	AQU	08.46	20.10	CAN	LEO	00.31	SCO	4
5	LEO	04.04	23.22	SAG	CAP	00.10	ARI	GEM	14.22	06.19	LIB	SCO	5
6	07.48	LIB	SCO	SAG	14.03	PIS	11.30	GEM	LEO	VIR	13.19	07.57	6
7	VIR	16.46	SCO	01.43	AQU	03.23	TAU	01.12	LEO	18.30	SCO	SAG	7
8	20.38	SCO	10.38	CAP	18.33	ARI	14.33	CAN	00.31	LIB	SCO	18.12	8
9	LIB	SCO	SAG	08.00	PIS	05.29	GEM	08.23	VIR	LIB	01.25	CAP	9
10	LIB	03.19	19.02	AQU	20.44	TAU	18.44	LEO	12.22	07.15	SAG	CAP	10
11	08.55	SAG	CAP	11.07	ARI	07.22	CAN	17.54	LIB	SCO	12.15	02.36	11
12	SCO	10.12	23.45	PIS	21.24	GEM	CAN	VIR	LIB	19.37	CAP	AQU	12
13	18.17	CAP	AQU	11.40	TAU	10.29	01.03	VIR	01.06	SAG	21.10	09.03	13
14	SAG	13.19	AQU	ARI	22.07	CAN	LEO	05.32	SCO	SAG	AQU	PIS	14
15	23.51	AQU	01.10	11.11	GEM	16.22	10.11	LIB	13.28	06.37	AQU	13.21	15
16	CAP	13.54	PIS	TAU	GEM	LEO	VIR	18.15	SAG	CAP	03.21	ARI	16
17	CAP	PIS	00.41	11.41	00.52	LEO	21.55	SCO	23.45	14.53	PIS	15.36	17
18	02.25	13.43	ARI	GEM	CAN	01.47	LIB	SCO	CAP	AQU	06.21	TAU	18
19	AQU	ARI	00.13	15.11	07.14	VIR	LIB	06.07	CAP	19.31	ARI	16.39	19
20	03.33	14.35	TAU	CAN	LEO	13.55	10.33	SAG	06.30	PIS	06.51	GEM	20
21	PIS	TAU	01.47	22.52	17.32	LIB	SCO	15.11	AQU	20.43	TAU	18.03	21
22	04.52	17.58	GEM	LEO	VIR	LIB	21.42	CAP	09.27	ARI	06.27	CAN	22
23	ARI	GEM	06.55	LEO	VIR	02.26	SAG	20.32	PIS	19.55	GEM	21.34	23
24	07.31	GEM	CAN	10.12	06.11	SCO	SAG	AQU	09.37	TAU	07.18	LEO	24
25	TAU	00.34	15.58	VIR	LIB	13.02	05.45	22.43	ARI	19.17	CAN	LEO	25
26	12.11	CAN	LEO	23.09	18.37	SAG	CAP	PIS	08.53	GEM	11.23	04.32	26
27	GEM	10.10	LEO	LIB	SCO	20.46	10.34	23.11	TAU	21.00	LEO	VIR	27
28	19.02	LEO	03.52	LIB	SCO	CAP	AQU	ARI	09.21	CAN	19.37	15.05	28
29	CAN	21.53	VIR	11.35	05.05	CAP	13.11	23.41	GEM	CAN	VIR	LIB	29
30	CAN		16.49	SCO	SAG	02.04	PIS	TAU	12.46	02.38	VIR	LIB	30
31	04.08		LIB		13.14		14.53	TAU		LEO		03.36	31

SUN

mth	dy	time → sign
JAN	1	00.00 → CAP
JAN	20	03.35 → AQU
FEB	18	17.52 → PIS
MAR	20	17.07 → ARI
APR	20	04.15 → TAU
MAY	21	03.39 → GEM
JUN	21	11.42 → CAN
JUL	22	22.40 → LEO
AUG	23	05.34 → VIR
SEP	23	03.05 → LIB
OCT	23	12.16 → SCO
NOV	22	09.33 → SAG
DEC	21	22.52 → CAP

SATURN

mth	dy	time → sign
JAN	1	00.00 → LIB

MERCURY

mth	dy	time → sign
JAN	1	00.00 → CAP
JAN	12	15.46 → AQU
JAN	31	17.34 → PIS
FEB	16	08.03 → AQU
MAR	18	04.33 → PIS
APR	8	09.13 → ARI
APR	24	05.31 → TAU
MAY	8	09.47 → GEM
MAY	28	17.04 → CAN
JUN	22	22.53 → GEM
JUL	12	21.08 → CAN
AUG	1	18.35 → LEO
AUG	16	12.44 → VIR
SEP	2	22.40 → LIB
SEP	27	11.04 → SCO
OCT	14	02.12 → LIB
NOV	9	13.14 → SCO
NOV	28	20.52 → SAG
DEC	17	22.21 → CAP

VENUS

mth	dy	time → sign
JAN	1	00.00 → SAG
JAN	11	06.46 → CAP
FEB	4	06.09 → AQU
FEB	28	06.04 → PIS
MAR	24	07.45 → ARI
APR	17	12.06 → TAU
MAY	11	19.44 → GEM
JUN	5	06.27 → CAN
JUN	29	20.20 → LEO
JUL	24	14.05 → VIR
AUG	18	13.45 → LIB
SEP	12	22.54 → SCO
OCT	9	00.04 → SAG
NOV	5	12.41 → CAP
DEC	8	20.56 → AQU

MARS

mth	dy	time → sign
JAN	1	00.00 → AQU
FEB	6	22.44 → PIS
MAR	17	02.25 → ARI
APR	25	07.17 → TAU
JUN	5	05.25 → GEM
JUL	18	08.43 → CAN
SEP	2	01.50 → LEO
OCT	21	01.47 → VIR
DEC	16	00.22 → LIB

JUPITER

mth	dy	time → sign
JAN	1	00.00 → LIB
NOV	27	02.33 → SCO

MOON

dy	jan	feb	mar	apr	may	jun	jul	aug	sep	oct	nov	dec	dy
1	SCO	10.37	CAP	18.41	06.57	16.48	02.57	18.54	LIB	SCO	12.46	07.09	1
2	15.42	CAP	CAP	PIS	ARI	GEM	CAN	VIR	21.10	16.59	CAP	AQU	2
3	SAG	17.55	03.51	20.25	06.59	16.38	04.47	VIR	SCO	SAG	CAP	17.16	3
4	SAG	AQU	AQU	ARI	TAU	CAN	LEO	02.24	SCO	SAG	00.51	23.49	4
5	01.41	22.21	08.12	20.04	06.01	18.43	09.26	LIB	09.24	05.49	AQU		5
6	CAP	PIS	PIS	TAU	GEM	LEO	VIR	12.58	SAG	CAP	09.52	ARI	6
7	09.12	PIS	09.48	19.47	06.18	LEO	17.42	SCO	21.48	17.01	PIS	ARI	7
8	AQU	01.01	ARI	GEM	CAN	00.25	LIB	SCO	CAP	AQU	14.38	02.31	8
9	14.42	ARI	10.22	21.34	09.40	LIB	LIB	01.22	CAP	AQU	ARI	TAU	9
10	PIS	03.11	TAU	CAN	LEO	09.55	05.02	SAG	07.58	00.32	15.44	02.30	10
11	18.43	TAU	11.42	CAN	16.55	LIB	SCO	13.20	AQU	PIS	TAU	GEM	11
12	ARI	05.51	GEM	02.36	VIR	21.54	17.35	CAP	14.34	04.01	14.59	01.40	12
13	21.45	GEM	15.06	LEO	VIR	SCO	SAG	22.56	PIS	ARI	GEM	CAN	13
14	TAU	09.43	CAN	10.56	03.24	SCO	SAG	AQU	17.55	04.43	14.37	02.08	14
15	TAU	CAN	21.02	VIR	LIB	10.31	05.19	AQU	ARI	TAU	CAN	LEO	15
16	00.17	15.10	LEO	21.38	15.37	SAG	CAP	05.34	19.30	04.41	16.33	05.38	16
17	GEM	LEO	LEO	LIB	SCO	22.21	15.02	PIS	TAU	GEM	LEO	VIR	17
18	03.08	22.34	05.20	LIB	SCO	CAP	AQU	09.49	20.59	05.52	21.53	12.58	18
19	CAN	VIR	VIR	09.39	04.14	CAP	22.26	ARI	GEM	CAN	VIR	LIB	19
20	07.21	VIR	15.31	SCO	SAG	08.36	PIS	12.43	23.39	09.34	VIR	23.39	20
21	LEO	08.12	LIB	22.50	16.20	AQU	PIS	TAU	CAN	LEO	06.33	SCO	21
22	14.02	LIB	LIB	SAG	CAP	16.44	03.43	15.18	CAN	16.05	LIB	SCO	22
23	VIR	19.54	03.14	SAG	CAP	PIS	ARI	GEM	04.08	VIR	17.36	12.11	23
24	23.45	SCO	SCO	10.31	03.00	22.18	07.18	18.17	LEO	VIR	SCO	SAG	24
25	LIB	SCO	15.51	CAP	AQU	ARI	TAU	CAN	10.29	00.56	SCO	SAG	25
26	LIB	08.29	SAG	20.57	11.05	ARI	09.42	22.10	VIR	LIB	06.00	00.59	26
27	11.49	SAG	SAG	AQU	PIS	01.16	GEM	LEO	18.40	11.38	SAG	CAP	27
28	SCO	19.46	03.52	AQU	15.44	TAU	11.41	LEO	LIB	SCO	18.53	12.53	28
29	SCO		CAP	03.56	ARI	02.21	CAN	03.31	LIB	23.48	CAP	AQU	29
30	00.11		13.15	PIS	17.10	GEM	14.20	VIR	04.53	SAG	CAP	23.01	30
31	SAG		AQU		TAU		LEO	11.02		SAG		PIS	31

SUN

mth	dy	time → sign
JAN	1	00.00 → CAP
JAN	20	09.33 → AQU
FEB	18	23.47 → PIS
MAR	20	22.53 → ARI
APR	20	10.08 → TAU
MAY	21	09.25 → GEM
JUN	21	17.23 → CAN
JUL	23	04.16 → LEO
AUG	23	11.15 → VIR
SEP	23	08.44 → LIB
OCT	23	17.58 → SCO
NOV	22	15.20 → SAG
DFC	22	04.36 → CAP

MERCURY

mth	dy	time → sign
JAN	1	00.00 → CAP
JAN	5	16.46 → AQU
MAR	13	19.14 → PIS
MAR	31	20.56 → ARI
APR	15	18.54 → TAU
MAY	1	13.25 → GEM
JUL	9	11.26 → CAN
JUL	24	08.47 → LEO
AUG	8	14.07 → VIR
AUG	28	03.26 → LIB
NOV	3	01.11 → SCO
NOV	21	14.24 → SAG
DEC	10	20.02 → CAP

VENUS

mth	dy	time → sign
JAN	1	00.00 → AQU
JAN	23	02.53 → CAP
MAR	2	11.25 → AQU
APR	6	12.23 → PIS
MAY	4	12.27 → ARI
MAY	30	21.06 → TAU
JUN	25	12.13 → GEM
JUL	20	16.25 → CAN
AUG	14	11.09 → LEO
SEP	7	21.35 → VIR
OCT	2	01.33 → LIB
OCT	26	01.14 → SCO
NOV	18	23.03 → SAG
DEC	12	20.25 → CAP

MARS

mth	dy	time → sign
JAN	1	00.00 → LIB
AUG	3	11.32 → SCO
SEP	20	01.29 → SAG
OCT	31	23.22 → CAP
DEC	10	06.02 → AQU

SATURN

mth	dy	time → sign
JAN	1	00.00 → LIB
NOV	29	10.13 → SCO

JUPITER

mth	dy	time → sign
JAN	1	00.00 → SCO
DEC	26	01.46 → SAG

MOON

dy	jan	feb	mar	apr	may	jun	jul	aug	sep	oct	nov	dec	dy
1	PIS	TAU	TAU	CAN	23.45	LIB	SCO	09.36	AQU	PIS	TAU	GEM	1
2	06.33	20.20	01.50	13.36	VIR	21.12	14.25	CAP	16.11	08.06	TAU	10.58	2
3	ARI	GEM	GEM	LEO	VIR	SCO	SAG	22.17	PIS	ARI	00.23	CAN	3
4	11.02	22.28	04.48	18.18	06.32	SCO	SAG	AQU	PIS	13.09	GEM	11.26	4
5	TAU	CAN	CAN	VIR	LIB	08.31	03.15	AQU	TAU	01.59	LEO	5
6	12.48	23.50	07.50	VIR	15.24	SAG	CAP	09.23	ARI	16.39	CAN	13.32	6
7	GEM	LEO	LEO	00.26	SCO	21.12	16.03	PIS	06.27	GEM	04.10	VIR	7
8	13.01	LEO	11.27	LIB	SCO	CAP	AQU	18.21	TAU	19.39	LEO	18.11	8
9	CAN	02.15	VIR	08.33	02.17	CAP	AQU	ARI	10.57	CAN	07.40	LIB	9
10	13.21	VIR	16.34	SCO	SAG	10.08	03.35	ARI	GEM	22.44	VIR	LIB	10
11	LEO	07.02	LIB	19.07	14.50	AQU	PIS	01.00	14.18	LEO	12.46	01.34	11
12	15.37	LIB	LIB	SAG	CAP	21.44	12.49	TAU	CAN	LEO	LIB	SCO	12
13	VIR	15.16	00.17	SAG	CAP	PIS	ARI	05.22	16.46	02.09	19.42	11.27	13
14	21.17	SCO	SCO	07.41	03.44	PIS	19.00	GEM	LEO	VIR	SCO	SAG	14
15	LIB	SCO	11.03	CAP	AQU	06.20	TAU	07.40	18.57	06.23	SCO	23.15	15
16	LIB	02.45	SAG	20.18	14.46	ARI	22.03	CAN	VIR	LIB	04.52	CAP	16
17	06.46	SAG	23.47	AQU	PIS	11.07	GEM	08.40	22.02	12.21	SAG	CAP	17
18	SCO	15.36	CAP	AQU	22.04	TAU	22.46	LEO	LIB	SCO	16.21	12.12	18
19	19.00	CAP	CAP	06.19	ARI	12.34	CAN	09.40	LIB	21.02	CAP	AQU	19
20	SAG	CAP	11.53	PIS	ARI	GEM	22.35	VIR	03.32	SAG	CAP	AQU	20
21	SAG	03.15	AQU	12.23	01.22	12.13	LEO	12.22	SCO	SAG	05.20	00.56	21
22	07.51	AQU	21.01	ARI	TAU	CAN	23.20	LIB	12.30	08.38	AQU	PIS	22
23	CAP	12.09	PIS	14.59	01.54	11.57	VIR	18.21	SAG	CAP	17.43	11.34	23
24	19.25	PIS	PIS	TAU	GEM	LEO	VIR	SCO	SAG	21.36	PIS	ARI	24
25	AQU	18.17	02.37	15.48	01.38	13.36	02.45	SCO	00.31	AQU	PIS	18.37	25
26	AQU	ARI	ARI	GEM	CAN	VIR	LIB	04.11	CAP	AQU	03.07	TAU	26
27	04.49	22.32	05.39	16.43	02.27	18.30	09.58	SAG	13.21	09.12	ARI	21.49	27
28	PIS	TAU	TAU	CAN	LEO	LIB	SCO	16.42	AQU	PIS	08.31	GEM	28
29	11.58		07.44	19.09	05.43	LIB	20.48	CAP	AQU	17.25	TAU	22.12	29
30	ARI		GEM	LEO	VIR	03.02	SAG	CAP	00.18	ARI	10.36	CAN	30
31	17.03		10.09		12.02		SAG	05.23		22.04		21.33	31

SUN		
mth	dy	time → sign
JAN	1	00.00 → CAP
JAN	20	15.14 → AQU
FEB	19	05.31 → PIS
MAR	21	04.36 → ARI
APR	20	15.50 → TAU
MAY	21	15.06 → GEM
JUN	21	23.07 → CAN
JUL	23	10.08 → LEO
AUG	23	17.07 → VIR
SEP	23	14.42 → LIB
OCT	23	23.56 → SCO
NOV	22	21.18 → SAG
DEC	22	10.32 → CAP

MERCURY		
mth	dy	time → sign
JAN	1	13.36 → AQU
JAN	12	06.55 → CAP
FEB	14	09.37 → AQU
MAR	7	04.28 → PIS
MAR	23	20.09 → ARI
APR	7	17.05 → TAU
JUN	14	08.06 → GEM
JUL	1	19.14 → CAN
JUL	15	20.57 → LEO
AUG	1	10.22 → VIR
AUG	29	06.06 → LIB
SEP	6	02.30 → VIR
OCT	8	23.42 → LIB
OCT	26	15.47 → SCO
NOV	14	08.56 → SAG
DEC	4	11.26 → CAP

VENUS		
mth	dy	time → sign
JAN	1	00.00 → CAP
JAN	5	17.56 → AQU
JAN	29	17.31 → PIS
FEB	22	21.32 → ARI
MAR	19	09.52 → TAU
APR	13	11.22 → GEM
MAY	9	10.57 → CAN
JUN	6	06.07 → LEO
JUL	10	05.25 → VIR
AUG	27	11.45 → LEO
OCT	5	19.33 → VIR
NOV	9	10.55 → LIB
DEC	6	16.14 → SCO

MARS		
mth	dy	time → sign
JAN	1	00.00 → AQU
JAN	17	13.24 → PIS
FEB	25	00.17 → ARI
APR	5	14.07 → TAU
MAY	16	21.40 → GEM
JUN	29	06.54 → CAN
AUG	13	16.51 → LEO
SEP	30	00.23 → VIR
NOV	18	10.21 → LIB

SATURN		
mth	dy	time → sign
JAN	1	00.00 → SCO
MAY	6	19.24 → LIB
AUG	24	11.43 → SCO

JUPITER		
mth	dy	time → sign
JAN	1	00.00 → SAG

MOON												
dy	jan	feb	mar	apr	may	jun	jul	aug	sep	oct	nov	dec	dy
1	LEO	09.47	LIB	16.20	11.01	AQU	PIS	07.37	GEM	12.54	23.31	09.41	1
2	21.49	LIB	23.51	SAG	CAP	19.42	14.47	TAU	02.53	LEO	LIB	SCO	2
3	VIR	14.32	SCO	SAG	23.09	PIS	14.43	CAN	14.15	LIB	14.56	3
4	VIR	SCO	SCO	02.30	AQU	PIS	ARI	GEM	04.47	VIR	01.53	SAG	4
5	00.44	23.28	07.15	CAP	AQU	06.59	00.05	18.09	LEO	14.42	SCO	22.28	5
6	LIB	SAG	SAG	15.06	11.44	ARI	TAU	CAN	04.36	LIB	06.09	CAP	6
7	07.16	SAG	18.29	AQU	PIS	15.05	05.41	18.37	VIR	16.06	SAG	CAP	7
8	SCO	11.33	CAP	AQU	22.16	TAU	GEM	LEO	04.13	SCO	13.31	08.39	8
9	17.14	CAP	CAP	03.30	ARI	19.37	07.50	17.49	LIB	20.21	CAP	AQU	9
10	SAG	CAP	07.30	PIS	ARI	GEM	CAN	VIR	05.49	SAG	CAP	20.53	10
11	SAG	00.40	AQU	13.37	05.36	21.32	07.54	17.51	SCO	SAG	00.10	PIS	11
12	05.26	AQU	19.47	ARI	TAU	CAN	LEO	LIB	11.08	CAP	04.30	AQU	PIS	12
13	CAP	13.02	PIS	20.59	10.03	22.21	07.43	20.44	SAG	12.41	PIS	09.17	13
14	18.26	PIS	PIS	TAU	GEM	LEO	VIR	SCO	20.34	16.00	PIS	ARI	14
15	AQU	23.46	06.00	TAU	12.48	23.38	09.10	SCO	CAP	AQU	PIS	19.33	15
16	AQU	ARI	ARI	02.15	CAN	VIR	LIB	03.33	CAP	AQU	00.36	TAU	16
17	07.02	ARI	14.04	GEM	15.01	VIR	13.38	SAG	08.45	04.41	ARI	TAU	17
18	PIS	08.30	TAU	06.14	LEO	02.36	SCO	13.59	AQU	PIS	10.06	02.23	18
19	18.08	TAU	20.20	CAN	17.37	LIB	21.31	CAP	21.30	16.18	TAU	GEM	19
20	ARI	14.52	GEM	09.26	VIR	07.59	SAG	CAP	PIS	ARI	16.45	06.02	20
21	ARI	GEM	GEM	LEO	21.11	SCO	SAG	02.25	PIS	ARI	GEM	CAN	21
22	02.36	18.31	00.52	12.12	LIB	15.55	08.11	AQU	09.10	01.47	21.10	07.44	22
23	TAU	CAN	CAN	VIR	LIB	SAG	CAP	15.10	ARI	TAU	CAN	LEO	23
24	07.40	19.46	03.43	14.04	02.17	SAG	20.26	PIS	19.12	09.10	CAN	09.01	24
25	GEM	LEO	LEO	LIB	SCO	02.08	AQU	PIS	TAU	GEM	00.19	VIR	25
26	09.28	19.49	05.18	19.04	09.27	CAP	AQU	03.08	TAU	14.47	LEO	11.18	26
27	CAN	VIR	VIR	SCO	SAG	14.07	09.11	ARI	03.24	CAN	03.02	LIB	27
28	09.10	20.30	06.48	SCO	19.07	AQU	PIS	13.38	GEM	18.50	VIR	15.27	28
29	LEO		LIB	01.28	CAP	AQU	21.21	TAU	09.24	LEO	05.57	SCO	29
30	08.35		09.57	SAG	CAP	02.52	ARI	21.49	CAN	21.33	LIB	21.44	30
31	VIR		SCO		07.00		ARI	GEM		VIR		SAG	31

SUN

mth	dy	time → sign
JAN	1	00.00 → CAP
JAN	20	21.04 → AQU
FEB	19	11.16 → PIS
MAR	20	10.22 → ARI
APR	19	21.38 → TAU
MAY	20	20.55 → GEM
JUN	21	05.02 → CAN
JUL	22	15.56 → LEO
AUG	22	23.00 → VIR
SEP	22	20.35 → LIB
OCT	23	05.43 → SCO
NOV	22	03.16 → SAG
DEC	21	16.22 → CAP

MERCURY

mth	dy	time → sign
JAN	1	00.00 → CAP
FEB	9	01.54 → AQU
FEB	27	18.07 → PIS
MAR	14	16.27 → ARI
MAR	31	20.25 → TAU
APR	25	11.45 → ARI
MAY	15	12.33 → TAU
JUN	7	15.42 → GEM
JUN	22	06.40 → CAN
JUL	6	18.53 → LEO
JUL	26	06.49 → VIR
SEP	30	19.41 → LIB
OCT	18	03.00 → SCO
NOV	6	12.09 → SAG
DEC	1	16.32 → CAP
DEC	7	20.46 → SAG

VENUS

mth	dy	time → sign
JAN	1	02.00 → SAG
JAN	25	18.49 → CAP
FEB	19	04.44 → AQU
MAR	14	12.36 → PIS
APR	7	20.13 → ARI
MAY	2	04.56 → TAU
MAY	26	14.40 → GEM
JUN	20	00.47 → CAN
JUL	14	10.31 → LEO
AUG	7	19.44 → VIR
SEP	1	05.07 → LIB
SEP	25	16.01 → SCO
OCT	20	05.46 → SAG
NOV	13	23.57 → CAP
DEC	9	03.26 → AQU

MARS

mth	dy	time → sign
JAN	1	00.00 → LIB
JAN	11	03.00 → SCO
AUG	17	19.38 → SAG
OCT	5	06.22 → CAP
NOV	15	18.18 → AQU
DEC	25	06.27 → PIS

SATURN

mth	dy	time → sign
JAN	1	00.00 → SCO

JUPITER

mth	dy	time → sign
JAN	1	00.00 → SAG
JAN	19	15.22 → CAP

MOON

dy	jan	feb	mar	apr	may	jun	jul	aug	sep	oct	nov	dec	dy
1	SAG	AQU	17.29	ARI	TAU	05.53	LEO	04.03	16.30	05.28	AQU	PIS	1
2	06.07	AQU	PIS	23.55	16.02	CAN	19.28	LIB	SAG	CAP	07.50	03.42	2
3	CAP	11.22	PIS	TAU	GEM	10.19	VIR	06.04	22.55	14.03	PIS	ARI	3
4	16.31	PIS	06.07	TAU	23.26	LEO	21.27	SCO	CAP	AQU	20.20	16.20	4
5	AQU	PIS	ARI	10.04	CAN	13.27	LIB	10.30	CAP	AQU	ARI	TAU	5
6	AQU	00.04	18.09	GEM	CAN	VIR	LIB	SAG	08.11	01.19	ARI	TAU	6
7	04.34	ARI	TAU	17.59	04.43	16.03	00.28	17.24	AQU	PIS	08.53	03.24	7
8	PIS	12.05	TAU	CAN	LEO	LIB	SCO	CAP	19.26	13.51	TAU	GEM	8
9	17.15	TAU	04.30	23.01	08.02	18.48	05.03	CAP	PIS	ARI	20.10	11.56	9
10	ARI	21.39	GEM	LEO	VIR	SCO	SAG	02.25	PIS	ARI	GEM	CAN	10
11	ARI	GEM	11.48	LEO	09.54	22.26	11.23	AQU	07.47	02.28	GEM	18.08	11
12	04.36	GEM	CAN	01.11	LIB	SAG	CAP	13.13	ARI	TAU	05.31	LEO	12
13	TAU	03.20	15.21	VIR	11.22	SAG	19.41	PIS	20.33	14.14	CAN	22.35	13
14	12.40	CAN	LEO	01.29	SCO	03.48	AQU	PIS	TAU	GEM	12.34	VIR	14
15	GEM	05.09	15.47	LIB	13.50	CAP	AQU	01.28	TAU	GEM	LEO	VIR	15
16	16.47	LEO	VIR	01.41	SAG	11.41	06.10	ARI	08.26	00.00	17.08	01.52	16
17	CAN	04.32	14.51	SCO	18.43	AQU	PIS	14.13	GEM	CAN	VIR	LIB	17
18	17.49	VIR	LIB	03.44	CAP	22.18	18.26	TAU	17.36	06.41	19.29	04.27	18
19	LEO	03.39	14.49	SAG	CAP	PIS	ARI	TAU	CAN	LIB	LIB	SCO	19
20	17.35	LIB	SCO	09.10	02.55	PIS	ARI	01.31	22.49	09.56	20.30	06.58	20
21	VIR	04.44	17.41	CAP	AQU	10.40	06.52	GEM	LEO	VIR	SCO	SAG	21
22	18.07	SCO	SAG	18.27	14.09	ARI	TAU	09.20	LEO	10.31	21.34	10.21	22
23	LIB	09.22	SAG	AQU	PIS	22.38	17.10	CAN	00.19>VIR	LIB	SAG	CAP	23
24	21.04	SAG	00.36	AQU	PIS	TAU	GEM	13.00	23.41	10.08	SAG	15.47	24
25	SCO	17.49	CAP	06.26	02.39	TAU	23.44	LEO	LIB	SCO	00.17	AQU	25
26	SCO	CAP	11.09	PIS	ARI	08.04	CAN	13.32	23.04	10.43	CAP	AQU	26
27	03.12	CAP	AQU	19.02	14.13	GEM	CAN	VIR	SCO	SAG	06.06	00.18	27
28	SAG	05.02	23.37	ARI	TAU	14.09	02.41	12.57	SCO	14.05	AQU	PIS	28
29	12.12	AQU	PIS	ARI	23.23	CAN	LEO	LIB	00.32	CAP	15.33	11.49	29
30	CAP		PIS	06.30	GEM	17.30	03.29	13.23	SAG	21.13	PIS	ARI	30
31	23.11		12.14		GEM		VIR	SCO		AQU		ARI	31

SUN

mth	dy	time	→	sign
JAN	1	00.00	→	CAP
JAN	20	02.55	→	AQU
FEB	18	17.08	→	PIS
MAR	20	16.15	→	ARI
APR	20	03.26	→	TAU
MAY	21	02.47	→	GEM
JUN	21	10.44	→	CAN
JUL	22	21.37	→	LEO
AUG	23	04.36	→	VIR
SEP	23	02.02	→	LIB
OCT	23	11.22	→	SCO
NOV	22	08.54	→	SAG
DEC	21	22.08	→	CAP

MERCURY

mth	dy	time	→	sign
JAN	1	00.00	→	SAG
JAN	11	18.28	→	CAP
FEB	1	07.49	→	AQU
FEB	18	23.42	→	PIS
MAR	7	00.07	→	ARI
MAY	14	02.11	→	TAU
MAY	30	19.47	→	GEM
JUN	13	16.11	→	CAN
JUN	29	19.37	→	LEO
SEP	6	19.39	→	VIR
SEP	22	23.14	→	LIB
OCT	10	18.54	→	SCO
OCT	31	16.44	→	SAG
DEC	4	19.20	→	SCO
DEC	12	11.04	→	SAG

VENUS

mth	dy	time	→	sign
JAN	1	00.00	→	AQU
JAN	4	06.22	→	PIS
FEB	2	08.25	→	ARI
JUN	6	08.52	→	TAU
JUL	6	08.06	→	GEM
AUG	2	09.10	→	CAN
AUG	28	03.36	→	LEO
SEP	22	02.53	→	VIR
OCT	16	13.07	→	LIB
NOV	9	15.08	→	SCO
DEC	3	13.02	→	SAG
DEC	27	09.13	→	CAP

MARS

mth	dy	time	→	sign
JAN	1	00.00	→	PIS
FEB	2	17.13	→	ARI
MAR	15	05.00	→	TAU
APR	26	09.24	→	GEM
JUN	9	10.42	→	CAN
JUL	25	04.14	→	LEO
SEP	10	01.45	→	VIR
OCT	27	15.31	→	LIB
DEC	14	18.48	→	SCO

SATURN

mth	dy	time	→	sign
JAN	1	00.00	→	SCO
NOV	17	02.23	→	SAG

JUPITER

mth	dy	time	→	sign
JAN	1	00.00	→	CAP
FEB	6	15.46	→	AQU

MOON

dy	jan	feb	mar	apr	may	jun	jul	aug	sep	oct	nov	dec	dy
1	00.36	GEM	15.23	LEO	21.21	SCO	18.22	AQU	05.42	00.35	GEM	CAN	1
2	TAU	05.59	CAN	10.25	LIB	07.33	CAP	12.33	ARI	TAU	08.31	00.59	2
3	12.00	CAN	21.28	VIR	21.17	SAG	21.36	PIS	17.28	13.36	CAN	LEO	3
4	GEM	11.02	LEO	10.54	SCO	08.34	AQU	21.43	TAU	GEM	19.04	09.14	4
5	20.18	LEO	23.43	LIB	20.56	CAP	AQU	ARI	TAU	GEM	LEO	VIR	5
6	CAN	13.09	VIR	10.10	SAG	11.52	03.40	ARI	06.27	01.59	LEO	14.33	6
7	CAN	VIR	23.47	SCO	22.11	AQU	PIS	09.41	GEM	CAN	02.18	LIB	7
8	01.28	14.10	LIB	10.18	CAP	18.47	13.21	TAU	18.10	11.33	VIR	16.56	8
9	LEO	LIB	23.47	SAG	CAP	PIS	ARI	22.31	CAN	LEO	05.52	SCO	9
10	04.40	15.49	SCO	12.57	02.38	PIS	ARI	GEM	CAN	17.09	LIB	17.13	10
11	VIR	SCO	SCO	CAP	AQU	05.24	01.44	GEM	02.27	VIR	06.31	SAG	11
12	07.13	19.09	01.29	19.04	10.56	ARI	TAU	09.28	LEO	19.12	SCO	16.59	12
13	LIB	SAG	SAG	AQU	PIS	18.11	14.23	CAN	06.52	LIB	05.52	CAP	13
14	10.07	SAG	05.55	AQU	22.25	TAU	GEM	16.57	VIR	19.13	SAG	18.15	14
15	SCO	00.27	CAP	04.30	ARI	TAU	GEM	LEO	08.34	SCO	05.53	AQU	15
16	13.48	CAP	13.11	PIS	ARI	06.45	00.54	21.15	LIB	19.06	CAP	22.50	16
17	SAG	07.36	AQU	16.18	11.23	GEM	CAN	VIR	09.17	SAG	08.25	PIS	17
18	18.29	AQU	22.50	ARI	TAU	17.22	08.25	23.44	SCO	20.35	AQU	PIS	18
19	CAP	16.38	PIS	ARI	TAU	CAN	LEO	LIB	10.40	CAP	14.42	07.36	19
20	CAP	PIS	PIS	05.12	00.01	CAN	13.29	LIB	SAG	CAP	PIS	ARI	20
21	00.38	PIS	10.20	TAU	GEM	01.32	VIR	01.51	13.49	00.54	PIS	19.41	21
22	AQU	03.43	ARI	18.01	11.05	LEO	17.10	SCO	CAP	AQU	00.42	TAU	22
23	09.02	ARI	23.06	GEM	CAN	07.32	LIB	04.36	19.11	08.27	ARI	TAU	23
24	PIS	16.27	TAU	GEM	19.54	VIR	20.16	SAG	AQU	PIS	13.07	08.45	24
25	20.05	TAU	TAU	05.26	LEO	11.48	SCO	08.24	AQU	18.47	TAU	GEM	25
26	ARI	TAU	12.02	CAN	LEO	LIB	23.12	CAP	02.50	ARI	TAU	20.44	26
27	ARI	05.11	GEM	14.10	02.06	14.37	SAG	13.31	PIS	ARI	02.08	CAN	27
28	08.53	GEM	23.13	LEO	VIR	SCO	SAG	AQU	12.43	06.59	GEM	CAN	28
29	TAU		CAN	19.24	05.40	16.30	02.21	20.25	ARI	TAU	14.23	06.44	29
30	21.01		CAN	VIR	LIB	SAG	CAP	PIS	ARI	19.59	CAN	LEO	30
31	GEM		06.51		07.07		06.25	PIS		GEM		14.43	31

SUN

mth	dy	time	→ sign
JAN	1	00.00	→ CAP
JAN	20	08.44	→ AQU
FEB	18	22.58	→ PIS
MAR	20	22.03	→ ARI
APR	20	09.16	→ TAU
MAY	21	08.28	→ GEM
JUN	21	16.30	→ CAN
JUL	23	03.25	→ LEO
AUG	23	10.26	→ VIR
SEP	23	07.57	→ LIB
OCT	23	17.11	→ SCO
NOV	22	14.45	→ SAG
DEC	22	04.05	→ CAP

MERCURY

mth	dy	time	→ sign
JAN	1	00.00	→ SAG
JAN	5	20.43	→ CAP
JAN	25	00.34	→ AQU
FEB	11	05.25	→ PIS
MAR	3	07.22	→ ARI
MAR	11	17.32	→ PIS
APR	17	12.33	→ ARI
MAY	7	12.34	→ TAU
MAY	22	07.22	→ GEM
JUN	5	14.06	→ CAN
JUN	26	14.15	→ LEO
JUL	23	21.53	→ CAN
AUG	11	21.09	→ LEO
AUG	30	03.28	→ VIR
SEP	15	02.26	→ LIB
OCT	4	00.19	→ SCO
DEC	10	00.34	→ SAG
DEC	29	23.14	→ CAP

VENUS

mth	dy	time	→ sign
JAN	1	00.00	→ CAP
JAN	20	05.34	→ AQU
FEB	13	03.11	→ PIS
MAR	9	03.35	→ ARI
APR	2	08.19	→ TAU
APR	26	19.11	→ GEM
MAY	21	13.46	→ CAN
JUN	15	18.55	→ LEO
JUL	11	16.23	→ VIR
AUG	7	20.44	→ LIB
SEP	7	10.11	→ SCO

MARS

mth	dy	time	→ sign
JAN	1	00.00	→ SCO
FEB	2	06.19	→ SAG
MAR	28	03.29	→ CAP
OCT	9	01.13	→ AQU
NOV	26	02.44	→ PIS

SATURN

mth	dy	time	→ sign
JAN	1	00.00	→ SAG

JUPITER

mth	dy	time	→ sign
JAN	1	00.00	→ AQU
FEB	20	16.28	→ PIS

MOON

dy	jan	feb	mar	apr	may	jun	jul	aug	sep	oct	nov	dec	dy
1	VIR	06.19	SCO	CAP	AQU	04.43	TAU	GEM	01.08	VIR	14.19	02.08	1
2	20.45	SCO	14.51	CAP	14.30	ARI	TAU	06.04	LEO	VIR	SCO	SAG	2
3	LIB	09.31	SAG	03.11	PIS	15.45	10.32	CAN	10.06	01.03	15.19	01.28	3
4	LIB	SAG	17.56	AQU	23.01	TAU	GEM	17.26	VIR	LIB	SAG	CAP	4
5	00.44	12.02	CAP	09.03	ARI	TAU	23.19	LEO	16.33	04.35	15.49	01.23	5
6	SCO	CAP	21.42	PIS	ARI	04.26	CAN	LEO	LIB	SCO	CAP	AQU	6
7	02.47	14.35	AQU	17.12	09.59	GEM	CAN	02.44	21.12	06.48	17.29	03.48	7
8	SAG	AQU	AQU	ARI	TAU	17.16	10.56	VIR	SCO	SAG	AQU	PIS	8
9	03.42	18.32	02.48	ARI	22.26	CAN	LEO	10.05	SCO	08.52	21.30	09.49	9
10	CAP	PIS	PIS	03.36	GEM	CAN	20.50	LIB	00.40	CAP	PIS	ARI	10
11	05.01	PIS	10.03	TAU	GEM	05.11	VIR	15.36	SAG	11.45	PIS	19.10	11
12	AQU	01.21	ARI	15.51	11.18	LEO	VIR	SCO	03.28	AQU	04.14	TAU	12
13	08.39	ARI	20.04	GEM	CAN	15.18	04.40	19.17	CAP	16.03	ARI	TAU	13
14	PIS	11.38	TAU	GEM	23.15	VIR	LIB	SAG	06.07	PIS	13.24	06.41	14
15	16.03	TAU	TAU	04.42	LEO	22.38	09.58	21.22	AQU	22.13	TAU	GEM	15
16	ARI	TAU	08.23	CAN	LEO	LIB	SCO	CAP	09.27	ARI	TAU	19.09	16
17	ARI	00.17	GEM	16.10	08.45	LIB	12.34	22.44	PIS	ARI	00.26	CAN	17
18	03.14	GEM	21.04	LEO	VIR	02.36	SAG	AQU	14.33	06.35	GEM	CAN	18
19	TAU	12.39	CAN	LEO	14.41	SCO	13.10	AQU	ARI	TAU	12.46	07.44	19
20	16.12	CAN	CAN	00.24	LIB	03.36	CAP	00.52	22.25	17.15	CAN	LEO	20
21	GEM	22.25	07.38	VIR	17.02	SAG	13.17	PIS	TAU	GEM	19.30	VIR	21
22	GEM	LEO	LEO	04.50	SCO	03.00	AQU	05.27	TAU	GEM	01.25	VIR	22
23	04.14	LEO	14.39	LIB	16.57	CAP	14.59	ARI	09.13	05.37	LEO	VIR	23
24	CAN	04.58	VIR	06.15	SAG	02.50	PIS	13.36	GEM	CAN	12.46	05.05	24
25	13.47	VIR	18.22	SCO	16.15	AQU	20.02	TAU	21.44	18.02	VIR	LIB	25
26	LEO	09.07	LIB	06.16	CAP	05.12	ARI	TAU	CAN	LEO	20.59	11.06	26
27	20.51	LIB	20.05	SAG	17.00	PIS	ARI	01.00	CAN	LEO	LIB	SCO	27
28	VIR	12.06	SCO	06.41	AQU	11.35	05.11	GEM	09.39	04.20	LIB	13.20	28
29	VIR		21.20	CAP	20.54	ARI	TAU	13.40	LEO	VIR	01.13	SAG	29
30	02.10		SAG	09.06	PIS	21.54	17.19	CAN	18.57	11.04	SCO	12.54	30
31	LIB		23.25		PIS		GEM	CAN		LIB		CAP	31

SUN

mth	dy	time → sign
JAN	1	00.00 → CAP
JAN	20	14.44 → AQU
FEB	19	04.52 → PIS
MAR	21	03.52 → ARI
APR	20	14.57 → TAU
MAY	21	14.10 → GEM
JUN	21	22.14 → CAN
JUL	23	09.06 → LEO
AUG	23	16.15 → VIR
SEP	23	13.46 → LIB
OCT	23	23.03 → SCO
NOV	22	20.29 → SAG
DEC	22	09.43 → CAP

MERCURY

mth	dy	time → sign
JAN	1	00.00 → CAP
JAN	17	13.11 → AQU
FEB	4	02.31 → PIS
MAR	11	21.54 → AQU
MAR	13	21.12 → PIS
APR	12	20.23 → ARI
APR	29	15.35 → TAU
MAY	13	17.50 → GEM
MAY	30	04.24 → CAN
AUG	6	21.20 → LEO
AUG	21	21.37 → VIR
SEP	7	13.52 → LIB
SEP	28	17.24 → SCO
NOV	1	01.57 → LIB
NOV	11	21.54 → SCO
DEC	3	13.33 → SAG
DEC	22	17.40 → CAP

VENUS

mth	dy	time → sign
JAN	1	00.00 → SCO
JAN	7	10.23 → SAG
FEB	5	03.07 → CAP
MAR	3	07.52 → AQU
MAR	28	16.20 → PIS
APR	22	16.03 → ARI
MAY	17	11.56 → TAU
JUN	11	05.14 → GEM
JUL	5	19.50 → CAN
JUL	30	06.52 → LEO
AUG	23	14.00 → VIR
SEP	16	18.15 → LIB
OCT	10	20.49 → SCO
NOV	3	23.07 → SAG
NOV	28	01.54 → CAP
DEC	22	06.31 → AQU

MARS

mth	dy	time → sign
JAN	1	00.00 → PIS
JAN	8	12.25 → ARI
FEB	20	14.42 → TAU
APR	5	16.37 → GEM
MAY	21	03.05 → CAN
JUL	6	16.43 → LEO
AUG	22	19.57 → VIR
OCT	8	19.19 → LIB
NOV	24	03.02 → SCO

SATURN

mth	dy	time → sign
JAN	1	00.00 → SAG

JUPITER

mth	dy	time → sign
JAN	1	00.00 → PIS
MAR	2	18.21 → ARI

MOON

dy	jan	feb	mar	apr	may	jun	jul	aug	sep	oct	nov	dec	dy
1	11.54	PIS	12.37	TAU	GEM	03.25	VIR	LIB	SAG	CAP	PIS	ARI	1
2	AQU	02.09	ARI	12.16	07.39	LEO	VIR	01.09	17.04	01.51	13.40	01.06	2
3	12.36	ARI	18.11	GEM	CAN	15.56	09.55	SCO	CAP	AQU	ARI	TAU	3
4	PIS	08.53	TAU	23.33	20.06	VIR	LIB	06.47	18.22	03.39	18.02	08.13	4
5	16.51	TAU	TAU	CAN	LEO	VIR	18.03	SAG	AQU	PIS	TAU	GEM	5
6	ARI	19.23	03.26	CAN	LEO	02.24	SCO	08.51	18.37	05.35	TAU	17.20	6
7	ARI	GEM	GEM	12.04	08.07	LIB	22.05	CAP	PIS	ARI	00.16	CAN	7
8	01.13	GEM	15.24	LEO	VIR	09.06	SAG	08.37	19.34	08.57	GEM	CAN	8
9	TAU	07.55	CAN	23.28	17.29	SCO	22.43	AQU	ARI	TAU	09.10	04.40	9
10	12.39	CAN	CAN	VIR	LIB	11.53	CAP	08.01	22.57	15.04	CAN	LEO	10
11	GEM	20.21	03.54	VIR	23.09	SAG	21.49	PIS	TAU	GEM	20.45	17.30	11
12	GEM	LEO	LEO	08.06	SCO	12.05	AQU	09.09	TAU	GEM	LEO	VIR	12
13	01.18	LEO	14.55	LIB	SCO	CAP	21.36	ARI	05.54	00.31	LEO	VIR	13
14	CAN	07.26	VIR	13.41	01.41	11.45	PIS	13.38	GEM	CAN	09.29	05.40	14
15	13.45	VIR	23.34	SCO	SAG	AQU	PIS	TAU	16.22	12.34	VIR	LIB	15
16	LEO	16.44	LIB	17.01	02.37	12.54	00.00	21.59	CAN	LEO	20.48	14.41	16
17	LEO	LIB	LIB	SAG	CAP	PIS	ARI	GEM	CAN	LEO	LIB	SCO	17
18	01.15	LIB	05.57	19.21	03.42	16.56	06.04	GEM	04.50	01.06	LIB	19.33	18
19	VIR	00.04	SCO	CAP	AQU	ARI	TAU	09.19	LEO	VIR	04.47	SAG	19
20	11.09	SCO	10.32	21.45	06.24	ARI	15.33	CAN	17.13	11.50	SCO	21.08	20
21	LIB	05.09	SAG	AQU	PIS	00.09	GEM	21.58	VIR	LIB	09.16	CAP	21
22	18.30	SAG	13.48	AQU	11.23	TAU	GEM	LEO	VIR	19.41	SAG	21.20	22
23	SCO	07.57	CAP	01.02	ARI	09.54	03.13	LEO	03.58	SCO	11.32	AQU	23
24	22.35	CAP	16.18	PIS	18.39	GEM	CAN	10.23	LIB	SCO	CAP	22.10	24
25	SAG	09.08	AQU	05.41	TAU	21.22	15.50	VIR	12.30	00.57	13.13	PIS	25
26	23.42	AQU	18.46	ARI	TAU	CAN	LEO	21.35	SCO	SAG	AQU	PIS	26
27	CAP	10.07	PIS	12.06	03.55	CAN	LEO	LIB	18.49	04.33	15.41	01.05	27
28	23.17	PIS	22.12	TAU	GEM	09.52	04.26	LIB	SAG	CAP	PIS	ARI	28
29	AQU		ARI	20.43	14.59	LEO	VIR	06.49	23.08	07.27	19.36	06.37	29
30	23.24		ARI	GEM	CAN	22.34	15.59	SCO	CAP	AQU	ARI	TAU	30
31	PIS		03.46		CAN		LIB	13.24		10.19		14.29	31

SUN

mth	dy	time	→ sign
JAN	1	00.00	→ CAP
JAN	20	20.23	→ AQU
FEB	19	10.35	→ PIS
MAR	20	09.36	→ ARI
APR	19	20.45	→ TAU
MAY	20	19.56	→ GEM
JUN	21	03.57	→ CAN
JUL	22	14.54	→ LEO
AUG	22	21.54	→ VIR
SEP	22	19.25	→ LIB
OCT	23	04.44	→ SCO
NOV	22	02.14	→ SAG
DEC	21	15.27	→ CAP

MERCURY

mth	dy	time	→ sign
JAN	1	00.00	→ CAP
JAN	10	05.27	→ AQU
MAR	16	10.13	→ PIS
APR	4	22.04	→ ARI
APR	20	06.44	→ TAU
MAY	4	19.40	→ GEM
JUL	12	06.40	→ CAN
JUL	28	21.19	→ LEO
AUG	12	17.26	→ VIR
AUG	30	20.25	→ LIB
NOV	6	14.52	→ SCO
NOV	25	10.04	→ SAG
DEC	14	11.51	→ CAP

VENUS

mth	dy	time	→ sign
JAN	1	00.00	→ AQU
JAN	15	16.00	→ PIS
FEB	9	13.01	→ ARI
MAR	6	10.21	→ TAU
APR	3	17.07	→ GEM
MAY	17	16.26	→ CAN
MAY	27	07.33	→ GEM
AUG	6	23.24	→ CAN
SEP	7	11.35	→ LEO
OCT	4	13.15	→ VIR
OCT	29	23.23	→ LIB
NOV	23	13.31	→ SCO
DEC	17	17.54	→ SAG

MARS

mth	dy	time	→ sign
JAN	1	00.00	→ SCO
JAN	8	15.17	→ SAG
FEB	22	10.28	→ CAP
APR	6	21.36	→ AQU
MAY	22	07.30	→ PIS
JUL	13	20.13	→ ARI
OCT	23	22.21	→ PIS
NOV	1	12.46	→ ARI

SATURN

mth	dy	time	→ sign
JAN	1	00.00	→ SAG
FEB	13	23.37	→ CAP
JUN	10	05.11	→ SAG
NOV	12	09.32	→ CAP

JUPITER

mth	dy	time	→ sign
JAN	1	00.00	→ ARI
MAR	8	15.32	→ TAU
JUL	21	23.45	→ GEM
NOV	30	20.37	→ TAU

MOON

dy	jan	feb	mar	apr	may	jun	jul	aug	sep	oct	nov	dec	dy
1	GEM	18.06	LEO	08.05	01.39	20.58	07.30	17.53	TAU	22.39	LEO	VIR	1
2	GEM	LEO	13.06	LIB	SCO	CAP	AQU	ARI	08.11	CAN	LEO	VIR	2
3	00.17	LEO	VIR	18.26	08.52	23.34	08.33	20.24	GEM	CAN	04.02	00.56	3
4	CAN	06.54	VIR	SCO	SAG	AQU	PIS	TAU	15.37	08.31	VIR	LIB	4
5	11.47	VIR	01.32	SCO	13.54	AQU	10.37	TAU	CAN	LEO	17.04	12.51	5
6	LEO	19.36	LIB	02.29	CAP	02.00	ARI	01.43	CAN	21.01	LIB	SCO	6
7	LEO	LIB	12.27	SAG	17.37	PIS	14.27	GEM	02.14	VIR	LIB	21.55	7
8	00.35	LIB	SCO	08.19	AQU	05.04	TAU	09.52	LEO	VIR	04.46	SAG	8
9	VIR	06.42	20.59	CAP	20.39	ARI	20.16	CAN	14.48	10.03	SCO	SAG	9
10	13.17	SCO	SAG	12.10	PIS	09.02	GEM	20.26	VIR	LIB	14.06	04.07	10
11	LIB	14.36	SAG	AQU	23.23	TAU	GEM	LEO	VIR	SAG	CAP	11
12	23.39	SAG	02.31	14.24	ARI	14.14	04.08	LEO	03.51	SCO	21.12	08.25	12
13	SCO	18.36	CAP	PIS	ARI	GEM	CAN	08.46	LIB	SCO	CAP	AQU	13
14	SCO	CAP	05.08	15.47	02.22	21.19	14.11	VIR	16.07	07.58	CAP	11.53	14
15	05.58	19.25	AQU	ARI	TAU	CAN	LEO	21.52	SCO	SAG	02.36	PIS	15
16	SAG	AQU	05.42	17.31	06.31	CAN	LEO	LIB	SCO	15.44	AQU	15.03	16
17	08.15	18.44	PIS	TAU	GEM	06.57	02.17	LIB	02.25	CAP	06.34	ARI	17
18	CAP	PIS	05.45	21.10	13.05	LEO	VIR	10.12	SAG	21.05	PIS	18.11	18
19	08.02	18.35	ARI	GEM	CAN	19.03	15.22	SCO	09.45	AQU	09.12	TAU	19
20	AQU	ARI	07.05	GEM	22.51	VIR	LIB	19.55	CAP	23.58	ARI	21.43	20
21	07.27	20.51	TAU	04.04	LEO	VIR	LIB	SAG	13.43	PIS	11.02	GEM	21
22	PIS	TAU	11.21	CAN	LEO	07.57	03.13	SAG	AQU	PIS	TAU	GEM	22
23	08.31	TAU	GEM	14.34	11.12	LIB	SCO	01.49	14.51	00.59	13.12	02.35	23
24	ARI	02.42	19.27	LEO	VIR	18.58	11.42	CAP	PIS	ARI	GEM	CAN	24
25	12.36	GEM	CAN	LEO	23.49	SCO	SAG	04.05	14.29	01.22	17.20	09.57	25
26	TAU	12.12	CAN	03.16	LIB	SCO	16.07	AQU	ARI	TAU	CAN	LEO	26
27	20.02	CAN	06.54	VIR	LIB	02.18	CAP	04.01	14.29	02.55	CAN	20.27	27
28	GEM	CAN	LEO	15.37	10.06	SAG	17.25	PIS	TAU	GEM	00.52	VIR	28
29	GEM	00.12	19.49	LIB	SCO	06.00	AQU	03.29	16.43	07.28	LEO	VIR	29
30	06.11		VIR	LIB	16.57	CAP	17.23	ARI	GEM	CAN	12.00	09.09	30
31	CAN		VIR		SAG		PIS	04.22		16.03		LIB	31

SUN

mth	dy	time	→ sign
JAN	1	00.00	→ CAP
JAN	20	02.06	→ AQU
FEB	18	16.24	→ PIS
MAR	20	15.29	→ ARI
APR	20	02.37	→ TAU
MAY	21	01.56	→ GEM
JUN	21	09.54	→ CAN
JUL	22	20.45	→ LEO
AUG	23	03.43	→ VIR
SEP	23	01.23	→ LIB
OCT	23	10.34	→ SCO
NOV	22	08.05	→ SAG
DEC	21	21.25	→ CAP

MERCURY

mth	dy	time	→ sign
JAN	1	00.00	→ CAP
JAN	2	19.41	→ AQU
JAN	29	04.04	→ CAP
FEB	14	18.11	→ AQU
MAR	10	18.06	→ PIS
MAR	28	03.16	→ ARI
APR	11	21.37	→ TAU
APR	29	19.52	→ GEM
MAY	28	22.53	→ TAU
JUN	12	08.52	→ GEM
JUL	6	00.51	→ CAN
JUL	20	09.05	→ LEO
AUG	5	00.54	→ VIR
AUG	26	06.14	→ LIB
SEP	26	15.28	→ VIR
OCT	11	06.12	→ LIB
OCT	30	13.53	→ SCO
NOV	18	03.10	→ SAG
DEC	7	14.32	→ CAP

VENUS

mth	dy	time	→ sign
JAN	1	00.00	→ SAG
JAN	10	18.10	→ CAP
FEB	3	17.11	→ AQU
FEB	27	16.59	→ PIS
MAR	23	18.37	→ ARI
APR	16	23.56	→ TAU
MAY	11	06.28	→ GEM
JUN	4	17.16	→ CAN
JUN	29	07.21	→ LEO
JUL	24	01.35	→ VIR
AUG	18	01.58	→ LIB
SEP	12	12.22	→ SCO
OCT	8	16.04	→ SAG
NOV	5	10.17	→ CAP
DEC	10	04.51	→ AQU

MARS

mth	dy	time	→ sign
JAN	1	00.00	→ ARI
JAN	19	08.02	→ TAU
MAR	11	08.43	→ GEM
APR	29	04.30	→ CAN
JUN	16	14.26	→ LEO
AUG	3	13.25	→ VIR
SEP	19	14.23	→ LIB
NOV	4	05.14	→ SCO
DEC	18	04.55	→ SAG

SATURN

mth	dy	time	→ sign
JAN	1	00.00	→ CAP

JUPITER

mth	dy	time	→ sign
JAN	1	00.00	→ TAU
MAR	11	03.39	→ GEM
JUL	30	23.22	→ CAN

MOON

dy	jan	feb	mar	apr	may	jun	jul	aug	sep	oct	nov	dec	dy
1	21.34	SAG	SAG	AQU	PIS	TAU	GEM	LEO	VIR	20.53	SAG	CAP	1
2	SCO	23.30	08.58	AQU	11.50	22.02	09.19	LEO	01.47	SCO	SAG	17.42	2
3	SCO	CAP	CAP	01.37	ARI	GEM	CAN	07.19	LIB	SCO	02.47	AQU	3
4	07.11	CAP	13.36	PIS	11.55	GEM	14.37	VIR	14.23	09.29	CAP	AQU	4
5	SAG	02.51	AQU	01.51	TAU	00.17	LEO	18.28	SCO	SAG	12.09	00.48	5
6	13.14	AQU	14.59	ARI	12.03	CAN	23.04	LIB	SCO	20.45	AQU	PIS	6
7	CAP	03.52	PIS	01.07	GEM	05.28	VIR	LIB	02.51	CAP	18.25	05.11	7
8	16.31	PIS	14.36	TAU	14.19	LEO	VIR	07.05	SAG	PIS	PIS	ARI	8
9	AQU	04.18	ARI	01.31	CAN	14.29	10.30	SCO	13.13	AQU	21.08	06.59	9
10	18.31	ARI	14.25	GEM	20.23	VIR	LIB	19.02	CAP	AQU	ARI	TAU	10
11	PIS	05.45	TAU	04.58	LEO	VIR	23.09	SAG	20.02	09.37	21.09	07.15	11
12	20.36	TAU	16.16	CAN	LEO	02.31	SCO	SAG	AQU	PIS	TAU	GEM	12
13	ARI	09.22	GEM	12.31	06.30	LIB	SCO	04.16	23.08	10.41	20.19	07.49	13
14	23.36	GEM	21.27	LEO	VIR	15.11	10.31	CAP	PIS	ARI	GEM	CAN	14
15	TAU	15.40	CAN	23.39	19.07	SCO	SAG	09.59	23.38	09.52	20.51	10.41	15
16	TAU	CAN	CAN	VIR	LIB	SCO	19.01	AQU	ARI	TAU	CAN	LEO	16
17	03.57	CAN	06.13	VIR	LIB	02.12	CAP	12.46	23.22	09.19	CAN	17.19	17
18	GEM	00.33	LEO	12.31	07.48	SAG	CAP	PIS	TAU	GEM	00.45	VIR	18
19	09.57	LEO	17.39	LIB	SCO	10.41	00.35	13.59	TAU	11.09	LEO	VIR	19
20	CAN	11.34	VIR	LIB	18.52	CAP	AQU	ARI	00.16	CAN	08.54	03.45	20
21	18.02	VIR	VIR	01.13	SAG	16.57	04.07	15.10	GEM	16.47	VIR	LIB	21
22	LEO	VIR	06.24	SCO	SAG	AQU	PIS	TAU	03.50	LEO	20.25	16.18	22
23	LEO	00.05	LIB	12.38	03.54	21.36	06.41	17.39	CAN	LEO	LIB	SCO	23
24	04.32	LIB	19.10	SAG	CAP	PIS	ARI	GEM	10.44	02.15	LIB	SCO	24
25	VIR	12.57	SCO	12.15	11.01	PIS	09.10	22.13	LEO	VIR	09.13	04.37	25
26	17.02	SCO	SCO	CAP	AQU	01.06	TAU	CAN	20.32	14.11	SCO	SAG	26
27	LIB	SCO	06.54	CAP	16.13	ARI	12.15	CAN	VIR	LIB	21.30	15.10	27
28	LIB	00.29	SAG	05.33	PIS	03.45	GEM	05.12	VIR	LIB	SAG	CAP	28
29	05.49		16.26	AQU	19.25	TAU	16.32	LEO	08.15	02.56	SAG	23.38	29
30	SCO		CAP	10.03	ARI	06.08	CAN	14.29	LIB	SCO	08.26	AQU	30
31	16.30		22.45		20.59		22.41	VIR		15.23		AQU	31

SUN

mth	dy	time → sign
JAN	1	00.00 → CAP
JAN	20	08.02 → AQU
FEB	18	22.14 → PIS
MAR	20	21.20 → ARI
APR	20	08.27 → TAU
MAY	21	07.38 → GEM
JUN	21	15.33 → CAN
JUL	23	02.22 → LEO
AUG	23	09.23 → VIR
SEP	23	06.56 → LIB
OCT	23	16.17 → SCO
NOV	22	13.47 → SAG
DEC	22	03.08 → CAP

MERCURY

mth	dy	time → sign
JAN	1	00.00 → CAP
FEB	12	01.14 → AQU
MAR	3	17.15 → PIS
MAR	20	00.06 → ARI
APR	4	07.37 → TAU
JUN	12	00.27 → GEM
JUN	27	20.44 → CAN
JUL	11	23.42 → LEO
JUL	29	11.11 → VIR
OCT	5	17.46 → LIB
OCT	23	01.48 → SCO
NOV	11	00.02 → SAG
DEC	2	00.12 → CAP
DEC	25	22.54 → SAG

VENUS

mth	dy	time → sign
JAN	1	00.00 → AQU
JAN	16	15.21 → CAP
MAR	3	17.51 → AQU
APR	6	09.15 → PIS
MAY	4	03.52 → ARI
MAY	30	10.14 → TAU
JUN	25	00.16 → GEM
JUL	20	03.41 → CAN
AUG	13	22.09 → LEO
SEP	7	08.21 → VIR
OCT	1	12.13 → LIB
OCT	25	12.04 → SCO
NOV	18	09.58 → SAG
DEC	12	07.19 → CAP

MARS

mth	dy	time → sign
JAN	1	00.00 → SAG
JAN	29	14.21 → CAP
MAR	11	15.45 → AQU
APR	20	22.19 → PIS
MAY	31	07.20 → ARI
JUL	12	14.34 → TAU
AUG	31	11.30 → GEM
DEC	14	07.49 → TAU

SATURN

mth	dy	time → sign
JAN	1	00.00 → CAP

JUPITER

mth	dy	time → sign
JAN	1	00.00 → CAN
AUG	18	07.51 → LEO

MOON

dy	jan	feb	mar	apr	may	jun	jul	aug	sep	oct	nov	dec	dy
1	06.12	19.27	01.43	12.50	00.08	23.31	18.01	SAG	20.51	13.42	ARI	16.23	1
2	PIS	TAU	TAU	CAN	LEO	LIB	SCO	SAG	AQU	PIS	05.31	GEM	2
3	10.58	22.12	03.37	17.50	07.18	LIB	SCO	02.09	AQU	17.42	TAU	15.27	3
4	ARI	GEM	GEM	LEO	VIR	11.21	06.35	CAP	04.06	ARI	05.06	CAN	4
5	14.04	GEM	07.04	LEO	17.28	SCO	SAG	12.21	PIS	19.06	GEM	16.00	5
6	TAU	01.27	CAN	01.42	LIB	23.59	18.39	AQU	08.23	TAU	05.07	LEO	6
7	16.02	CAN	12.24	VIR	LIB	SAG	CAP	19.54	ARI	19.47	CAN	19.39	7
8	GEM	05.51	LEO	11.44	05.23	SAG	CAP	PIS	10.55	GEM	07.24	VIR	8
9	17.52	LEO	19.47	LIB	SCO	12.12	05.07	PIS	21.29	LEO	VIR	9	
10	CAN	12.13	VIR	23.18	17.56	CAP	AQU	01.13	13.05	CAN	12.48	03.00	10
11	21.02	VIR	VIR	SCO	SAG	23.09	13.29	ARI	GEM	CAN	VIR	LIB	11
12	LEO	21.09	05.09	SCO	SAG	AQU	PIS	04.55	15.53	01.16	21.08	13.26	12
13	LEO	LIB	LIB	11.48	06.21	AQU	19.36	TAU	CAN	LEO	LIB	SCO	13
14	02.57	LIB	16.25	SAG	CAP	08.00	ARI	07.41	19.52	07.21	LIB	SCO	14
15	VIR	08.34	SCO	SAG	17.30	PIS	23.29	GEM	LEO	VIR	07.39	01.44	15
16	12.18	SCO	SCO	00.15	AQU	13.55	TAU	10.12	LEO	15.26	SCO	SAG	16
17	LIB	21.07	04.58	CAP	AQU	ARI	TAU	CAN	01.15	LIB	19.37	14.35	17
18	LIB	SAG	SAG	10.53	01.54	16.43	01.32	13.11	VIR	LIB	SAG	CAP	18
19	00.16	SAG	17.01	ARI	PIS	TAU	GEM	LEO	08.34	01.24	SAG	CAP	19
20	SCO	08.30	CAP	17.57	06.31	17.14	02.44	17.33	LIB	SCO	08.32	02.55	20
21	12.44	CAP	CAP	PIS	ARI	GEM	CAN	VIR	18.08	13.09	CAP	AQU	21
22	SAG	16.52	02.32	20.58	07.44	17.10	04.32	VIR	SAG	SAG	21.07	13.42	22
23	23.27	AQU	AQU	ARI	TAU	CAN	LEO	00.17	SCO	SAG	AQU	PIS	23
24	CAP	21.49	08.08	21.03	07.00	18.25	08.17	LIB	SCO	02.03	AQU	21.45	24
25	CAP	PIS	PIS	TAU	GEM	LEO	VIR	09.56	SAG	CAP	07.32	ARI	25
26	07.25	PIS	10.15	20.12	06.34	22.42	15.19	SCO	18.36	14.14	PIS	ARI	26
27	AQU	00.16	ARI	GEM	CAN	VIR	LIB	21.57	CAP	AQU	14.06	02.08	27
28	12.51	ARI	10.28	20.40	08.29	VIR	LIB	SAG	CAP	23.22	ARI	TAU	28
29	PIS		TAU	CAN	LEO	06.47	01.43	SAG	05.57	PIS	16.37	03.26	29
30	16.34		10.42	CAN	14.08	LIB	SCO	10.23	AQU	PIS	TAU	GEM	30
31	ARI		GEM		VIR		14.00	CAP		04.14		03.02	31

109

SUN

mth	dy	time → sign
JAN	1	00.00 → CAP
JAN	20	13.44 → AQU
FEB	19	03.55 → PIS
MAR	21	03.05 → ARI
APR	20	14.07 → TAU
MAY	21	13.20 → GEM
JUN	21	21.17 → CAN
JUL	23	08.11 → LEO
AUG	23	15.11 → VIR
SEP	23	12.48 → LIB
OCT	23	22.03 → SCO
NOV	22	19.36 → SAG
DEC	22	08.52 → CAP

MERCURY

mth	dy	time → sign
JAN	1	00.00 → SAG
JAN	14	08.05 → CAP
FEB	5	22.22 → AQU
FEB	24	02.38 → PIS
MAR	11	22.42 → ARI
MAY	16	22.45 → TAU
JUN	5	02.23 → GEM
JUN	19	05.40 → CAN
JUL	4	06.04 → LEO
JUL	26	13.00 → VIR
AUG	19	21.45 → LEO
SEP	10	17.14 → VIR
SEP	28	03.25 → LIB
OCT	15	14.01 → SCO
NOV	4	10.44 → SAG

VENUS

mth	dy	time → sign
JAN	1	00.00 → CAP
JAN	5	05.05 → AQU
JAN	29	04.47 → PIS
FEB	22	09.07 → ARI
MAR	18	21.43 → TAU
APR	13	00.13 → GEM
MAY	9	01.27 → CAN
JUN	6	01.16 → LEO
JUL	11	05.06 → VIR
AUG	21	15.09 → LEO
OCT	6	21.12 → VIR
NOV	9	06.34 → LIB
DEC	6	07.24 → SCO
DEC	31	15.18 → SAG

MARS

mth	dy	time → sign
JAN	1	00.00 → TAU
JAN	21	01.27 → GEM
APR	3	00.34 → CAN
MAY	26	12.29 → LEO
JUL	15	12.25 → VIR
SEP	1	06.34 → LIB
OCT	16	19.16 → SCO
NOV	29	02.11 → SAG

SATURN

mth	dy	time → sign
JAN	1	00.00 → CAP
FEB	6	18.40 → AQU

JUPITER

mth	dy	time → sign
JAN	1	00.00 → LEO
SEP	12	06.23 → VIR

MOON

dy	jan	feb	mar	apr	may	jun	jul	aug	sep	oct	nov	dec	dy
1	CAN	VIR	VIR	SCO	SAG	23.42	17.51	ARI	03.02	CAN	VIR	LIB	1
2	02.54	20.02	06.03	SCO	SAG	AQU	PIS	16.32	GEM	14.58	VIR	16.33	2
3	LEO	LIB	LIB	07.59	03.55	AQU	PIS	TAU	06.19	LEO	04.13	SCO	3
4	04.57	LIB	13.08	SAG	CAP	11.36	03.33	20.54	CAN	17.45	LIB	SCO	4
5	VIR	04.01	SCO	20.20	16.51	PIS	ARI	GEM	08.13	VIR	10.09	01.32	5
6	10.33	SCO	23.35	CAP	AQU	20.25	09.52	22.47	LEO	21.00	SCO	SAG	6
7	LIB	15.23	SAG	CAP	AQU	ARI	TAU	CAN	09.35	LIB	18.21	12.41	7
8	19.59	SAG	SAG	09.00	04.04	ARI	12.42	23.09	VIR	LIB	SAG	CAP	8
9	SCO	SAG	12.14	AQU	PIS	01.13	GEM	LEO	11.52	02.00	SAG	CAP	9
10	SCO	04.16	CAP	19.18	11.34	TAU	13.03	23.35	LIB	SCO	05.16	01.27	10
11	08.06	CAP	CAP	PIS	ARI	02.36	CAN	VIR	16.42	09.58	CAP	AQU	11
12	SAG	16.16	00.31	PIS	15.07	GEM	12.35	VIR	SCO	SAG	18.06	14.19	12
13	21.00	AQU	AQU	01.49	TAU	02.17	LEO	01.52	SCO	21.10	AQU	PIS	13
14	CAP	AQU	10.11	ARI	16.02	CAN	13.12	LIB	01.14	CAP	AQU	PIS	14
15	CAP	01.59	PIS	05.06	GEM	02.10	VIR	07.34	SAG	CAP	06.33	01.06	15
16	09.04	PIS	16.37	TAU	16.14	LEO	16.34	SCO	13.04	10.04	PIS	ARI	16
17	AQU	09.11	ARI	06.41	CAN	04.03	LIB	17.11	CAP	AQU	16.08	08.10	17
18	19.23	ARI	20.40	GEM	17.30	VIR	23.41	SAG	CAP	21.53	ARI	TAU	18
19	PIS	14.24	TAU	08.17	LEO	09.01	SCO	SAG	01.58	PIS	21.49	11.21	19
20	PIS	TAU	23.37	CAN	21.00	LIB	SCO	05.34	AQU	PIS	TAU	GEM	20
21	03.28	18.10	GEM	11.06	VIR	17.18	10.16	CAP	13.20	06.33	TAU	11.55	21
22	ARI	GEM	GEM	LEO	VIR	SCO	SAG	18.27	PIS	ARI	00.22	CAN	22
23	09.01	20.56	02.27	15.29	03.08	SCO	22.55	AQU	21.56	11.55	GEM	11.38	23
24	TAU	CAN	CAN	VIR	LIB	04.16	CAP	AQU	ARI	TAU	01.25	LEO	24
25	12.06	23.13	05.43	21.36	11.41	SAG	CAP	05.51	ARI	15.09	CAN	12.24	25
26	GEM	LEO	LEO	LIB	SCO	16.49	11.49	PIS	03.59	GEM	02.37	VIR	26
27	13.23	LEO	09.41	LIB	22.21	CAP	AQU	15.01	TAU	17.37	LEO	15.37	27
28	CAN	01.50	VIR	05.34	SAG	CAP	23.35	ARI	08.25	CAN	05.12	LIB	28
29	14.03		14.49	SCO	SAG	05.47	PIS	22.00	GEM	20.20	VIR	22.03	29
30	LEO		LIB	15.42	10.40	AQU	PIS	TAU	11.58	LEO	09.47	SCO	30
31	15.44		22.01		CAP		09.20	TAU		23.47		SCO	31

SUN

mth	dy	time	→ sign
JAN	1	00.00	→ CAP
JAN	20	19.36	→ AQU
FEB	19	09.47	→ PIS
MAR	20	08.47	→ ARI
APR	19	19.53	→ TAU
MAY	20	19.13	→ GEM
JUN	21	03.15	→ CAN
JUL	22	14.11	→ LEO
AUG	22	21.12	→ VIR
SEP	22	18.44	→ LIB
OCT	23	03.57	→ SCO
NOV	22	01.24	→ SAG
DEC	21	14.41	→ CAP

MERCURY

mth	dy	time	→ sign
JAN	1	00.00	→ SAG
JAN	10	01.48	→ CAP
JAN	29	21.13	→ AQU
FEB	16	07.04	→ PIS
MAR	3	21.43	→ ARI
APR	3	23.53	→ PIS
APR	14	17.38	→ ARI
MAY	11	04.11	→ TAU
MAY	26	21.15	→ GEM
JUN	9	18.27	→ CAN
JUN	27	05.14	→ LEO
SEP	3	08.03	→ VIR
SEP	19	05.44	→ LIB
OCT	7	10.12	→ SCO
OCT	29	17.03	→ SAG
NOV	21	19.43	→ SCO
DEC	12	08.02	→ SAG

VENUS

mth	dy	time	→ sign
JAN	1	00.00	→ SAG
JAN	25	07.17	→ CAP
FEB	18	16.43	→ AQU
MAR	13	23.57	→ PIS
APR	7	07.13	→ ARI
MAY	1	15.42	→ TAU
MAY	26	01.15	→ GEM
JUN	19	11.23	→ CAN
JUL	13	21.09	→ LEO
AUG	7	06.22	→ VIR
AUG	31	16.09	→ LIB
SEP	25	03.32	→ SCO
OCT	19	17.45	→ SAG
NOV	13	12.48	→ CAP
DEC	8	17.52	→ AQU

MARS

mth	dy	time	→ sign
JAN	1	00.00	→ SAG
JAN	9	09.32	→ CAP
FEB	18	04.30	→ AQU
MAR	28	02.15	→ PIS
MAY	5	21.28	→ ARI
JUN	14	15.56	→ TAU
JUL	26	18.55	→ GEM
SEP	12	06.11	→ CAN

SATURN

mth	dy	time	→ sign
JAN	1	00.00	→ AQU

JUPITER

mth	dy	time	→ sign
JAN	1	00.00	→ VIR
OCT	10	13.38	→ LIB

MOON

dy	Jan	feb	mar	apr	may	jun	jul	aug	sep	oct	nov	dec	dy
1	07.30	CAP	AQU	PIS	19.09	GEM	22.15	VIR	SCO	SAG	12.43	09.23	1
2	SAG	14.09	AQU	03.04	TAU	11.58	LEO	08.17	SCO	17.29	AQU	PIS	2
3	19.09	AQU	09.11	ARI	TAU	CAN	22.37	LIB	00.50	CAP	AQU	21.49	3
4	CAP	AQU	PIS	11.18	00.28	13.35	VIR	11.16	SAG	CAP	01.13	ARI	4
5	CAP	02.51	20.07	TAU	GEM	LEO	VIR	SCO	10.06	04.53	PIS	ARI	5
6	07.59	PIS	ARI	17.33	04.09	15.28	00.27	17.57	CAP	AQU	13.19	08.16	6
7	AQU	14.15	ARI	GEM	CAN	VIR	LIB	SAG	22.08	17.38	ARI	TAU	7
8	20.52	ARI	05.05	22.18	07.07	18.33	04.53	SAG	AQU	PIS	23.19	15.37	8
9	PIS	23.36	TAU	CAN	LEO	LIB	SCO	04.00	AQU	PIS	TAU	GEM	9
10	PIS	TAU	12.03	CAN	09.56	23.27	12.17	CAP	10.56	05.36	TAU	20.05	10
11	08.22	TAU	GEM	01.46	VIR	SCO	SAG	16.06	PIS	ARI	06.49	CAN	11
12	ARI	06.08	16.50	LEO	13.05	SCO	22.16	AQU	23.02	15.48	GEM	22.47	12
13	17.00	GEM	CAN	04.09	LIB	06.29	CAP	AQU	ARI	TAU	12.19	LEO	13
14	TAU	09.31	19.20	VIR	17.15	SAG	CAP	04.51	ARI	TAU	CAN	LEO	14
15	21.55	CAN	LEO	06.10	SCO	15.50	10.03	PIS	09.47	00.08	16.23	00.56	15
16	GEM	10.15	20.13	LIB	23.22	CAP	AQU	17.11	TAU	GEM	LEO	VIR	16
17	23.26	LEO	VIR	09.10	SAG	CAP	22.44	ARI	06.36	19.28	19.28	03.33	17
18	CAN	09.47	20.55	SCO	SAG	03.19	PIS	ARI	GEM	CAN	VIR	LIB	18
19	22.57	VIR	LIB	14.40	08.13	AQU	PIS	04.10	GEM	11.01	22.03	07.20	19
20	LEO	10.05	23.20	SAG	CAP	16.00	11.07	TAU	00.59	LEO	LIB	SCO	20
21	22.22	LIB	SCO	23.40	19.44	PIS	ARI	12.36	CAN	13.27	LIB	12.42	21
22	VIR	13.11	SCO	CAP	AQU	PIS	21.36	GEM	04.19	VIR	00.52	SAG	22
23	23.42	SCO	05.13	CAP	AQU	04.03	TAU	17.36	LEO	14.39	SCO	20.04	23
24	LIB	20.26	SAG	11.38	08.25	ARI	TAU	CAN	05.08	LIB	05.01	CAP	24
25	LIB	SAG	15.09	AQU	PIS	13.28	04.44	19.15	VIR	16.04	SAG	CAP	25
26	04.32	SAG	CAP	AQU	19.52	TAU	GEM	LEO	04.55	SCO	11.38	05.43	26
27	SCO	07.33	CAP	00.20	ARI	19.14	08.08	18.46	LIB	19.29	CAP	AQU	27
28	13.20	CAP	03.44	PIS	ARI	GEM	CAN	VIR	05.44	SAG	21.19	17.28	28
29	SAG	20.34	AQU	11.13	04.16	21.42	08.39	18.11	SCO	SAG	AQU	PIS	29
30	SAG		16.23	ARI	TAU	CAN	LEO	LIB	09.33	02.18	AQU	PIS	30
31	01.07		PIS		09.19		08.01	19.38		CAP		06.07	31

111

SUN

mth	dy	time	→ sign
JAN	1	00.00	→ CAP
JAN	20	01.21	→ AQU
FEB	18	15.35	→ PIS
MAR	20	14.44	→ ARI
APR	20	01.47	→ TAU
MAY	21	01.03	→ GEM
JUN	21	09.00	→ CAN
JUL	22	19.54	→ LEO
AUG	23	02.50	→ VIR
SEP	23	00.26	→ LIB
OCT	23	09.36	→ SCO
NOV	22	07.07	→ SAG
DEC	21	20.23	→ CAP

MERCURY

mth	dy	time	→ sign
JAN	1	00.00	→ SAG
JAN	2	14 47	→ CAP
JAN	21	11.23	→ AQU
FEB	7	16.21	→ PIS
APR	15	15.18	→ ARI
MAY	3	21.51	→ TAU
MAY	18	06.53	→ GEM
JUN	2	03.52	→ CAN
AUG	10	05.50	→ LEO
AUG	26	07.03	→ VIR
SEP	11	11.18	→ LIB
OCT	1	02.13	→ SCO
DEC	7	01.04	→ SAG
DEC	26	12.48	→ CAP

VENUS

mth	dy	time	→ sign
JAN	1	00.00	→ AQU
JAN	3	23.51	→ PIS
FEB	2	12.37	→ ARI
JUN	6	10.01	→ TAU
JUL	6	00.21	→ GEM
AUG	1	22.36	→ CAN
AUG	27	15.48	→ LEO
SEP	21	14.27	→ VIR
OCT	16	00.13	→ LIB
NOV	9	02.10	→ SCO
DEC	2	23.55	→ SAG
DEC	26	20.07	→ CAP

MARS

mth	dy	time	→ sign
JAN	1	00.00	→ CAN
APR	27	23.30	→ LEO
JUN	23	07.29	→ VIR
AUG	12	01.14	→ LIB
SEP	27	02.19	→ SCO
NOV	9	05.32	→ SAG
DEC	20	00.39	→ CAP

SATURN

mth	dy	time	→ sign
JAN	1	00.00	→ AQU
MAY	21	04.44	→ PIS
JUN	30	08.13	→ AQU

JUPITER

mth	dy	time	→ sign
JAN	1	00.00	→ LIB
NOV	10	08.27	→ SCO

MOON

dy	jan	feb	mar	apr	may	jun	jul	aug	sep	oct	nov	dec	dy
1	ARI	11.15	GEM	14.21	00.00	10.22	SAG	16.36	PIS	ARI	10.13	02.17	1
2	17.30	GEM	GEM	LEO	VIR	SCO	SAG	AQU	21.21	16.13	GEM	CAN	2
3	TAU	16.56	02.16	16.10	01.20	13.01	01.48	AQU	ARI	TAU	20.25	09.33	3
4	TAU	CAN	CAN	VIR	LIB	SAG	CAP	02.44	ARI	TAU	CAN	LEO	4
5	01.42	18.51	05.40	15.54	01.57	17.26	09.14	PIS	10.09	04.27	CAN	14.43	5
6	GEM	LEO	LEO	LIB	SCO	CAP	AQU	14.39	TAU	GEM	04.06	VIR	6
7	06.10	18.29	05.52	15.32	03.34	CAP	19.10	22.16	14.42	LEO	18.03	7
8	CAN	VIR	VIR	SCO	SAG	00.39	PIS	ARI	GEM	CAN	08.47	LIB	8
9	07.49	17.58	04.46	17.10	07.51	AQU	PIS	03.22	GEM	21.34	VIR	20.04	9
10	LEO	LIB	LIB	SAG	CAP	10.57	07.11	TAU	07.37	LEO	10.42	SCO	10
11	08.20	19.24	04.40	22.24	15.44	PIS	ARI	14.47	CAN	LEO	LIB	21.39	11
12	VIR	SCO	SCO	CAP	AQU	23.14	19.37	GEM	12.51	00.36	11.00	SAG	12
13	09.30	SCO	07.33	CAP	AQU	ARI	TAU	22.46	LEO	VIR	SCO	SAG	13
14	LIB	00.08	SAG	07.36	02.51	ARI	TAU	CAN	14.20	00.47	11.20	00.06	14
15	12.42	SAG	14.28	AQU	PIS	11.19	06.07	CAN	VIR	LIB	SAG	CAP	15
16	SCO	08.20	CAP	19.33	15.24	TAU	GEM	02.43	13.44	00.01	13.34	04.51	16
17	18.30	CAP	CAP	PIS	ARI	21.12	13.08	LEO	LIB	SCO	CAP	AQU	17
18	SAG	19.05	00.52	PIS	ARI	GEM	CAN	03.41	13.15	00.23	19.08	12.59	18
19	SAG	AQU	AQU	08.14	03.16	GEM	16.47	VIR	SCO	SAG	AQU	PIS	19
20	02.46	AQU	13.11	ARI	TAU	04.05	LEO	03.35	14.53	03.42	AQU	PIS	20
21	CAP	07.12	PIS	20.08	13.07	CAN	18.24	LIB	SAG	CAP	04.27	00.19	21
22	13.00	PIS	PIS	TAU	GEM	08.26	VIR	04.27	19.54	10.49	PIS	ARI	22
23	AQU	19.50	01.51	TAU	20.38	LEO	19.39	SCO	CAP	AQU	16.30	13.05	23
24	AQU	ARI	ARI	06.27	CAN	11.18	LIB	07.45	CAP	21.17	ARI	TAU	24
25	00.47	ARI	13.59	GEM	CAN	VIR	22.00	SAG	04.19	PIS	ARI	TAU	25
26	PIS	08.11	TAU	14.45	02.03	13.46	SCO	13.58	AQU	PIS	05.14	00.46	26
27	13.28	TAU	TAU	CAN	LEO	LIB	SCO	CAP	15.13	09.39	TAU	GEM	27
28	ARI	18.52	00.48	20.39	05.46	16.37	02.13	22.42	PIS	AQU	16.48	09.46	28
29	ARI		GEM	LEO	VIR	SCO	SAG	AQU	PIS	22.20	GEM	CAN	29
30	01.37		09.14	LEO	08.18	20.28	08.27	AQU	03.29	TAU	GEM	15.59	30
31	TAU		CAN		LIB		CAP	09.19		TAU		LEO	31

SUN

mth	dy	time → sign
JAN	1	00.00 → CAP
JAN	20	07.09 → AQU
FEB	18	21.22 → PIS
MAR	20	20.26 → ARI
APR	20	07.36 → TAU
MAY	21	06.46 → GEM
JUN	21	14.48 → CAN
JUL	23	01.44 → LEO
AUG	23	08.44 → VIR
SEP	23	06.16 → LIB
OCT	23	15.36 → SCO
NOV	22	13.09 → SAG
DEC	22	02.21 → CAP

MERCURY

mth	dy	time → sign
JAN	1	00.00 → CAP
JAN	14	00.28 → AQU
FEB	1	10.28 → PIS
FEB	21	15.18 → AQU
MAR	18	12.04 → PIS
APR	9	16.32 → ARI
APR	25	18.27 → TAU
MAY	9	21.05 → GEM
MAY	28	14.52 → CAN
JUL	2	23.18 → GEM
JUL	10	12.42 → CAN
AUG	3	06.09 → LEO
AUG	18	00.47 → VIR
SEP	4	04.56 → LIB
SEP	27	08.54 → SCO
OCT	19	06.19 → LIB
NOV	10	12.45 → SCO
NOV	30	04.39 → SAG
DEC	19	06.26 → CAP

VENUS

mth	dy	time → sign
JAN	1	00.00 → CAP
JAN	19	16.26 → AQU
FEB	12	14.05 → PIS
MAR	8	14.27 → ARI
APR	1	19.21 → TAU
APR	26	06.23 → GEM
MAY	21	01.27 → CAN
JUN	15	07.20 → LEO
JUL	11	06.30 → VIR
AUG	7	14.39 → LIB
SEP	7	17.11 → SCO

MARS

mth	dy	time → sign
JAN	1	00.00 → CAP
JAN	28	04.18 → AQU
MAR	7	11.20 → PIS
APR	14	18.13 → ARI
MAY	23	22.37 → TAU
JUL	3	22.34 → GEM
AUG	16	19.25 → CAN
OCT	4	15.53 → LEO
DEC	12	11.35 → VIR

SATURN

mth	dy	time → sign
JAN	1	00.00 → AQU
JAN	28	23.29 → PIS

JUPITER

mth	dy	time → sign
JAN	1	00.00 → SCO
DEC	9	10.43 → SAG

MOON

dy	jan	feb	mar	apr	may	jun	jul	aug	sep	oct	nov	dec	dy
1	20.15	LIB	14.43	SAG	16.34	PIS	ARI	11.05	CAN	LEO	LIB	SCO	1
2	VIR	07.49	SCO	03.38	AQU	18.31	14.23	GEM	15.37	06.39	20.19	07.13	2
3	23.31	SCO	16.54	CAP	AQU	ARI	TAU	22.22	LEO	VIR	SCO	SAG	3
4	LIB	11.14	SAG	09.45	00.47	ARI	TAU	CAN	20.33	08.56	19.46	06.43	4
5	LIB	SAG	21.24	AQU	PIS	07.14	03.12	CAN	VIR	LIB	SAG	CAP	5
6	02.29	16.02	CAP	18.51	12.01	TAU	GEM	06.31	22.57	09.22	20.02	07.52	6
7	SCO	CAP	CAP	PIS	ARI	20.03	14.17	LEO	LIB	SCO	CAP	AQU	7
8	05.34	22.16	04.15	PIS	ARI	GEM	CAN	11.42	LIB	09.47	22.48	12.24	8
9	SAG	AQU	AQU	06.09	00.50	GEM	22.43	VIR	00.26	SAG	AQU	PIS	9
10	09.16	AQU	13.09	ARI	TAU	07.22	LEO	15.07	SCO	11.44	AQU	21.03	10
11	CAP	06.23	PIS	18.48	13.43	CAN	LEO	LIB	02.25	CAP	05.04	ARI	11
12	14.25	PIS	23.59	TAU	GEM	16.29	04.48	17.56	SAG	16.09	PIS	ARI	12
13	AQU	16.49	ARI	TAU	GEM	LEO	VIR	SCO	05.44	AQU	14.44	08.56	13
14	22.04	ARI	ARI	04.48	01.27	23.16	09.15	20.53	CAP	23.18	ARI	TAU	14
15	PIS	ARI	12.27	GEM	CAN	VIR	LIB	SAG	10.42	PIS	ARI	22.00	15
16	PIS	05.20	TAU	19.41	10.58	VIR	12.35	SAG	AQU	PIS	02.44	GEM	16
17	08.42	TAU	TAU	CAN	LEO	03.48	SCO	00.18	17.31	08.56	TAU	GEM	17
18	ARI	18.05	01.29	CAN	17.31	LIB	15.09	CAP	PIS	ARI	15.41	10.25	18
19	21.22	GEM	GEM	04.45	VIR	06.20	SAG	04.34	PIS	20.34	GEM	CAN	19
20	TAU	GEM	12.54	LEO	20.54	SCO	17.30	AQU	02.30	TAU	GEM	21.13	20
21	TAU	04.27	CAN	09.58	LIB	07.32	CAP	10.27	ARI	TAU	04.21	LEO	21
22	09.35	CAN	20.39	VIR	21.51	SAG	PIS	13.47	TAU	09.28	CAN	LEO	22
23	GEM	10.48	LEO	11.40	SCO	08.37	AQU	18.55	TAU	15.33	06.01	VIR	23
24	18.55	LEO	LEO	LIB	21.43	CAP	AQU	ARI	TAU	22.15	LEO	12.27	24
25	CAN	13.27	00.14	11.18	SAG	11.10	01.56	ARI	02.41	CAN	LEO	25
26	CAN	VIR	VIR	SCO	22.17	AQU	PIS	06.13	GEM	CAN	00.09	LIB	26
27	08.38	14.06	00.46	10.48	CAP	16.44	10.31	TAU	15.12	09.05	VIR	16.17	27
28	LEO	LIB	LIB	SAG	CAP	PIS	ARI	19.07	CAN	LEO	05.22	SCO	28
29	03.39		00.15	12.05	01.19	PIS	22.13	GEM	CAN	16.21	LIB	17.45	29
30	VIR		SCO	CAP	AQU	02.07	TAU	GEM	00.55	VIR	07.21	SAG	30
31	05.34		00.41		08.03		TAU	07.00		19.46		17.57	31

SUN

mth	dy	time	→ sign
JAN	1	00.00	→ CAP
JAN	20	13.04	→ AQU
FEB	19	03.13	→ PIS
MAR	21	02.13	→ ARI
APR	20	13.26	→ TAU
MAY	21	12.36	→ GEM
JUN	21	20.32	→ CAN
JUL	23	07.32	→ LEO
AUG	23	14.37	→ VIR
SEP	23	12.13	→ LIB
OCT	23	21.32	→ SCO
NOV	22	19.03	→ SAG
DEC	22	08.19	→ CAP

MERCURY

mth	dy	time	→ sign
JAN	1	00.00	→ CAP
JAN	6	22.14	→ AQU
MAR	14	21.33	→ PIS
APR	2	07.29	→ ARI
APR	17	07.52	→ TAU
MAY	2	15.18	→ GEM
JUL	10	16.59	→ CAN
JUL	25	22.19	→ LEO
AUG	10	00.14	→ VIR
AUG	29	02.07	→ LIB
NOV	4	08.54	→ SCO
NOV	22	22.47	→ SAG
DEC	12	02.56	→ CAP

VENUS

mth	dy	time	→ sign
JAN	1	00.00	→ SCO
JAN	7	12.10	→ SAG
FEB	4	20.11	→ CAP
MAR	2	22.13	→ AQU
MAR	28	05.13	→ PIS
APR	22	04.10	→ ARI
MAY	16	23.26	→ TAU
JUN	10	16.17	→ GEM
JUL	5	06.39	→ CAN
JUL	29	17.32	→ LEO
AUG	23	00.45	→ VIR
SEP	16	05.03	→ LIB
OCT	10	07.48	→ SCO
NOV	3	10.17	→ SAG
NOV	27	13.24	→ CAP
DEC	21	18.21	→ AQU

MARS

mth	dy	time	→ sign
JAN	1	00.00	→ VIR
JAN	22	23.32	→ LEO
MAY	25	16.23	→ VIR
JUL	21	09.16	→ LIB
SEP	7	07.03	→ SCO
OCT	20	21.14	→ SAG
NOV	30	13.48	→ CAP

SATURN

mth	dy	time	→ sign
JAN	1	00.00	→ PIS

JUPITER

mth	dy	time	→ sign
JAN	1	00.00	→ SAG

MOON

dy	jan	feb	mar	apr	may	jun	jul	aug	sep	oct	nov	dec	dy
1	CAP	08.05	PIS	16.59	11.53	CAN	LEO	01.23	16.57	01.10	13.17	00.51	1
2	18.39	PIS	23.30	TAU	GEM	19.17	11.35	SAG	19.45	CAP	PIS	ARI	2
3	AQU	14.13	ARI	TAU	GEM	LEO	VIR	07.29	19.45	03.59	19.21	09.40	3
4	21.49	ARI	ARI	04.49	00.45	LEO	19.55	SCO	CAP	AQU	ARI	TAU	4
5	PIS	ARI	08.50	GEM	CAN	05.46	LIB	11.14	21.47	07.35	ARI	20.35	5
6	PIS	00.09	TAU	17.40	12.55	VIR	LIB	SAG	AQU	PIS	03.35	GEM	6
7	04.56	TAU	20.55	CAN	LEO	13.13	01.19	12.52	AQU	12.42	TAU	GEM	7
8	ARI	12.44	GEM	CAN	22.33	LIB	SCO	CAP	00.08	ARI	13.55	08.44	8
9	15.58	GEM	GEM	05.16	VIR	17.03	03.37	13.28	PIS	20.05	GEM	CAN	9
10	TAU	GEM	09.40	LEO	VIR	SCO	SAG	AQU	04.14	TAU	GEM	21.24	10
11	TAU	01.17	CAN	13.39	04.30	17.50	03.43	14.46	ARI	TAU	01.57	LEO	11
12	04.57	CAN	20.28	VIR	LIB	SAG	CAP	PIS	11.21	06.10	CAN	LEO	12
13	GEM	11.31	LEO	18.20	06.53	17.05	03.21	18.41	TAU	GEM	14.37	09.26	13
14	17.20	LEO	LEO	LIB	SCO	CAP	AQU	ARI	21.48	18.20	LEO	VIR	14
15	CAN	18.52	03.54	20.13	06.58	16.52	04.37	ARI	GEM	CAN	LEO	19.09	15
16	CAN	VIR	VIR	SCO	SAG	AQU	PIS	02.25	GEM	CAN	02.02	LIB	16
17	03.36	VIR	08.18	20.52	06.36	19.13	09.23	TAU	10.16	06.46	VIR	LIB	17
18	LEO	00.00	LIB	SAG	CAP	PIS	ARI	13.40	CAN	10.18	10.18	01.07	18
19	11.39	LIB	10.52	21.54	07.39	PIS	18.20	GEM	22.20	17.11	LIB	SCO	19
20	VIR	03.55	SCO	CAP	AQU	01.29	TAU	GEM	LEO	VIR	14.40	03.13	20
21	17.54	SCO	12.57	CAP	11.40	ARI	TAU	02.24	LEO	VIR	SCO	SAG	21
22	LIB	07.13	SAG	00.38	PIS	11.35	06.23	CAN	08.01	00.15	15.56	02.46	22
23	22.32	SAG	15.31	AQU	19.13	TAU	GEM	14.13	VIR	LIB	SAG	CAP	23
24	SCO	10.11	CAP	05.51	ARI	TAU	19.16	LEO	14.50	04.06	15.48	01.52	24
25	SCO	CAP	19.10	PIS	ARI	00.02	CAN	23.50	LIB	SCO	CAP	AQU	25
26	01.37	13.14	AQU	13.41	05.47	GEM	CAN	VIR	19.20	05.56	16.15	02.45	26
27	SAG	AQU	AQU	ARI	TAU	12.56	07.07	VIR	SCO	SAG	AQU	PIS	27
28	03.26	17.16	00.18	23.53	18.07	CAN	LEO	07.15	22.30	07.15	18.59	07.06	28
29	CAP		PIS	TAU	GEM	CAN	17.12	LIB	SAG	CAP	PIS	ARI	29
30	05.03		07.26	TAU	GEM	01.02	VIR	12.51	SAG	09.23	PIS	15.21	30
31	AQU		ARI		06.59		VIR	SCO		AQU		TAU	31

SUN

mth	dy	time → sign
JAN	1	00.00 → CAP
JAN	20	18.51 → AQU
FEB	19	09.04 → PIS
MAR	20	08.01 → ARI
APR	19	19.13 → TAU
MAY	20	18.23 → GEM
JUN	21	02.23 → CAN
JUL	22	13.19 → LEO
AUG	22	20.21 → VIR
SEP	22	18.00 → LIB
OCT	23	03.16 → SCO
NOV	22	00.49 → SAG
DEC	21	14.03 → CAP

MERCURY

mth	dy	time → sign
JAN	1	00.00 → CAP
JAN	1	18.08 → AQU
JAN	17	09.37 → CAP
FEB	15	02.46 → AQU
MAR	7	11.53 → PIS
MAR	24	08.02 → ARI
APR	8	03.12 → TAU
JUN	13	21.45 → GEM
JUL	2	07.35 → CAN
JUL	16	09.54 → LEO
AUG	1	16.17 → VIR
AUG	26	05.14 → LIB
SEP	12	09.31 → VIR
OCT	9	03.13 → LIB
OCT	27	01.01 → SCO
NOV	14	16.33 → SAG
DEC	4	13.48 → CAP

VENUS

mth	dy	time → sign
JAN	1	00.00 → AQU
JAN	15	04.32 → PIS
FEB	9	02.33 → ARI
MAR	6	02.04 → TAU
APR	3	15.24 → GEM
AUG	7	06.17 → CAN
SEP	7	05.05 → LEO
OCT	4	03.23 → VIR
OCT	29	12.02 → LIB
NOV	23	01.35 → SCO
DEC	17	05.34 → SAG

MARS

mth	dy	time → sign
JAN	1	00.00 → CAP
JAN	8	11.14 → AQU
FEB	15	11.36 → PIS
MAR	24	15.23 → ARI
MAY	2	18.26 → TAU
JUN	12	14.55 → GEM
JUL	25	18.35 → CAN
SEP	9	20.13 → LEO
OCT	30	07.20 → VIR

SATURN

mth	dy	time → sign
JAN	1	00.00 → PIS
APR	7	08.35 → ARI

JUPITER

mth	dy	time → sign
JAN	1	00.00 → SAG
JAN	3	07.01 → CAP

MOON

dy	jan	feb	mar	apr	may	jun	jul	aug	sep	oct	nov	dec	dy
1	TAU	CAN	16.47	VIR	LIB	01.43	CAP	PIS	12.19	04.01	CAN	LEO	1
2	02.29	CAN	LEO	21.26	12.43	SAG	12.05	23.05	TAU	GEM	09.16	06.11	2
3	GEM	09.46	LEO	LIB	SCO	02.29	AQU	ARI	19.08	13.14	LEO	VIR	3
4	14.56	LEO	04.13	LIB	16.05	CAP	12.07	ARI	GEM	CAN	21.57	18.23	4
5	CAN	21.22	VIR	03.57	SAG	02.44	PIS	03.33	GEM	CAN	VIR	LIB	5
6	CAN	VIR	13.40	SCO	17.54	AQU	14.47	TAU	05.29	01.12	VIR	LIB	6
7	03.30	VIR	LIB	08.21	CAP	04.19	ARI	11.49	CAN	LEO	09.29	03.39	7
8	LEO	07.30	21.05	SAG	19.39	PIS	20.43	GEM	17.54	13.49	LIB	SCO	8
9	15.29	LIB	SCO	11.30	AQU	08.23	TAU	22.57	LEO	VIR	18.02	08.59	9
10	VIR	15.35	SCO	CAP	22.29	ARI	TAU	CAN	LEO	VIR	SCO	SAG	10
11	VIR	SCO	02.32	14.09	PIS	15.11	05.52	CAN	01.00	23.27	23.27	11.15	11
12	01.55	20.58	SAG	AQU	PIS	TAU	GEM	11.29	VIR	LIB	SAG	CAP	12
13	LIB	SAG	06.08	17.00	03.00	TAU	17.08	LEO	17.51	09.46	SAG	12.14	13
14	09.30	23.30	CAP	PIS	ARI	00.16	CAN	LEO	LIB	SCO	02.44	AQU	14
15	SCO	CAP	08.15	20.43	09.25	GEM	CAN	00.07	LIB	16.07	CAP	13.44	15
16	13.25	CAP	AQU	ARI	TAU	11.08	05.31	VIR	03.20	SAG	05.14	PIS	16
17	SAG	00.01	09.50	ARI	17.48	CAN	LEO	11.55	SCO	20.37	AQU	16.55	17
18	14.07	AQU	PIS	02.05	GEM	23.22	18.16	LIB	10.31	CAP	08.00	ARI	18
19	CAP	00.09	12.15	TAU	GEM	LEO	VIR	21.50	SAG	23.51	PIS	22.10	19
20	13.15	PIS	ARI	09.54	04.16	LEO	VIR	SCO	15.12	AQU	11.34	TAU	20
21	AQU	01.58	16.59	GEM	CAN	12.07	06.14	SCO	CAP	AQU	ARI	TAU	21
22	13.02	ARI	TAU	20.25	16.28	VIR	LIB	04.38	17.39	02.22	16.12	05.17	22
23	PIS	07.08	TAU	CAN	LEO	23.37	15.43	SAG	AQU	PIS	TAU	GEM	23
24	15.37	TAU	00.59	CAN	LEO	LIB	SCO	08.22	18.43	04.50	22.20	14.14	24
25	ARI	16.14	GEM	08.44	04.58	LIB	21.24	CAP	PIS	ARI	GEM	CAN	25
26	22.16	GEM	12.06	LEO	VIR	07.54	SAG	09.10	19.46	08.11	GEM	CAN	26
27	TAU	GEM	CAN	20.49	15.33	SCO	23.17	AQU	ARI	TAU	06.37	01.09	27
28	TAU	04.10	CAN	VIR	LIB	12.01	CAP	08.49	22.24	13.34	CAN	LEO	28
29	08.43	CAN	00.37	VIR	22.30	SAG	22.47	PIS	TAU	GEM	17.30	13.45	29
30	GEM		LEO	06.27	SCO	12.47	AQU	09.15	TAU	21.56	LEO	VIR	30
31	21.11		12.15		SCO		22.00	ARI		CAN		VIR	31

SUN

mth	dy	time → sign
JAN	1	00.00 → CAP
JAN	20	00.41 → AQU
FEB	18	14.55 → PIS
MAR	20	13.53 → ARI
APR	20	01.03 → TAU
MAY	21	00.14 → GEM
JUN	21	08.20 → CAN
JUL	22	19.12 → LEO
AUG	23	02.19 → VIR
SEP	22	23.54 → LIB
OCT	23	09.15 → SCO
NOV	22	06.46 → SAG
DEC	21	20.05 → CAP

MERCURY

mth	dy	time → sign
JAN	1	00.00 → CAP
FEB	9	05.50 → AQU
FEB	28	03.51 → PIS
MAR	16	04.14 → ARI
APR	1	13.45 → TAU
MAY	5	01.44 → ARI
MAY	12	10.26 → TAU
JUN	8	23.22 → GEM
JUN	23	20.41 → CAN
JUL	8	05.27 → LEO
JUL	27	00.46 → VIR
OCT	2	05.38 → LIB
OCT	19	12.06 → SCO
NOV	7	17.43 → SAG
NOV	30	19.11 → CAP
DEC	13	18.03 → SAG

VENUS

mth	dy	time → sign
JAN	1	00.00 → SAG
JAN	10	05.35 → CAP
FEB	3	04.28 → AQU
FEB	27	04.03 → PIS
MAR	23	05.26 → ARI
APR	16	09.44 → TAU
MAY	10	17.20 → GEM
JUN	4	04.17 → CAN
JUN	28	18.38 → LEO
JUL	23	13.12 → VIR
AUG	17	14.32 → LIB
SEP	12	02.18 → SCO
OCT	8	08.25 → SAG
NOV	5	08.53 → CAP
DEC	12	04.39 → AQU

MARS

mth	dy	time → sign
JAN	1	00.00 → VIR
JAN	3	08.23 → LIB
MAR	8	19.32 → VIR
JUN	19	08.21 → LIB
AUG	14	08.22 → SCO
SEP	28	22.15 → SAG
NOV	9	05.26 → CAP
DEC	18	06.30 → AQU

SATURN

mth	dy	time → sign
JAN	1	00.00 → ARI

JUPITER

mth	dy	time → sign
JAN	1	00.00 → CAP
JAN	21	15.25 → AQU

MOON

dy	jan	feb	mar	apr	may	jun	jul	aug	sep	oct	nov	dec	dy
1	02.32	SCO	12.01	CAP	12.50	ARI	11.35	CAN	04.27	LIB	SCO	18.38	1
2	LIB	04.51	SAG	03.59	PIS	00.39	GEM	10.27	VIR	LIB	04.27	CAP	2
3	13.02	SAG	17.39	AQU	14.59	TAU	18.33	LEO	17.30	11.57	SAG	23.58	3
4	SCO	08.45	CAP	05.42	ARI	04.55	CAN	22.15	LIB	SCO	12.31	AQU	4
5	19.27	CAP	19.55	PIS	17.04	GEM	CAN	VIR	LIB	22.43	CAP	AQU	5
6	SAG	09.21	AQU	06.19	TAU	11.02	03.45	VIR	06.10	SAG	18.33	04.07	6
7	21.55	AQU	19.57	ARI	20.21	CAN	LEO	11.17	SCO	SAG	AQU	PIS	7
8	CAP	08.34	PIS	07.20	GEM	19.58	15.22	LIB	16.54	07.04	22.35	07.24	8
9	22.00	PIS	19.33	TAU	GEM	LEO	VIR	23.50	SAG	CAP	PIS	ARI	9
10	AQU	08.29	ARI	10.28	CAN	LEO	VIR	SCO	SAG	12.29	PIS	10.00	10
11	21.51	ARI	20.37	GEM	CAN	07.43	04.21	SCO	00.23	AQU	00.44	TAU	11
12	PIS	10.56	TAU	17.03	11.33	VIR	LIB	09.45	CAP	14.59	ARI	12.35	12
13	23.22	TAU	TAU	CAN	LEO	20.35	16.20	SAG	04.10	PIS	01.45	GEM	13
14	ARI	16.53	00.48	CAN	23.43	LIB	SCO	15.42	AQU	15.25	TAU	16.25	14
15	ARI	GEM	GEM	03.22	VIR	LIB	SCO	CAP	04.59	ARI	03.05	CAN	15
16	03.40	GEM	08.51	LEO	VIR	07.51	01.02	17.58	PIS	15.16	GEM	22.58	16
17	TAU	02.13	CAN	16.00	12.27	SCO	SAG	AQU	04.25	TAU	06.32	LEO	17
18	10.53	CAN	20.08	VIR	LIB	15.39	05.45	18.01	ARI	16.26	CAN	LEO	18
19	GEM	13.52	LEO	VIR	23.12	SAG	CAP	PIS	04.21	GEM	13.38	09.00	19
20	20.29	LEO	LEO	04.36	SCO	20.02	07.29	17.45	TAU	20.45	LEO	VIR	20
21	CAN	LEO	08.59	LIB	SCO	CAP	AQU	ARI	06.38	CAN	LEO	21.35	21
22	CAN	02.38	VIR	15.19	06.51	22.20	08.00	18.57	GEM	CAN	00.33	LIB	22
23	07.50	VIR	21.35	SCO	SAG	AQU	PIS	TAU	12.33	05.10	VIR	LIB	23
24	LEO	15.23	LIB	23.32	11.51	AQU	09.03	22.56	CAN	LEO	13.29	10.07	24
25	20.26	LIB	LIB	SAG	CAP	00.09	ARI	GEM	22.12	16.59	LIB	SCO	25
26	VIR	LIB	08.42	SAG	15.20	PIS	11.53	GEM	LEO	VIR	LIB	20.07	26
27	VIR	02.57	SCO	05.32	AQU	02.38	TAU	06.11	LEO	VIR	01.43	SAG	27
28	09.21	SCO	17.40	CAP	18.18	ARI	17.04	CAN	10.27	06.05	SCO	SAG	28
29	LIB		SAG	09.50	PIS	06.23	GEM	16.19	VIR	LIB	11.28	02.48	29
30	20.48		SAG	AQU	21.18	TAU	GEM	LEO	23.32	18.15	SAG	CAP	30
31	SCO		00.07		ARI		00.38	LEO		SCO		06.58	31

SUN

mth	dy	time → sign
JAN	1	00.00 → CAP
JAN	20	06.44 → AQU
FEB	18	20.55 → PIS
MAR	20	19.54 → ARI
APR	20	06.57 → TAU
MAY	21	06.02 → GEM
JUN	21	14.03 → CAN
JUL	23	00.52 → LEO
AUG	23	07.57 → VIR
SEP	23	05.34 → LIB
OCT	23	14.56 → SCO
NOV	22	12.31 → SAG
DEC	22	01.55 → CAP

MERCURY

mth	dy	time → sign
JAN	1	00.00 → SAG
JAN	12	16.23 → CAP
FEB	2	15.16 → AQU
FEB	20	10.22 → PIS
MAR	8	08.25 → ARI
MAY	15	02.10 → TAU
JUN	1	08.06 → GEM
JUN	15	05.33 → CAN
JUN	30	23.52 → LEO
SEP	8	01.56 → VIR
SEP	24	10.14 → LIB
OCT	12	02.45 → SCO
NOV	1	16.03 → SAG

VENUS

mth	dy	time → sign
JAN	1	00.00 → AQU
JAN	9	21.06 → CAP
MAR	4	16.14 → AQU
APR	6	05.36 → PIS
MAY	3	19.17 → ARI
MAY	29	23.32 → TAU
JUN	24	12.24 → GEM
JUL	19	15.14 → CAN
AUG	13	09.20 → LEO
SEP	6	19.26 → VIR
SEP	30	23.16 → LIB
OCT	24	23.03 → SCO
NOV	17	21.04 → SAG
DEC	11	18.33 → CAP

MARS

mth	dy	time → sign
JAN	1	00.00 → AQU
JAN	25	09.12 → PIS
MAR	4	16.10 → ARI
APR	13	01.21 → TAU
MAY	24	03.32 → GEM
JUL	6	09.09 → CAN
AUG	20	19.08 → LEO
OCT	7	12.17 → VIR
NOV	27	10.00 → LIB

SATURN

mth	dy	time → sign
JAN	1	00.00 → ARI
JUN	9	06.24 → TAU
OCT	25	18.55 → ARI

JUPITER

mth	dy	time → sign
JAN	1	00.00 → AQU
FEB	4	10.37 → PIS

MOON

dy	jan	feb	mar	apr	may	jun	jul	aug	sep	oct	nov	dec	dy
1	AQU	ARI	ARI	GEM	CAN	03.21	LIB	SCO	02.23	AQU	11.27	TAU	1
2	09.56	21.25	05.00	19.10	09.49	VIR	LIB	07.48	CAP	23.23	ARI	21.30	2
3	PIS	TAU	TAU	CAN	LEO	15.17	11.45	SAG	09.21	PIS	11.12	GEM	3
4	12.43	TAU	07.15	CAN	19.47	LIB	SCO	17.18	AQU	PIS	TAU	21.28	4
5	ARI	01.09	GEM	02.36	VIR	LIB	23.24	CAP	12.48	0032>ARI	10.11	CAN	5
6	15.52	GEM	12.27	LEO	VIR	04.06	SAG	23.31	PIS	23.57	GEM	23.55	6
7	TAU	06.57	CAN	13.25	08.19	SCO	SAG	AQU	13.52	TAU	10.39	LEO	7
8	19.42	CAN	20.46	VIR	LIB	15.34	08.27	AQU	ARI	23.44	CAN	LEO	8
9	GEM	14.57	LEO	VIR	21.10	SAG	CAP	03.04	14.16	GEM	14.33	06.21	9
10	GEM	LEO	LEO	02.04	SCO	SAG	14.52	PIS	TAU	GEM	LEO	VIR	10
11	00.43	LEO	07.35	LIB	SCO	00.50	AQU	05.10	15.40	01.48	22.37	16.43	11
12	CAN	01.09	VIR	14.56	08.48	CAP	19.22	ARI	GEM	CAN	VIR	LIB	12
13	07.45	VIR	19.58	SCO	SAG	08.03	PIS	07.04	19.20	07.25	VIR	LIB	13
14	LEO	13.17	LIB	SCO	18.39	AQU	22.45	TAU	CAN	LEO	09.58	05.16	14
15	17.31	LIB	LIB	02.52	CAP	13.31	ARI	09.46	CAN	16.32	LIB	SCO	15
16	VIR	LIB	08.51	SAG	CAP	PIS	ARI	GEM	01.48	VIR	22.41	17.47	16
17	VIR	02.13	SCO	13.05	02.30	17.23	01.33	13.55	LEO	VIR	SCO	SAG	17
18	05.44	SCO	20.56	CAP	AQU	ARI	TAU	CAN	10.52	04.02	SCO	SAG	18
19	LIB	13.56	SAG	20.41	08.03	19.47	04.18	20.01	VIR	LIB	11.13	04.55	19
20	18.34	SAG	SAG	AQU	PIS	TAU	GEM	LEO	21.57	16.36	SAG	CAP	20
21	SCO	22.30	06.43	AQU	11.06	21.26	07.43	LEO	LIB	SCO	22.45	14.17	21
22	SCO	CAP	CAP	01.06	ARI	GEM	CAN	04.21	LIB	SCO	CAP	AQU	22
23	05.25	CAP	13.02	PIS	12.06	23.39	12.48	VIR	10.22	05.16	CAP	21.45	23
24	SAG	03.10	AQU	02.31	TAU	CAN	LEO	15.02	SCO	SAG	08.43	PIS	24
25	12.39	AQU	15.43	ARI	12.25	CAN	20.34	LIB	23.05	17.05	AQU	PIS	25
26	CAP	04.42	PIS	02.09	GEM	04.04	VIR	LIB	SAG	CAP	16.14	03.04	26
27	16.27	PIS	15.49	TAU	13.58	LEO	VIR	03.25	SAG	CAP	PIS	ARI	27
28	AQU	04.42	ARI	01.55	CAN	11.54	07.14	SCO	10.30	02.44	20.34	06.05	28
29	18.08		15.06	GEM	18.38	VIR	LIB	15.55	CAP	AQU	ARI	TAU	29
30	PIS		TAU	03.57	LEO	23.05	19.44	SAG	18.53	08.58	21.53	07.22	30
31	19.21		15.37		LEO		SCO	SAG		PIS		GEM	31

SUN

mth	dy	time → sign
JAN	1	00.00 → CAP
JAN	20	12.34 → AQU
FEB	19	02.44 → PIS
MAR	21	01.43 → ARI
APR	20	12.43 → TAU
MAY	21	11.50 → GEM
JUN	21	19.49 → CAN
JUL	23	06.42 → LEO
AUG	23	13.51 → VIR
SEP	23	11.33 → LIB
OCT	23	20.52 → SCO
NOV	22	18.27 → SAG
DEC	22	07.44 → CAP

MERCURY

mth	dy	time → sign
JAN	1	00.00 → SAG
JAN	7	02.01 → CAP
JAN	26	09.32 → AQU
FEB	12	15.29 → PIS
MAR	2	22.54 → ARI
MAR	18	09.23 → PIS
APR	17	22.07 → ARI
MAY	8	21.22 → TAU
MAY	23	21.23 → GEM
JUN	7	00.16 → CAN
JUN	26	15.39 → LEO
JUL	31	18.43 → CAN
AUG	11	04.25 → LEO
AUG	31	15.12 → VIR
SEP	16	12.53 → LIB
OCT	5	05.11 → SCO
OCT	30	20.08 → SAG
NOV	9	20.10 → SCO
DEC	11	02.09 → SAG
DEC	31	06.50 → CAP

VENUS

mth	dy	time → sign
JAN	1	00.00 → CAP
JAN	4	16.23 → AQU
JAN	28	16.17 → PIS
FEB	21	20.46 → ARI
MAR	18	09.57 → TAU
APR	12	13.17 → GEM
MAY	8	16.26 → CAN
JUN	5	21.25 → LEO
JUL	12	15.16 → VIR
AUG	15	14.12 → LEO
OCT	7	16.54 → VIR
NOV	9	02.18 → LIB
DEC	5	22.42 → SCO
DEC	31	04.52 → SAG

MARS

mth	dy	time → sign
JAN	1	00.00 → LIB
JAN	26	11.37 → SCO
MAY	5	21.27 → LIB
JUL	5	03.50 → SCO
SEP	2	19.18 → SAG
OCT	17	01.30 → CAP
NOV	26	06.43 → AQU

SATURN

mth	dy	time → sign
JAN	1	00.00 → ARI
MAR	1	01.38 → TAU

JUPITER

mth	dy	time → sign
JAN	1	00.00 → PIS
FEB	13	01.35 → ARI
JUN	28	09.41 → TAU
OCT	23	05.58 → ARI

MOON

dy	jan	feb	mar	apr	may	jun	jul	aug	sep	oct	nov	dec	dy
1	08.15	LEO	10.05	LIB	SCO	02.06	AQU	16.47	TAU	13.31	LEO	17.29	1
2	CAN	01.37	VIR	12.49	07.36	CAP	AQU	ARI	05.25	CAN	04.07	LIB	2
3	10.31	VIR	18.34	SCO	SAG	13.37	04.34	21.09	VIR	17.13	VIR	LIB	3
4	LEO	09.56	LIB	SCO	20.12	AQU	PIS	TAU	08.10	LEO	11.57	03.35	4
5	15.49	LIB	LIB	01.07	CAP	23.01	11.21	23.57	CAN	22.40	LIB	SCO	5
6	VIR	21.06	05.22	SAG	CAP	PIS	ARI	GEM	11.29	VIR	21.46	15.27	6
7	VIR	SCO	SCO	13.39	07.40	PIS	15.22	GEM	LEO	SCO	SCO	SAG	7
8	00.53	SCO	17.46	CAP	AQU	05.08	TAU	01.53	15.57	05.52	SCO	SAG	8
9	LIB	09.38	SAG	CAP	16.16	ARI	17.00	CAN	VIR	LIB	09.15	04.14	9
10	12.49	SAG	SAG	00.24	PIS	07.44	GEM	03.55	22.16	15.01	SAG	CAP	10
11	SCO	21.10	05.54	AQU	20.53	TAU	17.27	LEO	LIB	SCO	22.00	16.59	11
12	SCO	CAP	CAP	07.35	ARI	07.48	CAN	07.22	LIB	SCO	CAP	AQU	12
13	01.23	CAP	15.32	PIS	21.56	GEM	18.26	VIR	07.08	02.18	CAP	AQU	13
14	SAG	05.57	AQU	10.46	TAU	07.14	LEO	13.24	SCO	SAG	10.46	04.18	14
15	12.29	AQU	21.30	ARI	21.07	CAN	21.39	LIB	18.35	15.04	AQU	PIS	15
16	CAP	11.40	PIS	11.07	GEM	08.07	VIR	22.40	SAG	CAP	21.21	12.30	16
17	21.11	PIS	PIS	TAU	20.39	LEO	VIR	SCO	SAG	CAP	PIS	ARI	17
18	AQU	15.06	00.13	10.39	CAN	12.12	04.19	SCO	07.13	03.17	PIS	16.45	18
19	AQU	ARI	ARI	GEM	22.37	VIR	LIB	10.32	CAP	AQU	03.57	TAU	19
20	03.40	17.29	01.09	11.27	LEO	20.10	14.30	SAG	18.38	12.33	ARI	17.39	20
21	PIS	TAU	TAU	CAN	LEO	LIB	SCO	22.59	AQU	PIS	06.26	GEM	21
22	08.25	19.54	02.05	15.06	04.15	LIB	SCO	CAP	AQU	17.42	TAU	16.52	22
23	ARI	GEM	GEM	LEO	VIR	07.18	02.48	CAP	02.51	ARI	06.14	CAN	23
24	11.52	23.09	04.33	22.04	13.29	SCO	SAG	09.49	PIS	19.25	GEM	16.32	24
25	TAU	CAN	CAN	VIR	LIB	19.51	15.08	AQU	07.34	TAU	05.29	LEO	25
26	14.29	CAN	09.22	VIR	LIB	SAG	CAP	17.50	ARI	19.33	CAN	18.34	26
27	GEM	03.44	LEO	07.46	01.05	SAG	CAP	PIS	09.51	GEM	06.19	VIR	27
28	16.57	LEO	16.34	LIB	SCO	08.12	01.54	23.09	TAU	20.09	LEO	VIR	28
29	CAN		VIR	19.13	13.37	CAP	AQU	ARI	11.21	CAN	10.11	00.14	29
30	20.16		VIR	SCO	SAG	19.19	10.27	ARI	GEM	22.47	VIR	LIB	30
31	LEO		01.49		SAG		PIS	02.41		LEO		09.36	31

SUN

mth	dy	time	→ sign
JAN	1	00.00	→ CAP
JAN	20	18.25	→ AQU
FEB	19	08.31	→ PIS
MAR	20	07.37	→ ARI
APR	19	18.42	→ TAU
MAY	20	17.49	→ GEM
JUN	21	01.45	→ CAN
JUL	22	12.43	→ LEO
AUG	22	19.47	→ VIR
SEP	22	17.25	→ LIB
OCT	23	02.46	→ SCO
NOV	22	00.16	→ SAG
DEC	21	13.34	→ CAP

MERCURY

mth	dy	time	→ sign
JAN	1	00.00	→ CAP
JAN	18	22.22	→ AQU
FEB	5	08.09	→ PIS
APR	13	00.14	→ ARI
APR	30	03.53	→ TAU
MAY	14	07.13	→ GEM
MAY	30	04.27	→ CAN
AUG	7	05.45	→ LEO
AUG	22	10.11	→ VIR
SEP	7	22.24	→ LIB
SEP	28	13.28	→ SCO
NOV	7	07.25	→ LIB
NOV	8	21.45	→ SCO
DEC	3	20.26	→ SAG
DEC	23	02.06	→ CAP

VENUS

mth	dy	time	→ sign
JAN	1	00.00	→ SAG
JAN	24	19.56	→ CAP
FEB	18	04.45	→ AQU
MAR	13	11.36	→ PIS
APR	6	18.36	→ ARI
MAY	1	02.47	→ TAU
MAY	25	12.15	→ GEM
JUN	18	22.18	→ CAN
JUL	13	08.03	→ LEO
AUG	6	17.33	→ VIR
AUG	31	03.36	→ LIB
SEP	24	15.28	→ SCO
OCT	19	06.16	→ SAG
NOV	13	02.11	→ CAP
DEC	8	08.46	→ AQU

MARS

mth	dy	time	→ sign
JAN	1	00.00	→ AQU
JAN	4	03.13	→ PIS
FEB	12	01.18	→ ARI
MAR	23	01.33	→ TAU
MAY	3	19.26	→ GEM
JUN	16	12.45	→ CAN
AUG	1	01.30	→ LEO
SEP	17	00.25	→ VIR
NOV	4	02.19	→ LIB
DEC	23	14.42	→ SCO

SATURN

mth	dy	time	→ sign
JAN	1	00.00	→ TAU
AUG	10	02.36	→ GEM
OCT	16	00.55	→ TAU

JUPITER

mth	dy	time	→ sign
JAN	1	00.00	→ ARI
FEB	14	21.31	→ TAU
JUN	30	07.22	→ GEM

MOON

dy	jan	feb	mar	apr	may	jun	jul	aug	sep	oct	nov	dec	dy
1	SCO	17.10	CAP	08.12	00.55	16.34	03.09	13.27	LIB	22.50	CAP	AQU	1
2	21.32	CAP	13.14	PIS	ARI	GEM	CAN	VIR	05.55	SAG	CAP	AQU	2
3	SAG	CAP	AQU	15.22	04.54	16.30	02.38	15.31	SCO	SAG	06.41	03.23	3
4	SAG	05.31	23.30	ARI	TAU	CAN	LEO	LIB	14.08	09.42	AQU	PIS	4
5	10.24	AQU	PIS	19.29	06.23	16.45	03.19	21.04	SAG	CAP	19.13	14.17	5
6	CAP	16.02	PIS	TAU	GEM	LEO	VIR	SCO	SAG	22.33	PIS	ARI	6
7	22.53	PIS	06.54	21.58	07.14	18.57	06.47	SCO	01.47	AQU	PIS	21.27	7
8	AQU	PIS	ARI	GEM	CAN	VIR	LIB	06.30	CAP	AQU	05.02	TAU	8
9	AQU	00.17	12.01	GEM	09.01	23.59	13.48	SAG	14.45	10.36	ARI	TAU	9
10	09.59	ARI	TAU	00.16	LEO	LIB	SCO	18.44	AQU	PIS	11.12	00.50	10
11	PIS	06.21	15.46	CAN	12.41	LIB	SCO	CAP	AQU	19.51	TAU	GEM	11
12	18.48	TAU	GEM	03.16	VIR	07.55	00.06	CAP	02.34	ARI	14.27	01.49	12
13	ARI	10.23	18.51	LEO	18.27	SCO	SAG	07.43	PIS	ARI	GEM	CAN	13
14	ARI	GEM	CAN	07.19	LIB	18.18	12.28	AQU	12.00	02.06	16.21	02.09	14
15	00.38	12.45	21.43	VIR	LIB	SAG	CAP	19.41	ARI	TAU	CAN	LEO	15
16	TAU	CAN	LEO	12.36	02.16	SAG	CAP	PIS	19.05	06.19	18.19	03.30	16
17	03.25	14.11	LEO	LIB	SCO	06.27	01.27	PIS	TAU	GEM	LEO	VIR	17
18	GEM	LEO	00.48	19.35	12.09	CAP	AQU	05.44	TAU	09.37	21.15	07.01	18
19	04.01	15.53	VIR	SCO	SAG	19.26	13.44	ARI	00.22	CAN	VIR	LIB	19
20	CAN	VIR	04.57	SCO	SAG	AQU	PIS	13.31	GEM	12.42	VIR	13.12	20
21	03.58	19.21	LIB	04.58	00.01	AQU	PIS	TAU	04.16	LEO	01.35	SCO	21
22	LEO	LIB	11.17	SAG	CAP	07.52	00.09	18.55	CAN	15.52	LIB	21.57	22
23	05.07	LIB	SCO	16.47	13.00	PIS	ARI	GEM	07.00	VIR	07.33	SAG	23
24	VIR	01.58	20.43	CAP	AQU	17.56	07.44	22.00	LEO	19.30	SCO	SAG	24
25	09.09	SCO	SAG	CAP	AQU	ARI	TAU	CAN	09.02	LIB	15.33	08.54	25
26	LIB	12.10	SAG	05.42	01.07	ARI	12.02	23.17	VIR	LIB	SAG	CAP	26
27	17.01	SAG	08.51	AQU	PIS	00.19	GEM	LEO	11.22	00.23	SAG	21.25	27
28	SCO	SAG	CAP	17.06	10.08	TAU	13.30	23.55	LIB	SCO	01.57	AQU	28
29	SCO	00.45	21.34	PIS	ARI	02.59	CAN	VIR	15.30	07.40	CAP	AQU	29
30	04.18		SAG	PIS	15.02	GEM	13.24	VIR	SCO	SAG	14.26	10.27	30
31	SAG		AQU		TAU		LEO	01.33		18.02		PIS	31

The Sun, Moon and Inner Planets Through the Twelve Signs of the Zodiac

THE SUN

Keyword: LIVING

The Sun is the CENTRE, HEART and LIFE-GIVING FORCE of our Solar System. So, astrologically, your Sun-Sign describes the CENTRE OF YOUR BEING — your WILL; what dwells in or lies close to your HEART and what gives your LIFE a SENSE OF CREATIVE PURPOSE. The Sun is symbolic of your SPIRIT.

Negative expressions of the Sun are traits such as CONCEIT and EGOTISM, according to which you attach too much or the wrong sort of IMPORTANCE to the qualities of the Sign in which your Sun is placed.

The Sun is the most important astrological energy because all of the Planets (including the Moon) revolve around it and draw their life from it. And so your Sun-Sign nature affects and VITALIZES your Moon-Sign and all your Planet-Sign positions. Expressing the Solar Will comes more naturally to males, so if you are female you may be attracted to males who embody your Sun-Sign qualities. Sooner or later, through life's experiences and relationships, you come to realize and to express consciously the power and nature of your OWN INDIVIDUALITY.

THE SUN IN ARIES

ESSENCE

Living through Doing
The Pioneer • The Champion

As the first Sign of the Zodiac, your role as an Arian is simply to get something started, which is why the Sun is Exalted in Aries, for here the Will has free rein to express itself. You could be doing this in some form of leadership, or by forcing others to look at themselves in a new way. You could accomplish this either consciously, by carrying out a deliberate act in the name of some cause, or unconsciously, by making it hard for others to relate to you as you are.

It is preferable to be consciously aware of your pioneering streak, for in this way not only do you enjoy life more, but you avoid feeling pushed around by others. And with Aries it's more or less a case of push or be pushed. This can be objectionable to others at times, but you must have the freedom to act, rather than just thinking about it and getting pent-up in the process. At all costs you need to avoid negative emotions like resentment, regret and self-pity, for they would deny you what is essential to your Arian nature: Straightforwardness.

As an Arian, you like a challenge that will stir you to action. This challenge may just be frustration; or at a more evolved and conscious level, you may know what or whom you're fighting for. If you don't, then ask yourself until you have an answer. An Arian without a direction in which to head or a cause to champion is more like a sheep than a Ram. The quest is all.

You should not be afraid to be forceful, for this is central to your nature. If you are afraid, then look for negative examples of force in your personal history, such as violence or abuse from others, or a tradition that negated independence and personal initiative, for this could have inhibited your natural urge to go forward into life in a direct and uncomplicated fashion. Conversely, such bad influences could also have led you to be overly forceful, or to be unsympathetic to your own needs and sensitivity. Much as you are the Ram, there is still the Lamb in you, which means that at times you would attain your goals more easily by gently falling in with the demands of a given social situation, rather than getting your horns entangled in something bigger and more powerful than yourself. This of course takes patience, the acquiring of which is definitely your greatest achievement – along with a sense of the strength of your inner softness.

You like extremes – physical, emotional and mental – and are all the better for experiencing them; but if your extremism goes too far beyond social acceptability, then expect to be extremely lonely. At your Arian best, you can inject new life into relationships and enterprises. Ever emerging like a fountain-head into the arena of life, you lead others from darkness into light.

LIKES
Action • Coming first • Challenges
Championing causes • The spur of the moment

DISLIKES
Waiting around • Admitting defeat
Lack of opposition • Tyranny • Taking advice

If you are a woman, this could be the kind of man to whom you are attracted – but it is really you, so realize it and express it.

THE SUN IN ARIES

TRANSFORMER

POSITIVE	NEGATIVE
Assertive Go-getting Crusading Enthusiastic	Aggressive Unreflective Fanatical Arrogant
Direct Frank One-pointed Straightforward	Blunt Tactless Blind to side-issues Simplistic
Spontaneous Energetic Stimulating Courageous	Impatient Restless Irritating Foolhardy
Good starter Warrior caste Leader type Confident	Bad finisher Argumentative Unco-operative Pompous
Independent Strong willed Single-minded Original being	Self-centred Headstrong Thoughtless Intolerant

SOLUTION	PROBLEM
Know that freedom and individuality are found in the narrowest passes and the loneliest places.	Feeling alone, with no external point of reference or source of comfort.
See your role as the ideas person, then inspire the other(s) to carry them through.	Projects that come to nothing. Partnerships that come to blows.
What springs from your body or mind is only as good as what dwells in your heart.	Lacking coherence and direction. Failing to contemplate, posing as decisiveness.
If you truly have a point, then they'll come back for more. If you don't – they won't!	Being deserted by others because they cannot make you notice them and their feelings any other way.
Learn to look before you leap, which means first finding out what you wish to make happen.	Always tripping over yourself, inviting conflict and harsh treatment. Getting deflated.

If you find yourself on the receiving end of negative traits, it is because you are not expressing the opposing positive traits.

125

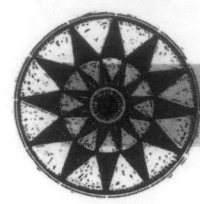

THE SUN IN TAURUS

ESSENCE

Living through Stabilizing
Mother Nature's Own • Beauty and the Beast

No sign is closer to the Earth than Taurus the Bull. It is as if the whole purpose of your Taurean Life is to maintain the Stability of Earthly things. However, you can go wrong by interpreting this only to mean having a substantial amount of money and possessions, or being assured of a predictable future in a purely tangible world. In fact, your main possession as a Taurean is your sense of Earthly harmony and wholesomeness. When you truly get in touch with this sense, you need worry no longer about blindly reassuring yourself with possessions and securities, for you will then know and feel that this sense, this art, attracts these very things.

Another of your solid virtues is the ability to endure change, while at the same time conserving those habits and traditions that are so important to a healthy and wholesome physical life. You have to be careful not to let this talent become blunted merely into the ability to resist change – even when it is for the good. Your broad Taurean back can carry more than you sometimes believe.

Taurus is the great provider. This is not just in the material sense, but more essentially it is your calm and unruffled vibration, along with a well-vitalized body, that can work wonders on the physical and emotional state of others, be it through sensuous affection, massage, good living, artistic expression, or just your sheer physical presence that emanates that aura of stability, that feeling that the Earth and Heaven are in their respective and proper places.

However, the other side of your Earthy wisdom and natural docility is probably your most dangerous state, that of sluggishness, inertia and grossness – the Beast – born of a fear of change or of what you cannot handle. When you fall into this state, it is only a matter of time before you attract someone or something that will make such immobility uncomfortable and compromising. It is then that a change has to be made, and something let go of. When you make such a change, you then discover how much more stable things become as a result!

Ultimately, as a Taurean, you have to discover your truest, deepest and highest values. This is symbolized by ascending terraces of sweeter and sweeter clover. When you know what is truly valuable, you are no longer chained to people and to things that have to do with lesser values. The greatest indication of value is beauty, which cannot be owned, but only appreciated. And as a Taurean you certainly know how to appreciate beauty, not only in the sense of being aware of its value, but also through implanting and increasing its value in the hearts and minds of others.

LIKES	**DISLIKES**
Stability • Being attracted • Things natural	Disruption • Being pushed • Synthetics
Time to ponder • Comfort and pleasure	Being hurried • Sensory deprivation

If you are a woman, this could be the kind of man to whom you are attracted – but it is really you, so realize it and express it.

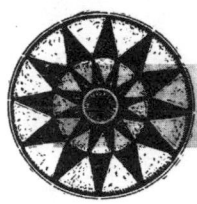

THE SUN IN TAURUS

TRANSFORMER

POSITIVE	NEGATIVE
Earthy Sensuous/artistic Productive Practical provider	Materialistic Hedonistic Gross and extravagant Prodigal
Steadfast and stable Unruffled and calm Even-tempered Soothing	Plodding and ponderous Sluggish and lazy Boneheaded Boring
Self-trusting Loyal Persevering Trustworthy	Self-satisfied Possessive Stubborn Bigoted/fanatical
Appreciative Admiring Affectionate Aesthetic	Self-gratifying Idolatrous Lecherous Aloof
Physically comforting Magnetically healing Attractive	Unaware of 'unseen' Sucker for good looks Easily attached
You are not just a body, but a set of vibrations that both attracts and is attracted.	Feeling that you are being manipulated, led a dance, taken for what you've got.
Discover your truest and highest values, then realize how well you can express them physically.	The world of the senses feels less and less appealing and more and more appalling.
You have the power to attract faithfulness, but being unable to let go signifies a lack of faith.	Fear of loss. Feeling of jealousy, of beliefs and/or followers turning against you.
Realize that during and after periods of stress you can be a source of reassurance to others.	Feeling of inertia and uneasiness. Fear of change. Others get bored and impatient with you.
Know that the value of Earthly things is simply that they serve to keep bodies happy and healthy.	Feelings of self-disgust and dissatisfaction, of life lacking any meaning. Addicted to sensations.
SOLUTION	PROBLEM

If you find yourself on the receiving end of negative traits, it is because you are not expressing the opposing positive traits.

THE SUN IN GEMINI

ESSENCE

Living through Communicating
The Contact-Maker ● Forever Young

Gemini may be likened to blossom and to the playful spring breezes that spread its petals hither and thither. Your touch is light but effective, broadcasting and collecting wit and knowledge over a wide area – although it can be shortlasting and superficial.

Gemini is famous for its dualistic or even contrary nature. This can be hugely fascinating because word and mind play is an endless source of amusement to you as synchronous events and paradoxical paradigms abound. On the other hand, it can only amount to a sort of psychological doodling which achieves nothing more than pushing air and nerve cells around. What your talent is really intended for is getting the message and putting it across.

You are aiming to avoid the logic trap of 'this' as opposed to 'that', and are potentially able to bridge the gap between two extremes, be they people, philosophies, beliefs, character traits or whatever. This you do by zipping back and forth between them with such speed and alacrity that the differences become like the two sides of a spinning coin. Intuitively, you see no difference between any one thing and another – everything is equally interesting (a favourite word!). Because of this, Gemini is probably the least prejudiced of all the Signs – and one of the friendliest.

Mythologically, the Heavenly Twins Castor and Pollux each divided their time between living in Heaven and on Earth. This means that as a Geminian, you can mentally dwell in pure abstraction, and at the same time be able to turn your hand to the most mundane of tasks. You are nothing if not versatile.

Other important dualities of Gemini are those of the Magician/Mimic and the Rogue/Villain: the former uses the quickness of hand, eye and tongue to create wondrous effects and illusions; the latter merely employs nimble fingers and the gift of the gab to make a relatively small profit. You are also the Juggler. You can keep a tricky issue up in the air, postponing coming down to Earth almost indefinitely. Just when it seems that you are going to crash, you suddenly appear on the other side of the street – still juggling. However, you are not infallible, even though you could talk your way out of a document shredder!

The last word is that as a Geminian you have a very lively imagination, and you are therefore one of the most artistically creative Signs. Conversely true to form though, you can lack the imagination to see that using the imagination draws you into a closer intimacy with life itself – and getting deeply involved is the Twins' weakest suit. After all, they themselves got separated between Heaven and Earth. Yet the answer to your eternal Geminian question still lies in the imagination, not the brain.

LIKES	DISLIKES
Reading and talking ● Being on the move	Mental stagnation ● Being tied down
More than one interest ● The quirky and the unusual	Lack of interest/education ● Ruts that turn into graves
Novelty and variety	Yesterday's papers

If you are a woman, this could be the kind of man to whom you are attracted – but it is really you, so realize it and express it.

THE SUN IN GEMINI

TRANSFORMER

POSITIVE	NEGATIVE
Amusing Perceptive Witty Eloquent	Cheap Glib Sarcastic Chatterbox
Swift Ingenious Quick on uptake Mobile	Fly Devious Shifty Evasive
Versatile Flexible Adaptable Imaginative	Dabbler Two-faced Fickle Chases rainbows
Non-dogmatic Sees both sides Light touch Objective	Non-committal Indecisive Superficial Aloof
Acquisitive mind Clever Informative Resourceful	Blind to whole picture Inane Gossip Bluffer

There is a need out there for what you know and how you express it – so meet it!	Becoming a mine of useless information with conflicting views that amount to little.
Appreciate how refreshing your stereoscopic vision of life is to others.	Identity crises. Beset by feelings of insubstantiality. Troubled conscience.
Respect your own dreams, and avoid cutting corners in the pursuit of them.	Jack of all trades, master of none. Plans that come to nothing.
Others aren't as speedy as you and don't jump to the same unlikely conclusions.	Constantly looking over your shoulder. Feeling the world's designed to catch you out.
Pay attention to the value of what you say; how you say it looks after itself – admirably.	Feelings of being ignored or not being taken seriously.

SOLUTION	PROBLEM

If you find yourself on the receiving end of negative traits, it is because you are not expressing the opposing positive traits.

129

THE SUN IN CANCER

ESSENCE

Living through Nurturing
Hold on with Love • My Family is Humanity

Everything about the Sign of Cancer may be tracked down to the experience of birth: the instinct for survival; the attachment to the mother; the baby's soft sensitivity to the world into which it is being born, and the utter dependence upon the mercy of that world; the mother's sensitivity to that dependency and the fear born of it; the innate enthusiasm to succeed gloriously in this world, or, sheer resentment at ever having being born into the harsh reality of this world at all.

Behind all these feelings lie the most fundamental urges of your curious and dreamy Sign – those to protect, nourish and nurture. As a child, you, like everyone else, needed to receive protection, nourishment and nurturing, but a denial or shortage of them would be more damaging to Cancer in later life than to any other Sign. This is because you would continue, vainly, to look for a 'mother' in your adult life, or would overdo being a mother – smothering – by way of compensation. In either case an unhealthy fear of revealing your inner self to the outside world is produced, along with a need to blame others.

Esoterically, it is written that all Souls are first born on to Planet Earth in the Sign of Cancer, simply because they know intuitively that the Cancerian Will is the one most likely to find a way of being looked after in their new home. Cancer has been called the 'Lighthouse of Welcome', which is something the individual Cancerian would do well to become. When you seek to protect rather than just seek protection, your essential qualities of neediness, sympathy and emotional receptivity then become a recognition of where nourishment and care are needed, along with the motivation and method required to give and sustain them, rather than an aching dependency in itself. What were clinging claws, that would clam up at the slightest sign of emotional intrusion, then become a pair of open arms that holds firmly and cradles gently. The acute awareness of another's feelings, which can be used negatively to exert emotional blackmail, becomes a ray of healing. Vulnerable side-stepping becomes sensitive approach.

Being such a maternal, home-making Sign, you probably find this easier to express if you are female. Male Cancerians can have a problem with laying themselves open emotionally, and can seek to protect themselves under a hard macho shell. Ironically, though, it is the soft sensitive meat within that is so attractive in both men and women. But, most importantly, and whatever your sex, you need to avoid being an apology for yourself as a result of feeling neglected or neglectful. The ultimate discovery for the Cancerian is that one is cared for all along by the greatest mother of them all – Mother Nature. As a Cancerian you need roots, and so you must go digging for your Sign's essential truth, which is that your Family is the Human Race itself. Mother Nature looks after her own.

LIKES	DISLIKES
Kindness and tenderness • To belong	Bluntness and direct confrontation • Uncertainty
Warmth and reassurance • Solitude and reminiscing	Discomfort • Soul-baring and bad memories
Being around strong people	Feeling weak and neglected

If you are a woman, this could be the kind of man to whom you are attracted – but it is really you, so realize it and express it.

THE SUN IN CANCER

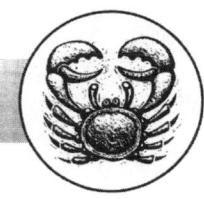

TRANSFORMER

POSITIVE	NEGATIVE
Tenacious	Clinging
Dependable	Dependent
Abiding	Apathetic
Thrifty	Hoarding
Protective	Smothering
Caring	Possessively doting
Home-maker	Stay-at-home
Hospitable	Anti-social
Tender and responsive	Oversensitive
Sympathetic	Self-pitying
Psychically aware	Touchy
Self-sacrificing	Self deluding
Subtly supportive	Devious and indirect
Kind and consoling	Argumentative
Emotionally encouraging	Emotionally blackmailing
Adaptable	Moody
Childlike	Childish
Watchful	Over-cautious
Enchanting	Sickly sentimental
Trust the Universe. Remember that all things must pass and that every day is new.	Feeling threatened by the future. Feeling haunted by the past, yet yearning for it.
Remember that your emotional awareness is more acute than that of most others – so use it, constructively.	Feeling avoided and victimized, resented and resentful.
Objective sensitivity to others rewards you. Exclusive sensitivity to yourself hurts you.	Feelings of melancholy and martyrdom. Irritable but out of touch.
Withdraw and contemplate exactly in what way and to what extent others need you. Affirm to yourself 'I belong'.	Feeling guilty and resentful, agoraphobic and unappreciated.
Establish and execute your responsibilities generously.	Feeling insecure and helpless. Sluggish. Alternately grudging and apologetic.
SOLUTION	PROBLEM

If you find yourself on the receiving end of negative traits, it is because you are not expressing the opposing positive traits.

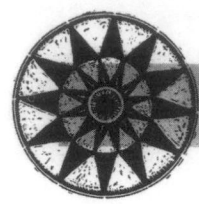

THE SUN IN LEO

ESSENCE

Living through Creating
Child of the Sun • I Am my Own Role Model

As the Sun is Dignified in Leo, your main qualities are best expressed and understood in terms of the Sun. You want to shine and be the centre of attention. No matter how shy or how lacking in confidence you might feel inwardly, you will want to be noticed in some way. For this reason, it is necessary for you to feel happy in the spotlight, which means that respect is vitally important, both for yourself and from others. In fact, respect from others is dependent upon self-respect, so for Leo honour really does have to be bright.

In effect, Leo shines in any event. How warm and bright, how noble and creative that light that radiates from you happens to be is the crucial point. You can bring warmth and illumination to situations where they are needed like no other Sign. And this radiant glow is often quite physically noticeable. In this way, you create a focal point and a generator for anything that is happening. As you do so, you imply Leo's well-known royal presence. Leo creates an 'Air of Certainty' that makes possible so many things – as if by royal decree. And you need to be aware of your royal presence. The apparent confidence that streams forth from your Heart gives the lie to the fact that you are highly dependent upon being appreciated. A king or queen without subjects or with no audience is not much of a monarch, just as the Sun cannot function without the sky around it.

This great Leonine possession – your natural ability to generate light, warmth and centrality in the form of creative, healing or commanding expressions – needs to be controlled. The Sun is, after all, an enormous nuclear reactor, and if it is not constantly checked, the Leonine ego can lead to a 'meltdown' (wild destructive passions) or to 'sunspots' (losing face or facial blemishes). This means that you need to pay as much attention to your critics as to your admirers, if you are to avoid the danger of being blinded by your own light, and destroying the very thing you originally sought to vitalize and maintain, be it a relationship, your home, health, profession, or even your own children. Again, like the Sun, Leo cannot see the shadows that it casts.

Your brightness can also blind others to your vulnerability. And when Leo is wounded, it is like the Sun disappearing behind a cloud; the world is a colder and duller place for it. Such sensitivity could, of course, be seen merely as vanity, which is your most dangerous negative quality as others are unlikely to praise and appreciate what appears as immodesty, and so a vicious circle can begin. At a certain critical stage, Leo has to realize that its power and influence shine through it, and not from it. Thus your undeniable brightness shows others their path to the glory of good, and so, ultimately, your own. Like Leo, the Sun as it is seen – as that shimmering disc called the photosphere – is not really the Sun itself, but just how it is seen by mortal eyes.

LIKES	DISLIKES
A good time • To rule well	Bad timing or repetition • Ruin or drudgery
To affect others • Gaining respect • Style	Being ignored • Losing face • Drabness

If you are a woman, this could be the kind of man to whom you are attracted – but it is really you, so realize it and express it.

THE SUN IN LEO

TRANSFORMER

POSITIVE	NEGATIVE
Noble Confident Generous Gracious	Pretentious Self-righteous Flamboyant Supercilious
Encouraging Commanding Ambitious Enterprising	Domineering Demanding Intolerant Overestimating
Proud Cultivated Dramatic sense Impressive	Vain Snobbish/Stuck-up Melodramatic Show-off
Self-expressive Wealth of ideas Fun to be with Warm	Self-centred Overbearing Overblown Scorching
Affectionate Loyal Irrepressible Romantic	Affected Fierce Impossible Unrealistic
Those who love you, love your inner glow more than your outer show.	Getting away with murder, and still feeling unwanted.
The Sun never tries to shine or set conditions – it just shines. So should you.	Crest-fallen as a result of expecting too much both of self and of others. Loss of dignity.
False pride comes before a fall – true pride comes after one.	Falling from grace. Excesses have invited a decrease in lifestyle.
Leo controls others as much as it controls itself. Rank imposes obligations.	Banishment. Close associates withdraw support or investment. Secret feelings of insecurity.
Recognize, appreciate, respect and pardon both yourself and others – they will then follow suit.	Fearful of humiliation and of not being recognized, appreciated or respected.
SOLUTION	PROBLEM

If you find yourself on the receiving end of negative traits, it is because you are not expressing the opposing positive traits.

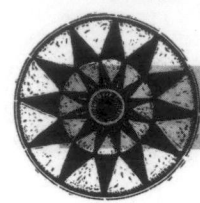

THE SUN IN VIRGO

ESSENCE

Living through Analysing
The Noble Helper • The Perfectionist

Virgo has its roots in the Vestal Virgin principle which stresses the importance of maintaining the purity of the individual – or anything else – and ensuring that it remains unsullied by society's polluting and corrupting ways. As the Sign of the harvest, your task is to separate the wheat from the chaff, the useful from the useless. Through such constant analysis you strive to reach a state of purity, of being a clear channel of expression.

There are two types of Virgoan: the Purist and the Puritan. The Puritan attempts to avoid anything regarded as physically unwholesome, emotionally threatening or mentally indigestible. This is the picky squeaky-clean type, who is not really pure in the sense of being 'you and only you'. The Purist, on the other hand, trusts his or her innate purity to not only withstand involvement with potentially corrupting elements, but actually attempts to influence them with that purity. It should be noted that as a Virgoan, you may have elements of both the Puritan and the Purist distributed through your personality. For example, the Purist could get involved on a mental and a physical level, but the Puritan could be uninvolved on an emotional level. There are, of course, other permutations here, but this is probably the most common one, which can lead to being abandoned by your mate – or to not having one at all. And although you can appear to be self-sufficient, you in fact need mutual caring and sharing – albeit of a very particular kind!

As a Virgoan, you must have a 'work' or be of some kind of service in order to make sense of life. You are constantly preparing for something, and unless you know or feel quite what that something is, you can become frustrated with an all-work-and-no-play-makes-for-a-dull-life type of situation. The task of Virgo is a difficult one, and so you need to perfect some form of technique, through study and training. This will minimize wear and tear (especially of the nervous system and the intestines) and will also equip you for an efficient work role, without which you are unhappy.

Virgo is the Sign of health which, in addition to technique, means giving yourself the time and the space to assimilate things properly through regular rest and retreat, and correct diet. More esoterically, Virgo's concern is where and how the psyche meets the soma, the Soul interacts with the body. So your body is very much the barometer of your psychological condition. However, you should endeavour not to allow your physical state to rule your life, but rather to understand that your body will serve you well if you observe carefully and inwardly what it is telling you.

Discover precisely what you are devoted to, and you will then realize that you need not be so hard on yourself. Blessed be.

LIKES	**DISLIKES**
Natural methods • Orderliness • Making lists	Being a 'Puritan' • Sloppiness • Making mistakes
Being helpful • Earthiness	Being a martyr • Crudity or violation

If you are a woman, this could be the kind of man to whom you are attracted – but it is really you, so realize it and express it.

THE SUN IN VIRGO

TRANSFORMER

POSITIVE	NEGATIVE
Thoughtful Analytical Lively mind Observant	Thinks too much Sceptical Worrier Critical
Scholarly Precise Pure intentions Discriminating	Dry Pedantic Too earnest Fault-finding
Helpful Problem-solving Wholesome Health-conscious	Interfering Problem-making Fusspot Hypochondriac
Industrious Methodical Efficient Reliable	Workaholic Inflexible Mechanistic Spoilsport
Dispassionate Modest Considerate Pure	Clinical Unsure Stand-offish Sterile
There must be passion there in order for you to purify it – so quietly express it.	The 'wallflower'. Left on the shelf. Intact but lonely.
Conceive of a more wonderful reason for striving. Put some 'madness' into your method.	Life becomes a meaningless drudge. Your efforts are taken for granted.
If it works don't try to fix it. Help where it isn't needed doesn't help.	Irritable and worried all the time. Unaware that a bit of chaos is 'in' order.
True perfection consists of being able to accept life's imperfections.	Life feels increasingly uncomfortable with every flaw you detect.
Regard your mind as a lens – not as a light, a film or a screen.	Living in your head – and the skull is one very cramped space.
SOLUTION	PROBLEM

If you find yourself on the receiving end of negative traits, it is because you are not expressing the opposing positive traits.

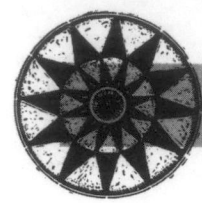

THE SUN IN LIBRA

ESSENCE

Living through Relating

A Question of Balance • My Law is my Will

As a Libran, your life is concerned with creating and maintaining a set of values that will guide you as you constantly endeavour to relate to one and all in a just and pleasant fashion. The Sun here, being in the Sign of its Fall, means that to a certain extent the expression of your individual Will is determined by others. However, the irony is that to be truly balanced you have to offset such an obliging manner with an edge as hard as the fulcrum upon which an actual set of scales balances. This means that when it comes to the common Libran problem of indecisiveness, making a hard and fast decision for its own sake – and keeping to it – is far better than no decision at all. Being unable to make up your mind can be more annoying and anti-social than most things! And on the subject of the Scales themselves, Libra is the only Sign whose symbol is an inanimate object rather than an animal or a human being. You can, therefore, be inclined to live life as an immaculate concept rather than as a living, breathing, fallible creature. You need to remember that it is all right to make mistakes. After all, it is only when you 'tip' the scales (put a definite measure of weight on one side) that the point of balance is determined and the desired result reached.

But for you as a Libran, the balancing act goes on and on, as the proverbial pendulum of life swings back and forth. And it is your ongoing relationships that give you the measure of your success here. Again, you must establish yourself as having a definite value or personality in the first place, in the knowledge that through relating you will change and grow. You can rely on your natural charm and your sense of harmony to attract relationships and to conduct them skilfully. But you should base these relationships on and maintain them according to your innate sense of balance – that is, your awareness of what is pleasing or fair both to yourself and to the other party. And 'relationships' mean interchanges with one person or between many, on a professional or on a private level – between your inner world and the outer world, or between one stage of life and another.

Like a bee, a Libran likes to taste many different flowers in order to arrive at the perfect 'honey', or way of relating and expressing him/herself. The danger is that this can become such a sweet lifestyle that you gloss over the nasty bits, or actually indulge in them, too. And so, to avoid or to get off such a not-so-merry-go-round of increasingly meaningless social dalliance, remember that pleasures got from sex and money are the means through which you seek to find the joy of union, the true balance that lies beyond what is merely pleasant. Libra is a 'cardinal' Sign, which means that you are supposed to be an initiator of social activities and values – not merely a response to them. Libra is also the Sign of the Peacemaker, which points to the fact that rather than ignoring areas of conflict, disharmony or injustice, you should realize that this is where your art is most needed and appreciated.

LIKES	**DISLIKES**
Pleasing surroundings • Peace and justice	Discordant atmospheres • Violence and injustice
A partner/Companions • Gentleness • Following fashion	Zero social feedback • Brutishness • Being a slave to fashion

If you are a woman, this could be the kind of man to whom you are attracted – but it is really you, so realize it and express it.

THE SUN IN LIBRA

TRANSFORMER

POSITIVE	NEGATIVE
Aesthetic Graceful Peaceful Calm	Affected Superficial Non-committal Lazy
Socially orientated Popular Co-operative Amenable	Lacks self-reliance Indulgent/Indulged Yes-person Insincere
Attractive Refined Subtle manner In tune with the times	Vain Easily upset Lacking confidence Style victim
High principles Idealistic Socially aspiring and aware	Compromising Peace at any price Elitist and class-conscious
Diplomatic Harmless Friendly Good counsellor	Indecisive Insipid Smarmy Ingratiating
Other people are not God. God is your awareness that life is manifestly both hard and soft.	Feeling like a nonentity; merely a human counterweight to other humans. Frustrating others.
Libra's role is to initiate social activities that blend the rough with the smooth.	Feeling taken advantage of. Feeling awkward in certain types of company.
To be both attractive and secure, sensitivity requires spiritual strength and awareness.	Uncomfortably delicate. Made to feel ill (at ease) by what to others is merely disagreeable.
Truly please yourself and you will truly please others.	If only you liked yourself as much as others appear to like you.
Your outward poise will remain as long as it subordinates itself to your inner values.	Finding yourself in social situations that have no depth and little real value. Divorce.
SOLUTION	PROBLEM

If you find yourself on the receiving end of negative traits, it is because you are not expressing the opposing positive traits.

137

THE SUN IN SCORPIO

ESSENCE

Living through Desiring
The Phoenix • The Urge to Merge

Scorpio is the most powerful Sign of the Zodiac. This is because you can sense what is going on beneath the surface in most situations, but especially where intimate relating or business dealing is concerned. So with such an emotional awareness of what is motivating someone or something, you have a certain 'inside knowledge' with which you are able to influence or to manipulate, to corrupt or to purge, to harm or to heal.

Once you have realized that you have this power, then two burning questions arise: How may such power be used, and is there anyone out to disempower you? This poses a moral dilemma, because if you use your inside knowledge to further low or mean intentions, you then fall into a downward spiral of defending yourself against something that you yourself started. On the other hand, when you get on top of your main weakness, which is simply a fear of admitting to having a chink in your armour, then, by using your penetrating insight you are capable, like no other Sign, of bringing to the surface what is causing trouble, be it a heartache, a disease, a financial problem, or anything else. The former or negative type of Scorpion is called the 'Serpent of Evil'; the latter or positive type is called the 'Serpent of Wisdom' or the 'Eagle'.

You have an awareness of what sex is for and what it is about. Again this is connected with your ability to penetrate beneath the surface. You can really get under people's skin, to the roots of feeling and desire. This can lead to a great intimacy with life itself – even brushing with death. The extent to which you are conscious of this sexual awareness can make the difference between deliverance and disaster. In any case, though, you thrive in a crisis; you achieve more when the going gets rough. Just think of the difficulty a Scorpion would have progressing across a smooth surface.

Your Scorpionic power can appear as a magnetic charm that can be totally disarming, or as downright cruelty, trampling others and striking unexpectedly. You can raise others from the depths – or hurl them down there! Behind this power is a kind of nuclear energy that can drive on through the night, literally or metaphorically. You also like to test such grit by indulging in the lowest levels of life experience, and then coming up not only intact but positively regenerated. Some don't come back, though.

You can be relied upon to possess deep and genuine emotions, and will unerringly test out the emotions of others, while hiding behind a 'smokescreen' that conceals your own depth. A probing and secretive person, you are emotionally frightening (or frightful) when invasion threatens. However, when you let go and allow someone or something in, a magical effect, an alchemical release occurs as your 'sting' is transformed from a defensive or self-destructive weapon into a healing lance.

LIKES	**DISLIKES**
Total involvement • Rooting out hidden causes	Superficial relationships • Scratching the surface • Being got
Being persuasive • Meaningful work • The untarnished truth	one over on • Demeaning tasks • Flattering and flattery

If you are a woman, this could be the kind of man to whom you are attracted – but it is really you, so realize it and express it.

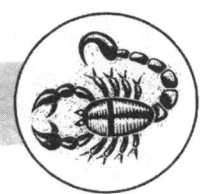

THE SUN IN SCORPIO

TRANSFORMER

POSITIVE	NEGATIVE
Intense Loyal Passionate Faith-inspiring	Obsessive Possessive Fanatical Emotionally sapping
Dynamic Regenerating Compelling Magnetic	Coercive Degrading Enforces allegiance Seductive
Penetrating insight Scrutinizing Shrewd Resourceful	Black looks Suspicious Cunning Revengeful
Compassionate Strong and deep Brave Firm views	Self-punishing Scornful of weakness Cruel Rigid outlook
Powerful Healing touch Self-sacrificing Intimate	Corrupt Manipulative Jealous Resentful
Power is not in you, but comes through you. If you hate, power kills. If you love, power heals.	Overstretched but not admitting it. Supplanted but not accepting it. Close but not seeing it.
Your greatest weakness is denying weakness; your greatest strength is forgiving weakness.	Descending down a dark spiral of self-disgust. Disdainful of help and of others.
Look deeply into anything or anyone and you will find only yourself and the power therein.	Attracting enemies who waste your energies. Feeling persecuted. Struggling with powers that be.
When you know how not to, you can show others how to – which they find irresistible.	You've got everyone where you want them but you still don't like it.
When you reach a point where you are no longer after anything, you begin to realize what you are after.	Obsessed and possessed to the point of acute anxiety. Driven blindly from bad to worse.
SOLUTION	PROBLEM

If you find yourself on the receiving end of negative traits, it is because you are not expressing the opposing positive traits.

THE SUN IN SAGITTARIUS

ESSENCE

Living through Seeking
The Adventurer • The Opener of Ways

Sagittarius is probably the most positive Sign of the Zodiac, for the simple reason that you see life as an opportunity. So it never matters just how hard the road ahead might look, for it is still a road, and roads go places! Sagittarius rules and loves the highways – literal and symbolic.

Your sense of 'going places' also gives you a strong sense of history and culture, and of where things are bound. This sense of trend can keep you abreast or ahead of the times, or locked into some sub-culture that's had its day. You can be embarked upon some genuinely spiritual quest, or merely be 'trendy'. In any event, you are adept at furthering anything and anyone that you believe in, but be careful not to take over everything and everyone in the process, or others will ultimately find your enthusiasm tiresome rather than awesome.

'Belief' is a Keyword for Sagittarius, and you are as believable as what you believe in. The dualistic nature of your Sign (the Centaur: animal and human) can make you appear hypocritical, as one moment you aspire to the Divine, with high-flown theories and philosophies, and the next, you get down with the beastly best of them in order to keep earthed. You are thus seeking to marry the Spirit with the Flesh, and reveal the one in the other, which is what your adventurous nature is really about. You have the power to proliferate, so attaching too much importance to the material side of life can either cause the physical rapidly to go out of control, such as in your becoming grossly overweight, or mean that you are denied something money cannot buy.

In whatever sphere or at whatever level you are functioning, you have a marvellously intuitive grasp of how life works. You are the 'manager' of the Zodiac. And, being half-horse, you cover a lot of ground and get to know the lie of the land. You also require the freedom and possess the energy to do this. It is your libidinous drive that also creates your main trouble, for such galloping get-up-and-go can find you overstretched, overbearing and over-confident. Sagittarius has the peculiar problem of the superiority complex, and you will resort to equally peculiar tactics to give yourself a more 'human' stature. In other words, because you are so aware of how society as a whole is shaping up, you have a comparatively weak sense of how you feel personally. So you resort to rubbing others up the wrong way in the hope of getting some kind of personal reaction. You also do this in order to get to the underlying truth of a given situation. This can be very effective for it clears the air and opens up the way ahead.

Like an Archer-Charioteer with a team of four spirited horses, you have great power at your disposal. If you let the horses run wildly, you have a great ride followed by a great crash, as a result of which you are torn apart. With reins held lightly, in touch with your animal drive, and with a high target to aim at, for Sagittarius, anything is possible!

LIKES	DISLIKES
Freedom and space • Travelling (fast and far)	Being constrained • Being domestically tied
Getting on with it • The general feel • Laws and meanings	Kicking your heels • Details • Glib theories

If you are a woman, this could be the kind of man to whom you are attracted – but it is really you, so realize it and express it.

THE SUN IN SAGITTARIUS

TRANSFORMER

POSITIVE	NEGATIVE
Benevolent Generous Enthusiastic Jovial	Promises too much Excessive Over-zealous Overbearing
Optimistic Lucky Far-sighted Positive thinker	Blind to details Jammy Jumps to conclusions Cocksure
Stimulating Outspoken Colourful Open and honest	Contentious Inconsiderate Exaggerative Embarrassing
Able Good Judgment Honourable Mobile	Boastful Moralizing Pompous Volatile
Expansive Adventurous Carefree Vitalistic	Scattered Irresponsible Careless Lascivious

SOLUTION	PROBLEM
Focus upon one thing that will satisfy you. Be true to it, and it'll be true to you.	Exhausted and exhausting. Exasperated and exasperating. Frustrated and frustrating.
Look down and you go down; look up and you go up. You know that ruts make poor runways.	You can't move: your feet are set in the concrete of dogma, or are not touching the ground at all.
Your target area is way beyond the boring, but just short of the unbelievable (or unbearable).	Others cease to confide in you or to take you seriously. What was warm now burns – there's the rub.
There's always a direction in which to head, and a 1,000-mile journey begins with the first step.	Feeling lost and disillusioned. Out of gas. No map. No compass.
Be sure you have a product to match your advertisement. Is it for a fact or for effect?	Too many irons in the fire. Others look askance at you and have no time for you.

If you find yourself on the receiving end of negative traits, it is because you are not expressing the opposing positive traits.

THE SUN IN CAPRICORN

ESSENCE
Living through Building
The Sea-Goat • The Pragmatist

Capricorn is concerned with making a success of life. This could be said of any Sign, but you aim to do this by getting the hang of how things actually 'work' down here on Planet Earth. You are, therefore, a decidedly down-to-earth person who won't cling to abstract concepts and lofty ideals in order to justify being here. What satisfies this urge in you is a sense of purpose and of responsibility. You feel a part of this world when you can feel its weight upon your shoulders and its ground beneath your feet.

Traditionally, you are interested in external, socially established values of life rather than inner ones. To be honest, you assess anything or anyone in terms of how useful they are. As your Sign's symbol, the Mountain Goat, implies, you make your way to the summit of material success by taking one sure-footed step after another. You fix your attention on a vantage point and secure it. Sometimes a foothold can be someone else's head! And as you build your pile, you want solid value and solid values. With regard to what you consume, you like the right brand-names and to have a sense of belonging to the upper echelons of society – at least in terms of how your particular section of society currently sees itself.

However, you are far more complex than this, and have more subtlety than to be concerned solely with the outside world and what can be got out of it, an attitude that runs the danger of acquiring a blind spot. This can be seen by looking at the original symbol of Capricorn, the Sea-goat. This creature is half-goat and half-fish. The upper, or goat, half represents what has been described above – the earthy and persistent climber. But when the climber stumbles or falls, or just begins to realize that there is more to life than can be physically sensed, you begin to acquaint yourself with that other world of the fish – the mystical, irrational, unconscious inner realm. And when Capricorn gets spiritual, it does so with the same pragmatic efficiency with which it dealt with the material world. In fact, at an evolved level, you do not see any difference.

And so you come to realize how truly useful an awareness of the reality of invisible forces (such as thoughts, feelings and, most importantly, the imagination) is, and that roots and foundations – upon which everything is actually built – are usually out of sight.

The Capricorn who does not tune into his/her fish-half and the watery realm in which it dwells, can slip up on it and smell decidedly fishy, like Richard Nixon, who was undone by something called Watergate! But when and if you are practically attuned to the underlying mystical realities of life on Earth, rather than just being superstitious, then you are truly able to reach the pinnacle of Earthly success, the highest point, from which the next step up is Heaven, a little bit of which you can then bring down to Earth, with which to guide and govern.

LIKES	DISLIKES
Being worldly • Knowing your limits	Feeling groundless • Feeling boundless
Order and control • Being busy • Traditions	Feeling helpless • Feeling useless • The untried

If you are a woman, this could be the kind of man to whom you are attracted – but it is really you, so realize it and express it.

THE SUN IN CAPRICORN

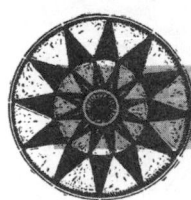

TRANSFORMER

POSITIVE	NEGATIVE
Materially aware Responsible Efficient Orderly	Status slave Unscrupulous Ingratiating Wet blanket
Ambitious Organizer Industrious Takes the reins	Cold Calculating Slave to self Dictatorial
Reserved Patient Thoughtful Deep understanding	Inhibited Intolerant Worrisome Inscrutable
Resourceful Canny Persevering Disciplined	Tight Suspicious Rigid Austere
Earthy Senses others' needs Employs others Solid	Philistine Opportunist Uses others Hard
Flood the market and you drown the demand. Elevate people's needs rather than increase them.	What started out as a good living has turned into a monster that cannot be satisfied.
Capricorn can get by on the smell of an oily rag – but only when it has to!	Life becomes existence. Work becomes drudge. Body becomes stiff. Friend becomes foe.
When you begin to appreciate fully your invisible qualities, so will others.	Nobody knows you – and they've almost given up trying to.
Indeed 'Ambition is the devil's own sin', unless you strive in a spirit of redemption.	The warm smell of success becomes an icy blast. Alone in your ivory tower with a white elephant.
Apply your talents to what is inferior and you go down, do so to what is superior and you go up.	Backed the wrong horse. Made your bed and having to lie in it. Only cold comfort available.
SOLUTION	PROBLEM

If you find yourself on the receiving end of negative traits, it is because you are not expressing the opposing positive traits.

143

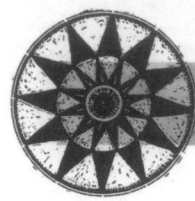

THE SUN IN AQUARIUS

ESSENCE
Living through Liberating
Befriend the Truth • High Mind – Low Profile

Aquarius is the Water-bearer, and Water symbolizes emotion. This means that your goal is to experience and to express your feelings without getting 'wet' – that is, emotionally biased, overly attached or upset. In order to accomplish this you strive to be free of whoever or whatever has an emotionally cramping influence over you. However, in your effort to liberate yourself, you run the danger of throwing the baby out with the bath water, by pretending not to have feelings for anything other than the reasonably manageable. Furthermore, your convoluted mind is able to detach itself from the very fact that you have detached yourself in the first place! This is why the Sun is in its Detriment in Aquarius, for your Will can lose itself in the 'sky' of your urge to be free.

This would not matter if it were not for the fact that more than any other Sign, you hold the key to what being a human being is. This has to do with the 'Truth' that originally there was nothing to fear, like a clear sky. But along with being born came the apparently unchosen situation of being emotionally involved with someone, like your father or your mother. As an Aquarian, you have chosen to free yourself (and others) from the family, class and racial and religious conditioning that holds the Truth in bondage. So you have to discover a way of loosening these bonds, which requires first having a good look at them.

Aquarius is said to put everything in the shop widow, and to keep nothing back in the shop. This means that in the attempt to present your ideal and most evolved but uninvolved self, you actually overlook much of your all too human goodness, a goodness that you keep out of sight, regarding it as too emotional or autocratic. This is one way, but not the right way, of 'bearing Water', or of containing and expressing emotion.

The positive, and most obvious, meaning of the Water-bearer symbol is that of refreshing the masses. With the Dawning of the Age of Aquarius, this is one of the main tasks on humanity's agenda for the next two thousand years. In order to accomplish this, the Aquarian qualities of teamwork and group effort have to be employed. So if you find that your life is a pointless struggle, it is probably because you are not enlisting yourself as part of a group, a flight of Souls aiming for the same goal. It appears necessary for you to place more importance on the sky than on the Sun, to put the requirement of the masses above your own individual desires. Yet paradoxically, it is equally necessary for you to maintain a firm sense of individuality in order to uphold and express the Aquarian democratic ideal, and not just be an ego-less space. Above all, you are seeking freedom for yourself and others through developing a greater sense of what life on this Planet is about.

LIKES		DISLIKES
Good companions • Rebellious causes		Excessive loneliness • Causeless rebels
Good times past • Future dreams		Mawkishness • Pie in the sky
Equality and originality		The ordinary and imitation

If you are a woman, this could be the kind of man to whom you are attracted – but it is really you, so realize it and express it.

144

THE SUN IN AQUARIUS

TRANSFORMER

POSITIVE	NEGATIVE
Impartial Cool Broad-minded Fair judge	Avoids intimacy Aloof Non-committal Emotionally inept
Friendly Gregarious Humanitarian Democratic	Impersonal Anti-social Lacks sympathy Hypocritical
Reformist Idealistic Inventive Original	Reactionary Impractical Cranky Elitist
Unaffected Convincing Intuitive Outwardly calm	Mocking Imposes ideas Cutting Secretly anxious
Clownish Free-thinking Free-loving Open-ended	Sarcastic Scatty Flighty Pointless

SOLUTION	PROBLEM
Life is a masquerade. Removing one mask merely reveals another. Enjoy the masquerade – live life.	Being afraid of presenting an emotional persona, you miss your role in the human drama.
To err is human, and your sense of the truth is all the more appreciated for being so.	As you observe and deride others' weaknesses, they leave you uncomfortably alone with your own.
Everyone is unique, and has the right to be so. Others' quirks are reminders of your own.	It annoys you when someone or something is either too odd or not odd enough.
The evolving personality turns fear into love; so first you have to acknowledge your fears.	You love humanity, but are not so keen on people. Such aversions are fears that bind you.
Treat yourself with as much understanding as you are afraid to expect of others.	Difficulty in relating to the opposite sex. Your mental guard becomes a mindless watchdog.

If you find yourself on the receiving end of negative traits, it is because you are not expressing the opposing positive traits.

THE SUN IN PISCES

ESSENCE

Living through Accepting

Life is a Mystery • I am a Mystery

There are two fishes: the upstream one and the downstream one. As the upstream fish, you make an effort, you fight against the current, looking for inspiration in order that you may give it. As the downstream fish, you foster the notion that everything and everyone will wind up where they're going to get to sooner or later, so what's the point in trying.

The upstream fish has a point, the downstream fish doesn't. However, the upstream fish can push so hard that it misses the point, which is that sensitivity and acceptance are essential to Pisces, whereas the downstream fish can go with the flow and wind up in the swim. The addictive personality that you can be (fishes get hooked!) is the escapist looking for a way out that in time may prove to be a way in. For example, ex-alcoholics founded Alcoholics Anonymous. Faith comes with acceptance, and vice versa.

Ideally, you are plotting a course while letting things take their course. Such a way of handling life can give many impressions of who you are, ranging from the genuine altruist to the subtle manipulator, from the mystic to the misfit. This all stems from your sense that all is one and one is all. You can be anything – or virtually nothing. But the inescapable fact is that you are definitely here as a feeling being, and so you devise many a disguise to camouflage your immense sensitivity, which is your greatest possession. And although your need to camouflage yourself is behind much of your incomprehensibility, it is also what enables you to present one thing as another, for example horror as beauty, or curse as blessing, and so you can enlighten or relieve those who look or listen. You might not be able to fathom yourself, but you are adept at understanding others and their failings. You have to contend with a greater emotional input than any other Sign, and to channel it or evade it.

You may also unconsciously protect such emotional sensitivity and universal awareness with fierce analysis and scientific rationalization. Although this is often highly necessary to offset the frequently indiscriminate 'anything goes' attitude of Pisces, it can also be an evasiveness of the most subtle kind, for it appears to be the opposite.

You are innately aware and appreciative of all walks of life. You may periodically protest and complain about the ways of certain others, but you eventually flip back into your more usual mode of ongoing acceptance. This makes you identify and side with the underdog. Fundamentally this is because you recognize that the Soul of anything or of anyone is synonymous with sensitivity, which is synonymous with suffering, which is something of which you are exquisitely aware. Joy and sorrow are one.

LIKES	**DISLIKES**
Dreamy solitude • Mystery • The discarded	Criticism • Pedantry • The obvious
Getting lost • The absurd	Feeling lost • Know-alls

If you are a woman, this could be the kind of man to whom you are attracted – but it is really you, so realize it and express it.

THE SUN IN PISCES

TRANSFORMER

POSITIVE	NEGATIVE
Compassionate Self-sacrificing Suffers artistically	Self-pitying The human doormat Suffers needlessly
Unassuming Self-effacing Gentle Still but stirring	Indecisive Self-limiting Wimpish Inwardly storm-tossed
Wise Accepting Adaptable Confided in	Inner doubts Oblivious Vague Unforthcoming
Sensitive Fascinating Mysterious Imaginative	Escapist Deceptive Self-mystifying Impressionable
Multi-talented Selfless Devoted Easygoing	Unenterprising Pointless Slaving Lazy
Give yourself a starting point and an end that endures; then trust in life's creative process.	Many possibilities dissolve Into many improbabilities. Life becomes a thankless task. Weary.
Your mystical allure, your ancient understanding – solidly express and appreciate them.	Adrift. At sea. Confusion reigns. Like a bucket of water without the bucket.
Learn to face the music, then you'll know the score – how you and others fit in.	Caught in the net of the fear of being caught. Every move you make gets you more entangled.
You inspire others, so don't forget to take some credit for it – then forget it.	Drowning in a sea of your own despair – and no one knows.
Be a part of what you feel for. Give yourself to yourself before anybody else. Illuminate.	Being walked all over leaves you flat. Are you cut out for crucifixion?
SOLUTION	PROBLEM

If you find yourself on the receiving end of negative traits, it is because you are not expressing the opposing positive traits.

THE MOON

Keyword: SECURITY

The Moon, as it reflects the light of the Sun, your will, symbolizes your FEELING RESPONSES to life in general, and being SUBJECTIVE to the will of others. In CHILDHOOD, while your will was still UNCONSCIOUS, having your SECURITY NEEDS met made you totally DEPENDENT upon others, especially your MOTHER.

Consequently, much of your PERSONALITY became conditioned by the HABITS and BIASES of your MOTHER, your FAMILY, CLASS, RACE etc., for good or ill. Positively this gives you a sense of BELONGING and INNER SUPPORT, whereas negatively it can amount to CLANNISHNESS, a FEAR OF THE UNKNOWN and CLINGING TO THE PAST, which can effectively eclipse your individual sense of being – the Sun.

Your Moon-Sign position therefore shows how you experience life subjectively, how you REACT to it as a result of maternal and other conditioning. It also shows how you INSTINCTUALLY seek to satisfy your own needs and SYMPATHIZE with those of others.

The Lunar sense comes more naturally to females, so if you are male you may be attracted to females who embody your Moon-Sign qualities. Sooner or later, through life's experiences and relationships, you come to realize and to express the qualities of your EMOTIONS.

THE MOON IN ARIES

ESSENCE

Security through Doing

The Eternal Youth • Be Here Now

You experience life as something that never stands still, which in the strictest sense it is. However, if you are feeling insecure about any part of your life, then this can prod you into attempting to resolve things more quickly than is naturally possible. So you are predisposed to racing around as if there is some ghastly time limit set upon you. And since Aries Moon makes for a strong personality, you can either precipitate predicaments where hurrying seems unavoidable, or use such forcefulness quickly to begin to slow down, decide what you are after, and then establish your own more comfortable pace.

However, what actually motivates you into doing anything in the first place is a sense of insecurity, which was very likely inherited from your mother. To feel peaceful can therefore be rather meaningless, even boring, to you. So you also have difficulty in being calm, and can wear yourself out before you know it. All the same, you have the marvellous ability to recover quickly from traumas, be they physical, mental or emotional. You have a large helping of that human capacity to recharge yourself in times of need, when alone in the wilderness. You could be regarded as the warrior or scout type of personality. Equally, your resilience is marked by being subject to emotional surges rather than lingering moods. You experience life as a thing of the moment, and should train and trust yourself to respond to the needs of that moment. Travel light. You have a temper than can frighten and amaze, but this too flares up and dies down suddenly, and this is born of frustration – again from/with your mother – rather than maliciousness.

The 'battle stations' mode is one that seems to prevail, and you actually thrive on conflict, even though other dimensions of your personality may suffer because of it, and refuse to accept it. You feel that there are only two alternatives – either breaking through or breaking down. This has a decidedly see-saw effect on your intimate involvements in particular, and on all relationships in general. Even so, everyone depends upon you to provide excitement and unpredictability. However, somewhere along the line you need to cultivate a steadier emotional rhythm, and remember that you are not under continual threat of hostile forces. Even though you like to regard life as a battle, bear in mind that 'like' should be the operative word.

Above all, you are after something that will last, which is quite a quest in itself, maybe *the* quest. As you view your probably rapid social or romantic turnover so far, you may leap to the conclusion that sustaining anything is just not part of your game-plan. But look again and you will see that what persists is persistence itself and, most of all, your childlike sense which inspires both you and others with the primary assumption that life is a thrilling and unique experience.

<table>
<tr><td align="center">**LIKES**</td><td align="center">**DISLIKES**</td></tr>
<tr><td align="center">The chase • New experiences • Leading • Honesty
Outdoor adventures</td><td align="center">Anti-climaxes • Inactivity • Being told what to do
Soppiness • Emotional confinement</td></tr>
</table>

If you are a man, this could be the kind of woman to whom you are attracted – but it is really you, so realize it and express it.

THE MOON IN ARIES

TRANSFORMER

POSITIVE	NEGATIVE
Spontaneous Direct Straightforward Sharp	Impetuous Brusque Unsubtle Blunt
Energetic Stimulating Quick responses Lively	Frenzied Too excitable Jumpy/Irritable Impatient
Open Daring Self-assertive Independent	Tactless Reckless Pushy Unco-operative
Trail-blazing Original Future sense Spirited	Ahead of self Inaccessible Tense Restless
Every-ready Arousing Unstoppable Unbeatable	Fit to burst Precipitous Bad finisher Sore loser
Know that whatever is required of you – but no more, and no less – is always possible.	Meteor-like, you spend yourself too soon, and create situations where you cannot win.
A fire must have fuel to burn on. To continue, recognize your needs as well as your wants.	Lonely and ill at ease with yourself.
Ensure that what you are after is consciously constructive, not unconsciously defensive.	People and things either get in your way or don't go along with you.
It's driving you. And it won't let you down, so there's no need to hurry unnecessarily.	Although your fiery energy can be fun, are you driving it, or is it driving you?
Between your refreshing outbursts, be mindful of others' finer feelings – and express your own.	Unaware of others' sensibilities, they cannot be aware of yours. Are you aware of this?!
SOLUTION	PROBLEM

If you find yourself on the receiving end of negative traits, it is because you are not expressing the opposing positive traits.

THE MOON IN TAURUS

ESSENCE

Security through Stabilizing
Child of Nature • Bounty or Burden

Security is sought through stability, which sounds straightforward enough, and indeed with Moon in Taurus you are usually known for your practical and materially dependable nature. A minimum of change is seen as equalling a maximum of security. This emotional stability is the reason for the Moon being Exalted in Taurus, but unless you are quite happy with a predictable, down-home sort of life, or have made the ultimate realization that the only totally consistent factor is change itself, then such a need for stability is not going to be so simply met. Complications are then likely to become manifest in a number of ways: someone else upon whom you are dependent creating a change; changes in your body state – especially diseases of the throat and the reproductive system; feelings of boredom and inertia; deadlock situations as you try to fulfil needs of security in one camp and of pleasure in another; becoming a beast of burden through failing to appreciate the value of your own broad back; staying too long in an unfruitful relationship.

Behind all of this is an issue of self-worth. If you are not sure what you are or what you are worth, then a never-ending search for some form of external value (material security being mistaken for emotional security) is going to try your decidedly persistent nature in a rather unrewarding fashion. In other words, peace with yourself has to be found before you can really expect it to occur on the outside. And even if it does, it comes at a very high price. As a child you possibly felt threatened by some kind of ominous disruption – or were actually a victim of it. Or perhaps your mother had such an anxiety which was transmitted to you and developed into a blind fear of change or a blind need for material security. Another cause of self-doubt could be that your mother had similar doubts about herself and therefore was not able to notice and affirm your worth.

So what is having Taurean Moon worth? Most essentially it is a feeling about you of physical substance and sensuousness that is very reassuring and attractive to others. Instinctively, you know how to identify and satisfy those needs. The personal applications of this talent are obvious; the professional ones include any activities that cater for physical needs, such as food and drink, comfort, property, management and production generally – also areas of healthcare that connect directly with the physical body, like massage, osteopathy etc. Artistic senses are pronounced, too – especially singing or country crafts. You also have a way with animals that could serve a useful purpose.

As Nature's child, you have deep, rich emotions as a result of being so close to the Earth. But there is no need to bury yourself in it through seeking too much material security. The gift of a Taurean Moon is that material supply will always be forthcoming – unless you doubt it.

LIKES	**DISLIKES**
Material security • Bargain-hunting • Quality	Change • Waste and extravagance • Letting go
Predictability • Ownership	The unknown • Borrowing

If you are a man, this could be the kind of woman to whom you are attracted – but it is really you, so realize it and express it.

THE MOON IN TAURUS

TRANSFORMER

POSITIVE	NEGATIVE
Dependable Consistent Pragmatic Robust	Stick-in-the-mud Habit-ruled Tunnel-visioned Dense
Methodical Painstaking Patient Persistent	Wooden Overloaded Slow-reacting Bulldozing
Affectionate Sensuous Generous Good-natured	Demanding Carnal Self-indulgent Hedonistic
Materially aware Organizer Good taste Thrifty	Money-minded Bossy Consumer snob Mean
Steady Placid Self-reliant Attuned to nature	Brooding Listless Insecure Melancholic
When you hit the bottom you'll know which way is up. Relax into your inner beauty.	Feeling very uncomfortable with yourself and the world. Feeling let down and hung up.
As you measure what things are worth, be mindful of what actually constitutes the quality of life.	Knowing the price of everything and the value of nothing, you are in charge but not in clover.
The rarer the gift, the more valuable it is. Your body is your most valuable physical possession.	Beset by demands that are physically impossible to meet – and they're consuming you.
Appreciate others' values and they will appreciate yours. Lend some weight and lose some.	Others seem to be either constantly resisting you and avoiding you, or forgetting you.
Look beyond your fears of loss and identify what you need and what you have right now.	Waiting in vain and unable to see your way ahead.
SOLUTION	PROBLEM

If you find yourself on the receiving end of negative traits, it is because you are not expressing the opposing positive traits.

153

THE MOON IN GEMINI

ESSENCE

Security through Communicating
Thinking is Feeling • Feeling is Thinking

Security is found through communicating your feelings not only to others but also to yourself. You have a knack of keeping difficult emotions on mental hooks, and thereby create an illusion of emotional lightness. This is just fine until you run out of hooks; you then have to start clearing the closet of all those unlooked-at doubts and fears – or hang-ups.

The bane and the boon of Gemini Moon is the constant flow of emotion through your mind. In a positive sense this means that your feelings can be readily and cleverly expressed through the written or spoken word. On the other hand, without a serious sense of purpose, what you are thinking or saying will be experienced like a television that is continually having its channels changed. However, you certainly have the gift of the gab. No one can compete with you when it comes to spontaneously holding forth. Your ability to verbalize a stream of consciousness is remarkable, and should prove itself in such fields as literature, journalism, counselling or public speaking.

You also have a talent for putting your finger on it when it comes to assessing the emotional state of a person or an occasion. However, accurate as such appraisals are, take care not to overlook deeper and more powerful emotional drives that are present. Similarly, a lack of commitment from another suggests that there is an area of your own feelings that is being skimmed over. Others (without Gemini Moon) do not find it so easy to take things at face value. Until you begin to discover and reveal deeper layers of your own personality, a partner is going to be equally evasive or hard to find.

Geminian duality is very marked here. For example, on the one hand you have a flair for making light of heavy emotions that can be quite relieving, but on the other, such a sticking-plaster approach can deceive both you yourself and others into thinking that everything is fine when really it is not. Also, your natural ability to intellectualize emotions may enable you to keep a cool head – but a cold heart, too, if you are not too careful. Others find a cool head good to have around, but with a cold heart there won't be anyone around!

Underlying your breezy emotional nature is a deep need to keep everyone informed of the fact that life is but a passing show, and that the world of opposites always prevails, in that there can be found joy in sadness, amusement in boredom, absurdity in profundity – and, of course, vice versa. What is important is the interplay between the main poles of thinking and feeling. This can often be just a case of your not knowing when to stop talking as you juggle and shunt your notions and emotions back and forth. But when you are aware that you are doing this, sparks of genius begin to fly.

LIKES	**DISLIKES**
Variety • Mental stimulation • Being in the know	Predictability • Clods • Being lost for words
Keeping on the move • Grooves	Being pinned down • Ruts

If you are a man, this could be the kind of woman to whom you are attracted – but it is really you, so realize it and express it.

THE MOON IN GEMINI

TRANSFORMER

POSITIVE	NEGATIVE
Easygoing Light touch Uncomplicated Lively	Heavy weather Superficial Simplistic Manic depressive
Mobile Witty Quick Live wire	Restless Worrisome Impatient Anxious
Versatile Multi-faceted Fast responses Fast learner	Spread too thin Two-faced Flip Sketchy
Good conversationalist Friendly Charming Delightful	Gossip Nosy Insincere Deceitful
Intelligent Broad-minded Interesting Perceptive	Too rational Shallow Dissatisfying Trivial

Trust your mind to express and understand feelings, not replace them.	Others can't feel for you – neither can you! Mistaking your reactions for reasons.
Think big as you talk small. Feed the grapevine with your sparkling mind.	Caught in the web of your own words and thoughts. The victim of your own curiosity.
Having too many irons in the fire slows you down. The ultimate string to your bow is thoroughness.	Projects take off but then disappear altogether. Feeling hard-pressed to maintain position.
Being habitually speedy is no joke. To be smart, avoid outrunning yourself.	Nervous exhaustion. Insomniac. Strung out.
Admitting to your contradictory nature is refreshing. Let others enjoy it, too.	Others cannot see where you're coming from or going to, so they don't wish to accompany you.

SOLUTION	PROBLEM

If you find yourself on the receiving end of negative traits, it is because you are not expressing the opposing positive traits.

155

THE MOON IN CANCER

ESSENCE

Security through Nurturing
Ebb and Flow • The World is my Home

Security is gained through classic security-producing traditions such as home and family – and the activities that are associated with them: cooking, gardening, domestic skills and supplies etc., so there is a homely, familiar feel about you that others are drawn towards. You should not underestimate or lose sight of such an attractiveness, for Cancer Moon's greatest weakness is being so subjective that you fail to notice your hearth-like warmth and focus – and then so do others.

As you exude this aura of strength and dependability, which is the hallmark of the Moon being Dignified in the Sign of the Crab, guard against its preventing you from showing your own hurts and doubts. Apart from causing such feelings to fester, this would actually inhibit rather than create the secure relationships that are so important to you. Partners and family can become habituated all too easily to your doing all the caring. This is more likely to be the case if you are female, whereas males are often inclined to doing the leaning. With both males and females, the ties to your mother are strong – for better or for worse. You may need to put some space between you and her.

Your feeling nature is well-developed, which can mean, on the one hand, a great ability to tune into the moods of others, and, on the other, being rather wrapped up in your own emotions. With a natural ability to nurture and protect, you make a good parent or a supportive friend. However, you have to watch overdoing this, for it can lead to being smothering or patronizing, which in turn can lead to others growing too dependent or feeling resentful. Your natural nurturing ability also extends to animal and plant life.

You have a sentimental nature, and a good memory – of both favours granted and wounds inflicted. Learning to forgive and forget is necessary in order to forestall spells of brooding, which can devolve into rank depression. In any event, you are prone to much emotional fluctuation, but this blesses you with a great ability to adapt to changing situations, and others depend on this. Recognizing and going with the ebb-and-flow pattern of your life is absolutely central to governing your emotions rather than allowing them to govern you. You can be melancholy, touchy and bemoaning your fate in the morning, and then a tower of strength in the afternoon. You also need to withdraw periodically to recharge your batteries in order to avoid exhausting your own – and others' – emotions. In some respects you tend to have a limited scope or viewpoint, but your rich emotional expression, which warms and reassures all within your sphere of influence, more than compensates. However, it would still be well to cultivate open-mindedness and a measure of detachment without any trace of rancour. Such nurturing as this truly creates a feeling of belonging in this world.

LIKES		**DISLIKES**
Your own patch • Secure home and home-life		Feeling rootless • Being uprooted • Carelessness
Peace and quiet • A family feel • The natural world		Unkindness • A plastic world

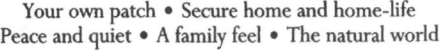

If you are a man, this could be the kind of woman to whom you are attracted – but it is really you, so realize it and express it.

THE MOON IN CANCER

TRANSFORMER

POSITIVE	NEGATIVE
Sympathetic Caring Devoted Accommodating	Oversensitive Clinging Fawning Harbours wounds
Tenacious Dependable Regular Self-reliant	Flogs dead horses One-sided Habit-prone Self-absorbed
Home-loving Home-making Family-conscious Firmly rooted	Agoraphobic Limited Clannish Entrenched
Enchanting Introspective Receptive Meditative	Lost Withdrawn Defensive Brooding
Emotionally attuned Deep feelings Responsive Nurturing	Manipulative Deeply needy Despondent Swamping
Identify the needs you feel cannot be met, then realize they represent others' needs for you.	Eventually others find it impossible to relate to your bottomless pit of neediness.
Retreat and regenerate with a strong, creative and deliberate purpose in mind.	Feeling controlled by your feelings, and a victim of circumstance.
Seek professional help to cut the ties that bind you to your negative past. Re-root yourself.	Tied to the home. Your horizons appear to get narrower and narrower.
Check that 'love' is not need in disguise. Be conscious of what you are holding on to, and why.	Apparently you have given your all, only to be taken for granted and even abandoned.
Let someone into your space, but leave the door open in case they want to go – then they'll stay.	Feeling desperately alone and unloved. Emotionally exhausting both to yourself and to others.
SOLUTION	PROBLEM

If you find yourself on the receiving end of negative traits, it is because you are not expressing the opposing positive traits.

THE MOON IN LEO

ESSENCE

Security through Creating
The Natural Thespian • The Closet Show-off

Security is sought through creating a definite impression and gaining some kind of acclaim. Often, however, when you eventually get caught in the spotlight you can feel uncomfortably self-conscious. Why should this be so? It is important that you feel good about this need for recognition for you have it in you to draw the limelight, and to hold it naturally and gracefully. Conversely, seeking attention and not really knowing what for can lead to all sorts of complications. Your liking for money and status is also strong – as is your ability to attain them. But again, if you are the 'closet' type of Moon in Leo, you may play down these matters, almost to the point of perversity.

If you suffer from any of the negative cases above, then look for the possibility of not wishing to repeat overt or negative expressions of ego as practised in the past – by your mother or by yourself. For example, as a child, insistent demands for attention may have been either always indulged or unavoidably ignored. Behind everything lies a fear of criticism and, consequently, an inability to take it. As the Moon is indicative of unconscious behaviour patterns, and since both negative and positive patterns are dramatized so grandly in Leo, it is necessary for feedback to be received, acknowledged and acted upon. Otherwise, such precious and self-justifying egocentricity can lead to others expressing their discomfort at it in a far more dramatically upsetting fashion than merely telling you what they think of you.

With such fiery and lively emotions you have a natural sense of drama and creativity. You are also a wow with children – being childlike yourself. You can overreact to relatively insignificant situations, but you can also make a dull situation into an exciting one. With this childlike sense of fun and games, you can find the absurd and ridiculous in everything – except yourself, perhaps. It is difficult for you to create a sense of detachment; everything is taken as personal praise or insult. So when it is essential to let go of something or of someone, it is best achieved in a spirit of grace rather than favour. In this way your all-important dignity may be kept intact, and your feathers remain unruffled.

On one level you are not quite sure if you have any right to have an ego at all. But on another, you can be highly perturbed and upset by the thought of being taken in vain. One way of expressing this is by appearing to be easygoing and flexible, when really you are not. On the other hand, too rarely do you show your sincerity, emotional warmth and generosity. No doubt someone or something made you feel small and insignificant in the past – or else you gained a false sense of pride. In any event, you'd best come out to play and meet both the embarrassment and the glory that go with having a human ego.

LIKES	DISLIKES
Being centre of attraction • Children and parties	Feeling self-conscious • Stuffy social occasions
Romantic involvements • Privilege and grandeur	Lack-lustre relationships • Going second class
An influential position	Being answerable to others

If you are a man, this could be the kind of woman to whom you are attracted – but it is really you, so realize it and express it.

THE MOON IN LEO

TRANSFORMER

POSITIVE	NEGATIVE
Impressive Self-confident Majestic Noble	Demanding Praise-seeking Subtly domineering Snobbish
Popular Lively Sunny Dignified	Easily flattered Easily hurt Self-centred Vain
Dramatic Leader Creative Persevering	Overbearing Power-tripper Self-important Stubborn
Cheerful Charming Magnetic Proud	Hedonistic Conceited Attention-seeking Arrogant
Loyal Sincere Warm Good-hearted	Possessive Inflexible Overreacts Prima donna
Find solace in your principles, and comfort in magnanimity.	Feeling threatened and about to be taken advantage of. Sulky. Wounded pride.
Even the bright Sun has spots! As you radiate show your doubts, too.	Feeling dissipated, unappreciated and misunderstood.
Try expressing yourself honestly rather than trying painfully to prove yourself.	Frightened that your insecurity will be found out and that you'll be shot down in flames.
Be aware of that light within; it can never be extinguished, so set no limits on it.	Feeling cheated and crestfallen, and being self-righteous only makes matters worse.
Recognize your obvious pride, then master it – and what it is in.	Feeling indignant. Rejected and avoided by others, but not openly.
SOLUTION	PROBLEM

If you find yourself on the receiving end of negative traits, it is because you are not expressing the opposing positive traits.

THE MOON IN VIRGO

ESSENCE

Security through Analysing
Security in Purity • Trust your Darker Side

Security is sought through analysing, which can lead either to a pure and well-ordered emotional lifestyle, whereby you consistently weed out influences that are detrimental to your well-being, or to one that is prudish and fastidious, whereby you try to govern feelings as if they were things to be tidied away. In either case you would need to cultivate some open-ended tolerance and acceptance of life's imperfections.

Behind such exacting emotional requirements as you feel subject to, there lies your mother's influence, which, on the positive side, was likely to have been clear and wholesome or, on the negative, may have been critical and narrow. In either case this could have led to your being afraid of your dark side showing – 'dark side' meaning anything that your mother or any other influential childhood figure found unacceptable. For example, your more Earthy or raw emotions possibly got branded as vulgar or crude, with the result that the healthy but sticky passions that keep relationships glued together became repressed, and devolved, instead, into a lurking urge. Apart from weakening bonds in this fundamental way, there is the added strain of constantly trying to maintain a goody-two-shoes image. Because such emotional fastidiousness can leave you on the shelf, or at least left alone too often, it is advisable for you to trust life to unfold according to itself, rather than how you think it ought to. Sanity is not always sanitary, and what is wholesome obviously includes everything.

A feeling of security can also be attained through being of service in some way, in particular with regard to health. You can go to great lengths to help others, as if you thrive on it – and you do. This sense of service can also satisfy your need for Purity, in that you are able, with great thoroughness, to clean up anything that is messy or polluted. Or else you can go around as if you have a bad smell under your nose – what could that be? Virgo is a Sign that can polarize; this strong need to be so orderly and clean can turn into the opposite: your being untidy or loose – either voluntarily or otherwise.

As a rule you have a liking for animals, especially small ones or pets. This is because they have a certain purity of being that humans seem to lack. But then observe how 'natural' animals are with their Earthy habits. This is an example of one of those grey areas that you can fail to see, or avoid seeing, as you are predisposed to seeing life in black and white. But it is to these grey, misty areas that your unconscious will always draw you, as it urges you to understand that there is as much purity in darkness as there is in light, and that you can trust the mysterious more than the logical. What you don't know is always greater than what you do.

LIKES	**DISLIKES**
Order and plans • Hygiene • Making lists	Uncertainty • Squalor • Sloppiness
Wholesomeness • Health aids	Sordidness • Health hazards

If you are a man, this could be the kind of woman to whom you are attracted – but it is really you, so realize it and express it.

THE MOON IN VIRGO

TRANSFORMER

POSITIVE	NEGATIVE
Conscientious Dutiful Straight Upright	Worrier Austere Prudish Rigid
Shrewd Methodical Precise Discriminating	Cold Exacting Pedantic Carping
Neat Clean Health-conscious Helpful	Neurotic Clinical Health freak Interfering
Modest Unassuming Gentle Light touch	Falsely modest Undemonstrative Timid Creepy
Finely tuned Keen instincts Analytical Concerned	Hypersensitive Prejudiced Labelling Anxious

SOLUTION	PROBLEM
Life ahead of you is a multi-coloured experience, so why switch to black and white?	Reducing life to a set of theories and pigeon-holes results in your being fearfully restricted.
It takes time to be aware of your true worth, but when you are, others will be so automatically.	Feeling underestimated and rejected. Afraid or unable to express your deepest feelings.
Healthy body = healthy mind? Not necessarily; but a pure heart emanates a healing aura.	Your well-intentioned preoccupation with health makes others avoid you like the plague.
Realize that the idea behind any method is to reduce wear and tear.	You no longer enjoy your full-time job maintaining the illusion of control.
Who or what are you serving? Are you devoted or enslaved?	Feeling that life is all uphill, and that everything will fall apart if you relax.

If you find yourself on the receiving end of negative traits, it is because you are not expressing the opposing positive traits.

161

THE MOON IN LIBRA

ESSENCE

Security through Relating
The Need for Balance • The Emotional Mirror

Security is sought through feeling socially involved – having a partner; having a definite social position. Your refined instincts are readily able to achieve this, but you can run the risk of finding yourself attempting to be all things to all people. Your undeniable social graces, like metaphorical clothing, need to be worn lightly in order to prevent this predisposition to please becoming unpleasantly restricting for you. Such a need to please – which can be very enjoyable to others – may merely have its roots in your having felt that you had to please your mother, father or whoever brought you up. However, sooner or later, what pleases you has to emerge and take priority – and that might not please anyone else at all!

Until then, all this makes you very difficult to dislike, which is both your boon and your bane, because although popularity has its obvious advantages, people can find it hard to confront you with what they don't like about you. You are then made to feel socially excluded or emotionally rejected for no apparent reason. When you realize that a Libran Moon attracts the kind of people and social situations that eventually force your individually held principles into conscious awareness, the instinctive sense of beauty and harmony that you most surely have will become a creative and dynamic expression of you, rather than a passive and insecure reflection of others that makes it hard for you to accept the consequences of your actions.

The need for balance and harmony is essential to your Moon position. This need can manifest itself negatively, in the form of abortive relationships and fickleness – in either yourself or your partner – that have resulted from your attempting to keep things 'nice' rather than getting down to the nitty gritty. This reluctance to look at and to express your darker and more powerful urges and feelings again probably stems from your sensing that your mother or father would not have liked it; or there could have been an incident in your childhood in which this darker side to your nature was thrust upon you in the form of a traumatic experience. The simplest, clearest, most rewarding and most relieving thing that you can do is to share both your good and your bad feelings with your partner. If this cannot be done, then seek counsel or therapy in order to disperse your fear of just being yourself as you are, as opposed to what you feel others expect you to be. Learning to trust your natural talent for making things appealing is all-important. This can take the form of a flair for cooking, décor, fashion, entertaining, or be expressed as the basic ability to make others feel they are a part of something. Perversely, not trusting this social sense can make you rather anti-social. Your soothing presence, which may even have the voice or musical ability to go with it, should be recognized as a powerful tool with which you can influence the social and emotional climate around you.

LIKES	DISLIKES
Fine people and fine things • Sharing	Coarseness and vulgarity • Emotional tight-fistedness
Knowing social pitch • Conviviality • Being agreeable	Feeling outcast • Inhospitality • Being misjudged

If you are a man, this could be the kind of woman to whom you are attracted – but it is really you, so realize it and express it.

THE MOON IN LIBRA

TRANSFORMER

POSITIVE	NEGATIVE
Romantic Charming Graceful Affectionate	Silly Insincere Superficial Unfaithful
Refined Aesthetic Gentle Kind	Shallow Glossy façade Limp Vague
Pleasing Richly expressive Attractive Friendly	Self-indulgent Affected Seductive Flirt
Tolerant Tactful Reasonable Gracious	Yes-person Indecisive Insipid Disappointing
Socially aware Hospitable Dependable Relaxing	Anti-social Neglectful Unreliable Lazy
Do not resist your basic need to feel liked, and put both others and yourself at ease.	Your need to please has exhausted itself rather than matured into a social skill.
Do not accept peace at any price; after all, you know what it takes to keep it.	Your fear of being thought badly of has created that very thing.
People who matter are attracted to all your qualities, not just to the ones you like.	No one seems able or available to please you because they cannot get to the real you.
You have a need to make nice what's nasty, so acknowledge what's nasty!	Feeling empty and unfulfilled. Reluctant to face life's deeper or harsher realities.
Know that your lightness attracts heaviness, thereby challenging your charms.	Failed relationships – either you become fickle or you invite fickleness. In love with love.
SOLUTION	PROBLEM

If you find yourself on the receiving end of negative traits, it is because you are not expressing the opposing positive traits.

163

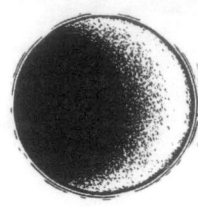

THE MOON IN SCORPIO

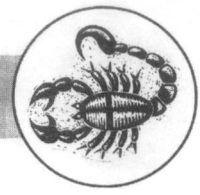

ESSENCE

Security through Desiring
A Soul Needs a Soul • Trust or Perish

Security is found in strong, deep feelings, which necessarily poses the acknowledgement of your equally deep need for a profound and gut-wrenching relationship. This is because the Moon is said to be in its Fall in Scorpio, which means that some kind of emotional death has to be experienced before you can begin to feel able to manage the intimate bond that is so important to you. Light-hearted affairs are, therefore, doomed to failure because they fail to purge you in this way. However, paradoxically, a failure to purge can be experienced as a purging in itself!

As your emotional experiences strike right to your heart and soul with great intensity, understandably you make great attempts to control your emotional environment. Such control is made possible by an intuition that is as profound as your feelings. Unfortunately, this need for control can lead to your using underhand means, such as hitting another person where it hurts before they hit you. The fact that they probably have no intention of striking you at all is a point worth considering.

Behind this lie experiences from childhood that made you feel at the mercy of traditions and attitudes that had no conception of your emotional sensitivity and of the nature of your desires. Consequently, you felt betrayed and abandoned, and may still continue to guard against such threats. You should grasp the fact that your emotional intensity and insight can put anyone where you want them. You need to let go of that fear of betrayal, because holding on to it will simply attract it – such is your power. Abandon your fears or be abandoned because of them.

You see yourself as a survivor. While it is true that you have great emotional stamina, be careful that it does not merely take the form of resisting involvement of an intimate kind. Being proud of your inscrutability is rather like being Houdini on a bad night – the audience can't see in, and you can't get out.

Not surprisingly you have an unerring ability to detect the emotional state of others, even when it is well hidden. Although this talent can sometimes be misused to drag them down into the hole that you are in yourself, at your best you cannot fail to see what has to be done in order to rectify or to quicken a given situation – even if it might result in your losing something or someone. Until you reach such a level of emotional awareness and expression, you are in danger of being driven by a self-destructive pressure to hedge your bets or to sublimate such strong emotions through overwork, alcohol, drugs or simply talking incessantly. More than any other Moon-Sign you are capable of seeing beyond the trivial, the cheap and the immediately attainable. 'It is a far, far better thing that I do, than I have ever done.'

LIKES	DISLIKES
Intimacy • Soul mates • Moving experiences	Superficiality • Meaningless ties • Being controlled
Profound feelings • A sense of finality	Insipidness • Dragging things out

---

If you are a man, this could be the kind of woman to whom you are attracted – but it is really you, so realize it and express it.

THE MOON IN SCORPIO

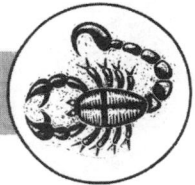

TRANSFORMER

POSITIVE	NEGATIVE
Magnetic Genuine feelings Intuitive Compassionate	Unyielding Apparently unfeeling Suspicious Scornful
Energetic Passionate Powerful Determined	Maniacal Jealous Gloating Obsessive
Self-sacrificing Just Persevering Stoical	Grudging Revengeful Unforgiving Emotionally denying
Inscrutable Self-reliant Deep Self-possessed	Unreachable Lonely Brooding Self-destructive
Complex Influential Shrewd Firm	Subtly dominating Manipulative Underhand Obstinate
Others fall easily under your spell, so bless and be blessed – or curse and be cursed.	Your security feels threatened by the very things you vainly use to gain it.
The true test and validation of your secret world is to let a chosen few into it.	Feeling abandoned, betrayed and misunderstood.
The price of getting what you want is exactly equal to what you give up.	Poisoned by your own bitterness. Gutted by your own emptiness.
Taking hold only in order to let go will continually absorb you.	After you have got what you want, you are quickly, if not immediately, dissatisfied.
Trust the depth of your feelings and insight to attract people to your level.	Fearful of submitting. Unable to trust others and to show your love.
SOLUTION	PROBLEM

If you find yourself on the receiving end of negative traits, it is because you are not expressing the opposing positive traits.

THE MOON IN SAGITTARIUS

ESSENCE

Security through Seeking

A Need to Roam • The Gypsy Soul

This is the Lunar position of the Soul that has sought for a long time. You are the natural philosopher – the habitual seeker. However, it is actually through habit that you may have forgotten that seeking is your greatest need, that you must find a system of belief, or a mission, that will guide and give meaning to your life. In the process of seeking you may well have to learn to make the distinction between your own beliefs and those that you were taught or that were bred into you as a child. Because you naturally prefer your spiritual or religious beliefs to be kept fluid and free, any dogmatic indoctrination in the past can be reacted against later, when you may completely reject any kind of spiritual or ethical code – or can result in your becoming even more dogmatic. But, for your security's sake, some kind of faith or philosophy is required. Insisting on being without any – a dogma in itself – is tantamount to cutting off your nose to spite your face.

You are also a gambler, looking for the big chance, the unique, the ideal, which ultimately could only be yourself. Without risk-taking, nothing is discovered or gained – a phrase that could be your personal motto. On the other hand, you can get into the habit of taking risks for the hell of it, as a kind of compensation for not taking more calculated risks in aid of furthering your quest – or, initially, of just discovering the nature of the quest itself.

You are basically a positive person, and you maintain that positivity most easily in a changing environment; no matter what darkness falls across your path, you will magically find a new direction to take, and will come up smelling of roses. As you believe in Providence, so she looks after you. Equally refreshing is your natural inclination to be spontaneous and outspoken – you clear the air, and the way, whenever confusion or despondency reigns. However, cheerful and optimistic as you are in company, unless you discover where such feelings are coming from, you can sometimes feel hollow and empty when on your own.

At root, you have an almost mystical sense of life's 'story' – that it is all going somewhere, and coming from somewhere. It is this innate and primitive faith that allows you to see the light at the end of the tunnel, when others are stumbling and crestfallen. This sense also gives you the desire to embrace more and more of life's meanings and experiences. To inhibit such a natural urge can give rise to blind indulgences and listlessness. So at all costs, if your feet feel itchy, hitch your caravan to the brightest star, your most inspiring thought-feeling, and embark upon another chapter in your life's history.

LIKES	DISLIKES
Freedom and adventure • Drama and story-telling	Restrictions and small thinking • Humdrum normality
Honesty • Extremes	Pretentiousness • Prejudice and pedantry
Travel and the outdoor life	Morbid soul-searching

If you are a man, this could be the kind of woman to whom you are attracted – but it is really you, so realize it and express it.

THE MOON IN SAGITTARIUS

TRANSFORMER

POSITIVE	NEGATIVE
Philosophical Enthusiastic Cheerful Sense of fun	Unrealistic Restless Hysterical Irresponsible
Sincere seeker Sense of mission Devout Concerned	Offhand Non-committal Amoral Careless
Wise and understanding Humanitarian Frank Outspoken	Pompous and narrow-minded Holier-than-thou Blunt Arrogant
Innocent Naturally trusting Open-minded Optimistic	Gullible Naïve Dizzy Unreliable
Alert Lively Playful Generous	Idle Listless Silly Self-indulgent

SOLUTION	PROBLEM
Stir yourself and give of yourself – and be the exception that proves the rule.	Feeling sluggish and tired, and that life is just an unfair game. Overweight.
Others learn to trust in life more by your example – as long as you get your facts right.	Feeling taken advantage of. Overstretched and out to lunch.
Learn to be receptive to others' feelings and viewpoints as your express your own.	Others feel unable to approach you. You feel lonely.
The only point that life has is the one you make or discover for yourself.	Feeling neglected and pointless. Others are indifferent to your predicament.
Treat life more adventurously, others more seriously, and yourself less seriously.	Feeling humiliated and anxious about your credibility. Distress and confusion reign.

If you find yourself on the receiving end of negative traits, it is because you are not expressing the opposing positive traits.

THE MOON IN CAPRICORN

ESSENCE

Security through Building
The Need to be Needed • The End Justifies the Means

Security is built upon a base of being useful to society and seeking justification in its eyes – for better or for worse. Such a need can incline you to undervalue what you want from and for yourself. This in turn can lead to feeling unloved, unwanted or inferior in some way. This is why the Moon is said to be in its Detriment in Capricorn, for seeking external approval to allay inner doubts proves detrimental to your personality as a whole.

Whether it shows or not, you have a great need to be needed. So others come to rely on you to keep things together materially in some way. This can make you indispensable, but if having this need met means losing sight of your inner worth, you can wind up feeling a bit of a slave. In other words, by not trusting the importance of your own inner values and subscribing to those that outside pressures seem to dictate, you are in danger of feeling let down, by both yourself and the state of affairs around you.

However, it is important to recognize how and why this distrust of your inner self occurred in the first place, and subsequently created a distrust of others. The Moon symbolizes the Child – both literally and in the sense of the 'Child within'. Capricorn is the Sign that governs the 'big, bad world out there' – concrete or man-made reality. So the Moon is not happy in Capricorn, for the Child is thrust harshly into the material world. This can mean that you literally had a hard or deprived childhood. Burdens were piled upon your small shoulders; austere and oppressive surroundings were your lot. There may have been something lacking in your father, or a lack of him altogether, and this could have cast a shadow over your mother that was passed on to you in some way. Whatever your childhood circumstances, you learnt, through their material or emotional difficulties, to become a survivor.

The most likely expression of this 'survivorship' is being able to function well in the material world, as a way of compensating for that inner emotional blight. Such a shrewd and businesslike streak can take you far up the socio-economic ladder. But at some stage the outer trappings that you have built up around you can no longer seal you off from that feeling that something is missing, and it is this very feeling that makes you reluctant to be the outright materialist go-getter that you have or could become. As this new type of 'survivor' you can turn into quite a special sort of human being, because you manage to combine your childlike charm with strong instincts of how the material world works. And just how it works, you discover, is built upon that real 'real world' within you. Ultimately, and usually after the age of thirty, you stand to become an influence over others, because you are an example of the no-nonsense human being who has survived against the odds.

LIKES	**DISLIKES**
The tried and the true • Strong people • Organization	Pie-in-the-sky • Spinelessness • Feeling out of control
Steadiness of purpose • Firm foundations	Having no purpose • Shaky set-ups

---

If you are a man, this could be the kind of woman to whom you are attracted – but it is really you, so realize it and express it.

THE MOON IN CAPRICORN

TRANSFORMER

POSITIVE	NEGATIVE
Self-controlled Cautious Modest Reserved	Repressed Distrustful Self-doubting Inhibited
Serious Disciplined Pragmatic Prudent	Depressive Austere Unimaginative Boring
Achiever Hardworking Determined Shrewd	Status-conscious Slave to system Cold-hearted Crafty
Loyal Influential Steadfast Respected	Sycophantic Name-dropper Unctuous Insincere
Sensitive Self-sacrificing Efficient helper Dignified	Insensitive Uses others Self-serving Conceited
To rule truly is to serve. Improving the lot of others improves your self-image.	For all your selfish attention to your ambitions, you are still dissatisfied.
Relate to others in the knowledge that they are after what you are after: respect.	Licking others' boots only gets you a kick in the face. Loss of self-respect.
When you realize that what you are after cannot be found in the outer world, look within.	Feeling that life is just a meaningless struggle. Disillusioned.
Seriously consider not taking yourself so seriously; humour is a necessity, not a luxury.	Feeling grey and downcast. Unable to see beyond your deeply furrowed brow.
What you need to keep under control is that voice from the past that says 'Not good enough'.	Feeling inadequate and unappreciated. Lonely and alienated.
SOLUTION	PROBLEM

If you find yourself on the receiving end of negative traits, it is because you are not expressing the opposing positive traits.

THE MOON IN AQUARIUS

ESSENCE

Security through Liberating
Invent Yourself • Long-Distance Love

Security is gained through liberation, which means that idealistically you aspire to be free of negative emotions such as greed, fear, anger, jealousy etc. But you should be careful not simply to pretend that you are so, for this can lead to others expecting you to be impossibly tolerant of their negative emotions. As Aquarius is the Sign of Humanity, with the Moon placed in it you should remember to be merely human, and not more than human. Being unaware of your feelings and natural instincts can mean that you will attract quite drastic upheavals and confrontations, as your unconscious mind makes a bid to get you in touch with who you truly are, as opposed to who you like to think you are.

Emotional experiences of your mother and your childhood have often been disruptive, alienating or out of the ordinary. Although these also helped to get you in touch with your individual feelings, they also probably initially distanced you from so-called normal social interplay. Thus you began to become an observer of rather than a participant in life, which gave you an awareness of human nature. Now, as the natural psychologist or counsellor, you are sought after, professionally or personally, for your fitting and impartial advice.

Another type of emotional response peculiar to Moon in Aquarius is usually experienced in adolescence, but leaves its mark for years to come. This is the inclination to think of yourself as more emotional than you in fact are, with the result that you become romantically attracted to others who are indifferent or unavailable in some way. This pattern persists until you realize that you are trying too hard, and that it is your own air of unavailability that is so attractive. However, this can be carried to the extreme where you are emotionally unreachable, and thus remain attracted to the unattainable or far-distant.

An important need of yours is to have a lover as a friend. It is vital for you to be able to share and to discuss views and feelings on an intellectual level. Until this kind of relationship is attained, you tend to be happier in a group situation, rather than an intimate one. In this way you are able to disguise or to forget your emotional fears, as things can be kept light and breezy. For this reason, a group situation is best for getting you in touch with your feelings. You can then get back into the one-to-one scene with a renewed sense that it is all right to be an emotional being.

Your need for freedom of expression is ever-present, and will consistently jolt others, as well as yourself, out of any complacency that has built up through mere illusions of freedom. This can produce much mood-swinging and unpredictability, but with an Aquarian Moon you know that in order to be moved to liberation, one first has to be stirred, if not shaken.

LIKES	**DISLIKES**
Being unique • Openness • The unusual	Being ordinary • Emotional confinement
Clear minds • Keeping cool	Stick-in-the-muds • Over-emotionalism • Show-offs

If you are a man, this could be the kind of woman to whom you are attracted – but it is really you, so realize it and express it.

THE MOON IN AQUARIUS

TRANSFORMER

POSITIVE	NEGATIVE
Impartial Dispassionate Broad-minded Candid	Impersonal Not earthed Indiscriminate Insubstantial
Courteous Friendly Human Good listener	Artificial Superficial Unreal Unresponsive
Reformist Progressive Intuitive Individualistic	Rebellious Unpredictable Insensitive Misfit
Own person Paradoxical Knowing Open	Stubborn Perverse Know-all Closed
Observant Cool Unbiased Detached	Aloof Icy Non-committal Remote
Look and you will see that there are others just as far out as you think you are. Befriend them.	It begins to bother you that you only seem to enjoy your 'freedom' on your own.
Knowing and accepting that feelings are irrational is your ticket to freedom.	Having both fixed ideas and a liberal attitude gives both you and others a tense time.
Your personal view of the world is both your cue and your clue to bettering it, not beating it.	At odds with yourself, you secretly dwell on the chances of getting even.
Remember: what you really like about people is that they belong to the same species as you.	Feeling very unsure of what you are feeling. Unable to show yourself.
Choose a standpoint that allows you to be fair and comfortable with yourself.	The unbearable lightness of being. Feeling that you are not quite here.
SOLUTION	PROBLEM

If you find yourself on the receiving end of negative traits, it is because you are not expressing the opposing positive traits.

171

THE MOON IN PISCES

ESSENCE

Security through Accepting

Got to have a Dream ● The Soul of Sensitivity

Of all the Moon-Sign positions, this one has the acutest emotional sensitivity – and, consequently, the most complex responses to life situations. You find a million and one ways to enhance or to evade whatever might present itself to your super-receptive nature.

Most positively, you have the qualities of the healer, poet or mystic. Most negatively, you are inclined to experience the refined senses that make this possible as a distaste for mundane existence and thus you seek to escape it. The notion of 'what you could be' is endlessly used as a means of keeping you in a fascinated state of being neither special nor ordinary. Owing to childhood feelings of being 'a fish out of water', you wind up 'at sea'. But when you truly embark upon a creative or spiritual quest, your fertile imagination is capable of transporting you (and others) to rare heights, and depths, of human experience. Fantasizing about such things as high hopes or morbid fears involves the illusion of not getting hurt. However, this is, in fact, a delusion, for you still feel pain even – or most of all – in your imagination. So eventually you pursue, or through some real crisis are forced to pursue, the lofty role that you originally envisaged falling into your lap. In effect, with a Piscean Moon you need a vision of a better life for one and all that not only will act as a focus for all your compassion, imagination and sensitivity, but also is practically attainable. Otherwise your fantasy overdrive will continue to get you nowhere.

You are malleable, seductive and seductable, and looking for a 'dreamboat' to take you away on the morning tide. Your imagination is, in fact, so vivid that this dreamboat actually appears to arrive. However, after a few months or years at sea, the dream evaporates and by contrast you seem to be living off hard-tack biscuits and brackish water – that is, your partner seems boring and emotionally tainted. In fact, of course, neither extreme was real; the ordinary, but sad and beautiful human being is what is real – which, naturally, includes yourself.

Not surprisingly you can have an addictive personality, be it to drink, drugs, cream cakes, seafood, men with beards or girls in turquoise rubber. An addiction is essentially a distraction; you are pulled towards something that your Soul desires, but because this poses a real sacrifice, you opt for the phoney sacrifice of throwing yourself away on something self-destructive, dissipating, fetishistic or insidiously inconsequential. However, sooner or later, you will have to go for the Soul's desire – no other drug will do. Poetically enough, that desire will eventually entail the relief or guidance of those mortals who, similarly, have lost sight of their Soul's desire. So rather than looking for a dreamboat, you become a lifeboat.

LIKES	**DISLIKES**
Highs and lows ● Music and poetry ● The fascinating	The commonplace ● Aesthetic starvation ● The obvious
Romantic quests ● Taking off	Confronting reality ● Coming down

If you are a man, this could be the kind of woman to whom you are attracted – but it is really you, so realize it and express it.

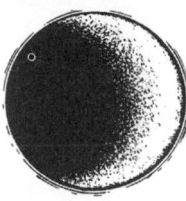

THE MOON IN PISCES

TRANSFORMER

POSITIVE	NEGATIVE
Imaginative Inspiring Mystical Creative	Escapist Deceptive Spaced out Wool-gathering
Empathetic Psychic Compassionate Mediumistic	Impressionable Too open Hypersensitive Easily drained
Devoted Highly adaptable Amiable Romantic	Idolatrous Self-doubting Seductable Unfaithful
Selless Kind Healer Yielding	Weak-willed Indiscriminate Victim Leaf-in-the-wind
Tolerant Gentle Relaxed Understanding	Too easygoing Weak Lazy Excuse-making

Making fewer allowances for shortcomings increases the value of your virtues.	Life has lost its shape and direction. Procrastination is stealing all your time.
Offer your services to an institution/movement that works quietly to relieve others.	Easily exploited and forced to carry the can for others, because you do not carry your own.
Look for the highest quality that you can find in yourself and develop it.	A slave to your senses and fantasies. Resentment grows as does your dependency.
Learn to locate – protect – use – your chakras or energy centres and they will serve, not sap you.	Prone to infection and invasion by lower astral phenomena. Easily irritated or upset.
Use your imagination or it will use you. Build castles in the air, but don't move in.	Confusion, self-pity and bitterness reign. Drug and alcohol abuse. Discontented.

SOLUTION	PROBLEM

If you find yourself on the receiving end of negative traits, it is because you are not expressing the opposing positive traits.

MERCURY

Keyword: THINKING

Mercury, the Messenger of the Gods, symbolizes your ability to CONNECT one thing to or with another — most particularly in your head, as RATIONAL THINKING, in your body, as your NERVOUS SYSTEM, and, externally, via COMMUNICATION, PERCEPTION and DEXTERITY.

So your Mercury Sign tells you how well and in what manner you think and communicate, what your nervous disposition is, how well 'WIRED' you are and your capacity to LEARN on an INTELLECTUAL level.

Negatively, Mercury can be expressed as OVER-RATIONALIZATION, which leads to DRYNESS and a LACK OF FEELING, which in turn can give rise to NERVOUSNESS.

Your Mercury-Sign can also give some indication of the kind of work that suits your MENTALITY, thereby providing clues to fruitful areas of EMPLOYMENT for both your MIND and your HANDS.

MERCURY IN ARIES

ESSENCE

Thinking through Doing

The Wrangler • Action Speaks Louder than Words

Yours is a mind that has to be active, and wants thoughts and words to become deeds rather than be left merely in the realm of ideas. So firstly, it is important for you to receive not only mental stimulation but also challenges, and secondly, it will probably be necessary to remain mindful of the fact that it takes time for an idea or an aim to be realized.

You have a terrier-like mentality that gets hold of a thought, word, idea or piece of information, and wants to push it forward as if it is the most important thing in the world. Positively, this signifies an ability to learn, communicate or teach quickly and effectively; it also confers on you a flair for selling. However, negatively, you can have a one-sided point of view and a tendency to make decisions and form opinions before all the facts available have been considered. For this reason, it should be no surprise that there can be a lack of follow-through with certain projects.

Your brisk and headstrong mentality is just as disinclined to dwell on old grievances as on outworn interests. This gives an impression of broad-mindedness, when it is actually more a case of not having the time or room for stuffy thoughts or feelings.

Without enough mental input or assertion of your intellectual outlook, there is a danger of nervous or physical restlessness that can develop into more serious mental or emotional conditions, with circumstances to match. You should never be afraid to argue a point, but you should also be aware that although arguing for its own sake will release tensions of the moment, it might simultaneously provoke in others antagonism that creates further tension. Your bellicose brain runs according to the formula that there is no stimulation without some aggravation, which is fine as long as you learn that the secret is to be good-hearted and to respect your opponent for being your opponent.

Needless to say, you often speak before thinking, which leads to your making *faux pas* at times, and coming refreshingly right to the point at others. At some stage it is more than likely that you will have to 'make the running', in the sense of taking the initiative workwise, setting a precedent, going out on a limb, or rattling a few cages in your neighbourhood. This is unavoidable in order for you to make some progress – or merely to get out from under.

LIKES	DISLIKES
Hot debate • Intellectual competition • Immediate reactions Brain-teasers • Straight talking	Delays • Lack of opposition • Slowcoaches Mind-games • Pussy-footing

Mercury is your tool for making connections and getting leads.

MERCURY IN ARIES

TRANSFORMER

POSITIVE	NEGATIVE
Quick-thinking Spontaneous Quick-acting Decisive	Impatient Irritable Quick-tempered Premature
Mentally forceful Stimulating Fighting spirit Fiery	Headstrong Hectoring Quarrelsome Spitting
Frank Witty To the point Observant	Thoughtless Sarcastic Terse Precocious
Initiates ideas Thinks on feet Mentally active and agile	Snap opinions Snap decisions Verbally/mentally restless
Eloquent Verbally assertive Intellectually confident	Strident One-sided viewpoint Intellectually arrogant
Your tongue is a sensitive muscle; hold it and appreciate what it's attached to.	Carried away by your own verbal powers, you're now overworked and your concentration is flagging.
You'd enjoy your mental muscles more if you flexed them less often. Where's the fire?	On a moving mental pavement and you can't get off. Nervy and bordering on the hysterical.
Add a dash of humility to your candour and others will more readily take your point.	Later regretting what you have said. Failing to cover this up with more blustering.
Make sure you have a cause to match your force. Be aware of your contentiousness.	You probably don't spot it, but others get out of your way when they see you coming.
Slow down enough to clarify your objectives, then trust that you'll rise to the occasion.	Out of step with yourself. Competing with yourself. Strife at work.
SOLUTION	PROBLEM

If you find yourself on the receiving end of negative traits, it is because you are not expressing the opposing positive traits.

177

MERCURY IN TAURUS

ESSENCE

Thinking through Stabilizing
The Concrete Mind • Seeing is Believing

Yours is a mind that likes to chew things over, and so you acquire depth of knowledge as a result of thoroughly enjoying the process of learning – rather as you would a good meal. A taste for the traditional rather than the newfangled is also in evidence. Once you have learnt and assimilated something, you will probably never forget it. However, should an idea come along that challenges an already existing concept, you are very reluctant to accept it. You are slow to form opinions, and equally slow to change them.

You are materially-minded, which means that you are a practical thinker and are not too happy with total abstractions. If it is really necessary mentally to digest complex theories, they are more easily understood when expressed or taught in a visual or a practical way.

In money matters you are either efficient, sometimes to the point of being a bit miserly, or lazy, at the price of someone else holding the purse-strings. This depends on the particular set of values that you are used to, and at some time or other these may be the very values that have to be changed.

As your mind works at a natural pace, you develop steady working habits, and are therefore thorough and produce solid results. Tasks are performed evenly from start to finish. From a more philosophical or spiritual point of view, your intellectual role in life is to keep matters of the mind running on an even keel, and to prevent the waste of resources through unwise investments and impractical ideas. For this reason, you can also make a good manager.

Dependable and reassuring as your conservative way of thinking is, if it is carried to extremes in resisting change, others might have to resort to more emotional methods of making their point. If you, in turn, regard this as unreasonable or even underhand, you are really asking to get buried in the very rut in which you insist on staying. With Mercury in Taurus it is supremely sensible to ensure that your firm grip on concrete reality does not set into mental obstinacy.

Above all you have the gift of being able to see how any plan will work out – if at all – in physical terms. And so you have a natural bent towards arts and crafts, and also towards construction skills such as carpentry and building. Quite simply, yours is the kind of mind that gives value for money – or for any other kind of energy.

LIKES	**DISLIKES**
Common sense • Good workmanship • Peace of mind	Airy-theory • Practical ineptitude • Being badgered
Time to ponder • Concrete evidence	Deadlines • Blind faith

Mercury is your tool for making connections and getting leads.

MERCURY IN TAURUS

TRANSFORMER

POSITIVE	NEGATIVE
Sound mind Thorough Patient Cautious	Slow mind Plodding Tardy Guarded
Shrewd Resourceful Sensible Realistic	Mean-minded Money-grubbing Boneheaded Purblind
Good concentration Mentally sure Deliberating	Blinkered One-track-minded Overburdened
Practical thinker Sense of form Steady mind Enduring	Limited thinker Mechanistic Stubborn mind Stodgy
Mentally laid-back Docile Ruminating Undemanding	Lazy-minded Dumb Misses point Couch potato
Give your wholesome mind something wholesome – and worthwhile – to chew on.	Feeling uncomfortably stuck in one of life's intellectual lay-bys.
Regard your strong concrete thinking as a foil or foundation to others' wilder ideas.	You find it hard to understand or accept abstract concepts and so reject them.
Take definite steps to add another string to your bow. Retrain.	Dissatisfied with your working life. Overworked and underemployed.
You have the ability to master money – by conquering your fear or love of it.	The material world gives you, or those with whom you are financially involved, a headache.
Take your time, and use visual aids to brush up on those areas of knowledge that you are unsure of.	Difficulty in grasping subjects that threaten to ridicule you.
SOLUTION	PROBLEM

If you find yourself on the receiving end of negative traits, it is because you are not expressing the opposing positive traits.

MERCURY IN GEMINI

ESSENCE

Thinking through Communicating
Wizard or Smart Alec • The Eclectic

Your mind is fed and furthered through making contact with as many people and as many subjects as possible. Your intellect is all wired up and raring to go; it more or less constantly needs to be occupied, otherwise nervous irritability or feeling restlessly at a loose end can result. Your brain, hands and nervous system can be likened to a highly sophisticated piece of electrical equipment. If there is not enough 'output' the whole thing gets too hot and a circuit blows. Your mind is efficient in that it is quick and acquisitive, but the quality of it is only as good as what is being fed into it via social, business and educational pursuits. Mercury in Gemini can be an eloquent speaker or a gossip, clever or facile, fluent or flippant. What you read and who you mix with have everything to do with this, so 'input' is just as important as output. Because you are quick-witted and articulate – no matter what anyone says – and because you possess a natural sense of curiosity, you should have no trouble in finding suitable friends and employment – once you put your mind to it!

You are capable of thinking on two or more levels at once, which can make you a whiz at work or at play. However, if there is not some serious direction or intention given to such mental acrobatics, there is a danger of your mind becoming confused in a sort of mental traffic jam. You require an absorbing and ongoing interest that has some emotional content that will keep your agile mind from revolving on its own spot and prevent you suffering from scattered energies, divided attention, or a lack of continuity of purpose.

You usually have a friendly attitude, for you are naturally interested in all walks of life. Such a light and unbiased touch is welcome in almost every place, and you would be wise to capitalize on this. This typically Mercurial talent for being able to talk about anything at any time anywhere stands you in good stead for activities that require this contact-making ability, such as journalism, publicity, buying and selling, transport, courier work etc. You are also proficient in the use of all basic mental functions, like communications and mathematics, and are naturally logical and dextrous – only some serious pathological affliction would contradict this.

Above all is that need to have a motivation or goal that organizes your undeniable dexterity and mental versatility. Then, rather than learning parrot-fashion and acquiring knowledge merely for its own sake, your mind becomes your servant and not a tyrannical master or rogue who blinds you to the fact that it is not so much a product or an end in itself, but rather a shining multi-purpose tool which you hold, so to speak, in your hands, to use as you see fit.

LIKES	DISLIKES
Mental stimulation • Facts and figures	Intellectual deserts • Biased opinions
A quick turnover • Getting around • Intellectual style	Slow thinking • Being tied down • Dead-heads

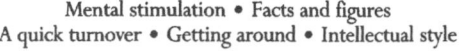

Mercury is your tool for making connections and getting leads.

MERCURY IN GEMINI

TRANSFORMER

POSITIVE	NEGATIVE
Articulate Curious Well-informed Widely read	Chatterbox Nosy Gossip Superficial knowledge
Quick-witted Lively mind Fast learner Dextrous	Highly strung Unruly mind Unpersevering Fidgety
Clever Humorous Sharp Fluent	Crafty Mischievous Flippant Facile
Inventive Versatile Original Handy	Makeshift Slipshod Imitative Simplistic
Interesting Agreeable Unbiased Logical	Trite Scatters energies Unfocused Misses point
Obviously you can only go in one direction – your own. This is what influences others.	Apparently going along with everyone while obviously no one goes along with you.
Do one thing at a time, well; then do another, better – as only you can.	Much that you do either falls apart or never comes together.
Learn to put and keep levity and gravity in their appropriate places.	Others either distrust you or fail to take you seriously.
Make your undeniably keen mind your servant, not your master. Learn correct breathing.	Irritable, irritated and irritating. Nervy. Working agitatedly. Unfinished tasks.
Respect the value and efficiency of your own mind: watch what goes into it and what comes out of it.	Prone to trivia: knowing a little about everything and a lot about nothing.
SOLUTION	PROBLEM

If you find yourself on the receiving end of negative traits, it is because you are not expressing the opposing positive traits.

181

MERCURY IN CANCER

ESSENCE

Thinking through Nurturing
The Caring Mind • Know Your Feelers

It is said that the eyes are actually an extension of the brain, but with Mercury in Cancer it is rather as if you have a set of feelers, like a moth ... or a crab ... that pick up the thoughts and feelings around you in a super-sensitive fashion. Because of this you need to take great care how you receive such information, and not to take everything personally; you also need to remind yourself to look at the facts rather than the opinions of the people concerned. These precautions would also help guard against being conditioned by having taken on board the erroneous ideas of others, which, left unchecked, can give rise to problems whose roots are hard to detect at a later date. In fact you are quite adept at sensing whether someone is genuine or not by the sound of their voice.

Positively speaking, such a sympathetic mind as yours can make you an effective speaker, as you can tune in to the listener's emotional and mental state. The way you speak and what you say have a 'stroking' quality that is persuasive and therapeutic. All of this mental sensitivity, your feelers, is due to your conscious mind being very close to the unconscious. You draw upon your awareness of what makes anything or anyone feel looked after and are able to express it – or deny it. It is, therefore, very important that such a talent is guided by a strong set of ethics, and is used with a constructive purpose in mind. Without this kind of deliberate intention to employ your feelers in some positive way, you are merely suggestible and prey to being or to feeling manipulated – consequently you yourself feel tempted to manipulate. The vicious circle of suspicion that this hatches is the polar opposite of the reassuring atmosphere that you are capable of creating, be it in a home environment, with your sheer physical presence, or whatever. Put another way, if you are aware of your own source of light and warmth, you are less likely to be drawn, like a moth, into someone else's flame.

Not surprisingly, you have a good memory – that serves and disserves. Conversations can be remembered almost word for word, and you can yank to the surface long 'forgotten' information in times of need. As long as you learn to let go of painful feelings and not to nurse them like a sore tooth, your memory will serve you well.

Fundamentally, you are concerned with creating good memories, which is a thought worth remembering in itself! Whereas bad memories create bad feelings which in turn lead to narrow and defensive thinking, collecting good memories through the caring use of your sensitive mind gives rise to good feelings, and to clear, positive thinking.

LIKES	**DISLIKES**
Gentle interactions • Sentimental surroundings	Verbal violence • Unfamiliar territory
Collecting (old things) • Reminiscing • Local interests	Breaks in continuity • Changing attitudes • Language barriers

Mercury is your tool for making connections and getting leads.

MERCURY IN CANCER

TRANSFORMER

POSITIVE	NEGATIVE
Mentally tenacious	Mentally habit-ridden
Good memory	Distracted
Reliable	Inflexible
Sensitive mind	Impressionable
Poetic	Impractical
Intuitive	Irrational
Agreeable	Yes-person
Absorbs information	Too open
Attuned to public opinion	Taking things too personally
Profound	Depressive
Polite	Self conscious
Softly-spoken	Unclear
Discreet	Incomprehensible
Diplomatic	Diffuse
Arouses sympathies	Prejudiced
Emotionally appealing	Capricious
Persuasive speaker	Untruthful

SOLUTION	PROBLEM
Your natural ability to influence others is worthy of only the highest motives.	A failure to look at the truth is followed by a failure to recognize it.
Reassure others of your doubts and intentions and they will be happy to reassure you.	Insecurity owing to difficulty in getting to the root of a problem. Foggy-brained.
A mind like yours is sensitive to bigger issues, so it must address itself to same.	Mentally confused and easily upset. Distraught and not quite knowing why.
Tuning in to your finer feelings and expressing them is bound to be rewarding.	So susceptible to the opinions of others, you rarely know your own mind.
Remember what you are after, who you are with and why – and stick with it.	Frustration as a result of clinging to outworn ideas and attitudes.

If you find yourself on the receiving end of negative traits, it is because you are not expressing the opposing positive traits.

MERCURY IN LEO

ESSENCE

Thinking through Creating

The Ideas Person • Honour Your Critics

With Mercury in Leo you are, or should be, proud of your intellectual talents and capabilities. Because your mind is, so to speak, close to your heart, you show great passion and strength, as well as originality, in the manner in which you think and communicate. But Leo, like all the Fire Signs, is actually quite often as insecure as it appears to be the opposite, that is, confident. This can lead to either your coming on too strong when expressing your ideas and opinions, or, conversely, your underestimating the power of your mind, and not making it clear either to yourself or to others what is going on in your head. In the first case you would be inclined to ignore any negative feedback, and in the latter, you would be paralysingly oversensitive to criticism.

Mercury, which symbolizes the logical ability to see things merely as they are, functions best when it is cool and detached from the ego, whose bias is towards getting what it thinks it wants. But this is difficult in self-conscious Leo, where your personal aims and intentions seem to be all-important, and other factors of far less importance. The danger here is that such egocentricity wants to bat and bowl at the same time, and so you cannot win because you are also busily but unconsciously trying to defeat yourself. The answer lies in finding a balance between the two extremes described above. Firstly, you can use your pronounced talent for mental concentration to focus upon the enthusiasm and vitality that is roaring away inside you, and which can so easily radiate warmth and wit in much of what you say and do. And secondly, like a wise king or queen – for you have a regal mind – you can take heed of the advice or comments given by trusted friends and associates. If they won't speak their minds to your face for fear of having their heads bitten off – or simply being ignored – they could well turn into your enemies, creep up behind you, and pinch your ideas! You would then have good reason to feel unappreciated. People soon give up trying to help someone who always thinks he/she knows better. On the other hand, combining your obviously creative and enterprising mind with an awareness of the ideas and attitudes of the other people involved in your drama will benefit everyone – and not least of all your own projects.

After all, you tackle problems imaginatively and energetically. You are also able to teach effectively because you encourage interest in a subject through your creative and dramatic treatment of it. The way you speak has authority built into it, and so others will automatically take you seriously. You have so many good ideas that giving them away and allowing them to be mixed with and slightly altered by the input of others will strengthen and enrich them. Rather than being a frustrated one-person show, your mind will thus become the vital spark that ignites a greater group endeavour.

LIKES	DISLIKES
Artistic pursuits • Being your own boss	Lack of recreation • Being answerable to others
Combining work with pleasure • A positive reaction	Not having your own work space • Dull people
A creative purpose	A meaningless production line

Mercury is your tool for making connections and getting leads.

MERCURY IN LEO

TRANSFORMER

POSITIVE	NEGATIVE
Mentally creative Distinctive verbal style Warmly articulate	Mentally conceited Likes sound of own voice Voluble
Identifies with popular ideas Grasps whole issue Intellectually confident	Only interested in own ideas Overlooks details Mentally arrogant
Focused concentration Fixed intentions Continuity of purpose Enthusiastic worker	Inflexible mind Stubborn and one-track mind Self-centred Feels superior at work
Convincing speaker Outspoken and optimistic Knows own mind	Craves appreciation Verbally overbearing Self-conscious
Teaching and planning ability Foresight Executive mind	Talks at others Wrapped up in pet projects and theories
Remember you teach what you wish to learn. Do your plans include others' plans?	Losing your place in midstream – falling from grace in midscheme.
You owe it to yourself to stand or fall by what you say and how you say it.	Compensating for fear of humiliation by saying too much or too little.
With your strong and creative mind, you could and should diversify your interests.	Trapped by putting all your eggs in one basket, especially at work.
Never ignore that 'still small voice' that plays such a vital part in the greater whole.	Projects falling apart at the seams, stitch by stitch. Lack of cohesiveness.
What springs from your lips is only as good as what dwells in your heart.	Turning around one day, you find that no one is listening to you.
SOLUTION	PROBLEM

If you find yourself on the receiving end of negative traits, it is because you are not expressing the opposing positive traits.

MERCURY IN VIRGO

ESSENCE

Thinking through Analysing
The Wordsmith • The Pure Mind

It is very unlikely that you lack intelligence, with Mercury placed in Virgo. The ability to reason functions well and easily in this precise and analytical Sign. Its failing is simply due to the fact that you find it easier to think than anything else – and than most other people, too. And so you can come to live in your head and not realize it, forgetting that there is a big difference between knowledge and experience. You can also be critical of others' lesser mental powers (how could they be otherwise?!), but this overlooks the fact that what they may be lacking intellectually is more than made up for by their emotional qualities.

Your amazing analytical ability tells you that everything has its place – hopefully, including your amazing analytical ability! In other words, you have the mind of the specialist and are able to excel in your chosen field of work because you make it your business to know precisely how a given thing operates. But at the same time it would be a mistake to apply your specialist knowledge to all other spheres of life. Brilliant as it is, the way you think is just the way you think, not the way of the world. This point is worth pondering, for your preoccupation with thinking life is only as you see it can give you much cause for anxiety, especially with regard to being more critical of yourself than of anyone else. In truth, what you are seeking is as clear a mental viewpoint as possible, with an absolute minimum of prejudice and misinformation. For this reason, you are particularly good at helping others to see more clearly. This can, of course, take many forms: writing, editing, counselling, teaching, drawing, translating, to name just a few.

Very little avoids your perceptive gaze, and your computer-like memory is very valuable. You are able to assimilate vast amounts of complex information and then represent it in a far more digestible form, with all repetitions and non-essentials removed. But, curiously, when it comes to expressing something close to your heart, you can obscure the very point that you are attempting to make with all manner of irrelevant references and dead-end data. At the top of each of your many lists there should be a reminder of exactly what you wish to express.

Having such a marvellous mental potential as yours, it is rather important that initially you gain a thorough grasp of a specific subject. Without training or education you are liable to suffer far more than others from being unemployed, underemployed or unemployable. However, paradoxically, the ultimate objective of your tidy mind is to tidy itself away, which means that eventually you appreciate that what gets in the way of understanding life is thinking about it too much. A totally clear mind is no mind at all.

LIKES	DISLIKES
Reading • Knowledge • Mental clarity	Idle conversation • Wasting time • Woolly thinking
Mental freedom • Being occasionally crazy	Intellectual regimentation • Being constantly reasonable

Mercury is your tool for making connections and getting leads.

MERCURY IN VIRGO

TRANSFORMER

POSITIVE	NEGATIVE
Analytical Objective Systematic Logical	Unfeeling Remote Clinical Cold and dry
Discerning Precise Meticulous Clever	Hypercritical Pedantic Trivial Worrisome
Eloquent Well-read Well-informed Accurate	Wordy Bookish Intellectual snob Misses point
Retentive memory Fast learner Highly efficient Good worker	Greedy mind Impatient Highly strung Workaholic
Modest Matter-of-fact Helpful Practical	Self-critical Sceptical Slave (to reason) Pointless
Mysterious axiom: the justification for just being what you are is just being what you are.	Trapped on the treadmill of trying to prove what cannot be proven. Nothing rhymes.
Remember the old formula for health: work, rest (give others some, too) and play.	Mentally overloaded. Irritated by your intolerance of your own and others' fallibility.
The point you wish to make: remember it, research it, rehearse it – then express it.	With all your hard work, others still do not appreciate what you say or do. Scorned even.
Make the best of what you know, and trust what you do not know to look after itself.	Not seeing the wood for the trees, you spend some lonely nights in the forest.
It's easy for you to work out that you are not just a mind, albeit a fine one.	Knowing everything and feeling nothing; others know what you think but not what you feel.
SOLUTION	PROBLEM

If you find yourself on the receiving end of negative traits, it is because you are not expressing the opposing positive traits.

187

MERCURY IN LIBRA

ESSENCE

Thinking through Relating
The Spokesperson • Agree to Differ

It is said that if Moses had formed a committee, the Children of Israel would still be in Egypt! So he probably did not have Mercury in Libra – but, then again, maybe he did, because when expressed positively this Planetary placement results in the ability to consider all the facts, and then to make a decision or lay down a law that is just and equitable. However, its weakness is to get stuck at the stage of forming that consensus of opinion, which gives rise to interminable stalemate situations in which no one feels satisfied or justified.

As the way you think is based largely on how you feel in relating to others, you are inclined, naturally enough, to agree at the expense of failing to contact how you yourself actually feel about a given issue. This results in the person to whom you relate most intimately becoming frustrated through not knowing which side of the fence you're on. What they don't see is that you are striving to keep the peace amongst a wide variety of people and opinions. However, the point that any close associate is trying to make is that you have to have a yardstick of your own, otherwise no one will get your measure, and consequently will find you hard to take seriously. And this would be a shame, considering that your decision – when finally made – is the one most likely to be the fairest.

You have the style to make another see things your way – and to get them to see things from a third party's point of view. But in your bid to gain approval, do not forget that it is your actual sense of justice that carries the weight, rather than having someone agree with you. Others are aware of your fair mind, and either they will seek to take advantage of it and to get you on their side, or they will respect it – therefore, so must you. The kind of work that suits a mind such as yours includes anything that requires an awareness of how people tick – something that fascinates you: public relations, politics, psychology, law, sociology, to name but a few. A guideline for you could be 'anything that appeals to the masses' – a phrase worth pondering.

What underlies much of your thinking is a desire for agreement. As you like to be honest – or like to be seen to be honest – reflecting upon what exactly it is that you want others to agree to is vitally important in order to maintain the integrity that you hold so dear. If this is vague, then others will also feel vague about what you are proposing. On the other hand, because you are so keen on mental balance and order, you can overlook the fact that others are not as disciplined in this respect as you. As others look to you for wise counsel, what or who you look to yourself hinges on something holy.

LIKES	DISLIKES
An honest reputation • Refined minds • Good manners	Being underestimated • Mob rule • Uncouthness
Moral justice • Learning through others	Rough justice • No one to talk with

Mercury is your tool for making connections and getting leads.

MERCURY IN LIBRA

TRANSFORMER

POSITIVE	NEGATIVE
Agreeable Flexible Diplomatic Prudent	Yes-person Weak-minded Non-committal Turncoat
Persuasive Charming Well-spoken Communicative	Smooth-talking Insincere Affected Prattling
Hardworking Disciplined Scholarly Orderly	Rat-racer Blindly obedient Doctrinaire Officious
Eclectic Fair judge Good arbitrator Reasonable	Unoriginal Insipid Indecisive Banal
Team-spirited Principled Honourable Open-minded	Sheep-like Cowardly Phoney Vacuous
Mentally striving to uphold your heartfelt principles inspires others.	The people who matter to you are wondering whether you matter to them.
Remember that your talent for deliberating is wholly in aid of making a fair decision.	To be honest, you often bore yourself. To be even more honest, others are bored by you.
There is! As long as the spirit of the law supersedes the letter of the law.	Secretly a voice in your head echoes: 'There has to be more to life than this!'
Make sure that your brilliant patter is matched by what you are promoting.	The more convincing you pretend to be, the emptier you feel inside.
Meeting others halfway is a good starting point for negotiations.	Torn between toeing the line and putting your best foot forward.
SOLUTION	PROBLEM

If you find yourself on the receiving end of negative traits, it is because you are not expressing the opposing positive traits.

MERCURY IN SCORPIO

ESSENCE
Thinking through Desiring
X-Ray Eyes • The Sleuth

What you want and what you fear are heavily entwined in your mind. This is because such a profound and probing intellect as yours is quite likely to have attracted attacks from others who have seen it as a threat. Such antagonists in your past may very well have been those who should have known better, like teachers or anyone else who had authority over you – even older brothers or sisters.

The essential point here is that yours is a mind that sees through people and situations, and as such can be satisfyingly employed digging out anything of trouble or of interest. This can include many occupations, but particularly favours psychological, political, research or detective work. However, if you are ruled by a hidden agenda of emotional vulnerability caused by the above-described intellectual disempowerment, you can misuse your own powers by stabbing at others' tender spots in order to pre-empt their having a poke at you first. This ensures that you are never insipid and that you have a mind of your own, but such cunning defensiveness can turn your mental state into a police state.

Your delving mind does not miss many tricks – hopefully including your own. This failing of Mercury in Scorpio to suspect malice of intent where there is none, can give rise to mental convolutions that are almost impossible to work out – except, maybe, for Mercury in Scorpio! Perhaps you create intrigue in order to keep your mind on its stealthy toes, which is fine just as long as you do not get foiled by your own mental swordplay. Looked at another way, yours is a fundamentally sharp and efficient mind as there is always something that needs looking into – and you cannot resist – so your mental muscle is constantly exercised.

However, learning to leave well enough alone is a talent that you also have, or that you should develop. This is a sign of real mental power and superiority. Equally, you are able to wait and watch silently which can be quite unnerving for others. In this way your insight is sharpened and confidential information is mysteriously absorbed.

Providing that they do not have the emotional truth unceremoniously thrust upon them (as a kind of indirect revenge on your part), other people benefit greatly from your penetrating insight. However, this is only one hundred per cent effective when you are not involved personally – keenness is therefore dependent upon detachment. This means that you are happiest when not ruled by personal fears and phobias, because they cloud your judgment. So with Mercury in Scorpio your powers of perception are ultimately proven by eliminating your own mental twists and ruses.

LIKES	DISLIKES
Brain-teasers • Mental control • Intrigues	Mental inactivity • Weak-mindedness • Lack of subtlety
Smoke-screens • Cut and thrust	Fudged issues • Mincing words

Mercury is your tool for making connections and getting leads.

MERCURY IN SCORPIO

TRANSFORMER

POSITIVE	NEGATIVE
Sharp Incisive Subtle Satirical	Cutting Acidic Sneaky Sarcastic
Perceptive Penetrating mind Stealthy Audacious	Suspicious Paranoid Intrusive Abusive
Accurate Investigative Punchy Emphatic	Uncharitable Grilling Scathing Overstated
Determined Good concentration Quick-minded Dextrous	Argumentative Mentally tense Presumptuous Meddlesome
Profound Confiding Insightful Strategic	Incomprehensible Secretive Devious Scheming
Secrecy is an art — not a game.	Your intrigues have become tangled webs that mystify you more than anyone else.
Use your ability to leave no stone unturned in order to find what you're really after — yourself.	Living on your nerves, you start at shadows — your own. Anxiety creates itself.
Pick a target worth your beady eyes. Push an idea worth your mental weight.	Deflating others' ideas and inflating your own is distrust that breeds distrust.
Your mental powers can transform your fear of being found out into a desire to find out.	It is no fun being on a 24-hour alert, and keeping on the outside what's already on the inside.
Just because you're able to get to the bottom of things, there's no need to be a creep.	All that acid is giving you indigestion, and your wit has sunk out of sight.
SOLUTION	PROBLEM

If you find yourself on the receiving end of negative traits, it is because you are not expressing the opposing positive traits.

MERCURY IN SAGITTARIUS

ESSENCE

Thinking through Seeking
The Eternal Student • Eyes of Wonder

You have a broad and active mind that is capable of cultivating itself and being aware of many different aspects of life. Work could or should involve travelling around or mixing with a wide assortment of people; and you should avoid being stuffed away in some corner. If there is no focus to the knowledge and experience that you readily gather, so that it becomes a personal philosophy of life, you are likely to have merely a scattered collection of disconnected thoughts and ideas.

Yours is a seeking mind; it is looking for a meaning to life – with and without the jokey connotation of such a pursuit. In fact, your sense of humour is second to none, for you appreciate that anything worth seeking had better be fun, too. For the same reason you make a wonderful travelling companion along the road of life. In the process of seeking, your mind can get involved with many different schools of thought, yet avoids settling for a 'ready-made' philosophy or belief system.

This mental or physical roaming gives you a feel for how society and human thought are developing. On the one hand, this bestows on you a prophetic insight and a sense of history; on the other, it can pose merely as being fashionable. So your mind has the makings of anything from a creator of religious, social or political opinion, to just being hip to the latest craze.

You speak your mind, and this is refreshing for it clears the air and allows you to see where you stand with others, and where they stand both with you and with themselves. At first such candour as you possess can give rise to embarrassing situations, but the essential fact is that you have lifted a matter out of the fog that obscures the truth, and have thereby created the opportunity to see things more clearly and to breathe more freely. Getting things off your chest is very important to you, otherwise you can have difficulties with breathing or with communication. However, equally, you are inclined to say too much. This is due mainly just to enthusiasm on your part, but others could read it as being gushing and mentally undisciplined – and they may have a point. Nevertheless, you have a lofty line of reasoning that can be an inspiration to others. At the same time you should be aware that to many people your far-sighted ideas border on the barmy, at least, or are just plain hypocritical, if you are committing your cardinal sin of being all mouth and no action.

Fundamentally, yours is a 'native intelligence' which is instinctively filled with wonder at all the world has to offer. To you, everything is there for the finding. With just the right amount of schooling, your natural mind has the world to offer – and to teach, in return.

LIKES	**DISLIKES**
Mental freedom • Hot debate • A laugh and a joke	Too many ideas • Tepid talk • Long faces
Great thoughts • Life's promise	Small minds • Wet blankets

Mercury is your tool for making connections and getting leads.

MERCURY IN SAGITTARIUS

TRANSFORMER

POSITIVE	NEGATIVE
Frank Sincere Open-minded Speaks mind	Indiscreet Gauche Irreverent Garrulous
Versatile mind Speculative Intuitive Noble-thinking	Scattered mind Irrelevant Illogical Poor concentration
Thinks big Learned Clever Far-sighted	Grandiose ideas Academic Impractical Short-sighted
Philosophical Fair judge Sees truth Enthusiastic	Sermonizing Opinionated States obvious High-handed
Cultured Eclectic Informed Well-connected	Trendy Fanciful Pedantic Pompous
A mind of its own knows that fashions are not facts but opinions.	You know the right faces and places, but secretly you still lack identity.
Ponder on what you feel most strongly about, then make a case for what opposes it.	For all your apparent confidence, you are not at all sure where you stand.
Complement your native intelligence with formal training, or vice versa. Look and listen.	Occupational difficulties: all experience and no knowledge, or vice versa. Missing the obvious.
Cleave your thoughts to an end that endures or a cause that inspires.	Disconnected thoughts rattle round your head, frustrating both you and others.
Your honesty is not in question, but the way you express it is. Think before speaking.	Social ineptitude finds you socially alienated and/or emotionally compromised.
SOLUTION	PROBLEM

If you find yourself on the receiving end of negative traits, it is because you are not expressing the opposing positive traits.

MERCURY IN CAPRICORN

ESSENCE

Thinking through Building
The Mind Rules Matter • The Organizer

'Thinking through Building' means two things mainly. Firstly, when building, you have to have a plan, which means that some sort of goal is essential. Your mind has to have something worthwhile to chew on, otherwise solving petty problems or dealing with endless paperwork could be your mental lot. Yours is either a dull or a constructive mind, depending on what you are directing it towards.

Secondly, building is always done in definite stages. On the one hand, this means that you have a decidedly methodical mind, the kind that can produce a good organizer and successful business person. But on the other, you can be inclined to get stuck on one level of thinking, which can lead to mental or professional stagnation. So keep building, but add a definite dash of idealism to your natural pragmatism.

As the motto reads, 'The Mind Rules Matter', not the other way around. In other words, if you let material considerations defeat or rule over you, you have missed the point of having the kind of mind that is designed to overcome just such difficulties.

You have most likely been conditioned to regard knowledge and your ability to think as the main assurances that you are on the right track and will get on in the world. If, however, you found formal or book learning painfully difficult, you could have lurched the other way and become quite scornful of intellectuality. On finding that this puts you at a social or professional disadvantage you might then strive to become a master of one particular subject – the more definite and structured, the better. For, in fact, when you put your mind to learning something, you do so with admirable thoroughness.

However, it is not the facts that your mind contains that determine its quality – and this is possibly why you were wary of filling it with them in the first place – any more than it is the architectural plans of a building that appeal to its occupants. It is how you use your mind and what you use it for that count. Being unaware of this can make you feel stiff and wooden at times, as you become afraid of using the wrong word, or obsessed with using the right one. Your essential lesson is to learn to use concrete facts and not to be weighed down by them.

When you have surmounted these inherent snags of Mercury in Capricorn, you will find that you'll be able to see the ultimate absurdity of being a slave to material status and belongings, and to the demands that they make. As a result of this, you are known for a wry humour that is based on a firm awareness of the vagaries and subtleties of physical existence. And through your sense of irony not a little wisdom shines.

LIKES
Time-tested values • Mental order and feasibility
Skill and efficiency • Economy and industriousness
Knowing your standpoint

DISLIKES
One-hit wonders and false ideals • Sloppy thinking
Poor workmanship and laziness • Wasting time and materials
Being taken for a ride

Mercury is your tool for making connections and getting leads.

MERCURY IN CAPRICORN

TRANSFORMER

POSITIVE	NEGATIVE
Good timing Mentally cautious Not easily fooled Retentive mind	Procrastinating Slow learner Sceptical Mentally overloaded
Methodical mind Orderly mind Serious when necessary Level-headed	Lacking originality and imagination Given to melancholy Boring and rigid Pedestrian
Canny Discriminating Shrewd Profits from little	Suspicious Censorious Devious Avaricious
Employs others Sober Clear and deliberating mind	Uses others Stern Dry and pigeon-holing mind
Strong concentration Painstaking Patient	Blinkered or narrow-minded Too exacting Intolerant
Inspire others with the goal that you should be able to see more clearly than they can.	Feeling frustrated and angry with others – especially co-workers.
You have the mind of the boss, so use it without doubt or rancour.	Dissatisfaction, even though everything and everyone are in their right place.
You will never lose what really counts – your resourcefulness.	Feeling that others are out to undo you, get the better of you and take advantage of you.
Give your mind a break – or it will! Loosen what's too tight. Tighten what's too loose.	You are constantly 'at work' and feel like a wet blanket.
It is better to appear a fool than it is to be one. You won't forget what's worth knowing.	Stuck in a rut. Afraid of losing your mental grip. Intellectually constipated.
SOLUTION	PROBLEM

If you find yourself on the receiving end of negative traits, it is because you are not expressing the opposing positive traits.

MERCURY IN AQUARIUS

ESSENCE

Thinking through Liberating
The Exalted Mind • The Free Thinker

'A paradox is the truth standing on its head to attract attention.' The bright spark who said this may or may not have had Mercury in Aquarius, but it expresses perfectly both the way in which you see the world and how you think. This is because your mind goes through the kind of processes that are 'plugged in' to what has been called the Universal Mind, and so you perceive things in a manner that to others can seem highly unlikely – even odd – because it often goes against the emotional bias or moral attitudes of your family, peer group, colleagues etc.

So often you have to stand and work alone with your original, but sometimes quirky, ideas. It is very important that you express them at the same time, for in this way you will attract people of like mind, who interpret reality from the same elevated viewpoint as you, and who occasionally experience exactly the same flashes of insight as you.

There is a definite streak of stubbornness running through your mind, which is part and parcel of having a sense of the Truth, of understanding how things really are. After all, this is how the Truth eventually gets through. You could be regarded as part of a team that aspires to making known the kind of thinking that is coming in with the New Age – the Age of Aquarius. The type of work that suits you includes anything that aims to reveal the Truth, or to see the bigger picture; a few examples would be: psychology, astrology, astronomy, the sciences, the mass media and anything that aims to make known a humanitarian viewpoint.

Your blind spot is where such detached objectivity as yours is inclined to miss the emotional 'count' in a given situation. You can overlook even your own feelings until they become an issue that challenges your airy vision of how things ought to be.

When you're as quick at understanding people's feelings as you are things of the mind, you are able to express your revolutionary ideas in a clear and appealing fashion. Yours can be the common touch that gets through to friends and co-workers – or even to the masses – because you are attuned to that Universal Mind and what it thinks. You are aware today of how others will think tomorrow. The challenge for you is to communicate that vision, to help others to see life from a point beyond their personal hopes and fears – or to see that those hopes and fears are not as personal as they think they are!

Your enthusiastic interest in all things new and full of Truth means that living a lie will sit very uncomfortably in your mind. The slightest shade of hypocrisy, whether in yourself or in others, is something that you'll root out vigorously. And, either consciously or unconsciously, you are attracted to people and to pursuits that force you to do just this.

LIKES	**DISLIKES**
New Age thinking • Mental stimulation	Chauvinism • Mental stagnation
Team or group work • Open-mindedness	No one to share ideas with • Closed minds
Emotional honesty	Emotional reactions

Mercury is your tool for making connections and getting leads.

MERCURY IN AQUARIUS

TRANSFORMER

POSITIVE	NEGATIVE
Original thinker Inventive Unorthodox Comprehensive	Way-out thinker Cranky Irrelevant Disjointed
Scientific Objective Concise Well-informed	Clinical Lacks warmth Abrupt Unfeeling
Unshockable Open-minded Truth-loving Perceptive	Indifferent Fixed opinions Contrary Emotionally blind
Progressive thinker Utopian Reformist Socially aware	Out of time Unrealistic Reactionary Anti-social
Intuitive Cosmically aware Telepathic and inspiring mind	Scatterbrained Spaced out Overactive mind
Tune out the 'static' by tuning in to what others need to hear.	Mentally distressed. Contradiction reigns. Everything is nothing is everything.
In other words, having the courage of your convictions depends on your convictions.	Either you are a rebel without a cause or a cause without a rebel.
The truth awakens like a flash of lightning. Are you ready to be struck by it?	As life tries to move or influence you, you toss between caring and not caring.
Knowing that knowing is but one side of the spinning coin of life is knowing indeed.	You can see it all so clearly but cannot get anyone else to.
As an independent mind you've chosen a lonely road and a high goal. Stick with it.	No one seems to understand or appreciate your ideas.
SOLUTION	PROBLEM

If you find yourself on the receiving end of negative traits, it is because you are not expressing the opposing positive traits.

197

MERCURY IN PISCES

ESSENCE

Thinking through Accepting
The Poetic Mind • Dreamer of Dreams

Yours is a sensitive mind that absorbs as much information as, if not more than, it learns. Ideas and solutions seem to surface, as opposed to actually being worked out. Because of this mental osmosis you are sometimes not quite sure whether it is your own mind that is doing the thinking. How this kind of receptive mentality is likely to be handled or experienced depends greatly on what kind of person you are generally, and whether you are left-brained/rational or right-brained/intuitive.

If your ego is the type that likes to maintain the illusion of being in command of everything that passes through the mind, you will put together a firm intellectual framework of facts and figures. Armed with this mental battery you present a formidable opponent to anyone whom you regard as a woolly thinker. However, you are in effect opposing the sensitivity of your own mind. Because certain thoughts and notions seem to come from 'somewhere else', you doubt their veracity. Eventually this leads to a form of mental exhaustion as a result of resisting your cerebral sensitivity.

If, however, you are not so concerned about whether the thoughts coming through your head have your ego's stamp of approval, then you let the ideas stream forth, and give them some kind of creative and inspiring form. Although yours is the mind of the poet rather than of the technician, you are able to 'dream up' both scientific and artistic visions. You think in pictures, and can profit much through drawing from your dream life.

However, the chances are that you waver somewhere between these two extremes of how Mercury in Pisces operates. But the fact remains that you are fortunate or unfortunate enough, depending on your attitude, to be in touch mentally with the Collective Unconscious, which is like a vast sea of all the thoughts and feelings that ever were or ever will be. Your mind, like a boat, can either trust and explore this ocean of notions and ancient wisdom, or distrust it and attempt to keep it out with a mental sea-wall of concrete knowledge, or with a sea-mist of fantasy, evasiveness, alcohol or drug abuse.

One way or the other, it is wise to accept and to understand the channel-like quality of your mind, and always to give expression to what is coming through it. Giving form your thoughts is the correct means of maintaining mental security. Keeping them to yourself because some appear to be quite weird, will eventually make you feel quite weird yourself. ('Weird' literally means 'what must be'.)

As a sign of your fluid-like mentality, you are ill-disposed to being pinned down to facts – other than those of your 'own' making, that is. Such 'facts' may even include this definition of Mercury in Pisces!

LIKES	**DISLIKES**
Dreaming • The mysterious • Nostalgia	Rude awakenings • Lack of imagination
Feeling inspired • Soft spots	Bad memories • Feeling invaded • Hard facts

Mercury is your tool for making connections and getting leads.

MERCURY IN PISCES

TRANSFORMER

POSITIVE	NEGATIVE
Imaginative Sensitive mind Visually aware Artistic	Suspicious Evasive Easily freaked out Lazy
Obliging Psychic Good instincts Receptive	Easily swayed Irrational Fearful Gullible
Humorous Versatile Good mimic Highly perceptive	Obscure Vague Parrots others Uncommunicative
Philosophical Dreamer Good long-term memory Accepting	Absent-minded Wool-gathering Bad short-term memory Elusive
Refined mind Contemplative Gentle Sympathetic	Weak-minded Slow Wimpish Sycophantic

SOLUTION	PROBLEM
What you lack in knowledge you make up for in understanding. Take your time.	Others' apparently superior mental powers making you feel at a disadvantage.
Seeing to the boring details of life will allow you to reflect on greater issues in peace.	Caught out or feeling threatened by what you have 'accidentally' forgotten.
Others are only too pleased to know your inspired version of the human condition.	Uncomfortably at a loss for words. Afraid of being pinned down or giving yourself away.
You have the power to choose what you take on board. Discover how to use it.	Feeling like a leaf in the wind. Invaded by the thoughts and opinions of others.
Use your imagination creatively rather than being a victim of it.	Disturbed by what others might be saying or thinking. Seeing things.

If you find yourself on the receiving end of negative traits, it is because you are not expressing the opposing positive traits.

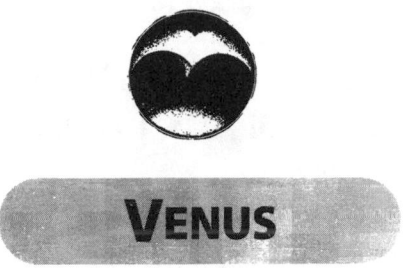

VENUS

Keyword: LOVING

Looked at more intuitively, Venus symbolizes ATTRACTION, in that your Venus-Sign shows what you are drawn towards so that you may give or receive by way of LOVE and AFFECTION, BEAUTY and HAPPINESS, VALUE and VALUES. Negatively it poses INDULGENCE and SUPERFICIALITY.

Venus also represents the way you RELATE, and create and appreciate HARMONY through SOCIAL or ARTISTIC expression. If you are an artist of any kind, your style will resemble your Venus-Sign manner of loving and relating. Venus is what you LIKE.

If you are a male, your Venus-Sign will intimate the kind of female to whom you are attracted — although it is actually a part of you. If you are a female, you express and embody the qualities of your Venus-Sign quite directly. With either sex, if you find that you are on the receiving end of negative Venus-Sign traits, it is because you are not expressing the positive ones.

VENUS IN ARIES

ESSENCE
Loving through Doing
Love at First Sight • Love Elemental

You love as a child loves, seeing human relationships as natural and uncomplicated – at least at first. You are generous, guileless and direct, and expect others to be the same. You are crestfallen when you find that they are not, but not, as a rule, heartbroken. You get back up again as quickly as you fell in love in the first place.

This impetuosity of yours certainly possesses a quality that is immediately attractive to others. They sense this innate notion of yours that love is a quest and deed for the doing. Essentially, you are absolutely right, but, unlike children, adults have a backlog of unmet needs and unresolved fears from their own childhood. So, although you have a talent for appealing to the child in others in a way that reminds them of an almost Eden-like simplicity, you also stimulate their more immature traits.

But the truth is that their immaturity is merely reflecting your own. If you fail or refuse to see this, you are headed for a precipitous life of loving and leaving, or of being left. But, then again, this could all be included in your feeling that love is a quest, and that your lovers are co-adventurers. Indeed, a companion-in-arms-like quality is very desirable to you – as long as you make sure that your partner sees it that way, too. Then you are on your way back to Eden – together – before the Fall.

In fact your love nature can be condensed into one small and simple word – imp. You are impish in that you are naughty and that you delight in getting others to misbehave. You are impudent in your manner of boldly and shamelessly pursuing the object of your desires. You are also impulsive and impatient in all matters of love and relating. An imp is, essentially, an elemental, or something that was there at the beginning. In other words, you have a rather primitive approach that can be either enchanting or disenchanting. More refined parts of your personality may try to suppress this, but there is something wild and gleeful in your manner of loving that should never be altogether eclipsed by so-called civilized behaviour – as long as you maintain some sensitivity to the sensibilities of others, while you tease their own impishness to the surface.

In affairs of the heart, not only are you trying to 'get back to the Garden', but also you sense that way back. The hunger that is born of this sense may well make you mistake sex for love more than once. Your greatest lesson is probably learning that sex is a flower that blooms in love far more often than the other way around. Know that as a romantic idealist you are looking for someone who can strike a blend of loyalty and elusiveness, vibrancy and veracity. Know also that this blend must first be found in yourself.

LIKES	**DISLIKES**
Independence in partner • The chase • A social whirl	Clinging vines • Being too cosy • Social inactivity
Spontaneous affection • Bold romance	Undemonstrativeness • Feeble advances

If you are a man, this could be the kind of woman to whom you are attracted – but it is really a part of you, so realize it.

VENUS IN ARIES

TRANSFORMER

POSITIVE	NEGATIVE
Erotic	Licentious
Winning style	Flirtatious
Passionate	Lustful
Playful	Irresponsible
Demonstrative	Blunt
Outgoing	Inconsiderate
Basic	Coarse
Straightforward	Unsubtle
Popular	Unenduring
Sparkling	Fanciful
Generous	Wanton
Appealing	Teasing
Childlike charm	Naïve in love
Romantic idealist	Fool in paradise
Easily roused	Easily hurt
Ingenuous	Clueless
Persuasive	Pushy
Ardent	Forces affections
Warm-hearted	Self-centred
Quick off the mark	Impatient in love

SOLUTION	PROBLEM
What keeps you in love is the chase. Go for it, but don't (imagine you can) catch it.	After you get what you want you don't want it, or you don't know what you've got till it's gone.
Falling in love with love – what else can you do?! Keep falling. Keep questing.	Feeling let down, disillusioned, trodden on, abused and confused.
Give your best to get the best.	The delightful has a habit of turning into the detestable.
It becomes you to come right out and say or ask what is and what isn't agreeable.	Either you feel the victim of a turn-off or a bore, or you're being one.
As you are so attractive, check out what you're actually attracting.	You may have a lot of fun – but a merry-go-round just goes round in circles.

If you find yourself on the receiving end of negative traits, it is because you are not expressing the opposing positive traits.

VENUS IN TAURUS

ESSENCE

Loving through Stabilizing
Nature's Connoisseur • Heart of Oak

You possess the best qualities of Venus as expressed in the physical or material sense, which means that in you the five senses are well-developed. So you have a strong sensuousness that others find attractive, although if this is allowed to become excessive, subsequent grossness can have the opposite effect. Such awareness as yours of what satisfies the physical senses can, of course, make you successful in a number of areas: art – you may be especially good at singing, or at least have a pleasant-sounding speaking voice; cooking, and other means of offering others comfort and enjoyment; consumerism – you may have a good market sense; healing – your sense of touch can be highly evolved.

Your wonderful feel for bodily and Earthly things also makes you dependent on physical evidence of your worth and desirability. You greatly need shows of physical affection in order to feel loved – mere words or implications will not suffice. However, the more aware you are of your physical charm, which is a kind of emanation rather than solely good looks, the more likely you are magnetically to satisfy your needs. Additionally, you must bear in mind that most others are not as naturally skilled in expressing affection, so you should take the lead here, ever teaching how to enjoy the body more.

Fundamentally, you have a sense of how Nature enjoys her own existence, her own poetic and seasonal interplay. This sense is reflected to a great extent in your emotional needs and sexual inclinations. You have such love for certain physical aspects of Nature, like another human being or a work of art, that you just have to have them. But you cannot really possess them, for Nature's gifts, like rain, come and go in their own time. The secret to obtaining the object of your desires and maintaining the kind of stable relationship that is so important to you, is to recognize that anything or anyone outside yourself will only become truly a part of your life when your value and values are a reflection of, and in harmony with, Nature herself. Until then, you will always be involved, either unconsciously or deliberately, in some sort of 'deal' whereby you foster the illusion that you're getting, or not getting, value for your 'investment'.

Venus in Taurus is one of the strongest Planet-Sign indications of a love of Nature. Apart from the above-described implications of what this means, you are also quite likely to be concerned with ecology and conservation. But the same Natural Truth persists here, namely that what you love and care about is only as sound and secure as you feel inside. After all, Nature is here to provide for our development. You are particularly trusting of, and entrusted with, Nature's gifts, which includes a true appreciation of Nature.

<table>
<tr><td align="center">LIKES</td><td align="center"></td><td align="center">DISLIKES</td></tr>
<tr><td align="center">Physical contact • Creature comforts
Beautiful surroundings
Being depended on • Natural products</td><td></td><td align="center">The physically distasteful
Scarcity • Spartan conditions
Gold-diggers • Synthetics</td></tr>
</table>

If you are a man, this could be the kind of woman to whom you are attracted – but it is really a part of you, so realize it.

VENUS IN TAURUS

TRANSFORMER

POSITIVE	NEGATIVE
Attractive	Avaricious
Earthy	Materialistic
Affectionate	Cupboard love
Artistic	Self-indulgent
Aesthetic	Hedonistic
Peaceful	Indolent
Sensuous	Sensual
Satisfying	Self-satisfied
Steadfast	Stubborn
Loyal	Possessive
Wholesome	Smug
Constant	Too abiding
Sympathetic	Sybaritic
Encouraging	Misguiding
Comforting	Dissipating
Pleasure-giving	Insatiable
Nature-loving	Limited viewpoint
Deeply trusting	Gullible
Sound values	Precious
Conservational	Green green

SOLUTION	PROBLEM
Deep down you know that Nature's needs reflect your own, therefore look to and after them.	Your concern for what you think matters is a cause for concern in itself.
Your undeniable awareness of what feels good should lead to what feels even better.	Believing you can't have too much of a good thing is becoming harmful both to you and to others.
What makes you feel loved is your persistent faith in your own love nature.	Your need to be loved posing as fidelity makes you feel threatened.
Follow your nose to what smells sweeter, whatever the cost.	Rotting in the rut of your own sense of what pleases – and it doesn't.
You have natural wealth and beauty, giving and receiving in their own time, like the seasons.	Your being greedy for something but not realizing it is creating an empty feeling.

♀ SOLUTION PROBLEM ♉

If you find yourself on the receiving end of negative traits, it is because you are not expressing the opposing positive traits.

VENUS IN GEMINI

ESSENCE

Loving through Communicating
Love in Bud • The Sparkling Personality

As Venus is the Planet of Love, and Gemini is the Sign of the Lovers, you would imagine this to make for rewarding relationships. However, if you are blindly expecting security and predictability in your love life, then you are in for a disappointment. This is because Gemini is the Sign of Youth, and as such you have a strong urge to prevent stagnation and maintain fluidity in your relationships. A partnership that is not allowed change and freedom is doomed to failure, whereas being true to your desire to pursue youthful dreams and ideas will literally rejuvenate flagging relationships.

Venus in Gemini is Love in Bud rather than in full bloom, so you have to give it a chance to develop, be more steadfast, and not abandon it or leave it to the winds of fate. You like variety, but it is better to seek diversity within a relationship than outside it, for obvious reasons. Similarly, do not allow your easygoing nature to be interpreted as a lack of commitment. Loving through Communicating means that if you feel love for someone, you should let it be known to them rather than sitting on the fence. You have a natural sparkle that is there to highlight your love and your loved one as you discover more and more bright facets of the Jewel of Love.

It is natural for you to make social contact in an easy and undemanding fashion. You like to get around – or to do the rounds. If you were to cut yourself off from a variety of friends and acquaintances this would exert pressure on you that would eventually cause you and your more intimate relationship to suffer. Sexual or family ties are your 'heart', but it is your diverse social relationships that are your 'lungs', that breathe life into your being. It is these ongoing communications that breathe fresh air into the lives of others as well.

Your love of communication can also bestow upon you a literary talent, or at least a love of the written and the spoken word. Having a wide range of knowledge should be something on which you can draw, for in this way you are able to discover and to express the ultimately important mental and spiritual aspects of love, as opposed to seeking superficial gratification, which can be a weakness of Venus in Gemini, as you attempt to keep things too breezy for your own good.

Gemini is the Sign of Duality, so you will experience not only the above-described opposition of security versus freedom, but also that of what you want versus what you think you want. In fact, you will only attract what you truly desire, and that is to meet your own shadow or alter ego, with which, like Narcissus, you are in love.

LIKES	DISLIKES
Poise • Keen minds • A lively partner • Social variety	Gracelessness • Dullards • 'Settling down'
The romantically unexpected	Tired relationships • Routine romance

If you are a man, this could be the kind of woman to whom you are attracted – but it is really a part of you, so realize it.

VENUS IN GEMINI

TRANSFORMER

POSITIVE	NEGATIVE
Amusing and friendly Coolly affectionate Light-hearted Emotionally objective	Flirtatious Flippant and flighty Makes light of others' feelings Emotionally distant
Socially at ease Emotionally buoyant Stimulating company	Social butterfly Superficial values Lack of commitment
Lively conversationalist Ear to the ground Good-humoured Expressive	Meaningless banter Shallow gossip Empty gestures Verbose
Agile and witty Socially adaptable Emotionally flexible Well-connected	Restless and fickle Double standards Inconsistent partner Social opportunist
Charming Courteous Tactful Co-operative	Ingratiating Insincere Insipid Easy come easy go
Others will truly appreciate you, if you truly appreciate them.	Feeling avoided and not taken seriously. Empty and dissatisfied.
Expressing your feelings verbally will break new ground both emotionally and socially.	Divided interests creating unstable personal relationships. Jilted – two-timed/two-timing.
Try listening to your heart rather than to your own and other people's voices.	Nil response from those who matter to you. Left out in the cold.
Show your dark side – and your light side will be brighter!	Afraid of intimacy. Uncomfortable with feelings or silences in company.
Trust your natural wit and appeal, and be the wiser for the asking.	Unsure of how others are 'reading' you, and of social or sexual direction.
SOLUTION	PROBLEM

If you find yourself on the receiving end of negative traits, it is because you are not expressing the opposing positive traits.

VENUS IN CANCER

ESSENCE

Loving through Nurturing
Home is Where the Heart Is • On the Sentimental Side

Your expressions of love are intricately tied up with your need to give or to receive comfort and security. The love, or the lack of love, forthcoming from your mother (or mother-figure) greatly affects both how you show and how you need affection. Being unsure of mother-love will make you cling blindly to partners, and possibly indulge your own children – or pretend to be indifferent towards them. Conversely, feeling sure of mother-love will give rise to a well-balanced fondness for and care of loved ones. Any kind of deprived family background is likely to have a serious influence on your love-life as an adult. Feelings of being misunderstood and unloved can be, well, Cancerous, for maudlin sentiments and sulky behaviour will be triggered off by normal emotional confrontations as a reaction to past hurts.

As with most Planets placed in Cancer, there is a strong subjectivity, which with Venus means that in being unconsciously so concerned with receiving love, you forget the quality and quantity of love you are actually giving. In a way your love is of the most instinctual kind, for it is characterized by an automatic nurturing of whatever needs it, be it the young, the sick, the weak or the needy. Feelings of insecurity on your part are in aid of furthering your awareness of the same in others, rather than laying you open to exploitation. Your value, like the home and hearth and Mother Nature herself, is all too easily taken for granted. So, occasionally, you may have to go on strike, make the earth quake, let them know which side their bread is buttered, then they'll come running!

Romantically you lean towards the sentimental. An intimate dinner for two at home is more likely to set your heart-strings playing than a night out on the tiles. You are also a bit old-fashioned, and like women to be ladylike and men to be chivalrous.

You have a changeable nature with regard to showing or accepting affection owing to inner feelings of doubt about your attractiveness. If this is a problem for you, then try to make the distinction between security needs and your innate lovability. In other words you should be loved for what you are, not for what you need.

The home and family are central to your happiness. You are, therefore, very sensitive to the needs and hurts of loved ones, and to the home or house atmosphere as a whole. It is also very likely that you possess cooking, decorating and other domestic skills. Naturally enough, a fear of change and disruption in the home and family scene can give rise to worry, which can be expressed physically, in the form of stomach or throat problems. Remind yourself that such worry has to do with the past rather than the future, and that Venus, as the Planet of Attraction, will always eventually favour you with the nest in which to nurture those you feel to be in need of your nurturing love.

LIKES	DISLIKES
Hearth and home harmony • The domestic scene • Familiar faces and places • Security before romance • Praise for caring	Domestic strife • Inhospitality • Alien territory Emotional threats • Being taken for granted

If you are a man, this could be the kind of woman to whom you are attracted – but it is really a part of you, so realize it.

VENUS IN CANCER

TRANSFORMER

POSITIVE	NEGATIVE
Gentle Kind Tender Romantic	Timid Soppy Fawning Gooey
Sentimental Sensitive Compassionate Dreamy	Maudlin Easily hurt Moody Muddle-headed
Devoted Loyal Unselfish Dependable	Clingy Too attached Weak-willed Dependent
Caring Protective Motherly Sympathetic	Doting Parsimonious Old-womanish Fuss-pot
Home-making Reassuring Familiar feel Comforting	Shy Insecure Fears unfamiliar Gluttonous

Knowing what it's like to be without, you cater well to the same plight in others.	The 'waif' in you is taking over – running and hiding, and gobbling down scraps and sweet things.
Use Mother Nature as your role model for how to nurture and nourish.	Acting like Old Mother Hubbard gets you a bare cupboard! What's called 'poverty consciousness'.
Gladly allowing others to lean on you will help stop you leaning on someone else.	Difficulty letting go of negative feelings and relationships.
Admitting to your hopes and hurts encourages others to do so – everyone then benefits.	Not looking at your emotional vulnerability gives rise to mental and emotional confusion.
Your softness is one of your most attractive features, so don't overstate or undersell it.	Others are either repelled by your ingratiating behaviour, or take advantage of it.

SOLUTION	PROBLEM

If you find yourself on the receiving end of negative traits, it is because you are not expressing the opposing positive traits.

VENUS IN LEO

ESSENCE

Loving through Creating
Courtly Love • Love Comes Shining

Venus in Leo makes for such a romantic nature that your love feelings would in some ways be better expressed in poem, picture or song than in real life. At least, to give some form of creative expression to your ardour would give personal relationships more chance of surviving. Otherwise, the expectations that you have of any mere mortal are very unlikely to be met.

At first your paramour cannot believe his or her luck at having found such an enthusiastic lover, then they realize that you have (unconsciously) written them into your own particular romantic script. You can also be fiercely loyal on the one hand – and expect the same from your mate – yet still feel entitled to flirt, and even to have an affair if such a passion seizes you. However, if there is the slightest sign of infidelity from your partner, then there is hell to pay. Rather than on love's terms, you very much want things on your own terms, alongside which a healthy emotional interplay cannot exist.

At the root of this dilemma is the same old Leo problem: a deep-seated doubt of your own lovability that is totally undetectable from the outside, as you come across as passion posing as confidence, or as aloof and dignified. Either you are desperately trying to prove your desirability by playing at being Romeo or Cleopatra, or you are pretending not to care. If, before it's too late, you get your pride into the proper perspective and give the object of your desires just a glimpse of the human being who is playing these roles, then they will be not only impressed, but relieved at not having to live up to such a figure as the one you're projecting. They will also be more able to meet your needs. You are certainly generous and warm-hearted – unless you have limped off to some lonely lair as a melodramatic consequence of playing one of the above roles. In a sense you are paying homage to romantic love, with your lover as the altar. As long as your partner is aware of and alive to this acting out a myth, and you do not lose sight of each other as individuals, you can create a very noble and rewarding relationship. Put another way, Venus in Leo needs to combine its sense of 'royal privilege' with a sense of equal rights; the 'queen' should regard her mate as the 'king' (and vice versa), with all the courtly respect and honour that this understanding entails.

Artistic sense is strong in you. Life is seen as an ongoing creative experience, which, of course, it is. This is what can be so sunny and wonderful and attractive about Venus in Leo. Pride in physical appearance and sexual prowess is also strong, which is fine provided it does not become neurotic. At a certain stage you must go looking for your inner beauty, which is beautiful indeed. 'I see Love shining in the shining Sun.'

LIKES
Admiration • Mutual respect • Lavish parties
Showing off your partner • Classic courtship

DISLIKES
Slightest rejection • Insulting behaviour • Second-rate 'do's
Being shown up • Lack-lustre love

If you are a man, this could be the kind of woman to whom you are attracted – but it is really a part of you, so realize it.

VENUS IN LEO

TRANSFORMER

POSITIVE	NEGATIVE
Romantic Ardent Passionate Loyal	Unrealistic Sexually obsessed Consuming Too loyal
Artistic Dramatic Entertaining Fun-loving	Prima donna Overbearing Demanding Inappropriate
Radiant Outgoing Warm Openly affectionate	Self-centred Showy Brassy Flirtatious
Charming Attractive Benevolent Gives a lot	Seducing Flaunting Patronizing Expects too much
Social pride Personal pride Number one Fun to be with	Snobbish Vain Competitive Game-playing
The only thing that you can be compared with is your own self-respect.	Preoccupied with physical appearance or social position. Jealousy.
What you have to give is priceless – so why put a price on it!	Doubting your charms and overstating them as you swing from too little to too much confidence.
Love – and be loved in return. Send out the waves, pause, and feel them come back.	Everyone can see what you've got going for you – except you.
Channel your larger-than-life energy into larger-than-life pursuits or pastimes.	Creating scenes that upset you more than they please you.
For better results, bestow your affections judiciously rather than squander them blindly.	Never getting back what you are putting in. Feeling let down and unappreciated.
SOLUTION	PROBLEM

If you find yourself on the receiving end of negative traits, it is because you are not expressing the opposing positive traits.

VENUS IN VIRGO

ESSENCE

Loving through Analysing
Behold the Beauty • Love Love's Paradox

Venus is said to be in its Fall in Virgo, because Love and Beauty do not really bear analysis, and so one or the other has to go. The choice is, as ever, up to you, but here we assume that a world of Love and Beauty is preferable to one of analysis.

The ultimate result of analysing love and art, or objects thereof, is that eventually you come to realize that you must surrender to their mystery and analyse no more. However, in the meantime, during your constant routine of spotting and removing the fly from the ointment, you acquire a finely tuned sense of social, emotional and artistic values. As far as love and relating are concerned, it could be said that you are going through a kind of cleansing process as you rid yourself of impure thoughts, feelings and values. However, the tendency is to see these impurities in others, and in sexual partners in particular. As a consequence of this you can place yourself either temporarily or permanently in bachelor- or spinsterhood. This may of course be entirely to your liking, but the critical question is, are you keeping yourself to yourself in order to have an unadulterated look at yourself, or are you just misguidedly condemning everything but yourself as being 'unclean'. If such self-denial is not to your liking, then you are prone to doing something apparently out of character, such as being promiscuous or unkempt. This is because the moral strait-jacket that you have fashioned for yourself becomes so horribly restricting that you streak from one end of the ethical spectrum to the other. As a result of being as loose as previously you were tight, you unconsciously think that you are getting what you desire. This reversal can occur the other way round, too, from being loose to being tight.

When you realize and admit to this perversity with regard to your sense of what pleases, you could then ask yourself: Who am I to judge or be critical of anyone else? However, the poles swing around swiftly here, for the fact is that you have a fine and valuable sense of discrimination. But ultimately one has to be discriminating about being discriminating. In learning this, as you analyse and sensitively balance your moral values with your emotional desires, you come closer to distilling the perfection that you originally envisioned, warts and all! Realizing the Paradox of Love, that perfection is the acceptance of imperfection, is the goal and the gold of Venus in Virgo.

All of the above can also apply to how you view or create art or craftwork. Be aware that you cannot prove that a rose is beautiful by pulling it apart petal by petal — on the contrary, this destroys it. When you can resist this temptation to tamper with what is already simply attractive, and let the technical take second place to the inspirational, you can be second to none in appreciating, expressing and upholding the exquisite fragility of Love and Beauty.

LIKES	DISLIKES
A spotless reputation	Mud being thrown at you
A working relationship • Good manners	A non-mental relationship • Feeling stiff
Sexual hygiene • Pure or natural art	Sordid affairs • Art hypes

If you are a man, this could be the kind of woman to whom you are attracted — but it is really a part of you, so realize it.

VENUS IN VIRGO

TRANSFORMER

POSITIVE	NEGATIVE
Knowing what you like Discriminating Fine aesthetic and design sense Artistic	Critical of partners Fussy and nagging Easily dissatisfied Neurotically artistic
Sincerely affectionate Subtle love signs Simple and clear	Inhibits affection Undemonstrative Dry and clinical
Quietly charming Strong character Impartially kind Coolly helpful	Socially stiff Hides sensitivity Emotionally absent Cold exterior
Precision worker Refreshing at work Specialist worker Painstaking	Too exacting Retreats into work Indecisive of work Restrained
Pure and modest lover High moral sense Socially discerning Privately sensuous	Feels sexually inferior Puritanical Social misfit Self-effacing
Be mindful that amidst today's murky moral quagmires, you are a refreshing spring.	Loneliness and frustration. Over-reacting to this with loose thinking or living.
Recognize that yours is a labour of love, so employ both feelings and judgment.	Frustrations as a result of divorcing personal feelings from working life – or vice versa.
It can be your quiet attention to social details that makes things go with a swing.	Lack of spontaneity means that others cannot relax in your presence. Party pooper.
Any emotional expression of how you feel is better than no expression at all.	(Fear of) being supplanted or spurned. Disappointment in love.
Concentrate on what pleases – not what displeases.	Eternal bachelor or spinster. Feeling that nothing and nobody is good enough.
SOLUTION	PROBLEM

If you find yourself on the receiving end of negative traits, it is because you are not expressing the opposing positive traits.

213

VENUS IN LIBRA

ESSENCE

Loving through Relating
The Aesthete • The Social Touchstone

You appreciate and understand art and society on their own levels. This means that you have an inner sense of harmony which, quite naturally, sees life in terms of Beauty and Justice. But this sensibility is essentially born of your mind, rather than of your emotions, so the nature of your feelings, security needs and cultural conditioning is possibly going to intrude on how you would like to express your artistic skills and social charms.

As you recognize that beauty is important, the question arises as to whether it is more than or merely skin-deep. The answer is both, as you are bound to find out sooner or later. If you are looking for a partner who is glamorous and blemish-free, and has all the social graces, then with your charms you are quite likely to attract such a person. In time and after getting to know them – and them you – something quite other than that vision of loveliness or handsomeness could emerge. At this point you either go looking elsewhere or start criticizing the contents of the product and forget the wrapping. Alternatively you could be attracted to someone's inner beauty, then find their outer appearance not up to magazine-myth standard.

The answer to this is to remember that 'Beauty is in the Eye of the Beholder' – and should not be misted up by some notion of beauty that has been devised and promulgated by the mass media. Be that as it may, it is very difficult to separate what you find truly attractive and lovable from what you have been led to believe to be so. This is precisely where Venus in Libra's sense of harmony and beauty must come into its own. At some point you become a leader rather than a follower of fashion. Unless you are faithful to your truest and deepest inner vision of grace, beauty and fair play, you will paradoxically find yourself either being guilty of boorishness, infidelity or indifference, or being the victim thereof. Ultimately others will look to you as a social or artistic success – or disaster! As you are in touch spiritually with what the Ancient Greeks called 'The Golden Mean', the perfect balance, others will measure themselves by you or against you.

As a result of this natural charm, you are likely to attract either popularity or wealth, or both. And because you enjoy the pleasures of art and society, you like to make sure that this wherewithal – in the form of money and looks – is ever-present. This can, of course, result in your being neurotic about money and extremely vain. In any event, what you are most probably afraid of is conflict and disharmony. But the ultimate proof of your undeniable Venusian sense is your ability to lend grace where there is awkwardness, and understanding where there is strife.

LIKES	DISLIKES
Social harmony • Tastefulness • Being in love	Ugly scenes • Philistines • Feeling unattractive
Beautiful surroundings • True marriage	Uncouth behaviour • Pretended love

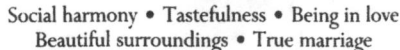

If you are a man, this could be the kind of woman to whom you are attracted – but it is really a part of you, so realize it.

VENUS IN LIBRA

TRANSFORMER

POSITIVE	NEGATIVE
Eye for beauty Strong colour sense Good ear Artistic	Hung up on appearances Oversensitive Music snob Art snob
Affectionate Likeable Magnetic Fair-looking	Takes liberties Frivolous Seducing Vain
Refined Graceful Pleasant Socially correct	Foppish Affected Phoney Etiquette freak
Romantically steadfast Relates well Harmonious	Conventionally superficial Insincere Avoids conflict
Just Empathetic Broad-minded Social touchstone	Indifferent Cold Cynical Social outcast
Such a fine social sense as yours, at some stage, just has to be tempered by tolerance.	Your innate understanding of human society finds you at a loss. Familiarity has bred contempt.
Relationships prosper on love – of the best *and* the worst.	Not showing how you really feel leads to your not knowing how you really feel.
Manners maketh not man. Others can benefit from your style – but only if they want to.	Limited, compromised and agitated by others who are apparently not up to your standard.
You need not indulge in your obvious charms, unless you doubt them – and doubt breeds itself.	Strife in personal relationships through your arousing insecurity in your partner.
Your ideal is something to strive towards not insist on. It may even lie beyond the human.	There is always something out of place or not quite right.
SOLUTION	PROBLEM

If you find yourself on the receiving end of negative traits, it is because you are not expressing the opposing positive traits.

VENUS IN SCORPIO

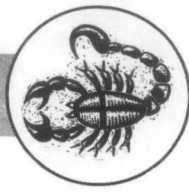

ESSENCE

Loving through Desiring
All or Nothing • Harmony through Conflict

As the song said, 'You've got what it takes – but it takes a lot to give it away'. With Venus in Scorpio it is as necessary for you to control your strong emotional awareness of what turns people on – or off – as it is hard for others to resist it. With a sexual bag of tricks such as this you might think that, like Svengali or Mata Hari, you could get anyone to do your bidding. But the catch with Venus in Scorpio is that it has you in its trap more than you have anyone in yours. In other words, the Power of Love is what Venus in Scorpio is about, and it will ultimately have its way with you, rather than the other way round.

Your feelings of love always have an undeniable streak of desire running through them, which means that there is something desperate or fated about your love life. You exude a strongly attractive sexual power, matched by that deep sense of another's emotional nature and sexuality. The danger arises either when you use this power blindly to build a feeling of security, or when you resist this power because you know it will attract relationships that will force you to change your lifestyle.

In the first case it can lead to a Faustian situation in which the source of your emotional security or the object of your affections exerts a definite but invisible power over you, because they know that the deal is 'Don't prod me and I won't prod you – at least, not so you'd notice it' (other than a vague sense of being trapped). In the second case your avoidance of emotional transformation can lead you down a sleazy trail of desire trying to get the better of love.

Fundamentally you have a deep desire to find love – true, genuine love, the love that purges you of petty values, that transforms your life from travesty to destiny, via tragedy and ecstasy. Such a deep and fulfilling love could already be with you. However, the surge of Venus in Scorpio does not ever really rest for it is seeking out your depths, and, more particularly, what can and must be given from those depths. As a result of this emotional delving, you may feel that you have to be quite guarded about your intimate life, throwing up a smokescreen to maintain secrecy. That smokescreen could even be an apparent openness, for you are nothing if not subtle. You may withhold love in order to control your partner, because you are unsure of how to handle your own depths of emotion and the vulnerability that goes with them. All you need to remember is that the trust comes with the depth!

Yet, in the end, all these expressions of Venus in Scorpio lead to the same thing: an inescapable intimacy with yourself, where all taboos must be broken and you become the purged and faithful exponent of the Power of Love.

LIKES	DISLIKES
Heartfelt emotions • Gutsy experiences	Insipidness • A banal lifestyle
Sexual revelation • Depth of aliveness • Plenty of soul	Exposure to ridicule • Superficial beings • Lack of soul

If you are a man, this could be the kind of woman to whom you are attracted – but it is really a part of you, so realize it.

VENUS IN SCORPIO

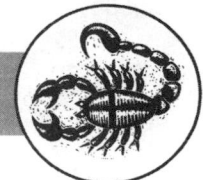

TRANSFORMER

POSITIVE	NEGATIVE
Sexually aware Sensuous Colourful Rapturous	Sexually obsessed Licentious Blue Depraved
Stimulating Fruity Magnetic Influential	Hurtful Bitter Hateful Poisonous
Sultry Subtle Self-controlled Self-sacrificing	Immoral Underhand Manipulative Self-destructive
Dignified Confiding Sense of secrecy Intimate	Tight-lipped Unforthcoming Conspiratorial Close
Faithful Passionate Gives all Intense	Possessive Jealous Expects all Fanatical

SOLUTION	PROBLEM
When you find you cannot get enough, start giving all you can.	Your appetite for love is a bottomless pit – with you at the bottom of it.
For every secret you keep, respectfully reveal one of your own. Break a taboo today.	Keeping doubts and desires to yourself and a few other moles is creating emotional claustrophobia.
Your invasive charms ultimately have to be used for more than just sating your desires.	Misusing your subtle powers finds you subtly disadvantaged; on the road to dereliction.
You see your own unrealized potential in others. Bring it to life – don't beat it to death.	Attracting figures who reflect your self-disdain in order to scorn them is doing you in.
Sex without love goes nowhere – except down. What price carnal knowledge and experience?	Finding yourself in degrading relationships or scenes. Sexual diseases.

If you find yourself on the receiving end of negative traits, it is because you are not expressing the opposing positive traits.

VENUS IN SAGITTARIUS

ESSENCE

Loving through Seeking
The Joy of Love • The Bon Vivant

Above all you are aware of Love's bounty and inexhaustibility. As such this can mean either that you have an enthusiastic appetite for love – or lust – that never actually seems to amount to much, or that through thick and thin you never lose faith that love is always bound for glory. Philosophically you know that you cannot have good times without bad, and that good times here mean better times down the road. As you look back down your life track, you will appreciate your heart's experience more when you consider it in terms of quality rather than quantity, of love gained rather than love lost.

You see love as an adventure, a true romance, and seeking it can – and should – lead you far afield. Fortune or the one you crave could well be found some way beyond your original and possibly limited horizon. A homey and predictable love life or partner is not really to your taste, until you have spread your wings and sown enough wild oats to appreciate that love is an adventure wherever you are and whoever you are with. Indeed, it is your expansive and unbounded sense of love and pleasure that can inspire and warm another's heart when it has become a little cold and damp along the way. In your natural awareness of Love's infinite supply, it is important that you really give something of value to others. Promising and not delivering can be your most common and infuriating fault. When you express your sense of Love's bounty in a focused and discriminating fashion, you truly teach and convey Love's majesty and wonder, and this is what truly satisfies you. This also applies to any artistic expression, in that you can and must put across something of lasting and eternal value.

Venus in Sagittarius is basically concerned with the bonding, or rather the inseparability, of physical love and spiritual love. However, as you prefer to learn from experience rather than from a book, it is quite likely that initially you will try to keep the two apart; if not, you will find it hard to keep them together. In other words, either your physical need for love can somehow divorce itself from a moral sense of social behaviour, which could lead to separation and divorce itself; or your need for sanctity in intimacy can be unmet by your partner, or forced by yourself, with the same unhappy result. Another alternative could be to find a philosophy to justify your sexual escapades or emotional shortcomings.

However, eventually a set of beliefs and principles that dictate your manner of loving and relating is essential to your happiness. So in a relationship you should discover and establish an agreed moral/spiritual basis of understanding – and keep to it – otherwise love will fly out of the same window through which it flew in.

LIKES	**DISLIKES**
Quick emotional responses	Hanging back • Leaving things unsaid
Honest, upfront relating • 'Religious' art	Meaningless fashions • Restraint and inactivity
Horsing around • Gallantry and philanthropy	Flattery and empty façades

If you are a man, this could be the kind of woman to whom you are attracted – but it is really a part of you, so realize it.

VENUS IN SAGITTARIUS

TRANSFORMER

POSITIVE	NEGATIVE
Romantic imagination Light-hearted Warmly affectionate Generous	Easily attracted Impressionable Flirtatious Unkept promises
Guided by definite standards Benevolent and loyal	Forces beliefs on to partner Cannot face emotional truth
Idealistic Ardent feelings Demonstrative Non-possessive	Hard to please Escapist Scatters emotions Fickle
Emotionally frank Honest with lover Broad-minded	Brutally and offensively tactless Impersonally affectionate Licentious and amoral
Socially active Vivacious Popular Friendly	Name-dropper Promiscuous 'Groupie' Squanders affections
Set a higher value on yourself and you'll be that much more appreciated by others.	You feel 'The more I give the less I get'. Feeling unloved and unlovable.
You will be truly loved for expressing how you truly feel about yourself.	Feeling secretly disliked, you tease and taunt as a vain compensation.
Identify your ideals and your needs and seek to express them, then you will find love.	Feeling that there is no one in the world who can love and understand you.
Recognize that love grows through its trials. Don't expect too much too soon.	Love never lives up to your expectations; something always seems to spoil it.
Giving should be its own reward – and you have a lot to give.	Feeling taken for granted. Good-time girl/guy reputation.
SOLUTION	PROBLEM

If you find yourself on the receiving end of negative traits, it is because you are not expressing the opposing positive traits.

VENUS IN CAPRICORN

ESSENCE

Loving through Building
The Test of Time • Love is No Business

You have an apparently restrained love nature, and, as a rule, are not given to being openly affectionate – at least, not when you really mean it. You can be formally fond, in the sense of being tactile and gracious in the current socially accepted manner, but where your true amorous intentions are concerned, only one person will know about them for quite a while. This is because basically you are not inclined to commit yourself to a relationship until some form of commitment has been shown by the other party. This points to the likelihood of your being attracted to someone who is more demonstrative and more direct than yourself, otherwise a mutual attraction might never lead to anything, despite itself.

You look for the traditional values in a relationship, like fidelity and constancy, and until a partnership has stood the test of time, distrustfulness can be in evidence. To prevent this in itself becoming a blight on the survival of the relationship, you may need to get to the root of why you can be so lacking in trust. Once these formalities have been observed, you then reveal a rather passionate, if somewhat sculptured, kind of love nature, with an enduring relationship (probably marriage) to match.

As there is a measure of unreachability about you emotionally, you are perennially attracted to those who also exude a certain mystique. It is as if you find pleasure in seeking a balance between total reliability and eternal elusiveness. This can mean that you stray from the very path that you originally insisted everyone keep to – and this would be in direct proportion to how much you were keeping certain feelings too close to your chest. In other words, not giving expression to your wilder and less conventional desires would, at some stage, attract you to someone wild and unconventional. The secret to all this is that the partner you already have probably has similar urges just waiting to be identified and unearthed – by you! However, if not, then making off into the romantic undergrowth will be both necessary and unavoidable.

On those other Venusian subjects of art and values, you are someone who can either carefully blend them through expressing yourself artistically in a valid and substantial fashion, or appreciate art and perhaps even deal in it. However, on the negative side, you could either fail to place the right value on your social or artistic merits, or, conversely, attempt to use your charms to gain money and status. But, fundamentally, you know that neither love nor art is a business. The paradox with Venus in Capricorn is seen in the fact that really you want a deeply spiritual kind of love relationship – with a person or with your creations – but unless you open up and surrender your heart, all you will feel is short-changed.

LIKES	**DISLIKES**
Mature relationships	Romantic illusions
Knowing social pitch • Working spouse	Embarrassments • Bimbos/Toy-boys
Traditional/classical art • Testing the water	So-called 'Art' • Love at first sight

If you are a man, this could be the kind of woman to whom you are attracted – but it is really a part of you, so realize it.

VENUS IN CAPRICORN

TRANSFORMER

POSITIVE	NEGATIVE
Committed Serious lover Steadfast Constant	Possessive Jealous Inflexible Self-righteous
Cautious Trustworthy Disciplined Objective	Inhibited Distrustful Stern Indifferent
Genuine affections Modest Cool exterior Reserved	Undemonstrative Mean Cold manner Unfeeling
Dignified Sense of composure Self-controlled Upright	Snobbish Too formal Self-contained Stiff
Practical Resourceful Affluent Self-made	Materialistic Money-grubbing Penny-pinching Selfish

SOLUTION	PROBLEM
Establish what you are worth and feel good about it, then you are bound to obtain it.	Money problems as a result of attaching too much or too little importance to it.
Your strength of character need not be forced, for it will show itself in the course of time.	Trying to conceal your social shortcomings only serves to perpetuate them.
When you let someone know how you feel, they really know how you feel.	Feeling cut-off and unappreciated. Others' ignorance of your plight only exacerbates this.
Temper your self-restraint with the knowledge that the better things are worth waiting for.	Life feels a joyless and lack-lustre affair. Everything seems flat and pointless.
You can only be true to love, as you see and feel it – not to the loved one.	Fretting over what – or rather who – you think is 'yours'. Uncomfortably justified.

If you find yourself on the receiving end of negative traits, it is because you are not expressing the opposing positive traits.

221

VENUS IN AQUARIUS

ESSENCE

Loving through Liberating
Set Your Love Free • Beauty Awakens

With the Planet of Love and Beauty in Aquarius, you have an open and experimental approach to relating and to artistic expression. On the one hand this can be both relaxing and stimulating, as it allows others to loosen up and be more themselves, but then again it can make it rather difficult for others to know where you're coming from emotionally, as your style can be disconcerting, even shocking, or just plain odd.

You have a liberal attitude that aspires to accommodating all types of people, but unless you actually devise some kind of individual moral code, relationships can float away on the breeze as your free-and-easiness turns out to be a case of hedging your bets. Your coolly and impersonally affectionate nature goes down very well with friends and at social gatherings, but it can also make it quite easy for someone closer than a friend to up and leave.

With such a blithe and deceptively undemanding air about you, it may be difficult for you to comprehend why you experience so much heat and hassle in emotional relationships. The key to understanding how your personal magnetism and manner of relating attract such dilemmas hinges on the meaning of the word 'freedom'. Your problem is that you want to allow a partner the freedom and the space to do as they please, but if you give them too much then they think you don't care. Alternatively, you will put it the other way round and pretend that it is you who doesn't care, which makes your opposite number feel so insecure that he/she begins to impinge upon your freedom.

The secret is to reveal, in a heartfelt way, your opinions and questions concerning freedom of love for the person or persons to whom you feel the closest. They will then feel included in your quest for freedom. It they should hotly disagree with or reject your views then you can grant them the freedom to do and to think as they please – but tell them to remember that it is you who wanted to find freedom with them. Furthermore, you can help to awaken them to the nature of their own love and values by enquiring, in your charming manner, what exactly it is that they think freedom means. But, above all, show your love, otherwise anything done in the name of freedom will just be a sham, that is, the freedom not to love.

You can be socially inventive and creatively innovative, and you are naturally drawn towards the forefront of artistic styles and cultural values. If your partner does not share similar views or does not feel able to express such differences in a friendly way, then sudden disaster could strike. Conversely, sharing a 'contemporary' lifestyle should not be a substitute for a genuine emotional rapport. With Venus in Aquarius, love and friendship must coexist; and freedom loves to be found by two people at once in the midst of the beauty of both their joy and their sorrow.

LIKES	DISLIKES
Lover to be a friend • Personal code of ethics	Not sharing everything • Being tied down
Freedom in marriage • Social experimentation • Openness	Being clung to • Outworn social values • Jealousy

If you are a man, this could be the kind of woman to whom you are attracted – but it is really a part of you, so realize it.

VENUS IN AQUARIUS

TRANSFORMER

POSITIVE	NEGATIVE
Free-loving Idealistic Easygoing Liberal	Lacks feeling Naïve Indiscriminate Erratic
Original lover Non-possessive Unique Mild	Odd lover Unfeeling Peculiar Touchy
Cultured Experimental Progressive Eclectic	Insincere Kinky Superficial Promiscuous
Sparkling Popular Friendly Tongue-in-cheek	Scatty Impersonal Flattering Sarcastic
Convincing Refined Quietly persevering Humane	Stubborn Manipulative Uncompromising Reactionary
The values that you espouse are only as effective as they are gentle and considerate.	Mania posing as morality is totally immoral and leaves others no choice but to leave – suddenly.
A sense of self-ridicule is the critical ingredient that makes you utterly attractive.	To make you to their liking, others have to take you with a pinch of salt.
Through it all, you discover ultimately that healthy sexuality blooms most of all in love.	Your attempts to be sexually enlightened/enlightening founder on reefs of sexual self-doubt.
Letting it be known that only one side of you is that cool will make others warm towards you.	Relating to you is like hugging thin air that occasionally and unaccountably crackles.
True liberalism is about telling the difference between your fears and your principles.	Your ideas on how to relate seem to create more misunderstanding than understanding.
SOLUTION	PROBLEM

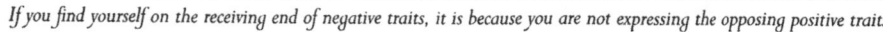

If you find yourself on the receiving end of negative traits, it is because you are not expressing the opposing positive traits.

VENUS IN PISCES

ESSENCE

Loving through Accepting
Love of All • Love is All

Venus is said to be Exalted in Pisces because Love and Beauty can find their fullest expression in this sensitive, imaginative and compassionate Sign. But, as ever, to reach great highs you may first have to encounter great lows – lows that are the result of your expression of love being too full, your expectations of love too naïve. At heart you know and feel that love is everything, but the world as it currently is still puts things like money and self-preservation at the top of the list. So you have to learn some discrimination and awareness of how best to express such a universal love sense as yours, otherwise you are prone to being too vulnerable and impressionable, and to having your fundamentally caring nature taken advantage of.

You regard everything as being alive and sacred, from a minute insect to a human being, from a fluffy toy to an angel. As a result of this lover-of-the-universe quality that you have about you, one-to-one relationships can run into trouble through your trying either to give or to get all this sense of love to or from one person. This is the gallon-in-a-pint-pot syndrome, whereby either your partner can be drowned by your love and affection, feel unable to live up to it, and possibly then go off with someone else who they feel is not so demanding; or, you yourself can become so frustrated that your partner does not meet all your needs and longings that you are then unfaithful (which is rather ironic) – or promiscuous, which is a rather wonky way of loving the world!

Venus in Pisces makes for a complex love nature. This is mainly because, on the one hand, you have a highly evolved sense of love as unconditional and of beauty as a healing property; and, on the other, your fears and doubts as an ordinary, fallible human being are inclined to make you see love as something you need and beauty as something to get or to own. The truth is that you are already a thing of love and beauty, but if you doubt this because of emotional and social conditioning, you then lay yourself open to being used and abused.

So, in order to channel and express appropriately such a love nature as yours, some form of art or service should be practised, in such forms as painting, music, nursing, animal welfare or any other that enlightens or relieves. This in turn gives you an increased sense of self-worth, a lack of which is what lies behind the pain, confusion and hopeless longings that arise from your looking for something in someone else which you have inside you. This yearning can also be experienced as a religious fervour in which you worship someone or something as a substitute for loving your Self, which you doubt. Venus is Exalted in Pisces because you are intuitively aware that God and Love are within you, even though the path to such Exaltation can be strewn with false gods and goddesses – of your own making.

LIKES	DISLIKES
All living things • Relieving suffering	Insensitivity • Witnessing suffering
Romance and exotica	Pedestrian love life
Poetry of the soul • A peaceful touch	Commercial hypes • Rough handling

If you are a man, this could be the kind of woman to whom you are attracted – but it is really a part of you, so realize it.

VENUS IN PISCES

TRANSFORMER

POSITIVE	NEGATIVE
Compassionate Sympathetic Appreciates unity of all life	Martyr Too sentimental Fanciful choice of lover
Congenial Evocative Sensitive lover Easygoing	Too passive Seducing Idealizes lover Lazy lover
Artistically inspired Natural healer Self-sacrificing	Romantically deluding Hypersensitive Self-pitying
Selfless Highly affectionate Altruistic Very generous	Weak-willed Wanton No self-value Undiscerning
Loves unconditionally Gentle Philanthropic Peaceful	Fears rejection Soppy Indulging Evasive

Yours is a case of learning to turn the other cheek, and accepting pain as a way to, not of, love.	Fear of involvement. Enforced isolation. Subjected to emotional cruelty.
When you love for love's sake rather than your own there are no bounds to your love.	Pretending to fall or be in love in the vain hope of feeling loved and worth something.
Redirect your sensitivity and imagination towards pursuits that relieve or enlighten.	Feeling disillusioned. Unrequited love. Suffering for love. Lovesick.
Remember that, in truth, you associate love less with the body and more with the Soul.	Unsure of love aims and your lovability. Confusing love with sex or need. Lovelorn.
You can only love the world as much as you love yourself as a part of the world.	Feeling taken advantage of, and that others are too dependent on your selflessness.

SOLUTION	PROBLEM

If you find yourself on the receiving end of negative traits, it is because you are not expressing the opposing positive traits.

Keyword: GETTING

Mars symbolizes the urge to GET what you WANT. This takes DRIVE, which includes SEXUAL DRIVE, INITIATIVE and COURAGE. But Mars is RAW ENERGY, and as such needs Direction and Consideration. Without these, Mars is merely SELFISHNESS, ABUSE and, at its most extreme, VIOLENCE.

Your Mars-Sign shows how you best express your DESIRES, without being PUSHY or feeling PUSHED.

If you are female, your Mars-Sign will point to the kind of male to whom you are attracted — although it is actually a part of you. If you are male, you express and embody quite directly the qualities of your Mars-Sign. With either sex, if you find that you are on the receiving end of negative Mars-Sign traits, then it is because you are not expressing the positive ones.

MARS IN ARIES

ESSENCE
Getting through Doing
The Doer • The Ramrod

The best and the worst expressions of Mars's self-assertion burst forth in Aries. You have a reliable but uncontainable supply of raw energy which must have an outlet and, more importantly, a direction. Unless you have some more introverted personality traits, you are unlikely to see the complications to life that seem to beset so many others. This enables you to get on with things without being side-tracked by the pros and cons.

Simple and straightforward as this no-nonsense approach and unfettered style of yours is, it can cause you to miss more subtle points and undercurrents. If you are as thick-skinned as you are hard-nosed, then this probably doesn't bother you. However, if you feel that in not grasping some vitally important element you are failing to get what you want out of life, then it would be wise to stop and ask yourself 'What am I actually after?' But this simple question is unlikely to be asked until quite a few spills and collisions have occurred with both animate and inanimate objects. You certainly have plenty of get-up-and-go, and hard knocks are taken in your stride – or charge, more like.

Courage and initiative are firmly on your list of virtues, but love and patience are not, and may need to be learned. And the combative or even soldier-like quality of Mars in Aries can have a get-sex-while-I-can kind of attitude. Sexual stamina is in abundance, as a rule, and if you are female you may well be attracted to military-, macho- or even violent-type males.

You can spark enthusiasm in others, and your confidence and daring set an effective example. However, unless there are more steady and persevering qualities present, such as indicated by Planets in Taurus or Capricorn, you could be poor on follow-through. You can and should learn to finish tasks through recognizing what it is about yourself that you are unsure of, and doing something about it. Many of your troubles are the result of using your undeniable energy to go forward in pursuit of some external challenge in order to evade an internal conflict. What you then end up with is an external conflict. Your obvious courage will be needed at a certain stage to penetrate your psychological jungle – rather than a green, fleshy or concrete one. This stage is very noticeable when you – or your partner – begin to react more and more hotly to anything that points to any feelings of inferiority.

You are very much the 'warrior' or 'Amazon' – or supersalesperson. The worst expression of this is a coarse or bullying nature that interferes and dominates with sheer physical force, and is insensitive to the feelings of others. The best expression is as the untiring champion of the underdog, when you use both word and deed to promote your cause, cutting through obstacles and red tape like a machete through hollow green stems.

LIKES	**DISLIKES**
Fast satisfaction • Quick returns • Competition	Watching and waiting • Complicated conditions
Action • Getting your own way	Opposition • Kicking your heels • Interference

If you are a woman, this could be the kind of man to whom you are attracted – but it is really a part of you, so realize it.

MARS IN ARIES

TRANSFORMER

POSITIVE	NEGATIVE
Self-assured Self-willed Independent Survivor	Inner doubt Egocentric Unco-operative Selfish
Bold Energetic Fighter Fearless	Aggressive Pushy Militant Violent
Direct Brisk Championing Outspoken	Unsubtle Intolerant Irascible Quarrelsome
Daring Dashing Exhilarating Spirited	Foolhardy Bumptious Exhausting Ostentatious
Leader-type Strong stamina Enthusiastic Self-starting	Bullying Insensitive Insatiable Self-defeating

Showing people what you can do – rather than what they should do – sets an inspiring example.	Dissatisfaction with others as a result of seeing them as objects of your unsatisfied desires.
When you've discovered what you're driving at you'll have no trouble getting there.	In your hurry to get 'it' and give the impression you've got 'it', you've forgotten what 'it' is!
It benefits you to direct your energies into a worthwhile cause rather than badgering others.	Feeling raw and uncomfortable with yourself. Others are as short with you as you are on patience.
Take up a pursuit that suits your martial nature, but that isn't unnecessarily harmful.	You are making some part of your life or being into a horrific battlefield.
Knowing who and what you are dependent on both emancipates and supports you.	Being left to your own devices but not getting very far. Lack of staying power.

SOLUTION	PROBLEM

If you find yourself on the receiving end of negative traits, it is because you are not expressing the opposing positive traits.

MARS IN TAURUS

ESSENCE

Getting through Stabilizing

Share Your Wealth • Lighten Your Load

Getting what you want means laying your hands on conventionally recognizable assets, such as money and property. With Mars in Taurus you are able to progress easily and steadily in the material sphere of life, and use your patience and worldliness (or someone else's) to make your pile, or at least to secure a quiet corner somewhere.

However, as is often the case with seemingly uncomplicated Taurus, there is a snag. In the case of Mars the snag is that whatever you initially set in motion in order to achieve these material ends – and this you may have done quite unconsciously, through marriage or inheritance, for example – cannot easily change direction. It just keeps chugging along, churning out what eventually can be meaningless and frustrating. Where you were once close to the Earth, you could, at a later date, find your feet stuck in clay. What was obtained in the name of stability becomes a millstone around your neck. Alternatively, the money-making-machine could just grind to a halt.

As you are basically intent on achieving stability, the secret lies in your establishing what truly constitutes stability, rather than blindly conforming to an overly materialistic society's idea of it. This strongly implies a need for the change in direction that you hitherto found so difficult to negotiate. In making the change, two points should be borne in mind.

Firstly, the nature of the change in how you view material stability could be said to hinge on the Law of Infinite Supply, which states that in order to keep supply flowing in, you must keep it flowing out. In other words, continually investing whatever you possess in people or in causes in which you believe, without just thinking of gain for yourself, will ensure that your incoming supply line is maintained. Secondly, you cannot be expected to make such changes overnight, because you are rather like a very low-geared vehicle – you have great pulling and pushing power, but are a devil to stop or to steer. Nevertheless, you have the strength to hold steady as you turn, so to speak. For this reason, whenever you make a change, be it personal or professional, there is no going back.

Your sexual drive could also be likened to this 'low-geared vehicle', in that it is slow to start but hard to stop – and has great pulling and pushing power! Yet, like a bull, you can sometimes be led by the nose. Your decidedly sensuous nature should also find appealing the notion that ploughing back into the Earth what you have gained from it, in the form of possessions, pleasures or experience, will naturally yield fresh fruits.

<table>
<tr><td align="center">LIKES</td><td align="center"></td><td align="center">DISLIKES</td></tr>
<tr><td align="center">Wealth and comfort • Concrete results
Being dominant or dominated • Taking your time
Planning and foresight</td><td></td><td align="center">Scarcity or just making do
Abstract objectives • Wishy-washy relationships
Being pushed • Sudden changes</td></tr>
</table>

If you are a woman, this could be the kind of man to whom you are attracted – but it is really a part of you, so realize it.

MARS IN TAURUS

TRANSFORMER

POSITIVE	NEGATIVE
Capacity for work Earning power Productive/Industrious	Materialistic Avaricious Wealth for wealth's sake
Methodical Practical Persistent Patient	Plodding Boring Slow to change Slow to act
Close to nature Craftsperson Mechanically skilled and able	Cloddish/Brutish Philistine Mechanical and thick-headed
Dependable Sexually attractive Sensuous Passionate	Jealous and possessive Smouldering Carnal Intense
Executive ability Formidable Powerful reserves of strength	Vindictive Bullying Violent when pushed
Identify your 'beast' and re-channel its energy; transform its nature. Be strong with yourself.	Getting into violent and distressing situations. Trouble with the Law.
Your Earthy appeal is at its best when you enjoy it for what it is yet observe its limitations.	Sexual frustration. Acute and persistent emotional pain.
Search for, recognize and express your sense of beauty and physical order.	A dull and unrewarding time. No ray of hope or sign of meaning.
You know that you must make a change. You know that in time it will work out for the better.	Lack of direction. The agony of indecision born of inertia and boredom.
Focus on how your material awareness or position could benefit others.	Successful but not satisfied. Meaningless material pursuits. Financial dilemmas.
SOLUTION	PROBLEM

If you find yourself on the receiving end of negative traits, it is because you are not expressing the opposing positive traits.

MARS IN GEMINI

ESSENCE

Getting through Communicating
The Live Wire • Touch and Go

'Those who don't ask, don't get' is a saying that could apply to Mars in Gemini, for a couple of reasons. If you want or want to know something, it won't be too long before you go and ask. If you find yourself hanging back, then possibly it's for the other reason – that unless you've asked yourself what you want in the first place, you're unlikely to ask anybody else. However, since your desire nature, your tongue and your nervous system seem to be wired up to each other, you can find yourself quite impulsively getting something – or someone – and then wondering what to do with it – or with him/her. So it won't be long before your restless mind and mobile body start looking for something else, getting it, and, again, not quite knowing why – and so on.

Your sexual drive has almost as much to do with nervous energy as with anything else. Attaining the object of your desires and satisfying them can be achieved quickly, and often in the same deft stroke. The relief at having made some kind of definite contact is very important to you, because it both eases your nervous tension and makes you feel desirable – until you next need topping up. However, what you are in fact experiencing is that initially described urge to find out what it is you really want, for if you don't, you're likely to get trapped in a round of tasting the 'goods', not feeling too sure and sitting on the fence as you try to have your cake and eat it, then coming back on second thoughts and finding the goods gone. Ideally you need to slow things down in order to see what is happening so that you might discover what your heart desires. This does not mean slowing down to the point where you are always at the talking/thinking stage, because that can leave you very tense or testy – and still with no answer.

As is ever the case with Planets in Gemini, the contact you are truly trying to make is with yourself. You can talk the hind legs off a donkey, dazzle any sexual target with your personal light-show, and sell something that nobody wants to anyone. Yet until you concentrate your attention and distinguish between what you want, what you have, and what you can't have, you will be at the mercy of your nervous system running the show, which is like setting a chimpanzee loose in a telephone exchange.

Your highly-strung energies need an almost constant outlet, examples of which may be ferreting out information, or intense mental or physical activity. Alcohol abuse would be a sign that you were trying to suppress these energies, but then so would too much self-denial, especially sexual, for you can cerebralize your urges only too well. Whenever you have made contact with someone who absorbs, preoccupies or frustrates your energies, you must follow the 'current' back to the 'generator': ask what it is about them that is really driving you – be it upwards, downwards, forwards, backwards, wild or just plain crazy – for it'll really be something inside you.

LIKES	DISLIKES
Intellectual contests • Thrills and spills • Variety	Dull company • Nothing happening • Routine
Being kept guessing • Keeping them guessing	The predictable • Being pinned down

If you are a woman, this could be the kind of man to whom you are attracted – but it is really a part of you, so realize it.

MARS IN GEMINI

TRANSFORMER

POSITIVE	NEGATIVE
Sharp-witted Humorous Droll Stimulating	Sharp-tongued Sarcastic Irreverent Argumentative
Ingenious Dextrous Resourceful Adaptable	Mischievous Light-fingered Meddlesome Unreliable
Quick Agile Lively Mobile	Hasty Jumpy Unrelaxing Restless
Eloquent Inquisitive Communicative Contact-maker	Verbose Nosy Rambling Gets wires crossed
Versatile mind Flexible Full of ideas Multi-talented	Scatters thoughts Changeable Lacks perseverance Motley
Focus your attention on developing one talent; the rest will progressively cleave to this.	Strung out, spread too thinly, nothing hanging together. Getting nowhere fast.
When you've made it clear to yourself what's going on, make it crystal-clear to others.	Your nervous desire to be in the know disguises your fear of being known. Misunderstandings.
Find a pursuit that involves both danger and discipline, speed and judgment.	The thrills you seek are not worth the havoc they wreak. Irritation breeds Irritation.
The devil need only make work for idle hands (and minds) – not ones as capable as yours.	Getting involved in dubious schemes and affairs. Hairy, touch-and-go situations.
You're the most amusing person to be with – when you see your own joke.	Mocking what you cannot understand gets plenty of reaction, but no respect.
SOLUTION	PROBLEM

If you find yourself on the receiving end of negative traits, it is because you are not expressing the opposing positive traits.

MARS IN CANCER

ESSENCE

Getting through Nurturing
Fight or Flight • Bury the Hatchet

Direct, forceful and uncomplicated Mars is not too happy in Cancer, with its deep and convoluted emotions. You want to make your desires known but not at the expense of laying yourself open to insecurity or embarrassment. Consequently, those desires – or fears – are all too often not clearly expressed and not recognized by others, with the end result exactly as you feared – neither party knowing where the other stands. For this reason the Red Planet is said to be in its Fall in the Sign of the Crab, meaning that your old way of getting what you want out of life has to 'die', and a new way be devised.

Quite simply, when you really care about something you want, you can get it. On the one hand this means taking the trouble to separate carefully your desires from your fears, and to discover how your desires unerringly put you in touch with your fears. In this case you may have to seek help in tracking down what it is from your past that drives you both towards and away from the object of your desires. On the other hand, you need to get in touch tenderly with the fears and needs of the ones who matter to you, which is why you already have the ability to seep into another's most private and hidden areas – an ability that should only be trusted as long as it has honourable intent behind it. In effect, you are able to heal other people of their doubts and fears, and, in so doing, achieve the same for yourself. This is where the indirectness of Mars in Cancer becomes a positive quality, because you can get alongside a sensitive area without its running away and hiding. Having the courage to push on into the emotional heartland, in the face of pain and vulnerability, is the essential challenge here.

You are fiercely protective, particularly of your family. However, unconscious motivations are strong in Cancer, which means that in protecting others close to you, you may also be attempting to conceal what you're unsure of within yourself. For this reason you will attract relationships that force such fears into the open. What these fears most often contain is a certain amount of unconscious anger, which in turn can draw bad temper, strife or even fire or violence down on you, especially in the family/domestic sphere, for this is where such anger probably originated, in your own childhood. For a more peaceful life you have to bury the hatchet – but in order to do so you have first to dig it up.

Your sex drive is strong, largely because it has emotional need behind it, which is both a good and a bad thing. Bad, because when your insecurities overshadow your desires, sexual indolence and doubt occur, which can be very frustrating, and can lead to insecurity for both you and your partner. Positively, though, you are able to tune in keenly to the needs of your mate, making him/her feel both excited and secure at the same time, which is very special.

LIKES	**DISLIKES**
Close involvements • Secure sex life	Lukewarm emotions • 'Unsafe' sex
Striving for your kin	Distressing the family
Active home life • Rooting around	Domestic conflagrations • Inner doubts

---

If you are a woman, this could be the kind of man to whom you are attracted – but it is really a part of you, so realize it.

MARS IN CANCER

TRANSFORMER

POSITIVE	NEGATIVE
Sensuous Provocative Passionate Sexually subtle	Irritable Evasive Too intense Sexually unsure
Tenacious Protective Bold Hardworking	Possessive Defensive Surreptitious Compulsive
Complex Adaptable Sensitive Healing	Neurotic Moody Quarrelsome Confusing
Instinctual Intuitive Original Occultist	Unaware of urges Fatalistic Weird Spooky/Spooked
Binds family Strongly sympathetic Fights for security	Splits family Blind allegiance Domestically domineering

SOLUTION	PROBLEM
A happy person makes a happy family, so go for what makes you happy, but not guilty.	Domestic strife through not distinguishing between emotional priorities and passing desires.
Deliberately going upstream to seek the source of your desires will reveal hidden depths.	Allowing yourself just to float downstream has found you at sea.
Find out what's really making you angry. Recognizing your own quirks helps others to do so, too.	Suppressed anger wells up, and causes temper tantrums that blow things just at the wrong moment.
Ascertain what or who you really care about, and make it known in a direct and energetic fashion.	Your hidden fear of losing someone or something is causing exactly that.
Learn to recognize the fine line between stimulation and aggravation.	Sexual involvement puts you in touch with problems by exploding them in your face.

If you find yourself on the receiving end of negative traits, it is because you are not expressing the opposing positive traits.

MARS IN LEO

ESSENCE

Getting through Creating
All the World's a Stage • The Warrior King or Queen

There is nothing tepid about Mars in Leo. Whatever else is present in your personality, this makes for a hot and fiery streak that should find some form of dramatic, creative or romantic expression.

Mars in Leo lends a very 'masculine' influence, which means that if you are a male you lean towards the macho and chauvinistic. If you are a female you find this kind of man irresistable, often despite yourself. If this expression of such rank masculinity invites trouble, then it needs to be taken to a higher, more sophisticated, level. Perhaps Carl Jung's definition of the masculine principle, which is present in both men and women, will be of help here: masculinity is the desire to get what you want and the ability to do so.

You are determined and confident – at least, outwardly. But the impression you give is what's important to you – and you don't get a second chance to make a good first impression! It is crucial, therefore, to know your pitch and to be able to call the shots. And, as you wish to soar to the heights, you need a head for them, which includes being prepared to be shot down.

You love to be seen to shine and excel. Although this can lead to a neurotic need for admiration, it also demands that you have the honour, dignity and ability that command respect. You can be tempted to enforce respect and obedience in others, which is 'creating' in the wrong sense, and this leads to extreme humiliation, which is something that you dislike, nay fear, more than anything else. You can definitely be an inspiring figure, for you have a strong sense of personal power, which you should maintain through being loved rather than feared. You may well occupy a position of authority, for such vitality and will-power as yours cannot, or should not, go unnoticed.

You are a gallant or gracious lover. To you the opposite sex is the most attractive thing in the world, which keeps the 'royal blood' coursing through your veins until the end. Your desire nature is very reliable, and, although it inclines you to possessiveness, makes sure that you get your man or your maid.

You have a feeling of invincibility within you and without you. If you interpret this in a selfish or small way, you then overact and overreact to everything, which can lead to heart trouble, be it of the medical or the romantic kind. When you recognize this triumphant feeling as an expression of the Eternal Spirit (symbolized by the Sun, the Planetary ruler of Leo) your sense of glory goes beyond petty ego drives, and the way in which you set about getting is truly creative, for it becomes a gift.

LIKES	**DISLIKES**
Centre stage • Pride in partner • Respect	Feeling insignificant • A dowdy partner • Humiliation
Excitement • Honesty	Losing control • Small-mindedness

If you are a woman, this could be the kind of man to whom you are attracted – but it is really a part of you, so realize it.

MARS IN LEO

TRANSFORMER

POSITIVE	NEGATIVE
High-spirited Passionate Ardent lover Energetic	Melodramatic Possessive Jealous lover Coercive
Dignified Zealous Proud Heroic	Pompous Self-righteous Vain Tyrannical
Enthusiastic Vital Speculative Exciting	Offensive Brutal Wild gambler Over-excited
Self-assured Determined Strong-willed Leader-type	Feels infallible Quarrelsome Domineering Egoistic
Consistent desire Ambitious Magnetic Fearless	Overbearing Ruthless Conceited Arrogant
'When the going gets tough, the tough get going' is all.	A force greater than you has got you in its sights – or has already opened fire.
Your way out is your way forward, is what you are absolutely sure you do best.	As long as you don't admit that you're cornered, you'll stay cornered.
Staking your life on following your life and harming no other, is your best – your only – bet.	Feeling threatened or humiliated – or just hoping against hope. Accused and accursed.
As you hold your head high and take over, make sure there's no egg on your face.	Embarrassing or intimidating others so that they either ignore or oppose you.
If you're as magnificent and unique as you make out – and you do have style – then fear no rivals.	Haunted by a monster, a green-eyed monster – a monster that is you!
SOLUTION	PROBLEM

If you find yourself on the receiving end of negative traits, it is because you are not expressing the opposing positive traits.

MARS IN VIRGO

ESSENCE

Getting through Analysing
Slave-Driver or Slave-Driven • Health is Efficiency

Mars in Virgo can make for such an exacting nature, both in yourself and in others, that there comes a time when it is necessary to give it a break and to begin to let life live itself, according to its own rules. Although your accuracy at work and at play is something to be marvelled at, you tend to forget that you are only supposed to be doing your best, not the impossible!

As is often the case with Planets placed in Virgo, a lesson needs to be learnt from the opposite Sign of Pisces. This means giving in to the mystery of life, the world, sex etc., and putting everything on automatic pilot for a while. This will mean asking yourself the question: What exactly am I striving for? When analysing what it is that you wish to get, you will be surprised to discover either that it is very simple or that you haven't got a clue. Next question: So why all the hassle?

If you do not get this Piscean message written in Virgoan script, then it is more than likely that you will find yourself involved in some sort of reversal of the usual expression of your desires. For example, where you are normally so in charge of your physical well-being, you could be subject to ill-health (relating to nerves, stomach, guts, muscle cramps or to some more mysterious complaint). Or, you could be making a hash of things at work, when you pride yourself on taking pains to be efficient. In either case, this reversal is mainly due to loss of energy and concentration, as a result of thinking you have to keep tabs on every little issue, or to unsatisfied desire mixed with consequent irritation. You may even end up being work-shy, as opposed to workaholic. In general, where work is concerned you are very reliable, but prefer not to be responsible for the whole show: you are happier serving than ruling. However, you can be so utterly efficient that it can go painfully unnoticed, as there is no sign that the work had to be done in the first place. If this should ever be the case, then go 'on strike' for a bit.

Probably the most interesting area of this character reversal is your sexuality. A Virgoan Mars can zip between chastity and promiscuity like no other. For a start, if there is any sexual repression lurking in the past, you won't miss it. You can sit on it, but it's better to have an experimental attitude and sort it out. Taboos won't get laid until they are so! There is quite likely to be more sexual guilt in you than in most, but you are very good at disguising it in some way, through promiscuity, for instance. Desire (Mars) and Purity (Virgo) have always been uneasy bedfellows, and given rise to extremes as they react to each other. One way of being sexually involved but 'untouched' at the same time would be voyeurism, or seeing yourself doing it as if in a film, while you take notes. But sex is essentially a trip into the unknown, so you need to keep a wary eye on it, but avoid judging or keeping score, for this smacks of repressed desires.

LIKES	DISLIKES
Fine precision work • The professional touch	Inaccuracies • Bodging • Those who do not try
Getting it right • Sexual hygiene • Technique	Tacky sex • Ham-fistedness

If you are a woman, this could be the kind of man to whom you are attracted — but it is really a part of you, so realize it.

MARS IN VIRGO

TRANSFORMER

POSITIVE	NEGATIVE
Fine sexuality Hits the spot Watchful Even-tempered	Frustrating Sexually exacting Voyeuristic Repressed
Helpful Healing ability Attentive Subtle touch	Interfering Hypochondriac Neurotic Precious
Industrious Methodical Energy-saving Thorough	Workaholic Inflexible Energy-wasting Never finishes
Shrewd Correct in procedure Clever Ingenious	Exploitative Sanctimonious Wheedling Cantankerous
Precise Accurate Clean Economical	Critical Fussy Clinical Niggardly
Allowing room for human error will actually create less of it. Take it easy.	Difficult or even impossible to work with or to be with.
The first step towards getting something is learning how to get it – but don't try too hard.	Feeling lonely and isolated, and uncomfortable with your ways of trying to resolve this.
For best results, apply your fine awareness of efficiency to your own mind and body.	Feeling exhausted and run-down. Overworked but under-productive.
'Physician heal thyself' – and then anyone else who asks.	Being a pain in the neck, butt etc., both to yourself and to others.
Allow yourself the time, grace and opportunity to explore your sexual mystery.	Frustration from being sexually inhibited and inhibiting. Feeling undesirable.
SOLUTION	PROBLEM

If you find yourself on the receiving end of negative traits, it is because you are not expressing the opposing positive traits.

239

MARS IN LIBRA

ESSENCE

Getting through Relating

The Social Mover • Balance Your Impulses

As Mars symbolizes the urge to be independent and assertive, it has its wings clipped in socially-conscious Libra. If you are wanting to make a decisive move or statement, you find it cannot easily be done without some prior sanction or approval from others in general, or from one person in particular. So the challenge is to get what you want but to fit it in with social values and emotional requirements. This is challenging indeed, and the dynamics of Mars in Libra seem to force you into finding this balance one way or the other ...

Until you are able to adjust your needs and values to your desires, and vice versa, you are liable to be controlled by whoever you are sexually involved with, or want to be sexually involved with. In effect, you are attracting a conflict of wills in order that your desires be tested and realized. Additionally, and for the same reason, you are likely to attract an aggressive, energetic or quick-tempered partner. One difficulty here might be that of confusing your own desires with those of the other party, which is one reason why they will appear to have you dangling on a string, like a set of scales!

Libra also has the effect on Mars of softening its hard-cutting edge. This is particularly hard-going on the male ego, but, of all the planetary influences, selfish and hard-headed Mars has probably been most responsible for the harm and strife in the world. So it can be very worthwhile (indeed manly) to use such force and drive sensitively, rather then selfishly.

This is a subtle placement because you could be seeking approval of a kind that has nothing to do with your own values. For example, feeling that you have to live up to some social or sexual role that is being created by your peers, when in truth such a standard is not your style at all. So . . .

Essentially, you are an initiator of social activities and new social values. Your desires spring from a feeling of wanting everyone to be in harmony and to pull together. So your forceful and impatient qualities really have to be expressed in a graceful or aesthetic fashion in order for you to make your point. However, what can happen is that your own wishes and opinions do not get put across at all for fear of social ridicule or sexual rejection. The anger and resentment that can mount up as a result of this may then come out in an anything but graceful way. You can see both sides of an argument, but this should not be regarded as a reason for not acting at all. In fact, at an evolved level, Mars in Libra often finds itself with the casting vote, which is when you have to be aware of your own moral convictions, and have the courage of them, which is what Mars in Libra is truly all about.

LIKES	**DISLIKES**
Togetherness • Doing it with style • The social whirl	Injustice • Being blunt • Social vacuums
Knowing your desires • Equal partnerships	Indecisiveness • Being dominant or dominated

If you are a woman, this could be the kind of man to whom you are attracted — but it is really a part of you, so realize it.

MARS IN LIBRA

TRANSFORMER

POSITIVE	NEGATIVE
Attentive lover Enthusiastic Skilful lover Gentle	Fawning Idolizing Impersonal Tentative
Fair Easygoing Diplomatic Co-operative	Bland Indecisive Insincere Misleading
Persuasive Binding Discreet Perceptive	Devious Separative Awkward Judgmental
Idealistic Intuitive Principled Measured	Unreal Unfeeling Self-limiting Inhibited
Polite Considerate Agreeable Sedate	Vulgar Selfish Disputatious Impulsive

True good manners naturally follow when you consider the ways of others and yourself equally.	As a reaction to your forced good behaviour, you now see yourself as behaving badly.
Your concept of a better life and society has to be based on a vision – not a need.	Narrowing your social horizons for the sake of maintaining your security needs proves unrewarding.
Quietly achieve your objectives through being sure of yourself – not so much of others.	Juggling people and situations towards your idea of harmony is having the opposite effect.
You are learning the art of diplomacy – but sometimes at the expense of being ill at ease.	Caught in a netherworld of not knowing your social values from your individual desires.
To gain the object of your desires, focus on what they really are, not what you presume they are.	Whatever you try in order to gain the object of your desires still finds you at a disadvantage.

SOLUTION	PROBLEM

If you find yourself on the receiving end of negative traits, it is because you are not expressing the opposing positive traits.

MARS IN SCORPIO

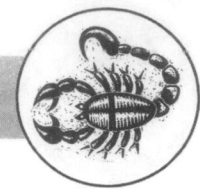

ESSENCE

Getting through Desiring
Do or Die • The Front-Liner

This indicates a primal nature of the highest – or lowest – order. In other words, you have a powerful sense of survival and sexuality, as well as how these two drives become intertwined. This amounts to a kind of magnetic intensity about you that has such an effect on your surroundings that you never elicit a bland response from others – you always get to them in some way, whether you mean to or not. This underlying 'poke' that you have was just as apparent when you were a child, in fact it was probably more so for you may since have tried to conceal it, and so it is likely that you invited extreme friendship or extreme hostility from quite early on. It was, and still is, as if you strongly and automatically challenge or champion other people's most basic hopes and fears.

The psychological effect that this has had on you is important to consider, for it will have similarly coloured all your subsequent relationships, especially those of an intimate nature. It is vital for you to admit to possessing this provocative energy that continually hums around and about you, and to understand its qualities and conditions. You are not about to get or to go for anything unless you really desire it: merely liking, needing or, least of all, going along with something is not sufficient for you. Your defiant aura, be it active or passive, will always attract great loyalty or great enmity, and not much in between. For you it is a case of either get or be got, or have or be had. Metaphorically speaking, your safety-catch is permanently in the 'off' position.

You are thus capable of creating quite a stir, and gaining the object of your desires in the process. However, what can queer your pitch is a reluctance to assert yourself in this powerful way as a result of having been abused in some way yourself, or having a strong urge to get your own back for this reason. In either case you are likely to be filled with a degree of self-disgust, or at least self-criticism. In turn, you will express or disguise this with an air of politeness, or the complete opposite.

Ultimately, therefore, the inherent strength and power of Mars in Scorpio are best used to heal or to transform your environment in some way, beginning with your own self-image. Merely trying to keep yourself to yourself, often in a smugly unassailable way, is a result of that previously-felt threat of destruction. However, a fear of being destroyed can lead to self-destruction – witness a cornered Scorpion! In ancient times, astrologers would instruct army generals to put troops with Mars in Scorpio in the front-line of battle. Even today you have no equal when it comes to pushing for changes and improvements where they are most needed, be they for your personal evolution or for society in general.

LIKES	DISLIKES
Intimate involvement	Indifference
Emotional intensity • Being influential	Compromising • Being manipulated
Firing from the hip • Winning against the odds	Going down on your knees • Giving up

If you are a woman, this could be the kind of man to whom you are attracted – but it is really a part of you, so realize it.

MARS IN SCORPIO

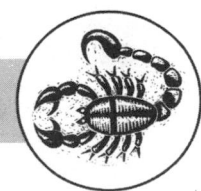

TRANSFORMER

POSITIVE	NEGATIVE
Charismatic Highly sexed Irresistible Emotionally rich	Megalomaniac Degrading Dissipated Resentful
Strong-willed Indestructible Forceful Courageous	Stubborn Self-destructive Brutal Seething
Thorough Exhaustive Determined Ambitious	Cruel Exhausting Unrelenting Ruthless
Probing Healing Discreet Perceptive	Prying Manipulative Devious Caustic
Passionate Deep Red-blooded Powerful	Jealous Dark Cold-blooded Revengeful
The life-force is omnipotent, omniscient and omnipresent – it has you, go with it.	Feeling very depressed, meaning that you are fighting against the life-force.
Discovering that you are able to get the best out of others allows you to do the same for yourself.	Not being prepared to find your own better nature, you look for the damnable in others.
Tempering your taking to task with a measure of affection is what successfully completes it.	Taxing, scorning or denying others is a sign that you have no love for yourself.
You also know there is a power in life that is for the good, and you feel it at the core of you.	Stuck in the pit of your own bloody-mindedness – and you know it.
There is something about you that others look to or are drawn to – you can and must live up to it.	Dissatisfaction with yourself, which is reflected in perverting yourself or others.
SOLUTION	PROBLEM

If you find yourself on the receiving end of negative traits, it is because you are not expressing the opposing positive traits.

MARS IN SAGITTARIUS

ESSENCE

Getting through Seeking
Defender of the Faith • Is Might Right?

Mars in Sagittarius gives you a built-in sense that freedom of movement is your birthright, that you should be able to make off over some distant horizon in any direction whenever you feel the urge to do so. Furthermore, you usually possess the energy and enthusiasm to take you there. However, the operative phrase is 'in any direction', or, more precisely, it's a burning question of 'in what direction?' For Mars in the Sign of the Centaur is essentially a very raw and untamed kind of energy, and, as such, needs directing and controlling, rather like a team of spirited horses, otherwise you are liable to feel torn apart by conflicting urges, or, even worse, to bottle them up, in which case the very least you can do is to get plenty of physical exercise.

For you to get what you want in life you have to have a definite goal. What should guide your 'team of horses' is a strong sense of crusading for some ideal, be it religious, artistic, scientific or whatever you believe to be worthy of your considerable energy, for it is really only something 'big' that satisfies Mars in Sagittarius. Without this cause to consume your exuberance, you could be driven to merely raging around, both physically and emotionally, or to being the armchair philosopher, forever holding forth about this and that opinion, but never acting upon any.

Not surprisingly, your sex life has a lot to do with how you channel your vibrant libido. When you want sex you want a lot of it, right there and then. But, at other times, you can be curiously matter of fact, take it or leave it. It all depends what is currently calling you onward, a sense of mission or a sense of frustration, an absorbing relationship or a habitual one.

When you avoid getting carried away on your own fanatical wave of beliefs, or being stuck in the mud of not having any beliefs at all, you excel at rallying others (and yourself) out of apathy, and exhorting them to act out their sense of adventure or to reveal what is inhibiting it. This could be in the living room or in the world at large. You enjoy the splendour and majesty of being on the march towards some lofty goal, or, at least, the idea of it.

Yes, without a dream on which to focus your energies, you can be a very wild Centaur indeed, and might well wind up 'hobbled' by something that Saturn cooked up that forces you to find a new direction – or indeed, any direction. In other words, if you feel constricted by any of life's situations, is it because you have not considered what you actually want freedom for? There is something mighty about you, but might without just cause can never be right. Imagine that you have a personal banner – and what is emblazoned upon it!

LIKES	DISLIKES
Firm and fiery principles	Lukewarm beliefs
Honesty and hot debate • Outdoor activities	Lies and small-talk • Being cooped up
Sports and games • Pageantry	Physical inactivity • The humdrum

If you are a woman, this could be the kind of man to whom you are attracted – but it is really a part of you, so realize it.

MARS IN SAGITTARIUS

TRANSFORMER

POSITIVE	NEGATIVE
Independent Far-sighted Espouses and grants freedom	Opinionated Overlooks obvious Demands unlimited freedom
Explorative Daring and bold Adventurous Optimistic	Tangential Impetuous Scatters energies Wildly hopeful
Forcefully convincing Crusading Effective teacher Active idealist	Self-righteous Fanatical Ear-bashing Preaching
Frank and open To the point Clears the air Enthusiastic	Tactless and rude Harsh Argumentative Extremist
Lusty and vigorous Mobile Spirited Very friendly	Lustful and carnal Restless Boisterous Lecherous
Your concerted energies are as uplifting as your rampant energies are disturbing.	Feverishly frustrated when your desires are not met or when you feel baulked.
Allowing others to come out with what's bothering them will release what's bothering you.	Confusion and resentment resulting from others feeling reluctant to confront your hotheadedness.
Your visions and ideals are as good as others' understanding of them.	Out of touch with prevailing trends. Blinded by your own beliefs.
The ultimate adventure: getting lost in order to discover where, who and what you are.	Biting off more than you can chew. Lost for direction. Constantly shifting objectives.
Are your beliefs allowing you the freedom you desire in order to further yourself?	Missing the point, and frustrated by your inappropriate convictions.
SOLUTION	PROBLEM

If you find yourself on the receiving end of negative traits, it is because you are not expressing the opposing positive traits.

MARS IN CAPRICORN

ESSENCE

Getting through Building
The Master-Builder • The Executive

Mars is said to be Exalted in Capricorn, which means that, ideally, you go about getting what you want in such a deliberate, pragmatic and sure-footed fashion that what you get stays got. In effect, you are basing your achievements on firm foundations, and are not, as a rule, inclined to taking short cuts, for you know that they end up being the long way round. However, it is highly possible that you do not fully realize just how broad and deep are those foundations on which you are building your endeavours, especially if there is an impatient streak somewhere in your personality. The key to appreciating that you are getting somewhere is to trust that 'building work' is going on, even though it could be taking place unconsciously, beneath the surface, where foundations are based.

You are also aware of the facilities and structures society and business have to offer, and should make use of them in order to further your ambitions. However, although one secret of your success is an evolved sense of how various systems work, this can also be your downfall if you allow them to eclipse your own independent methods and values. Alternatively, your Exalted sense of what achieving really means could well necessitate your having to go it alone, without even being able to subscribe to the standard procedures that others follow. Mars in Capricorn is a great indication of the self-made person, sooner or later.

Sexually you are quite passionate, but only someone whom you have allowed yourself to become intimately involved with would or need be aware of this. Essentially, your Earthiness ensures that you understand both the gross and the subtle nature of the human body. Again, the Exalted status of Mars in Capricorn more or less demands that you do this, and not just indulge in a body for its own sake, without appreciating that it houses a Soul.

Conversely, or even perversely, you can suppress your passion and curb your drive with your basically disciplined nature. But, potentially, you are more capable than most of determining the fine line between being sexually aware and being just plain sexy, between sexual restraint and sexual inhibition.

The ability to delegate and regulate is an essential quality of Mars in Capricorn. This applies both to the professional and the personal spheres of your life. This ability rests mainly on having a purpose and a plan, and a sense of timing. You know, or learn, that everything can be accomplished, using time as your instrument. So, whether they concern a business deal or a sexual relationship, your ends can be achieved as long as you pace yourself and do not allow yourself to be hypnotized and pressured into meeting a deadline or target that is a convention of others, born of their fear of failure, as opposed to your certainty of ultimate success.

LIKES	DISLIKES
Knowing your pitch	Vagueness • Ridicule and ignominy
Professionalism and status • Direction and purpose	Dead-end jobs • Being fantasy-ruled
Sexual reliability • Firm foundations	Hare-brained schemes

If you are a woman, this could be the kind of man to whom you are attracted – but it is really a part of you, so realize it.

MARS IN CAPRICORN

TRANSFORMER

POSITIVE	NEGATIVE
Persistent Single-minded Nobody's fool Industrious	Pig-headed Disagreeable Dog-eat-dog attitude Workaholic
Works according to plan Earthy and practical	Cold and calculating Insists on material results
Authoritative Respects order Disciplined Commands respect	Uses others Lust for control Disregards others' rights Slave-driving
Sexually disciplined Capable of celibacy Strong sex drive Self-reliant	Sexually controlling/controlled Suppresses libido Lacking affection Lonely
Energetic worker Decisive Cuts red tape Inscrutable	Restless at work Agonizing Bucks system Self-mystifying
Avoid wasting time and energy seeking external approval – and realize your ability to organize yourself.	Feeling thwarted and down-trodden, underemployed and directionless.
Your fears create an austere love life, whereas prudence would create a well-regulated one.	Feeling unapproachable and emotionally dried-up. Impotent or frigid. Lonely.
Balance your sense of order with that of others. Self-discipline comes before order.	Feeling that others are not being efficient or co-operative. Rejected advances.
Base your plans or ideas on what is practical and expedient – and then stick to them.	Getting bogged down in your own system – or your lack of one. Progress slow or halted.
Rather than fighting the way of the world, you are able to tailor your ambitions to suit it.	Feeling all alone in the world. Working very hard merely to keep the wheels going round.
SOLUTION	PROBLEM

If you find yourself on the receiving end of negative traits, it is because you are not expressing the opposing positive traits.

247

MARS IN AQUARIUS

ESSENCE

Getting through Liberating
The Freedom Fighter • Leader of the Pack

'If you wish to get the fruit – you have to go out on a limb' is a suitable maxim for Mars in Aquarius. In other words, for you to be moved to get what you want, your actions have to involve an element of the unusual, something that sets you apart from the crowd. If they suggest doing what everyone else is doing then you become quite inactive, even withdrawn. Whatever the case, what truly motivates you is having some kind of system to buck, and 'system' can mean family, state, partner, friends or anything that appears to be limiting your freedom. In fact, as you can also be rather disinclined to stick your neck out without good reason, it may have to be the sudden realization that you have got yourself hemmed in that forces you to act for yourself. For without sufficient freedom you are the first person to suffer, as your vital energies get dammed up inside you.

At a more evolved level, getting what you want entails doing something that helps beings with less freedom of thought and movement. You can be a social activist on a small or great, an individual or collective scale. You are motivated by goals for the common good, which can include benefiting all forms of life, not just the human. It is also highly likely that, at some stage, you will begin to appreciate that certain goals cannot be attained other than through teamwork. You may even be unconsciously aware of this, and be a compulsive joiner of groups and clubs – and an unpredictable leaver of them, because you have yet to discover your own act. However, ultimately, your interest in yourself has be to aligned with the interest of others. Owing to this desire both to do your own thing and to be a part of a team, you are quite difficult to understand. But mucking in with others is your true métier, whereas being selfish is justifiable only when you are developing yourself in order to find your social niche, rather than being reluctant to have one at all, owing to a fear of getting lost in the grey mass of human society.

This complex reserve that you possess is very marked in your manner of relating sexually. You are more capable than most of enjoying sex, free of guilt and other negative conditions, and will demand the freedom to do so. However, you are also capable of keeping your desires locked up in your head, as a result of being afraid to bring your emotional needs into the sphere of sexual intimacy. But, then again, you may enjoy sex entirely as an expression of freedom rather than of love or of the senses.

All in all, you just don't want to do things the way others do. Although you are prone to throwing the baby out with the bath water when a given situation becomes stale, your inventiveness, especially in emergencies, and the quickness with which you learn from your mistakes, are a strong example to others of how a human being can best get along in this world.

<table>
<tr><td align="center">LIKES</td><td align="center">DISLIKES</td></tr>
<tr><td align="center">New methods • Teamwork • Just causes
Freedom • Unusual activities</td><td align="center">Outworn methods • Blind dependence • Blind authority
Rigid conservatism • Predictability</td></tr>
</table>

If you are a woman, this could be the kind of man to whom you are attracted – but it is really a part of you, so realize it.

MARS IN AQUARIUS

TRANSFORMER

POSITIVE	NEGATIVE
Independent Unconventional Complex Original	Cantankerous Perverse Contrary Peculiar
Progressive Reformist Humanitarian Idealistic	Impatient Rebellious Superficial Escapist
Resolute Resourceful Group leader Co-operative	Inconstant Insular Loner Unco-operative
Surprising High-spirited Very active Stimulating	Erratic Disruptive Indolent Shocking
Sexually free Sexually experimental Non-possessive Cool	Sexually loose Sexually irresponsible Unfeeling Cold
You are after knowing what strings are attached – not for having no strings attached at all.	You put no human or emotional value on what you want, so what you get seems valueless.
As you jolt others out of their complacency, point to a more attractive alternative.	You make your point, but your way of making it appeals to nobody. Being in a majority of one.
The purpose of being alone (all-one) is to discover that one is for all and all is for one.	On your own but not liking it. Maybe you've not noticed this, but then neither have many others.
Make it known both to yourself and to others what you want freedom for, not from.	Surrounded by people who are irritatingly unaware of your way of acting and being.
When and where there is no precedent – make one. Don't expect immediate understanding.	Getting yourself into situations that have no apparent meaning or way out or way through.
SOLUTION	PROBLEM

If you find yourself on the receiving end of negative traits, it is because you are not expressing the opposing positive traits.

249

MARS IN PISCES

ESSENCE

Getting through Accepting
Tease or Tonic • The Soft Touch

You get what you want through subtle or indirect means. This can be likened to the angler who baits and casts his line, and then sits and waits, ready to accept what Life's current will bring. Yet strong emotional undercurrents are influencing your actions, so you need to discover what these are if you are to avoid being tugged this way and that, which in turn can compromise your asserting yourself. The resentments or regrets that build up as a result of this can lead to unconscious ways of expressing your anger or desire, such as sarcasm or secret liaisons. This kind of underhandedness ultimately meets with equally obscure reactions from others, and confusion then begins to reign.

What's really going on with Mars in Pisces is that you have an uncanny ability to drift and seep into the feelings of others. But what enables you to do this is something that is invisible, rather as moods are infectious. It is as if you emanate a subtle aura that others respond to hypnotically. However, unless you tune in to this subtle aspect of your being, and endeavour to refine your coarser or more material desires, you are likely to be seduced by your own seductiveness.

As much as your moods are infectious, so too are you easily infected, both clinically and psychologically. Being aware of this is half the battle won; making sure you are not over-exposed to people and situations with whom or in which you feel uncomfortable. So much here depends on your being sure of what you actually want, and not giving in to your vagueness, which you use as a kind of get-out clause in case you fail to achieve your objective. The activities that galvanize you are ones that employ imagination or compassion. Occupations that do not cater to your finer feelings will tend to find you listless and easily fatigued. Yoga, Tai Chi and other subtle forms of exercise are most suited to keeping your body and energy supply healthy. Dancing or water sports are also things that you thrive on and can also be particularly good at. Work that involves mental or physical healing is something else to which you are well-suited; and working behind the scenes will also appeal to your somewhat shy and self-effacing nature. This could also include activities that require you to be present but not too noticeable, like photography.

Where your sexuality is concerned, either these finer feelings can lend a delicate and delicious quality to your style of love-making, or they can cause you to be quite confused or misled. It is best to remember that your sexual drive is highly dependent on your emotional state, which means that you can resort to pretence, fantasy or artificial stimulants in an effort to simulate excitement. But what is so exciting about Mars in Pisces is something you possess that is more emotional than physical, of the Soul rather than of the body. Tune in to that, and so will others.

LIKES	**DISLIKES**
Quiet surroundings	Being pressured • Banal sex
Sexual mysteries • Subtle stimulation	Coarseness • Anything mundane
Exotica • Creating illusions	Direct confrontation

If you are a woman, this could be the kind of man to whom you are attracted – but it is really a part of you, so realize it.

MARS IN PISCES

TRANSFORMER

POSITIVE	NEGATIVE
Fascinating Charismatic Subtle Diffuse	Neurotic Volatile Evasive Unfocused
Charitable Congenial Self-sacrificing Tender	Seductable Malleable Self-deluding Weak/Lazy
Inspiring Imaginative Generous Psychic	Gushing Fanciful Indiscriminate Temperamental
Stealthy Sensuous Healing Intuitive	Furtive Treacherous Confusing Invasive
Compassionate Diplomatic Humorous Fluid	Resentful Frustrating Absurd Inconsistent

SOLUTION	PROBLEM
When you have admitted to your anger, lust or whatever, you will make room for your finer points.	Frustrated by others who are frustrated by your not being honest about negative feelings.
Employ your talent for gently asserting yourself and subtly revealing the soul of the matter.	Involved in or the victim of secret affairs, leading to social scandal or emotional confusion.
Something sublime and wonderful is calling from your imagination – not from someone else's personality.	Not knowing where you're coming from or going to. Tossed upon your own wave of imagined desire.
Check your motives before giving yourself away – but give yourself you must, eventually.	Feeling listless or dominated, impotent or frigid. Throwing yourself away gets you dumped on.
Identify that part of you to which others are drawn and which you, too, must follow. Surrender.	Psychosomatic complaints – usually as a result of misdirected energy; for example, work versus play.

If you find yourself on the receiving end of negative traits, it is because you are not expressing the opposing positive traits.

JUPITER

Keyword: GROWING

Jupiter symbolizes GROWTH and the LAWS, BELIEFS and ETHICS that govern it and make it possible. Jupiter is also a sense of EXPANSION and FURTHERANCE that leads to OPPORTUNITY, WEALTH and FAITH.

So your Jupiter-Sign will show the way in which you seek to BROADEN your knowledge, horizons and UNDERSTANDING, through such pursuits as HIGHER EDUCATION, TRAVEL, RELIGION, PHILOSOPHY etc. Negatively, Jupiter's Sign will point to ways in which you can be EXCESSIVE and OVER-something (over-indulgent, overweight, over-optimistic, over-careful, over-zealous, over-the-top etc.). At its highest level, Jupiter and thus your Jupiter-Sign indicate how you actually, or how you may, express and experience JOY and GOODWILL, and what you hold to be your 'Image of God'.

Note: Jupiter takes twelve years to orbit the Sun and to go through the twelve Signs of the Zodiac, therefore it takes a year to pass through one Sign. Because of this, everyone born in the same twelve-month period will share the same Jupiter-Sign. This in itself indicates the fact that Jupiterian qualities such as Beliefs and Moral Values depend to quite a degree on the social climate into which you were born. However, the more you study and understand all your Planet-Sign qualities, the more able you will be to make your Jupiter-Sign qualities very much your own.

JUPITER IN ARIES

ESSENCE

Growing through Doing

Fools Rush in...   ...Where Angels Fear to Tread

You have the enthusiasm and faith of a child, whatever age you actually are, and because of this you can go far in life. However, you need to be careful that your natural eagerness does not become arrogance, or that your magnanimity does not get swallowed up by extravagance.

Your faith rests on the principle that Life looks after those who live it; trusting spontaneously is your most positive mode of being. When things go wrong this philosophy tells you that there is always more to come, that Life's supply of opportunity and experience is inexhaustible.

Not surprisingly, Jupiter in Aries invites quite a few knocks and falls, mainly because you are inclined to bite off more than you can chew as a result of a surfeit of enthusiasm but a lack of know-how, plus a failure to appreciate or to enlist the abilities of others. Nevertheless, high hopes and high spirits invariably carry you through, and, most importantly, it is your readiness to plunge into an experience that leads to your learning what you need to know. Your Soul ever precipitates challenges that demand growth on all levels, and, by the same token, major developments usually occur on the spur of the moment.

Your Image of God is a force that is always up and at it, abandoning or renewing what is outmoded and unworkable, forever marching on to the next step forward, and to the next, and the next ... So you strongly and continually need to feel that your life is going somewhere, and will invest great amounts of time, money and energy to ensure this. Such an attitude will attract followers, especially if there are other leadership traits in your personality (indicated by your other Planet-Sign positions).

This can, of course, also attract lame ducks and sheep, with the result that you appear to have to do almost everything. But really it is for you to get things going and to make sure that certain others will keep them going, while you lead on – and on – following your youthful star. Joy for you is found in experiencing Life as a procession with you at, or somewhere near, the head of it. Your goodwill is expressed as you pass back and down the vision you behold that lies forever ahead.

LIKES	**DISLIKES**
Active occupations • Travel	Sitting around • Being housebound
Forward-looking people	Dead-ends and dead-wood
Optimism • The Pageant of Life	Pessimism • Faint-heartedness

Jupiter is your clue to making more of life.

JUPITER IN ARIES

TRANSFORMER

POSITIVE	NEGATIVE
Crusading Exhorting Adventurous Aspiring	Self-righteous Bullying Overbearing High-handed
Enthusiastic Quick grasp of whole Zestful Honourable	Over-optimistic Ill-prepared Rash Naïve
Generous Thinks big Enterprising Unshakable	Gives to impress Extravagant Boastful Over-confident
Innovative Self-sufficient Carefree Noble	Precocious Pig-headed Careless Stupid

In all matters relating to Jupiter, a critical point of development occurs every twelve years when it returns to the Sign in which it was placed at the time of your birth. In effect, this marks the beginning of a new cycle of growth and understanding.

SOLUTION	PROBLEM
Your ability to overcome even the direst dilemmas gives rise to new ideas and strengths.	Finding yourself in seemingly impossible situations – often alone.
Keeping something back is proof that you have even more to offer and to rely on.	Self importance – apparent or real – arouses resentment in others that leads to harsh treatment.
Any high-flier checks his/her instruments before taking off – then the sky's the limit.	Dubious speculations. Overspending. Losses in business and in friendship.
What inspires you is where you're going. What inspires others is how you get there.	Getting others' backs up when you want them to back you up.

If you feel subjected to the negative traits or values, you will overcome this by accentuating the positive ones.

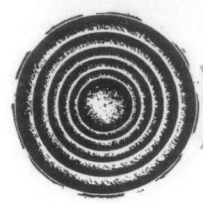

JUPITER IN TAURUS

ESSENCE

Growing through Stabilizing
The Trustee • The Fund-Raiser

Material possessions and development, together with the position and comfort that they give, is what you believe in. And, to a greater or lesser degree, you are also quite able to attract wealth in some way or other. However, as our society currently bases its beliefs on material values, it is important for you to understand the Cosmic Law that governs the accumulation of material things. Failure to do so would mean that you were possibly going to amass wealth, wallow in it, and then lose it or lose control of it, or be dogged by a fear of losing it or by a need for something that money cannot buy. Alternatively, you could find it excessively difficult to make much at all in material terms.

In the first case, there is a lack of understanding of the Law of Infinite Supply, which states that in order to maintain wealth you must invest what you have in furthering others, and not just hang on to it for its own sake. In the second case, you are not aware that, if you need and use it for something worthwhile, material wherewithal will always be forthcoming. Jupiter in Taurus poses the issue of what you do with money. Growing through Stabilizing means that the improvement in your material circumstances has everything to do with understanding that stability is a natural state that everyone is entitled to, and that it is maintained by keeping resources flowing in through keeping them flowing out. Meanness just does not suit you.

When you have begun to appreciate this wisdom that Jupiter in Taurus offers, you are likely to find yourself in a position of management or trust, or one in which you are actually responsible for fund-raising. Yet 'all that glistens is not gold', and sooner or later you become aware that it is a sense of wealth, rather than wealth itself, that really matters.

For this reason your expression of Jupiter's joy is quite obvious and tangible as you are usually merry and generous. However, this feeling of bounty can be abused through various forms of physical indulgence, or by frittering away funds that have come your way too easily. When you have got through or around this area of prodigality, you are capable of embodying your Image of God, which could be said to resemble Father Christmas, Old King Cole or Mother Nature's Horn of Plenty.

LIKES	**DISLIKES**
Good things of life • Being the provider	Bare existence • Wastefulness
Material wealth • Traditional values	Being in debt • New-fangled ideas
Warmth and comfort	Sparseness and scarcity

Jupiter is your clue to making more of life.

JUPITER IN TAURUS

TRANSFORMER

POSITIVE	NEGATIVE
Sound judgment Contemplative Practical philosopher	Self-opinionated Too cautious Blinkered philosopher
Comfortable Gives stability Steady progress Trusting	Smug Expects ease Stick-in-the-mud Cynical
Jovial Good-humoured Generous Good appetite	Hedonistic Irresponsible Wasteful Gluttonous
Affluent Moneywise Furthers economy Charitable	Greedy Penny-pinching Exploitative Status-conscious

In all matters relating to Jupiter, a critical point of development occurs every twelve years when it returns to the Sign in which it was placed at the time of your birth. In effect, this marks the beginning of a new cycle of growth and understanding.

SOLUTION	PROBLEM
The wiser your use of material resources, the more available those resources become.	The more material position means to you, the more you feel threatened by material collapse.
You have a sense of life being infinitely abundant – but your lack of faith tries to prove it otherwise.	Physical or material degeneration – or both – through misunderstanding the meaning of abundance.
Believing that there is more to life than you know, would find you – and others – so much better off.	Resisting or failing to see changes in the world around you finds you at a dead-end.
When you've weighed all the odds in your inimitable style, you realize that life is good.	Obsessed with your own viewpoint, you fail to see how others can figure positively in your life.

If you feel subjected to the negative traits or values, you will overcome this by accentuating the positive ones.

JUPITER IN GEMINI

ESSENCE

Growing through Communicating
The Further One Travels...   ...The Less One Knows

Your natural enthusiasm for encountering as many facets of life as possible is in aid of getting to know the one who's getting to know – that is, yourself. The trouble with Jupiter in Gemini is that it can get so caught up with the endless attractions and distractions that life has to offer that it can forget this vital point. Who is being attracted? Why are you seeking distraction?

In effect, you are gathering information in order to weave it into a comprehensive whole, gathering knowledge to attain understanding, and drawing a circle to find its centre. In the process of doing this you naturally acquire many contacts which would serve you well as any kind of agent (for travel, employment, services etc., or for something more unusual). At a more intellectual level your 'gathering' can enable you to see the general trends of society, as well as its individual points of interest; this has the qualities of the social commentator or historian. At any rate, being a mine of information in one or more areas is central to your capabilities.

You are rather like a tree with many broad, shallow roots rather than one narrow, deep root. In addition to the possibility of being the intellectual dilettante described above, you can also subscribe to two or more philosophies or sets of morals simultaneously. On the surface this may seem quite convenient, but it could also mean having to lead a double life, which, in turn, could mean falling between two stools, but then again this might suit you nicely. You are mobile and adaptable, but also easily uprooted.

So your widespread roots should be employed to give you a broad grasp of life, through which your faith in life will be established. This is preferable to merely skimming the surface of a subject or a culture, as if life were some kind of package tour. Your Image of God resembles an infinitely large library in which everything that needs to be known can be found, as long as you are prepared to open the book, and to see yourself reflected in what you find. Your joy is the joy of making things known and available to others, which at some point necessarily involves your becoming known and available to yourself, and to others, too. Gemini's paradox here is that there is always more to know, but only ever you to know it.

LIKES	**DISLIKES**
Travel and literature	Lack of variety and interest
Human networks • Being in the know	Lack of communication • Being out of circulation
Food for thought • Analogies and mental models	Idle chatter • Disconnected thoughts

Jupiter is your clue to making more of life.

JUPITER IN GEMINI

TRANSFORMER

POSITIVE	NEGATIVE
Well-travelled Well-connected Popular Sociable	Scattered interests Disconnected Not known Restless
Knowledge-seeker Broad-minded Grasps general outline	Mere dabbler Shallow interest Sketchy knowledge
Knowledgeable Scholarly Mentally alert Many-sided	Academic Intellectual snob Verbose Tangential
Obliging Well-mannered Witty Cheerful	Hypocritical Crafty Indiscreet Empty

In all matters relating to Jupiter, a critical point of development occurs every twelve years when it returns to the Sign in which it was placed at the time of your birth. In effect, this marks the beginning of a new cycle of growth and understanding.

SOLUTION	PROBLEM
Amusingly let it be known that you are only prepared to be light and breezy up to a point.	Your semblance of acceptability is not acceptable to yourself. Too many twists to your turn.
You are after something that is worth knowing – that would be worth saying.	Saying a lot but communicating little, or saying nothing and communicating even less.
Travel broadens the mind – knowing where you are deepens it. You're the centre of your own circle.	Curiosity killed the cat. Your intelligence is severely limited by a fear of discovering yourself.
Realize that you are as interesting and as appealing as any place or face you come across.	After all the faces and places you've got to know, both you and others still have no idea who you are.

If you feel subjected to the negative traits or values, you will overcome this by accentuating the positive ones.

JUPITER IN CANCER

ESSENCE

Growing through Nurturing
The Philanthropist • Root and Branch

As the Keyphrase 'Growing through Nurturing' implies, you possess the highest standards when it comes to developing anything or anyone, for you understand the most basic of Nature's laws, that what is cared for usually prospers. For this reason, Jupiter is described as being Exalted in the Sign of Cancer.

Your feeling nature is both broad and deep, and you try to accommodate everyone. But wherever Jupiter is there lies the possibility of excess. So you can be overly emotional and sentimental and, literally, too kind. People are inclined either to run away from you or to walk all over you. This 'over-care' is often a compensation for the emotional understanding and nurturing that you did not receive from your own mother and family. If this is the case you need to be as kind and considerate towards yourself as you are towards others. If you are often a 'port in a storm' for others, believe in always having a safe haven for yourself, and you shall.

The wisdom that Jupiter in Cancer represents, as implied by Nature, can be expressed in a number of ways. Perhaps most importantly, because of the tendency to 'over-care', you should be aware that at a certain stage a being needs to be 'hardened off', in the same way as a gardener will put young plants outside, in order that they might gain the strength they need to survive in the outside world. This is Nurturing in the highest sense because the concern is for the ultimate welfare, rather than just the seemingly unselfish satisfaction of taking care of someone or something.

In truth, your undeniable sense of goodwill rests upon a belief, conscious or otherwise, that we all spring from the same root, that the Family of Man has one family tree. At one level you could experience this as a great sense of closeness to your immediate family or to your country, but this could lead to your feeling rather limited by it. At a move evolved level you begin to realize that all living things are related and need the same care and consideration. You greatly enjoy the family scene or your sense of nationality, but you can, and maybe must, find a greater joy in the sense of our common ancestry. Your Image of God is of the World Mother, of the Planet Earth, as a living, caring being, Gaia, and is most profoundly felt and expressed by you as the Milk of Human Kindness.

LIKES	**DISLIKES**
A caring society	A dog-eat-dog world
Quiet, homely pleasures • A home to be proud of	Nowhere to go • Bad accommodation
Domestic skills • A home from home	Inhospitality • Feeling rootless

Jupiter is your clue to making more of life.

JUPITER IN CANCER

TRANSFORMER

POSITIVE	NEGATIVE
Hospitable Protective Caring Becoming	Too accommodating Spoiling Doting Indulging
Charitable Sympathetic Super-receptive Friendly	Conscience-stricken Soppy Touchy Gushing
Loyal to family Patriotic Abundant feelings Exuberant	Biased Prejudiced Sickly sentimental Overdone
Good-natured Kind Sharing Generous	Affected Too kind Self-effacing Mean with self

In all matters relating to Jupiter, a critical point of development occurs every twelve years when it returns to the Sign in which it was placed at the time of your birth. In effect, this marks the beginning of a new cycle of growth and understanding.

SOLUTION	PROBLEM
Having a good impression of Nature's fullness, you can give a good impression of it.	Not trusting what you actually believe in, you give too much to others and not enough to yourself.
Your deep love of your heritage must lead you ultimately to a realization of our common ancestry.	Being overly attached to what you are familiar with drives the familiar away.
Charity begins at home: when you feel at home with yourself you'll feel at home with others.	Continually bothered by what you have to do – or avoid doing – in order to be appreciated.
Caring for everyone has to include yourself – and 'hardening off the young ones'.	Others expecting too much of you – or you of yourself. Weight problems for self or others.

If you feel subjected to the negative traits or values, you will overcome this by accentuating the positive ones.

JUPITER IN LEO

ESSENCE

Growing through Creating
Thine is the Kingdom...   ...The Power and the Glory

There is something very self-evident about Jupiter in Leo, for you believe that your sheer existence is a testament to your worth. So it could be said that growth and development are achieved simply through an enthusiasm for yourself. There is a danger here of egotism and self-importance, but in some ways this is better than being falsely modest or shrewish.

However, although your sense of grandeur can lead to great displays of confidence and wealth, it can also lead to a fall from grace. But, then again, thinking or acting small could find you equally pressured to pull something extra out of the bag. So with Jupiter in Leo there comes a time when the nature of greatness has to be properly understood.

As with other placements in Leo, looking at it in terms of the Sun can be very illuminating. The Sun just pours out energy all day and every day, but it can also scorch and cause things to wilt. Likewise, your enthusiasm can miss the point that energy supply is one thing, but the nature of what it is feeding is another. In other words the people and the things in which you invest your time, money and feelings have certain qualities, requirements and limitations that can be easily overlooked by you, with consequent disappointment either on your part or on theirs, or on both. When you stop for long or often enough to note what real effect you are having on others, you will get a far better idea of just how powerful you are, and will then avoid your most common mistake, which is to overplay your hand. For the same reason, not being aware of your potential can cause you to underplay your hand.

'The more you make, the more you get' could be a reliable golden rule for you, as long as you appreciate that what you get is in aid of serving others, rather than merely so that you can bask in its glory. Joy for you is similar to the satisfaction that a king or queen would take from being the benevolent monarch who appreciates his or her subjects – friends, partners, subordinates etc. – as being what make him/her feel great. Your Image of God is therefore of the Sun-King or the Sun-Queen who is the Earthly expression of Divine Will, who bestows with wisdom, governs with compassion, and pledges his/her all to the glory of something greater than his/her ego. For you, God is like the Sun who shines for all.

<table>
<tr><td align="center">LIKES</td><td align="center">DISLIKES</td></tr>
<tr><td align="center">Gambling and speculation
Pageantry and ceremony • Drama and grandeur
Children • Lavishness</td><td align="center">Playing it safe • The dull and the ordinary
Mean-heartedness/ Small-mindedness
Having no dependents • Penny-pinching</td></tr>
</table>

Jupiter is your clue to making more of life.

JUPITER IN LEO

TRANSFORMER

POSITIVE	NEGATIVE
Big-hearted Benevolent Altruistic Inspiring	Big-headed Pretentious Self-serving Misleading
Sense of glory Prestigious Honourable Noble	Vainglorious Self-aggrandizing Unkept promises Hollow
Self-confident Radiates warmth Energetic Strong stamina	Egomaniac Ostentatious Overbearing Intolerant
Self-assured Generous Entrepreneurial Thinks big	Over-confident Spendthrift Overblown Unrealistic

In all matters relating to Jupiter, a critical point of development occurs every twelve years when it returns to the Sign in which it was placed at the time of your birth. In effect, this marks the beginning of a new cycle of growth and understanding.

SOLUTION	PROBLEM
Basing your expectations on what you can give rather than get has the desired effect.	Unwise speculations, possibly leading to financial ruin. Losses in love/children.
Once you've stopped trying to gain attention you'll find yourself doing so – but in the right way.	Others find you impossible to get through to – so neither can you get through to them.
What ultimately impresses others is what initially impresses you. What is that?	The impression you have given is an act you are finding hard to live up to.
What you really have is a sense of greatness. Walk tall by looking up to what is greater than you.	Others are demanding that you deliver more than you really have.

If you feel subjected to the negative traits or values, you will overcome this by accentuating the positive ones.

JUPITER IN VIRGO

ESSENCE

Growing through Analysing
Slow But Sure • The Faithful Servant

This is not the easiest Sign in which to have Jupiter placed, as the analytical and perfectionist nature of Virgo can, at times, make the Jupiterian growth and expansion almost imperceptible. The resolution of your frustration here rests on making a choice between either scaling down whatever your projects might be so that some sort of readily noticeable and therefore encouraging advances are made possible, or, philosophically accepting the notion that you have got a large and complex exercise in operation and that the 'tale will grow in the telling'. Additionally, analysing what it is that is growing through your efforts will help you become aware of the vital but relatively small role that you are playing in some greater operation that possibly involves many other people. On this score, a part of your work could very likely involve the enlisting of men and women to take part in that 'greater operation' that serves the common welfare.

However, because the first and lesser choice of scaling down could lead to your becoming a big fish in a small pond, the increasing confidence but diminishing satisfaction that would arise from this would inevitably urge you to launch into being a part of that greater endeavour, which is the latter alternative. It helps you to understand that the next step up from being, so to speak, at the top of the second division is being at the bottom of the first. Indeed, perceiving the pattern and manner of (your) growth and development leads to a greater sense of understanding, which is growth in itself, but on a mental rather than a material level, and that is what Jupiter in Virgo is largely about.

In this respect you are also peculiarly able to make an orderly whole out of a sea of apparently unrelated details. In fact you experience joy in doing this for your Image of God is of some gigantic but precise Plan to which life and evolution are keeping. So your religious persuasions can amount to being puritanical, but they can also be profoundly practical and relevant. However, as a reaction to this possible over-concern for physical correctness, you can swing towards being quite the opposite by way of relief, so your hedonistic behaviour and pie-in-the-sky beliefs can surprise others. Yet as a result of this pendulum-like process of development, you arrive at an increasingly workable philosophy of life.

LIKES	**DISLIKES**
Encouraging others • Cleanliness and order	Bad working atmosphere • Being over-organized
A practical philosophy • Sense of long-term purpose	Armchair philosophy • Meaningless labour
A philosophy of health	Superficial healthcare

Jupiter is your clue to making more of life.

JUPITER IN VIRGO

TRANSFORMER

POSITIVE	NEGATIVE
Urge to learn	Too studious
Organized progress	Self-limiting
Persevering	Brain-bashing
Professional	Materialistic
Pragmatic	Cynical
Realistic	Pedantic
Judicious	Petulant
Methodical	Too analytical
Ethical	Prudish
Philosphical	Moralizing
Virtuous	Narrow-minded
Honest	Glib
Practical helper	Solicitous
Conscientious	Sanctimonious
Upstanding	Priggish
Thorough	Mean

In all matters relating to Jupiter, a critical point of development occurs every twelve years when it returns to the Sign in which it was placed at the time of your birth. In effect, this marks the beginning of a new cycle of growth and understanding.

Use your fine awareness to ascertain precisely where, when and how you are needed.	Rejected offers of your help and your opinion find you feeling offended and unappreciated.
In truth, something is only right and good if it both looks and feels right and good.	You think you are right but you are not enjoying it one bit. Bottled-up emotions.
Know that trying to work things out both in detail and way into the future is counter-productive.	You make mountains out of molehills, and cannot see the wood for the trees. Overworked.
Be aware that you are moving ahead – but on a broad front, and for a far-reaching purpose.	Working very hard but apparently getting nowhere.
SOLUTION	PROBLEM

If you feel subjected to the negative traits or values, you will overcome this by accentuating the positive ones.

JUPITER IN LIBRA

ESSENCE

Growing through Relating
The Social Animal • The Peacemaker

As the Keyphrase suggests, you take your greatest strides forward in life through learning to relate in a manner that is wise and fair. As ever with Jupiter, your moral values, which are the basic guideline to relationships, are not so much your own as you might think; and this is particularly the case with socially-conscious Libra. The ethical/religious influences in your life have a direct bearing on the success of your personal relationships. Furthermore, you are inclined to take on board the more conventional moral attitude. If you are comfortable with this then well and good, and you probably have or will have a stable marriage, forever guided by the yardstick provided by your cultural background.

If, on the other hand, you find that this is not suitable to your needs and desires, then you will probably encounter at least one emotional upheaval that involves a major shift in your moral philosophy and sense of fair play, and possibly even includes some kind of litigation. For with Jupiter in Libra you are effectively standing in judgment – either consciously or unconsciously – both of yourself and of others. If your own 'inner' judge is not being objective enough, then your 'case' comes before a 'real' judge.

And so you are constantly weighing your needs and desires against your beliefs and values. Sometimes the former is the heavier influence, and you are the regular socialite, being very much the person on everyone's guest list, and sometimes being quite intemperate. At other times you become immersed in trying to justify what you are and how you behave. You make the effort to be mild and temperate, but if your blood is on the red side you soon swing back into being taken up with the highs and lows of socializing and interpersonal relationships. This pendulum-like lifestyle can continue for some time, swinging between the intemperate, fun-loving but somewhat superficial you that craves social position and adulation, and the well-behaved, temperate you that places both you and others in the dock to be judged.

Eventually, joy comes your way when you realize that you are actually your own lawmaker and lawgiver, and that the God that judges you has the Image of the Peacemaker, which you yourself can become, when you realize that peace is simply an end to conflict, inner conflict, created by an imbalance between pleasures and moral values.

LIKES	**DISLIKES**
Feeling socially 'in' • Art and culture	Being alone • Cultural deserts
Good companions • Romantic journeys	Feeling unwanted • No sense of occasion
An attractive belief system	Harsh self-denial

Jupiter is your clue to making more of life.

JUPITER IN LIBRA

TRANSFORMER

POSITIVE	NEGATIVE
Cultured Cultivates others Encouraging Shares riches	Snobbish Patronizing Flattering Toadying
Well-meaning Benign Conciliatory Grandly sympathetic	Superficial Too nice Ingratiating Expects too much
Sense of justice Sound morality Obliging and considerate	Too conceptual Misguided standards Double standards
Honourable partner Idealistic Enduring lover Sociable	Fanciful Promises too much Too abiding Juggles options

In all matters relating to Jupiter, a critical point of development occurs every twelve years when it returns to the Sign in which it was placed at the time of your birth. In effect, this marks the beginning of a new cycle of growth and understanding.

SOLUTION	PROBLEM
Either stick to your principles or change them – then you'll live up to them admirably.	Suddenly finding yourself being disloyal – or suspected of being so. Too many close ties.
When you've gained a truly impartial viewpoint, you're just as you'd like to think you are.	Legal or moral difficulties arise as a result of what you think being different from what you do.
Base your good intentions on what you believe, not what you need, and good you'll feel.	Your excessive need for praise makes you untrue to yourself, and thus others are untrue to you.
When you know a culture is something you grow in, not jump in or stay in, you set a fine example.	Being out of touch with your own values causes you blindly to subscribe to those of others.

If you feel subjected to the negative traits or values, you will overcome this by accentuating the positive ones.

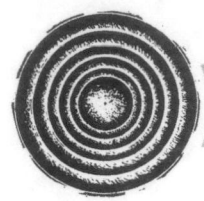

JUPITER IN SCORPIO

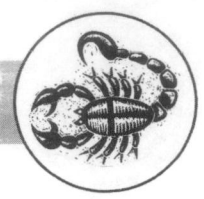

ESSENCE

Growing through Desiring

As One Door Closes...   ...Another One Opens

Who or what you find irresistible will push you to your limits. Whether you know it or not, your philosophy is of the 'no gain without pain' variety, and that gain can apply to either your material or your emotional life. In fact, the two have a natural inclination to become heavily intertwined. However, to be more precise, it is really a case of 'no gain without loss – of what you no longer need'.

The desire that springs from this philosophy is powerful indeed, for it makes you hunger after the deep, the dark and the mysterious, and eventually leads you to find it. Alternatively, you are the one who is deep, dark and mysterious, and someone will find you out! So Jupiter in Scorpio does not gladly suffer superficial displays from other people, or from yourself, either. The dark side of your nature is where the gold lies, and one way or another you will go through hell and high water to knock off the soppy or wobbly bits that inhibit or compromise the discovery of that 'gold'.

The sexual dimensions of experience offer you the most opportunity in your search for the profound and cathartic. In the process you are likely to over-emphasize sex in some way, in order that it get your bigger wheels going round. Unusual sensations and reckless experimentation are also likely to be on your erotic menu, which could lead to 'indigestion' in the form of degradation, complaints of the sexual organs and emotional destabilization. However, this is all par for the course for you, grist to the mill. The darker it gets, the brighter one has to be.

Another – although probably less conscious – way of living dangerously is through financial involvements that stand to make or ruin you. This also gives you this sense of being close to the edge, of dicing with death. The belief that you gain through some kind of loss can be expressed more simply as making money through inheritance or settlement. At its 'tamest' level, Jupiter in Scorpio can manifest itself as a lack of enterprise, owing to a fear of the transformation that growth would bring.

A more direct, and more dangerous, method of delving to satisfy your intense feeling, to confirm your deep convictions, is through involvement with the Occult – black, white or off-white. It will be found that your Image of God is like Isis Unveiled, which is life as it truly is at the core, not as we have fearfully and superficially disguised it. The joy that issues from this ongoing search is being able to help others through deep and dark places and periods. But, most importantly, you yourself should learn to transcend life's difficulties in a disciplined, informed and organized fashion.

LIKES	DISLIKES
Fateful challenges • The occult and the mysterious	An uneventful life • Superficiality
Sexual adventures • A philosophy of the soul	Automatic sex • Passionless philosophies
Deep joy through deep sorrow	Lukewarm lifestyles

Jupiter is your clue to making more of life.

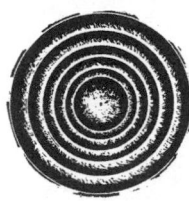

JUPITER IN SCORPIO

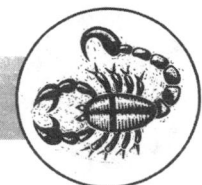

TRANSFORMER

POSITIVE	NEGATIVE
Full-bodied	Heavy-going
Provocative	Dangerous
Intriguing	Scheming
Subtle strengths	Subtle weaknesses
Ambitious	Materialistic
Shrewd	Uses others
Flair for business	Power gamester
Resourceful	Devious
Inner strength	Obsessive and fanatical
See things through	Unrelenting
Healing	Exacerbating
Occultist	Dabbler
Efficient	Intolerant
Confident	Dogmatic
Keen judgment	Judgmental
Utterly truthful	Fanatically blind

In all matters relating to Jupiter, a critical point of development occurs every twelve years when it returns to the Sign in which it was placed at the time of your birth. In effect, this marks the beginning of a new cycle of growth and understanding.

SOLUTION	PROBLEM
Being as convinced as you are, you can afford to show your doubts, and be even more convincing.	Your anger at yourself for trying to be too strong is reflected in others' weaknesses.
Remember the harder you push the harder you pull. You know that a rebirth means a death of some kind.	Unwise involvements that are hard to get out of. Attracting what you cannot cope with drains you.
You know that being feeble doesn't suit you – so get down to developing the muscles you need.	Emotional or money troubles through over- or under-estimating the powers you're dealing with.
Discover and accept hidden weaknesses, and you will find and use hidden strengths.	Getting out of your depth, or someone else out of theirs – or both. Degradation.

If you feel subjected to the negative traits or values, you will overcome this by accentuating the positive ones.

JUPITER IN SAGITTARIUS

ESSENCE

Growing through Seeking
Lucky? • You'd Better Believe It!

To one degree or another, you subscribe to the ultimate philosophy that 'life is what you make it'. Accordingly you have a natural yearning to broaden your horizons, be it through travel, academic experience or just living itself, for you know that one thing leads to another, and that one lap of your journey will furnish you with what you need for the next, and so on. Consciously or otherwise, you believe in Providence, and your Image of God is the Golden-haired Goddess of Opportunity.

The real question that arises is how aware you are of this good relationship with Providence. At one level you could regard it merely as something that never leaves you wanting for too much, and often seems to provide you with the right thing at the right time. At a lower level you may just rely on it to get you out of a scrape, knowing that 'something will always turn up'. However, in a more evolved sense you are aware that Providence is much more than merely some sort of cosmic nanny who is forever making sure that you don't fall over and hurt yourself. You recognize that the Golden-haired Goddess of Opportunity is someone who can see around the curve of Time, and prepare you and others for the future by providing you with whatever is necessary. And so you believe, or at least feel the urge to believe, that there is some form of overall Intelligence System governing and furthering existence.

However, depending on other components of your personality, this System could be seen in somewhat narrower terms than those described above, as a dogmatic religious belief, for example, or as an inflexible set of morals, which at the same time professes to be the opposite. Alternatively, you may have no system of belief at all, for this is one way of keeping your options open, as open as the arms of Providence herself, maybe. You could also go overboard for some philosophy that says there is no plan, no limits, no nothing, just never-ending expansion.

What is common to all these views, irrespective of whatever your own might be, is that there is 'something', some 'rule' that binds everything together, that there is something common to everything. You therefore have some measure of interest in history, law, publishing, religion or any subject that concerns the search for a common and meaningful thread. And you find your joy in discovering this thread, in experiencing what it can show you and give you, and in revealing its truth, as you see it, to others.

LIKES	**DISLIKES**
Big questions • Philosophizing	Small talk • Pointlessness
To believe in luck • Travel	Negative thinking
Anything that furthers	Being confined • Stasis

Jupiter is your clue to making more of life.

JUPITER IN SAGITTARIUS

TRANSFORMER

POSITIVE	NEGATIVE
Philosophical	Opinionated
Aspiring	Self-justifying
Explorative	Irresponsible
Strong beliefs	Irreverent
Liberal-minded	Cavalier
Tolerant	Wasteful
Ethical	Self-righteous
Just	Narrow
Far-reaching mind	Wool-gathering
Prophetic	Superstitious
Speculative	Fanciful
Optimistic	Unrealistic
Jovial	Preposterous
Enthusiastic	Extravagant
Noble-hearted	Pretentious
Kindly	Indulgent

In all matters relating to Jupiter, a critical point of development occurs every twelve years when it returns to the Sign in which it was placed at the time of your birth. In effect, this marks the beginning of a new cycle of growth and understanding.

SOLUTION	PROBLEM
The secret of freedom lies in limitations, the secret of joy in sorrow. Rejoice in these and others.	Your limited sense of the unlimited finds you disappearing into infinitely confusing scenarios.
To come down from the mountain you first have to climb it.	Excessive expectations have given rise to excessive fears. False prophecy.
Believing the Universe to be just, you confess your doubts, are pardoned – then become an example of it.	Making vaguely generous gestures to conceal your doubts proves both restrictive and unprofitable.
Understanding that one set of beliefs eventually takes you to the next makes you quite believable.	Others keep trying to knock you off your high horse – or find it hard to take you seriously.

If you feel subjected to the negative traits or values, you will overcome this by accentuating the positive ones.

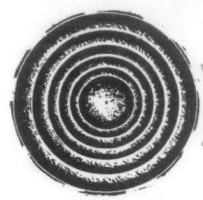

JUPITER IN CAPRICORN

ESSENCE

Growing through Building
Step by Step...   ...And the Occasional Leap

You inherited a traditional set of beliefs and values that serve you well in the ordinary day-to-day sense. However, when change, even in the form of opportunity, comes your way, what normally holds you in good stead holds you back. The Keyphrase 'Growing through Building' suggests that you have a reliable way of progressing in life, but your life is a building of more than one storey, and so, occasionally, you have to put aside one set of plans or beliefs, and look for another that will serve and guide you appropriately for the next storey or the next chapter in your life.

The foundation upon which you are building your life – your cultural background – was most likely quite well-established, in its own way. This solid base is therefore something that you can probably always fall back on, be it a certain type of education, a religious, communal or professional tradition, material wealth, or something quite unusual, but nevertheless long-standing. However, this background, although it provides the backbone of society, is something than can keep you chained to its limitations as well as reassured by its traditions.

Any radical or highly individualistic streak in your personality will force you to free yourself from the negative tradition that is a part of your background. However, 'the town may change but the well doesn't', which means that you may have shaken off that drab set of beliefs and morals, but you are still going to need some kind of belief system, or a rebuilding programme. An ongoing danger with Jupiter in Capricorn is the tendency, as a reaction to your cultural conditioning, to believe in nothing that cannot be proved. In the process, you'll settle for whatever the 'system' says is so, and blindly mould yourself to fit in with it, while at the same time jealously preserving a few personal quirks to foster the illusion that you are your own person.

These difficulties are due to Jupiter being in its Fall in the Sign of Capricorn, which means that unless you drop your inclination to subscribe to the letter of the law rather than the spirit of it, your sense of joy in life will be as meagre as your ethics are narrow and confining, reliable though they may be. Your Image of God is all too likely to be non-existent, or of the most conventional and bigoted kind, or of Mammon. To get your rebuilding under way, and to put a spring in your step, a blend of Earth Magic and Common Sense would serve you well.

LIKES	**DISLIKES**
A position in life • A practical philosophy	Lack of direction
Physical evidence of beliefs	Pie-in-the-sky • Fanciful cults
The traditional • A sound plan	The newfangled • No plan

Jupiter is your clue to making more of life.

JUPITER IN CAPRICORN

TRANSFORMER

POSITIVE	NEGATIVE
Conscientious Loyal Conservative Correctly behaved	Austere Bigoted Hide-bound Stiff
Productive Industrious Disciplined Capable	Pointless Slogging Self-restricting Dull
Highly esteemed Authoritative Successful Delegating	Sycophantic Brow-beaten/beating Status slave Buck-passing
Attracts wealth Prudent Philanthropic Economical	Avaricious Miserly Gives conditionally Penny-pinching

In all matters relating to Jupiter, a critical point of development occurs every twelve years when it returns to the Sign in which it was placed at the time of your birth. In effect, this marks the beginning of a new cycle of growth and understanding.

You only get out what you put in. And man does not live by bread alone.	Always on the breadline, or feeling threatened by the prospect of it.
Use the system to further yourself – but don't let it use you or take you over.	Either you've fallen from grace, or you never seem able to rise at all.
Developing your talent for meeting a collective need for growth satisfies your earnest beliefs.	Working merely to keep body and Soul together – but not recognizing the Soul's real needs.
You are honourable and responsible – but to what? Make sure it is worth your while.	Feeling you're wasting your life and time. Your mean idea of life is self-perpetuating.
SOLUTION	PROBLEM

If you feel subjected to the negative traits or values, you will overcome this by accentuating the positive ones.

JUPITER IN AQUARIUS

ESSENCE

Growing through Liberating
Share and Share Alike • The Call of the New

With Jupiter in Aquarius the question arises of how the World ought to be. This makes you want to view life in as open and democratic a way as possible. In effect, you feel that in order to plot a course into the future, some form of consensus of opinion is necessary, that everyone should agree with everyone else, or at least agree to differ. This idealistic and humanitarian philosophy of yours therefore has to develop and make itself real through your sharing your individual views with others, through friendships, teams, groups or any form of association.

But the paradoxical and vitally important point is that you have to start out with a belief of your own before you can offer it up to others. And then, by getting it mixed in with their beliefs, a 'new' set of beliefs is arrived at that suits the aims and intentions of the group. The idea is that, taking this a number of steps further, all of humanity will eventually subscribe to a common ideology. So your Image of God is of a World Religion. Your philosophy is very much that of the New Age – The Age of Aquarius. So this is a long-term plan.

The catch to the wonderful idea that humanity can be together as One is that you have to have the 'one' first, that is, one's own only too human and imperfect self. In other words, in order to further this aim, as you initially put forward your own beliefs, you should do so in the knowledge that there is bound to be some dogmatic and unrealistic content in them. This involves applying to yourself the same high standards of tolerance and openness to debate that your principles themselves engender. The weakness that arises here is the common Aquarian one of using an ideal with which all your friends or associates agree, in order that your personal shortcomings may be ignored in the fervid pursuit of the 'cause'. Such associations inevitably become unreliable and fall apart because they are built on a desire to escape rather than to liberate.

Joy for you is arrived at by recognizing that we all have something in common, and that through sharing both our hopes and our fears we will reach that common consciousness, an agreement based on the knowledge that love and acceptance are the beginning and end of human existence. It will be reached in no other way, and will take a long time. Your joy is also in knowing that we and you are on our way.

LIKES	**DISLIKES**
Brotherhood/Sisterhood • Democracy • Sharing all	Inhumanity • Fascism · Fear and greed
Universal morality • Feelings of togetherness	Dogmatism • Factionalism

Jupiter is your clue to making more of life.

JUPITER IN AQUARIUS

TRANSFORMER

POSITIVE	NEGATIVE
Broad-minded Impartial Unprejudiced Intuitive	Amoral Offhand Undisciplined Tactless
Idealistic High principles Reformist Innovative	Spaced out Aims too high Rebellious Upstart
Liberal Tolerant Congenial Friendly	Woolly Wimpish Impersonal Too casual
Philanthropic Humanitarian Non-dogmatic Diplomatic	Patronizing Self-righteous Dogmatic Insincere

In all matters relating to Jupiter, a critical point of development occurs every twelve years when it returns to the Sign in which it was placed at the time of your birth. In effect, this marks the beginning of a new cycle of growth and understanding.

SOLUTION	PROBLEM
Allow yourself the same rights and understanding that you are insisting everyone should have.	Your good intentions have become a mask for bad feelings, and the mask is slipping.
The naturally soft standards to which you subscribe gain effectiveness with a hard edge.	Others find it hard to relate to a human marshmallow – so you feel easily squashed. Ignored.
Return to first principles; first know yourself – then you and everything else will change.	Blindly following some lofty revolutionary concept has left you hanging in mid-air.
Be open to the possibility that something will happen – not just that anything can happen.	Anything goes – but nothing new comes along. You relieve pointlessness with pointed remarks.

If you feel subjected to the negative traits or values, you will overcome this by accentuating the positive ones.

JUPITER IN PISCES

ESSENCE

Growing through Accepting
Blessed are the Meek... • The Metaphysician

The word 'meek' is very appropriate for you because, like you, it is commonly misinterpreted as feeble or wimpish. What it really means is soft, mild and gentle, and this truly describes your philosophy of life and the beliefs to which you subscribe. It does not mean that you have to be a self-effacing push-over, which is possibly an uncomfortable image you have of yourself, and it is very likely that in the past you have been too obliging and consequently had too much expected of you. As a result, you may have become self-indulgent, suspicious of religious doctrines and others' intentions, and prone to exaggerating your own difficulties in a rather crooked attempt to reveal your misunderstood sensitivity.

Yet in typically Piscean fashion, this can all be flipped over to reveal that your growth and development in life hinge on trusting in the power of your sensitivity and goodwill. For the positive qualities of Jupiter in Pisces are essentially of the spiritual kind. The joy that can be yours rests on an unshakable belief in the beauty and goodness of the Universe. Your tragedy is the waste, indolence and frustration that can result from not maintaining this belief. The danger of this happening is due to your confusing your natural acceptance of things with a reluctance to take a stand until you feel cornered. Passive resistance can be both your best and your worst policy.

Inclined as you are to be the visionary artist or teacher, and someone who is often moved to help the underdog, it is important that you retreat regularly from society, especially into Nature, in order to recharge your spiritual batteries. However, this retreat should not take the form of wrapping yourself up in a security blanket that seals you off from past misunderstandings, for you are thus liable to find yourself sealed off from almost everything.

Likewise, some form of structured spiritual search is advisable, as opposed to free-wheeling in a self-comforting but meaningless fashion. However, on the other hand, you can easily be drawn to 'follow' someone or something that you elevate to god- or goddess-like status, only to be ultimately disillusioned. Wrapping yourself up in your own pet beliefs is a very likely reaction to this possibility.

Your true Image of God is of the 'Master', the Christ or Messiah. God in human form, in fact. And the winding road of life leads you to the realization that this human form is your own.

LIKES	**DISLIKES**
Beauty in simple things	Lack of subtlety
Feeling great feelings • Mystical adventures	Lack of inspiration • Workaday existence
Sensitive friends • Peace and quiet	Being misunderstood • Oppressive noise

Jupiter is your clue to making more of life.

JUPITER IN PISCES

TRANSFORMER

POSITIVE	NEGATIVE
Mystical Visionary Imaginative Subtle humour	Peculiar Self-deceiving Paranoid Too obscure
Altruistic Compassionate Selfless Understanding	Parasitical Indiscriminate Self-indulgent Evasive
Mysterious Reclusive Sagacious Inner contentment	Unsociable Inaccessible Incomprehensible Self-contained
Unmercenary Flexible Good value Fair	Undervalues self Wishy-washy Self-effacing Weak

In all matters relating to Jupiter, a critical point of development occurs every twelve years when it returns to the Sign in which it was placed at the time of your birth. In effect, this marks the beginning of a new cycle of growth and understanding.

SOLUTION	PROBLEM
Money is merely a symbol of worth. What anything is actually worth is entirely up to you.	Not putting a price on anything to avoid putting a price on yourself finds you hard-up.
Remember you originally retreated to re-evaluate, then to re-emerge and reveal what you'd remembered.	The living human fossil disguising your longing to be discovered as quite the opposite.
Sooner or later you find that living for others is the perfect complement to furthering yourself.	Either you look to others for the world, or you wallow in your own. Spinning in your own pond.
Your great sense of the wonder of the Universe should take you closer to it – not away from it.	Submerged in your own safe little backwater, which is self-comforting but self-defeating.

If you feel subjected to the negative traits or values, you will overcome this by accentuating the positive ones.

SATURN

Keyword: TESTED

Saturn symbolizes the LESSONS we have to LEARN in life. So, naturally enough, it also represents what we are least sure of, or, more simply, what we FEAR. Through FORCE OF CIRCUMSTANCES we are driven to find the DISCIPLINE, EFFORT and SENSE OF ORDER to overcome LIMITATIONS and OBSTACLES, and to pass the TESTS that Saturn sets us.

So your Saturn-Sign will show how you encounter the above through your experience of CONCRETE REALITY, the STATUS QUO and AUTHORITY FIGURES (especially your FATHER). It also suggests a way in which you cope with and pass these tests, with the result that in TIME you become an authority in your own fashion, and become the author of your own destiny. Saturn also describes in what way you are AMBITIOUS, and what you regard as valid MATERIAL STATUS. It shows what your TASK is, and what you have to WORK at and how.

As Saturn is symbolic of your SHADOW — the dark side of yourself about which you have doubts — there is a tendency to conceal your DOUBT, even to the point of giving the impression of doing quite the opposite, in the form of a polished VENEER. Your Saturn-Sign will also indicate the way in which you might become RIGID through being held back by such a SUPERFICIAL DEFENCE SYSTEM, and how you may overcome this.

Saturn symbolizes the metal LEAD, and through passing its heavy tests (major ones every twenty-nine and a half years, lesser ones every seven years or so) we reach the Gold that is the radiance and confidence represented by your Sun-Sign.

SATURN IN ARIES

ESSENCE

Tested in Doing

The Spartan • That Lonesome Road

This is basically a case of learning to be self-assertive and sure of your standpoint, whatever that might be, as indicated by your Sun-, Moon- and other Planet-Sign positions. In order that this lesson be learnt, you will often find yourself left to your own devices. It could be said that the first lesson here is one of learning to enjoy and make use of the freedom of movement and expression that this offers – or rather imposes.

Saturn is said to be in its Fall in Aries, which means that any form of order other than that which you have won through your own efforts will not stand up. You are having to drive in the first post and blaze the first trail. 'Beaten paths are for beaten people', as a leader once said.

One of the main problems that can result from this kind of test is a lack of feedback, which can make it difficult for you to ascertain how well you're doing in your own right. This can, in turn, lead to bad timing and pushing too hard. Furthermore, provocation and defensiveness may be present in your effort to elicit any sort of response. But this is self-defeating, because the very sense of inadequacy that you are trying to appease or excuse is what others then take a poke at.

So being a bit hard-nosed – but not hard-bitten – will, at times, be the only way in which progress can be made. There is no need to feel bad about this as long as there is some justification, some point down that lonesome road of self-discovery or self-expression on which you have fixed your gaze. Gaining and not losing sight of this point is of paramount importance as otherwise such a need for self-justification becomes habitual and neurotic. The noble but lonesome traveller should not be allowed to become a mumbling, shambling vagabond – at least, not for too long a stretch of the road.

Not surprisingly you are hard to please, because you know deep down that this can only be done by you. On the other hand, the simplest of things can delight you for hours. But ultimately, the only thing that satisfies you is the development of your own will, like a polished sword of tempered steel glinting in the first light of your day.

LIKES	DISLIKES
Physical activity • Arguments	Being out of condition • Losing
Overcoming the odds	Push-overs • Lack of direction
Having a goal • Self-discipline	Imposed discipline

Saturn says: 'Time is your instrument – not your enemy. So take your time.'

SATURN IN ARIES

TRANSFORMER

POSITIVE	NEGATIVE
Self-reliant Singular Independent One-pointed	Self-justifying Egocentric Hard to please Headstrong
Enduring Determined Persistent Strong	Austere Hard-hearted Unsubtle Cruel
Bold Assertive Strategic Self-assured	Defiant Reactionary Impatient Defensive
Disciplined Self-denying Resourceful Reserved	Restrained Mean with self Unsympathetic Unapproachable

With all matters relating to Saturn, a critical point is reached every twenty-nine and a half years, when it returns to the Sign position in which it was placed at the time of your birth. This is a life-progress report, when inner and outer pressures serve to demolish what is weak in you, and to consolidate what is strong.

SOLUTION	PROBLEM
Learn to trust the value of limitations, but avoid making a hair shirt out of them.	Expecting the worst allows very little room for the best. Tightness squeezes.
The more you learn the secret of timing and gradual development, the more confident your actions will be.	Your intense expectation of opposition actually invites it, thereby frustrating your plans.
Surviving should not be an end in itself, but a means to an end that endures.	Feeling raw and uncomfortable, more grim than determined.
Once you've convinced yourself of yourself, others will follow, as a flight does an arrowhead.	Lonely. Insisting that others recognize your standpoint merely drives them away.

If you seem oppressed by any of the negative traits in others, it is because you are not taking responsibility for them in yourself and transforming them into the positive.

SATURN IN TAURUS

ESSENCE

Tested in Stabilizing
The Banker • For What It's Worth

You are learning to set the correct value on things. Initially, this usually means that you have a particularly good sense of material values, but tend to undervalue intangibles or 'invisible assets': qualities in life, yourself, and others that are not immediately obvious.

Naturally enough, money can be a critical source of worry or concern, either because you are frightened of losing what you already possess, or because you are in debt, or funds seem hard to come by. In the first case you are probably attaching too much importance to material possessions; in the second you have probably not taken them seriously enough; and in the third you need to understand that cash flow has not so much to do with external circumstances as with how well-off you feel inside that you ought to be. At the root of this preoccupation with material worth is a fear resulting from an impecunious situation in early life, most likely due to your father. And so you feel that this area of life needs to be sorted out above all others. But, as ever with Saturn, an essential part of the test is gaining a sense of balance, and not overcompensating by evaluating life in purely material terms, or by being cavalier about it.

You are, or are seriously seeking to be, physically reliable and financially stable. Even if you appear to be laid-back about money matters, you quietly keep a wary eye on finances and subscribe to the usual investments like deposit accounts, stocks and shares, insurance etc.

If ever you find yourself counting the cost of things to such an extent that there ceases to be any real enjoyment of life – or that you feel tied to whoever or whatever it might be that is determining your material stability – then the time has come to review just what is worth what. Left unattended to, such a need for major re-evaluation could quite possibly involve the very loss you feared.

In order to pass Saturn's test in Taurus, it must never be forgotten that what is on trial is your sense of material and physical values, and not so much what you possess of material and physical value. Underlying the failure or success in this test is really only one of two issues: either a fear of (being without) money, or a sound understanding of its proper place in the scheme of things.

LIKES	**DISLIKES**
Material stability • Practical methods	Material limitations • Abstract reasoning
Dependable people • Physical proof	Wishy-washy people • Emotional doubt
Business and bargaining	Being unproductive

Saturn says: 'Time is your instrument – not your enemy. So take your time.'

SATURN IN TAURUS

TRANSFORMER

POSITIVE	NEGATIVE
Economical Wise buyer Frugal Realistic	Miserly Penny-pinching Grudging Dour
Financially stable and aware Acquisitive Affluent Earthy	Mercenary Grasping Avaricious Materialistic
Patient Persevering Imperturbable Concentrated	Inhibited Plodding Unobservant Limited
Constructive Purposeful Methodical Conservative	Stubborn Restricted Leaden Dull

With all matters relating to Saturn, a critical point is reached every twenty-nine and a half years, when it returns to the Sign position in which it was placed at the time of your birth. This is a life-progress report, when inner and outer pressures serve to demolish what is weak in you, and to consolidate what is strong.

With a purpose in mind nothing can stop you. Without one nothing can start you.	Stalemate and inertia. Consistently resisting change leaves you feeling like a lump.
Your discipline and hard work can be a pleasure in themselves, but should also be justly rewarded.	Head down and yoked to the task, you find that life is passing you by.
In reality you are making the choice between trusting and not trusting yourself.	Weighed down by your material considerations, you're making the simplest decision a heavy one.
The worth of what you give and get is exactly equivalent to what you think to be your own worth.	So afraid of being short-changed that your desire to get your money's worth just isn't worth it!

SOLUTION	PROBLEM

If you seem oppressed by any of the negative traits in others, it is because you are not taking responsibility for them in yourself and transforming them into the positive.

SATURN IN GEMINI

ESSENCE
Tested in Communicating
Riddle My Riddle • A Matter of Mind

Saturn indicates what one is least sure of, and therefore needs to become more versed in. When this Planet is placed in Gemini the issue becomes one of learning to use your mind efficiently and correctly. However, as rational thought has dominated our society for several hundred years, you must be careful to ascribe the right value to Reason – to use it, not to be ruled by it.

As is typical with the Sign of Gemini, it can go to one of two extremes: either you are the type who virtually worships the intellect, and for whom everything has to have a logical explanation, or you are hampered by not being able to reason things through.

If you belong to the first, and more common, type then you have the obvious advantage of being able to fit in fairly comfortably with the status quo. The conventional job market with its clearly defined roles that involve the use of minds and hands offers opportunities and few complications. This is especially so because you probably got fed through the educational system in the way that was intended: to produce citizens to fill the jobs available.

If you fall into the second category, you probably have an intuitive type of personality, and therefore your idiosyncratic mentality can encounter many difficulties and set-backs at school and in securing a stable job. However, this dilemma breeds in you a very resourceful and versatile mind that can rise to many different occasions.

Nevertheless, Geminian duality persists, and either type can split yet again, or turn into the other. The intellectual type can become too rigid and specialized, and suddenly find him/herself out of a job or feeling uncomfortable in our fast-changing world. This would lead to his/her having to become more flexible and intuitive. Alternatively, the intuitive type can become so suspicious of clever-clever intellectualism and so stuck with lots of opinions but no practical or broader knowledge, that he/she is forced to knuckle down to gaining just that.

The riddle of Saturn in Gemini becomes clearer upon pondering the Keyphrase 'Tested in Communicating'. The mark of an efficient mind is that it communicates, both to others and within itself. This entails having one side of the brain complementing and in contact with the other, the intuitive with the logical. If you cannot work it out, then let it work itself out, and, as ever, vice versa.

LIKES
Brain-teasers • Well-defined thoughts
Things in black and white • Facts and figures
Recognition of mental ability

DISLIKES
Mental quandaries • Keeping your options open
Grey areas • Being mentally pinned down
Feeling awkward or ridiculed

Saturn says: 'Time is your instrument – not your enemy. So take your time.'

SATURN IN GEMINI

TRANSFORMER

POSITIVE	NEGATIVE
Good intellect Literary Learned Clever	Doubts intuition Bookish Unoriginal Boring
Scientific Systematic Disciplined thinker Practical mind	Sceptical Rigid attitude Pedantic Cynical
Problem-solver Mentally resourceful Painstaking Serious	Problem-maker Mentally inundated Painful Pessimistic
Steady nerves Cool Observant Versatile	Tense Cold Critical Devious

With all matters relating to Saturn, a critical point is reached every twenty-nine and a half years, when it returns to the Sign position in which it was placed at the time of your birth. This is a life-progress report, when inner and outer pressures serve to demolish what is weak in you, and to consolidate what is strong.

Like the riddle of the Sphinx, the answer is not to attempt to find an answer. Wait and watch.	Awkwardly stretched between thinking you should have the answer and not knowing the question.
In addition to your mental deliberations, trusting what time will bring will attract a resolution.	Seemingly insoluble dilemmas. Damned if you do and damned if you don't.
Knowing the limitations of the logical mind lends a power to your mind as a whole.	Being suspicious of anything that cannot be proved is proving to be a serious limitation.
Trusting your wits gives them a lightness that lends weight to what you say and how you think.	For all your knowledge you still fear being caught out and ridiculed.

SOLUTION	PROBLEM

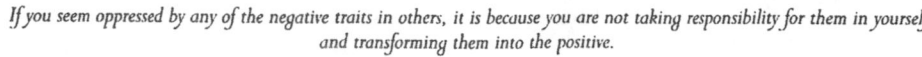

If you seem oppressed by any of the negative traits in others, it is because you are not taking responsibility for them in yourself and transforming them into the positive.

SATURN IN CANCER

ESSENCE

Tested in Nurturing

Cool but Caring • I Rise Above Myself

As a rule, feeling responses do not come easily to Saturn in Cancer. It is as if you have to take a step back from emotional involvement, be it with family, partners, friends or the world in general. Cancer represents an uninhibited emotional flow/response that is instinctual and naturally caring. However, with Saturn in this Sign, this would be denied you unless you had learnt what you truly feel and feel for. In other words, you have to become very sure of what your emotional values are, what or who you consciously care about in life, and what actually gives you a sense of belonging.

None of this comes easily, a fact that could possibly stem from and account for your early life having lacked a certain kind of emotional support, which in turn has led to your withdrawing your feelings in a certain way. Such deep insecurity can also make it hard to muster the discipline and perseverance necessary to make or to maintain progress in the professional world outside. So, in order that you be made aware of your feelings, you are at times made to feel again unsupported and cut off from sympathies and sentiments. The trick here is not to react too emotionally, yet at the same time to avoid not reacting at all. Show that you care, and need caring for, for a denial of both underlies your withdrawn and inhibited feelings.

Obviously this truly is a test, which is why Saturn is in its Detriment in Cancer, for expressing nurturing is very difficult when you have little or only a distorted idea of what it means. It is therefore important that you frequently make the attempt, even though it might prove abortive, to re-enter the emotional fray, and do not feel morbidly self-justified in self-imposed isolation, when your mawkishly or awkwardly expressed feelings are met with misunderstanding, or even scorn.

You are looking for a very real sense of belonging. When found, others come to rely on this greatly, and you become known for a matter-of-fact type of caring attitude that more than makes up for what could be interpreted as a lack of empathy. Ultimately Saturn in Cancer demands a sincere and selfless response to life and to the needs of the world around you. When you are successful in this expression of care, which is what confers true status upon you, there are usually no fanfares, just a quiet but sure sense of your being in the right place at the right time.

LIKES
Genuine sentiments • Being highly motivated
Material security • Domestic order
Knowing the emotional score

DISLIKES
False emotions • Meaningless commitments
The rat race • Feelings of rootlessness
Being compromised by feelings

Saturn says: 'Time is your instrument – not your enemy. So take your time.'

SATURN IN CANCER

TRANSFORMER

POSITIVE	NEGATIVE
Emotional self-control Dignified Strength of character	Emotionally inhibited Hides feelings Lack of warmth
Subtly kind Practically protective Unsensationally supportive	Self-pitying Preoccupied with self Mistrusts feelings
Concern for public welfare Aids humanity Paternal/Maternal	Avoids own feelings Blind to others' feelings Self-serving
Quietly persevering Shrewd Ambitious Economical	Lack of discipline Lack of empathy Self-centred Miserly

With all matters relating to Saturn, a critical point is reached every twenty-nine and a half years, when it returns to the Sign position in which it was placed at the time of your birth. This is a life-progress report, when inner and outer pressures serve to demolish what is weak in you, and to consolidate what is strong.

Forget yourself and direct your attention and talents outwards to the needs of the world.	Feeling unable to make your way in life. Feeling unprovided for.
Instead of being stricken by your conscience, listen to it and act upon it.	Feeling guilty and paranoid. Merely worrying about loved ones or the world.
You must discover what and who you truly care about, and how you may express that care.	Feeling inadequate (as partner or parent). Difficult family life.
Eventually such trials will have earned you a true and deep sense of inner security.	Feeling cut-off, lonely and misunderstood. Emotionally crippled.

SOLUTION	PROBLEM

If you seem oppressed by any of the negative traits in others, it is because you are not taking responsibility for them in yourself and transforming them into the positive.

SATURN IN LEO

ESSENCE

Tested in Creating

Rule Thyself...   ...Or Be Ruled Over

The task here is one of expressing Saturn's limiting and conservative nature through bright and expansive Leo. The test is to establish self-esteem without getting too big for your boots, and to command respect without being dictatorial. Self-importance when carried too far attracts a fall from grace.

However, since Saturn frequently represents doubt, fear and what we're not sure of, there is a strong likelihood of your being so anxious about that possible fall from grace that you hide your light under a bushel. But this is hardly putting yourself to the test, so Saturn makes sure that something else comes into your life, in some form of authority, such as parent, partner, school, church or government, or a certain imposed responsibility, that forces you either to develop your creative potentials or merely to bemoan your fate.

However, whatever the case, as Leo is such a powerful Sign you are bound to attempt to attain some form of respect. The arch-enemy here is self-doubt, probably caused by early suppression or lack of a positive example of self-expression. Apart from the down-trodden feeling that this creates, it would also cause you to be defensively puffed-up. Self-assuredness needs to be flexible, not brittle, and pretending to be confident shows like skin disease, but because of your vanity no one would tell you.

You need to take command of all that you have at your disposal as an individual human being, and to express it creatively, heart and Soul. Don't be afraid to be proud, but avoid feeling stiff. Enjoying having an ego is the antidote to Saturn's stern presence. However, carrying it too far the other way, and being autocratic and too full of yourself, would bring Saturn's rod down on your back in the form of some kind of loss or affliction. Saturn in Leo states that what is important is the act of creation, not so much the creator or the creations themselves, be they of an artistic or business nature, or children.

Saturn in Leo demands true strength of will and nobility of character. Living in the knowledge that this is what you are working towards is the guarantee of its attainment.

LIKES	DISLIKES
Lasting respect • Recognition of efforts	False praise • Living in someone's shadow
Feeling truly entitled • Being in command	Snatched pleasures • Being ruled by pride
Responsibility	Lack of dependants

Saturn says: 'Time is your instrument — not your enemy. So take your time.'

SATURN IN LEO

TRANSFORMER

POSITIVE	NEGATIVE
Controlled self-expression Brilliant, warts and all Commanding	Inhibited self-expression Dogmatic and demanding Hypocritical
Self-assured Strong-willed Composed Dignified	Self-contained Stubborn Defensive Stands apart
Authoritative Organizer Impressive Centred	Autocratic Dictatorial Imperious Egotistical
Responsible Efficient Contented Good-hearted	Anxious workaholic Self-conscious Strained

With all matters relating to Saturn, a critical point is reached every twenty nine and a half years, when it returns to the Sign position in which it was placed at the time of your birth. This is a life-progress report, when inner and outer pressures serve to demolish what is weak in you, and to consolidate what is strong.

Taking pride in your self-development will attract and maintain all that you desire.	Being ruled by your fear of losing someone or something is taking the pleasure out of life.
Getting rid of your self-importance reveals your true self and vanquishes your doubts and foes.	One dictator deserves another. The tyrant in your life is a reflection of your own inner tyrant.
Involvement with others on their own level reveals the true measure of your self-esteem.	Isolation. Locked inside yourself with only your pride for company.
You are your own power station. Take responsibility for it and turn on the lights.	Dissatisfied with your life. One person or another seems to be responsible for this.

SOLUTION	PROBLEM

If you seem oppressed by any of the negative traits in others, it is because you are not taking responsibility for them in yourself and transforming them into the positive.

SATURN IN VIRGO

ESSENCE

Tested in Analysing
The Hermit • The Scholar

You are learning to distinguish between essentials and non-essentials, between what is 'good' and what is 'bad' for you. Such tests, as this implies, can drive you to extremes of self-denial, and of self-indulgence, by way of compensation. At times your conscience is like an altar at which all desires for Earthly pleasures are sacrificed; at other times you busily set about desecrating it.

The task before you is therefore one of establishing a certain purity of being without it becoming so exacting as to be almost masochistic, of living simply without stripping yourself down to less than the bare essentials. However, the 'bare essentials' may well be the circumstances you find yourself in with regard to a particular area of your life, most likely an emotional area, that is possibly reflected in a certain sparseness domestically. In your industrious efforts to separate the wheat from the chaff, at some point you find yourself with only a 'husk'. This is a critical stage because you are now able to see what you are, stripped of the trappings and influences of society. But unless you grasp that this was your objective in the first place, the self-denial can become so obsessive as to find you branding more and more things and people as impure, not good enough, stupid, improper, unhealthy, etc.

Saturn is about control. When it is placed in Virgo you are controlling the impulse to purify through keeping a weather-eye upon that very impulse. So allowing yourself consciously to take a break from your 'duties', introducing playtime into your work schedule, and hanging loose occasionally, will prevent you from descending into a dark and self-justifying spiral of withdrawal and misanthropy. 'Laugh and the world laughs with you; weep, and you weep alone.'

If you really feel that a cloistered life of study and self-abnegation is the one for you, then pursue it gladly as a necessary path, rather than allowing it to be suffered by yourself (and others) as an imposed punishment. But before doing either, check back on your experience of authority figures in your life, in order to ascertain who was too strict or not strict enough, for this will be a clue to your own inclination to austerity, or your rakish reaction to it. The real objective of Saturn in Virgo is for you to be an example of living simply yet enjoyably.

LIKES	DISLIKES
Rites and rituals • Orderliness • Purity of intent	Meaningless formalities • Feeling constrained
Knowing the odds • A clear conscience	Waywardness • Taking risks • False impressions

Saturn says: 'Time is your instrument – not your enemy. So take your time.'

SATURN IN VIRGO

TRANSFORMER

POSITIVE	NEGATIVE
Ascetic	Austere
Morally upright	Too strict
Prudent	Priggish
Cautious	Misanthropic
Meticulous	Punctilious
Attentive	Hypercritical
Precise	Pedantic
Efficient	Workaholic
Serious	Humourless
Concerned	Worrier
Health-conscious	Valetudinarian
Wise	Aloof
Discreet	Tight-lipped
Orderly	Stiff
Conscientious	Guilt-ridden
Well-measured	Restrained

With all matters relating to Saturn, a critical point is reached every twenty nine and a half years, when it returns to the Sign position in which it was placed at the time of your birth. This is a life-progress report, when inner and outer pressures serve to demolish what is weak in you, and to consolidate what is strong.

SOLUTION	PROBLEM
The controlled and occasional bite from 'forbidden fruit' forestalls your choking on it.	Keeping your wilder instincts and ideas bottled up mounts to collapse or explosion.
Seriously consider not being so serious. A true panacea includes something of its opposite.	Depression or ill-health. Inner conflict created by suppression of physical desires.
Your exacting nature eventually discovers that being less exacting is exactly what's required.	Keeping busy seems to be an answer to everything — except overwork.
Not merely self-denying, the true ascetic works upon what underlies the need for self-denial.	Feeling lonely and misunderstood.

If you seem oppressed by any of the negative traits in others, it is because you are not taking responsibility for them in yourself and transforming them into the positive.

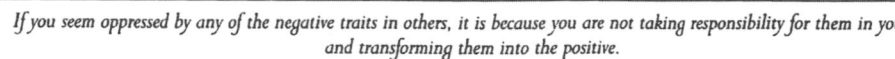

SATURN IN LIBRA

ESSENCE

Tested in Relating
Duty to Love • Love of Duty

It could be stated that Saturn in Libra represents that point where all other Planet-Sign positions converge, or, put another way, where a focus or point of balance has to be found between the needs and urges of the individual on the one hand, and the demands and conditions of life and society on the other. The most essential test of all is that of Relating, of establishing right relations between oneself and anything or anyone outside of oneself. For this reason Saturn is said to be Exalted in Libra; Order and Authority are best expressed through the qualities of Balance and Justice.

You are thus learning the most important lesson in life: Balance, such a simple word that can be skipped over with hardly a thought. But if you apply a sense of Balance to any situation with some imagination and objectivity, then a solution or guiding principle will begin to take shape. For example, if someone appears not to be giving you enough of their time, then it is probably because you are giving them too much of yours. The remedy is, therefore, to give more time to yourself, and then others will begin to have more time for you. Conversely, if another is paying too much attention to you, increase your attention to them through getting to know what they're really after, and then their attentions will eventually decrease or become more appropriate and manageable. There are, of course, many degrees and combinations possible with such 'balancing acts', and the ability to make fine adjustments is an art that you can develop and profit from.

How well you do this will determine and establish your place in the professional and personal scheme of things. With time well-spent and tests dutifully submitted to, you can become quite a paragon of human grace and social skill. On whatever level you are having to make an effort, you can be sure the external reality is reflecting exactly your inner reality. As love and marriage are the main testing grounds for Saturn in Libra, it should be noted that you are unerringly attracted to people who display those qualities that are over- or under-emphasized in your own personality. In effect, your duty to love is to tune in to what the relationship itself is telling you, rather than to force another into being some conventionally romantic ideal, which would only make them want to escape such a pressuresome expectation. Saturn in Libra teaches that 'another' is simply a reference point to which you are drawn, by love, and that enables you to establish your own identity and exalt your place in the world.

LIKES	**DISLIKES**
Feeling committed • A 'worthy opponent'	Being without relationship • Being unevenly matched
A serious partner • Learning through love	Flippant relationships • Unresolved relationships
Establishing right relations	Leaving relationships to chance

Saturn says: 'Time is your instrument – not your enemy. So take your time.'

SATURN IN LIBRA

TRANSFORMER

POSITIVE	NEGATIVE
Sense of moral obligation Loyal Honourable and co-operative	Over-committed Blind trust Weak sense of self
Just Impartial Diplomatic Tactful	Unforgiving Indecisive Insincere Stiff
Socially aware Good timing Well-mannered Composed	Socially unsure Bad timing Unrelaxed Rigid
Abiding partner Esteemed Idealistic Responsible	Insecure partner Resented Unrealistic Too particular

With all matters relating to Saturn, a critical point is reached every twenty-nine and a half years, when it returns to the Sign position in which it was placed at the time of your birth. This is a life-progress report, when inner and outer pressures serve to demolish what is weak in you, and to consolidate what is strong.

As the perfect partner you recognize that a perfect partnership is only as perfect as you are.	Sorrow in love owing to your stubbornly insisting that some impossible standard be maintained.
Know that where you are and who you are with is your reality. Harmonize with that and no other.	Confusion over where you fit in. Being with the wrong person at the right time, or vice versa.
Being fair to yourself and others is a balance created between your views and theirs.	Arousing enmity, frustration or awkwardness in others.
Assessing the exact nature of a relationship determines your exact role in it – and out of it.	Loss of marital or social status as a result of being unmindful of your own needs.

SOLUTION	PROBLEM

If you seem oppressed by any of the negative traits in others, it is because you are not taking responsibility for them in yourself and transforming them into the positive.

SATURN IN SCORPIO

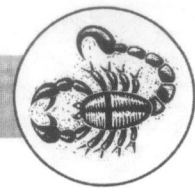

ESSENCE

Tested in Desiring
To Use or Abuse • The Masterstroke

This is really about learning effectively to express any kind of power, be it sexual, political, financial or whatever. You have a sense of power, but whether you experience it as oppressive or creative is another matter. In any case, there is an intensity about the way you pursue your aims and the objects of your desire, and it is very hard to stop you once you have decided on a particular course of action. Equally, and maybe because of this, you can agonize over what course of action to take; this is understandable considering the damage that could be wrought if your energies were misdirected.

You could not – or should not – ever be described as insipid. Attempting to hedge your bets or pull your punches would have an almost retrogressive effect, and you'd gain the reputation of a shrew or a weasel into the bargain. However, at the other extreme you can be quite fanatical about your individually-held principles.

This is an ambitious position for Saturn because both this Planet and the Sign of Scorpio like to have a sense of control. Here lies a killer instinct which can be expressed in a ruthless and scheming way. You may be the victim rather than the perpetrator of such, but it still points to the necessity of looking at your own repressed desires, for, as it is said, 'If you don't do it, someone else will do it for you – and to you.' Saturn always points to what we are learning about in life, and therefore what we are least sure of – but potentially may become masters of. Scorpio is about Power and Influence, Sex and Death. You therefore draw your authority from decidedly deep levels; superficial motivations and so-called civilized attitudes come to naught. Yet you are also aware of the value of cultivating and maintaining secret bonds that enable the execution of your plans. Additionally, you know the value of keeping others guessing while at the same time acquiring inside information. Saturn in Scorpio means business.

The fervour with which you hold to what you believe in can give rise to rigidity, in the form of arthritis and stones. But such physical complaints can also result from not letting some deep conviction be known, in which case skin problems could be in evidence. The insight and ability that belong to Saturn in Scorpio should not be allowed to go to seed or be used up in mere posturing. You are capable of achieving a great deal when your convictions are identified and acted upon.

LIKES	DISLIKES
Organized power • Intense commitment	Losing control • Half-heartedness
Knowing secrets • Sanctioned intimacy	Not being in the know
Strong characters	Philandering • Weak characters

Saturn says: 'Time is your instrument – not your enemy. So take your time.'

SATURN IN SCORPIO

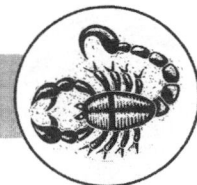

TRANSFORMER

POSITIVE	NEGATIVE
Purposeful Eye for main chance Persistent Disciplined	Ruthlessly ambitious Opportunist Obstinate Rigid
Sexually disciplined Sexually self-assured Intriguing Sexually aware	Sexually controlling Sexually controlled Jealous Twisted
Uses system to advantage Improves status quo Iron-willed	Slave-driver Impatient of weakness in others Megalomaniac
Serious Capable Resourceful Insightful	Morose Burdens self Constipated Sceptical

With all matters relating to Saturn, a critical point is reached every twenty-nine and a half years, when it returns to the Sign position in which it was placed at the time of your birth. This is a life-progress report, when inner and outer pressures serve to demolish what is weak in you, and to consolidate what is strong.

SOLUTION	PROBLEM
Look for a power to your life that goes beyond a mere secret yen for superiority.	Losing sight of a deep sense of purpose makes you feel as if destiny has abandoned you.
A brave awareness of your and others' failings enables you positively to transform a situation.	Frightened of putting a foot wrong you continually tread on everyone else's feet.
Regarding sexual activity as a friendly bout of psychological wrestling is mutually empowering.	Regarding sex as some kind of lever or emotional trade-off is progressively more dissatisfying.
Be mindful that your particular kind of forward push depends on who you have behind you.	The enemies you make on the way up, you meet up with on the way down. Stalemates.

If you seem oppressed by any of the negative traits in others, it is because you are not taking responsibility for them in yourself and transforming them into the positive.

295

SATURN IN SAGITTARIUS

ESSENCE

Tested in Seeking

The Serious Seeker • Devil's Advocate

The task of Saturn in Sagittarius is to build a sound set of religious and moral principles that will guide and give meaning to your life, and thereby to the lives of others. As if to force this issue, it is quite likely that you have a background of religious dogma which to one degree or another has had the effect of limiting your sense of scope in life. Or, in your past you may have been dealt with unjustly, giving rise on the one hand to resentment, but on the other to a sense of how not to go about the business of living. Or, yet again, it may be merely that social and cultural influences have kept you to the straight and narrow at the expense of experiencing something that might have broadened your concept of Self and Life. Although you may have done many exciting things and been to many faraway places, the lack of a feeling that you solidly believe in something, or something in you, persists.

This lack can amount to a great need for social and educational sanction, qualifications etc. You feel that this will 'put you on the map', and, indeed, because of this need such honours are very likely to be won. However, without an understanding of what 'Tested in Seeking' really means, the fear of moral or social censure lingers on. Having a handle to your name does not necessarily give you something to hold on to when the chips are down emotionally.

Tested in Seeking means exploring thoroughly as many avenues of furtherance as possible — mentally, emotionally, physically and spiritually — so that you progressively formulate and reformulate what is 'right' for you. You are more than likely to believe you've arrived at such a conclusion whenever someone or something offers a more comprehensive and impressive philosophy or lifestyle, and you will energetically propound such newly discovered beliefs. Alternatively, and in some ways more significantly, you will play Devil's Advocate to the spoutings of ardently emotional 'believers'. This kind of testing of other people's beliefs and opinions, providing it is not merely masking a lack of your own, plays a particularly valid role in making sure that feet are kept firmly on the ground when minds are seeking higher meaning.

LIKES

Searching for truth • Further education
Purposeful adventures • A good reputation
Physical and metaphysical exercise

DISLIKES

Blocks to discovery • Being a non-runner
Aimlessness • Being dishonoured
Vegetating

Saturn says: 'Time is your instrument — not your enemy. So take your time.'

SATURN IN SAGITTARIUS

TRANSFORMER

POSITIVE	NEGATIVE
High moral fibre	High-minded
Honourable	Self-righteous
Prudent	Priggish
Superior	Superior
Philosophical	Intellectual pride
Reflects on life's meaning	Tritely theoretical
Ascetic	Hypocritical
Devoted	Too easily hurt
Fearless	Tactless
Earnest	Insincere
Trustworthy	Fears disapproval
Good teacher	Lays down law
Well-informed	Merely academic
Focused attention	Brow-beating
Deft	Smug

With all matters relating to Saturn, a critical point is reached every twenty-nine and a half years, when it returns to the Sign position in which it was placed at the time of your birth. This is a life-progress report, when inner and outer pressures serve to demolish what is weak in you, and to consolidate what is strong.

SOLUTION	PROBLEM
You know that the most valid knowledge comes from within. Contemplate. Meditate. Be sure.	You don't feel as satisfied as you sound. An open-and-shut case you and life ain't.
Putting beliefs to the test with a view to accepting what is valid creates guidance and support.	Defensively shaking up others' beliefs to protect the shakiness of your own serves no one.
Knowing that one has to take both the high road and the low road leads to where it's at.	Religious problems. Conflicts of belief. Not being taken seriously.
Bearing your doubts gives you a dignified bearing. Respecting others' means they respect yours.	Insisting that others subscribe to your beliefs is having the opposite effect.

If you seem oppressed by any of the negative traits in others, it is because you are not taking responsibility for them in yourself and transforming them into the positive.

297

SATURN IN CAPRICORN

ESSENCE

Tested in Building
True or False Integrity • Build Your Own

Being placed in the Sign that it rules, and therefore said to be Dignified, Saturn in Capricorn poses a task which is simply that of Saturn itself: to know your place. However, this can be interpreted in two ways.

Negatively expressed, 'knowing your place' can mean anything but. In other words, you can be inclined to succumb to what society expects from your particular class, creed, race, material standing etc. However, there could be a compensatory reaction to this whereby you avoid and resist what these things demand of you, or brand you as, but without actually doing your own thing, either. So both of these interpretations would find you subjected to restrictions – self-imposed or otherwise.

Alternatively, you realize that the place you find in the world is what you establish through your own efforts. And with Saturn in Capricorn there is definitely a strong streak of self-determination at some level of your being, together with an inherent sense of discipline and structure.

First of all you have to establish a starting point, a foundation. This would mean building on whatever you have at hand, as opposed to getting bogged down in it. You instinctively make use of the materials that exist about you, in the form of business or governmental agencies, for example. This can take time, and you could get sucked back into anonymity. So not only is patience an essential part of Saturn in Capricorn's test, but so too is diligence. In effect, you are able – and are rather supposed – to make more order out of the existing order; and this also employs your liking for helping those who help themselves.

You go to meet reality with a healthy sense of ambition, of making your mark and amounting to something, or you are plagued with a sense of inadequacy. Saturn demands here that you be objective in the face of life's adversities, for feeling overcome by them is liable to invite creeping and self-perpetuating pessimism. With Saturn in Capricorn, its positive and negative qualities can therefore become sharply divided. It is very much up to you, and the image you have of the material world, which way it goes.

LIKES	**DISLIKES**
Professionalism • Successful people	Amateurishness • Dead-heads
Making a social contribution	Going to waste • Loss of status
Prestige • Firm objectives	Impractical advice

Saturn says: 'Time is your instrument – not your enemy. So take your time.'

SATURN IN CAPRICORN

TRANSFORMER

POSITIVE	NEGATIVE
Disciplined Hardworking Serious-minded Dutiful	Programmed Slave to system Depressed Repressed
Businesslike Career-minded Ambitious Industrious	Hard and cold Status freak Ruthless Unscrupulous
Self-sufficient Economical Capable Dignified	Lonely Austere Under-employed Stuck-up
Self-controlled Canny Helps others Patient	Controlling Suspicious Uses others Restrained

With all matters relating to Saturn, a critical point is reached every twenty-nine and a half years, when it returns to the Sign position in which it was placed at the time of your birth. This is a life-progress report, when inner and outer pressures serve to demolish what is weak in you, and to consolidate what is strong.

SOLUTION	PROBLEM
You notice that your and society's progress are inextricably linked, so you aid both.	Seeing the world as a hostile place finds you constantly on the offensive or defensive.
Know that your respectful place in the scheme of things is based on meeting mutual needs.	Fear-induced ignorance of the nature of society is preventing you from utilizing what it has to offer.
Trust that your time and effort will bring you to your rightful place.	The more you (try to) attain, the more dissatisfied and uncomfortable you feel.
Use the status quo to further yourself — with a view to being true to something greater.	Stuck with the lowest common denominator of what the state dishes out.

If you seem oppressed by any of the negative traits in others, it is because you are not taking responsibility for them in yourself and transforming them into the positive.

SATURN IN AQUARIUS

ESSENCE
Tested in Liberating
The Practical Idealist • Redemption Is

This position of Saturn makes for a complex set of rules in life, because somehow you want Freedom and Order rolled up together. You can get into a bind when you find yourself, or others, struggling against the very principles that you devised in order to attain your liberation. You then make adjustments that will accommodate your actions or those of others. This pattern continues until another adjustment has to be made, and then another, until you are seemingly surrounded by ideals and circumstances that are painfully at odds with one another.

Truly to free yourself from whatever is inhibiting you, which is the task of Saturn in Aquarius, you need first and foremost to identify what it is from your past conditioning that is preventing you from contacting or maintaining a consistent flow of emotion, for this is what lies at the root of your difficulty in finding freedom, and not some external factor in your present life. A very likely source of this dilemma would be a father – or father-figure – who did not give you a clear sense of authority or affection because he did not recognize you as an individual in your own right.

So you now create certain principles, be they moral, political, psychological or whatever, as a substitute for that lack of a strong feeling about yourself, your rights and your place in the world. Indeed these intellectual concepts can develop into real ideologies and a scientific and impartial view of life, which in turn can serve you and society well in the professional, but non-emotional, areas of life.

However, the freedom that you are striving to make a reality will not become so until you tear down all those social concepts and rationalizations about yourself and life, and get right down to the wood, which is the real, unique you that was originally seen as just plain odd. The challenge is to transform the odd into the ordinary, but not at the expense of your natural peculiarities, which are the hallmark of individuality. What follows on from this transformation is your becoming a very solid example not only of the supreme power of individuality, but also of the fact that one is redeemed simply through being what one essentially is.

LIKES		**DISLIKES**
The impartial truth		Misrepresentation
Human nature • Freedom		Distortion of nature • Suppression
The common touch • Living ideals		Elitism • Compromise

Saturn says: 'Time is your instrument – not your enemy. So take your time.'

SATURN IN AQUARIUS

TRANSFORMER

POSITIVE	NEGATIVE
Scientific	Pseudo-scientific
Observant	Clinical
Level-headed	Cunning
Open-minded	Bends rules
Individualistic	Elitist
Cool but friendly	Apparently friendly
Genuine	Hollow
Deliberate	Too formal
Humane	Intolerant
Unresentful	Belligerent
Impartial	Indifferent
Thoughtful	Insensitive
Visionary	Airy-theory
Idealistic	Unrealistic
Just	Dogmatic
Sincere	Glib

With all matters relating to Saturn, a critical point is reached every twenty-nine and a half years, when it returns to the Sign position in which it was placed at the time of your birth. This is a life-progress report, when inner and outer pressures serve to demolish what is weak in you, and to consolidate what is strong.

SOLUTION	PROBLEM
When your thoughts are matched by how you feel and what you do, you are utterly convincing.	Your suppositions know no limits — except that your suppositions are limitations in themselves.
If you cannot forget yourself, forgive yourself. Your blessing is your appreciation of the absurd.	Your crankiness is bordering on craziness is bordering on your being impossible to know or be with.
Make friends with yourself as if you were the most socially desirable person in the world.	Feeling alienated. Friendships built on false hopes or rigid expectations prove unreliable.
You have a talent for spotting what obscures the truth. If the mote's in your own eye, remove it.	Having devised your own but suspect version of reality, you are hard-put to maintain it.

If you seem oppressed by any of the negative traits in others, it is because you are not taking responsibility for them in yourself and transforming them into the positive.

SATURN IN PISCES

ESSENCE
Tested in Accepting
The Ancient Soul • Mystic or Misfit

There is a deep understanding and inner seriousness with Saturn in Pisces. You could be described as an Ancient Soul, with all its woes and wisdom. You have suffered at the hands of others, and are therefore sympathetic to others' suffering; you emanate a gentle and somewhat solemn light that guides and comforts in a very subtle way.

Indeed, there is a subtlety to your character that is connected in some way with the necessity simultaneously to dissolve inhibitions and stabilize your sensitive spots. This can be expressed in a number of ways, from camouflaging them as some oddity that has barely anything to do with you at all, to being able to rise above doubts and fears and see them for the illusions that they are. In addition to this there can be indiscriminate limiting of your potentials, as a kind of mock humility, while on the positive side, you express your talents and shortcomings, your joys and sorrows, as being of equal value.

'Tested in Accepting' therefore sets you the task of striking a balance between being oblivious of life's demands and being far too ready to take on unconditionally the problems of other people, between turning a blind eye and turning the other cheek, in fact. To plot this middle course sooner or later you (have to) find a way of drawing on the wisdom of that Ancient Soul of yours. To accomplish this, and to avoid getting caught in a sort of psychological whirlpool of despair, you need first to allow yourself regular quiet and solitude, and then to plumb your indigo depths through meditation, creative inspiration, psychoanalysis, or some other form of inner guided tour. The results of such disciplined introversion bring forth much relief and enlightenment, both to you and to others. It is also equally important that you offer up your discoveries in a certain way, and turn your attention to the outer world as well as the inner one, for even when you are enjoying your private spaces, that 'psychological whirlpool' can suck you under. In any case, you are a natural in helping others discover, investigate and escape from their own whirlpools. You have to go down there in order to discover what's been lost (treasures such as wisdom, vision and insight), or to release what may be trapped, like a tail in a long-forgotten net (a nagging pain from the past). The Ancient Soul longs for that Ancient Peace.

LIKES	**DISLIKES**
Peace and quiet	Constant uproar
Grotto-like places • Deliberate diffusion	Feeling trapped • Being pigeon-holed
Composure • A clean sheet	Being discountenanced • A murky past

Saturn says: 'Time is your instrument — not your enemy. So take your time.'

SATURN IN PISCES

TRANSFORMER

POSITIVE	NEGATIVE
Humble Modest Self-sacrificing Retiring	Self-negating Falsely modest Self-defeating Withdrawn
Enlightening Philanthropic Easygoing Accepting	Indecisive Undervalues self Lacks discipline Fears failure
Gentle Sensitive to suffering Understanding Concerned	Timid Suffers needlessly Too abiding Fretful
Meditative Imaginative Receptive Thoughtful	Morose Paranoid Disorderly Wool-gathering

*With all matters relating to Saturn, a critical point
is reached every twenty-nine and a half years,
when it returns to the Sign position in which it was
placed at the time of your birth. This is a life-progress
report, when inner and outer pressures serve to
demolish what is weak in you, and to consolidate
what is strong.*

SOLUTION	PROBLEM
Peace of mind is always here now – somewhere inside you. Look for it – it's looking for you.	Trapped in the past between the memories that haunt you and the times you pine for.
When you've quietly patched up your own boat, you can and do go quietly rescuing others.	Drowning in a sea of (others') troubles. Feeling hopelessly weak in the face of adversity.
Gradually you learn how to keep life's treadmill turning with one toe, and teach others how to, as well.	Struggling in vain, leading to regret. Dogged by regrets, you struggle in vain.
When you've eliminated a false sense of yourself, the real thing emerges, quietly and naturally.	Feeling joyless, hopeless and useless. Undoing yourself and feeling a perverse sense of achievement.

*If you seem oppressed by any of the negative traits in others, it is because you are not taking responsibility for them in yourself
and transforming them into the positive*

303

THE OUTER PLANETS

The Outer Planets are Uranus, Neptune and Pluto. They are also called the Trans-Saturnian Planets as they orbit beyond Saturn, which is symbolic of the limit described by conventional and material reality. And so the Outer Planets represent those forces which could be described as extra-ordinary or paranormal – that is, outside of what we regard as ordinary, beyond normality.

Put in simpler terms they are forces of Change, and of the Collective Unconscious (the totally interconnected sum-total of Humanity's feelings and memories) and the Unknown.

The famous astrologer Dane Rudhyar dubbed the Outer Planets 'Ambassadors of the Galaxy' for it is they that draw in and process cosmic influences from beyond our Solar System. Having done this, these influences are projected at the Sun which, having also collected and processed them, then radiates them out to all the Inner Planets up to Saturn. Sunspot cycles are the pulse of this process. What this all amounts to is the process of growth and evolution of our Solar System itself, much as you or I grow and evolve through being subject to the influences of everyday life. But, seeing as we live upon the Earth which is a part of the Solar System, we too are subject to the influences of the Outer Planets.

These influences, like the Sun, Moon and Inner Planets, affect us in three ways: by Sign, by House and by Aspect.

When seen as operating through the Signs of the Zodiac, because the Outer Planets appear to travel through the sky slowly, their influences are felt over a longer period of time than, say, Mars or Jupiter. And so they will affect an entire generation: Uranus spends seven years in a Sign, Neptune spends on average thirteen years, and Pluto on average twenty years. (Tables for the Outer Planet-Sign positions are on page 311.)

However, if Uranus, Neptune or Pluto occupies a significant position by House or Aspect, then their influences may be experienced and expressed far more personally. With regard to Houses I have put together a Planet-House Chart (see page 368) which will help you to approximate the Outer Planets' House positions and meanings in your individual birth chart, once you have determined your Rising Sign.

Aspects are precise angular relationships between one Planet and another. To be sure of your Inner to Outer Planet Aspects you should really have your birth chart properly calculated, for these show how the 'personal you' connects with the 'cosmic you'. But for those of you that just cannot wait to find out how you personally are a 'galactic being', just use the same, but approximate, method described for the Sun, Moon and Inner Planet Aspects under Internal Compatibility on page 100. By way of example, if you had Sun in Gemini and Uranus in that Sign too, your LIVING through COMMUNICATING (Sun in Gemini Keyphrase) would be of an UNUSUAL and INVENTIVE (Uranus Keywords) kind, and your LIFE IN GENERAL would encompass much of what Uranus and Uranus in Gemini stand for.

Likewise, you may determine External Compatibility in the same way as described in the section that follows Internal Compatibility. If, say, you had your Mars in Aries in Opposition to someone else's Neptune in Libra (Aries and Libra being Opposing Signs) you could possibly find out that your GETTING through DOING (Mars in Aries Keyphrase) was CONFUSED and UNDERMINED (*negative* Neptune Keywords because the Opposition is CONFRONTATIONAL) by their Neptune – making your usual style of assertion ineffective, causing you to SURRENDER and use your IMAGINATION and SENSITIVITY more (all *positive* Neptune Keywords).

KEYWORDS

As stated earlier on, the use of Keywords is the most effective bridge between symbolic and literal meaning. Keywords for the Sun, Moon and all Planets are given in CAPITALS on the Introduction page for each Planet. The main Keyword for each Sign (and Planet) is given in the Index on page 329. All keywords (and more) used in this book are given in the Glossary on page 375. Feel free to use the Keywords flexibly, allowing your intuition and common sense to arrive at a fruitful meaning.

Finally, I have noticed that over the years of my being an

astrological consultant there has been a distinct increase in people's sensitivity to and awareness of Outer Planet energies. This I believe is owing to the fact that we have simply (been) evolved to a point where we are more in tune with the very processes of evolution, plus the fact that the evolving forces are themselves being intensified by certain developments within our galaxy, the Milky Way.

Page 310 gives instructions for using the Outer Planet-Sign Tables, and is followed by the Tables themselves and descriptions of the actual Sign positions. Having accomplished all of this, don't forget to enter your Outer Planets information on your ongoing SUN M.A.P.S. LIFE PLAN form, and to include it in your Element Distribution (page 6).

Tables for the
Outer Planet-Sign Positions
for the 20th Century

HOW TO READ THE TABLES FOR THE OUTER PLANETS

Sign-Name Abbreviations

Aries	ARI	Libra	LIB
Taurus	TAU	Scorpio	SCO
Gemini	GEM	Sagittarius	SAG
Cancer	CAN	Capricorn	CAP
Leo	LEO	Aquarius	AQU
Virgo	VIR	Pisces	PIS

Our **EXAMPLE BIRTH TIME AND DATE** is the same as that used for the Inner Planets (see page 18): 22 July 1945 at 4.10pm British Summer Time (BST).

1) Again we convert Birth Time to Greenwich Mean Time (GMT), as necessary. In our example we subtract one hour to give 3.10pm (BST being one hour ahead of GMT).

2) All times given in the Tables are in 24-hour clock time, so, as before, our example becomes 15.10 GMT.

3) Each of the tables for URANUS, NEPTUNE and PLUTO gives the YEAR (year), MONTH (mth), DAY (dy) and TIME (time) when the relevant planet changed or entered a Sign. Using our example then, we look at the URANUS table and see that this time and day fell between 1942 on 15 MAY at 04.13 when URANUS entered the Sign of GEMini, and 1948 on 30 AUGUST at 15.40 when URANUS left GEMini and entered CANcer. At our example time and day, URANUS was in GEMini.

Using the tables for NEPTUNE and PLUTO in the same way as for URANUS will give for our example: NEPTUNE in LIBra, and PLUTO in LEO.

4) After you have looked up the Sign positions of the Outer Planets for the date of birth in question, and consulted the Index on page 329, turn to the pages containing the relevant texts for the Sign positions of URANUS, NEPTUNE and PLUTO.

OUTER PLANET SIGN TABLES

year	mth	dy	time → sign
1900	JAN	1	00.00 → SAG
1904	DEC	20	13.01 → CAP
1912	JAN	30	22.50 → AQU
1912	SEP	4	16.28 → CAP
1912	NOV	12	08.32 → AQU
1919	APR	1	01.20 → PIS
1919	AUG	16	21.51 → AQU
1920	JAN	22	07.45 → PIS
1927	MAR	31	17.14 → ARI
1927	NOV	4	10.41 → PIS
1928	JAN	13	08.10 → ARI
1934	JUN	6	15.41 → TAU
1934	OCT	10	00.07 → ARI
1935	MAR	28	02.37 → TAU
1941	AUG	7	15.30 → GEM
1941	OCT	5	02.00 → TAU
1942	MAY	15	04.13 → GEM
1948	AUG	30	15.40 → CAN
1948	NOV	12	13.20 → GEM
1949	JUN	10	04.04 → CAN
1955	AUG	24	17.57 → LEO
1956	JAN	28	01.50 → CAN
1956	JUN	10	01.42 → LEO
1961	NOV	1	16.00 → VIR
1962	JAN	10	05.54 → LEO
1962	AUG	10	01.13 → VIR
1968	SEP	28	16.01 → LIB
1969	MAY	20	21.21 → VIR
1969	JUN	24	10.26 → LIB
1974	NOV	21	09.30 → SCO
1975	MAY	1	17.41 → LIB
1975	SEP	8	05.05 → SCO
1981	FEB	17	08.42 → SAG
1981	MAR	20	23.23 → SCO
1981	NOV	16	12.07 → SAG
1988	FEB	15	00.07 → CAP
1988	MAY	27	01.20 → SAG
1988	DEC	2	15.33 → CAP
1995	APR	1	12.07 → AQU
1995	JUN	9	01.42 → CAP
1996	JAN	12	07.13 → AQU

year	mth	dy	time → sign
1900	JAN	1	00.00 → GEM
1901	JUL	19	23.45 → CAN
1901	DEC	25	13.20 → GEM
1902	MAY	21	13.33 → CAN
1914	SEP	23	20.20 → LEO
1914	DEC	14	20.13 → CAN
1915	JUL	19	13.30 → LEO
1916	MAR	19	15.22 → CAN
1916	MAY	2	10.38 → LEO
1928	SEP	21	12.00 → VIR
1929	FEB	19	11.21 → LEO
1929	JUL	24	15.07 → VIR
1942	OCT	3	17.10 → LIB
1943	APR	17	10.55 → VIR
1943	AUG	2	19.10 → LIB
1955	DEC	24	15.23 → SCO
1956	MAR	12	01.55 → LIB
1956	OCT	19	09.21 → SCO
1957	JUN	15	20.06 → LIB
1957	AUG	6	08.23 → SCO
1970	JAN	4	19.55 → SAG
1970	MAY	3	01.30 → SCO
1970	NOV	6	16.26 → SAG
1984	JAN	19	02.31 → CAP
1984	JUN	23	01.20 → SAG
1984	NOV	21	13.20 → CAP
1998	JAN	29	02.33 → AQU
1998	AUG	23	00.26 → CAP
1998	NOV	28	01.08 → AQU

year	mth	dy	time → sign
1900	JAN	1	00.00 → GEM
1912	SEP	10	16.00 → CAN
1912	OCT	20	08.30 → GEM
1913	JUL	9	22.11 → CAN
1913	DEC	28	04.23 → GEM
1914	MAY	26	20.42 → CAN
1937	OCT	7	12.26 → LEO
1937	NOV	25	09.13 → CAN
1938	AUG	3	18.20 → LEO
1939	FEB	7	12.59 → CAN
1939	JUN	14	04.50 → LEO
1956	OCT	20	06.57 → VIR
1957	JAN	15	02.19 → LEO
1957	AUG	19	04.35 → VIR
1958	APR	11	14.24 → LEO
1958	JUN	10	19.26 → VIR
1971	OCT	5	05.55 → LIB
1972	APR	17	08.02 → VIR
1972	JUL	30	11.13 → LIB
1983	NOV	5	21.11 → SCO
1984	MAY	18	14.47 → LIB
1984	AUG	28	04.59 → SCO
1995	JAN	17	10.10 → SAG
1995	APR	21	01.38 → SCO
1995	NOV	10	19.40 → SAG

The Outer Planets Through the Twelve Signs of the Zodiac

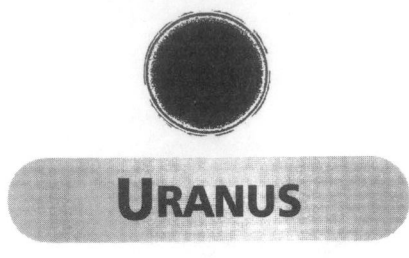

URANUS

Keyword: AWAKENING

Uranus is the force of AWAKENING which often amounts to some form of DISRUPTION taking place. Uranus introduces us to the UNUSUAL, INVENTIVE and INNOVATIVE, pointing the way ahead into the FUTURE, to what is UNIQUE about you as an INDIVIDUAL HUMAN BEING, and ultimately towards the recognition of the goals of the HUMAN RACE itself. This has much to do with the TEAM SPIRIT and OPENNESS that is the mark of FRIENDSHIP and GROUPS. Uranian events and personalities are UNEXPECTED or ERRATIC, ALTERNATIVE or IRREGULAR, for if you could see some of the CHANGES they were bringing you would probably avoid them as they force you to make all things NEW and to face the TRUTH of any given matter.

As well as the truth of any given matter, Uranus shows to what lengths you will go to reach FREEDOM, be it through REBELLION, REFORM or even REVOLUTION. Uranus governs PROCESS, especially that of EVOLUTION. For the same reason it also has rulership over the dynamics and laws of how things operate, which includes therefore SCIENCE, METAPHYSICS, and virtually anything with -OLOGY on the end of it – including ASTROLOGY. Similarly, Uranus concerns all types of CODE and SYMBOLISM.

In your Chart, Uranus by Sign position indicates how some or all of these qualities and powers come to be expressed and experienced by you individually and as a part of a whole seven-year generation of people. Most significantly, it shows the kind of social climate you were born into and consequently became a product of. A more personal interpretation may be arrived at by considering the House position of Uranus as well. For example, Uranus in Cancer in the Second House could mean that Financial (Second House) Security (Cancer) was acquired through Science (Uranus) – that is, a living was earned by practising or teaching some form of science. Or, alternatively, income could be irregular or earned from something unusual.

CRITICAL POINTS IN THE URANUS CYCLE

As Uranus takes 84 years to orbit the Sun, the critical points, which are determined by quartering the cycle, are approximately (due to certain irregularities) at a) 21 years, b) 38–42 years, c) 62–64 years and d) 84 years. a) is when we 'come of age' and (are meant to) break free from parental and familial ties in order to find ourselves as individual beings. b) is the so-called mid-life crisis when we (feel a need to) break away from our domestic or professional routines in an attempt to reconnect with our true purpose in life. c) is around retirement age when we are confronted with a dramatic break in life-style, when we possibly view life in a new way as old age and death approach. d), if you reach it, is actually the symbolic astrological lifetime. At this age you should ideally have arrived at some overall sense of what (your) life is or has been about; otherwise you would be vulnerable to forces or feelings of chaos.

URANUS IN ARIES

Awakening through Doing

You belong to a generation (born during the late 1920s to mid 1930s) whose intention is to re-assert a most basic human right: the freedom to do what you want to do. Such a raw and primary impulse can give rise to extremes: from being obstreperous and reactionary at one end of the scale, to, at the other end, having the courage and stamina to stick to your guns as you fight to establish a new beginning in some field of human endeavour.

Such a straightforward expression of human rights as Aries affords Uranus was evidenced at that time by strikes and labour movements, and going against state rulings on quite a large and uninhibited scale with such activities as bootlegging and gangsters leading society (Uranus governs outsiders and outlaws).

URANUS IN TAURUS

Awakening through Stabilizing

You belong to a generation (born during the mid 1930s to early 1940s) whose intention is to reform attitudes to money and the material side of life generally. You discover that your sense of freedom and the means of promoting new ideas is greatly inhibited by your attachment to material considerations. On the other hand, though, you invent new means of making money in order to further revolutionary concepts and practices. From still another point of view, the idea – or perhaps delusion – that money buys you freedom is a strong possibility. Basically, speedy and experimental Uranus is deprived of much of its essential energy and erratic expression in steady, slow and cautious Taurus.

Like the World War that marks this generation, it is evident in your life that old forms have to be destroyed in order to build anew. World War II also gave rise to enormous advances in the production of goods as part of the war effort, yet at the same time created a very real state of material shortage – hence your concern with money and freedom.

URANUS IN GEMINI

Awakening through Communicating

You belong to a generation (born during the early to late 1940s) whose intention is to reform thinking patterns, and the use of the written and spoken word, or to institute social change and mental outlook through the use of the written and spoken word. Your generation also aims to bring the fruits of science, technology and metaphysics into the everyday sphere of human activity. For example, a computer genius could have this placement. You have an unusual mode of thinking, or at least, you gravitate towards people who do. Brothers and sisters, or the lack of them, would contribute to your standing alone mentally in some way.

Gemini rules primary and secondary education, so freedom of choice was an issue as the class barriers that hitherto prevailed in schools began to be broken down. The great social and attitude changes created by World War II encouraged pupils to question the authority of teachers, giving rise to a more individual mind-set, but also setting a precedent for increased truancy.

 # URANUS IN CANCER

Awakening through Nurturing

You belong to a generation (born during the late 1940s to mid 1950s) whose intention is to reform attitudes towards security and family values. This period heralded both the break-up of the traditional family unit and increased freedom for women. Factors which contributed to the latter included more efficient birth control, and devices to help with grim and time-consuming household chores – both thanks to technology. All this has had far-reaching effects upon ideas of what life is about and has to offer. Significantly, this includes experiencing both the confusion and the pleasure which comes with having a

greater sense of choice. For example, sexual roles and family duties are no longer so clearly defined. This can be seen as a result of changeful and unpredictable Uranus being rather unwelcome in security-conscious Cancer as it breaks us away from the continuity of past customs and standards.

And so on an individual level it is very likely that you are torn between family and friends, or that you are able to skilfully and unselfconsciously blend the two. More often than not, though, there is an oscillating between the security but limitation that the family offers and the open-ended values of your peer group.

 # URANUS IN LEO

Awakening through Creating

You belong to a generation (born between the mid 1950s and early 1960s) whose intention is to reform attitudes towards romantic involvement and creative self-expression. This arose from the experimentation in these areas of life that were occurring then – especially as seen in modern art, beatniks, Jack Kerouac, Alan Ginsberg, James Dean, and the birth of the Swinging Sixties.

There is a stubbornness here, marked by an insistence upon going your own way on the one hand, and a strong sense of being in a distinctive kind of creative accord with your peers on the other. You sow

the seeds of self-rule.

The use of art – be it audio, visual or something like cooking – began at this time to reach the masses, and put them in touch with unusual or foreign styles. Advertising really started to take off – waking people up to the wealth of sights, tastes and sounds that were previously the realm of the bohemian or esoteric. And, of course, there was more television – and in colour too. Leonine dramatization used technology to take it to new heights – and eventually new depths as it swamped and replaced more natural forms of entertainment and recreation.

 # URANUS IN VIRGO

Awakening through Analysing

You belong to a generation (born during the 1960s) whose intention is to reform work methods and attitudes towards health. During this period, technology revolutionized the employment situation with automation and computers. You therefore are quite likely to encounter difficulties and sudden changes on your own employment scene as new requirements arise and certain occupations become obsolete. You may wish to modernize office systems or overthrow bureaucracy.

As Virgo, at least on one level, is about being clean and correct, a profound rebellion against such values was one of the main thrusts of the continuation of the Swinging Sixties. You, your generation, and the period in which you were born, comprised a strong reaction to what it regarded as middle-class fussiness and narrowness – witness Punk. On the other hand, however, Virgo may have got the upper hand with such licentiousness being kept at a distance.

URANUS IN LIBRA

Awakening through Relating

You belong to a generation (born during the late 1960s to mid 1970s) whose intention is to reform attitudes towards marriage, relating and social conduct in general. If you have a strong degree of social conscience, you will want to find some way of changing the laws and principles that guide and govern the people. Initially, this all may find itself being expressed in a somewhat chaotic fashion as you are oblivious to the social norms that you are awkwardly attempting to overthrow. The sharp increase in divorce rates that occurred during this time was one expression and cause of this. But this was all a necessary part of the process of realization – and led to your putting together your own highly personalized social philosophy.

The down side to Uranus in Libra is where the righteous reform of Uranus is neutralized by what can be the colourless sense of social nicety that Libra is sometimes prone to. The end result is political correctness – a strange animal which tries to enforce equality at the expense of limiting free expression.

When you can avoid this contradiction in terms that is the major pitfall of Uranus in Libra, you and your generation are very alive to the fact – or can be easily awakened to it – that a single powerful idea can change the face of society, or even the world.

URANUS IN SCORPIO

Awakening through Desiring

You belong to a generation (born during the mid 1970s to early 1980s) whose intention was to reform attitudes towards sexuality and intimacy, as well as other kinds of hidden power. During this period, these elements of life started to reach a critical state, be it the advent of dangerously defiant sexual freedom or a nuclear power station blowing up. Mount St Helens, the volcano in Washington state, USA, also blew its top in 1980, and right at the time when Uranus opposed the Sun in the Fixed Earth Sign of Taurus! Because of all this, your generation is basically having to wake up to what power actually is.

During the process of this awakening, some quite horrific expressions of the abuse – or is it just the misunderstanding – of power and sexuality have arisen. The most obvious is Aids. There has also been the waking up to how science has abused its power – the damage to the ozone layer, deforestation, the greenhouse effect, etc. But it is the way of Scorpio to bring matters into awareness through crisis. In other words, desires attract crises, and crises force an awakening. For this reason, more than most, you have the potential to wake others up to what is really happening – which to most people means that which is about to happen!

URANUS IN SAGITTARIUS

Awakening through Seeking

You belong to a generation (born during the first five years of the twentieth century or the early to late 1980s) whose intention is to reform religious, legal, cultural and academic attitudes. As an individual you could either be on the receiving end in that you fall foul of and rebel against these aspects of life as you encounter them, or (and possibly as a consequence of this) you seek to force changes in one or more of these areas. Whether you are conscious of it or not, a recognition of universal laws and the freedom to believe in what you wish is what fires your own convictions.

An example of some of the effects of the later Uranus in Sagittarius period has been the retrial and subsequent release of people convicted for rebellious acts (terrorism). These occurrences, plus the ongoing farce of law not imposing any order, has bred, and is still breeding, in people a profound distrust of the legal system – and the Church. What is really trying to emerge – through the efforts of your generation as it comes of age – is a true knowledge of what is right or true and what is wrong or false. The merging or colliding of Science and Religion is a significant issue beginning at this time.

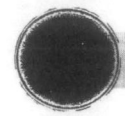 ## URANUS IN CAPRICORN

Awakening through Building

You belong to a generation (born between 1905 and 1912, or during the late 1980s to mid 1990s) whose intention was or is to reform business and governmental practices. There is an inherent danger of an apparently double standard with your generation because the loosening of authority's grip on the status quo can undermine one's own position (witness Mikhail Gorbachev's demise during the latter period). In other words, you are caught with having to create a balance between conserving old and trusted standards, and introducing new and potentially disruptive ones.

The earlier period just before World War I could be seen as a time of destabilization following the end of the Victorian era. This of course presaged the horror and chaos of the Great War, which in itself was largely because of the abuse of authority. It is as if the second and recent transit of Uranus through Capricorn is saying, almost poetically, that politicians and governments can no longer command such blind and stupid obedience. Hopefully, as this generation comes of age the world will begin building its institutions on new and more humanitarian and psychologically-aware foundations.

 ## URANUS IN AQUARIUS

Awakening through Liberating

You belong to a generation (born between 1912 and 1920, or during the late 1990s to the first years of the twenty-first century) whose intention was or is to reform and shed light upon the human condition. This means that the very essence of human nature is what concerns you deep down. Negatively or unconsciously, this could just amount to feeling odd and a bit of a misfit – simply because Humanity as a whole is off-track and at odds with its true nature. Positively, though, you are aware of the importance of individuality, brother/sisterhood and the essential uniqueness, freedom and inventiveness of the human being.

The first period bore witness to the revolutionary thrust of Uranus travelling through its own Sign in the form of the Great War and the Russian Revolution. In the first case, human beings had to be used as cannon-fodder before we stood up and noticed that this was not what human beings and human rights are for and about. The second case was archetypally Uranian/Aquarian in that it was revolution in the classic sense: the liberators and radicals of the day becoming the future oppressors and conservatives.

This second period should and will be a lot more positive, conscious and creative, with amazing happenings to match – occurring above and below, within and without – that will jog us into remembering what Humanity and human nature actually are: sensitivity as an essential quality rather than a painful liability; consideration for all as the only way of continuing to exist rather than merely as some lofty ideal.

 ## URANUS IN PISCES

Awakening through Accepting

You belong to a generation (born during the 1920s) whose intention was to awaken to the mysteries of life and the unconscious and thereby gain some release from and acceptance of the mundane. By and large however, this was expressed in the rather dissolute and 'anything goes' atmos-phere into which you were born (the Roaring Twenties). Consequently, unless you have taken definite steps to look at the mystical side of life, you are culturally inclined to avoid facing the music – you would have been too busy dancing to it! But after World War I no one could really blame you.

Neptune

Keyword: UNIFYING

Neptune is the realm of the SPIRITUAL, the UNIVERSAL, and the ETHEREAL. It is the 'NAGUAL', which means everything that cannot be named, in the sense that there is something 'in there' and 'out there' that is MYSTERIOUS and MYSTICAL – and way beyond the rational in the normally accepted sense of the word.

Neptune is where all is AT ONE. This 'in-touchness' of Neptune therefore gives rise to feeling more than what just the five senses are capable of. Such PSYCHIC powers can amount to anything from ENLIGHTENMENT to DELUSION, depending on how firmly feet are kept on the ground. One could view the saying 'We are all from a grander place' as a key to Mankind's SALVATION or as just a PIPE-DREAM.

So wherever Neptune is in your Chart you will find SENSITIVITY and IMAGINATION, whether it is expressed as a BLIND-SPOT or a VISION; as ESCAPE or RELEASE; as GIVING UP or SURRENDER; as SACRIFICE or as being a VICTIM; as VAGUENESS or SUBTLETY; as COMPASSION or PITY (the former includes respect, the latter does not). Neptune is the soul in the hard cold world in the sense that it is SUFFERING. How conscious that suffering is proves critical, for it can be regarded as a necessary experience as one seeks TRANSCENDENCE of how and what everything seems to be (through CONFINEMENT, HUMILITY, MEDITATION, HYPNOSIS, ASCETICISM, HEALING, ARTISTIC INSPIRATION, MUSIC, etc.). On the other hand, suffering can seem a pointless struggle and relief is sought through DRUGS, ALCOHOL, GLAMOUR, FANTASY, RELIGIOUS FERVOUR, ROMANTIC LOVE, FILMS, etc.

So Neptune has a lot to do with ALTERED STATES of consciousness. But everything depends upon the state of consciousness that is actually seeking to alter itself! Perhaps the root meaning of the word GIDDY – our simplest and earliest means of altering consciousness – points to the exquisitely two-sided nature of this Planet. It comes from the Old English gidig, which means INSANE – or LIKE GOD.

In the end, though, because Neptune is all about there being NO BOUNDARIES, it is quite difficult to draw distinct demarcation lines between one meaning and another, or where you end and someone else begins. How you experience Neptune in your Chart therefore has much to do with whether you find its DISSOLVING influence UPLIFTING or CONFUSING, CONSOLING or UNDERMINING. The Sign position shows how your generation translated these qualities. A more personal interpretation can be arrived at by ascertaining the House position of Neptune. For example, Neptune in Scorpio in the Sixth House could mean that Health and Work (Sixth House) are powerful and intensely (Scorpio) sensitive issues and/or that the use of psychic abilities are an integral part of them; or that learning humility through/at work and service are very necessary steps in one's spiritual development.

CRITICAL POINTS IN THE NEPTUNE CYCLE

As Neptune takes 165 years to orbit the Sun and critical points are determined by quartering the cycle, there is usually only one critical point – at 41–42 years, that is unless you reach your mid 80s which is the midpoint. As 41–42 is also the midpoint of the Uranus Cycle, this adds to the confusion of this time. In effect Neptune is saying 'what is it that you are missing, overlooking or being deluded by?' At this time you can – or have to – get far more in touch with the subtle and sensitive dimensions of your personality and of life in general; if you do not you can severely complicate matters that lie in the future. If you should reach the midpoint, which is also near the complete cycle of Uranus (84 years), then you are either enlightened or on painkillers – or somewhere in between!

NEPTUNE IN GEMINI
Unifying through Communicating

You belong to the Neptunian generation born between 1887 and 1902. You therefore came into being during a time that sought to express spiritual ideas and mystical visions in the written and spoken word – or tried to find rational explanations for them. When coming of age, such inspiration was probably best expressed through the Great War poets, like Wilfred Owen and Rupert Brooke.

NEPTUNE IN CANCER
Unifying through Nurturing

You belong to the Neptunian generation born between 1901 and 1916. You therefore came into being during a time which engendered a profound sentiment for Nature, family and all things concerning one's roots or origins. There are strong psychic tendencies in evidence, which when misguided gave rise to an unhealthy yearning for what was or what never can be.

Such nostalgia is hardly surprising and very under-standable considering that to a large degree it would have stemmed from the monumental loss of life during World War I, robbing families of their young men. Perhaps such suffering was, from Neptune's long-term viewpoint, a necessary spiritual and collectively emotional landmark for Humanity to refer back to, again and again, taking the form of such things as Remembrance Sunday. In other words, unification is nurtured through time and memory.

NEPTUNE IN LEO
Unifying through Creating

You belong to the Neptunian generation born between 1914 and 1929. You therefore came into being during a period that gave birth to glamour and good times – the Roaring Twenties. Although this gave rise to great fun and artistic creativity, with the birth of Jazz and Blues and Hollywood, it also created a very unreal sense of what love and emotion are about.

Be that as it may, creative inspiration is what Neptune in Leo is all about, and the moral and psychological aspects are something which Leo tends to regard as inhibitory to the creative process. Stopping too much to ponder the rights and wrongs or political correctness of things does indeed diminish the richness of Art.

This period also witnessed the Russian Revolution (1917) which in Neptune in Leo terms means, quite appropriately, the Dissolution of Royalty. Maybe this set a trend for the whole century with one Royal Family after another having to give up much or all of its power and influence.

For you as an individual this all points to your having a sense of the dramatic flow of feelings, but the price can be that of ultimate humiliation.

NEPTUNE IN VIRGO

Unifying through Analysing

You belong to the Neptunian generation born between 1928 and 1943. You therefore came into being during a time when economic chaos prevailed, resulting from the prodigality of the previous Neptune in Leo generation of the Roaring Twenties. And so you were instilled with a rather parsimonious attitude towards life, along with a distrust of spiritual notions and wild promises of better days.

Confusion over what actually constitutes health, along with the first chemical contamination of food, also arose during this period. We are still paying to this day for this misconception. The damage to the subtle nature of the human body, especially the immune system, was overlooked by the black-and-white, strictly logical and 'efficient' approach of Virgo. This serious misuse of chemicals (which Neptune governs) and also of synthetic drugs, which members of this generation

were either the perpetrators or victims of, unleashed elemental forces upon an environment where they do not belong – ours.

Essentially, your generation has the task of employing ideals to more practical ends. After all, the analytical quality that is Virgo is not that conducive to the free flow of Neptune. However, such Virgoan separating and categorizing is the very necessary discriminatory process that ultimately makes sure that what is eventually unified – be it in the form of a work of art or a spiritual philosophy – has been done so painstakingly and thoroughly, and not in a vain Neptunian hope that it will somehow hold up. In other words, you should be aware that preparation is the key to perfection. If you are not, then you would be rather inclined to give up. On the other hand, preparation should not be allowed to go on interminably so that nothing is ever finished.

NEPTUNE IN LIBRA

Unifying through Relating

You belong to the Neptunian generation born between 1942 and 1957. As this generation came of age, the whole Libran realm of love and marriage, art and music, and society in general, came under Neptune's subtle spell. This gave rise to an increased sensitivity to relating and sexual equality, with confusion and soaring divorce rates not far behind. Whether or not you see yourself as an active part of it, or regard it as a good or bad thing, this was the 'love' generation who marched for peace, gathered in great numbers at music festivals, experimented with psychedelic drugs, and embarked upon a more universal quest for spiritual meaning – or for an escape from mundane reality.

The period itself, being the end of conflict and the

post-war years, gives very appropriate form to the essential peace-making meaning of Neptune in Libra. However, it is just here where we see also the downside of Neptune in action. This is the old cliché of good intentions paving the road to hell. Libra is not known for its profundity, being a Sign that tends towards elegance of form and appearance rather than uncompromising inner convictions.

And so you are culturally inclined to fall in love with love, and having to repent at leisure. All in all, though, gentleness is your very basic trait, but as such can be reacted to by more dynamic or aggressive sides of your personality (or of others) that other Planet-Sign positions indicate.

 # NEPTUNE IN SCORPIO

Unifying through Desiring

You belong to the Neptunian generation born between the mid-1950s and 1970. As this generation came of age, established musical forms and the use of drugs took on more self-destructive and sexually explicit undertones. The seeking of highs became heavier, and also involved the underworld of crime more. The lack of Mankind's spiritual awareness which had been prevalent for some time became a more critical issue, with material status symbols becoming gods, and sexual diseases – especially Aids – becoming more threatening as the result of a lack of awareness as to the true and subtle nature of what intimacy means. The challenge to your generation is great indeed: to prevent degeneration. After all, encoded in your being is an intuitive sense of how sex and power operate in a true and healthy manner.

Considering the permissive period in which you were born – what we could simply call the Rock 'n' Roll Years – it is not surprising that there is little sense of a need to set any limits upon your desires, except perhaps in the form of death itself. But then Scorpio never does anything by halves – like forcing us into strong feelings of compassion as the result of having to behold the young, talented or beautiful being cut down in their prime. To paraphrase Oscar Wilde, nothing unifies human beings so much as the prospect of death. The question is, will that unified mass be a panicking mob or a harmonious and spiritually attuned group?

 # NEPTUNE IN SAGITTARIUS

Unifying through Seeking

You belong to the Neptunian generation born between 1970 and the mid 1980s. During this period, confusion was experienced with regard to what is right or wrong. As this generation comes of age, the underlying reason for this manifests as a want of distinction between the Law of Man and the Law of God.

In other words, this generation, and the time they are growing up in, has to contact a more spiritual and less material, yet at the same time practical, means of directing human morals and appetites. A real and combined sense of the divine and the quantum begins to emerge now.

By the end of this millennium and during the beginning of the next, members of this generation will start showing the world in no uncertain terms the magnificence and wonder that is Life on Earth. This will not only include human beings, but how we subtly interact with the animal and vegetable kingdoms in ways that hitherto would have been regarded as fantastic. The merging of world religions will also begin to take place, which will mean a far more flexible and accepting idea of the individual's image of god/goddess or concept of the Divine. This will, however, necessitate a reaching of fever pitch amongst fundamentalists as they burn themselves out.

NEPTUNE IN CAPRICORN

Unifying through Building

You belong to the Neptunian generation born between 1984 and 1998. You therefore came into being during a time when humanity officially began to realize how subtle but very powerful forces affect our Earthly environment – and how we could all be doomed if we did not begin to pull together as a species. This time sees the beginning of world government with regard to global environmental issues and the ascertaining of what spirituality and sensitivity mean in the most practical sense. Disillusionment with existing governmental agencies and figures also begins to increase exponentially now.

The most important aspect of this period for everyone living through it is that we are finding that getting things right on Planet Earth cannot be done overnight – yet it has to be started today! There is no longer any time or room for woolly New Age theories and practices. At this time there has to be a very real means of enlightening ourselves. Capricorn rules the skeleton, and this points to the possibility that 'feeling it in one's bones' means more than we thought. In other words, it will become an established fact – during this time and as this generation matures – that everyone is carrying around in their bone marrow access codes to the real reality of living on this Planet. But before this kind of realization can occur, many a false structure will have to fade away. Neptune in Capricorn is rather like having to build brand new sandcastles as the incoming tide dissolves away the old ones. Your generation is specifically designed to perform this formidable task.

NEPTUNE IN AQUARIUS

Unifying through Liberating

You belong to the Neptunian generation born between 1998 and 2012. You therefore came into being during a time when humanity had barely avoided terminating itself. Out of this crisis and the realizations born of it, your generation truly heralds the New Age – the Age of Aquarius. This arrives at the very end of this period, but /==the beginning of it will see the human race sharply divided between those who see the Light because they had prepared themselves to do so, and those that cannot because they had not. In real terms, this could see the one ascending to a far more enlightened sense of reality, and the other descending into mental and/or physical disorder.

Put quite simply, the best way to unify is to liberate. This means that when anyone attains a true sense of what freedom is, they then become automatically attuned to and united with fellow human beings. It all has to do with critical mass. When a certain number of individuals reach liberation – from fear, basically – then this rapidly 'infects' the rest of civilization. 'When the whole World can weep in each others' arms and fall asleep, we'll wake up to a bright new day.'

PLUTO

Keyword: EMPOWERING

Pluto is the SEED of POWER within. This can amount to a sense of DESTINY or just an OBSESSION. All this can be seen as a deep inner programme, rather like an acorn is the blueprint and POTENTIAL of an oak tree. Pluto is a force to be reckoned with, for being the Lord of the Underworld, it urges you to PENETRATE to HIDDEN CAUSES and more PROFOUND levels of consciousness. It is the power of DEATH and TRANSFORMATION and of SEXU-ALITY and the SECRET of BIRTH and REBIRTH and many other things. So Pluto either REGENERATES or DESTROYS – nothing in between. More than any other Planetary force, it has the power to HARM or HEAL – and by the same token it shows your DEPTH and INSIGHT.

Pluto's main modes of operation are those of INTENSIFICATION (of what must and shall be) and ELIMINATION (of what is outworn). In other words, in order for your destiny to fulfil itself there are certain times of your life and parts of your personality that in a very UNCOMPROMISING fashion force you to connect with the INNER TRUTH of your being in particular and of life in general, often by destroying anything that is getting in the way of this. Unfortunately, most of us have been led to believe that it is a TABOO to own and express such powers. So what Pluto so frequently has to eliminate is our very resistance to our own power, something that was MANIPULATED out of us a long time ago in order to control us. HORROR is what is commonly used to keep us fearful of the power within, rather like the enormous three-headed dog, Cerberus, who guarded the gates of HELL. But 'hell' can be seen as simply the underside of life that actually feeds the topside, just as it is the slimy, rotting, creepy-crawly infested earth that nourishes the flowers and trees. Ponder on this.

The Sign position of Pluto will give some idea of how you experience – individually or as part of a generation – some or all of these qualities. To get a more personal sense determine the House position of Pluto. For example, Pluto in Gemini in the First House could express itself as a powerfully (Pluto) communicative (Gemini) physical presence (First House). Laurence Olivier had this placement. This could also mean a penetrating look that is also hard to see through.

CRITICAL POINTS IN THE PLUTO CYCLE

As Pluto takes 248 years to orbit the Sun and critical points are determined by quartering the cycle, there is usually only one critical point. This occurs, owing to the very irregular orbit of Pluto, as early as your late 40s (which is usual for twentieth-century births), or some years later. At this time then, you are liable to be subject to pressures that force you to let go of the past in some way. The chances are that you will blame this necessity on something that is apparently outside of your control – like the government or the climate (economic, meteorological, etc.). Really, though, it is something deep inside of you that has got itself stuck, so you will need to dig around to find out what it is. As a result of rooting out what is holding you back, you then find that a previously unseen door of opportunity opens for you.

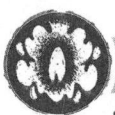

PLUTO IN GEMINI

Empowering through Communicating

You are a member of the Plutonian generation (1884–1913) which witnessed the birth of new and powerful communications and transport, like the telephone, automobile and aeroplane. Whole books could be written (and they probably have been) about the effects these devices have had upon human beings, individually and collectively. It probably won't be until the next transit of Pluto through Gemini 248 years later that we will have a true perspective upon the gigantic impact they have made on us.

For you personally, a great deal can depend on how much you appreciate and involve yourself with one form of communication or the other. The most common form, the spoken and written word, will have determined how you have fared in life – possibly far more than you think. The saying 'Sticks and stones may break my bones but words will never hurt me' could not be less true with Pluto in Gemini. A poorly considered or ill-timed remark can affect a whole lifetime. The irony is that someone with more Gemini than Pluto probably first said this – that is, they made light of the fact that words and thoughts are powerful things. Conversely, not speaking up when you really feel you should can have similarly destructive effects. If, on the other hand, you have been heedful and aware of word- and thought-power, you will probably be dearly remembered for what you have said – and what you did not say.

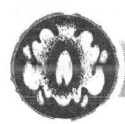

PLUTO IN CANCER

Empowering through Nurturing

You are a member of the Plutonian generation (1912–1939) which witnessed World War I and the beginnings of World War II. Essentially this was a struggle for power and omnipotence which threatened the security to which humanity had hitherto grown accustomed, and transformed our concept of personal and national security for good – or ill.

The destruction of homes by bombing – never before witnessed in known history – and the wholesale murder of family members (especially young males) is something that we should all ponder on. Ethnological races come under the rulership of Cancer, hence the holocaust and the so-called ethnic cleansing that began to peak at the close of this period – and is still with us. For you as a member of the Pluto in Cancer generation, this will have affected you in a deeply unconscious way. This does not mean to say that you are unaware of your intense concern for domestic, family and racial security – far from it – but the degree to which this impinges upon your entire outlook on life is something that has possibly influenced you more than you think.

A statistical effect is witnessed in the enormous increase in home-ownership since that time. But the psychological impact has been one of keeping your deepest feelings to yourself, which curiously can undermine the very feelings that domestic security is supposed to nurture. But when this point is realized, often after some subsequent threat to home and family, you excel at keeping intimately in touch with kith and kin. And this is so very important, for a failure to achieve this is one of the factors behind the post-war demise of the traditional family structure.

A deep and powerful sense and expression of caring is your destiny's keynote. A disenchantment with war is your generation's legacy. Pluto in Cancer brought home to us the very existence of power – used and misused, personal and collective – synchronistic with the discovery of Pluto itself in 1930.

PLUTO IN LEO

Empowering through Creating

You are a member of the Plutonian generation (1937–1958) which, apart from many other things, saw World War II and the advent of nuclear power and the atomic bomb. All this shifted the world into a process of transformation from which it can no more retreat than a nuclear power station can be closed down overnight. This transformative power which forces us to contact the hidden origins of all things – not least of all our very selves – is now unleashed, and your personal role in this global psychodrama is very real if you want it to be – or even if you don't.

What is meant by this last statement? Well, Pluto is the Planet of Power and Influence, and Leo is the Sign in which the individual expresses his or her personal strength and impact on others, be it locally or globally. In other words, when anything powerful is discovered it just has to be given some form of expression – good or bad. Metaphorically, this is rather like an actor with a fine strong voice who makes sure that it is heard by as many people as possible.

In real, and super-dramatic terms, when Pluto entered the fixed and fiery Sign of the Lion, such unbridled desire to express power culminated in the first atomic bomb being exploded. For those of you who like word-magic, the word 'pollution' is an anagram of Pluto and Lion! And there has been more fall-out than the obvious kind thanks to this and other events occurring during this time. The more subtle, yet equally far-reaching, effect is that of the realization within your generation of an increased sense that everyone should count for something in this world, should not just be an 'also ran', and that everyone should have his or her 'fifteen minutes of fame'. Obviously this is not the case for all of you, nor is it possible, but it has been a prevalent enough phenomenon to influence the collective consciousness and subsequent generations. What manifested as everyone from every class having the chance to become a star (Beatlemania), or as an unhealthy and even criminally destructive desire to be noticed, is now slowly becoming a conviction that an individual's unique creative input and output *does* affect the whole world. So make yours bright and good! In you it has been made known that human beings have the power of the Cosmos coursing through them – and so you need to become increasingly aware of Cosmic Intent or Divine Will.

PLUTO IN VIRGO

Empowering through Analysing

You are a member of the Plutonian generation (1956–1972) which grew up into a world where revolutionary changes began to take place with regard to the food that we eat and the way we work. Processing and pre-packaging of food has led to impurities and health hazards. Work has been automated and depersonalized. The introduction of more efficient means of birth control gave rise to an illusion of sexual inviolability when quite the opposite (sexual abuse) has increased, or rather has been brought to the surface. All these matters were in fact just crises waiting to happen so that they could be – or, rather, had to be – duly dealt with.

You personally, as a member of this generation, are a bristle in a gigantic new broom that will sweep clean. At some point you may well get obsessed over work and health as a deep sense of service and purity arises from your unconscious mind. Needless to say, an obsession is an unhealthy thing for it prevents you from seeing matters objectively.

That Virgoan monster, bureaucracy, unfortunately grew in size during this period, especially with the increased power of computers. This Sign's negative inclination to systemize as much as possible has led to a diminishing of personal touch and bedside manner. Your individual experience of this could be either that you are a part of it, or that you feel alienated and consequently inadequate. In both cases there is a need to step back and study the possibility that systemizing things is a way of keeping heavy or uncomfortable feelings at bay – rather like tidying a room gives one a feeling of order. But Pluto is concerned with the fact that the only true order is that which is deep within one's own being – and through your generation and its influence it will make this point only too clear as systems start to break down. And you begin to find profound solutions to profound problems – probably by having to.

 ## PLUTO IN LIBRA

Empowering through Relating

You are a member of the Plutonian generation (1971–1984) which grew up into a world where revolutionary changes began to take place with regard to marriage and social values. Being a child of a single-parent family would be a typical example of your generation's social conditions. In any event, you grew up in an atmosphere of great uncertainty as to what social justice and the social norm were. Essentially, your generation are re-writing the social rule-book, which unavoidably means being without, or refusing to observe, the old rule-book.

During this time therefore, social disorder became more prevalent. Crime and a lack of common decency increased. But new social values were birthing as this apparent deterioration occurred. Or, quite simply, an intense awareness of the importance of sound existing social values began to arise.

This period also saw an increase in the general use of psychotherapy and counselling. Whereas hitherto only certain strata of society had regarded such a practice as necessary, people who previously would have frowned at unloading their private lives on a stranger, came to recognize the value of looking beyond the apparent state of a relationship or attitude. The effects that this is going to have in the future, especially when your generation comes of age, will be profound. The majority of superficial social airs and graces will cease to exist. For example, saying 'How are you?' won't be said unless a genuine reply is expected. This is already beginning to happen.

That other Libran subject, fashion, also takes on a more intense aspect. Even the term 'power-dressing' came into being at this time. Possibly though, fashion – and this includes art and entertainment – experienced a few death throes as styles became simply rehashes of previous ones. Also, Plutonian obsession with Libran looks gave rise to the more common occurrence of anorexia and other so-called slimming diseases. It is as if this time, and its generation's influence that followed, marked the end of fashion as we know it. Pluto in Libra is a contradiction in terms in some respects for it is a case of deep and profound inner content trying to express itself through superficial form and appearance. Pluto should win in that no amount of haute couture, face-lifts or breast implants can hide or prevent the outing of inner and biological realities.

 ## PLUTO IN SCORPIO

Empowering through Desiring

You are a member of the Plutonian generation (1983–1995) which witnesses the inevitable consequence of mankind's mishandling of power and resources. During this period crises threatened our very existence, and it is only through a true and deep understanding of what power and transformation actually mean that we avert disaster and deliver ourselves into a new era. Pluto is Scorpio's Ruling Planet, and so this is rather like a power-ful machine performing on a track designed especially for it.

As a member of this generation you can be particu-larly uncompromising in your manner of expression. Even Pluto's trump card, death itself, has been used as a means of creating a profound influence through the apparently inexplicable phenomenon of 'cot-death'. This has been put down to things like urine reacting with certain types of bedding materials to give off a fatal gas. However, from Pluto's point of view such deaths were 'intended' by the babies themselves. From less esoteric points of view this would appear absurd, but the very thrust of Pluto in Scorpio is that of driving home the fact that there are not only deep and hidden reasons for things, but that there is intent and intelligence beneath the earth, before the womb, and beyond the grave. Witness, during this time, the plethora of Near Death Experiences and the Crop Circle phenomenon which increased so profoundly. The whole world knows of them – but not much about them.

It has been said that, astrologically, no planet is more like the Earth than Pluto. The deep power and mystery, the cycles of decay and rebirth, are, amongst other things, qualities they share. And so it is the Earthly Powers that during this period we begin to understand, assist and utilize; the generation born of it will take this further as they mature. The recognition of the true meaning of Sacred Sites around the globe, and the reactivating of them, is one example of this.

Potentially, your generation has a far greater sense of the power that lies within, and an equally great opportunity and necessity for expressing it and using it. Whatever you desire shall be attained – so you have to be very careful what you desire.

Last, but not least, Aids, brewed previously by Uranus and Neptune in Scorpio (see pages 317 and 322) manifested during this period, Pluto and Scorpio being both the Planet and Sign of Sex and Hidden Causes.

PLUTO IN SAGITTARIUS

Empowering through Seeking

You are a member of the Plutonian generation (1995–2008) which eventually sees a coming together of the essence of all valid world religions, and the demise of the false or negative ones as they burn out self-destructively. This marks the birth of a world religion which transforms our attitude to life through a combination of science and mysticism.

One of the most important agents in this process will be the realization of the true nature and significance of certain ancient civilizations. Chief among these will be the Mayans, a culture of pyramid city states that flourished for thousands of years and apparently came to an abrupt halt a thousand years ago. The Mayans venerated (and those that still exist continue to venerate) two things: the Sun and Time. Furthermore, they are connected by the phenomenon of Sunspot Cycles, and the Mayans, through an intimate awareness of them, were, and are, able to understand and predict the ebb and flow of Earthly and Human processes.

What all this means is that during Pluto's transit through Sagittarius we shall discover what is really determining our destiny. And then by learning to relate to it – the Sun – we may secure a positive fate. What would have previously appeared abstruse and mystical will be seen to be linked to scientific fact. Already, for example, a formula for everything has been scientifically discovered. In the process of determining this formula, two numbers, 10 and 26, kept occurring. The Mayan Sacred Calendar – their main means for plotting the Sun's 'life' – comprises 260 units, the product of those two numbers.

It could be said that seeking will find more than we bargained for during this time. Some people will hotly resist and deny new discoveries – particularly concerning public figures and archaeological finds – but others, like Olympic runners with their torches, will take them all the way to lighting the flame of the future. And it is those born of this generation that will run the final leg.

INDEX FOR SUN, MOON AND PLANETS THROUGH THE SIGNS

PLANETS

ZODIAC SIGNS	Page	SUN • LIVING	MOON • SECURITY	MERCURY • THINKING	VENUS • LOVING	MARS • GETTING	JUPITER • GROWING	SATURN • TESTED	URANUS • AWAKENING	NEPTUNE • UNIFYING	PLUTO • EMPOWERING
ARIES • DOING	124	150	176	202	228	254	280	315	–	–	
TAURUS • STABILIZING	126	152	178	204	230	256	282	315	–	–	
GEMINI • COMMUNICATING	128	154	180	206	232	258	284	315	320	325	
CANCER • NURTURING	130	156	182	208	234	260	286	316	320	325	
LEO • CREATING	132	158	184	210	236	262	288	316	320	326	
VIRGO • ANALYSING	134	160	186	212	238	264	290	316	321	326	
LIBRA • RELATING	136	162	188	214	240	266	292	317	321	327	
SCORPIO • DESIRING	138	164	190	216	242	268	294	317	322	327	
SAGITTARIUS • SEEKING	140	166	192	218	244	270	296	317	322	328	
CAPRICORN • BUILDING	142	168	194	220	246	272	298	318	323	–	
AQUARIUS • LIBERATING	144	170	196	222	248	274	300	318	323	–	
PISCES • ACCEPTING	146	172	198	224	250	276	302	318	–	–	

Your Ascendant or Rising Sign

The Ascendant or Rising Sign is the Sign that is rising on the Eastern Horizon at your Time and Place of Birth. The quality of that Sign, and of any Planet that might be placed around or in the area just below the Eastern Horizon (an area called the First House) symbolizes the manner of your SELF-PRESENTATION and SELF-EXPRESSION. It is your individual window on the world, and also the world's window on you as an individual. It is a very important astrological indication because it shows how you are seeking to establish an IDENTITY and what or who you identify with. It can also describe your APPEARANCE and PHYSICAL LOOKS. The Sun is what your life is about – the Rising Sign (and any First House Planet) represents the apparent way that you go about living it.

The qualities that characterize each Rising Sign are described in the pages following the Tables for looking up your Rising Sign (starting on page 336). In each case, the Planet which is said to rule your Rising Sign is also mentioned, and you are referred to the Sign and House position of that Planet. This Planet is called your RULING PLANET for it rules the whole of your Chart and carries great weight and significance. (This is not to be confused with the Planet which rules your Sun-Sign.) With regard to its Sign position you simply refer to the text concerning that Planet-Sign position. The House position refers to where any Planet, not just your Ruling Planet, is in the sky in relation to the Horizon. In turn this will affect where, in what area of your life, you *experience* that Planet's influence. In order to determine precisely the House positions, your Chart should be properly drawn up by an experienced astrologer. Indeed, to be absolutely sure of your Rising Sign you should use a similar method. There are many astrological computing services available nowadays who will calculate exactly both your Rising Sign and House positions for little cost. (See Further Information on page 379).

For this reason I have not given detailed descriptions of Planet-House positions. However, as the House position can quite dramatically affect your experience and expression of any particular Planet, I have put together a Chart which you will find on page 368. This Planet-House Chart enables you at a glance to discover in what field and mode any particular Planet is most likely to be felt and seen. I believe that you will find this very revealing, especially in cases where you find that a part of your personality that you thought was a secret is indicated astrologically. Or that a trait which is actually your own (that is, in your Chart) is seen to belong to, or is experienced through, someone close to you, like a partner or child!

Finally, in considering your Rising Sign, I also look at your *SETTING SIGN*, which is always opposite to your Rising Sign, as the Western Horizon is always opposite the Eastern Horizon. Your Setting Sign is important for it signifies the kind of people and *RELATIONSHIPS* that you attract. For this reason, quite often your *PARTNER* will actually have the Sun in that Sign, or the Moon or a number of Planets. In addition, I also refer you to the Planet which rules that Sign – the SETTING RULER – as this will tell you more about the types of partnership and partner you have. In both cases, simply refer to the page where that particular Planet's or Sign's qualities are described. Your Setting Sign and the Planet that rules it can also describe a part of your *SHADOW*, that dimension of your personality that you tend to see in others because for some reason you find it hard to accept or own as being in yourself – be it positive or negative.

DETERMINING YOUR RISING SIGN

In order to work out your Rising Sign you need to know your Birth Time. If you do not know this already, then the obvious people to ask are, if possible, your mother, father, near relatives or anyone else who was around at the time. Even if you get a vague response or an absolute blank, in my experience it pays to do a little prodding and probing. Ask whether it was day or night, near a mealtime, when it was in relation to family going to or coming home from work or school. You'll be surprised how this can jog their memories. Failing this, in many countries (but not England) it is the law to enter the time of birth on your birth certificate – so dig that out or consult the hospital at which you were born. If all this draws a blank too, consult a reliable dowser. However, I would regard this as a definite last resort because I have found that, after the correct birth time has been found by the usual means, dowsing has proved to be inaccurate.

So, once you are in possession of your Birth Time, be it to the minute or within half an hour either way, turn to page 336 where you will find instructions that enable you to determine your Rising Sign from the Tables that follow. Having done this, turn to the section starting on page 349, where you will find descriptions for all Rising Signs.

VAGUE BIRTH TIMES – Even if your Birth Time is within a few hours of being accurate, pick the two extremes and the average time, and then use the Tables to ascertain the Rising Sign for all three. From these results you may be able to work out your Rising Sign by reading all the descriptions and seeing which rings true for you.

Remember to enter your Rising Sign on your SUN M.A.P.S. LIFE PLAN. Also include it when determining your Element Distribution (page 6).

Tables for the Rising Signs

HOW TO READ THE RISING SIGN TABLES

Sign-Name Abbreviations

Aries	ARI	Libra	LIB
Taurus	TAU	Scorpio	SCO
Gemini	GEM	Sagittarius	SAG
Cancer	CAN	Capricorn	CAP
Leo	LEO	Aquarius	AQU
Virgo	VIR	Pisces	PIS

The Tables show Rising Signs for each hour of the day, on the hour. And for our purposes here it is only necessary to list them for every three days.

Once again we will use the same **EXAMPLE BIRTH TIME AND DATE:** 22 July 1945 at 4.10pm British Summer Time (BST) in London, England.

1) If you were born during Summer Time (or during some out of the ordinary time standard such as when the United Kingdom went over to Central European Time between 1968 and 1972), it is best to convert this back to the usual Standard Time – that is, the time as it was before being changed to Summer Time or some other time standard (War Time, for example). Such is the case with our example, so we take off one hour as BST is one hour ahead of GMT. This gives us 3.10pm.

2) Go to the Tables and look for the date nearest to the one in question. For our example this will be 21 JULY.

You will see that there are two strips of entries for all dates. The upper or shaded strip has AM birth times in the top half of it, and the corresponding Rising Sign and its Degree in the bottom half. The lower or non-shaded strip has PM birth times in the top half of it, and again, Rising Sign and Degree in the bottom half.

In our example we look along the lower strip, as the birth time is PM, for the Hour nearest 3.10pm. This is 3, and the Rising Sign given below this hour is SCO 29. Using the Sign-Name Abbreviations given above, we know this to be SCOrpio. So our example person was born with the Sign of Scorpio Rising.

3) Now for the Degree. There are 30 degrees of arc to each Sign of the Zodiac. This is because there are 360 degrees to a circle, and 12 Signs in the Zodiac (360 divided by 12 = 30). The first degree, or 01, is just past the thirtieth degree of the previous Sign.

4) Because this method of Rising Sign calculation has been greatly simplified, and is therefore approximate, if the Rising Sign you come up with is near the beginning (01–05 degrees) of a Sign, or near the end of one (26–30) then consider that, in the former case, the preceding Sign may be your Rising Sign, and, in the latter, the following Sign may be your Rising Sign. Read the texts for both and see which one is most suitable (see Figure 1 on page 5 for order of signs).

In our example we have SCO 29, which means that it is 29 degrees of Scorpio Rising. This is very near the end of this Sign, so it would be advisable to also look at the following Sign, SAGittarius, as being the possible Rising Sign.

If our example was 3.10am rather than pm (after having removed the hour for Summer Time) we would look on the upper or AM strip for 21 July, and find that the Rising Sign and Degree is CAN 04 or 4 degrees of Cancer Rising. Being near the beginning of the Sign there is also the possibility of the Ascendant being in the Sign before, which is GEMini.

5) **INTERPOLATION** If you know what this means then use it to determine a more accurate Rising Sign and Degree – that is, adjust the intervals between the birth times and between the birth dates, and, respectively, between the times, dates and degrees given in the Tables.

JAN 1 – AM	1	2	3	4	5	6	7	8	9	10	11	12noon
Sign/Degree	LIB 20	SCO 02	SCO 14	SCO 26	SAG 08	SAG 21	CAP 04	CAP 19	AQU 07	AQU 28	PIS 23	ARI 18

JAN 1 – PM	1	2	3	4	5	6	7	8	9	10	11	12midnight
Sign/Degree	TAU 12	GEM 01	GEM 18	CAN 02	CAN 15	CAN 28	LEO 09	LEO 21	VIR 03	VIR 15	VIR 27	LIB 09

JAN 4 – AM	1	2	3	4	5	6	7	8	9	10	11	12noon
Sign/Degree	LIB 23	SCO 04	SCO 16	SCO 28	SAG 10	SAG 23	CAP 07	CAP 22	AQU 11	PIS 03	PIS 28	ARI 23

JAN 4 – PM	1	2	3	4	5	6	7	8	9	10	11	12midnight
Sign/Degree	TAU 16	GEM 05	GEM 21	CAN 05	CAN 17	LEO 01	LEO 12	LEO 23	VIR 05	VIR 17	VIR 29	LIB 11

JAN 7 – AM	1	2	3	4	5	6	7	8	9	10	11	12noon
Sign/Degree	LIB 25	SCO 07	SCO 18	SAG 01	SAG 13	SAG 26	CAP 10	CAP 26	AQU 15	PIS 07	ARI 03	ARI 28

JAN 7 – PM	1	2	3	4	5	6	7	8	9	10	11	12midnight
Sign/Degree	TAU 20	GEM 08	GEM 23	CAN 07	CAN 20	LEO 02	LEO 14	LEO 26	VIR 08	VIR 20	LIB 02	LIB 14

JAN 10 – AM	1	2	3	4	5	6	7	8	9	10	11	12noon
Sign/Degree	LIB 27	SCO 09	SCO 21	SAG 03	SAG 15	SAG 28	CAP 13	CAP 29	AQU 19	PIS 12	ARI 08	TAU 02

JAN 10 – PM	1	2	3	4	5	6	7	8	9	10	11	12midnight
Sign/Degree	TAU 23	GEM 11	GEM 26	CAN 10	CAN 22	LEO 04	LEO 16	LEO 28	VIR 10	VIR 22	LIB 04	LIB 16

JAN 13 – AM	1	2	3	4	5	6	7	8	9	10	11	12noon
Sign/Degree	LIB 29	SCO 11	SCO 23	SAG 05	SAG 18	CAP 01	CAP 16	AQU 03	AQU 23	PIS 17	ARI 14	TAU 07

JAN 13 – PM	1	2	3	4	5	6	7	8	9	10	11	12midnight
Sign/Degree	TAU 27	GEM 14	GEM 29	CAN 12	CAN 25	LEO 07	LEO 19	VIR 01	VIR 12	VIR 24	LIB 06	LIB 18

JAN 16 – AM	1	2	3	4	5	6	7	8	9	10	11	12noon
Sign/Degree	SCO 02	SCO 14	SCO 26	SAG 08	SAG 20	CAP 04	CAP 19	AQU 07	AQU 28	PIS 22	ARI 18	TAU 11

JAN 16 – PM	1	2	3	4	5	6	7	8	9	10	11	12midnight
Sign/Degree	GEM 01	GEM 17	CAN 02	CAN 15	CAN 27	LEO 09	LEO 21	VIR 03	VIR 15	VIR 27	LIB 09	LIB 21

JAN 19 – AM	1	2	3	4	5	6	7	8	9	10	11	12noon
Sign/Degree	SCO 04	SCO 16	SCO 28	SAG 10	SAG 23	CAP 07	CAP 22	AQU 10	PIS 02	PIS 27	ARI 22	TAU 15

JAN 19 – PM	1	2	3	4	5	6	7	8	9	10	11	12midnight
Sign/Degree	GEM 04	GEM 20	CAN 04	CAN 17	LEO 01	LEO 11	LEO 23	VIR 05	VIR 17	VIR 29	LIB 11	LIB 23

JAN 22 – AM	1	2	3	4	5	6	7	8	9	10	11	12noon
Sign/Degree	SCO 06	SCO 18	SAG 01	SAG 12	SAG 25	CAP 09	CAP 25	AQU 14	PIS 07	ARI 02	ARI 27	TAU 19

JAN 22 – PM	1	2	3	4	5	6	7	8	9	10	11	12midnight
Sign/Degree	GEM 08	GEM 23	CAN 07	CAN 20	LEO 02	LEO 14	LEO 26	VIR 08	VIR 19	LIB 01	LIB 13	LIB 25

JAN 25 – AM	1	2	3	4	5	6	7	8	9	10	11	12noon
Sign/Degree	SCO 09	SCO 21	SAG 03	SAG 15	SAG 28	CAP 12	CAP 29	AQU 18	PIS 12	ARI 07	TAU 02	TAU 23

JAN 25 – PM	1	2	3	4	5	6	7	8	9	10	11	12midnight
Sign/Degree	GEM 11	GEM 26	CAN 10	CAN 22	LEO 04	LEO 16	LEO 28	VIR 10	VIR 22	LIB 04	LIB 16	LIB 28

JAN 28 – AM	1	2	3	4	5	6	7	8	9	10	11	12noon
Sign/Degree	SCO 11	SCO 23	SAG 05	SAG 17	CAP 01	CAP 15	AQU 02	AQU 23	PIS 17	ARI 12	TAU 06	TAU 27

JAN 28 – PM	1	2	3	4	5	6	7	8	9	10	11	12midnight
Sign/Degree	GEM 14	GEM 29	CAN 12	CAN 25	LEO 07	LEO 18	VIR 01	VIR 12	VIR 24	LIB 06	LIB 18	SCO 01

JAN 31 – AM	1	2	3	4	5	6	7	8	9	10	11	12noon
Sign/Degree	SCO 13	SCO 25	SAG 07	SAG 20	CAP 03	CAP 18	AQU 06	AQU 27	PIS 22	ARI 17	TAU 11	GEM 01

JAN 31 – PM	1	2	3	4	5	6	7	8	9	10	11	12midnight
Sign/Degree	GEM 17	CAN 02	CAN 15	CAN 27	LEO 09	LEO 21	VIR 03	VIR 14	VIR 26	LIB 09	LIB 21	SCO 02

FEBRUARY

FEB 3 – AM	1	2	3	4	5	6	7	8	9	10	11	12noon
Sign/Degree	SCO 16	SCO 28	SAG 10	SAG 22	CAP 06	CAP 22	AQU 10	PIS 02	PIS 27	ARI 22	TAU 15	GEM 04

FEB 3 – PM	1	2	3	4	5	6	7	8	9	10	11	12midnight
Sign/Degree	GEM 20	CAN 04	CAN 17	CAN 29	LEO 11	LEO 23	VIR 05	VIR 17	VIR 29	LIB 11	LIB 23	SCO 05

FEB 6 – AM	1	2	3	4	5	6	7	8	9	10	11	12noon
Sign/Degree	SCO 18	SAG 02	SAG 12	SAG 25	CAP 09	CAP 25	AQU 14	PIS 06	ARI 02	ARI 27	TAU 19	GEM 07

FEB 6 – PM	1	2	3	4	5	6	7	8	9	10	11	12midnight
Sign/Degree	GEM 23	CAN 07	CAN 20	LEO 02	LEO 14	LEO 25	VIR 07	VIR 19	LIB 01	LIB 13	LIB 25	SCO 07

FEB 9 – AM	1	2	3	4	5	6	7	8	9	10	11	12noon
Sign/Degree	SCO 20	SAG 02	SAG 15	SAG 28	CAP 12	CAP 29	AQU 18	PIS 11	ARI 07	TAU 02	TAU 23	GEM 11

FEB 9 – PM	1	2	3	4	5	6	7	8	9	10	11	12midnight
Sign/Degree	GEM 26	CAN 09	CAN 22	LEO 04	LEO 16	LEO 28	VIR 10	VIR 22	LIB 04	LIB 16	LIB 28	SCO 09

FEB 12 – AM	1	2	3	4	5	6	7	8	9	10	11	12noon
Sign/Degree	SCO 23	SAG 05	SAG 17	CAP 01	CAP 15	AQU 02	AQU 22	PIS 16	ARI 12	TAU 06	TAU 26	GEM 14

FEB 12 – PM	1	2	3	4	5	6	7	8	9	10	11	12midnight
Sign/Degree	GEM 29	CAN 12	CAN 24	LEO 06	LEO 18	VIR 01	VIR 12	VIR 24	LIB 06	LIB 18	SCO 01	SCO 12

FEB 15 – AM	1	2	3	4	5	6	7	8	9	10	11	12noon
Sign/Degree	SCO 25	SAG 07	SAG 20	CAP 03	CAP 18	AQU 06	AQU 27	PIS 21	ARI 17	TAU 10	GEM 01	GEM 17

FEB 15 – PM	1	2	3	4	5	6	7	8	9	10	11	12midnight
Sign/Degree	CAN 02	CAN 14	CAN 27	LEO 09	LEO 21	VIR 02	VIR 14	VIR 26	LIB 08	LIB 20	SCO 02	SCO 14

FEB 18 – AM	1	2	3	4	5	6	7	8	9	10	11	12noon
Sign/Degree	SCO 27	SAG 10	SAG 22	CAP 06	CAP 21	AQU 10	PIS 01	PIS 26	ARI 22	TAU 14	GEM 04	GEM 20

FEB 18 – PM	1	2	3	4	5	6	7	8	9	10	11	12midnight
Sign/Degree	CAN 04	CAN 17	LEO 01	LEO 11	LEO 23	VIR 05	VIR 17	VIR 29	LIB 11	LIB 23	SCO 05	SCO 16

FEB 21 – AM	1	2	3	4	5	6	7	8	9	10	11	12noon
Sign/Degree	SAG 01	SAG 12	SAG 25	CAP 09	CAP 25	AQU 14	PIS 06	ARI 01	ARI 26	TAU 19	GEM 07	GEM 23

FEB 21 – PM	1	2	3	4	5	6	7	8	9	10	11	12midnight
Sign/Degree	CAN 07	CAN 19	LEO 02	LEO 13	LEO 25	VIR 07	VIR 19	LIB 01	LIB 13	LIB 25	SCO 07	SCO 19

FEB 24 – AM	1	2	3	4	5	6	7	8	9	10	11	12noon
Sign/Degree	SAG 02	SAG 14	SAG 27	CAP 12	CAP 28	AQU 18	PIS 11	ARI 06	TAU 01	TAU 22	GEM 10	GEM 26

FEB 24 – PM	1	2	3	4	5	6	7	8	9	10	11	12midnight
Sign/Degree	CAN 09	CAN 22	LEO 04	LEO 16	LEO 27	VIR 09	VIR 21	LIB 03	LIB 15	LIB 27	SCO 09	SCO 21

FEB 27 – AM	1	2	3	4	5	6	7	8	9	10	11	12noon
Sign/Degree	SAG 05	SAG 17	CAP 01	CAP 15	AQU 02	AQU 22	PIS 16	ARI 11	TAU 06	TAU 26	GEM 14	GEM 28

FEB 27 – PM	1	2	3	4	5	6	7	8	9	10	11	12midnight
Sign/Degree	CAN 12	CAN 24	LEO 06	LEO 18	VIR 01	VIR 12	VIR 24	LIB 06	LIB 18	SCO 01	SCO 11	SCO 23

MARCH

MAR 2 – AM	1	2	3	4	5	6	7	8	9	10	11	12noon
Sign/Degree	SAG 07	SAG 20	CAP 03	CAP 18	AQU 05	AQU 26	PIS 21	ARI 16	TAU 10	GEM 01	GEM 17	CAN 01

MAR 2 – PM	1	2	3	4	5	6	7	8	9	10	11	12midnight
Sign/Degree	CAN 14	CAN 27	LEO 08	LEO 20	VIR 02	VIR 14	VIR 26	LIB 08	LIB 20	SCO 02	SCO 14	SCO 26

MAR 5 – AM	1	2	3	4	5	6	7	8	9	10	11	12noon
Sign/Degree	SAG 09	SAG 22	CAP 06	CAP 21	AQU 09	PIS 01	PIS 26	ARI 21	TAU 14	GEM 03	GEM 20	CAN 04

MAR 5 – PM	1	2	3	4	5	6	7	8	9	10	11	12midnight
Sign/Degree	CAN 17	CAN 29	LEO 11	LEO 23	VIR 04	VIR 16	VIR 28	LIB 10	LIB 22	SCO 04	SCO 16	SCO 28

MAR 8 – AM	1	2	3	4	5	6	7	8	9	10	11	12noon
Sign/Degree	SAG 12	SAG 25	CAP 09	CAP 24	AQU 13	PIS 06	ARI 01	ARI 26	TAU 18	GEM 07	GEM 22	CAN 06

MAR 8 – PM	1	2	3	4	5	6	7	8	9	10	11	12midnight
Sign/Degree	CAN 19	LEO 01	LEO 13	LEO 25	VIR 07	VIR 19	LIB 01	LIB 13	LIB 25	SCO 07	SCO 18	SAG 01

MAR 11 – AM	1	2	3	4	5	6	7	8	9	10	11	12noon
Sign/Degree	SAG 14	SAG 27	CAP 12	CAP 28	AQU 17	PIS 10	ARI 06	TAU 01	TAU 22	GEM 10	GEM 25	CAN 09

MAR 11 – PM	1	2	3	4	5	6	7	8	9	10	11	12midnight
Sign/Degree	CAN 22	LEO 04	LEO 15	LEO 27	VIR 09	VIR 21	LIB 03	LIB 15	LIB 27	SCO 09	SCO 21	SAG 03

MAR 14 – AM	1	2	3	4	5	6	7	8	9	10	11	12noon
Sign/Degree	SAG 17	CAP 01	CAP 15	AQU 02	AQU 22	PIS 15	ARI 11	TAU 05	TAU 26	GEM 13	GEM 28	CAN 11

MAR 14 – PM	1	2	3	4	5	6	7	8	9	10	11	12midnight
Sign/Degree	CAN 24	LEO 06	LEO 18	VIR 01	VIR 12	VIR 24	LIB 06	LIB 18	SCO 01	SCO 11	SCO 23	SAG 05

MAR 17 – AM	1	2	3	4	5	6	7	8	9	10	11	12noon
Sign/Degree	SAG 19	CAP 03	CAP 18	AQU 05	AQU 26	PIS 20	ARI 16	TAU 10	GEM 01	GEM 16	CAN 01	CAN 14

MAR 17 – PM	1	2	3	4	5	6	7	8	9	10	11	12midnight
Sign/Degree	CAN 26	LEO 08	LEO 20	VIR 02	VIR 14	VIR 26	LIB 08	LIB 20	SCO 02	SCO 14	SCO 25	SAG 08

MAR 20 – AM	1	2	3	4	5	6	7	8	9	10	11	12noon
Sign/Degree	SAG 22	CAP 05	CAP 21	AQU 09	PIS 01	PIS 26	ARI 21	TAU 14	GEM 03	GEM 19	CAN 03	CAN 16

MAR 20 – PM	1	2	3	4	5	6	7	8	9	10	11	12midnight
Sign/Degree	CAN 29	LEO 11	LEO 22	VIR 04	VIR 16	VIR 28	LIB 10	LIB 22	SCO 04	SCO 16	SCO 28	SAG 10

MAR 23 – AM	1	2	3	4	5	6	7	8	9	10	11	12noon
Sign/Degree	SAG 24	CAP 08	CAP 24	AQU 13	PIS 05	ARI 01	ARI 26	TAU 18	GEM 06	GEM 22	CAN 06	CAN 19

MAR 23 – PM	1	2	3	4	5	6	7	8	9	10	11	12midnight
Sign/Degree	LEO 01	LEO 13	LEO 25	VIR 07	VIR 19	LIB 01	LIB 13	LIB 25	SCO 06	SCO 18	SAG 01	SAG 12

MAR 26 – AM	1	2	3	4	5	6	7	8	9	10	11	12noon
Sign/Degree	SAG 27	CAP 11	CAP 28	AQU 17	PIS 10	ARI 06	TAU 01	TAU 22	GEM 10	GEM 25	CAN 09	CAN 21

MAR 26 – PM	1	2	3	4	5	6	7	8	9	10	11	12midnight
Sign/Degree	LEO 03	LEO 15	LEO 27	VIR 09	VIR 21	LIB 03	LIB 15	LIB 27	SCO 09	SCO 21	SAG 03	SAG 15

MAR 29 – AM	1	2	3	4	5	6	7	8	9	10	11	12noon
Sign/Degree	CAP 01	CAP 14	AQU 01	AQU 21	PIS 15	ARI 11	TAU 05	TAU 26	GEM 13	GEM 28	CAN 11	CAN 24

MAR 29 – PM	1	2	3	4	5	6	7	8	9	10	11	12midnight
Sign/Degree	LEO 06	LEO 18	VIR 01	VIR 11	VIR 23	LIB 05	LIB 17	LIB 29	SCO 11	SCO 23	SAG 05	SAG 17

APRIL

	1	2	3	4	5	6	7	8	9	10	11	12noon
APR 1 – AM Sign/Degree	CAP 03	CAP 17	AQU 05	AQU 26	PIS 20	ARI 16	TAU 09	TAU 29	GEM 16	CAN 01	CAN 14	CAN 26

	1	2	3	4	5	6	7	8	9	10	11	12midnight
APR 1 – PM Sign/Degree	LEO 08	LEO 20	VIR 02	VIR 14	VIR 26	LIB 08	LIB 20	SCO 02	SCO 13	SCO 25	SAG 07	SAG 20

	1	2	3	4	5	6	7	8	9	10	11	12noon
APR 4 – AM Sign/Degree	CAP 05	CAP 21	AQU 09	PIS 01	PIS 25	ARI 20	TAU 13	GEM 03	GEM 19	CAN 03	CAN 16	CAN 28

	1	2	3	4	5	6	7	8	9	10	11	12midnight
APR 4 – PM Sign/Degree	LEO 10	LEO 22	VIR 04	VIR 16	VIR 28	LIB 10	LIB 22	SCO 04	SCO 16	SCO 28	SAG 10	SAG 22

	1	2	3	4	5	6	7	8	9	10	11	12noon
APR 7 – AM Sign/Degree	CAP 08	CAP 24	AQU 13	PIS 05	ARI 01	ARI 25	TAU 17	GEM 06	GEM 22	CAN 06	CAN 19	LEO 01

	1	2	3	4	5	6	7	8	9	10	11	12midnight
APR 7 – PM Sign/Degree	LEO 13	LEO 25	VIR 06	VIR 18	LIB 01	LIB 12	LIB 24	SCO 06	SCO 18	SAG 01	SAG 12	SAG 25

	1	2	3	4	5	6	7	8	9	10	11	12noon
APR 10 – AM Sign/Degree	CAP 11	CAP 27	AQU 17	PIS 10	ARI 05	TAU 01	TAU 22	GEM 09	GEM 25	CAN 08	CAN 21	LEO 03

	1	2	3	4	5	6	7	8	9	10	11	12midnight
APR 10 – PM Sign/Degree	LEO 15	LEO 27	VIR 09	VIR 21	LIB 03	LIB 15	LIB 27	SCO 09	SCO 20	SAG 02	SAG 15	SAG 28

	1	2	3	4	5	6	7	8	9	10	11	12noon
APR 13 – AM Sign/Degree	CAP 14	AQU 01	AQU 21	PIS 15	ARI 10	TAU 04	TAU 25	GEM 13	GEM 28	CAN 11	CAN 24	LEO 06

	1	2	3	4	5	6	7	8	9	10	11	12midnight
APR 13 – PM Sign/Degree	LEO 17	LEO 29	VIR 11	VIR 23	LIB 05	LIB 17	LIB 29	SCO 11	SCO 23	SAG 05	SAG 17	CAP 01

	1	2	3	4	5	6	7	8	9	10	11	12noon
APR 16 – AM Sign/Degree	CAP 17	AQU 04	AQU 25	PIS 19	ARI 15	TAU 09	TAU 29	GEM 16	CAN 01	CAN 14	CAN 26	LEO 08

	1	2	3	4	5	6	7	8	9	10	11	12midnight
APR 16 – PM Sign/Degree	LEO 20	VIR 02	VIR 13	VIR 25	LIB 07	LIB 19	SCO 01	SCO 13	SCO 25	SAG 07	SAG 20	CAP 03

	1	2	3	4	5	6	7	8	9	10	11	12noon
APR 19 – AM Sign/Degree	CAP 20	AQU 08	AQU 29	PIS 25	ARI 20	TAU 13	GEM 02	GEM 19	CAN 03	CAN 16	CAN 28	LEO 10

	1	2	3	4	5	6	7	8	9	10	11	12midnight
APR 19 – PM Sign/Degree	LEO 22	VIR 04	VIR 16	VIR 28	LIB 10	LIB 22	SCO 04	SCO 16	SCO 27	SAG 10	SAG 22	CAP 06

	1	2	3	4	5	6	7	8	9	10	11	12noon
APR 22 – AM Sign/Degree	CAP 24	AQU 12	PIS 04	ARI 01	ARI 25	TAU 17	GEM 06	GEM 22	CAN 06	CAN 18	LEO 01	LEO 13

	1	2	3	4	5	6	7	8	9	10	11	12midnight
APR 22 – PM Sign/Degree	LEO 24	VIR 06	VIR 18	LIB 01	LIB 12	LIB 24	SCO 06	SCO 18	SAG 01	SAG 12	SAG 25	CAP 09

	1	2	3	4	5	6	7	8	9	10	11	12noon
APR 25 – AM Sign/Degree	CAP 27	AQU 16	PIS 09	ARI 05	ARI 29	TAU 21	GEM 09	GEM 25	CAN 08	CAN 21	LEO 03	LEO 15

	1	2	3	4	5	6	7	8	9	10	11	12midnight
APR 25 – PM Sign/Degree	LEO 27	VIR 09	VIR 21	LIB 03	LIB 15	LIB 27	SCO 08	SCO 20	SAG 02	SAG 14	SAG 27	CAP 12

	1	2	3	4	5	6	7	8	9	10	11	12noon
APR 28 – AM Sign/Degree	AQU 01	AQU 21	PIS 14	ARI 10	TAU 04	TAU 25	GEM 12	GEM 27	CAN 11	CAN 23	LEO 05	LEO 17

	1	2	3	4	5	6	7	8	9	10	11	12midnight
APR 28 – PM Sign/Degree	LEO 29	VIR 11	VIR 23	LIB 05	LIB 17	LIB 29	SCO 11	SCO 23	SAG 05	SAG 17	CAP 01	CAP 15

MAY

MAY 1 – AM	1	2	3	4	5	6	7	8	9	10	11	12noon
Sign/Degree	AQU 04	AQU 25	PIS 19	ARI 15	TAU 09	TAU 29	GEM 15	CAN 01	CAN 13	CAN 26	LEO 08	LEO 20

MAY 1 – PM	1	2	3	4	5	6	7	8	9	10	11	12midnight
Sign/Degree	VIR 01	VIR 13	VIR 25	LIB 07	LIB 19	SCO 01	SCO 13	SCO 25	SAG 07	SAG 19	CAP 03	CAP 18

MAY 4 – AM	1	2	3	4	5	6	7	8	9	10	11	12noon
Sign/Degree	AQU 08	AQU 29	PIS 24	ARI 20	TAU 13	GEM 02	GEM 19	CAN 03	CAN 16	CAN 28	LEO 10	LEO 22

MAY 4 – PM	1	2	3	4	5	6	7	8	9	10	11	12midnight
Sign/Degree	VIR 04	VIR 16	VIR 28	LIB 10	LIB 22	SCO 04	SCO 15	SCO 27	SAG 09	SAG 22	CAP 06	CAP 21

MAY 7 – AM	1	2	3	4	5	6	7	8	9	10	11	12noon
Sign/Degree	AQU 12	PIS 04	PIS 29	ARI 24	TAU 17	GEM 06	GEM 21	CAN 05	CAN 18	LEO 01	LEO 12	LEO 24

MAY 7 – PM	1	2	3	4	5	6	7	8	9	10	11	12midnight
Sign/Degree	VIR 06	VIR 18	LIB 01	LIB 12	LIB 24	SCO 06	SCO 18	SAG 01	SAG 12	SAG 25	CAP 09	CAP 24

MAY 10 – AM	1	2	3	4	5	6	7	8	9	10	11	12noon
Sign/Degree	AQU 16	PIS 09	ARI 04	ARI 29	TAU 21	GEM 09	GEM 24	CAN 08	CAN 21	LEO 03	LEO 15	LEO 26

MAY 10 – PM	1	2	3	4	5	6	7	8	9	10	11	12midnight
Sign/Degree	VIR 08	VIR 20	LIB 02	LIB 14	LIB 26	SCO 08	SCO 20	SAG 02	SAG 14	SAG 27	CAP 11	CAP 28

MAY 13 – AM	1	2	3	4	5	6	7	8	9	10	11	12noon
Sign/Degree	AQU 20	PIS 14	ARI 09	TAU 04	TAU 25	GEM 12	GEM 27	CAN 11	CAN 23	LEO 05	LEO 17	LEO 29

MAY 13 – PM	1	2	3	4	5	6	7	8	9	10	11	12midnight
Sign/Degree	VIR 11	VIR 23	LIB 05	LIB 17	LIB 29	SCO 10	SCO 22	SAG 04	SAG 17	CAP 01	CAP 14	AQU 01

MAY 16 – AM	1	2	3	4	5	6	7	8	9	10	11	12noon
Sign/Degree	AQU 24	PIS 19	ARI 14	TAU 08	TAU 28	GEM 15	CAN 01	CAN 13	CAN 25	LEO 07	LEO 19	VIR 01

MAY 16 – PM	1	2	3	4	5	6	7	8	9	10	11	12midnight
Sign/Degree	VIR 13	VIR 25	LIB 07	LIB 19	SCO 01	SCO 13	SCO 25	SAG 07	SAG 19	CAP 03	CAP 18	AQU 05

MAY 19 – AM	1	2	3	4	5	6	7	8	9	10	11	12noon
Sign/Degree	AQU 29	PIS 24	ARI 19	TAU 12	GEM 02	GEM 18	CAN 03	CAN 16	CAN 28	LEO 10	LEO 22	VIR 03

MAY 19 – PM	1	2	3	4	5	6	7	8	9	10	11	12midnight
Sign/Degree	VIR 15	VIR 27	LIB 09	LIB 21	SCO 03	SCO 15	SCO 27	SAG 09	SAG 22	CAP 05	CAP 21	AQU 09

MAY 22 – AM	1	2	3	4	5	6	7	8	9	10	11	12noon
Sign/Degree	PIS 04	PIS 29	ARI 24	TAU 16	GEM 05	GEM 21	CAN 05	CAN 18	LEO 01	LEO 12	LEO 24	VIR 06

MAY 22 – PM	1	2	3	4	5	6	7	8	9	10	11	12midnight
Sign/Degree	VIR 18	LIB 01	LIB 12	LIB 24	SCO 06	SCO 17	SCO 29	SAG 12	SAG 24	CAP 08	CAP 24	AQU 13

MAY 25 – AM	1	2	3	4	5	6	7	8	9	10	11	12noon
Sign/Degree	PIS 08	ARI 04	ARI 29	TAU 20	GEM 09	GEM 24	CAN 08	CAN 20	LEO 03	LEO 14	LEO 26	VIR 08

MAY 25 – PM	1	2	3	4	5	6	7	8	9	10	11	12midnight
Sign/Degree	VIR 20	LIB 02	LIB 14	LIB 26	SCO 08	SCO 20	SAG 02	SAG 14	SAG 27	CAP 11	CAP 28	AQU 17

MAY 28 – AM	1	2	3	4	5	6	7	8	9	10	11	12noon
Sign/Degree	PIS 13	ARI 09	TAU 03	TAU 24	GEM 12	GEM 27	CAN 10	CAN 23	LEO 05	LEO 17	LEO 29	VIR 11

MAY 28 – PM	1	2	3	4	5	6	7	8	9	10	11	12midnight
Sign/Degree	VIR 23	LIB 05	LIB 17	LIB 28	SCO 10	SCO 22	SAG 04	SAG 16	CAP 01	CAP 14	AQU 01	AQU 21

MAY 31 – AM	1	2	3	4	5	6	7	8	9	10	11	12noon
Sign/Degree	PIS 18	ARI 14	TAU 08	TAU 28	GEM 15	CAN 01	CAN 13	CAN 25	LEO 07	LEO 19	VIR 01	VIR 13

MAY 31 – PM	1	2	3	4	5	6	7	8	9	10	11	12midnight
Sign/Degree	VIR 25	LIB 07	LIB 19	SCO 01	SCO 13	SCO 24	SAG 06	SAG 19	CAP 02	CAP 17	AQU 05	AQU 26

JUNE

JUN 3 – AM	1	2	3	4	5	6	7	8	9	10	11	12noon
Sign/Degree	PIS 23	ARI 19	TAU 12	GEM 02	GEM 18	CAN 02	CAN 15	CAN 28	LEO 10	LEO 21	VIR 03	VIR 15

JUN 3 – PM	1	2	3	4	5	6	7	8	9	10	11	12midnight
Sign/Degree	VIR 27	LIB 09	LIB 21	SCO 03	SCO 15	SCO 27	SAG 09	SAG 21	CAP 05	CAP 21	AQU 09	PIS 01

JUN 6 – AM	1	2	3	4	5	6	7	8	9	10	11	12noon
Sign/Degree	PIS 28	ARI 24	TAU 16	GEM 05	GEM 21	CAN 05	CAN 18	LEO 01	LEO 12	LEO 24	VIR 06	VIR 18

JUN 6 – PM	1	2	3	4	5	6	7	8	9	10	11	12midnight
Sign/Degree	LIB 01	LIB 12	LIB 24	SCO 05	SCO 17	SCO 29	SAG 11	SAG 24	CAP 08	CAP 24	AQU 12	PIS 05

JUN 9 – AM	1	2	3	4	5	6	7	8	9	10	11	12noon
Sign/Degree	ARI 03	ARI 28	TAU 20	GEM 08	GEM 24	CAN 08	CAN 20	LEO 02	LEO 14	LEO 26	VIR 08	VIR 20

JUN 9 – PM	1	2	3	4	5	6	7	8	9	10	11	12midnight
Sign/Degree	LIB 02	LIB 14	LIB 26	SCO 08	SCO 20	SAG 02	SAG 14	SAG 27	CAP 11	CAP 27	AQU 17	PIS 10

JUN 12 – AM	1	2	3	4	5	6	7	8	9	10	11	12noon
Sign/Degree	ARI 08	TAU 03	TAU 24	GEM 12	GEM 27	CAN 10	CAN 23	LEO 05	LEO 17	LEO 28	VIR 10	VIR 22

JUN 12 – PM	1	2	3	4	5	6	7	8	9	10	11	12midnight
Sign/Degree	LIB 04	LIB 16	LIB 28	SCO 10	SCO 22	SAG 04	SAG 16	SAG 29	CAP 14	AQU 01	AQU 21	PIS 14

JUN 15 – AM	1	2	3	4	5	6	7	8	9	10	11	12noon
Sign/Degree	ARI 13	TAU 07	TAU 28	GEM 15	GEM 29	CAN 13	CAN 25	LEO 07	LEO 19	VIR 01	VIR 13	VIR 25

JUN 15 – PM	1	2	3	4	5	6	7	8	9	10	11	12midnight
Sign/Degree	LIB 07	LIB 19	SCO 01	SCO 12	SCO 24	SAG 06	SAG 19	CAP 02	CAP 17	AQU 04	AQU 25	PIS 19

JUN 18 – AM	1	2	3	4	5	6	7	8	9	10	11	12noon
Sign/Degree	ARI 18	TAU 12	GEM 01	GEM 18	CAN 02	CAN 15	CAN 27	LEO 09	LEO 21	VIR 03	VIR 15	VIR 27

JUN 18 – PM	1	2	3	4	5	6	7	8	9	10	11	12midnight
Sign/Degree	LIB 09	LIB 21	SCO 03	SCO 15	SCO 27	SAG 09	SAG 21	CAP 05	CAP 20	AQU 08	PIS 01	PIS 24

JUN 21 – AM	1	2	3	4	5	6	7	8	9	10	11	12noon
Sign/Degree	ARI 23	TAU 16	GEM 05	GEM 21	CAN 05	CAN 18	LEO 01	LEO 12	LEO 24	VIR 05	VIR 17	LIB 01

JUN 21 – PM	1	2	3	4	5	6	7	8	9	10	11	12midnight
Sign/Degree	LIB 11	LIB 23	SCO 05	SCO 17	SCO 29	SAG 11	SAG 24	CAP 08	CAP 24	AQU 12	PIS 04	ARI 01

JUN 24 – AM	1	2	3	4	5	6	7	8	9	10	11	12noon
Sign/Degree	ARI 28	TAU 20	GEM 08	GEM 24	CAN 07	CAN 20	LEO 03	LEO 14	LEO 26	VIR 08	VIR 20	LIB 02

JUN 24 – PM	1	2	3	4	5	6	7	8	9	10	11	12midnight
Sign/Degree	LIB 14	LIB 26	SCO 08	SCO 19	SAG 01	SAG 14	SAG 26	CAP 11	CAP 27	AQU 16	PIS 09	ARI 05

JUN 27 – AM	1	2	3	4	5	6	7	8	9	10	11	12noon
Sign/Degree	TAU 02	TAU 24	GEM 11	GEM 26	CAN 10	CAN 22	LEO 05	LEO 16	LEO 28	VIR 10	VIR 22	LIB 04

JUN 27 – PM	1	2	3	4	5	6	7	8	9	10	11	12midnight
Sign/Degree	LIB 16	LIB 28	SCO 10	SCO 22	SAG 04	SAG 16	SAG 29	CAP 14	AQU 01	AQU 21	PIS 14	ARI 10

JUN 30 – AM	1	2	3	4	5	6	7	8	9	10	11	12noon
Sign/Degree	TAU 07	TAU 27	GEM 14	GEM 29	CAN 12	CAN 25	LEO 07	LEO 19	VIR 01	VIR 12	VIR 24	LIB 06

JUN 30 – PM	1	2	3	4	5	6	7	8	9	10	11	12midnight
Sign/Degree	LIB 18	SCO 01	SCO 12	SCO 24	SAG 06	SAG 19	CAP 02	CAP 17	AQU 04	AQU 25	PIS 19	ARI 15

JUL 3 – AM	1	2	3	4	5	6	7	8	9	10	11	12noon
Sign/Degree	TAU 11	GEM 01	GEM 17	CAN 02	CAN 15	CAN 27	LEO 09	LEO 21	VIR 03	VIR 15	VIR 27	LIB 09
JUL 3 – PM	1	2	3	4	5	6	7	8	9	10	11	12midnight
Sign/Degree	LIB 21	SCO 03	SCO 15	SCO 26	SAG 08	SAG 21	CAP 05	CAP 20	AQU 08	AQU 29	PIS 24	ARI 19
JUL 6 – AM	1	2	3	4	5	6	7	8	9	10	11	12noon
Sign/Degree	TAU 15	GEM 04	GEM 20	CAN 05	CAN 17	LEO 01	LEO 12	LEO 23	VIR 05	VIR 17	VIR 29	LIB 11
JUL 6 – PM	1	2	3	4	5	6	7	8	9	10	11	12midnight
Sign/Degree	LIB 23	SCO 05	SCO 17	SCO 29	SAG 11	SAG 24	CAP 08	CAP 23	AQU 12	PIS 04	PIS 29	ARI 24
JUL 9 – AM	1	2	3	4	5	6	7	8	9	10	11	12noon
Sign/Degree	TAU 19	GEM 08	GEM 23	CAN 07	CAN 20	LEO 02	LEO 14	LEO 26	VIR 08	VIR 20	LIB 02	LIB 14
JUL 9 – PM	1	2	3	4	5	6	7	8	9	10	11	12midnight
Sign/Degree	LIB 25	SCO 07	SCO 19	SAG 01	SAG 13	SAG 26	CAP 10	CAP 27	AQU 16	PIS 09	ARI 04	ARI 29
JUL 12 – AM	1	2	3	4	5	6	7	8	9	10	11	12noon
Sign/Degree	TAU 23	GEM 11	GEM 26	CAN 10	CAN 22	LEO 04	LEO 16	LEO 28	VIR 10	VIR 22	LIB 04	LIB 16
JUL 12 – PM	1	2	3	4	5	6	7	8	9	10	11	12midnight
Sign/Degree	LIB 28	SCO 10	SCO 21	SAG 03	SAG 16	SAG 29	CAP 13	AQU 01	AQU 20	PIS 14	ARI 09	TAU 04
JUL 15 – AM	1	2	3	4	5	6	7	8	9	10	11	12noon
Sign/Degree	TAU 27	GEM 14	GEM 29	CAN 12	CAN 25	LEO 07	LEO 18	VIR 01	VIR 12	VIR 24	LIB 06	LIB 18
JUL 15 – PM	1	2	3	4	5	6	7	8	9	10	11	12midnight
Sign/Degree	SCO 01	SCO 12	SCO 24	SAG 06	SAG 18	CAP 02	CAP 16	AQU 04	AQU 24	PIS 19	ARI 14	TAU 08
JUL 18 – AM	1	2	3	4	5	6	7	8	9	10	11	12noon
Sign/Degree	GEM 01	GEM 17	CAN 02	CAN 15	CAN 27	LEO 09	LEO 21	VIR 03	VIR 15	VIR 27	LIB 09	LIB 21
JUL 18 – PM	1	2	3	4	5	6	7	8	9	10	11	12midnight
Sign/Degree	SCO 03	SCO 14	SCO 26	SAG 08	SAG 21	CAP 04	CAP 20	AQU 08	AQU 29	PIS 24	ARI 19	TAU 12
JUL 21 – AM	1	2	3	4	5	6	7	8	9	10	11	12noon
Sign/Degree	GEM 04	GEM 20	CAN 04	CAN 17	CAN 29	LEO 11	LEO 23	VIR 05	VIR 17	VIR 29	LIB 11	LIB 23
JUL 21 – PM	1	2	3	4	5	6	7	8	9	10	11	12midnight
Sign/Degree	SCO 05	SCO 17	SCO 29	SAG 11	SAG 23	CAP 07	CAP 23	AQU 11	PIS 04	PIS 29	ARI 24	TAU 16
JUL 24 – AM	1	2	3	4	5	6	7	8	9	10	11	12noon
Sign/Degree	GEM 07	GEM 23	CAN 07	CAN 20	LEO 02	LEO 14	LEO 25	VIR 07	VIR 19	LIB 01	LIB 13	LIB 25
JUL 24 – PM	1	2	3	4	5	6	7	8	9	10	11	12midnight
Sign/Degree	SCO 07	SCO 19	SAG 01	SAG 13	SAG 26	CAP 10	CAP 26	AQU 16	PIS 08	ARI 04	ARI 29	TAU 20
JUL 27 – AM	1	2	3	4	5	6	7	8	9	10	11	12noon
Sign/Degree	GEM 11	GEM 26	CAN 09	CAN 22	LEO 04	LEO 16	LEO 28	VIR 10	VIR 22	LIB 04	LIB 16	LIB 28
JUL 27 – PM	1	2	3	4	5	6	7	8	9	10	11	12midnight
Sign/Degree	SCO 09	SCO 21	SAG 03	SAG 16	SAG 29	CAP 13	AQU 01	AQU 20	PIS 13	ARI 09	TAU 03	TAU 24
JUL 30 – AM	1	2	3	4	5	6	7	8	9	10	11	12noon
Sign/Degree	GEM 14	GEM 29	CAN 12	CAN 24	LEO 06	LEO 18	VIR 01	VIR 12	VIR 24	LIB 06	LIB 18	SCO 01
JUL 30 – PM	1	2	3	4	5	6	7	8	9	10	11	12midnight
Sign/Degree	SCO 12	SCO 24	SAG 06	SAG 18	CAP 01	CAP 16	AQU 03	AQU 24	PIS 18	ARI 14	TAU 08	TAU 28

AUGUST

AUG 2 – AM	1	2	3	4	5	6	7	8	9	10	11	12noon
Sign/Degree	GEM 17	CAN 01	CAN 14	CAN 27	LEO 09	LEO 21	VIR 03	VIR 14	VIR 26	LIB 08	LIB 20	SCO 02

AUG 2 – PM	1	2	3	4	5	6	7	8	9	10	11	12midnight
Sign/Degree	SCO 14	SCO 26	SAG 08	SAG 21	CAP 04	CAP 19	AQU 07	AQU 29	PIS 23	ARI 19	TAU 12	GEM 01

AUG 5 – AM	1	2	3	4	5	6	7	8	9	10	11	12noon
Sign/Degree	GEM 20	CAN 04	CAN 17	CAN 29	LEO 11	LEO 23	VIR 05	VIR 17	VIR 29	LIB 11	LIB 23	SCO 05

AUG 5 – PM	1	2	3	4	5	6	7	8	9	10	11	12midnight
Sign/Degree	SCO 16	SCO 28	SAG 10	SAG 23	CAP 07	CAP 23	AQU 11	PIS 03	PIS 28	ARI 25	TAU 16	GEM 05

AUG 8 – AM	1	2	3	4	5	6	7	8	9	10	11	12noon
Sign/Degree	GEM 23	CAN 07	CAN 19	LEO 02	LEO 13	LEO 25	VIR 07	VIR 19	LIB 01	LIB 13	LIB 25	SCO 07

AUG 8 – PM	1	2	3	4	5	6	7	8	9	10	11	12midnight
Sign/Degree	SCO 19	SAG 01	SAG 13	SAG 26	CAP 10	CAP 26	AQU 15	PIS 08	ARI 03	ARI 28	TAU 20	GEM 08

AUG 11 – AM	1	2	3	4	5	6	7	8	9	10	11	12noon
Sign/Degree	GEM 26	CAN 09	CAN 22	LEO 04	LEO 16	LEO 28	VIR 10	VIR 21	LIB 03	LIB 15	LIB 27	SCO 09

AUG 11 – PM	1	2	3	4	5	6	7	8	9	10	11	12midnight
Sign/Degree	SCO 21	SAG 03	SAG 15	SAG 28	CAP 13	AQU 01	AQU 19	PIS 13	ARI 08	TAU 03	TAU 24	GEM 12

AUG 14 – AM	1	2	3	4	5	6	7	8	9	10	11	12noon
Sign/Degree	GEM 28	CAN 12	CAN 24	LEO 06	LEO 18	VIR 01	VIR 12	VIR 24	LIB 06	LIB 18	SCO 01	SCO 12

AUG 14 – PM	1	2	3	4	5	6	7	8	9	10	11	12midnight
Sign/Degree	SCO 23	SAG 05	SAG 18	CAP 01	CAP 16	AQU 03	AQU 24	PIS 18	ARI 13	TAU 07	TAU 28	GEM 15

AUG 17 – AM	1	2	3	4	5	6	7	8	9	10	11	12noon
Sign/Degree	CAN 01	CAN 14	CAN 27	LEO 09	LEO 20	VIR 02	VIR 14	VIR 26	LIB 08	LIB 20	SCO 02	SCO 14

AUG 17 – PM	1	2	3	4	5	6	7	8	9	10	11	12midnight
Sign/Degree	SCO 26	SAG 08	SAG 20	CAP 04	CAP 19	AQU 07	AQU 28	PIS 23	ARI 18	TAU 11	GEM 01	GEM 18

AUG 20 – AM	1	2	3	4	5	6	7	8	9	10	11	12noon
Sign/Degree	CAN 04	CAN 17	CAN 29	LEO 11	LEO 23	VIR 05	VIR 17	VIR 29	LIB 11	LIB 23	SCO 04	SCO 16

AUG 20 – PM	1	2	3	4	5	6	7	8	9	10	11	12midnight
Sign/Degree	SCO 28	SAG 10	SAG 23	CAP 07	CAP 22	AQU 11	PIS 03	PIS 28	ARI 23	TAU 16	GEM 05	GEM 21

AUG 23 – AM	1	2	3	4	5	6	7	8	9	10	11	12noon
Sign/Degree	CAN 06	CAN 19	LEO 01	LEO 13	LEO 25	VIR 07	VIR 19	LIB 01	LIB 13	LIB 25	SCO 07	SCO 19

AUG 23 – PM	1	2	3	4	5	6	7	8	9	10	11	12midnight
Sign/Degree	SAG 01	SAG 13	SAG 26	CAP 10	CAP 26	AQU 15	PIS 07	ARI 03	ARI 28	TAU 20	GEM 08	GEM 24

AUG 26 – AM	1	2	3	4	5	6	7	8	9	10	11	12noon
Sign/Degree	CAN 09	CAN 22	LEO 04	LEO 16	LEO 28	VIR 09	VIR 21	LIB 03	LIB 15	LIB 27	SCO 09	SCO 21

AUG 26 – PM	1	2	3	4	5	6	7	8	9	10	11	12midnight
Sign/Degree	SAG 03	SAG 15	SAG 28	CAP 13	CAP 29	AQU 19	PIS 12	ARI 08	TAU 02	TAU 24	GEM 11	GEM 26

AUG 29 – AM	1	2	3	4	5	6	7	8	9	10	11	12noon
Sign/Degree	CAN 12	CAN 24	LEO 06	LEO 18	VIR 01	VIR 12	VIR 24	LIB 06	LIB 18	SCO 01	SCO 11	SCO 23

AUG 29 – PM	1	2	3	4	5	6	7	8	9	10	11	12midnight
Sign/Degree	SAG 05	SAG 18	CAP 01	CAP 16	AQU 03	AQU 23	PIS 17	ARI 13	TAU 07	TAU 27	GEM 14	GEM 29

SEPTEMBER

	1	2	3	4	5	6	7	8	9	10	11	12noon
SEP 1 – AM Sign/Degree	CAN 14	CAN 27	LEO 08	LEO 20	VIR 02	VIR 14	VIR 26	LIB 08	LIB 20	SCO 02	SCO 14	SCO 26

	1	2	3	4	5	6	7	8	9	10	11	12midnight
SEP 1 – PM Sign/Degree	SAG 08	SAG 20	CAP 04	CAP 19	AQU 07	AQU 28	PIS 22	ARI 18	TAU 11	GEM 01	GEM 17	CAN 02

	1	2	3	4	5	6	7	8	9	10	11	12noon
SEP 4 – AM Sign/Degree	CAN 17	CAN 28	LEO 11	LEO 23	VIR 04	VIR 16	VIR 28	LIB 10	LIB 22	SCO 04	SCO 16	SCO 28

	1	2	3	4	5	6	7	8	9	10	11	12midnight
SEP 4 – PM Sign/Degree	SAG 10	SAG 23	CAP 07	CAP 22	AQU 10	PIS 02	PIS 27	ARI 23	TAU 15	GEM 04	GEM 20	CAN 04

	1	2	3	4	5	6	7	8	9	10	11	12noon
SEP 7 – AM Sign/Degree	CAN 19	LEO 01	LEO 13	LEO 25	VIR 07	VIR 19	LIB 01	LIB 13	LIB 25	SCO 07	SCO 18	SAG 01

	1	2	3	4	5	6	7	8	9	10	11	12midnight
SEP 7 – PM Sign/Degree	SAG 12	SAG 25	CAP 09	CAP 25	AQU 14	PIS 07	ARI 02	ARI 27	TAU 19	GEM 08	GEM 23	CAN 07

	1	2	3	4	5	6	7	8	9	10	11	12noon
SEP 10 – AM Sign/Degree	CAN 21	LEO 04	LEO 15	LEO 27	VIR 09	VIR 21	LIB 03	LIB 16	LIB 27	SCO 09	SCO 21	SAG 03

	1	2	3	4	5	6	7	8	9	10	11	12midnight
SEP 10 – PM Sign/Degree	SAG 15	SAG 28	CAP 12	CAP 29	AQU 19	PIS 12	ARI 07	TAU 02	TAU 23	GEM 11	GEM 26	CAN 10

	1	2	3	4	5	6	7	8	9	10	11	12noon
SEP 13 – AM Sign/Degree	CAN 24	LEO 06	LEO 18	VIR 01	VIR 11	VIR 23	LIB 05	LIB 17	LIB 29	SCO 11	SCO 23	SAG 05

	1	2	3	4	5	6	7	8	9	10	11	12midnight
SEP 13 – PM Sign/Degree	SAG 17	CAP 01	CAP 15	AQU 03	AQU 23	PIS 17	ARI 12	TAU 06	TAU 27	GEM 14	GEM 29	CAN 12

	1	2	3	4	5	6	7	8	9	10	11	12noon
SEP 16 – AM Sign/Degree	CAN 26	LEO 08	LEO 20	VIR 02	VIR 14	VIR 26	LIB 08	LIB 20	SCO 02	SCO 14	SCO 25	SAG 07

	1	2	3	4	5	6	7	8	9	10	11	12midnight
SEP 16 – PM Sign/Degree	SAG 20	CAP 03	CAP 19	AQU 06	AQU 27	PIS 22	ARI 17	TAU 11	GEM 01	GEM 17	CAN 02	CAN 15

	1	2	3	4	5	6	7	8	9	10	11	12noon
SEP 19 – AM Sign/Degree	CAN 29	LEO 11	LEO 22	VIR 04	VIR 16	VIR 28	LIB 10	LIB 22	SCO 04	SCO 16	SCO 28	SAG 10

	1	2	3	4	5	6	7	8	9	10	11	12midnight
SEP 19 – PM Sign/Degree	SAG 23	CAP 06	CAP 22	AQU 10	PIS 02	PIS 27	ARI 22	TAU 15	GEM 04	GEM 20	CAN 04	CAN 17

	1	2	3	4	5	6	7	8	9	10	11	12noon
SEP 22 – AM Sign/Degree	LEO 01	LEO 13	LEO 25	VIR 07	VIR 19	LIB 01	LIB 13	LIB 24	SCO 06	SCO 18	SAG 01	SAG 12

	1	2	3	4	5	6	7	8	9	10	11	12midnight
SEP 22 – PM Sign/Degree	SAG 25	CAP 09	CAP 25	AQU 14	PIS 07	ARI 02	ARI 27	TAU 19	GEM 07	GEM 23	CAN 07	CAN 20

	1	2	3	4	5	6	7	8	9	10	11	12noon
SEP 25 – AM Sign/Degree	LEO 03	LEO 15	LEO 27	VIR 09	VIR 21	LIB 03	LIB 15	LIB 27	SCO 09	SCO 20	SAG 02	SAG 15

	1	2	3	4	5	6	7	8	9	10	11	12midnight
SEP 25 – PM Sign/Degree	SAG 28	CAP 12	CAP 29	AQU 18	PIS 11	ARI 07	TAU 02	TAU 23	GEM 11	GEM 26	CAN 09	CAN 22

	1	2	3	4	5	6	7	8	9	10	11	12noon
SEP 28 – AM Sign/Degree	LEO 06	LEO 18	LEO 29	VIR 11	VIR 23	LIB 05	LIB 17	LIB 29	SCO 11	SCO 23	SAG 05	SAG 17

	1	2	3	4	5	6	7	8	9	10	11	12midnight
SEP 28 – PM Sign/Degree	CAP 01	CAP 15	AQU 02	AQU 23	PIS 16	ARI 12	TAU 06	TAU 27	GEM 14	GEM 29	CAN 12	CAN 24

OCTOBER

OCT 1 – AM	1	2	3	4	5	6	7	8	9	10	11	12noon
Sign/Degree	LEO 08	LEO 20	VIR 02	VIR 14	VIR 26	LIB 08	LIB 20	SCO 02	SCO 13	SCO 25	SAG 07	SAG 20

OCT 1 – PM	1	2	3	4	5	6	7	8	9	10	11	12midnight
Sign/Degree	CAP 03	CAP 18	AQU 06	AQU 27	PIS 21	ARI 16	TAU 10	GEM 01	GEM 17	CAN 02	CAN 14	CAN 27

OCT 4 – AM	1	2	3	4	5	6	7	8	9	10	11	12noon
Sign/Degree	LEO 10	LEO 22	VIR 04	VIR 16	VIR 28	LIB 10	LIB 22	SCO 04	SCO 16	SCO 28	SAG 10	SAG 22

OCT 4 – PM	1	2	3	4	5	6	7	8	9	10	11	12midnight
Sign/Degree	CAP 06	CAP 22	AQU 10	PIS 02	PIS 26	ARI 22	TAU 15	GEM 04	GEM 20	CAN 04	CAN 17	CAN 29

OCT 7 – AM	1	2	3	4	5	6	7	8	9	10	11	12noon
Sign/Degree	LEO 13	LEO 24	VIR 06	VIR 18	LIB 01	LIB 12	LIB 24	SCO 06	SCO 18	SAG 01	SAG 12	SAG 25

OCT 7 – PM	1	2	3	4	5	6	7	8	9	10	11	12midnight
Sign/Degree	CAP 09	CAP 25	AQU 14	PIS 06	ARI 01	ARI 27	TAU 19	GEM 07	GEM 23	CAN 07	CAN 19	LEO 02

OCT 10 – AM	1	2	3	4	5	6	7	8	9	10	11	12noon
Sign/Degree	LEO 15	LEO 27	VIR 09	VIR 21	LIB 03	LIB 15	LIB 27	SCO 08	SCO 20	SAG 02	SAG 15	SAG 28

OCT 10 – PM	1	2	3	4	5	6	7	8	9	10	11	12midnight
Sign/Degree	CAP 12	CAP 28	AQU 18	PIS 11	ARI 07	TAU 01	TAU 23	GEM 10	GEM 26	CAN 09	CAN 22	LEO 04

OCT 13 – AM	1	2	3	4	5	6	7	8	9	10	11	12noon
Sign/Degree	LEO 17	LEO 29	VIR 11	VIR 23	LIB 05	LIB 17	LIB 29	SCO 11	SCO 23	SAG 05	SAG 17	CAP 01

OCT 13 – PM	1	2	3	4	5	6	7	8	9	10	11	12midnight
Sign/Degree	CAP 15	AQU 02	AQU 22	PIS 16	ARI 12	TAU 06	TAU 26	GEM 14	GEM 28	CAN 12	CAN 24	LEO 06

OCT 16 – AM	1	2	3	4	5	6	7	8	9	10	11	12noon
Sign/Degree	LEO 20	VIR 01	VIR 13	VIR 25	LIB 08	LIB 19	SCO 01	SCO 13	SCO 25	SAG 07	SAG 20	CAP 03

OCT 16 – PM	1	2	3	4	5	6	7	8	9	10	11	12midnight
Sign/Degree	CAP 18	AQU 06	AQU 27	PIS 21	ARI 17	TAU 10	GEM 01	GEM 17	CAN 01	CAN 14	CAN 27	LEO 09

OCT 19 – AM	1	2	3	4	5	6	7	8	9	10	11	12noon
Sign/Degree	LEO 22	VIR 04	VIR 16	VIR 28	LIB 10	LIB 22	SCO 04	SCO 15	SCO 27	SAG 09	SAG 22	CAP 06

OCT 19 – PM	1	2	3	4	5	6	7	8	9	10	11	12midnight
Sign/Degree	CAP 21	AQU 09	PIS 01	PIS 26	ARI 21	TAU 14	GEM 03	GEM 20	CAN 04	CAN 17	CAN 29	LEO 11

OCT 22 – AM	1	2	3	4	5	6	7	8	9	10	11	12noon
Sign/Degree	LEO 24	VIR 06	VIR 18	LIB 01	LIB 12	LIB 24	SCO 06	SCO 18	SAG 01	SAG 12	SAG 25	CAP 09

OCT 22 – PM	1	2	3	4	5	6	7	8	9	10	11	12midnight
Sign/Degree	CAP 25	AQU 13	PIS 06	ARI 01	ARI 26	TAU 18	GEM 07	GEM 23	CAN 06	CAN 19	LEO 01	LEO 13

OCT 25 – AM	1	2	3	4	5	6	7	8	9	10	11	12noon
Sign/Degree	LEO 27	VIR 08	VIR 20	LIB 02	LIB 14	LIB 26	SCO 08	SCO 20	SAG 02	SAG 14	SAG 27	CAP 12

OCT 25 – PM	1	2	3	4	5	6	7	8	9	10	11	12midnight
Sign/Degree	CAP 28	AQU 18	PIS 11	ARI 06	TAU 17	TAU 22	GEM 10	GEM 25	CAN 09	CAN 22	LEO 04	LEO 16

OCT 28 – AM	1	2	3	4	5	6	7	8	9	10	11	12noon
Sign/Degree	LEO 29	VIR 11	VIR 23	LIB 05	LIB 17	LIB 29	SCO 11	SCO 22	SAG 04	SAG 17	CAP 01	CAP 15

OCT 28 – PM	1	2	3	4	5	6	7	8	9	10	11	12midnight
Sign/Degree	AQU 02	AQU 22	PIS 16	ARI 11	TAU 05	TAU 26	GEM 13	GEM 28	CAN 12	CAN 24	LEO 06	LEO 18

OCT 31 – AM	1	2	3	4	5	6	7	8	9	10	11	12noon
Sign/Degree	VIR 01	VIR 13	VIR 25	LIB 07	LIB 19	SCO 01	SCO 13	SCO 25	SAG 07	SAG 19	CAP 03	CAP 18

OCT 31 – PM	1	2	3	4	5	6	7	8	9	10	11	12midnight
Sign/Degree	AQU 05	AQU 26	PIS 21	ARI 16	TAU 10	GEM 01	GEM 16	CAN 01	CAN 14	CAN 26	LEO 08	LEO 20

NOV 3 – AM	1	2	3	4	5	6	7	8	9	10	11	12noon
Sign/Degree	VIR 04	VIR 16	VIR 28	LIB 10	LIB 22	SCO 03	SCO 15	SCO 27	SAG 09	SAG 22	CAP 06	CAP 21

NOV 3 – PM	1	2	3	4	5	6	7	8	9	10	11	12midnight
Sign/Degree	AQU 09	PIS 01	PIS 26	ARI 21	TAU 14	GEM 03	GEM 19	CAN 04	CAN 17	CAN 29	LEO 11	LEO 23

NOV 6 – AM	1	2	3	4	5	6	7	8	9	10	11	12noon
Sign/Degree	VIR 06	VIR 18	LIB 01	LIB 12	LIB 24	SCO 06	SCO 18	SCO 29	SAG 12	SAG 24	CAP 08	CAP 24

NOV 6 – PM	1	2	3	4	5	6	7	8	9	10	11	12midnight
Sign/Degree	AQU 13	PIS 05	ARI 01	ARI 26	TAU 18	GEM 07	GEM 23	CAN 06	CAN 19	LEO 01	LEO 13	LEO 25

NOV 9 – AM	1	2	3	4	5	6	7	8	9	10	11	12noon
Sign/Degree	VIR 08	VIR 20	LIB 02	LIB 14	LIB 26	SCO 08	SCO 20	SAG 02	SAG 14	SAG 27	CAP 11	CAP 28

NOV 9 – PM	1	2	3	4	5	6	7	8	9	10	11	12midnight
Sign/Degree	AQU 17	PIS 10	ARI 06	TAU 01	TAU 22	GEM 10	GEM 25	CAN 09	CAN 21	LEO 03	LEO 15	LEO 27

NOV 12 – AM	1	2	3	4	5	6	7	8	9	10	11	12noon
Sign/Degree	VIR 11	VIR 23	LIB 05	LIB 17	LIB 29	SCO 10	SCO 22	SAG 04	SAG 17	CAP 01	CAP 14	AQU 01

NOV 12 – PM	1	2	3	4	5	6	7	8	9	10	11	12midnight
Sign/Degree	AQU 21	PIS 15	ARI 11	TAU 05	TAU 26	GEM 13	GEM 28	CAN 11	CAN 24	LEO 06	LEO 18	LEO 29

NOV 15 – AM	1	2	3	4	5	6	7	8	9	10	11	12noon
Sign/Degree	VIR 13	VIR 25	LIB 07	LIB 19	SCO 01	SCO 13	SCO 24	SAG 07	SAG 19	CAP 02	CAP 17	AQU 05

NOV 15 – PM	1	2	3	4	5	6	7	8	9	10	11	12midnight
Sign/Degree	AQU 26	PIS 20	ARI 16	TAU 09	TAU 29	GEM 16	CAN 01	CAN 14	CAN 26	LEO 08	LEO 20	VIR 02

NOV 18 – AM	1	2	3	4	5	6	7	8	9	10	11	12noon
Sign/Degree	VIR 15	VIR 27	LIB 09	LIB 21	SCO 03	SCO 15	SCO 27	SAG 09	SAG 22	CAP 05	CAP 21	AQU 09

NOV 18 – PM	1	2	3	4	5	6	7	8	9	10	11	12midnight
Sign/Degree	PIS 01	PIS 25	ARI 21	TAU 14	GEM 03	GEM 19	CAN 03	CAN 16	CAN 29	LEO 10	LEO 22	VIR 04

NOV 21 – AM	1	2	3	4	5	6	7	8	9	10	11	12noon
Sign/Degree	VIR 18	LIB 01	LIB 12	LIB 24	SCO 06	SCO 17	SCO 29	SAG 11	SAG 24	CAP 08	CAP 24	AQU 13

NOV 21 – PM	1	2	3	4	5	6	7	8	9	10	11	12midnight
Sign/Degree	PIS 05	ARI 01	ARI 25	TAU 18	GEM 06	GEM 22	CAN 06	CAN 19	LEO 01	LEO 13	LEO 25	VIR 07

NOV 24 – AM	1	2	3	4	5	6	7	8	9	10	11	12noon
Sign/Degree	VIR 20	LIB 02	LIB 14	LIB 26	SCO 08	SCO 20	SAG 02	SAG 14	SAG 27	CAP 11	CAP 27	AQU 17

NOV 24 – PM	1	2	3	4	5	6	7	8	9	10	11	12midnight
Sign/Degree	PIS 10	ARI 05	TAU 01	TAU 22	GEM 10	GEM 25	CAN 09	CAN 21	LEO 03	LEO 15	LEO 27	VIR 09

NOV 27 – AM	1	2	3	4	5	6	7	8	9	10	11	12noon
Sign/Degree	VIR 22	LIB 04	LIB 16	LIB 28	SCO 10	SCO 22	SAG 04	SAG 16	CAP 01	CAP 14	AQU 01	AQU 21

NOV 27 – PM	1	2	3	4	5	6	7	8	9	10	11	12midnight
Sign/Degree	PIS 15	ARI 10	TAU 05	TAU 25	GEM 13	GEM 28	CAN 11	CAN 24	LEO 06	LEO 17	LEO 29	VIR 11

NOV 30 – AM	1	2	3	4	5	6	7	8	9	10	11	12noon
Sign/Degree	VIR 25	LIB 07	LIB 19	SCO 01	SCO 12	SCO 24	SAG 06	SAG 19	CAP 02	CAP 17	AQU 05	AQU 25

NOV 30 – PM	1	2	3	4	5	6	7	8	9	10	11	12midnight
Sign/Degree	PIS 20	ARI 15	TAU 09	GEM 01	GEM 16	CAN 01	CAN 14	CAN 26	LEO 08	LEO 20	VIR 02	VIR 14

DECEMBER

DEC 3 – AM	1	2	3	4	5	6	7	8	9	10	11	12noon
Sign/Degree	VIR 27	LIB 09	LIB 21	SCO 03	SCO 15	SCO 27	SAG 09	SAG 21	CAP 05	CAP 20	AQU 08	PIS 01

DEC 3 – PM	1	2	3	4	5	6	7	8	9	10	11	12midnight
Sign/Degree	PIS 25	ARI 20	TAU 13	GEM 03	GEM 19	CAN 03	CAN 16	CAN 28	LEO 10	LEO 22	VIR 04	VIR 16

DEC 6 – AM	1	2	3	4	5	6	7	8	9	10	11	12noon
Sign/Degree	LIB 01	LIB 12	LIB 23	SCO 05	SCO 17	SCO 29	SAG 11	SAG 24	CAP 08	CAP 24	AQU 12	PIS 04

DEC 6 – PM	1	2	3	4	5	6	7	8	9	10	11	12midnight
Sign/Degree	ARI 01	ARI 25	TAU 17	GEM 06	GEM 22	CAN 06	CAN 19	LEO 01	LEO 13	LEO 24	VIR 06	VIR 18

DEC 9 – AM	1	2	3	4	5	6	7	8	9	10	11	12noon
Sign/Degree	LIB 02	LIB 14	LIB 26	SCO 08	SCO 19	SAG 01	SAG 14	SAG 27	CAP 11	CAP 27	AQU 16	PIS 09

DEC 9 – PM	1	2	3	4	5	6	7	8	9	10	11	12midnight
Sign/Degree	ARI 05	TAU 01	TAU 21	GEM 09	GEM 25	CAN 08	CAN 21	LEO 03	LEO 15	LEO 27	VIR 09	VIR 21

DEC 12 – AM	1	2	3	4	5	6	7	8	9	10	11	12noon
Sign/Degree	LIB 04	LIB 16	LIB 28	SCO 10	SCO 22	SAG 04	SAG 16	SAG 29	CAP 14	AQU 01	AQU 21	PIS 14

DEC 12 – PM	1	2	3	4	5	6	7	8	9	10	11	12midnight
Sign/Degree	ARI 10	TAU 04	TAU 25	GEM 12	GEM 27	CAN 11	CAN 23	LEO 05	LEO 17	LEO 29	VIR 11	VIR 23

DEC 15 – AM	1	2	3	4	5	6	7	8	9	10	11	12noon
Sign/Degree	LIB 07	LIB 19	SCO 01	SCO 12	SCO 24	SAG 06	SAG 19	CAP 02	CAP 17	AQU 04	AQU 25	PIS 19

DEC 15 – PM	1	2	3	4	5	6	7	8	9	10	11	12midnight
Sign/Degree	ARI 15	TAU 09	TAU 29	GEM 16	CAN 01	CAN 13	CAN 26	LEO 08	LEO 20	VIR 01	VIR 13	VIR 25

DEC 18 – AM	1	2	3	4	5	6	7	8	9	10	11	12noon
Sign/Degree	LIB 09	LIB 21	SCO 03	SCO 15	SCO 26	SAG 09	SAG 21	CAP 05	CAP 20	AQU 08	PIS 01	PIS 24

DEC 18 – PM	1	2	3	4	5	6	7	8	9	10	11	12midnight
Sign/Degree	ARI 20	TAU 13	GEM 02	GEM 19	CAN 03	CAN 16	CAN 28	LEO 10	LEO 22	VIR 04	VIR 16	VIR 28

DEC 21 – AM	1	2	3	4	5	6	7	8	9	10	11	12noon
Sign/Degree	LIB 11	LIB 23	SCO 05	SCO 17	SCO 29	SAG 11	SAG 24	CAP 08	CAP 23	AQU 12	PIS 04	ARI 01

DEC 21 – PM	1	2	3	4	5	6	7	8	9	10	11	12midnight
Sign/Degree	ARI 25	TAU 17	GEM 06	GEM 22	CAN 06	CAN 18	LEO 01	LEO 12	LEO 24	VIR 06	VIR 18	LIB 01

DEC 24 – AM	1	2	3	4	5	6	7	8	9	10	11	12noon
Sign/Degree	LIB 14	LIB 26	SCO 08	SCO 19	SAG 01	SAG 14	SAG 26	CAP 11	CAP 27	AQU 16	PIS 09	ARI 04

DEC 24 – PM	1	2	3	4	5	6	7	8	9	10	11	12midnight
Sign/Degree	ARI 29	TAU 21	GEM 09	GEM 25	CAN 08	CAN 21	LEO 03	LEO 15	LEO 27	VIR 08	VIR 20	LIB 02

DEC 27 – AM	1	2	3	4	5	6	7	8	9	10	11	12noon
Sign/Degree	LIB 16	LIB 28	SCO 10	SCO 22	SAG 04	SAG 16	SAG 29	CAP 14	AQU 01	AQU 20	PIS 14	ARI 09

DEC 27 – PM	1	2	3	4	5	6	7	8	9	10	11	12midnight
Sign/Degree	TAU 04	TAU 25	GEM 12	GEM 27	CAN 11	CAN 23	LEO 05	LEO 17	LEO 29	VIR 11	VIR 23	LIB 05

DEC 30 – AM	1	2	3	4	5	6	7	8	9	10	11	12noon
Sign/Degree	LIB 18	SCO 01	SCO 12	SCO 24	SAG 06	SAG 18	CAP 02	CAP 17	AQU 04	AQU 25	PIS 19	ARI 14

DEC 30 – PM	1	2	3	4	5	6	7	8	9	10	11	12midnight
Sign/Degree	TAU 08	TAU 28	GEM 15	CAN 01	CAN 13	CAN 25	LEO 08	LEO 19	VIR 01	VIR 13	VIR 25	LIB 07

Rising Signs
Through the Zodiac

ARIES RISING

Expressing through Doing

You find identity simply through putting yourself forward. Initially at least, it does not matter in what way you do this – just so long as you do. With Aries in the Ascendant, just letting life go by will achieve that, and only that – until something happens that jolts you out of such hanging back and holding in. Through thick and thin, though, most of the time you present a chirpy or childlike external image, spontaneously going to the front.

The Keyword here is self-actualization. As far as you are concerned, to act, to physically do something, is what creates the Self. Nothing else will – except being acted upon by someone else in a typically Arian forceful or even violent fashion, which is more likely to be destructive to you. If this is the case, then it is a strong indication that independence must be sought and maintained.

Simply being impulsive is a strong alternative to being self-actualizing – or, in some cases, one could say that it is a precursor to it. It might take quite a few years before you stop and consider what you want, rather than energetically and possibly impudently pushing for what you want – or what you think you want at the time. You can come across as quite valiant in the process however, as you perennially put yourself forward as a champion of the underdog.

Your Ruling Planet is MARS. Its condition by Sign and House is very important here, because this will show in more detail the best way in which you can assert yourself – or how this is possibly being blocked or compromised.

Physically you appear to be quite energized – as if something was about to pop. This is particularly notice-able in your eyes, which have an intense, pointed quality – rather like a bird's. And they dart about rather than hold a fixed stare. However, all physical features can also be affected by any First House Planets if you have any (see Planet-House Chart on page 368), or again, Mars' placement.

Aries Rising means that you have the opposite sign of Libra Setting, which indicates that your possibly over-forceful attitude and self-presentation would benefit from being toned down by some social consideration and sense of harmony if you wish to maintain agreeable relationships. The Sign and House of VENUS will reveal more concerning the nature and quality of your relationships and partner(s). Recognize that you are likely to come across as arrogant, pushy or cheeky – even if you do not actually feel that way inside. Whatever the case, you are likely to attract sociable, considerate types who could be seen as trying to get you to take a leaf out of their book. Conversely, if you feel held back for some reason, then formulating some social purpose or ideal will help to mobilize your being.

If in doubt – Act! 'Courage is not merely one of the virtues – but every virtue at its testing point'.

• *TIP Considering any connections (Aspects) of the Planets mentioned above (MARS and VENUS) to other Planets in your Chart – by consulting the section entitled Compatibility on page 10 – will tell you more about the impression you give of yourself to others and about your relationships/partner(s).*
• *TIP Reading the double-page spread for SUN in ARIES (pages 124–125) will further describe the qualities of your persona or self-presentation.*

TAURUS RISING

Expressing through Stabilizing

You find identity through seeking for yourself a sense of substance. This is usually material in as much as you like to own things in the form of property, investments, credit, etc. But it could also mean something purely biological, such as a having a baby – and this is particularly significant if you are a female who has not found any other meaning to her life. On the literally earthy level of expression, you are at home with yourself while gardening or involved with Nature in some way.

As stability is very important to you, you do not entertain too broad a scope of possibilities as a rule, because this would complicate matters or create a 'top-heaviness'. You like to keep things at a manageable level. This approach can cause you to limit yourself unnecessarily, expressed as being mean (with yourself or others), or not seeing the whole picture – tunnel vision, or hanging on to what is known and tangible for too long. On a purely physical level this can manifest as astigmatism or myopia. However, limited as the field of endeavour may be, you are thorough and efficient and dependable within that field.

You have a liking for things of the flesh – food, drink, sex, etc. Also art or crafts figure in some way. Your Ruling Planet Is VENUS, and its position by Sign and House will reveal more concerning the sensuous and aesthetic qualities of your being, which are quite pronounced – and also regarding your financial fortunes, which are very important to you.

Your physical looks fall into one of two distinctive types. The more obvious one is the earthy, thick-necked, curly-haired kind who exudes a strongly physical aura – often attractive to the opposite sex. The other type is more fine-featured, but maybe slightly fleshy in parts – full-lipped for instance. This type is also usually sexually attractive, but not in such an obvious way.

Being ruled by material considerations at the expense of the more intangible or spiritual dimensions of life is an inclination you have that can lead to a sort of thick-headed confusion. Taurus Rising then needs to remind itself that it is designed to seek, experience and give stability and beauty on a physical level, but not at the expense of the spirit or sentiment within. Taken to its extreme, this materialistic type can wind up having everything but enjoying little or nothing.

With the opposite Sign of Scorpio Setting, you attract or are attracted to people and relationships that force you to feel and look at a deeper level. Your partner may not be aware of doing this, but one way or the other, you can feel either the beneficiary or the victim of his or her powers. In this way your awareness of the significance of the non-tangible or psychological qualities of life is encouraged or forced to develop. Sexual influences exert an especially strong pull – for good or ill. The Sign and House of PLUTO will reveal more concerning the nature of your relationships and partner(s), as well as a more profound way of relating.

• TIP *Considering any connections (Aspects) of the Planets mentioned above (VENUS and PLUTO) to other Planets in your Chart – by consulting the section entitled Compatibility on page 10 and the Introduction to the Outer Planets on page 307 – will tell you more about the impression you give of yourself to others and about your relationships/partner(s).*
• TIP *Reading the double-page spread for SUN in TAURUS (pages 126–127) will further describe the qualities of your persona or self-presentation.*

GEMINI RISING

Expressing through Communicating

You find your identity through making as many contacts as possible, for having interesting facts, useful people and witty anecdotes at your fingertips gives you an impression of 'being here'. To others this can come across as the party or conversation maker, or as a kind of blur of cerebral activity which makes them wonder what it is you are hiding or really trying to express. Your body expressions, especially hand and facial ones, are as agile as your mind. Your physical build is usually wiry or slim – but of course there may be other astrological indications to the contrary. And being so light and airy, you may put weight on as sheer ballast!

The condition of your Ruling Planet, MERCURY, by Sign and House is extremely important with Gemini Rising. You tend to stand or fall by your mental abilities or social and business contacts. A poorly placed Mercury, or an emphasis on its negative traits, will diminish your confidence more than usual, so in effect this Ascendant really forces you to get your mental or social act together. A positively expressed Mercury, on the other hand, will enable you to come across clear and strong.

You can get side-tracked by the individual points of any given issue, and overlook what it means as a whole. With Gemini Rising you have the opposite Sign of Sagittarius Setting, which means that ideally you attract a partner who is expansive and understanding and able to grasp the wider and emotional implications. The Sign and House of JUPITER will reveal more concerning the nature and quality of your relationships and partner(s), and the wisest way of relating. You yourself are more inclined to indulge in gossip and banter – at least where everyday intercourse is concerned. And it is your sparkling sense of humour that allows you to get away with murder. You can readily adapt to various types of company or situation, but thereby run the risk of appearing two-faced. Indeed, you may well have two or more names that you go by in different circles. Mimicking can also be a particularly special and amusing talent of yours.

You are a communicator, so being able to make your thoughts and feelings known through the benefit of a good education is rather important – particularly in languages. Fortunately, you are naturally inquisitive, which is essential for someone to whom assimilating facts and figures is as important as breathing. A lack of curiosity on your part would usually be a sign that there is some serious inner doubt going on.

You are dextrous and versatile, and have a light touch. Potentially, this makes you very relaxing yet also stimulating to be with. However, this might hide something more dark and delving – especially if there are Scorpio or Eighth House placements, or a prominent Pluto in your Chart – and this could amount to one reason for your being occasionally two-faced. You do not enter emotional involvements that easily because they pose the threat of limiting your other involvements, or forcing you to face your own contradictions. This dilemma is best handled by treating all experiences, particularly intimate relationships, as vital to the power and depth of your communications, unless you wish to be known as a lightweight – that is, not really being in touch with what is going on.

• TIP *Considering any connections (Aspects) of the Planets mentioned above (MERCURY and JUPITER) to other Planets in your Chart – by consulting the section entitled Compatibility on page 10 – will tell you more about the impression you give of yourself to others and about your relationships/partner(s).*
• TIP *Reading the double-page spread for SUN in GEMINI (pages 130–131) will further describe the qualities of your persona or self-presentation.*

CANCER RISING

Expressing through Nurturing

You find your identity through responding to the needs of yourself and others. You are therefore protective and are able to sense those needs in others. This is naturally useful and valuable in many fields – commerce, education, parenthood, etc. However, in order that you do not get overstretched it is advisable that you set limits upon your responses to the requirements of others.

You have a caring and receptive aura, and look for or act naturally as a mother figure, be you male or female. In fact, mother complexes are common with this Ascendant; it is important to establish whether or not such strong ties with her – and with your family in general – are completely healthy.

Yours is a very personal and soft approach – and therefore it feels easy to approach you. But this can be quite deceptive because there is a shell protecting the source of your vulnerable softness. So with Cancer Rising, you like being close – but not too close. This Ascendant has been described as the 'Emotional Waste Paper Basket', for you can be 'dumped upon' as a result of appearing too available emotionally. This may resemble a feeling of security through being needed, but some discrimination and increased sense of self-worth are eventually called for.

The Sign and House of your Ruling Planet, the MOON, will show in more detail how your much-needed security may be found, along with how the instinct to nurture may be utilized profitably and in a balanced fashion.

In truth, you best find and express yourself by realizing, meeting and promoting the 'family' need in everyone – be it your actual nuclear family or that of the human race, or any section of society with which you sympathize. Considering that this Rising Sign exudes such soft familiarity this should not be too hard – unless your shell is allowed to get in the way!

You also have a closeness to Nature herself, expressed as an ability to tune in to natural rhythms, methods and sources that may in turn be used to attain that much-needed security as an innate trust in all life processes (social, physical, emotional, mental, biological, ecological, etc.).

Crab-like, you approach matters and people in a sideways, indirect fashion. This can be very consoling to someone who needs to be dealt with in such a softly-softly fashion; but if there is an emotionally sticky issue that needs confronting, it can prove exasperating for those involved.

With Cancer Rising you have the opposite Sign of Capricorn Setting, which means that you generally like or attract a partner that lays down definite limits and a structural framework to which you can keep. Security is thus bought with reduced freedom, but this may paradoxically lead to your wanting more freedom. The Sign and House of SATURN will reveal more concerning the nature and quality of your relationships and partner(s), and how you may learn to relate more objectively and realistically. This is important because your emotional receptivity – which is your major asset – can cause you to take things too personally.

• TIP *Considering any connections (Aspects) of the Planets mentioned above (MOON and SATURN) to other Planets in your Chart – by consulting the section entitled Compatibility on page 10 – will tell you more about the impression you give of yourself to others and about your relationships/partner(s).*
• TIP *Reading the double-page spread for SUN in CANCER (pages 130–131) will further describe the qualities of your persona or self-presentation.*

LEO RISING

Expressing through Creating

This Ascendant gives you a winning, confident and usually sunny exterior. But how much your inner being is living up to this outer show can be another story entirely. It is as if you project a successful image which the rest of your personality has to live up to somehow. This can prove to be a very effective means of self-development, as long as you do not weaken. Pride in your appearance is therefore significant and important.

The commanding impression observed by others should not be underestimated or overlooked – because it is either convincing and effective or overbearing and affected. And responses from others that vindicate your own actions or attitudes are easily believed. So beware flatterers and bootlickers, for they could give you a false impression of yourself. All the same, you do need approval and praise from others in order to maintain your confidence. You have the persona of the actor – which you may actually be – or royalty, so a good 'audience response' is important.

But your need to be admired can also give rise to a fear of failure, which in turn poses as not even trying to live up to your sense or image of specialness. This can lead to your being gripped by a very uncharacteristic resentment towards a world that has not recognized that specialness. As a rule then, it is essential to obtain feedback in order that your sense of self-worth and power may become a reality rather than remaining a fantasy. And it is important to bear in mind that the desire of Leo Rising to lead, rule and impress is rooted in uncertainty. Where would the Sun be without the sky? What is a monarch without subjects? So, properly expressed, Leo Rising should also include the revealing of your doubts and fears to a trusted friend, partner or professional.

The pursuit of individual self-expression is what Leo Rising is mainly about. There are plenty of opportunities to prove, modify and stand up for this – one reason being that such overt egoism will attract others that either admire it or attack it, or both. Success and admiration are most likely to be found in the qualities of expression and areas of experience signified by the Sign and House position of your Ruling Planet, the SUN. And like the Sun which rules Leo, your personality is best seen as something that is constantly radiating light and warmth. Concentrating on the source of this (your heart) can be literally enlightening. Generosity lights the way. You should possess a proud and noble bearing, and celebrate all individuality, not just your own. In this way, true respect is won.

With Leo Rising you have the opposite sign of Aquarius Setting, which means that you will attract unusual or unstable relationships and people that require a certain amount of detachment and freedom/non-possessiveness. This is in aid of balancing out the Leonine self-centredness which you appear to have. The Sign and House of URANUS will reveal more concerning the nature and quality of your relationships and partner(s), as well as how you may evolve that all-important detached manner of relating – but without being insular.

• TIP *Considering any connections (Aspects) of the Planets mentioned above (SUN and URANUS) to other Planets in your Chart – by consulting the section entitled Compatibility on page 10 and the Introduction to the Outer Planets on page 307 – will tell you more about the impression you give of yourself to others and about your relationships/partner(s).*
• TIP *Reading the double-page spread for SUN in LEO (pages 132–133) will further describe the qualities of your persona or self-presentation.*

VIRGO RISING

Expressing through Analysing

You find your identity through a constant process of self-improvement and discrimination. It is also very helpful for you to develop or be trained in a definite skill or technique, and to be of some kind of service to others. Being usefully employed is essential to your sense of self. The Sign and House of your Ruling Planet, MERCURY, will further indicate work nature and difficulties, as well as your general manner of self-presentation.

You can have a 'slave' consciousness which leads to your being taken for granted and/or holding a grudge at feeling so menial. In the first case it may be necessary to 'go on strike'; in the second case you should cultivate a sense of service to others. There is a modesty or subtle shyness about your person that is very becoming. Beware false modesty, though – that is, underplaying your hand for fear of not living up to it.

You are usually clean and neatly turned out, or dishevelled in a studied kind of way. You appear younger than your actual age, or at least, your eyes (as distinct from the surrounding skin) are especially clear and unlived-in. This could be owing to the fact that you are quite health conscious – if not downright obsessive about it! Whatever the case, this should not be ignored in any way, for with Virgo Rising, you do have a keen awareness of what actually constitutes a healthy life. At a more extreme level of expression, such health-consciousness can cause you to be quite insular. Such insularity is also in aid of emotionally protecting yourself. You then develop a strong preoccupation with things being 'just so', characterized by an ongoing criticism of what and who is happening around you. This in turn can lead to your being rigidly self-contained and having a justification for not becoming involved with life – even though you might appear to be otherwise.

Looked at in another way, at least one area of your life has to be kept untainted by anything that is unwholesome or not entirely of your own choosing. This 'island of purity' is very important for it creates for you a feeling of keeping some vital part of yourself intact. In physical terms this could apply to your own body, or to an actual place to which you may retreat – like your home. Psychologically, it could be a highly individualistic attitude of mind that others could be aware of, but are very unlikely to pin down.

There is a certain clinical detachment in the way that you approach things. Professionally this can give a positively efficient impression. On a more intimate level, such a laboratory attitude may seem disenchanting – even creepy. You can appear to be watching every slightest move or detail. Others can find this reassuring or bothersome; it very much depends on what the feeling is behind such a perceptive gaze. Is it critical or caring?

With Virgo Rising you have the opposite Sign of Pisces Setting. This means that on the positive side you will attract sensitive or artistic folk. Negatively, it means that you become a target for lame-ducks or disorderly people. But in actual fact, this acts as a balance or challenge to the above described reserve or need to aid and assist where necessary. The condition of NEPTUNE by Sign and House will reveal much about the subtleties and difficulties of your relationships, partner(s) and manner of relating.

• *TIP Considering any connections (Aspects) of the Planets mentioned above (MERCURY and NEPTUNE) to other Planets in your Chart – by consulting the section entitled Compatibility on page 10 and the Introduction to the Outer Planets on page 307 – will tell you more about the impression you give of yourself to others and about your relationships/partner(s).*
• *TIP Reading the double-page spread for SUN in VIRGO (pages 134–135) will further describe the qualities of your persona or self-presentation.*

LIBRA RISING

Expressing through Relating

Even though the rest of your Chart/Personality may be quite independent and self-determining, with Libra Rising you will attempt to find your identity as a counterweight to whatever is going on around and about you. Usually this is a matter of adjusting yourself to fit in and harmonize, and to consistently put forward 'the case for the opposition'. It can also mean that if things are socially a bit dull, then a few caustic remarks may be in order. Or, conversely, a touch of seriousness could be introduced by you when the going gets too frivolous.

This is all very well, but who is this person, this human counterweight? What are his or her own values, beliefs, convictions? It is very important that these are arrived at and acted upon if you are to avoid becoming a cipher who finds it impossible to get off the fence and make a decision that does not need the approval of whoever you regard as the 'approving body'.

It is especially important for you to have and maintain a relationship – or even relationships. This is in order to have a counterweight to your own counterweight, with a view to finding your mettle through a 'worthy opponent'. The condition by Sign and House of your Ruling Planet, VENUS, will show how you might find a balanced individual identity – and a partner to match it and help you to create it. It will also reveal more about your artistic sense and abilities, things which are very significant to you because you attach much importance to the look of things. But as balance is the vital factor, make sure that beauty of form is matched by beauty or value of content, otherwise you will become greatly disappointed when something or someone (which includes yourself) turns out to be less than their appearance suggests.

You are always trying to be fair, and often you have the looks to match. But to be a successful social animal you have to have firm social principles if you are to discover and establish your own ground, rather than just teeter on the spot. The undeniable social or political outlook that is present with Libra Rising should become a dynamic expression, rather than a two-dimensional response that can earn you a reputation for indecisiveness, insincerity or moral cowardice – or for lacking any individual identity.

With Libra Rising, you have the opposite Sign of Aries Setting, which means that you tend to attract quite assertive partners. You either accept this as desirable, or eventually you realize that this is an imbalance, or even an injustice, in itself, and that you must get off that fence and start making your own standpoint firm and clear. However, if you are used to being the one who makes the decisions, you are probably not inclined to trust your partner or others to do so. As a result of this failure to delegate, others may have to resort to being troublesome in some way – from being aggressive or to being feeble. The Sign and House of MARS will reveal more concerning the nature and quality of your relationships and partner(s), and how they and your style of relating have everything to do with your manner of self-assertion.

• *TIP Considering any connections (Aspects) of the Planets mentioned above (VENUS and MARS) to other Planets in your Chart – by consulting the section entitled Compatibility on page 10 – will tell you more about the impression you give of yourself to others and about your relationships/partner(s).*
• *TIP Reading the double-page spread for SUN in LIBRA (pages 136–137) will further describe the qualities of your persona or self-presentation.*

SCORPIO RISING

Expressing through Desiring

You emanate a strong emotional and sexual force-field that can transform your surroundings, be they personal or even global, to a far better or far worse state. Notable examples include Gandhi, Mussolini, Lenin, Stalin, Margaret Thatcher. You base your identity on power and influence, and consequently have to wrestle with the dark side of life and of yourself. Failure to do so creates an unpleasant atmosphere.

This dark side, or the Id or the 'Beast', should be exorcized and expressed artistically or psychotherapeutically, or through sexual love – or a combination of these. You need a stable and resolute mate to balance out this intensity. This is indicated by having the opposite Sign of Taurus Setting, for the Bull is noted for its stability. But you should endeavour to develop your own stable qualities. The Sign and House of VENUS will reveal more concerning the nature and quality of your relationships and partner(s) – and how to relate more positively and openly.

You usually have a penetrating gaze – as if you are seeing life through X-ray eyes. These match your strong sexual vibration and sense. You also have the ability to become quite unnoticeable, yet still emanate that intense atmosphere. Some might regard this as the 'Evil Eye'.

You like secrecy and all that it involves. As such, you make an excellent confidante, for possessing a secret is far more enjoyable to you than spreading gossip. However, you can get caught on a power trip of belonging to a 'chosen few', like a secret society.

Or your sense of secrecy could be expressed as keeping your deepest doubts and feelings to yourself, with the consequence being that no one can really get close to you – which is actually what you desire deep down. So use this natural 'cloaking device' sparingly and consciously, not as 'standard dress'. Otherwise, you might get it stuck, so to speak, to your face. Scorpio, after all, is the intimate Sign that is able to get in genuinely close to life and others. That is why Scorpio has such strong intuition, so that you might feel your way through to a healthy intimacy – as opposed to using that intuition to avoid such a thing.

You can or should, in a constructive way, draw power from your partner or the mechanisms that society has to offer. Negative or unconscious expressions of this could be megalomania or 'vampirism'. Failure to recognize or use such power can result in feeling lonely and uninvolved with life's inherent energies. On the other hand, you could sap someone so much that they become a dead weight, or simply leave you or be unfaithful to you.

The condition of your Ruling Planet, PLUTO, by Sign and House will reveal more concerning the manner of your self-expression, the nature of your life's transformations and intimate attachments, as well as the matters with which you identify most intensely.

• *TIP Considering any connections (Aspects) of the Planets mentioned above (PLUTO and VENUS) to other Planets in your Chart – by consulting the section entitled Compatibility on page 10 and the Introduction to the Outer Planets on page 307 – will tell you more about the impression you give of yourself to others and about your relationships/partner(s).*
• *TIP Reading the double-page spread for SUN in SCORPIO (pages 138–139) will further describe the qualities of your persona or self-presentation.*

SAGITTARIUS RISING

Expressing through Seeking

With Sagittarius in the Ascendant you are likely to constantly see the world as your oyster. Life is always full of great possibilities, extraordinary experiences and horizons to disappear over.

Such an outgoing and adventurous outlook is obviously an asset – providing it eventually becomes more than just an outlook. This is because there is the danger with Sagittarius of promising yourself and others the world and delivering practically nothing. You can be great at exhorting others to do more and gain more out of life, but if after a time all your enthusiasms turn out to be just a string of wild schemes, others are liable to grin politely and then raise their eyebrows when your back is turned.

You stir people up one way or another – almost whether you want to or not. Your friction-producing character is as unavoidable as actually being here. Some kind of philosophical or enterprising end has to be in sight so that there is an intelligent and appealing direction to justify your arousing nature. Put in another way, you have to have a product to match your advertisement. On a social level, you are a good party person. In fact you are often the spirit of enjoyment itself. You excel at gathering people together for any reason, be it in the role of teacher, preacher or reveller.

Your physical features are usually broad, or at least there is a certain breadth of character that is both exciting and relaxing to be with; somewhat similar to standing next to a horse. Your physique can be rangy or lanky, or compact and lively, but your expansive nature can manifest as a weight problem when not properly expressed. A long prominent jaw, with a horse-like grin, can also be in evidence.

This vibrant physical presence of yours can sometimes be downright impossible to ignore. This is expressive of the horse half of the Centaur – the loping and libidinous animal drive. The upper or human half of Sagittarius represents your idealistic and truth-seeking self which is ever at pains to keep the lower half from galloping off on its own and getting up to mischief. In any event, though, travel and freedom of movement are very necessary; how else could you carry on seeking?!

The condition of your Ruling Planet, JUPITER, by Sign and House will indicate in what way, and with how much ease or difficulty, your aims, adventures and aspirations are furthered and satisfied.

With Sagittarius Rising you have the opposite Sign of Gemini Setting, which means that you are liable to attract people that wish to provide you with the facts and figures of life in order to complement your adventurous projects. This may be experienced as them checking your progress and limiting your freedom with tiresome trivia – but in fact they are probably making that vitally practical contribution which you can so easily overlook. Gemini, being the Sign of Duality, can also mean that you are inclined to have more than one relationship on the go at the same time. If you can maintain this, then okay. But there could well come a time when what amounts to a double standard has to be faced and sorted out. The Sign and House of MERCURY will reveal more concerning the nature and quality of your relationships and partner(s).

• TIP Considering any connections (Aspects) of the Planets mentioned above (JUPITER and MERCURY) to other Planets in your Chart – by consulting the section entitled Compatibility on page 10 – will tell you more about the impression you give of yourself to others and about your relationships/partner(s).
• TIP Reading the double-page spread for SUN in SAGITTARIUS (pages 140–141) will further describe the qualities of your persona or self-presentation.

CAPRICORN RISING

Expressing through Building

With Capricorn there is always a need for order and usefulness, so with this Sign placed here on your Ascendant the flow of your self-expression greatly depends on whether these criteria are being met. So your approach to life is decidedly industrious, no-nonsense and geared to weighing yourself down with what you regard as worthwhile responsibilities.

However, there is another side to Capricorn other than this rather serious and inhibiting one, and this has to do with the Goat's closeness to Nature. A good way to appreciate this is to think of Pan (the Goat-footed God) who is the Deity of the fruits of the Earth, which are to be both enjoyed and employed. Indeed, considering your hard-working nature, you should enjoy the senses simply because you deserve to.

With regard to your physical appearance you can appear quite earthy, rock-like, with a prominent brow – or even a little devilish (Pan again!). Or you might incline to the lean and bony, reflecting the hard-working and sometimes self-denying quality of this Sign.

While on the bleak side you can sometimes be a wet blanket in company, at your best other people feel happy and secure at work or at play when they are in your presence, for you give off an impression of having the material situation under control. Even though this could be somewhat illusory, you should regard this image that you project of order and efficiency as your own role model, rather than blindly modelling yourself on external standards. This is something which, with Capricorn Rising, you are in danger of doing and thereby losing sight of your true self. You are more than just the work you do and the position you maintain in the outside world.

However, having a figure or element of authority in life is very important to you. Initially you usually look to your father for this, but if he is weak or absent then this can leave you feeling that your life lacks authority and structure. In turn this can make you uncharacteristically feckless, even rebellious, as a result of lacking confidence. On the other hand a strong and healthy father image does much to prepare Capricorn Rising for taking on the material world – something which your innate ambition requires. The condition by Sign and House of your Ruling Planet, SATURN, will reveal more regarding your finding or being that figure of strength and authority that proves so important in making you feel able to present an authoritative image to the outside world and thereby amount to something in it.

Ultimately, whatever the case concerning this essential need for having a sense of authority and control over your environment, you do need to develop it. In some cases, especially if you are male, you might have to take on a fatherly role quite early on in life.

As a balance to the somewhat austere and even harsh demeanour of Capricorn Rising, you are attracted to a partner who embodies the soft, homely and protective characteristics which are symbolized by the opposite and complementary Sign that is setting, Cancer. Being sympathetic and emotionally receptive is also an advisable way of relating to your mate in particular, and others in general. The Sign and House of the MOON will reveal more concerning the nature and quality of your relationships and partner(s), and how to relate through a more natural response.

• TIP *Considering any connections (Aspects) of the Planets mentioned above (SATURN and MOON) to other Planets in your Chart – by consulting the section entitled Compatibility on page 10 – will tell you more about the impression you give of yourself to others and about your relationships/partner(s).*
• TIP *Reading the double-page spread for SUN in CAPRICORN (pages 142–143) will further describe the qualities of your persona or self-presentation.*

AQUARIUS RISING

Expressing through Liberating

You have a decidedly detached outlook and out of the ordinary air about you. Life is initially seen as a process to be observed coolly and impartially. This can lead to either a strong awareness of how society and life functions as a whole (through, on your part, an absence of subjectivity or emotional bias), or an inability to become involved on a personal level (often going no further than presenting to others a 'civilized idea' of what you think you are supposed to be – and this may even include a 'politically correct wildness').

With Aquarius Rising, you have the opposite Sign of Leo Setting, which means that as a compensatory reaction to your cool exterior you attract passionate or even explosive relationships and situations which are in aid of burning through to the heart of the matter which is hidden behind that idealistic and conceptualized façade. Your ability to chill out and cut off when the emotional going gets too rough is remarkable; but use it carefully, for one day you might find it both difficult and desirable to switch it – or the person you want – on again. The Sign and House of the SUN will reveal more concerning the nature and quality of your relationships and partner(s), and recommended style of relating.

You look to groups and friendships to gain a sense of identity, and if you suffer a loss of friendship, this can lead to a loss of identity. Ultimately, you wish to see yourself in the context of something that goes beyond social norms and acceptability. You are therefore attuned to any movements or styles that are in the forefront of evolution, be it computers, space, way-out fashions, the avant garde, New Age thought, etc. You also like to cultivate an unusual or individual appearance – which may often be what is currently laid down as looking 'unusual'. This embodies the paradox of being as individualistic as everyone else is being! On the other hand, you can look naturally and physically unusual, yet at the same time quintessentially 'human'.

You are inventive and like to set trends amongst your peers. Being so future orientated, you therefore need to have some goal or vision to work towards. You identify with freedom and equality – as far as you understand such principles. Sooner or later, one way or the other, these qualities are promoted or furthered by you. At the same time, though, this can make you a bit blind to the fact that consciously-held ideals in society are not as common as you like to imagine. The Utopian visions that Aquarius Rising can behold do not easily survive or get understood by the masses (those of Karl Marx and Abraham Lincoln, for example). Yet for you, hope always springs eternal, and you do have the ability to see the shape and pattern of things to come.

The condition by Sign and House of your Ruling Planet, URANUS, will indicate in what way, and with how much ease or difficulty, your individual identity and sense of freedom and future vision may be found and forged.

• TIP Considering any connections (Aspects) of the Planets mentioned above (URANUS and SUN) to other Planets in your Chart – by consulting the section entitled Compatibility on page 10 and the Introduction to the Outer Planets on page 307 – will tell you more about the impression you give of yourself to others and about your relationships/partner(s).
• TIP Reading the double-page spread for SUN in AQUARIUS (pages 144–145) will further describe the qualities of your persona or self-presentation.

PISCES RISING

Expressing through Accepting

Because you experience your body as one big feeler or antenna, you are very open to pleasure and pain, and therefore you identify with whatever stimulus seems the most appropriate to your ever-shifting outlook. If you feel like languishing ecstatically, then you become an exotic hedonist; if guilt prevails, then you are drawn to pain and punishment, or purity and asceticism. When feeling positive and noble, the artist or the healer appears as your persona. The list is endless.

Sooner or later your life has to be organized in a fashion that stops your various identities constantly changing into one another, for this breeds some confusion in others, and oceans of it in yourself. It's a good idea to bear In mind that a human kaleidoscope can be as boring as the real thing after a while. In order to acquire this integrated identity, you should embark upon a definite task or service in order that your supersensitivity be positively employed and enjoyed, otherwise you are in danger of dissolving into the boundless.

Such sensitivity could be divided into three types: Intuitive-Healing; Imaginative-Inspiring; Mystical-Enlightening. In the first case, it is a soft and soothing presence, which is also deep and powerful, like the sea, and this can give rise to a healing ability. It is as if others bathe in your aura, and are buoyed up and relaxed by it. In fact, the nature of the sea is embodied in Pisces Rising – calm on the surface and stormy beneath – or vice versa, engulfing, enchanting, fascinating, downsucking, surging, far-reaching, etc.

In the second case, the myriad impressions you receive from your inner and outer environments can be translated into sound, vision or words – or a combination of same. You sense the soul of a matter only too easily.

In the third case, your psychic awareness allows you to tune into presences, atmospheres and ethereal realms in such a way as to broaden and enrich your own and others' sense of what constitutes reality. You are possibly able to leave your physical body quite easily – for escapist or inspirational reasons.

But as you search the seven seas of your ultra-sensitive emotions for some lasting sense of identity, your very intent can be undermined by a need to dissolve any sense of being a separate entity with all the problems and pain that go with it. Fishes after all can get hooked – on a person, drugs, alcohol, a cult, etc. Beware of easy answers. The condition by Sign and House of your Ruling Planet, NEPTUNE, will reveal more about the visions and blindspots that constantly inspire or delude you.

With Pisces Rising you have the opposite Sign of Virgo Setting, which means that you will usually attract partners or certain people who are discriminating and helpful. And you either learn from these types to be more so yourself and thereby find a more singular direction in life, or you try to sabotage and undermine such a mentally-discerning approach. You can both cry for help and seduce at the same time. The Sign and House of MERCURY will reveal more concerning your way of relating and the quality of your relationships and partner(s).

You are apparently easygoing, non-judgmental and tolerant. But this should not mean you becoming a human doormat. Too much other-cheek-turning will make you dizzy.

• *TIP Considering any connections (Aspects) of the Planets mentioned above (NEPTUNE and MERCURY) to other Planets in your Chart – by consulting the section entitled Compatibility on page 10 and the Introduction to the Outer Planets on page 307 – will tell you more about the impression you give of yourself to others and about your relationships/partner(s).*
• *TIP Reading the double-page spread for SUN in PISCES (pages 146–147) will further describe the qualities of your persona or self-presentation.*

RISING SIGN/SUN-SIGN COMPATIBILITY

Now that you have established your Rising Sign, you can identify the Element of your Sun-Sign and Rising Sign by consulting the following and using Figure 1 (page 5). This will give you an idea of how well or in what way the manner of presenting yourself (Rising Sign) combines with who you actually are on the inside (Sun-Sign).

SAME RISING SIGN AS SUN-SIGN

If you were born around Dawn then the chances are that this will be the case. Put simply it means that you are what you appear to be, and because of this you mostly attract a positive, clear and direct response from others. But there are in fact two types here: those born before Sunrise and those born after it. If you are the former you are more true to type, and wear you heart on your sleeve. If you are the latter, then despite the fact that you seem to be upfront, there is a part of you that is kept very definitely out of sight – so you have quite a subtle persona. In either case, however, always bear in mind the actual nature of the Sign that is rising. For example, Leo Rising always appears to be showing everything, whereas Scorpio Rising is concealing something more often than not.

SAME ELEMENT RISING SIGN AS SUN-SIGN

This makes for a harmonious link between your outer show and inner reality, and is determined by the nature of the Element concerned. A Rising Sign and Sun-Sign in:

FIRE (Aries, Leo and Sagittarius) will make for a very compelling and forceful nature that has enormous supplies of energy. However, there can be a danger of burnout if material, physical or emotional limitations are not taken into consideration.

EARTH (Taurus, Virgo and Capricorn) will make for a reliable and dependable nature. What is promised is usually delivered. You may be a bit slow and stuck-in-the-mud at times, though.

AIR (Gemini, Libra and Aquarius) will make for a distinctly light and cerebral being that is able to move from one person or subject to another with comparative ease. Sometimes you can be up in the clouds and out of touch with the material or emotional side of life.

WATER (Cancer, Scorpio and Pisces) will make for a fluid and emotionally responsive and adaptable make-up. Being awash with unrestrained or uncontained feelings can be a problem though.

RISING SIGN AND SUN-SIGN IN COMPATIBLE ELEMENTS

These are FIRE WITH AIR and EARTH WITH WATER. With Rising Sign in one and Sun-Sign in the other, there is a fairly efficient and constructive link between inner intention and the way it is expressed. The exception to this is when Rising Sign and Sun-Sign are in OPPOSITE SIGNS. This would mean that you were born at or around Sunset. If you are a 'Sunset Baby' you come across very differently to how you actually are, or as a confounding and contradictory expression of both! Ultimately, though, you are aiming to achieve a very balanced expression of the positive qualities of both the Signs involved.

RISING SIGN AND SUN-SIGN IN INCOMPATIBLE SIGNS

These challenging combinations are as follows:

FIRE WITH WATER A Fire Sun-Sign with a Water Rising Sign will incline you to dampen and compromise yourself. Steady passion without boiling over is the recipe to aim for. With a Water Sun-Sign and a Fire Rising Sign you can exhaust yourself and others through a lack of awareness of limitations. Maybe very exciting and impressive – but at a price. You require 'good management'.

FIRE WITH EARTH With a Fire Sun-Sign and an Earth Rising Sign you have to find and forge a practical expression of some ideal or vision, otherwise a self-defeating attitude would be the depressing result. With an Earth Sun-Sign and a Fire Rising Sign you are someone who can appear more confident than you actually are, with disappointment ensuing. However, when used as a means of living up to something better, there can be steady growth.

AIR WITH WATER An Air Sun-Sign with a Water Rising Sign can actually make you into someone who is a good counsellor, professionally or otherwise, because of the combination of emotional sensitivity backed by mental awareness. First however, you will have to live through struggles of emotions getting the better of mind, or vice versa. A Water Sun-Sign with an Air Rising Sign is similar, but with the accent on the need for mental objectivity.

AIR WITH EARTH This is not really that much of a problem – other than the possibility that others' problems are not easily recognized or appreciated by you. This is because this is a 'dry' combination that cannot easily understand an emotional or excitable type.

The Planet-House Chart

WARNING! You are now entering the zone of real astrological complexities. If you do not think you are up to it yet, then do not venture further until you are! It is on further probing and grappling with a few figures, symbols and images that deeper and more detailed information concerning your own and others' personalities may be discovered. However, if your Rising Sign and House positions have been accurately calculated by more technical means, then you would only need to use the House Effects listed on page 369.

The Planet-House Chart on page 368 allows you to roughly assess the House Position of any particular Planet in your Birth Chart. All you do is look down the far LEFT-HAND COLUMN for your RISING SIGN. Next, look along the top of the Chart for the SIGN position of the PLANET in question. Where these two – Rising Sign and Planet-Sign position – intersect, you will find a number. This is the House Position of that Planet.

For example, say you are LEO RISING and you want to know the House position number for your SATURN, which you have in CANCER. By looking at the Chart you will see that the number where Leo Rising and Cancer intersect is 12. In other words, your Saturn is placed in the Twelfth House.

Note: If you wish to know what this means in terms of where the Twelfth House actually is in the sky and in relationship to the Horizon, turn to Figure 1 on page 5. Imagine that the cusp of Pisces and Aries (far left) is the Eastern Horizon, and the cusp of Virgo and Libra (far right) is the Western Horizon. Join the two together with a line to form the Horizon itself, and what is above it is the VISIBLE sky when you were born, and what is below it is the NON-VISIBLE sky when you were born – that is, the other side of the Earth. Now simply substitute Aries for the First House, Taurus for the Second House, and so on, until you get to Pisces, which you call the Twelfth House. So, in our example, Saturn will be placed just above the Eastern Horizon at birth – the Twelfth House.

Having established the House Position/Number, now refer to the list that follows the Planet-House Chart. Against the House Number you will find the HOUSE EFFECTS upon that Planet (and also the Sign it is placed in). Keywords for helping you get to grips with this are EXPERIENCED, EXPRESSED and/or MANIFESTED (THROUGH or AS). So, in our example, Saturn in Cancer in the Twelfth House is experienced, expressed and/or manifested (through/as) VAGUELY – REPRESSIVELY – BEFORE BIRTH (IN WOMB/KARMIC EFFECT) – INWARDLY – MEDITATION – RETREAT – CONFINEMENT – BEHIND THE SCENES – UNCONSCIOUS REALM.

To break this all down and delve deeper, simply take the Keywords or Meanings for Saturn itself and for Saturn in Cancer from the Saturn Section (beginning on page 279). To start off with, simply realize that being TESTED IN NURTURING (Saturn in Cancer Keyphrase) would/could have been EXPERIENCED IN THE WOMB. This could have meant a difficult pregnancy! It could also mean that learning to nurture, and be nurtured, was a karmic lesson; that discipline (Saturn keyword) had to be used inwardly, behind the scenes – perhaps as meditation (Twelfth House effects or modes); or that the caring nature was not that obvious to the outside observer.

By using the Planet, Sign and House in this way, endless and fascinating discoveries can be made regarding yourself and others. It is worth taking your time with this, and perhaps discussing it with others if you get stuck.

IMPORTANT! Because the above is only an approximation of House Position, (which is why I recommend you have your Planet-House positions precisely calculated) you may find that the House Number for a particular Planet is one side or the other of the number given. In our example, Saturn happens to be in the Eleventh House – but it could not be in the First House because for it to be so, it would just have to be in Leo (look at Figure 1 in order to understand this point). But in most cases the Planet could be in the House either side. Read the relevant descriptions and see which fits. Also, just because one Planet shifts Houses does not mean to say that all will do so. This sounds complicated – and it is! If astrological students have trouble with anything at first it is usually the Houses! So don't think you're dim or get frustrated if you have trouble with them – it is just a steep learning curve.

However, if you do find it all fairly easy to grasp, then you can become a lot more accurate by taking into account the *Degree* of the Rising Sign that is given in the Tables. Above, I have greatly simplified everything by assuming that your Rising Sign will be positioned near the beginning of the Sign. In reality this is not the case. For example, supposing your Rising Sign Degree was LEO 28, which is near the end of the Sign (there being 30 degrees to each and every Sign), then that Saturn in Cancer is more than likely to be in the Eleventh (or even Tenth) House. Again, look at Figure 1 and visualize or pencil things in and you will get the picture.

Having determined the House numbers for all of the Planets, enter them on your SUN M.A.P.S. LIFE PLAN in the column headed HOUSE, along with a note of their individual effect in the column headed MANIFESTING (thru).

ADVANCED STAR-TRACKING

By taking any particular Planet and looking at it closely you may discover quite detailed and highly individualistic information. Taking a closer look at your Ruling Planet (the one that rules your Rising Sign and therefore your whole Birth Chart) and the Planet that rules your Setting Sign (Relationships and Others), will tell you a great deal about how you and another will interact. In other words, it will give you a greater insight into what is the most common concern of most people: how to attain love and harmony between yourself and another.

So, let us take Leo Rising again as our example, who we'll call JACK. This means that Jack's Ruling Planet is the Sun, and the one that rules his Setting Sign (Aquarius) is Uranus. Looking at Jack's Planetary positions we see that his Sun is in Virgo and his Uranus is in Gemini. This means that they are Square to one another by Aspect, which means that they are CHALLENGING one another. So, right away, Jack is going to attract challenging relationships, and probably very UNUSUAL (Uranus) types of partner and relationship that challenge his Virgoan sense of CORRECTNESS and PURITY. But we also see that Jack has Venus, Mars and Neptune in Libra. Because Libra is an Air Sign like Gemini, these are Trine or in Harmony with his Uranus. So although relationships are difficult, he is able to make

or keep them PLEASANT and HARMONIOUS (Trine and Libra and Air). But then we see that he has that Saturn in Cancer in the Twelfth House (see above example for Planet-House use). Cancer and Libra are both Cardinal in Mode, so they are Square and Challenging one another. We have also noted that Saturn is the only Planet in the Water Element in his Chart. So emotionally relating is difficult for him, and although he manages to harmonize with another because of those Air (Libra and Gemini) Planets, Saturn will keep reminding him that he is not necessarily opening up emotionally. That Saturn in Cancer in the Twelfth House is inclined to make him keep his FEELINGS (Cancer) to himself or REPRESSED (Twelfth House). So Uranus the Awakener, Ruler of his Setting Sign or House of Relationships, finds this Planetary Route to waking him up to his innermost feelings.

Now let us look at a relationship that Jack is having with another, who we'll call JILL, and gain an astrological insight into a positive planetary connection between two people.

Looking at Jill's Chart we see that she has Sun in Aquarius (Jack's Setting Sign of Relationships) and Gemini Rising (the Sign placement of Jack's Uranus, the Ruler of his Setting Sign, which in turn is Trine to his Venus, Mars and Neptune in Libra). This means that through thoughts and words (Gemini) Jack awakens (Uranus) Jill's sense of self (Rising Sign), aided by it all taking place in the mental and aesthetic harmony provided by all the Air Signs (Gemini, Libra and Aquarius). Now we observe that Jill's Setting Sign is Sagittarius, and ruled therefore by Jupiter. Her Jupiter, we find, is positioned in Libra (Conjunct to Jack's Venus, Mars and Neptune) along with her Uranus. This means that she will attract and be attracted to Jupiterian types (EXPANSIVE, PHILOSOPHICAL) who are also unusual (Uranus). Going back to Jack's Sun in Virgo, we see that it is Conjunct to Jupiter – so he is a Jupiterian type, and both these Planets are Square to that Uranus in Gemini – so he would be unusual. To round it all off, we note that the Ruler of Jack's Setting Sign, Uranus, is Trine or Harmonizes with the Ruler of Jill's Setting Sign, Jupiter – because they are both in Air Signs, Gemini and Libra.

Underlying all this we must consider the Moon. The Moon is always very important in considering relationships (perhaps more so than the Sun) for it symbolizes feelings, familiarity, security and comfort. Jack has the Moon in Aries (Fire Sign) and Jill has the Moon in Leo (also a Fire Sign and also Jack's Rising Sign). These Moon positions are complementary mainly in that they both have a childlike sense of fun and games.

The above is not the whole planetary picture of Jack and Jill's relationship, but it goes to show that there is a relationship because of this subtle synchronization of their respective planetary positions. One swallow does not make a summer – or, in other words, because Jack has Aquarius Setting and therefore ruling his relationships, it is not enough that Jill be simply an Aquarian. There has to be a more comprehensive 'knit' to make a relationship manifest and progress before further rewards and challenges can happen at all within that relationship.

In studying your own and another's Planets in this way, you will find that the actual energy of the relationship will become more refined and highly attuned – simply because you have begun to look at it and harmonize with it on its own level. This is true Astrology.

THE PLANET-HOUSE CHART

Rising Sign	Planet's sign position											
	ARI	TAU	GEM	CAN	LEO	VIR	LIB	SCO	SAG	CAP	AQU	PIS
ARIES	1	2	3	4	5	6	7	8	9	10	11	12
TAURUS	12	1	2	3	4	5	6	7	8	9	10	11
GEMINI	11	12	1	2	3	4	5	6	7	8	9	10
CANCER	10	11	12	1	2	3	4	5	6	7	8	9
LEO	9	10	11	12	1	2	3	4	5	6	7	8
VIRGO	8	9	10	11	12	1	2	3	4	5	6	7
LIBRA	7	8	9	10	11	12	1	2	3	4	5	6
SCORPIO	6	7	8	9	10	11	12	1	2	3	4	5
SAGITTARIUS	5	6	7	8	9	10	11	12	1	2	3	4
CAPRICORN	4	5	6	7	8	9	10	11	12	1	2	3
AQUARIUS	3	4	5	6	7	8	9	10	11	12	1	2
PISCES	2	3	4	5	6	7	8	9	10	11	12	1

HOUSE EFFECTS

House	Qualities of Planet/Sign Experienced – Expressed – Manifesting (through/as)
1	Physical Appearance – Persona – Obviously – At Birth – Embodiment of Planet/Sign Qualities
2	Issues of Personal Worth/Resources – Property – Possessions – Finances
3	Daily Occurrences, Trips and Encounters – Verbally – Communications – Siblings – Primary and Secondary Schooling
4	Domestically – Background/Roots – Privately – Subjectively – Buried – Father's (or sometimes Mother's) Influence/Character
5	Creatively – Romantically – Children – Recreationally – Speculatively – Sexually – Fun/Pastimes – Entertainment/Dramatically
6	Work – Service – Body/Mind State (Health) – Colleagues/Employees – Methods
7	Relationships – Partner's Influence/Character – Others – The Public – Projections on to Another/Others
8	Intimately – Others' Resources – Investments/Taxes/Inheritances/Business – Intensely – Secretly – Crises (Death) – Transformatively – The Occult
9	Foreign Places/People – Adventurously – Religiously – Higher Education – Philosophically – Conceptually – Prophetically
10	Professionally – Publicly – Authority – Status – World Stage – Material World – Mother's (or sometimes Father's) Influence/Character
11	Friends – Groups – Ideals – Politically – Social values – Teamwork
12	Vaguely – Repressively – Before Birth (Womb/Karmic Effect) – Inwardly – Meditation/Retreat/Confinement – Behind the Scenes – Unconscious Realm

SUN M.A.P.S. LIFE PLAN

Example

NAME: Jill				DATE OF BIRTH: 3 February 1969 TIME OF BIRTH: 1pm PLACE OF BIRTH: England		
Planet (Dig, Det, Exal, Fall)	**Sign** (Element points)	**Planet-Sign Keyphrase**	**House**	**Manifesting** (through)	**Notes** (Personal Reality, Compatibility etc.)	
SUN (Detriment)	Aquarius (Air = 4)	Living through Liberating	10	Professionally	Professional Healer. Same Sign as his Setting Sign	
MOON	Leo (Fire = 4)	Security through Creating	4	Privately	Music-making at home comforts/grounds me. Same Element as his Moon.	
(R) MERCURY (Exalted)	Aquarius (Air = 3)	Thinking through Liberating	9	Prophetically	Premonitions in dreams and awake. Trine his Venus, Mars and Neptune.	
VENUS (Detriment)	Aries (Fire = 3)	Loving through Doing	11	Groups and Friends	Met partner at a group gathering. Same Sign as his Moon, but Opposite Venus.	
MARS (Dignity)	Scorpio (Water = 3)	Getting through Desiring	6	Work (Effort)	Have to work hard at getting what I want. Same Element as his Saturn. Square Pluto.	
(S) JUPITER	Libra (Air = 2)	Growing through Relating	5	Romantically	Partner broadened my horizons. Same Sign as his Venus, Mars and Neptune.	
SATURN (Fall)	Aries (Fire = 2)	Tested in Doing	12	Behind the scenes	Real efforts not seen by others. Same Sign as his Moon – Fated!	
URANUS	Libra (Air = 1)	Awakening through Relating	5	Sexually	Turned me on to my female power. Same Sign as his Venus, Mars and Neptune.	
NEPTUNE	Scorpio (Water = 1)	Unifying through Desiring	6	Health/Methods	Reiki practitioner. Dedication important. Trine his Saturn – work together.	
PLUTO	Virgo (Earth = 1)	Empowering through Analysing	5	Creatively	Singing helped cure stammering. Same Sign as his Sun, Mercury and Jupiter.	
ASCENDANT	Gemini (Air = 4)	Expressing through Communicating	n/a	n/a	Speaking my truth is everything to me. Same Sign as his Uranus – not judged!	

(R) = Ruling Planet   (S) = Setting Ruler

ELEMENT TOTALS:	FIRE = 9	AIR = 14	WATER = 4	EARTH = 1
and EMPHASIS:	Balanced	Over-emphasized	Borderline/Under	Under-emphasized

Sun M.A.P

Planet (Dig, Det, Exal, Fall)	Sign (Element points)	Planet-Sign Keyphrase	House
NAME:		DATE OF BIRTH:	
SUN	(= 4)	Living through	
MOON	(= 4)	Security through	
MERCURY	(= 3)	Thinking through	
VENUS	(= 3)	Loving through	
MARS	(= 3)	Getting through	
JUPITER	(= 2)	Growing through	
SATURN	(= 2)	Tested in	
URANUS	(= 1)	Awakening through	
NEPTUNE	(= 1)	Unifying through	
PLUTO	(= 1)	Empowering through	
ASCENDANT	(= 4)	Expressing through	n/a

Ⓡ = Ruling Planet   Ⓢ = Setting Ruler

ELEMENT TOTALS:	FIRE =	AIR =
and EMPHASIS:		

Life Plan

TIME OF BIRTH:	PLACE OF BIRTH:
Manifesting (thru)	**Notes (Personal Reality,Compatibility, etc.)**
n/a	

ELEMENT TOTALS:	WATER =	EARTH =
and EMPHASIS:		

GLOSSARY AND KEYWORD MEANINGS

PLANET – The 'WHAT' of Astrology

What ENERGY and INFLUENCE operates through the Signs, Houses and Aspects
The Sun and Moon are included in this term.

PLANETS – INDIVIDUAL KEYWORDS

SUN – Living – Centre (of your Being)- Heart – Life-giving Force – Will – Intention – Life (in general) – Sense of Creative Purpose – Spirit – Conceit – Ego(tism) – Vitalizes – Importance – Individuality – Illuminated – Outshone – Dominating – Warming – Gold – Exposed – Strengthened – Father

MOON – Security – Feeling Responses – Subjective – Child(hood) – Unconscious – Needs – Dependent – Mother – Habits – Biases – Family – Class – Race – Belonging – Inner Support – Clannishness – Fear of Unknown – Clinging – Past – Reaction – Instinct – Sympathy – Emotions – Reflection – Home/Domesticity – Nurturing – Familiarity – Comfort

MERCURY – Thinking – Connection – Rationality – Nervous System – Communication – Perception – Dexterity – Wired – Learning (ability) – Intellectual – Dryness – Over-rationalization – Lack of Feeling – Nervousness – Verbal – Mentality – Employment – Mind – Hands – Voice – Thought Processes

VENUS – Loving – Attraction – Affection – Beauty – Happiness – Indulgence – Superficiality – Relate – Social – Artistic – Like – Harmony – Sensual – Value – Values

MARS – Getting – Want – Drive – Initiative – Courage – Raw Energy – Violence – Selfishness – Abuse – Desires – Push(ed) – Stimulate – Sex(ually) – Aggression – Exciting – Threatening – Impulsive – Assertion – Force

JUPITER – Growing – Laws – Beliefs – Ethics – Expansion – Furtherance – Opportunity – Wealth – Faith – Broad(en) – Understanding – Travel – Higher Education – Philosophy – Excessive – Overbearing – Over-the-top – Joy – Goodwill – Image of God – Moral Values – Enthusiasm – Optimistic

SATURN – Tested – Lessons – Learn – Fear – Force of Circumstances – Discipline – Effort – Order – Limitations – Obstacles – Concrete Reality – Status Quo – Authority Figures – Father – Time – Ambitious – Task – Material Status – Work – Shadow – Veneer – Superficial Defence System – Lead – Consolidated – Restricted – Inadequate – Rigid – Inhibited – Doubt – Repressed

URANUS – Awakening – Disruption – Unusual – Inventive – Innovative – Future – Unique – Individual Human Being – Human Race – Team Spirit – Openness – Friendship – Groups – Unexpected – Erratic – Alternative – Irregular – Changes – Truth – Freedom – Rebellion – Reform – Revolution – Process – Evolution – Science – Metaphysics – Astrology – Code – Symbolism – Chaos – Outsiders – Outlaws

NEPTUNE – Unifying – Spiritual – Universal – Ethereal – Nagual – Mysterious – Mystical – At One – Psychic – Enlightenment – Delusion – Salvation – Pipe-dream – Sensitivity – Imagination – Blind-spot – Vision – Escape – Release – Giving Up – Surrender – Sacrifice – Victim – Vagueness – Subtlety – Compassion – Pity – Suffering – Transcendence – Confinement – Humility – Meditation – Hypnosis – Asceticism – Healing – (Artistic) Inspiration – Music – Drugs – Alcohol – Glamour – Fantasy – Religious Fervour – Films – Romantic Love – Altered States – Giddy – Insane – Like God – No Boundaries – Dissolving – Uplifting – Confusing – Consoling – Undermining

PLUTO – Empowering – Seed/Power – Destiny – Obsession – Potential – Penetrate – Hidden Causes – Profound – Death – Transformation – Sexuality – Secret – Birth – Rebirth – Regenerates – Destroys – Harm – Heal – Depth – Insight – Intensification – Elimination – Uncompromising – Inner Truth – Taboo – Manipulated – Horror – Hell

SIGN – The 'HOW' of Astrology

How the Planets seek to express and make their energies felt through the twelve QUALITIES which are the twelve Signs of the Zodiac.

SIGNS – INDIVIDUAL KEYWORDS

ARIES – Doing – Independence – Championing – Pioneering – Winning – Selling – Starting (Over) – Fighting – Precipitating – Acting – Leading – Being – Emerging

TAURUS – Stabilizing – Producing – Possessing – Maintaining – Holding – Insisting – Enduring – Enjoying – Having

GEMINI – Communicating – Thinking – Diversifying – Learning – Trading – Amusing – Interesting – Inquiring – Connecting

CANCER – Nurturing – Protecting – Securing – Clinging – Reflecting – Feeling – Responding – Dreaming – Sympathizing

LEO – Creating – Showing – Ruling – Respecting – Impressing – Dramatizing – Teaching – Entertaining – Playing – Giving

VIRGO – Analysing – Improving – Serving – Working – Criticizing – Purifying – Preparing – Cleaning – Studying – Correcting

LIBRA – Relating – Balancing – Pleasing – Socializing – Harmonizing – Beautifying

SCORPIO – Desiring – Delving – Concealing – Transforming – Controlling – Absorbing – Dealing – Probing – Influencing

SAGITTARIUS – Seeking – Exploring – Travelling – Understanding – Promising – Believing – Preaching – Enthusing – Advertising – Publishing

CAPRICORN – Building – Using – Organizing – Achieving – Upholding – Presiding – Establishing – Ordering – Structuring – Climbing

AQUARIUS – Liberating – Knowing – Reforming – Innovating – Befriending – Researching – Envisaging

PISCES – Accepting – Inspiring – Loving – Relieving – Empathizing – Fantasizing – Visualizing – Camouflaging

HOUSE – The 'WHERE' of Astrology.

Where the Planets in the Signs MANIFEST and make themselves felt in the actual AREAS or FIELDS OF EXPERIENCE of Earthly life.

HOUSES – INDIVIDUAL KEYWORDS (see PLANET-HOUSE CHART on page 368.)

ASPECT

A particular angular relationship that is made from one Planet (or point, such as the Ascendant) at one degree of the circle or Zodiac to another Planet at another (or the same) degree in the Zodiac.

ASPECTS – INDIVIDUAL KEYWORDS (and degree of angle)

CONJUNCTION (0°) – Uniting – Blending – Joining – Bound

OPPOSITION (180°) – Opposing – Confronting – Awareness – Projection

SQUARE (90°) – Challenging – Conflicting

TRINE (120°) – Harmonizing – Supporting – Flowing – Comfortable With

SEXTILE (60°) – Working Well With

RULING PLANETS

Each Planet is said to Rule a Sign or two. This means that the nature of the Planet corresponds to the Sign(s) that it Rules. This in turn gives rise to Planets expressing themselves well or easily in some Signs, and with difficulty in others. Ruling Planets also tell you how one area of your life (HOUSE) is managed or expressed by the Planet that Rules that House. For example, the Planet which Rules your Rising Sign, which is the beginning or Cusp of your First House, governs the way you Express your Self (First House issues), and therefore its position by Sign, House and Aspect tells you more about how and where you do this – that is, express yourself. The Planet which Rules your Rising Sign is called *your* RULING PLANET.

RULING PLANETS AND THE SIGNS THEY RULE

(see RULING PLANETS on page 14.)

RISING SIGN

The Sign that is Rising in the East at the Time of Birth. It is indicated by the ASCENDANT, or East Point/Eastern Horizon, and symbolizes how you present yourself to the world around you. The Ascendant is the Cusp/beginning of the First House.

RISING SIGN – KEYWORDS

Self-Expression – Self-Presentation – Identity – Appearance – Physical Looks

SETTING SIGN

The Sign that is Setting in the West at the Time of Birth. It is indicated by the DESCENDANT, or West Point/Western Horizon, and symbolizes what relationships you attract to yourself. The Descendant is the Cusp/beginning of the Seventh House.

SETTING SIGN – KEYWORDS

Relationships – Partner – Shadow – Others

SETTING RULER

The Planet which rules your Setting Sign, thereby revealing (through its Sign, House and Aspects) more about your relationships and manner of relating.

ASCENDANT (see RISING SIGN.)

DESCENDANT (see SETTING SIGN.)

ELEMENTS The Four Basic Qualities of Life (see page 6).

MODES

The Three Basic Modes of Life:
CARDINAL = Initiating
FIXED = Persistent
MUTABLE = Adaptive

MODES AND ELEMENTS

By stringing together the Mode and Element of any given Sign you will determine the basic nature of that Sign. For example, Scorpio is the Fixed Water Sign, and so it is the Sign of Persistent Feelings (that is, loyal but unforgiving).

DIGNITY, DETRIMENT, EXALTATION and FALL

The various classifications or states of Planets in Signs (see page 13).

FURTHER INFORMATION

If you wish to take your interest in astrology further, I recommend that you contact:

AUSTRALIA

**Federation of
Australian Astrologers**
Lynda Hill
20 Harley Road
Avalon NSW 2107
Tel: +61-2-918-9539

CANADA

**Association Canadiennes
des Astrologues
Francophones**
Denise Chrzanowska,
President
CP 1715
Succ 'B'
Montreal, H3B 3LB
Tel: +1-514-831-4153
Fax: +1-514-521-1502

Astrolinguistics Institute
Anne Black, Director
Astrolinguistics Institute
2182 Cubbon Drive
VICTORIA
British Columbia V8R 1R5
Tel: +1-604-370-1874
Fax: +1-604-370-1891
e-mail: ablack@islandnet.com

NEW ZEALAND

**Astrological Society
of New Zealand**
Joy Dowler, President
5266 Wellesley Street
AUCKLAND 1003

**Astrology Foundation
Incorporated**
Hamish Saunders, President
41 New North Road
Eden Terrace
AUCKLAND 1003
Tel/Fax: +64-9-373-5304

SOUTH AFRICA

**Astrological Society
of South Africa**
Cynthia Thorburn,
Chairperson
PO Box 2968
RIVONIA 2128
Tel: +27-11-864-1436

UK

**The Astrological
Association**
396 Caledonian Road
London N1 1DN

USA

**American Federation
of Astrologers**
Robert Cooper,
Executive Secretary
PO Box 22040
Tempe
AZ 85285-2040
Tel: 602-838-1751
Fax: 602-838-8293

**Association for
Astrological Networking**
8306 Wilshire Blvd
Suite 537
Beverley Hills
CA 90211

If you wish to obtain more technically detailed astro-data – such as the exact positions of Planets, Rising Signs, etc. – or to have further information such as the meaning of individual Aspects, the nature of your Birth Chart as a unique whole, and Transits and Progressions (past, future and present Planetary influences), then send a stamped addressed envelope to:

**Lyn Birkbeck (FIQ)
c/o Element Books Ltd, The Old Schoolhouse, The Courtyard,
Bell Street, SHAFTESBURY, Dorset SP7 8BP, England**